# The Force of Comparison

# New German Historical Perspectives

*Series Editor:* Paul Betts (Executive Editor)

Established in 1987, this St Antony's Series showcases pioneering new work by leading German historians on a range of topics concerning the history of Modern Germany and Europe. Publications address pressing problems of political, economic, social and intellectual history informed by contemporary debates about German and European identity, providing fresh conceptual, international and transnational interpretations of the recent past.

*Recent volumes:*

**Volume 11**
*The Force of Comparison: A New Perspective on Modern European History and the Contemporary World*
Edited by Willibald Steinmetz

**Volume 10**
*Negotiating the Secular and the Religious in the German Empire: Transnational Approaches*
Edited by Rebekka Habermas

**Volume 9**
*Humanitarianism and Media, 1900 to the Present*
Edited by Johannes Paulmann

**Volume 8**
*Space and Spatiality in Modern German-Jewish History*
Edited by Simone Lässig and Miriam Rürup

**Volume 7**
*Poverty and Welfare in Modern German History*
Edited by Lutz Raphael

**Volume 6**
*Anti-Liberal Europe: A Neglected Story of Europeanization*
Edited by Dieter Gosewinkel

**Volume 5**
*A Revolution of Perception? Consequences and Echoes of 1968*
Edited by Ingrid Gilcher-Holtey

**Volume 4**
*Popular Historiographies in the 19th and 20th Centuries: Cultural Meanings, Social Practices*
Edited by Sylvia Paletschek

**Volume 3**
*Work in a Modern Society: The German Historical Experience in Comparative Perspective*
Edited by Jürgen Kocka

**Volume 2**
*Crises in European Integration: Challenges and Responses, 1945–2005*
Edited by Ludger Kühnhardt

*For a full volume listing, please see the series page on our website:*
*http://www.berghahnbooks.com/series/new-german-historical-perspectives*

# The Force of Comparison
## A New Perspective on Modern European History and the Contemporary World

*Edited by Willibald Steinmetz*

berghahn
NEW YORK • OXFORD
www.berghahnbooks.com

First published in 2019 by
Berghahn Books
www.berghahnbooks.com

© 2019, 2026 Willibald Steinmetz
First paperback edition published in 2026

All rights reserved. Except for the quotation of short passages
for the purposes of criticism and review, no part of this book
may be reproduced in any form or by any means, electronic or
mechanical, including photocopying, recording, or any information
storage and retrieval system now known or to be invented,
without written permission of the publisher.

**Library of Congress Cataloging-in-Publication Data**

A C.I.P. cataloging record is available from the Library of Congress
Library of Congress Cataloging in Publication Control Number:
2019026285

**British Library Cataloguing in Publication Data**

A catalogue record for this book is available from the British Library

**EU GPSR Authorized Representative**

LOGOS EUROPE, 9 rue Nicolas Poussin, 17000, LA ROCHELLE, France
Email: Contact@logoseurope.eu

ISBN 978-1-78920-335-6 hardback
ISBN 978-1-83695-395-1 paperback
ISBN 978-1-80758-947-9 epub
ISBN 978-1-78920-336-3 web pdf

https://doi.org/10.3167/9781789203356

# Contents

*List of Figures and Tables*     vii

**Introduction.** Concepts and Practices of Comparison in Modern History     1
*Willibald Steinmetz*

1. Outlines of a Historical Epistemology of Comparison: From Descartes to the Early Nineteenth Century     33
*Michael Eggers*

2. Comparative Practices and Their Implications: The Case of Comparative Viewing     53
*Johannes Grave*

3. Above/Below, Better/Worse or Simply Different? Metamorphoses of Social Comparison, 1600–1900     80
*Willibald Steinmetz*

4. Empowering Comparisons? The Making of Republics in the Early Modern Period     113
*Lars Behrisch*

5. Comparing Europe and the Americas: The Dispute of the New World between the Sixteenth and Nineteenth Centuries     137
*Angelika Epple*

6. European Colonial Empires and Victorian Imperial Exceptionalism     164
*Alex Middleton*

7. Comparison and the Welfare State in Modern Europe, c. 1880–1945     191
*Julia Moses*

8. Comparison, Rivalry and Competition under Neoliberalism and State Socialism     214
*David Priestland*

9. Comparing Economic Activities on a Global Level in the 1920s
   and 1930s: Motives and Consequences    242
   *Martin Bemmann*

10. In Search of a Global Centre of Calculation:
    The Washington Statistical Conferences of 1947    266
    *Daniel Speich Chassé*

11. Formalized Comparisons: Rankings and Status in Higher Education    288
    *Wendy Espeland*

12. Good – Better – Best: Comparisons and the Power of
    Ranking Orders    306
    *Bettina Heintz*

*Index*    333

# Figures and Tables

**Figures**

Figure 2.1 Johann Peter Langer, Saint Thomas, after Marcantonio Raimondi, c. 1789. — 62

Figure 2.2 Marcantonio Raimondi, Saint Thomas, c. 1520. — 63

Figure 2.3 Ivan Lermolieff (i.e. Giovanni Morelli), *Kunstkritische Studien über italienische Malerei* (1890). — 68

Figure 3.1 Gerard de Lairesse, Body postures, gestures and manners of persons of different rank in similar situations, *Groot Schilderboek* (1712). — 87

Figure 3.2 William Hogarth, *Industry and Idleness* (1747), plate no. 1: The Fellow 'Prentices at their Looms. — 90

Figure 3.3 Daniel Chodowiecki, *Natural and Affected Forms of Conduct in Life*, 2nd series (1780), no. 7: Connoisseurship of Art. — 92

Figure 3.4 Daniel Chodowiecki, *Natural and Affected Forms of Conduct in Life*, 2nd series (1780), no. 8: Connoisseurship of Art. — 92

Figure 12.1 GDP per capita, growth rate, *United Nations Statistical Yearbook* (2016). — 312

Figure 12.2 'Balance des peintres' (extract), Roger de Piles, *Cours de peinture par principe* (1708). — 314

Figure 12.3 'Le rang scientifique des nations', Alphonse de Candolle, *Histoire des Sciences et des Savants depuis deux Siècles* (1873). — 315

Figure 12.4 British exports of cotton piece goods to European countries (1913 – 1919 – 1920 – 1921), *Manchester Guardian Commercial* (1922). — 316

Figure 12.5 Academic Ranking of World Universities 2017. — 319

Figure 12.6 Fractal spectrum of ranking orders. — 321

## Table

Table 12.1 List of countries by GDP per capita (2016). 313

# Introduction
# Concepts and Practices of Comparison in Modern History

Willibald Steinmetz

## The Importance and Impertinence of Comparison

This is the 'age of comparison'. Friedrich Nietzsche's remark is even more valid today than at the time when he jotted it down in his collection *Human, All Too Human* (1878).[1] Comparisons are ubiquitous in our daily experience. All over the globe, consumers make use of web portals to compare the quality of goods, services or tourist destinations. University administrations have developed sophisticated strategies to secure a good place for their own institution in the annually published league tables. The same is true for hospital trusts or city councils. And even governments and national publics are not indifferent to the practice of grading nation states by means of indices that claim to measure human development, the reading capabilities of pupils, degrees of corruption, or compliance with human rights declarations. Such comparisons are neither neutral nor harmless. Comparisons affect the ways in which individuals, organizations or nation states behave and relate to others. Comparisons are driven by strong emotions and in turn are a stimulus to fresh emotions such as envy, pride or shame. They are embedded in competitions and elicit new competitive games. They may provoke shifts in the priority of values and change the outlook of institutions. In short, comparisons have powerful effects and – sometimes perverse – side-effects.

Moulding a habit of competitive comparisons among individuals and companies may become a technique of governance. The most extreme case is present-day China, where a state-run Social Credit System is being implemented by which businesses and private citizens will be rated and receive scores not just for their creditworthiness, as if from a credit rating agency, but for the degree to which they meet certain behavioural standards defined by the Chinese government. Open exposure and punishment of wrongdoers, public praise and material rewards for those who receive the best scores are part of the programme. Pilot schemes in several Chinese cities have already been put in place. These schemes rely on citizens and businesses voluntarily supplying their data on a range of activities in the hope of reaping benefits or avoiding disadvantages such as being shut out from fast-train journeys.[2] Using carrots and sticks, the Chinese policy is similar to that used by health insurance companies in Western countries that want to induce their customers to lead a healthy lifestyle. However, the Chinese government's policy is much more comprehensive and radical in publicly communicating score tables that will enable China's citizens and businesses to compare themselves with others and outperform them in the future. At present, it seems that there is hardly any public criticism in China of the government's claim to set the standards according to which people's behaviour is evaluated. Nor is there any open debate on the need or justification for such a system of state-controlled governance by comparison. Most concerns limit themselves to the technical issues of how to guarantee a correct collection of the data and prevent their misuse by corrupt agencies or hackers.[3] It may well be that the mere public announcement of China's Social Credit System by an openly accessible state document in 2014 had already begun to direct the citizens' behaviour towards the goals desired by the government.[4]

These examples provide ample proof that comparisons are an important social practice that leads to changes in behaviour and creates new routines. At the same time, comparisons can also be *impertinent* in both senses of the word. Comparisons may deceive because the units compared are not genuinely comparable or because the criteria applied are misleading. Comparisons may also be deeply disturbing because they can destroy the social fabric and cause envious emotions or unfair competitive practices among the individuals, groups or states being compared. There is a long tradition of criticizing comparisons not just as a methodology with many pitfalls in the social sciences and humanities, but also as a potentially disruptive practice in all walks of life from private social intercourse up to international relations. *Comparaison n'est pas raison* – comparison is not reason – is an ancient French pun and proverb that sums up common reservations against comparisons. The allegation is that comparisons are not disclosing but hiding the truth. *Toute comparaison est odieuse* – comparisons are odious – is another old French proverb, also used in England from the fifteenth century onwards, to articulate the thought that comparisons may be emotionally hurtful to those being compared, or indeed hurtful to reason itself because they treat units as equal or similar that should not be equated in such a way. Sir John Fortescue (c. 1395–c. 1477) felt a need to defend himself against such a reproach when he compared the laws of England with those of continental Europe in a didactic dialogue written some time before 1471 and addressed to the young Prince

Edward, son of King Henry VI, while in exile in France: 'Comparisons, indeed, Prince, as I remember you said at one time, are reputed odious, and so I am not fond of making them but you will be able to gather more effectively whether both of these laws are of equal merit, or whether one more richly deserves praise than the other, not from my opinion, but from those points wherein their judgments differ.'[5] The Chancellor who addresses the Prince with these words in Fortescue's dialogue implies that it might be sufficient to hold back one's own opinion and just let 'the facts' speak for themselves so that the interlocutor may conclude which of the two entities compared is the superior one. In Fortescue's fictitious dialogue, the impartiality claim inherent in the Chancellor's words has the desired effect on the Prince, for towards the end of the first part of the book ('In Praise of the Laws of England'), he declares himself satisfied 'that these laws are not only good but the best'.[6]

Not all readers of Fortescue's book may have been so easily convinced as the young Prince. The practice of comparing laws or institutions, nation states, civilizations or famous historical figures across time and space with the intention of ranking them in relation to their respective achievements has rarely been uncontentious. Sooner or later, those deemed inferior in such comparisons have always cast doubt on the criteria used by the comparers and have tried to replace them with other criteria more favourable to them. More fundamentally, and increasingly from the late eighteenth century onwards, comparisons in general were criticized as irrelevant and misleading. Around 1800, uniqueness became an ideal that was applied to individual persons as well as collective entities or historical periods. The English literary critic William Hazlitt (1778–1830) resumed the scepticism expressed by many early nineteenth-century romanticists and historicists against comparisons. In his essay *On Thought and Action*, published in 1821 as part of his collection *Table Talk*, Hazlitt took up the old proverb and gave it a more sweeping turn: 'Comparisons are odious, because they are impertinent, and lead only to the discovery of defects by making one thing the standard of another which has no relation to it.' As an example, Hazlitt discusses comparisons between famous figures including artists and military leaders in order to explain his view that any ranking of such figures tends to miss the unique excellence of each of them: 'The mind is not well competent to take in the full impression of more than one style of excellence or one extraordinary character at once.' Therefore, he concludes, that if asked 'which is the greatest of those who have been the greatest in different ways', his answer would be 'the one that we happen to be thinking of at the time'.[7] Judging historical figures, peoples or periods by the standards of their own self and their own times only, not by any later standard that shows them to be defective in some point: this historicist formula was an option that was often chosen by historians, literary scholars and art critics from the early nineteenth century onwards.

In structural terms, Hazlitt's argument is not very distant from that of contemporary postcolonial critics who argue that comparisons between imagined entities such as nations, societies, empires or civilizations, past or present, are always at risk of discovering nothing but defects if the conceptual world of one of the compared entities ('Europe', 'the West') is taken as the point of departure for the comparison. In nineteenth-century Europe, the risk of finding that other cultures were 'lacking' something, or were 'arrested in development', was exacerbated when evolutionary conceptions of history came to the fore. The West European travellers, philologists and imperialists whose writings are analysed in Edward Said's classic study *Orientalism* (1978) are cases in point. Ernest Renan (1823–91), one of the orientalist authors studied by Said, was particularly outspoken with regard to the fantasies of power involved in the act of comparing: 'Me, being there at the center, inhaling the perfume of everything, judging, comparing, combining, inducing – in this way I shall arrive at the very system of things.'[8] Ordering the world by comparison, this vision of Renan, a philologist and scholar of religion, lay at the heart of all the comparative sciences and humanities that began to flourish in Europe from the late eighteenth century onwards. In the context of evolutionary thought, these attempts at ordering the world always had a temporal dimension using West European standards as yardsticks for progress or backwardness. The rhetorical figure of the noncontemporaneousness of the contemporary was one way to articulate that kind of comparative thinking. It often served to relegate non-Western societies to what Dipesh Chakrabarty famously called the 'waiting room of history'.[9]

Our eclectic introductory survey has revealed a puzzling spectrum of voices on comparison as practised and conceptualized in European history and the contemporary world. The anonymous French and English proverbs; Fortescue's early defence of comparing medieval institutions; Hazlitt's romanticist rejection of all comparisons; Renan's visions of ordering the world through comparison; Nietzsche's intuition that the late nineteenth century in particular could be called an 'age of comparison'; our present-day tension between postcolonial criticism of comparison on the one hand, and the ubiquity of comparative ranking and rating practices, embracing not only individual countries or sectors but the whole globe, on the other hand – all these instances of the importance and impertinence of comparison suggest that comparisons as a social practice have a history of their own that deserves to be explored. Yet surprisingly little research has been done on the changing relationship between the comparers and the objects or persons compared, on the different motives for and social effects of comparisons, on the variable criteria and commensurability assumptions applied, and on when and why the craze for subjecting almost everything and everyone to comparative rankings or ratings started. Except for comparison as a methodological issue, there is no reasonably coherent research tradition that deals with *comparisons as practices and concepts* that have a history of their own and indeed also *make* history in a very tangible way.[10]

This volume will open up new perspectives on how to research the changing forms, motives and impacts of comparison. Comparison is treated here not as a methodological problem, but as an object of inquiry in its own right and with far-reaching historical significance. The book's main hypothesis, expressed in its title, is that comparisons have been, and still are, a major driving force that has contributed to the dynamism of modern European history and contemporary world society. The topic is explored from several disciplinary angles: history and sociology, literary studies and the history of the visual arts. The temporal scope of the volume is broad, with examples ranging from the sixteenth to the twenty-first centuries. Geographically, the book's main focus is on modern and contemporary Europe and the Americas, but the chapters on twentieth- and twenty-first-century statistics and ranking practices (Chapters 9–12) extend the view to global linkages by means of contact or mutual observation.

While the initial chapters deal with historical conceptualizations and changing theoretical frameworks of comparative practices in literature, the sciences and the visual arts (Chapters 1 and 2), the subsequent chapters are long-range overviews or case studies on comparative practices in particular fields: comparisons in social intercourse (Chapter 3), comparisons between state constitutions, forms of imperial rule and patterns of governance in welfare and work regimes (Chapters 4–8), and finally comparisons through modern statistics (Chapters 9 and 10) and contemporary rankings (Chapters 11 and 12). The fields covered are not exhaustive, but exemplary in the sense that they expose typical, reiterated forms of comparison and describe their powerful effects in the modern and contemporary world.

## Investigating Comparisons in Theory and Practice

Until very recently, the only coherent line of inquiry on comparisons has been concerned with the methodological issue of how to use them, or whether to use them at all, as a tool in the humanities and social sciences. All disciplines within that broad field have carried on their own particular controversies about that problem, and it is impossible and unnecessary here to follow their course in detail.[11] However, within those debates, one can discern a handful of basic ideas that have crossed disciplinary boundaries and, taken together, circumscribe the range of possible positions on whether and how to use comparisons. Although this volume is not intended to be yet another contribution to methodology, a brief discussion of those basic positions may be necessary, not least because comparative practices outside the academic field are often, and increasingly, informed by the conversations in the various branches of the sciences and humanities.

Roughly speaking, there are those who argue against and those who defend comparisons. The most radical critics reject comparisons more or less completely because they believe that any (nontrivial) comparison inevitably commensurates the incommensurable. It does so, they claim, by the very act of establishing the categories needed to make two or more things comparable at all. The trivial example is that we need a category like 'fruit' to compare apples and oranges. A nontrivial example is that we use a category like 'religion' to compare Buddhism, Hinduism and Islam. According to the critics, this is an unsound procedure because the category 'religion', as we use it today, is a European invention of the early modern period and imposes an artificial similarity and uniformity on belief systems and ritual practices that in reality should be seen as far more apart from each other and as much more porous and multifarious.[12] A similar argument could be made for the category 'culture'/'civilization'.[13] Following on from this, even the compared entities themselves (Buddhism, Hinduism, Islam) are said to be artificially homogenized formations of rather recent origin, only created by an interplay between European powers who demanded clear boundaries in accordance with their category of 'religion', and movements for 'purity' among the non-Christian communities who found the European demands useful for their own agenda.[14] Such historicizations of a category like 'religion' and entities such as Buddhism, Hinduism or Islam would make all comparisons applied to earlier periods than the colonial age appear highly problematic. Moreover, postcolonial critics can point out that 'religion' itself is a concept of Latin-European origin and therefore imbued with the semantic baggage of that particular tradition whose experiences should not be elevated to a general touchstone for allegedly similar phenomena in other cultures.

The crucial point of this line of criticism is not the familiar one of Eurocentrism or Western conceptual imperialism. The real challenge is that any practitioner of (nontrivial) comparison is inevitably bound to construct the compared units, as well as the categories needed to make the units comparable, by drawing on the conceptual apparatus of one particular language, usually his or her own. Hence, in the eyes of the radical critics, it is the very process of category-making and unit-construction that makes cross-cultural, or even diachronic comparison within one's own culture, a dubious enterprise. Compared to that fundamental objection, the contingent fact that most analytic concepts nowadays used in the humanities and social sciences happen to be of Western origin is of secondary importance. Theoretically, the objection could also be raised against Sinocentric comparisons. It is an objection against the modus operandi of comparison as such, and the fundamental nature of the objection makes it difficult to refute.

In response, defenders of comparison have followed several – mutually supportive – lines of argument. One of them confronts head-on the implicit or explicit incommensurability claim lying at the bottom of the radical critics' rejection of comparison. Are peoples, societies or other collective entities as well as their languages, institutions or belief systems really so quintessentially different that no common ground whatsoever can be found that would allow meaningful comparisons? And is not absolute incommensurability among human beings a much more unlikely assumption than similarity in at least some, if only elementary, respects? If the question is reformulated in that way we are getting closer to a position that postulates anthropological universals or at least stable features over a very *longue durée* and extended space. Many defenders of comparison admit that such a position is no definitive solution to the problems of category-making and unit-construction. The more flexible defenders of comparison therefore propose that historical events or different societies, although apparently similar on a phenomenal level, should indeed be studied as unique cases first. Small-number comparisons of such case studies should then only enter the stage as a kind of second-order inquiry on a theoretical level, designed to test hypotheses about the possible workings of causal mechanisms or structural effects.[15]

Comparing individual case studies from a distant, critical standpoint still leaves scholars with the problem of finding a neutral 'metalanguage' that might bridge the conceptual worlds of the societies compared and of the comparer. However, such a metalanguage, as Reinhart Koselleck once remarked, does not exist.[16] It seems futile to hope that the analytic terms of scholarly discourse could ever reach a sufficient degree of neutrality. The problem of being dependent on a particular linguistic tradition when defining the categories, units and *tertia comparationis* needed for any comparison still remains. One pragmatic way out of this dilemma is to organize – and present – the research process itself as an exercise in translation that involves both sides, the comparer and the societies compared. Cultural anthropologists can achieve nonunilateral translations by entering into a dialogue with those they observe. Historians, whose sources cannot 'speak' for themselves, may approximate that ideal by continuously discussing their translational activity, 'pointing out different ways of conceptualising and of drawing boundaries'. Such an explicit discussion of translation and its limitations may lead to a reciprocal semantic enrichment of the terms used for the analysis and, ideally, result in 'more elastic concepts representative of cultural plurality'.[17] Another pragmatic way to avoid the danger of hastily familiarizing the other by using one's own conceptual apparatus is to centre comparative inquiries around recurrent elementary problems or challenges, such as the ways in which societies include or exclude people, attribute positions or contend with past, present and future. The trick consists in starting the comparative inquiry at the most elementary level of meaning production through signs (semiosis), i.e. at the level of basic sentences in language or nonverbal sign usages that articulate the problem without naming or addressing it explicitly. This 'onomasiological' procedure at least has the advantage of not imposing the relevant abstract terms in advance, but making the finding of those terms one objective (*explanandum*) of the comparative investigation.[18] Admittedly, both solutions sketched here are pragmatic makeshifts only and cannot get rid of the comparer's dependency on his or her own conceptual world completely. Postcolonial critics therefore have a point when they stress that asymmetrical power relations between the comparer and the people or objects compared may still remain.[19] However, the alternative of relinquishing comparisons altogether seems no less unsatisfactory.

Another line of criticism engages with the ways in which comparative scholars have dealt with the problem of choosing the units and spatial scales of their comparisons. An obvious point is to reject the cruder varieties of methodological nationalism still to be encountered in some niches of political science departments or historical scholarship. Yet the critical issue is that any comparison, however self-reflective, requires an artificial, quasi-experimental, if only temporary, immobilization and homogenization of the units compared, whether they be called nation states, regions, societies, empires, civilizations or even transnational spaces. Those who raise that critical point usually call for a shift of focus from comparative studies to the historical examination of intersections, connections and circular movements of people, knowledge and things. Shifting the focus in that way to a 'crossed history', they claim, will help to elucidate and *historicize* the processes of boundary-drawing that have constituted and constantly rearranged the units and objects that comparative scholars tend to artificially immobilize.[20] While most comparative scholars concede the point, their counterclaims are that historicizing everything at the same time is practically impossible and that concentrating on intercrossings and entanglements will produce its own blind spots too. In particular, they say, comparisons are still needed when it comes to evaluating the relative impact (or even absence) of connections and circular movements within and between various nations, empires, world regions or other spaces and settings.[21]

The dilemmas posed by scholarly comparisons have thus brought some of its practitioners to demand yet another shift of perspective that gets very close to the objective pursued in this book: the study of *practices of comparison* not only in various scientific disciplines, but also in diverse social fields in which the scientists are one group of agents among others. Thus, in their book on *Comparative Political Thought*, Michael Freeden and Andrew Vincent turn our attention to 'the intriguing issue of the comparative study of practices of comparison or, in other words, the epistemologies through which comparison is effected'. They also suggest that we should ask where 'the quest for comparison' comes from, whether it is 'itself indicative of a particular view of the world' and whether we may 'distinguish between keen comparison and reluctant comparison as a cultural trait'.[22] Even more germane to this book's concerns is Ann Laura Stoler's call to historicize and investigate comparisons as conceptualized and practised by nineteenth- and twentieth-century travellers, anthropologists, sociologists, imperialists and, indeed, the colonial governments themselves: 'We might historicize the *politics of comparison*, tracing the changing stakes for polities and their bureaucratic apparatuses. What did agents of empire think to compare and what political projects made them do so? What did comparison as a state project entail?' Stoler also proposes looking at how categories like 'mixed bloods' or 'poor whites' were fabricated, and how these categories 'produced cross-colonial equivalencies' that made imperialists in various countries and participants at international conferences believe 'that they were in the same conversation, if not always talking about the same thing'.[23]

Angelika Epple's chapter in this volume builds on these suggestions when she proposes a model of how to study practices of comparing historically. Epple exemplifies her suggestions by looking at how natural historians, travellers and political observers made comparisons between Europe and the Americas from the sixteenth to the early nineteenth centuries. By dissecting the operations involved in the comparison process (unit-construction, invention of *tertia comparationis*, creation of racial or other categories), she highlights the mechanisms through which some comparisons were able to acquire a 'truth effect' that made them hegemonic, while other, formerly accepted comparisons lost in credibility. Over the period observed, Epple traces an 'increasing differentiation' of comparative practices, resulting in ever more 'second-order comparisons' and engendering a 'dynamic process' in which one comparison provoked further comparisons.[24] Alex Middleton's chapter on British imperialists in the Victorian period and the ways in which they compared their own methods of imperial rule with those of continental Europeans shows this dynamic process in full swing. In particular, Middleton places emphasis on two additional factors that helped to maintain the comparative drive: competition among European colonial powers on the one hand, and the needs to arouse or appease domestic public opinion with regard to the British imperial project on the other hand. Moreover, Middleton shows that when Victorian imperialists asserted the superiority of British rule over that of continental Europeans in all respects (moral as well as institutional or economic), they not only pursued a deliberate legitimizing agenda but also accentuated the distinctiveness of the British style of imperial rule itself as compared to others.[25]

As we have seen, criticism of comparison as a methodological tool has helped to effect the shift of perspective proposed in this book from the (normative) criticism of method to the (empirical) analysis of practice. The beginnings of such a shift are not only discernible in (post)colonial and crossed-history studies, but also in the fields of philosophical epistemology, aesthetics, literature, the visual arts and the natural sciences. Some rather intuitive remarks by Michel Foucault in *Les mots et les choses* (1966) have been an important inspiration for this shift of focus. In that book Foucault claimed that comparisons, from the mid seventeenth century onwards, began to exhibit a significant change in format and function. In lieu of being quests to prove resemblance and a god-given harmony by means of similes and analogies, comparisons now increasingly emphasized difference or identity by means of contrasts. Except for poetry and the fine arts proper, literary forms of comparison based on the figures of ancient rhetoric were now increasingly superseded and ultimately replaced by scientific forms of comparison based on logical reasoning and observation. Measurement and classification became the instruments by which these new forms of comparison were effected and gained prestige as the preferred way to achieve certain knowledge.[26] Recent studies have confirmed Foucault's basic hypothesis on the changing formats and functions of comparison, while providing a much more nuanced picture with regard to the timing, intensity and propagation of the transformation. Thus, a magisterial study by the literary comparativist Michael Eggers with in-depth analyses of key texts on the epistemology and practical uses of comparison from René Descartes and Carl Linnaeus to Friedrich Schlegel and Honoré de Balzac has relativized some of Foucault's insights. Eggers' findings, summarized here for an anglophone readership in the first chapter of this book, reveal that adjustments are particularly necessary with regard to Foucault's assertions about the supposed devaluation and decline of analogy as a means to acquire and certify knowledge.[27] Eggers shows that analogies, although indeed criticized early on, continued to be used side by side with the more 'scientific' forms of comparison as defined by Foucault far into the nineteenth century.[28] Other recent studies on the explosion of comparative studies in a variety of disciplines around and after 1800 (aesthetics, natural history/biology, anatomy, linguistics, anthropology, etc.) corroborate Eggers' discoveries. The American historian Devin Griffiths, without being aware of Eggers (and vice versa), even speaks of an 'Age of Analogy'.[29]

In art history, the fluid boundaries between comparison as a methodological tool of analysis and comparative practices that involve bodily movements and technical artefacts are particularly pertinent. There is a long tradition of rivalrous comparisons between different forms of art (painting, sculpture, poetry), all taking their cue from the allegation of resemblance between painting and poetry (*ut pictura poiesis*) in Horace's *Ars poetica* (19 BC). Since the Italian Renaissance, these comparisons have become a genre of their own under the designation of *paragone*. The tension between quests for superiority and definitions of specificity has been an inherent feature of this genre, which can thus be seen as an early template for similar controversies in other humanities.[30] From the early modern period onwards, art collectors and connoisseurs have used techniques such as the juxtaposition and cataloguing of pictures, drawings, prints and artefacts ever more extensively to distinguish between 'originals' and 'copies', to classify works by 'style' or to attribute particular works to an individual artist. More recently, the technique of parallel slide projection for teaching purposes and in mass entertainment has again reinforced the long-established routines of a comparative gaze among professional art historians as well as amateur beholders of art works.[31] More perhaps than in other human sciences, the comparative routines in art history have come under attack as being conducive to narrowing the view, but they have also found their defenders. Johannes Grave's chapter in this book engages with the arguments of both sides – critics and defenders – while pleading himself for an intense look, informed by sociological practice theories, at what beholders of art works, connoisseurs, professional art historians, curators of exhibitions and artists themselves actually *do* when they compare. This means paying close attention to the performative aspects, the material objects involved in, and the situatedness of, comparative viewing practices. Case studies on Johann Wolfgang Goethe and other eighteenth- and nineteenth-century commentators and collectors of engravings exemplify Grave's conclusion that comparative viewing practices have a double-edged effect: on the one hand, they may sharpen the perception to enable a viewer's understanding of even the smallest details in an image, such as the folds of a robe, as bearing significance; on the other hand, they may lead to a conditioning of the eye movements in such a way as to isolate the individual units of meaning from their visual context, thus promoting a 'latent semiotic reading of images'.[32]

## The Emergence of Competitive Comparisons: Individuals and Political Regimes

Debates about comparison as a method in the sciences and humanities are not the only pathway towards the empirical study of *practices of comparison* proposed in this book. Another starting point is the study of *competition* on various levels and stages.[33] Social psychologists and historical sociologists have analysed envious comparisons and confident emulation among individuals and groups competing for prestige, material advantages or sportive success.[34] Explaining economic competition among businesses is a classical object in economics and in sociological inquiries into the structure of markets.[35] And the manifestations of rivalry among empires, nation states and political regimes in all conceivable respects – military strength, economic power, cultural prestige – have occupied historians and political scientists for a long time.[36] In all these competitive settings, self-comparisons of the agents play a crucial role, yet in most works on competition, those comparisons are only mentioned in passing, as if their functioning and specific forms were a matter of course. Several chapters in this book therefore address the intertwinement of comparison and competition in a more explicit way.

Useful hints for the study of comparison in the context of competitions can be gathered in Georg Simmel's chapter on conflict ('Der Streit') in his general *Sociology* (1908).[37] In particular, Simmel draws attention to the decisive impact of a third party in all pure forms of competition. Pure competition, he says, is not just a fight between two or more parties for a certain good or a position, but a contest for the favour of a third party. Businesspeople, public intellectuals or professional football teams do not just engage in a combat against each other; rather, they strive for recognition and acceptance of their products, capacities or efficiency by a *third party*. The third party may be customers in the case of businesses, the reading public, students or the mass media in the case of intellectuals, and spectators and potential employers in the case of football players. These third parties, whose attention is courted by the competitors, are incessantly comparing the products and performances of those who compete. Hence, the success of the competitors does not depend on any absolute quality of their own, but first and foremost on the judgement of the third party about their *relative* value in relation to someone else's performance. The third parties set the standards for the comparisons, and it is through their continuous comparative activity that the competitors must learn how to compare themselves. They do so by estimating and continuously re-adjusting their own position in relation to others with respect to the known (or presumed) quality criteria of the third parties.

Building on Simmel's insights, Tobias Werron and Bettina Heintz have pointed to the fact that the third parties in modern world society may, or may not be, visible persons or agencies. In fact, competitors nowadays feel increasingly called to conform to what they suspect to be the comparative criteria of largely anonymous audiences. Thus, global 'comparison horizons' (*Vergleichshorizonte*) are spreading even without any previous direct contact between the competitors themselves or the (presumed) third parties to whose criteria they respond.[38] In a pioneering article of 2007, Wendy Espeland and Michael Sauder made similar points with regard to the effect of national and international ranking and rating practices in the field of higher education.[39] Wendy Espeland's and Bettina Heintz's chapters in this book expand their respective earlier research on the reasons for, and the consequences of, ranking and rating practices.[40] Both chapters – Espeland's on the case of higher education and Heintz's on a broad variety of social fields – arrive at a more fine-grained typology, to be further explained below, with regard to competitive comparisons, their form, function and ever more acutely felt presence in contemporary world society.

In abstract terms, one might conceive the relationship between competition and comparison as one of mutual reinforcement. Competitions necessitate comparisons, and comparisons may enhance existing competitions and entail new ones. The relation is best described as a circular movement where it is impossible to tell which of the two – comparison or competition – comes first. However, in *historical* terms, it seems appropriate to ask whether the intensity of that circular movement of mutual reinforcement has grown since the onset of modernity and, more particularly, to what degree it presupposes the existence of societies based on the principles of economic and political freedom. Competition, as conceived by Simmel, seems to require a certain amount of freedom of choice and can only flourish in the absence of regulations or unwritten conventions that inhibit it. Although competition in personal interaction (for example, children's play) can probably be considered an anthropological universal, there are reasons to assume that as a practice invading nearly all spheres of life in politics, economics and culture, it could be a phenomenon of more recent origin. One might hypothesize that the form of competitive comparison identified by Simmel was less relevant in a society in which the position, wealth and sociopolitical function of individuals and groups depended mainly on preordained rank or *status* rather than on free competition. In an article on 'Personal Competition' (1899), the American sociologist Charles Horton Cooley came to a conclusion along those lines: 'There is but one alternative to competition as a means of determining the place of the individual in the social system, and that is some form of *status*, some fixed, mechanical rule, usually a rule of inheritance, which decides the function of the individual without reference to his personal traits, *and thus dispenses with any process of comparison.*'[41]

But is it true that there is no personal competition, and hence no comparison among, or between, individuals and groups in a society based on status? Cooley at least takes care not to associate too closely the principles of status on the one hand and competition on the other with particular historical periods or stages. While he posits that the 'general tendency in modern times has been toward the relative increase of the free or competitive principle', he sees a persistence of status in some respects 'even in the freest countries' – and also vice versa, instances of competition in premodern societies.[42] However, as a historian of comparison and competition, one should go beyond these cautious reservations and question more radically the habitual assertion that competition is coextensive with modern market societies of a Western, liberal type.

In this book, David Priestland does exactly that in a long-range survey, encompassing the period from the sixteenth to the twenty-first centuries, on the metamorphoses of competition and the comparisons underlying it.[43] His main arguments are that we should think of competition as situated 'both within and outside the context of markets and economic liberalism', and that even within liberalism, as well as 'neoliberalism', one should distinguish several types of competition. For a provocative start, Priestland points to the (perhaps not so) strange resemblances between the regulated forms of 'socialist emulation' (*sorevnovanie*) in Stalinist Russia and the 'neo-liberal methods of performance-measurement by comparisons' in English and other Western universities. Moving on from these observations, he unfolds a differentiated tableau of conceptions of competition in time and space. He starts with a distinction into three basic, reiterable and combinable types of competition, each originally related to the ethos of a social group: the first a competition of merchants relying on values such as self-discipline and turning around buying cheap and selling dear, the second a competition of warrior aristocrats turning around codes of rivalry, honour and courage, and the third a preoccupation of technocrats and officials with regulating and overseeing competition.[44]

Priestland interprets the long-term history of competition as a struggle between these different conceptions and the groups supporting them, but his main point is that, from the late nineteenth century onwards, hybrid forms of the basic types became increasingly common both in liberal and socialist economic theory *and* in governmental practices of states, bureaucracies and private enterprises. In that way, Priestland arrives at a more subtle explanation of rivalrous conceptions of competition. And thus he can also explain why there are those strange resemblances between Soviet efforts to stimulate 'socialist emulation' in an otherwise extremely regulated economy on the one hand, and various shades of neoliberal visions geared to educate economic subjects to behave competitively and yet also to conform to the rules of quasi-markets dictated by New Public Management on the other hand.

Willibald Steinmetz's chapter in this volume also takes a long-range view on the intertwinements between comparison and competition, but he concentrates on the changing modes and forms of social comparison among individuals in social intercourse and other pursuits of ordinary life.[45] His particular focus is on the long transitional period from a society regulated by rank and inherited status to one based primarily on competition. With regard to that period, reaching from the late sixteenth to the turn of the twentieth centuries, Steinmetz distinguishes three types of social comparison, which in abbreviated language he calls 'above/below', 'better/worse' and 'simply different'. His main findings are, first, that social comparisons between persons of higher and lower rank (above/below), although theoretically illicit, were indeed common practice in early modern Europe and further on until the turn of the twentieth century; second, that the competitive (better/worse) variant of social comparison has been on the increase, as one might expect, from the mid eighteenth century onwards; but, third, that it found a vigorous counterpart almost simultaneously in explicit assertions of individuals to be 'simply different' – in other words, in emphatic assertions of uniqueness. Up to the present day, Steinmetz concludes, modernity is characterized by a tense and sometimes uneasy co-presence of all three types of social comparison that may come to the fore, or recede, depending on the situation.

In today's world, comparisons in a competitive context not only affect individuals or small groups, but also large collective entities, particularly nation states. It is obvious that contemporary nation states compete for material advantages, but they also compete at least as much for 'soft goods' administered by third parties. Examples are quests by national governments (and various other agents who claim to represent their nations) for cultural prestige in the eyes of global publics or for positive evaluations by professional comparing agencies.[46] Yet it is less clear whether, *historically speaking*, the practices of comparing states or empires have followed a logic and timing resembling that which has governed social comparisons between individuals. However, the indications are strong that, as far as England is concerned, there was a growing awareness, and pride, already at work in the later Elizabethan period of being in advance of continental European nations that were seen as commercial and military rivals, in particular France and the Dutch Republic. Moreover, as Paul Slack has shown, the seventeenth-century English comparisons with continental European states had a strong temporal bias in envisioning the contest with the competitors as an open-ended race towards 'infinite improvement' in the future.[47] For all their apparent modernity, one has to bear in mind that these early modern progressive comparisons extended above all to the fields of commerce and the general wellbeing of citizens and also, increasingly in the eighteenth century, to the fiscal-military complex – the state's capacity to raise taxes and loans for sustaining military effort. On the other hand, the political system itself, the constitution and legal order, was hardly touched by the progressive-competitive mode of comparison, despite a long tradition, reaching back to Sir John Fortescue, of comparing English and continental European laws. The standard by which Fortescue and his early modern followers 'measured' the relative excellency of laws was an ideal of absolute justice, not a capacity to improve infinitely.

The assumption that the political field did not lend itself so easily to the progressive-competitive mode of comparison is underscored by Lars Behrisch's chapter in this book.[48] In a broad sweep ranging from the sixteenth-century Dutch revolt to the late eighteenth-century American and French Revolutions, Behrisch investigates how early modern revolutionaries, mostly republicans, drew parallels between their own endeavours and those of earlier or contemporaneous revolutionaries elsewhere. Comparing the comparisons made by the Dutch, English, French and American revolutionaries with foreign attempts to establish a republican government, Behrisch finds almost as many different kinds of comparison as there were situations. While he can indeed point to several instances in which the parallels were meant to encourage positive emulation, as when some Dutch revolutionaries recommended following the model of the Swiss confederacy, he discovers many more comparisons that served the opposite purpose. Comparisons were either plainly discouraging, as in the case of the French *Frondeurs* who assured themselves and the public that they would never follow the course of the English regicides, or they were made to buttress claims that proved the uniqueness, exceptionalism or absolute novelty of one's own situation and goals, as in the case of the American Federalists during the debate about the U.S. Constitution or the Abbé Sieyès' proposals for a new French constitution. Until the end of the eighteenth century, then, and in some cases further into the nineteenth century, comparisons in the field of legal and political institutions were not predominantly framed in a logic of competing for progress with other, supposedly more 'advanced' states along an imagined, commonly accepted scale of what would nowadays be called 'best practices'. As Behrisch demonstrates, comparisons could just as well belong to a type that stressed above all differences, if not incommensurability.

However, comparisons among nation states and empires changed significantly in the course of the nineteenth century, especially towards its end. Vulgarized versions of Charles Darwin's supposed dictum of the 'survival of the fittest' (in fact coined by Herbert Spencer) were increasingly mobilized to underpin comparisons that put existing institutions, including political systems, under closer scrutiny. The most important *tertium comparationis* now became the 'efficiency' of nations in comparison to other major powers that were seen as competitors. On all sides, state agencies supported by statistical bureaus were busy figuring out why competing nations or empires were more successful than others, whether in military, economic or technological terms. The cultural and moral prestige of a nation, made visible and audible at world exhibitions or international expert congresses, became another asset in the (perceived) struggle of nations for supremacy. The important watchword here was 'civilization'. Belonging to the club of 'civilized' nations, being recognized as 'civilized' by others, was a precondition for deserving to be comparable at all – as Julia Moses demonstrates in her chapter in this book on international debates about the issue of accidents at work around 1900.[49] While the technological, military and commercial exploits of the most successful nations served as points of comparison for 'efficiency', the relevant benchmarks for 'civilization' were soft goods such as a well-educated population, a low crime rate, a high level of health, hygiene and morality among the working classes, the degree of emancipation of women, the absence of coercion, a great amount of personal freedom, effective suppression of slavery and violence in the colonies, the existence of provisions for the sick, the old or the victims of workplace accidents at home, and ultimately a political system that could be described as self-government of the people.

Pride and shame became the prime movers of international and inter-imperial comparisons on the levels of both efficiency and civilization. Alex Middleton's chapter in this book provides examples of a British sense of pride, mixed with complacency, in comparisons with imperial rivals, while Julia Moses discusses the German government's indefatigable, yet only moderately successful, efforts to propagate the Bismarckian social insurance legislation as a model.[50] On the other hand, being noticeably backwards in one, or several, of the fields mentioned was considered a reason for shame. Thus, in his 1908 State of the Union Address to the U.S. Congress, President Theodore Roosevelt called it 'humiliating that at European international congresses on accidents the United States should be singled out as the most belated among the nations in respect to employers' liability legislation'.[51] Julia Moses' chapter examines the congresses alluded to by Roosevelt at work.[52] The main role of these international expert gatherings (twelve alone on workplace accidents between 1889 and 1912) was to promote the exchange of regular – and comparable – information in the shape of statistics along uniform principles, to define the problems to be solved (including the agreement on the meaning of key terms such as 'professional risk') and to reach a consensus on the broad goals of legislation, in this case some scheme of compensation for accident victims, without however recommending any specific national scheme as a model. Generalizing Moses' findings, one might say that international expert congresses around 1900 were at best able to make problems *comparable* by finding a common (numerical and verbal) language and developing a broad idea of what might constitute best practices in a certain field, but much less effective when it came to advocate concrete solutions.[53] Legislation remained entirely the domain of nation states. Moses analyses the comparisons made in domestic British and Italian debates on compensation schemes. Here she finds that older ideas of national specificity and path-dependency often prevailed over anxieties of falling behind a certain standard. This was especially the case if that proclaimed standard, as in the case of workmen's compensation, originated from a country like Wilhelmine Germany, which in political respects was considered as authoritarian and militaristic – in other words, 'backwards'. Comparisons used in the realm of *political* argument, one might conclude, often followed another logic than the progressive one and were also far removed from the allegedly unpolitical language used in expert discussions on legal or technical issues.

Throughout the twentieth century, comparisons of welfare legislation and labour laws in particular continued to attract much attention from state bureaucracies, professional observers and international bodies like the International Labour Organization (ILO).[54] In the 1950s and 1960s, Scandinavians were particularly eager to praise the 'Nordic model' as an item for export. As Julia Moses also shows, historical and sociological studies of the welfare state, often comparativist themselves, should be interpreted as an integral part of, and a stimulating factor for, welfare state expansion in the twentieth century.[55] And as Pauli Kettunen remarks, even recent comparative research on welfare state models is 'often associated with comparative concerns about economic competitiveness' – with the important difference that growing competitiveness is nowadays often equated with a reduction of welfare provision.[56] Since the 1970s, comparisons of welfare state models have rarely served as an incentive for expansion, but much more frequently as a justification for less generous welfare regulations. Yet, a driving force they have remained – one way or the other.

## The Seductive Power of Numbers and the Suggestiveness of Rankings

It makes a difference whether comparisons are communicated through language, bodily performance, images or numbers. Even if language often intervenes in performative, pictorial or numerical communication, these nonverbal communication media possess an intrinsic logic that affects their potential effectiveness, outreach, clarity or ambiguity; in short, the meaning of the message. Following art historians who postulate an 'iconic difference' with regard to the specific operating mode of images,[57] Bettina Heintz speaks of a 'numerical difference' to stress the remarkable qualities (and hidden drawbacks) of communication by numbers.[58] Quantitative comparisons, she explains, are complex operations as soon as they go beyond simple statements of 'more' or 'less', expressed in isolated figures. Before one can even begin to calculate average scores, growth rates over time, relative increase or decrease in view of certain units, one has to be sure that these units (for instance, 'industrial workers', 'states', or 'universities') are indeed comparable, i.e. sufficiently similar in at least one relevant respect. This act of category-making, which social scientists generally refer to as the operationalization of variables, is far from self-evident and may give rise to all kinds of controversies. The steps are, first, to fix the criteria for the comparison (for example, 'relative backwardness'), second, to define the specific countable and calculable indicators that allow to measure it (for example, ratio of 'industrial workers' per general workforce) and, third, to determine the practical methods of data collection. All these steps involve further acts of abstracting from specific, local qualities in the interest of making things countable, calculable and hence numerically comparable across space and time. In a short formula, Wendy Espeland and Mitchell Stevens have called the entire sequence of these steps 'commensuration'. They define it as the 'transformation of different qualities into a common metric'. They thereby emphasize the fact that numerical comparisons inevitably simplify and reduce the complexity of the reality they pretend to present, yet in fact actually produce to a large extent.[59]

The seductive power of numbers and statistics, once established, consists above all in their capacity to be removed from the original contexts from which they were derived. Statistics and their representations in tables or charts tend to conceal the complex sequence of steps that were needed to fabricate them. The figures acquire a life of their own and may be used without reference to their sources or to the objects they once represented. Another advantage of numbers is that they can be decontextualized and translated much more easily than verbal language. For the knowledgeable, the language of mathematics is universally understandable, and even laypersons may read the figures of a chart or league table. Numbers also seem to be more unambiguous than images and less open to intercultural misunderstanding than body language or other nonverbal signs. Taken together, these specific qualities make up what Bettina Heintz calls the 'numerical difference' as compared with other communication media (language, images, performances). Ultimately, she argues, it is the 'decontextualizing effect' of numbers and statistics that has made the numerical comparisons based on them a moving force of globalization.[60]

The ease with which numbers and statistics circulate in today's world obscures the fact that their historical development was a protracted process.[61] Each of the steps involved in 'commensuration' described above required the buildup of a complicated infrastructure and the achievement of a consensus on difficult epistemological questions. Pioneer historical studies on the growth of statistics have mostly focused on these infrastructural and epistemological problems: the setup of national statistical bureaus, the formation of international expert networks, the methods of calculation, and the use of statistics in the natural and social sciences.[62] In recent years, scholars have paid more attention to aspects that are relevant for a history of the practices and politics of numerical comparison, both within nation states and across borders. There are now numerous case studies, covering individual countries as well as transnational actors in nineteenth- and twentieth-century Europe and the world, that deal with the construction of units to be counted, the formation of categories to make units comparable and the definition of the criteria for comparisons.[63] Of particular interest here is the laborious invention of numerical indicators such as Gross National Product (GNP), a conflict-ridden story told by Daniel Speich Chassé.[64] Stepping back in time, Lars Behrisch's impressive work on eighteenth-century Germany and France has highlighted how statistics already in their early days relied on, and helped to substantiate, a new conception of a national economy that was seen as a complex mechanism, capable of improvement and to be managed by the state. Already in their eighteenth-century beginnings, then, statistics were a modernizing project of welfare promotion combined with biopolitics. To proceed towards that goal, the early French and German statistical bureaucrats created uniformity, reduced complexity and suppressed particularities. Their sometimes ruthless neglect of local knowledge and habits of measuring things explains why they met with massive obstacles and passive popular resistance.[65]

Two nineteenth-century innovations were crucial for facilitating numerical comparisons: the institutionalization of official statistics and their publication at regular intervals in a standardized printed format. The regularization of the practice accustomed the population to being counted and to accepting the categories used by the statisticians as self-descriptions – a feedback effect that in the long run helped to secure comparability. The open accessibility of the printed statistics allowed businesspeople and other interest groups to use them for their own purposes and learn to argue numerically – another feedback effect. Moreover, the expansion of counting and calculating to ever more fields, including moral issues such as crime and suicide, meant that the statistical results for several sectors could now be interrelated to make new, experimental calculations. And the longer the series of published statistics became, the more it was also possible to widen the *temporal* horizons of numerical comparisons. Historical change could now be described in quantitative terms.

However, what remained a problem and could not be solved in a satisfactory way before the mid twentieth century was to make statistics comparable across national borders. It has already been mentioned how international expert congresses on workplace accidents could only reach modest progress in terms of agreeing about the definition of criteria and terminology. The same was true for other efforts to fit national statistics on particular issues to a common standard. It is only after the First World War that these efforts became more successful. Two interlocking chapters in this volume by Martin Bemmann on the 1920s and 1930s and by Daniel Speich Chassé on the 1940s address the intricacies and obstacles to be surmounted by statistical experts and politicians committed to construct economic statistics on a global scale.

Bemmann examines the reasons why the efforts of the international experts, against all odds, found more positive resonance in the crisis years of the interwar period than in the last decades before the First World War, which in many other respects saw a massive drift towards globalization.[66] One reason he finds for the 'cacophony' of international statistics before 1914 was, paradoxically, the successful implementation and firm entrenchment of national statistics. This, he argues, raised the threshold for the national statisticians to depart from their routines, a departure that would also have been regarded at home as a loss of prestige and an interference with internal affairs. By contrast, the years after 1919 saw the establishment of international organizations such as the ILO with at least some competencies under the umbrella of the League of Nations. These organizations not only augmented the need for comparable statistical data, but also, by their very mode of operation, strengthened the willingness of nation states to cooperate. Since a majority of state representatives in the ILO's governing body was to be nominated by the eight member states 'of the chief industrial importance', national governments had a strong incentive to partake in the debates about the indicators supposed to measure 'industrial importance' and then make their national statistics conform to these demands. Thus, a primitive ranking mechanism among states was introduced that had effects similar to those known from university or other rankings today. In addition, the financial weakness even of powerful states such as Britain after the war made them more inclined to abandon regular parts of their own prewar statistics and pool resources with other member states for international statistical ventures. Furthermore, it became a matter of national prestige for newly created states such as Poland and Czechoslovakia, as well as for colonial or semi-colonial countries like India, to build up their own statistical apparatuses, and they did so from scratch in accordance with the rules set by the expert gatherings. Coupled with the demands by private businesses for reliable comparative information, and technocratic visions of government officials to steer the economy through the crisis years, these motives were sufficient to give the efforts of the international statisticians a boost they had not known in the prewar decades. Despite their relative success in relation to achieving comparability, Bemmann concludes, global economic statistics in the interwar years still remained limited to separate series of data for particular economic aspects such as foreign trade, industrial production or state finances.

Global statistical comparisons became a key issue again after the Second World War, particularly at the World Statistical Conferences at Washington DC in 1947, discussed in Daniel Speich Chassé's chapter.[67] The awareness of the pitfalls of statistical comparability as well as the willingness, technocratic fantasies and institutional pressures to erect a global 'centre of calculation' (an expression coined by Bruno Latour) were perhaps even stronger after 1945 than after the First World War. Yet, as Speich Chassé shows, the several hundred experts and government officials gathered at Washington DC could reach no agreement to create such a centre or to invest an existing organization, whether the then already sixty-year-old International Statistical Institute (ISI) or some new organization under the umbrella of the United Nations, with that function. Apart from the rivalries between possible candidates, the main reason for this failure were disagreements about the priorities to be attained between academic experts like the economist Simon Kuznets on the one hand and political pragmatists closer to the concerns of governments, in particular the U.S. government, on the other hand. While the academic experts insisted on the elaboration of categories and criteria that could stand up to rigorous scientific testing, the pragmatists pushed towards solving the problems of comparability through 'compromise', as one U.S. government delegate put it. What happened, Speich Chassé says, was that the 'science-policy-nexus' changed in the course of the Washington Conferences and in the following years. Despite the protests of the scientists, numerous statistical indicators began to be used for comparative purposes and proliferated in an uncontrolled, incremental way, driven largely by political demands. No recognized global 'centre of calculation' developed after 1945, and until today no such centre exists. Consequently, national governments, nongovernmental organizations (NGOs) and institutions like the World Bank and the International Monetary Fund have to use a plethora of statistical indices from a wide range of sources to produce their comparisons and rankings, with tangible effects for those who are being compared.

It is at this point that the final chapters of this volume by Wendy Espeland and Bettina Heintz take up the thread to explore the origins and portent of rankings in our contemporary world. Drawing on Georg Simmel's sociology of social forms, Espeland interprets rankings as a 'historical, globalized and consequential *specific* symbolic form of social life, one grounded in comparison, hierarchy and exchange', as well as a 'commodity form' that is characteristic for Simmel's (and our own) understanding of the 'tragedy and freedom of modern life'.[68] Referring to Kenneth Burke's *Rhetoric of Motives*, Espeland also underlines the capacity of forms such as rankings to 'channel cognition and emotion in patterned ways' as well as their specific 'dramatism'. It makes sense, she says, to analyse rankings not just with regard to their method that produces 'many layers of commensuration' resulting in 'reductions of reductions of reductions', but also in terms of their rhetoric and aesthetics and even their entertainment value, for instance, the ways in which rankings are graphically visualized to make them look attractive and elegant, if one wishes to fully understand why they have proliferated and become so seductive. On the other hand, she also points to social and political reasons – the expansion of choice in the systems of education and the introduction of neoliberal performance measurement policies – to account for the emergence of rankings in the particular field of higher education. A closer look at the ways in which American law schools or Chinese universities deal with, and try to manipulate, rankings – for example, when they have to decide whether or not to admit students who tend to score less well on standardized tests – then allows her to explain how the 'feedback loop between rankings and effects' functions in practice.[69] The case studies substantiate her point that rankings, despite producing many negative feelings such as anxiety, create an almost irresistible appeal because of their formal qualities.

While most contemporary ranking orders make use of numbers or symbols that are akin to numbers (such as stars), not all rankings are actually based on numbers in the strict sense that any calculating operation has taken place. In fact, as Bettina Heintz stresses in this book's final chapter, many ranking orders rest entirely on qualitative assessments ('connoisseurial reviews').[70] Rankings, Heintz argues, should be seen above all as 'comparative devices'. Thus, not all rankings presuppose commensuration as defined by Wendy Espeland, but comparison is the indispensable foundation and purpose of all ranking orders. The first part of Heintz's chapter contains useful terminological clarifications.[71] Analogies are a less complex operation than comparisons because they produce knowledge by stressing similarities only, not similarities *and* differences. Category-making is a necessary step in comparisons, and new categories may induce new comparisons, but categorization is not itself a complete comparison. The same is true for classifications that may be described as hierarchically organized systems of categories and also for dichotomies that are a special case of classification, and again for asymmetric dichotomies (or counterconcepts in Reinhart Koselleck's sense) that are a special case of a dichotomy. Heintz goes on to distinguish between neutral (nonevaluative) comparisons, evaluative (better/worse) comparisons and progressive comparisons (evaluative comparisons with a temporal index). Statistical tables that merely present the information, but hide the valuation, may be described as neutral comparisons, whereas ranking orders are evaluative comparisons – with or without a temporal index.

On the basis of her terminological clarifications, Heintz briefly reviews the historical development of ranking orders since the eighteenth century to demonstrate that many rankings until today are nothing other than qualitative judgements expressed in a numeral or symbolic form, not valuations based on statistical operations. On the other hand, many early statistics were not transformed into ranking orders. Only by the late nineteenth century was there the appearance of the first truly quantifying ranking orders based on indicators that were counted and compared, and since then, and especially from the 1980s onwards, they have spread all over the world. Still, different forms of ranking orders are to be distinguished. Thus, in ratings, the entities are judged individually and only then compared and assigned to quality classes that are not exclusive: many states may receive a 'triple A'. By contrast, in rankings, the entities are directly compared to each other, and these comparisons are zero-sum games: the rise of the one entails the fall of the other. Both ratings and rankings may rely on qualitative assessments or quantifying procedures – or combine both methods in a sequence of steps. Applying Andrew Abbott's concept of 'fractal distinctions'[72] to supposedly 'qualitative' and 'quantitative' ranking orders, Heintz ends up with a more fine-grained heuristic that shows a continuum of steps and procedures rather than a clear-cut distinction. While the belief in numbers – and their seductive power – may have grown, quantification as a procedure in the strict sense is only present in a much smaller fraction of ranking orders. The suggestiveness of ranking orders, Heintz concludes, does not primarily (and sometimes not at all) reside in quantification, but in their 'promise to tame human subjectivity and to replace it by an objective assessment'. Ranking orders are a device to bridge the gap between the claims for uniqueness and quests for comparability at the same time. They thus deal with a tension that is typical for our own contemporary world, which, according to Bettina Heintz, is no longer just an 'age of comparison', as it was for Friedrich Nietzsche, but an age that glorifies the superlative in which excellence is elevated to a norm for everyone.

## Concluding Remarks: For an Integral History of Conceptualizations and Practices of Comparison

This book wants to give a new impulse for the study of comparisons. It draws together research traditions that hitherto have existed only unconnected to each other: the history of ideas about comparisons; present-day criticism and praise of comparison; the history of competition in various settings and spatial scales; and the history of statistics and rankings. The common thread that binds the overviews and case studies of this volume together is the question as to what people actually do, think, say or show when they compare.[73] The media they use, the emotions they encounter and the purposes they pursue must occupy an important place in that new history of comparative practices as proposed in this volume. Whether comparisons are communicated by means of script, print, verbal acts, bodily performance, visual images, numbers, statistical tables, maps, infographs or interactive websites, and whether they are kept secret or published makes a huge difference. Comparisons may be used to politicize issues, but may also be part of efforts to depoliticize contested problems, for instance, if they appear embedded in technocratic visions.

Apart from the experiences and expectations of the agents, the unintended effects of comparisons – in particular, their apparently irresistible mobilizing force in the last two hundred years of European and world history – need to be investigated. The interplay of competition and comparison has undoubtedly been responsible for much of that dynamism. On the other hand, comparisons can also be brought about by a mere curiosity to know and result in peaceful encounters or even cooperation. The history of comparative practices and conceptualizations of comparison is thus not a linear story of the emergence of one particular kind of comparison, the progressive-competitive variant being the obvious candidate. There were always countermovements to being compared, or at least to being compared in a specific way: claims for uniqueness or absolute incommensurability, radical individualism or fundamentalisms, and more limited contests about the categories or criteria applied.

If there is anything specific about the history of comparisons since the eighteenth century, it seems to be precisely the intensification of such conflicts about the use and misuse, meaningfulness or impertinence, legitimacy or outlawing of particular kinds of comparisons or even comparison in general. The more comparisons have become a key method in the sciences and humanities, the more they have been an object of explicit reflection and sometimes vehement rejection. Since the advent of print and other media of preserving and distributing knowledge, comparisons have been a means to cope with growing amounts of available information by category-making, unit-construction and ordering the world through criteria and standards. On the other hand, it is important not to forget the possibility of a reluctance to compare or the demise of an urge to compare where, formerly, comparison was a frequently used and hotly contested practice. Comparisons may be routinized in such a way that they are no longer recognizable as comparisons, for example, when once explicit comparisons congeal into stereotypes or fixed classifications that are no longer questioned by anyone. The history of the vocabularies of comparison in different languages as well as the history of inconspicuous basic sentences that perform comparisons may be one way to elucidate the changing degrees of reflexivity in the history of comparison. The new history of comparisons as advocated here should therefore be an integral one, combining the history of conceptualizations and practices of comparison.

**Willibald Steinmetz** is Professor of Modern and Contemporary Political History at Bielefeld University. He has published widely on political languages, parliamentary rhetoric and the use of sociopolitical concepts. His current research interests include the history of comparison as a practice in modern and contemporary history. Among his publications in English are three edited collections of essays: *Political Languages in the Age of Extremes* (2nd edn, 2012); *Writing Political History Today* (2013); and *Conceptual History in the European Space* (coedited with M. Freeden and J. Fernández-Sebastián, Berghahn Books, 2017).

## Notes

1. F. Nietzsche, *Human, All Too Human: A Book for Free Spirits* (1878), A. Harvey (trans.) (Chicago: Charles H. Kerr & Co., 1908), 49–50 (number 23 'Age of Comparison').
2. M. Meissner, 'China's Social Credit System: A Big-Data Enabled Approach to Market Regulation with Broad Implication for Doing Business in China', *Mercator Institute for China Studies, China Monitor*, 24 May 2017.
3. M. Ohlberg et al., 'Central Planning, Local Experiments: The Complex Implementation of China's Social Credit System', *Mercator Institute for China Studies, China Monitor*, 12 December 2017.
4. State Council Notice Concerning Issuance of the Planning Outline for the Construction of a Social Credit System (2014–2020), R. Creemers (trans.) (University of Oxford), retrieved 18 February 2019 from https://chinacopyrightandmedia.wordpress.com/2014/06/14/planning-outline-for-the-construction-of-a-social-credit-system-2014-2020.
5. Sir John Fortescue, *On the Laws and Governance of England* (c. 1463–71), S. Lockwood (ed.) (Cambridge: Cambridge University Press, 1997), 29.
6. Ibid., 78.
7. W. Hazlitt, *Table-Talk: Essays on Men and Manners* (1821–22) (London: Henry Frowde, 1905), 141–42.
8. E. Renan, *L'avenir de la science* (1848/1890), quoted and trans. by E.W. Said, *Orientalism* (Harmondsworth: Penguin, 1995), 132.
9. D. Chakrabarty, *Provincialising Europe: Postcolonial Thought and Historical Difference* (Princeton: Princeton University Press, 2000), 9.
10. For an outline of such a research programme, see A. Epple and W. Erhart (eds), *Die Welt beobachten: Praktiken des Vergleichens* (Frankfurt am Main: Campus Verlag, 2015).
11. For a useful overview on debates in sociology, history, anthropology and political science, see G. Steinmetz, 'Comparative History and its Critics: A Genealogy and a Possible Solution', in P. Duara, V. Murthy and A. Sartori (eds), *A Companion to Global Historical Thought* (Chichester: John Wiley & Sons, 2014), 412–36. A variety of positions within the fields of literature and cultural studies is documented in R. Felski and S.S. Friedman (eds), *Comparison: Theories, Approaches, Uses* (Baltimore: Johns Hopkins University Press, 2013).
12. A clear statement of this position is T. Asad, 'The Construction of Religion as an Anthropological Category', in *Genealogies of Religion. Discipline and Reasons of Power in Christianity and Islam* (Baltimore: Johns Hopkins University Press, 1993), 27–54. On the beginnings of comparative religious studies in early modern Europe, see L. Hunt, M. Jacob and W. Mijnhardt (eds), *Bernard Picart and the First Global Vision of Religion* (Los Angeles: Getty Publications, 2010).
13. On the genesis of the 'culture' concept out of comparisons and its feedback effects on comparisons, see N. Luhmann, 'Kultur als historischer Begriff', in *Gesellschaftsstruktur und Semantik*, vol. 4 (Frankfurt am Main: Suhrkamp Verlag, 1993), 31–54.
14. M. Pernau, *Ashraf into Middle Classes: Muslims in Nineteenth-Century Delhi* (New Delhi: Oxford University Press, 2013), esp. xvii–xviii, 43–51, 190–204, 287–95 and 429–34. For an argument against the view that 'Hinduism' was the creation of European interference, see D.N. Lorenzen, *Who Invented Hinduism? Essays on Religion in History* (New Delhi: Yoda Press, 2006), esp. 1–36 (Chapter 1, 'Who Invented Hinduism?').

15. For an extended argument along that line, see G. Steinmetz, 'Odious Comparisons: Incommensurability, the Case Study, and "Small N's" in Sociology', *Sociological Theory* 22 (2004), 371–400.
16. R. Koselleck, 'Three *bürgerliche* Worlds? Preliminary Theoretical-Historical Remarks on the Comparative Semantics of Civil Society in Germany, England, and France', in *The Practice of Conceptual History: Timing History, Spacing Concepts* (Stanford: Stanford University Press, 2002), 208–17, at 217.
17. M. Juneja and M. Pernau, 'Lost in Translation: Transcending Boundaries in Comparative History', in H.-G. Haupt and J. Kocka (eds), *Comparative and Transnational History: Central European Approaches and New Perspectives* (New York: Berghahn Books, 2009), 105–29 (quotations at 114 and 119).
18. W. Steinmetz and M. Freeden, 'Conceptual History: Challenges, Conundrums, Complexities', in W. Steinmetz, M. Freeden and J. Fernández-Sebastián (eds), *Conceptual History in the European Space* (New York: Berghahn Books, 2017), 1–46, at 22–23.
19. See e.g. G.C. Spivak, 'Rethinking Comparativism', in Felski and Friedman, *Comparison*, 253–70; and also her earlier seminal essay: G.C. Spivak, 'Can the Subaltern Speak?', in C. Nelson and L. Grossberg (eds), *Marxism and the Interpretation of Culture* (Urbana: University of Illinois Press, 1988), 271–313.
20. For a discussion of various approaches along that line, see M. Werner and B. Zimmermann, 'Beyond Comparison: *Histoire croisée* and the Challenge of Reflexivity', *History and Theory* 45 (2006), 30–50.
21. Juneja and Pernau, 'Lost in Translation', 118–19.
22. M. Freeden and A. Vincent, 'Introduction: The Study of Comparative Political Thought', in M. Freeden and A. Vincent (eds), *Comparative Political Thought: Theorizing Practices* (London: Routledge, 2013), 1–23, at 13–14.
23. A.L. Stoler, 'Tense and Tender Ties: The Politics of Comparison in North American History and (Post)Colonial Studies', *Journal of American History* 88 (2001), 829–65, at 862–63.
24. See below, Chapter 5. For an explanation of the analytical model, see also A. Epple, 'Doing Comparisons: Ein praxeologischer Zugang zur Geschichte der Globalisierung/en', in Epple and Erhart (eds), *Die Welt beobachten*, 161–99.
25. See below, Chapter 6. For an extended case study see also A. Middleton, 'French Algeria in British Imperial Thought, 1830–1870', *Journal of Colonialism and Colonial History* 16 (2015), n.p.
26. M. Foucault, *The Order of Things: An Archaeology of the Human Sciences* (London: Routledge, 1989), esp. 19–28, 51–64 and 74–76.
27. See below, Chapter 1.
28. M. Eggers, *Vergleichendes Erkennen: Zur Wissenschaftsgeschichte und Epistemologie des Vergleichs und zur Genealogie der Komparatistik* (Heidelberg: Universitätsverlag Winter, 2016).
29. O. Breidbach, 'Analoge Anthropologien: Zur Reanimierung des Mikro-Makrokosmos-Denkens im 19. Jahrhundert', in M. Eggers (ed.), *Von Ähnlichkeiten und Unterschieden: Vergleich, Analogie und Klassifikation in Wissenschaft und Literatur (18./19. Jahrhundert)* (Heidelberg: Universitätsverlag Winter, 2011), 33–55; S. Willer, 'Die Allgemeinheit des Vergleichs: Ein komparatistisches Problem und seine Entstehung um 1800', in Eggers (ed.), *Von Ähnlichkeiten und Unterschieden*, 143–65; D. Griffiths, *The Age of Analogy: Science and Literature between the Darwins* (Baltimore: Johns Hopkins University Press, 2016); Eggers's chapter was finished before Griffith's book came out.

30. For edited collections of the Italian debates in French and German translation, see L. Fallay d'Este (ed.), *Le Paragone : Le parallèle des arts* (Paris: éditions Klincksieck, 1992); O. Bätschmann and T. Weddigen (eds), *Benedetto Varchi: Paragone. Rangstreit der Künste* (Darmstadt: Wissenschaftliche Buchgesellschaft, 2013).
31. For broader discussions of the instances and implications of comparative viewing in art history, other humanities and the sciences, see L. Bader, M. Gaier and F. Wolf (eds), *Vergleichendes Sehen* (Munich: Fink, 2010); M. Bruhn and G. Scholtz (eds), *Der vergleichende Blick: Formanalyse in Natur- und Kulturwissenschaften* (Berlin: Dietrich Reimer Verlag, 2017).
32. See below, Chapter 2.
33. For historical views on competition in various fields, see R. Jessen (ed.), *Konkurrenz in der Geschichte: Praktiken – Werte – Institutionalisierungen* (Frankfurt am Main: Campus Verlag, 2014).
34. The starting point for social-psychological theories of social comparison is L. Festinger, 'A Theory of Social Comparison Processes', *Human Relations* 7 (1954), 117–40; for a more recent summary, see M.B. Brewer, *Intergroup Relations*, 2nd edn (Buckingham: Open University Press, 2003). A historical survey of sociological views on competitive comparison is to be found in F. Nullmeier, *Politische Theorie des Sozialstaats* (Frankfurt am Main: Campus Verlag, 2000). The case of sports is discussed by T. Werron, 'World Sport and its Public: On Historical Relations of Modern Sport and the Media', in U. Wagner, R. Storm and J. Hoberman (eds), *Observing Sport: Modern System Theoretical Approaches* (Schorndorf: Hofmann, 2010), 33–60.
35. See e.g. R.E. Backhouse, 'Competition', in J. Creedy (ed.), *Foundations of Economic Thought* (Oxford: Blackwell Publishers, 1990), 58–86; J. Beckert, 'The Social Order of Markets', *Theory and Society* 38 (2009), 245–69; and see also David Priestland's chapter in this volume, below Chapter 8.
36. See e.g. I. Hont, *Jealousy of Trade: International Competition and the Nation-State in Historical Perspective* (Cambridge, MA: Belknap Press of Harvard University Press, 2005); G.R. Searle, *The Quest for National Efficiency: A Study in British Politics and Political Thought, 1899–1914* (Oxford: Basil Blackwell, 1971); T. Werron, 'What Do Nation States Compete for? A World-Societal Perspective on Competition for "Soft" Global Goods', in B. Holzer, F. Kastner and T. Werron (eds), *From Globalization to World Society: Neo-institutional and Systems-Theoretical Perspectives* (London: Routledge, 2015), 85–106.
37. G. Simmel, *Soziologie: Untersuchungen über die Formen der Vergesellschaftung*, O. Rammstedt (ed.) (Frankfurt am Main: Suhrkamp 1992), 284–382, esp. 323–49.
38. B. Heintz and T. Werron, 'Wie ist Globalisierung möglich? Zur Entstehung globaler Vergleichshorizonte am Beispiel von Wissenschaft und Sport', *Kölner Zeitschrift für Soziologie und Sozialpsychologie* 63 (2011), 359–94; see also T. Werron, 'Universalized Third Parties: The Role of "Scienticized" Observers in the Construction of Global Competition between Nation States', in A. Jansen, A. Franzmann and P. Münte (eds), *Legitimizing Science: National and Global Publics (1800–2010)* (Frankfurt am Main: Campus Verlag, 2016), 307–26.
39. W.N. Espeland and M. Sauder, 'Rankings and Reactivity: How Public Measures Recreate Social Worlds', *American Journal of Sociology* 113 (2007), 1–40; see also S. Kette, 'Prognostische Leistungsvergleiche: Ratings zwischen Performanz und Performativität', in C. Dorn and V. Tacke (eds), *Vergleich und Leistung in der funktional differenzierten Gesellschaft* (Wiesbaden: Springer, 2018), 73–98.
40. See below, Chapters 11 and 12.

41. C.H. Cooley, 'Personal Competition' (1899), in *Sociological Theory and Social Research*, R. Cooley Angell (ed.) (New York: Augustus R. Kelley Publishers, 1969), 163–226, at 165 (emphasis added).
42. Ibid., 167.
43. See below, Chapter 8.
44. For an inspiring historical overview based on that typology, see D. Priestland, *Merchant, Soldier, Sage: A New History of Power* (London: Penguin, 2013).
45. See below, Chapter 3.
46. See Werron, 'What Do Nation States Compete for?'
47. P. Slack, *The Invention of Improvement. Information and Material Progress in Seventeenth-Century England* (Oxford: Oxford University Press, 2015).
48. See below, Chapter 4.
49. See below, Chapter 7.
50. See below, Chapters 6 and 7.
51. T. Roosevelt, State of the Union Address, Part I, 8 December 1908, retrieved 18 February 2019 from http://teachingamericanhistory.org/library/document/state-of-the-union-address-part-i-13; see also Werron, 'What Do Nation States Compete for?'; and D.T. Rodgers, *Atlantic Crossings: Social Politics in a Progressive Age* (Cambridge, MA: Harvard University Press, 2000).
52. See below, Chapter 7.
53. On the limited success of international efforts to standardize statistics before the First World War, see also the chapters by Martin Bemmann and Daniel Speich Chassé in Chapters 9 and 10 in this volume, below.
54. On practices of global comparisons in the ILO, see T. Wobbe, 'Das Globalwerden der Menschenrechte in der ILO: Die Umdeutung von Arbeitsrechten im Kontext weltgesellschaftlicher Strukturprobleme von den 1930er bis 1950er Jahren', in B. Heintz and B. Leisering (eds), *Menschenrechte in der Weltgesellschaft: Deutungswandel und Wirkungsweise eines globalen Leitwerts* (Frankfurt am Main: Campus Verlag, 2015), 283–316.
55. See below, Chapter 7; see also C. Conrad, 'Wohlfahrtsstaaten im Vergleich: Historische und sozialwissenschaftliche Ansätze', in H.-G. Haupt and J. Kocka (eds), *Ansätze und Ergebnisse international vergleichender Geschichtsschreibung* (Frankfurt am Main: Campus Verlag, 1996), 155–80.
56. P. Kettunen and K. Petersen, 'Introduction: Rethinking Welfare State Models', in P. Kettunen and K. Petersen, *Beyond Welfare State Models: Transnational Historical Perspectives on Social Policy* (Cheltenham: Edward Elgar, 2011), 1–15, at 2.
57. The term 'iconic difference' was coined by Gottfried Boehm; see G. Boehm, 'Ikonische Differenz', *Rheinsprung 11 – Zeitschrift für Bildkritik* 1 (2011), 171–76, retrieved 19 February 2019 from https://rheinsprung11.unibas.ch/fileadmin/documents/Edition_PDF/Ausgabe1/glossar-boehm.pdf.
58. B. Heintz, 'Numerische Differenz: Überlegungen zu einer Soziologie des (quantitativen) Vergleichs', *Zeitschrift für Soziologie* 39 (2010), 162–81.
59. W.N. Espeland and M. Stevens, 'Commensuration as a Social Process', *Annual Review of Sociology* 24 (1998), 312–43, at 314; see also W.N. Espeland and M. Stevens, 'A Sociology of Quantification', *European Journal of Sociology* 49 (2008), 401–36, esp. 408.
60. Heintz, 'Numerische Differenz', 175–8.
61. See also M. Poovey, *A History of the Modern Fact: Problems of Knowledge in the Sciences of Wealth and Society* (Chicago: University of Chicago Press, 1998).

62. T. Porter, *Trust in Numbers: The Pursuit of Objectivity in Science and Public Life* (Princeton: Princeton University Press, 1995); A. Desrosières, *La politique des grands nombres : Histoire de la raison statistique* (Paris: La Découverte, 1993).
63. A. Tooze, *Statistics and the German State, 1900–1945* (Cambridge: Cambridge University Press, 2001); K. Brückweh, *Menschen zählen: Wissensproduktion durch britische Volkszählungen und Umfragen vom 19. Jahrhundert bis ins digitale Zeitalter* (Berlin: De Gruyter Oldenbourg, 2015); B. Zimmermann, 'Semantiken der Nicht-Arbeit an der Wende vom 19. zum 20. Jahrhundert: "Arbeitslosigkeit" und "chômage" im Vergleich', in J. Leonhard and W. Steinmetz (eds), *Semantiken von Arbeit: Diachrone und vergleichende Perspektiven* (Cologne: Böhlau, 2016), 269–88.
64. D. Speich Chassé, *Die Erfindung des Bruttosozialprodukts: Globale Ungleichheit in der Wissensgeschichte der Ökonomie* (Göttingen: Vandenhoeck & Ruprecht, 2013).
65. L. Behrisch, *Die Berechnung der Glückseligkeit: Statistik und Politik in Deutschland und Frankreich im späten Ancien Régime* (Ostfildern: Thorbecke Verlag, 2016).
66. See below, Chapter 9.
67. See below, Chapter 10.
68. See below, Chapter 11.
69. See also W.N. Espeland and M. Sauder, *Engines of Anxiety: Academic Rankings, Reputation, and Accountability* (New York: Russell Sage Foundation, 2016); for a historical view on the changing forms of competition, including rankings, between universities in nineteenth and twentieth-century Germany, see M. Szöllösi-Janze, '"Eine Art *pole position* im Kampf um die Futtertröge": Thesen zum Wettbewerb zwischen Universitäten im 19. und 20. Jahrhundert', in Jessen (ed.), *Konkurrenz in der Geschichte*, 317–51.
70. See below, Chapter 12.
71. See also B. Heintz, '"Wir leben im Zeitalter der Vergleichung": Perspektiven einer Soziologie des Vergleichs', *Zeitschrift für Soziologie* 45 (2016), 305–23.
72. A. Abbott, *Chaos of Disciplines* (Chicago: University of Chicago Press, 2001).
73. This introduction and chapters 2 (Grave), 3 (Steinmetz) and 5 (Epple) have been written within the framework of the Collaborative Research Centre (SFB 1288) 'Practices of Comparing: Ordering and Changing the World' at Bielefeld University, funded by the German Research Foundation (DFG).

# Bibliography

Abbott, A., *Chaos of Disciplines* (Chicago: University of Chicago Press, 2001).
Asad, T., 'The Construction of Religion as an Anthropological Category', in *Genealogies of Religion: Discipline and Reasons of Power in Christianity and Islam* (Baltimore: Johns Hopkins University Press, 1993), 27–54.
Backhouse, R.E., 'Competition', in Creedy, J. (ed.), *Foundations of Economic Thought* (Oxford: Blackwell, 1990), 58–86.
Bader, L., Gaier, M. and Wolf, F. (eds), *Vergleichendes Sehen* (Munich: Fink, 2010).
Bätschmann, O., and Weddigen, T. (eds), *Benedetto Varchi: Paragone. Rangstreit der Künste* (Darmstadt: Wissenschaftliche Buchgesellschaft, 2013).
Beckert, J., 'The Social Order of Markets', *Theory and Society* 38 (2009), 245–69.
Behrisch, L., *Die Berechnung der Glückseligkeit: Statistik und Politik in Deutschland und Frankreich im späten Ancien Régime* (Ostfildern: Thorbecke Verlag, 2016).

Boehm, G., 'Ikonische Differenz', *Rheinsprung 11 – Zeitschrift für Bildkritik* 1 (2011), 171–76, retrieved 18 February 2019 from https://rheinsprung11.unibas.ch/fileadmin/documents/Edition_PDF/Ausgabe1/glossar-boehm.pdf.

Breidbach, O., 'Analoge Anthropologien: Zur Reanimierung des Mikro-Makrokosmos-Denkens im 19. Jahrhundert', in Eggers, M. (ed.), *Von Ähnlichkeiten und Unterschieden. Vergleich, Analogie und Klassifikation in Wissenschaft und Literatur (18./19. Jahrhundert)* (Heidelberg: Universitätsverlag Winter, 2011), 33–55.

Brewer, M.B., *Intergroup Relations*, 2nd edn (Buckingham: Open University Press, 2003).

Brückweh, K., *Menschen zählen: Wissensproduktion durch britische Volkszählungen und Umfragen vom 19. Jahrhundert bis ins digitale Zeitalter* (Berlin: De Gruyter Oldenbourg, 2015).

Bruhn, M., and Scholtz, G. (eds), *Der vergleichende Blick: Formanalyse in Natur- und Kulturwissenschaften* (Berlin: Dietrich Reimer Verlag, 2017).

Chakrabarty, D., *Provincialising Europe: Postcolonial Thought and Historical Difference* (Princeton: Princeton University Press, 2000).

Conrad, C., 'Wohlfahrtsstaaten im Vergleich: Historische und sozialwissenschaftliche Ansätze', in Haupt, H.-G. and Kocka, J. (eds), *Ansätze und Ergebnisse international vergleichender Geschichtsschreibung* (Frankfurt am Main: Campus Verlag, 1996), 155–80.

Cooley, C.H., 'Personal Competition' (1899), in *Sociological Theory and Social Research*, Cooley Angell, R. (ed.) (New York: Augustus R. Kelley Publishers, 1969), 163–226.

Desrosières, A., *La politique des grands nombres : Histoire de la raison statistique* (Paris: La Découverte, 1993).

Eggers, M., *Vergleichendes Erkennen: Zur Wissenschaftsgeschichte und Epistemologie des Vergleichs und zur Genealogie der Komparatistik* (Heidelberg: Universitätsverlag Winter, 2016).

Epple, A., 'Doing Comparisons: Ein praxeologischer Zugang zur Geschichte der Globalisierung/en', in Epple, A. and Erhart, W. (eds), *Die Welt beobachten: Praktiken des Vergleichens* (Frankfurt am Main: Campus Verlag, 2015), 161–99.

Epple, A., and Erhart, W. (eds), *Die Welt beobachten: Praktiken des Vergleichens* (Frankfurt am Main: Campus Verlag, 2015).

Espeland, W.N. and Sauder, M., 'Rankings and Reactivity: How Public Measures Recreate Social Worlds', *American Journal of Sociology* 113 (2007), 1–40.

Espeland, W.N., and Stevens, M., 'Commensuration as a Social Process', *Annual Review of Sociology* 24 (1998), 312–43.

———. 'A Sociology of Quantification', *European Journal of Sociology* 49 (2008), 401–36.

———. *Engines of Anxiety: Academic Rankings, Reputation, and Accountability* (New York: Russell Sage Foundation, 2016).

Fallay d'Este, L. (ed.), *Le Paragone: Le parallèle des arts* (Paris: éditions Klincksieck, 1992).

Felski, R., and Friedman, S.S. (eds), *Comparison: Theories, Approaches, Uses* (Baltimore: Johns Hopkins University Press, 2013).

Festinger, L., 'A Theory of Social Comparison Processes', *Human Relations* 7 (1954), 117–40.

Fortescue, Sir J., *On the Laws and Governance of England* (c. 1463–71), Lockwood, S. (ed.) (Cambridge: Cambridge University Press, 1997).

Foucault, M., *The Order of Things: An Archaeology of the Human Sciences* (London: Routledge, 1989).

Freeden, M., and Vincent, A., 'Introduction: The Study of Comparative Political Thought', in Freeden, M. and Vincent, A. (eds), *Comparative Political Thought: Theorizing Practices* (London: Routledge, 2013), 1–23.

Griffiths, D., *The Age of Analogy: Science and Literature between the Darwins* (Baltimore: Johns Hopkins University Press, 2016).

Hazlitt, W., *Table-Talk: Essays on Men and Manners* (1821–22) (London: Henry Frowde, 1905)
Heintz, B., 'Numerische Differenz: Überlegungen zu einer Soziologie des (quantitativen) Vergleichs', *Zeitschrift für Soziologie* 39 (2010), 162–81.
———. '"Wir leben im Zeitalter der Vergleichung": Perspektiven einer Soziologie des Vergleichs', *Zeitschrift für Soziologie* 45 (2016), 305–23.
Heintz, B., and Werron, T., 'Wie ist Globalisierung möglich? Zur Entstehung globaler Vergleichshorizonte am Beispiel von Wissenschaft und Sport', *Kölner Zeitschrift für Soziologie und Sozialpsychologie* 63 (2011), 359–94.
Hont, I., *Jealousy of Trade: International Competition and the Nation-State in Historical Perspective* (Cambridge, MA: Belknap Press of Harvard University Press, 2005).
Hunt, L., Jacob, M. and Mijnhardt, W. (eds), *Bernard Picart and the First Global Vision of Religion* (Los Angeles: Getty Publications, 2010).
Jessen, R. (ed.), *Konkurrenz in der Geschichte: Praktiken – Werte – Institutionalisierungen* (Frankfurt am Main: Campus Verlag, 2014).
Juneja, M., and Pernau, M., 'Lost in Translation: Transcending Boundaries in Comparative History', in Haupt, H.-G. and Kocka, J. (eds), *Comparative and Transnational History: Central European Approaches and New Perspectives* (New York: Berghahn Books, 2009), 105–29.
Kette, S., 'Prognostische Leistungsvergleiche: Ratings zwischen Performanz und Performativität', in Dorn, C. and Tacke, V. (eds), *Vergleich und Leistung in der funktional differenzierten Gesellschaft* (Wiesbaden: Springer, 2018), 73–98.
Kettunen, P., and Petersen, K., 'Introduction: Rethinking Welfare State Models', in P. Kettunen and K. Petersen, *Beyond Welfare State Models: Transnational Historical Perspectives on Social Policy* (Cheltenham: Edward Elgar, 2011), 1–15.
Koselleck, R., 'Three *Bürgerliche* Worlds? Preliminary Theoretical-Historical Remarks on the Comparative Semantics of Civil Society in Germany, England, and France', in *The Practice of Conceptual History: Timing History, Spacing Concepts* (Stanford: Stanford University Press, 2002), 208–17.
Lorenzen, D.N., *Who Invented Hinduism? Essays on Religion in History* (New Delhi: Yoda Press, 2006).
Luhmann, N., 'Kultur als historischer Begriff', in *Gesellschaftsstruktur und Semantik*, vol. 4 (Frankfurt am Main: Suhrkamp Verlag, 1993), 31–54.
Meissner, M., 'China's Social Credit System: A Big-Data Enabled Approach to Market Regulation with Broad Implication for Doing Business in China', *Mercator Institute for China Studies, China Monitor*, 24 May 2017.
Middleton, A., 'French Algeria in British Imperial Thought, 1830–1870', *Journal of Colonialism and Colonial History* 16 (2015), n.p.
Nietzsche, F., *Human, All Too Human: A Book for Free Spirits* (1878), Harvey, A. (trans.) (Chicago: Charles H. Kerr & Co., 1908).
Nullmeier, F., *Politische Theorie des Sozialstaats* (Frankfurt am Main: Campus Verlag, 2000).
Ohlberg, M. et al., 'Central Planning, Local Experiments: The Complex Implementation of China's Social Credit System', *Mercator Institute for China Studies, China Monitor*, 12 December 2017.
Pernau, M., *Ashraf into Middle Classes: Muslims in Nineteenth-Century Delhi* (New Delhi: Oxford University Press, 2013).
Poovey, M., *A History of the Modern Fact: Problems of Knowledge in the Sciences of Wealth and Society* (Chicago: University of Chicago Press, 1998).

Porter, T., *Trust in Numbers: The Pursuit of Objectivity in Science and Public Life* (Princeton: Princeton University Press, 1995).
Priestland, D., *Merchant, Soldier, Sage: A New History of Power* (London, Penguin Books, 2013).
Rodgers, D.T., *Atlantic Crossings: Social Politics in a Progressive Age* (Cambridge, MA: Harvard University Press, 2000).
Roosevelt, T., State of the Union Address, Part I, 8 December 1908, retrieved 18 February 2019 from http://teachingamericanhistory.org/library/document/state-of-the-union-address-part-i-13.
Said, E.W., *Orientalism* (Harmondsworth: Penguin, 1995).
Searle, G.R., *The Quest for National Efficiency: A Study in British Politics and Political Thought, 1899–1914* (Oxford: Basil Blackwell, 1971).
Simmel, G., *Soziologie: Untersuchungen über die Formen der Vergesellschaftung*, Rammstedt, O. (ed.) (Frankfurt am Main: Suhrkamp 1992).
Slack, P., *The Invention of Improvement: Information and Material Progress in Seventeenth-Century England* (Oxford: Oxford University Press, 2015).
Speich Chassé, D., *Die Erfindung des Bruttosozialprodukts: Globale Ungleichheit in der Wissensgeschichte der Ökonomie* (Göttingen: Vandenhoeck & Ruprecht, 2013).
Spivak, G.C., 'Can the Subaltern Speak?', in Nelson, C. and Grossberg, L. (eds), *Marxism and the Interpretation of Culture* (Urbana: University of Illinois Press, 1988), 271–313.
———. 'Rethinking Comparativism', in Felski, R. and Friedman, S.S. (eds), *Comparison: Theories, Approaches, Uses* (Baltimore: Johns Hopkins University Press, 2013), 253–70.
State Council Notice Concerning Issuance of the Planning Outline for the Construction of a Social Credit System (2014–2020), Creemers, R. (trans.) (University of Oxford), retrieved 18 February 2019 from https://chinacopyrightandmedia.wordpress.com/2014/06/14/planning-outline-for-the-construction-of-a-social-credit-system-2014-2020.
Steinmetz, G., 'Odious Comparisons: Incommensurability, the Case Study, and "Small N's" in Sociology', *Sociological Theory* 22 (2004), 371–400.
———. 'Comparative History and its Critics: A Genealogy and a Possible Solution', in Duara, P., Murthy, V. and Sartori, A. (eds), *A Companion to Global Historical Thought* (Chichester: John Wiley & Sons, 2014), 412–36.
Steinmetz, W., and Freeden, M., 'Conceptual History: Challenges, Conundrums, Complexities', in Steinmetz, W., Freeden, M. and Fernández-Sebastián, J. (eds), *Conceptual History in the European Space* (New York: Berghahn Books, 2017), 1–46.
Stoler, A.L., 'Tense and Tender Ties: The Politics of Comparison in North American History and (Post)Colonial Studies', *Journal of American History* 88 (2001), 829–65.
Szöllösi-Janze, M., '"Eine Art *pole position* im Kampf um die Futtertröge": Thesen zum Wettbewerb zwischen Universitäten im 19. und 20. Jahrhundert', in Jessen, R. (ed.), *Konkurrenz in der Geschichte: Praktiken – Werte – Institutionalisierungen* (Frankfurt am Main: Campus Verlag, 2014), 317–51.
Tooze, A., *Statistics and the German State, 1900–1945* (Cambridge: Cambridge University Press, 2001).
Werner, M., and Zimmermann, B., 'Beyond Comparison: *Histoire croisée* and the Challenge of Reflexivity', *History and Theory* 45 (2006), 30–50.
Werron, T., 'World Sport and its Public: On Historical Relations of Modern Sport and the Media', in Wagner, U., Storm, R. and Hoberman, J. (eds), *Observing Sport: Modern System Theoretical Approaches* (Schorndorf: Hofmann, 2010), 33–60.

———. 'What Do Nation States Compete for? A World-Societal Perspective on Competition for "Soft" Global Goods', in Holzer, B., Kastner, F. and Werron, T. (eds), *From Globalization to World Society: Neo-institutional and Systems-Theoretical Perspectives* (London: Routledge, 2015), 85–106.

———. 'Universalized Third Parties: The Role of "Scienticized" Observers in the Construction of Global Competition between Nation States', in Jansen, A., Franzmann, A. and Münte, P. (eds), *Legitimizing Science: National and Global Publics (1800–2010)* (Frankfurt am Main: Campus Verlag, 2016), 307–26.

Willer, S., 'Die Allgemeinheit des Vergleichs: Ein komparatistisches Problem und seine Entstehung um 1800', in Eggers, M. (ed.), *Von Ähnlichkeiten und Unterschieden: Vergleich, Analogie und Klassifikation in Wissenschaft und Literatur (18./19. Jahrhundert)* (Heidelberg: Universitätsverlag Winter, 2011), 143–65.

Wobbe, T., 'Das Globalwerden der Menschenrechte in der ILO: Die Umdeutung von Arbeitsrechten im Kontext weltgesellschaftlicher Strukturprobleme von den 1930er bis 1950er Jahren', in Heintz, B. and Leisering, B. (eds), *Menschenrechte in der Weltgesellschaft: Deutungswandel und Wirkungsweise eines globalen Leitwerts* (Frankfurt am Main: Campus Verlag, 2015), 283–316.

Zimmermann, B., 'Semantiken der Nicht-Arbeit an der Wende vom 19. zum 20. Jahrhundert: "Arbeitslosigkeit" und "chômage" im Vergleich', in Leonhard, J. and Steinmetz, W. (eds), *Semantiken von Arbeit: Diachrone und vergleichende Perspektiven* (Cologne: Böhlau, 2016), 269–88.

# 1
# Outlines of a Historical Epistemology of Comparison

*From Descartes to the Early Nineteenth Century*

Michael Eggers

The mental act of comparison must count as one of the most basic intellectual operations. It is an act we cannot avoid performing when trying to cope with our everyday experience. Since antiquity, comparison has been dealt with as one of the key movements of thought and method, in philosophy as well as in the sciences. However, it is precisely this elementary function of comparison that makes it difficult to analyse its variable forms and appearances through time and space. How can we adequately conceptualize and historicize something that is so ubiquitous and so inevitable? Something that is constantly being applied in everyday life as well as the sciences, be it deliberately, subconsciously or simply by habit? For just as obvious as comparison's generality are its differences in form and purpose. The history of philosophical thought and of scientific method, which I will scrutinize in this chapter, offers ample evidence: it is not the same when Carl Linnaeus compares the reproductive organs of two flowers in order to classify them, when Alexander Gottlieb Baumgarten compares the rhetorical effect of two poetic phrases or when Étienne Bonnot de Condillac describes the comparison of the first sensory perceptions of a human being as the origin of thought. To notice the existence of such differences may be the first step towards escaping the conceptual dilemma. Starting from the differences, we can identify important historical types of comparison and specify their use with respect to particular contexts. As a result, it should be possible to sketch a historical epistemology of comparative models that inform the beginnings of the modern system of academic disciplines and that shape our understanding of scientific thought.[1]

Why 'historical epistemology'? On the one hand, my approach is a *historical* one, because all comparisons discussed in this chapter refer to comparative acts defined or performed in philosophical, historical or scientific texts *of the past*. On the other hand, my approach is an *epistemological* one, referring both to the English sense and the French sense of the word 'epistemological'. The most prominent methodological conceptions of comparison have been elaborated within the context of theories of the acquisition and organization of knowledge, and continue to be part of what is called *Erkenntnistheorie* in German or epistemology in English. I refer to the French concept of épistémologie at the same time, because it allows us to point out qualities of comparison shared by several scientific branches or registers of knowledge, notwithstanding their apparent diversity. What comes into view are structures of knowledge that apply across disciplinary boundaries of academic fields at specific points in time. A discursive archaeology of comparison of this kind becomes comparative in itself.[2]

To delimit the material at hand, I only consider comparisons that have the theoretical capacity to constitute their respective fields of knowledge. In other words, the focus is on theoretical knowledge that, at specific points in time, counts as reliable because it has been brought about by comparative measures. In many of these cases, authors expressly declare that they use comparative methods, but in other cases they do not, even if the method in question does depend on comparison. In addition to these positive instances, the negative side, i.e. those opinions that remain sceptical towards or openly criticize comparative procedures, should not be neglected. Scepticism or reluctance turns out to be an important element that opposes, but also testifies to, the temporary dominance of comparison. We will cover the historical period beginning with the early Enlightenment and ending in the decades around 1800.

## Comparison vs. Analogy

Following Michel Foucault, the most prominent thinker of an épistémologie à la française, I take René Descartes as a starting point. Foucault claims that the Cartesian philosophy marks a shift in Western thinking because it treats comparison as the most reliable method that we can use to establish truths about the world. According to Descartes, everything we may securely know either comes to us by intuition or must be calculated by our mind by means of comparison. With his theoretical efforts, he aims at a universal science of which the mathematical method is the privileged form and comparison the essential tool. In his *Regulae ad directionem ingenii* (*Rules for the Direction of the Mind*, 1628), he describes what Foucault identifies as a signal for the end of the age of analogy that had prevailed up to this point, giving human conceptions of the world the shape of a network of similarities.[3] By contrast, Descartes proposes that every problem the mind wants to solve should be reduced to simple equations, referring to one common quality. This quality serves as a *tertium comparationis* and must be determined beforehand by means of abstraction. 'This common idea is carried over from one subject to the other solely by means of a simple comparison, which enables us to state that the thing we are seeking is in this or that respect similar to, or identical with, or equal to, some given thing. Accordingly, in all reasoning, it is only by means of comparison that we attain an exact knowledge of the truth.'[4]

A close reading of Descartes' essay would be necessary to verify Foucault's account and to explain in detail how Descartes conceived the process of abstraction that leads up to comparison.[5] Assuming that Foucault is right in pointing out the epochal significance of the method of mathematical comparison that starts from here, we should still be careful about declaring Descartes *the* founder of modern scientific thought, all the more so since Foucault himself always refused to attribute historical inventions to single authors.[6] Furthermore, it should be noted, as André Rudolph, Claus Zittel and Peter Galison have also shown,[7] that Foucault very much underestimates the enduring persistence of analogy, not only in Descartes' writings, but throughout the seventeenth and eighteenth centuries in general.

As Galison has pointed out, Descartes' position is contradictory. On the one hand, he stresses the importance of the faculty of imagination that assists the mind whenever it sets out to acquire knowledge. Thus, Rule Number Twelve claims: 'It is of course only the intellect that is capable of perceiving the truth, but it has to be assisted by imagination, sense perception and memory.'[8] On the other hand, in his *Principles of Philosophy* (1644), where Descartes makes the well-known definitions of clear and distinct (*clare et distincte*) knowledge, he warns us not to let deceptive similarities mislead us, e.g. when we imagine a specific object to be the cause of an acute bodily pain even if we are unable to actually determine, by vision or touch, what triggers the sensation. Reliable knowledge, Descartes says, should be based on evidence, and the most evident facts are mathematical ones that have to do with facts like proportions of size. But this restriction, which certainly is still in accordance with contemporary scientific beliefs, does not prevent him from making use of analogies himself in order to prove assumptions that cannot be demonstrated and perceived with the senses, as when he explains his theory that the world is composed of invisible, minute particles. According to his mechanistic worldview, sequences of physical movement of visible objects, which may also be repeated experimentally, can serve as models for analogous events, even if the latter are located *within* bodies or if they are of an immensely smaller scale. In Descartes' own words:

> No one who uses his reason will, I think, deny the advantage of using what happens in large bodies, as perceived by our senses, as a model [exemplum] for our ideas about what happens in tiny bodies which elude our senses merely because of their small size. This is much better than explaining matters by inventing all sorts of strange objects which have no resemblance to what is perceived by the senses.[9]

Here, Descartes propagates the very modes of proof and demonstration, i.e. analogy and sense perception, that he had suspected of yielding false evidence earlier in his *Rules*. In general, he claims that convincing truths have to be evident, like simple mathematical facts that we can comprehend by intuition and without further reasoning. But here those truths serve as a basis for speculative, analogical comparisons. Notwithstanding his modernizing project of doubt and methodical reflection, Descartes still invokes the age-old idea of a correspondence of microcosm and macrocosm.[10] While he praises the significance of mathematical comparisons, he still constructs analogies by making use of the same faculty of imagination that he treats quite sceptically in his *Rules*. With these contradictions in mind, it becomes difficult to distinguish neatly between mathematical comparisons on the one hand and analogies that remain within the realm of imagination on the other hand.

The history of the concepts of 'comparison' and 'analogy' during the following two centuries shows that they function both as antagonistic models of knowledge and as complements that need each other in order to distinguish themselves as coherent methods.[11] In some cases, as in Descartes, there is no clear-cut terminological differentiation, and sometimes what is called 'comparison' turns out to be an analogy on closer inspection. However, there can be no doubt that, when it comes to questions of evident knowledge, a preference for comparison and a devaluation of analogy dominate Enlightenment philosophy. John Locke unmistakably lists the advantages of judgement, which he defines as the capability to carefully separate one idea from another and thus 'to avoid being misled by Similitude, and by affinity to take one thing for another'.[12] Knowledge, according to his *Essay Concerning Human Understanding* (1690), is based on simple ideas that the mind intuitively and doubtlessly identifies, such as the basic colours or geometrical shapes, whether they be actually perceived by the senses or just in imagination:

> Some of the *Ideas* that are in the Mind, are so there, that they can be, by themselves, immediately compared, one with another: And in these, the mind is able to perceive, that they agree or disagree, as clearly, as that it has them ... And this, therefore, as has been said, I call *Intuitive Knowledge*; which is certain, beyond all Doubt, and needs no Probation, nor can have any; this being the highest of all Humane Certainty.[13]

Again, we have a theory of knowledge built on intuition and comparison that treats the latter as the decisive mental act that constitutes this kind of knowledge. Discussing the different degrees of evidence, Locke describes the immediately perceptible difference between, e.g. white and black or between a circle and a triangle as the 'the clearest and most certain [kind of knowledge] that human frailty is capable of'.[14] The results of such comparisons should even be rated higher than the evidence of a *single* idea being perceived or brought to mind. For Locke, similarity counts as deceptive; analogies, which we can treat as the epistemological instruments that rely on similarity, may be helpful in certain cases, but do not attain the same degree of evidence.[15] Locke's attitude towards figurative language is well known and mirrors his distrust of similarity. Rhetorical figures of speech like metaphors, which Aristotle defines as analogies,[16] embellish our speech and entertain us, but they 'indeed are perfect cheat' because, he says, they 'insinuate wrong *Ideas*, move the Passions, and thereby mislead the Judgment'.[17]

## Empirical and Logical Comparisons

In the course of the eighteenth century, modern historical and developmental thinking was beginning to take hold, and natural phenomena too were increasingly regarded on a temporal scale. There is no need here to decide whether Wolf Lepenies is right to suggest that the rising tendency to explain things historically was a reaction to the modern growth of empirical knowledge.[18] Undoubtedly, however, the eighteenth century saw tendencies of temporalization emerging in many disciplines and at various levels. In philosophy, authors like Jean-Jacques Rousseau or Étienne Bonnot de Condillac tried to understand their subject matter by reconstructing its historical development. Long before Nietzsche and Foucault, who used genealogical derivations to question established cultural beliefs and social institutions, they began to speculate about origins to shed new light on seemingly well-known phenomena.

Just like Descartes and Locke, Condillac aimed at understanding human thought. He conceived mental activity to rest on primary physical sensations that serve as the basis of and the material for our understanding of the world and ourselves. Without sensations, there would be no attention of the mind and no thought. Every sensation, Condillac claims, creates a perception in the mind that we are able to remember. As memories, these perceptions serve as signs that refer back to the original sensations. The emergence of the second perception that follows a physical sensation is a key moment in Condillac's theory of knowledge, because from that point on, each subject is mentally active. While the first perception is a merely passive consequence of human physical receptiveness, the subject now operates actively with mental material: it compares. It experiences its sensations as being comfortable to a greater or lesser extent and, having experienced more than one sensation, spontaneously begins to weigh them in order to find out which one better meets his needs. This is the onset of the capacity of comparison and judgement, or, to use another word for the same activity, reflexion. Condillac puts it simply and unmistakably: 'When there is comparison, there is judgment.'[19] Within the history of comparison as a method, Condillac's sensualist position is significant because here comparison becomes one of the activities that constitute subjectivity. Many philosophers of the eighteenth century elaborate on the antique psychology of faculties, adding numerous mental faculties to those already specified by Aristotle himself. For

Condillac, they all emerge from, or are triggered by, physical sensation, and comparing is one of them.[20]

The fact that philosophers like Locke and Condillac stressed the importance of sense data for any and all knowledge correlates with a growing prominence of empirical research within natural history at the same time. The publication history of Carl Linnaeus' epochal *Systema Naturae* runs from its first edition in 1735 to the twelfth in 1768 (considering only those editions of which Linnaeus himself is the sole author). The systems of objects that natural historians like Linnaeus conceived obviously relied on comparison as a crucial method. Within such a system, each object – animals, plants or minerals – is classified according to its specific identifying character, following the pattern of *genus proximum et differentias specificas*.[21] For plants, Linnaeus defined the twenty-six parts of fructification as those characteristics that help to identify any species by comparison. Scientific methods that aim at classificatory systems like these need comparison as their most important tool, whether or not they constitute strictly logical systems or diverse classifications and arrangements.[22] Empiricism and sensualism can count as philosophical positions that fostered the kind of empirical research that natural historians undertook during the eighteenth century, leading to the emergence of a whole range of new scientific disciplines. The rational significance that comparison gained on the philosophical level corresponded to its methodical implementation in empirical disciplines and its application to specific features of natural objects. Towards the end of the eighteenth century, empirical research worked independently of the kind of metaphysical superstructure that had always been part of natural history before.

A multitalented philosopher like Johann Heinrich Lambert, who, in addition to his philosophical writings, undertook mathematical, cosmological, physical and technological research, combined empirical methods and rationalist philosophy to create an epistemological perspectivism, based on the idea that we have to compare each optical or semiotic representation with the truth of things to become aware of our limited human perception. According to Lambert, our visual images of things are no more real than the words we use to describe them. He regards both as signs that have to be transcended. Whether it is his cosmological view of the planetary system,[23] his optical and phenomenological theory about our limited perception of the world or his complex system of propositional logic,[24] he always assumes that comparative steps have to be taken to advance our knowledge: comparisons of perspective, of concrete words, abstract words and metaphors, of appearances and their causes. In spite of the fact that – or maybe just because? – Lambert shares a fundamental epistemological scepticism with Kant, he has unjustly fallen into oblivion in favour of his colleague from Königsberg, with whom he was in correspondence.[25] Apart from his multifaceted contribution to a comprehensive comparative epistemology, his achievements are the establishment of semiotics as well as of phenomenology as disciplines.[26]

## The Limits of Comparison

In philosophy, the 1750s must count as the height of comparative thinking. The fact that, in the same decade, an important strand of scepticism towards comparison sets in is further evidence of this high tide. Contemporaneously with Condillac, and on his part testifying to the trend of temporalization, Rousseau publishes his highly influential philosophical essays. In his history of human development, the early natural state or condition, which is a state of absolute happiness, comes to an end when human beings begin to make use of their capacity to reflect. In his *Essay on the Origin of Languages* (1753), Rousseau, just like Condillac,[27] describes the emergence of signs and emphasizes the importance of comparison for this landmark in cultural evolution:

> Reflection is born of compared ideas, and it is the multiplicity of ideas that leads to their comparison. He who sees only a single object has no comparison to make. He who sees from his childhood only a small number and always the same ones still does not compare them, because the habit of seeing them deprives him of the attention needed to examine them; but as a new object strikes us, we want to know it; it is in this way that we learn to consider what is before our eyes, and how what is foreign to us leads us to examine what touches us.[28]

Only when men and women have to deal with many things at once and when they reconsider those things that they have met with before do they begin to compare them among each other. This is, in Rousseau's story, the point at which the need of words and languages arises. When, in his *Discourse on the Origin and Foundation of the Inequality among Mankind* (1755), he brings to bear these ideas to explain the emergence of social structures, it becomes clear that this is also the point when the first state of happiness that humanity experienced in its beginnings must end. When individuals begin to compare each other, themselves with each other and their own belongings with those of others, they start to construct social rank orders and single out qualities that some have and others do not have. It is the beginning of social inequality, of envy and jealousy, all resulting from the transformation of the feelings of *amour de soi*, which Rousseau defines as a subject's completely natural feeling of estimation for the own self, into the socially induced *amour-propre*: the kind of self-love that is aroused by vanity and pride. 'Men begin to consider different Objects, and to make Comparisons; they insensibly acquire Ideas of Merit and Beauty, and these soon produce Sentiments of Preference.'[29] Rousseau leaves no doubt that *amour-propre*, as a 'Sentiment arising from Comparisons',[30] is the source of social corruption and moral decadence. Whereas epistemological philosophers of the Enlightenment period valorize comparison as an important part of rational thought, Rousseau takes a negative stand and blames the human mental disposition to compare for the social and cultural decline of modernity.

Yet, it is the philosophical discipline of aesthetics that after its invention in the 1750s much more enduringly questioned and eroded the strong position of comparison. Whereas rationalistic philosophy had emphasized the significance of reason for all human efforts to conceptualize and explain the world, Alexander Gottlieb Baumgarten turned to the realm below the 'clear and distinct', defined by Descartes as the epistemological norm. In the two volumes of his *Aesthetica* from 1750/1758, Baumgarten concentrates on what he describes as sensuous thought, a capacity to complement reason by indistinct and confused (*confusus*) knowledge. He calls this capacity *ars analogi rationis*, the art of thinking analogous to reason.[31] This is the philosophical foundation of aesthetics as an affective and, as Baumgarten's *Aesthetica* demonstrates elaborately, rhetorical mode of cognition below rationalization and calculation. Aesthetic thought, as conceptualized by Baumgarten, is a mode of perception in its own right, even if strictly analogous to reason. As a new and necessary complement to logics, it appears in Baumgarten's writings for the first time. Nevertheless, its goal remains to achieve knowledge, but the quality of such knowledge can no longer be measured according to its clearness and distinctness. It has to be aesthetically – that is to say, affectively – evident. Its model is rhetoric and poetry, it deals with the sensations and affections that are aroused by the literary examples of the old Latin poets, i.e. by artistic language.[32] The fact that Baumgarten has constructed the *Aesthetica* as a counterpart to his own textbook of logics[33] implies a first comparison: the analogy between reason and affection offers the opportunity to relate one to the other step by step.

Baumgarten leaves the system of traditional logics intact, but suggests a few decisive changes in order to establish aesthetics alongside. Logical *diairesis* with its terminological classification relies on abstractions to determine the place of the thing in question. To find out what an object or an activity actually is, it is necessary to classify it according to a given system of hierarchical categories and on the basis of its likeness or difference to neighbouring categories. Predetermined, abstract criteria must be used to assign a given thing to its terminological place in the system. Baumgarten departs from this established scheme and places the focus on individuality or, rather, singularity instead. For him, to think aesthetically means to be interested in all major and minor facets of the object; in short, in diversification. 'While the logical and scientific mode of thinking considers its preferred objects ... in abstraction, those who think beautifully with the analogue of reason contemplate their matters not only concretely but in the highest possible determination, hence in singularities, in persons and things, as often as it is possible.'[34] Such a manner of thought still relies on comparisons, but it directs the attention to similarities and analogies as they may be presented in figurative speech, in metaphors and similes. And such a manner of thought is no longer interested in terms, in the sense of the general categories that logical thought seeks to define. Rhetorically refined speech and poetry make use of a large number of different stylistic comparative instruments to create an image in the mind that is vivid but not exact, in the sense of Descartes' 'clear and distinct'. Accordingly, aesthetic thinking is concerned with illustration and exemplification. Its comparisons are not only manifold, but let the thing in question stand out as singular, as just the thing it actually is. Within aesthetic thought, the more we compare, the more our comparisons become obsolete because they no longer help to classify, but create a different, nonterminological perception. In this sense, Baumgarten's innovation anticipates idealist and romantic positions of aesthetical autonomy.

Despite the fact that rhetorical comparisons are at the core of Baumgarten's aesthetics, his writings and those of Rousseau indicate a vein of thought that, in the middle of the century, was beginning to set a limit to the reach of comparative methods. Such a limitation became an integral part of the architecture of the most prominent and influential German aesthetic theory after Baumgarten, Immanuel Kant's *Critique of the Power of Judgment* (1790). While comparison has its place in the basic and more traditional classificatory logics of what Kant calls 'reflective judgment', it is practised in the judgement of taste, which is crucial for the project of aesthetic theory, only to a certain extent. In several of his intricate phrasings, Kant emphasizes what happens when we consult our sensation of taste to find out whether something is beautiful or not: imagination and understanding enter into a free play that resembles the process of cognition. But because it only *resembles* cognition, it does not lead to a determinate scientific (terminological) conclusion that is binding. It does claim to be valid for everyone ('I assume that what I find beautiful must be so for everyone else, too'), but it is impossible to prove this validity:

> The subjective universal communicability of the kind of representation in a judgment of taste, since it is supposed to occur without presupposing a determinate concept, can be nothing other than the state of mind in the free play of the imagination and the understanding (so far as they agree with each other as is requisite for a cognition in general): for we are conscious that this subjective relation suited to cognition in general must be valid for everyone and consequently universally communicable.[35]

It is important to note that the 'free play' only *resembles* cognition because this marks the judgement of taste as something that is not scientific. Here, Kant differs from Baumgarten, whose aim is to establish aesthetics as a science, according to the contemporary understanding of what an academic science can be.[36] To form a judgement means, in Kantian philosophy, to compare things (or, rather, mental representations of things) with each other in order to find out which concept they belong to. However, for an aesthetical judgement, i.e. a judgement of taste, it is not necessary to conclude a reflection with a concept that subsumes the thing under consideration. To put it differently: judgements of taste remain subjective, they correspond to the feelings and perceptions of one subject at a time, and do not necessarily fit into a given and valid conceptual system. They stop short just before they reach this point, because they only claim to be common ground for everybody. But again, it is important to note that they *only claim* to be so. This means that judgements of taste need no comparison; they are triggered by representations that remain 'singular and without comparison to others'.[37]

With his theory of the sublime, one of the most famous parts of the book, Kant introduces an even more determined restriction. The sublime he declares to be 'great beyond all comparison'.[38] While aesthetical judgements have no need of comparisons, the experience of the sublime is absolutely incompatible with comparative thought. Indeed, this idea is Kant's effort to describe something that is beyond the reach of logic.

Aesthetic theory's systematic limitation of comparison answers the sceptical position of Johann Gottfried Herder, and prepares the ground for Romantics like Friedrich Schlegel and Wilhelm Heinrich Wackenroder. In his writings, Herder regularly has recourse to comparison's more liberal counterparts, to analogies, as links that secure the coherence of the world as a holistic creation. This does not prevent him from repeatedly articulating deep misgivings about the idea of measuring one national literature or culture against another by means of comparison. What Herder – in this respect a follower of Rousseau – seeks to avoid are any *evaluative* comparisons directed at anthropological, i.e. social or cultural matters.[39] It is the idiosyncrasy of his writings that, because of his ample knowledge of other European literatures and cultures, he passes on to the German public as an early intercultural mediator and, notwithstanding his scepticism about comparisons, he may rightly count as one of the most important forerunners of the discipline of comparative literature. His aversion to comparisons is counterbalanced by his own repeated comparisons, e.g. between German and other European literatures, and by the fact that he emphasizes the benefit that such critical parallels may have for communication between, and the improvement of, cultures – an idea that generally gained much ground around 1800.[40] Yet, it is not surprising that Herder gets entangled in contradictions because any (aesthetical, ethical or other) postulation of incomparabilities is paradoxical: any incomparability might be considered as absolute, but the recognition of its uniqueness is in itself a tacit comparison. Later in the century, authors of German Romanticism like Wackenroder and Friedrich Schlegel expressed their doubts as to the possibility and legitimacy to grasp aesthetical and cultural parameters by comparison. For Wackenroder's fictitious and romantic, yet autobiographical friar who confesses his enthusiasm for Renaissance painting: 'Comparison is a serious impediment to any appreciation, and even the most sublime beauty in art makes its full and proper impact on us only when our gaze is not distracted by other beauties.'[41] And for Schlegel too, art works cannot and should not be made the object of comparisons: '[f]or the infinite does not tolerate comparison; the enjoyment of the beautiful has unconditional value.'[42]

## The Comparative Paradigm

The period around 1800 is dominated by two versions of the comparative episteme. The first is that an *empirical* use of comparison helps to create new scientific disciplines. Natural history becomes divided into several sciences like biology or chemistry and increasingly makes use of empirical methods. Classificatory systems are reinterpreted from a historical and genealogical perspective. The single most prominent success of all comparative sciences is Georges Cuvier's comparative anatomy: Cuvier's invention of the science of palaeontology and the possibility to reconstruct extinct species by comparing their fossil remains is a spectacular event of the time and, being taught and debated in postrevolutionary Paris, receives much attention.[43] Countless authors take this as a model for their own efforts to establish new disciplines: Joseph-Marie de Gérando refers to the natural sciences and to Condillac's sensualism to introduce his comparative history of philosophy[44] and his methodological sketch of comparative anthropology.[45] Likewise, Marc-Antoine Jullien sees comparative anatomy as the example for his fragmentary project of comparative education, which was published in 1816 and fell into oblivion until the twentieth century.[46] De Gérando's and Jullien's influence is small, but their efforts must count as the first attempts to conceptualize comparative social and ethnographic sciences with an international and intercultural scope. Wilhelm von Humboldt and Friedrich Schlegel both spent a few years in Paris around the turn of the century and witnessed the breakthrough of comparative anatomy themselves. Both authors were eager to participate in the rising fame that surrounded this discipline, which they pointed to as a model for their efforts to establish comparative anthropology and comparative linguistics.[47]

In the second version of comparison prevalent around 1800, comparative anatomy is the point of reference too. Notwithstanding Foucault's claim that already in the early seventeenth century comparison put an end to 'the age of resemblance',[48] yet another revitalization of analogy was taking place: I already mentioned Herder, whose manifold writings touch upon philosophy, natural history, history, literary criticism, anthropology and theology, and whose thinking is an impressive example of how strong the attraction of the epistemological pattern of analogy still was towards the end of the eighteenth century. The romantic movement adopted this pattern, albeit sometimes disguised as comparison: in his groundbreaking linguistic study of the etymology and grammar of Sanskrit, Schlegel cites comparative anatomy as an example for historical linguistics, making ample use of verbal resemblances in his etymological interpretations. And the whole trend of natural philosophy that comes up in Germany at that time relies on analogical arguments, even if its protagonists like F.W.J. Schelling, Novalis, Lorenz Oken, Carl Gustav Carus or Friedrich Burdach use the terminology of *vergleichende Wissenschaften*[49] or attempt to institute new disciplines like 'Vergleichende Psychologie'.[50]

In fact, the debate as to whether comparison or analogy had more to offer to intellectual and scientific reasoning was at the heart of some of the key disciplines of the time. Kant accused Herder of overestimating the epistemological use of analogy in his work on natural history and of taking for facts what, in Kant's eyes, were mere interpretations.[51] And the public dispute between Cuvier and his rival Étienne Geoffroy St. Hilaire in front of the French Academy of the Sciences in 1830 concerned the question whether there was one basic type that, as a pattern, morphologically united all animal organisms (Geoffroy's position) or whether there were four *embranchements* (as Cuvier called them) of the animal kingdom, i.e. different types of organisms that disproved the traditional assumption of a great chain of being.[52] Cuvier regarded differences 'as arising from the very essence of organic nature', whereas he held analogies to be only 'somewhat fortuitous combinations which remained after differences had been identified'.[53] In other words, during the historical period when the separation of philosophy and biology, which Kant still related to each other in his *Critique of Judgment*, was only just beginning, both disciplines distinguished between approaches that pointed out differences between the objects to be compared and analogical arguments that rather emphasized affinities and similarities. In around 1800, the theoretical framework of many academic subjects was organized according to one of these two comparative approaches.

## Conclusion

What I have tried to sketch is the emergence and establishment of comparison as one of the elementary and defining scientific methods of modernity. In around 1800, the scientific history of comparison, of which I have singled out some of the most distinctive examples, was in fact only beginning to take hold with the institutionalization of comparative anatomy in France. Most of the approaches mentioned above stuck to comparative procedures in the decades and centuries that followed, and the fact that there is hardly another method that has been adopted for the titles of so many and so diverse subjects testifies to its prominence up to this day (comparative literature, comparative mythology, comparative philosophy, comparative theology, etc.). With Charles Darwin's theory of evolution, the paradigm of biological classification had to be reinterpreted historically. Of course, this did not make the comparative method obsolete (in fact, the reverse was true), but it diverted the attention to the temporal dimension of nature.

Yet, the nineteenth century became, in Friedrich Nietzsche's words, the 'age of comparison'[54] in another field: the method was adapted by the social sciences and was one of the theoretical cornerstones of sociology. For Auguste Comte and Émile Durkheim, comparison was one of the key methods of their subject, and with the growing interest in the international and ethnographic dimensions of culture after the beginnings of anthropology as a discipline in the eighteenth century,[55] scientific comparison began to fulfil its role as a tool for intercultural studies. Most of the inventions of new comparative disciplines, like the advent of comparative literature, is a result of this shift in emphasis from general epistemology and natural history to society and culture.

I took Foucault's *Order of Things* as a starting point and have tried to elaborate on some of his ideas, without adopting all of the methodical implications of his poststructuralist approach. The above overview assembles some of the most significant developments in comparative epistemology, opening the field for further related study in these or other epochs and areas of knowledge. The names and titles admittedly represent a very canonical part of the Western history of ideas, but there is no doubt that it would be possible to delve deeper into the written records of intellectual history and to collect countless less well-known examples of comparative approaches in line with those that have been presented here. The sum of these conceptions across several disciplines constitutes something that may be called, in Foucaultian terminology, a comparative *episteme* that asserted itself in scientific and intellectual thought between the Enlightenment and the Romantic period, and shaped much of the historical and social sciences in the nineteenth century. Alternatively, we might as well speak of a 'style of reasoning', using a concept that Alistair Crombie introduced and Ian Hacking adopted. Crombie distinguishes six of these *Styles of Scientific Thinking in the European Tradition* from antiquity to the nineteenth century.[56] Number three concerns 'hypothetical modelling … by the construction of analogies', while number four is about 'taxonomy … as a logical method of ordering variety … by comparison and differentiation'.[57] The conceptualizations discussed in this chapter confirm Crombie's hypothesis that analogy and comparison belong to the basic theoretical instruments in the sciences as well as in the humanities of the Western tradition. In the period from the seventeenth to the nineteenth centuries, comparison took the lead to support the establishment and differentiation of a large number of empirical subjects, while analogy never ceased to be a fundamental tool to organize and interpret nature as well as human perceptions and sensations. We can conclude that comparison is more than an essential intellectual operation of the human mind. During the eighteenth and nineteenth centuries, it was one of the most significant patterns that helped to define an argument or a subject matter as scientific.

**Michael Eggers** is a lecturer at the Institute for German Language and Literature at the University of Cologne. He has published widely on comparative literature. His most important recent publications are *Vergleichendes Erkennen: Zur Wissenschaftsgeschichte und Epistemologie des Vergleichs und zur Genealogie der Komparatistik* (2016); *Komparatistik und Didaktik* (coedited with Christof Hamann, 2018); and 'Das Wissen der Anderen. Zur Notwendigkeit einer wissenspoetologischen Komparatistik', in L. Simonis (ed.), *Kulturen des Vergleichs: Komparative Erkenntnis in Literaturwissenschaft, Philosophie, Sozial- und Kulturwissenschaften* (2016), 127–40.

## Notes

1. This chapter is a condensed summary of my book *Vergleichendes Erkennen: Zur Wissenschaftsgeschichte und Epistemologie des Vergleichs und zur Genealogie der Komparatistik* (Heidelberg: Universitätsverlag Winter, 2016). I refer to that publication for a more extensive explanation of the individual theories mentioned.

2. Cf. M. Foucault, *The Archaeology of Knowledge and the Discourse on Language* (New York: Pantheon Books, 1972), 157–65.
3. M. Foucault, *The Order of Things: An Archaeology of the Human Sciences* (New York: Pantheon Books, 1970), 50–58.
4. R. Descartes, 'Rules for the Direction of the Mind', in *The Philosophical Writings of Descartes* (Cambridge: Cambridge University Press, 1985), vol. I, 57 (Rule Fourteen).
5. For such a close reading, see H. Gutschmidt, *Objektive Ideen: Untersuchungen zum Verhältnis von Idee, Begriff und Begründung bei René Descartes und in der nachkartesischen Philosophie des 17. Jahrhunderts* (Tübingen: Mohr Siebeck, 2014), 56–65.
6. Foucault, *The Archaeology of Knowledge*, 221–22; M. Foucault, 'What is an Author?', in D. Bouchard (ed.), *Language, Counter-memory and Practice: Selected Essays and Interviews by Michel Foucault* (Ithaca, NY: Cornell University Press, 1977), 113–38.
7. A. Rudolph, *Figuren der Ähnlichkeit: Johann Georg Hamanns Analogiedenken im Kontext des 18. Jahrhunderts* (Tübingen: Niemeyer, 2006), 7–14; C. Zittel, *Theatrum philosophicum: Descartes und die Rolle ästhetischer Formen in der Wissenschaft* (Berlin: Akademie Verlag, 2009); P. Galison, 'Descartes' Comparisons: From the Invisible to the Visible', *ISIS* 75 (1984), 311–26.
8. Descartes, 'Rules', 39 (Rule Twelve).
9. R. Descartes, 'Principles of Philosophy', in *The Philosophical Writings of Descartes* (Cambridge: Cambridge University Press, 1985), vol. I, 287 (Part IV.201).
10. Zittel, *Theatrum philosophicum*, 156ff.
11. W. Steinmetz, '"Vergleich" – eine begriffsgeschichtliche Skizze', in A. Epple and W. Erhart (eds), *Die Welt beobachten: Praktiken des Vergleichens* (Frankfurt am Main: Campus, 2015), 85–134, at 100–4.
12. J. Locke, *An Essay Concerning Human Understanding* (1690), P.H. Nidditch (ed.) (Oxford: Clarendon Press, 1975) Book II, ch. XI, §2, 156. See also E. Knörer, *Entfernte Ähnlichkeiten: Zur Geschichte von Witz und ingenium* (Munich: Fink Verlag, 2007), 158–62: 'Das philosophische Phantasma Lockes ist das eines von der Vernunft aufzuklärenden Strukturhintergrunds von Identitäten und Differenzen. Der Vordergrund der Ähnlichkeiten ist ein Produkt von Gedächtnis und Einbildungskraft und Witz und erzeugt werden so nur Evidenzen, deren Wesen der Schein ist. Zur Wahrheit gelangt man, so Locke, gerade nicht auf dem Wege sich nahelegender Ähnlichkeiten, sondern "umgekehrt": durch sorgfältiges Unterscheiden' (at 160) ('It was Locke's presumptive idea that reason had to illuminate the entanglements of identity and difference. Memory, imagination and wit would only produce superficial similarities and misleading evidences. According to Locke, truth can be reached only by differentiating carefully and not by following apparent similarities' – my translation); cf. also O.F. Best, *Der Witz als Erkenntniskraft und Formprinzip* (Darmstadt: Wissenschaftliche Buchgesellschaft, 1989).
13. Locke, *An Essay*, Book IV, ch. XVII, §14, 683.
14. Ibid., ch. II, §1, 531.
15. Ibid., ch. XVI, §12, 665–67.
16. Aristotle, *Poetics*, S. Halliwell (ed.) (Cambridge, MA: Harvard University Press, 2014) 1457b, 104–6.
17. Locke, *An Essay*, Book III, ch. X, §34, 508.
18. W. Lepenies, *Das Ende der Naturgeschichte: Verzeitlichung und Enthistorisierung in der Wissenschaftsgeschichte des 18. und 19. Jahrhunderts* (Munich: Hanser, 1976), 16–20. See also L.C. Eiseley, *The Firmament of Time* (New York: Atheneum, 1975); and S. Toulmin and J. Goodfield, *The Discovery of Time* (Chicago: University of Chicago Press, 1982).

19. É.B. de Condillac, *Treatise on Sensations* (1754), M.G. Carr (trans.) (London: Favil Press, 1930), 9, I.2, §15.
20. De Condillac, *Treatise on Sensations*, I.7, §2.
21. Aristotle, *Topics*, Book IV. See H. M. Nobis, 'Definition I', in J. Ritter et al. (eds), *Historisches Wörterbuch der Philosophie* (Basel: Schwabe, 1971–2007), vol. 2, 31–35, at 31; cf. Locke, *An Essay*, Book III, ch. III, §9–10, 412–13.
22. S. Müller-Wille, *Botanik und weltweiter Handel: Zur Begründung eines natürlichen Systems der Pflanzen durch Carl von Linné (1707–78)* (Berlin: Verlag für wissenschaftliche Bildung, 1999), 46–48. Müller-Wille convincingly argues that the Linnaean system cannot be understood as simply corresponding to a logical hierarchy.
23. J.H. Lambert, *Kosmologische Briefe über die Einrichtung des Weltbaues* (1761), *Philosophische Schriften*, 10 vols (Hildesheim: Olms, 1965–2008), vol. 5.
24. J.H. Lambert, *Neues Organon (oder Gedanken über die Erforschung und Beziehung des Wahren und dessen Unterscheidung vom Irrthum und Schein)* (1764), *Philosophische Schriften*, 10 vols (Hildesheim: Olms 1965–2008), vols 1 and 2. The *Neues Organon* is Lambert's main work and is divided into four parts: *Dianoiologie* (about the forms of knowledge), *Alethiologie* (about logical truth), *Semiotik* (about signs) and *Phänomenologie* (about truth and appearance).
25. J. Bernoulli (ed.), *Johann Heinrich Lamberts Deutscher gelehrter Briefwechsel* (Berlin, 1782), 333–68.
26. For introductions to Lambert, see G.L. Schiewer, *Cognitio symbolica: Lamberts semiotische Wissenschaft und ihre Diskussion bei Herder, Jean Paul und Novalis* (Tübingen: Niemeyer, 1996); S. Metzger, *Die Konjektur des Organismus: Wahrscheinlichkeitsdenken und Performanz im 18. Jahrhundert* (Munich: Fink, 2002). See also the chapter on Lambert in Eggers, *Vergleichendes Erkennen*, 119–78.
27. Cf. É. B. de Condillac, *An essay on the origin of human knowledge. Being a supplement to Mr. Locke's essay on the human understanding. Translated from the French of the Abbé de Condillac, Member of the Royal Academy of Berlin. By Mr. Nugent* (London: J. Nourse, 1756), ch. I.4: 'That the use of signs is the real cause of the progress of the imagination, contemplation and memory.'
28. J.-J. Rousseau, *The Collected Writings of Rousseau*, vol. 7: *Essay on the Origin of Languages and Writings Related to Music*, J.T. Scott (trans. and ed.) (Hanover: University Press of New England, 1998), 313.
29. J.-J. Rousseau, *Discourse upon the Origin and Foundation of the Inequality among Mankind* (London: R. and J. Dodsley, 1761), 112–13.
30. Ibid., 251.
31. 'The science of knowing and presenting [*proponendi*] with regard to the senses is AESTHETICS (the logic of the inferior cognitive faculty, the philosophy of graces and muses, inferior gnoseology, the art of thinking beautifully, the art of the analogue of reason).' A. Baumgarten, *Metaphysics: A Critical Translation with Kant's Elucidations, Selected Notes, and Related Materials*, trans. and ed. with an introduction by C.D. Fugate and J. Hymers (London; Bloomsbury, 2013), 205, §533. With Baumgarten, the notion of 'art' is at the beginning of the historical episode after which it no longer mainly designates 'skill' or 'craft', but rather 'fine arts'.
32. In the essay in which he conceives many of his important aesthetical ideas for the first time, Baumgarten is concerned with poetry only: A.G. Baumgarten, *Reflexions on poetry: Alexander Gottlieb Baumgarten's Meditationes philosophicae de nonnullis ad poema*

*pertinentibus* (1735), trans., with the original text, an introduction and notes, by K. Aschenbrenner (Berkeley: University of California Press, 1954).

33. F. Solms, *Disciplina aesthetica: Zur Frühgeschichte der ästhetischen Theorie bei Baumgarten und Herder* (Stuttgart: Klett-Cotta, 1990), 30–31. Cf. A.G. Baumgarten, *Acroasis logica* (Halle: Hemmerde, 1761).
34. A.G. Baumgarten, Ästhetik (Latin-German), D. Mirbach (trans. and ed.) (Hamburg: Felix Meiner, 2007), 754, §752. There is no published English translation of this seminal work; the above and the following quote (fn. 36) are my own attempts. The original reads: 'Si genus cogitandi logicum et scientificum obiecta sua primaria ... lubentius in abstracto considerat: pulcre cogitaturus analogo rationis suas materias praecipuas non in concreto solum, sed etiam in determinatissimis, in quibus potest, hinc in singularibus, suppositis, personis, factis, quoties datur, lubentissime contempletur.'
35. I. Kant, *Critique of the Power of Judgment*, Paul Guyer (ed.) (Cambridge: Cambridge University Press, 2000), 103, §9.
36. Baumgarten, Ästhetik, 11, §1: 'AESTHETICS (theory of free arts, lower cognition, art of thinking beautifully, art of the analogue of reason) is the science of sensible cognition.' 'AESTHETICA (theoria liberalium artium, gnoseologia inferior, ars pulcre cogitandi, ars analogi rationis) est scientia cognitionis sensitivae' (at 10).
37. Kant, *Critique of the Power of Judgment*, 104, §9.
38. Ibid., 132, §25.
39. The following is one of many examples from Herder's writings: 'For if, again, human nature is no container of an absolute, independent, unchangeable happiness as the philosopher defines it, but it everywhere attracts as much happiness as it can ... – then at bottom all comparison proves to be problematic ... – who can compare the different satisfaction of different senses in different worlds? – the shepherd and father of the Orient, the farmer and artist, the sailor, competitive runner, conqueror of the world – who can compare them? ... Each nation has its *center* of happiness *in itself*, like every sphere its center of gravity!' J.G. Herder, 'This Too a Philosophy of History for the Formation of Humanity' (1774), in *Philosophical Writings*, M.N. Forster (ed.) (Cambridge: Cambridge University Press, 2002), 272–360, at 296–97.
40. Steinmetz, 'Vergleich', 119 and 126–29.
41. W.H. Wackenroder and L. Tieck, *Outpourings of an Art-Loving Friar* (1796), trans. from the German and with an introduction by E. Mornin (New York: Frederick Ungar, 1975), 58.
42. F. Schlegel, *On the Study of Greek Poetry* (1797), trans., ed. and with a critical introduction by S. Barnett (Albany, NY: State University of New York Press, 2001), 59.
43. See G. Cuvier, *Lectures in Comparative Anatomy*, W. Ross (trans.) (London: T.N. Longman and O. Rees, 1802) and many other publications.
44. J.-M. de Gérando, *Histoire comparée des systèmes de philosophie, relativement aux principes des connaissances humaines* (Paris: Chez Henrichs, 1804).
45. J.-M. de Gérando, *The Observation of Savage Peoples* (1800), trans. from the French by F.C.T. Moore, with a preface by E.E. Evans-Pritchard (London: Routledge, 1969).
46. Jullien's text is printed in S. Fraser (ed.), *Jullien's Plan for Comparative Education, 1816–1817* (New York: Bureau of Publications, Teachers College, Columbia University, 1964).
47. 'There is, however, one single point, the investigation of which ought to decide every doubt, and elucidate every difficulty; the structure of comparative grammar of the languages furnishes as certain a key to their general analogy, as the study of comparative anatomy has done to the loftiest branch of natural science.' F. Schlegel, 'On the

Language and Philosophy of the Indians' (1808), in *The Aesthetic and Miscellaneous Works of Friedrich von Schlegel*, trans. from the German by E.J. Millington (London: George Bell & Sons, 1900), 425–64, at 439; cf. also W. von Humboldt, 'Plan einer vergleichenden Anthropologie' (1795), in H.-J. Wagner (ed.), *Wilhelm von Humboldt: Anthropologie und Theorie der Menschenkenntnis* (Darmstadt: Wissenschaftliche Buchgesellschaft, 2002), 9.
48. Foucault, *Order of Things*, 51.
49. S. Willer, 'Die Allgemeinheit des Vergleichs. Ein komparatistisches Problem und seine Entstehung um 1800', in M. Eggers (ed.), *Von Ähnlichkeiten und Unterschieden: Vergleich, Analogie und Klassifikation in Wissenschaft und Literatur (18./19. Jahrhundert)* (Heidelberg: Universitätsverlag Winter, 2011), 143–65, at 153–57.
50. C.G. Carus, *Vergleichende Psychologie oder Geschichte der Seele in der Reihenfolge der Thierwelt* (Vienna: Braumüller, 1866); K.F. Burdach, *Comparative Psychologie*, 2 vols (Leipzig: Voß, 1842).
51. I. Kant, 'Review of J.G. Herder's *Ideas for the Philosophy of the History of Humanity*. Parts 1 and 2 (1785)', in I. Kant, *Anthropology, History and Education*, G. Zöller and R.B. Louden (eds) (Cambridge: Cambridge University Press, 2007), 121–42.
52. T.A. Appel, *The Cuvier-Geoffroy Debate: French Biology in the Decades before Darwin* (New York: Oxford University Press, 1987). Cf. A.O. Lovejoy, *The Great Chain of Being: A Study of the History of an Idea* (Cambridge, MA: Harvard University Press, 1936). For Cuvier's scientific methods, see W. Coleman, *Georges Cuvier, Zoologist: A Study in the History of Evolution Theory* (Cambridge, MA: Harvard University Press, 1964).
53. Coleman, *Georges Cuvier*, 157.
54. F. Nietzsche, *Human, All Too Human: A Book for Free Spirits* (1878–80) (Chicago: Charles H. Kerr & Co., 1908), 49–51 (no. 23).
55. For an overview, see L. M. Gisi, *Einbildungskraft und Mythologie: die Verschränkung von Anthropologie und Geschichte im 18. Jahrhundert* (Berlin: de Gruyter, 2007).
56. A.C. Crombie, *Styles of Scientific Thinking in the European Tradition: The History of Argument and Explanation Especially in the Mathematical and Biomedical Sciences and Arts* (London: Duckworth, 1994), 83–85. The full list of Crombie's six styles comprises (in my rephrasing of his more elaborate explanations): (1) the method of postulation exemplified by the Greek mathematical sciences; (2) the scientific experimental method as the strategy of searching for principles in the observable relations of more complex subject matters; (3) hypothetical modelling by the construction of analogies; (4) taxonomy as a logical method of ordering variety by comparison and differentiation; (5) the probabilistic and statistical analysis of expectation and choice; and (6) the method of historical derivation, or the analysis and synthesis of genetic development. Cf. also I. Hacking, 'Styles of Scientific Reasoning', in J. Rajchman and C. West (eds), *Post-analytic philosophy* (New York: Columbia University Press, 1985), 145–65, at 147.
57. Crombie, *Styles*, 84.

# Bibliography

Appel, T.A., *The Cuvier-Geoffroy Debate: French Biology in the Decades before Darwin* (New York: Oxford University Press, 1987).
Aristotle, *Poetics*, Halliwell, S. (ed.) (Cambridge, MA: Harvard University Press, 2014).

Baumgarten, A.G., *Reflexions on poetry: Alexander Gottlieb Baumgarten's Meditationes philosophicae de nonnullis ad poema pertinentibus* (1735), trans., with the original text, an introduction and notes, by Aschenbrenner, K. (Berkeley: University of California Press, 1954).

———. *Acroasis logica* (Halle: Hemmerde, 1761).

———. Ästhetik, Latin-German, Mirbach, B. (trans. and ed.) (Hamburg: Felix Meiner, 2007).

———. *Metaphysics: A Critical Translation with Kant's Elucidations, Selected Notes, and Related Materials*, trans. and ed. with an introduction by Fugate, C.D. and Hymers, J. (London: Bloomsbury, 2013).

Bernoulli, J. (ed.), *Johann Heinrich Lamberts Deutscher gelehrter Briefwechsel* (Berlin, 1782).

Best, O.F., *Der Witz als Erkenntniskraft und Formprinzip* (Darmstadt: Wissenschaftliche Buchgesellschaft, 1989).

Burdach, K.F., *Comparative Psychologie*, 2 vols (Leipzig: Voß, 1842).

Carus, C.G., *Vergleichende Psychologie oder Geschichte der Seele in der Reihenfolge der Thierwelt* (Vienna: Braumüller, 1866).

Coleman, W., *Georges Cuvier, Zoologist: A Study in the History of Evolution Theory* (Cambridge, MA: Harvard University Press, 1964).

Crombie, A.C., *Styles of Scientific Thinking in the European Tradition: The History of Argument and Explanation Especially in the Mathematical and Biomedical Sciences and Arts* (London: Duckworth, 1994).

Cuvier, G., *Lectures in Comparative Anatomy*, Ross, W. (trans.) (London: T.N. Longman and O. Rees, 1802).

De Condillac, É. B., *Treatise on Sensations* (1754), Carr, M.G. (trans.) (London: Favil Press, 1930).

———. *An essay on the origin of human knowledge. Being a supplement to Mr. Locke's essay on the human understanding. Translated from the French of the Abbé de Condillac, Member of the Royal Academy of Berlin. By Mr. Nugent* (London: J. Nourse, 1756).

De Gérando, J.-M., *Histoire comparée des systèmes de philosophie, relativement aux principes des connaissances humaines* (Paris: Chez Henrichs, 1804).

———. *The Observation of Savage Peoples* (1800), trans. from the French by Moore, F.C.T., with a preface by Evans-Pritchard, E.E. (London: Routledge, 1969).

Descartes, R., 'Principles of Philosophy', in *The Philosophical Writings of Descartes* (Cambridge: Cambridge University Press, 1985), vol. I, 177–292.

———. 'Rules for the Direction of the Mind', in *The Philosophical Writings of Descartes* (Cambridge: Cambridge University Press, 1985), vol. I, 7–78.

Eggers, M., *Vergleichendes Erkennen: Zur Wissenschaftsgeschichte und Epistemologie des Vergleichs und zur Genealogie der Komparatistik* (Heidelberg: Universitätsverlag Winter, 2016).

Eiseley, L.C., *The Firmament of Time* (New York: Atheneum, 1975).

Foucault, M., *The Order of Things: An Archaeology of the Human Sciences* (New York: Pantheon Books, 1970).

———. *The Archaeology of Knowledge and the Discourse on Language* (New York: Pantheon Books, 1972).

———. 'What is an Author?', in Bouchard, D. (ed.), *Language, Counter-memory and Practice: Selected Essays and Interviews by Michel Foucault* (Ithaca, NY: Cornell University Press, 1977), 113–38.

Fraser, S. (ed.), *Jullien's Plan for Comparative Education, 1816–1817* (New York: Bureau of Publications, Teachers College, Columbia University, 1964).

Galison, P., 'Descartes' Comparisons: From the Invisible to the Visible', *ISIS* 75 (1984), 311–26.

Gisi, L.M., *Einbildungskraft und Mythologie: die Verschränkung von Anthropologie und Geschichte im 18. Jahrhundert* (Berlin: de Gruyter, 2007).

Gutschmidt, H., *Objektive Ideen: Untersuchungen zum Verhältnis von Idee, Begriff und Begründung bei René Descartes und in der nachkartesischen Philosophie des 17. Jahrhunderts* (Tübingen: Mohr Siebeck, 2014).

Hacking, I., 'Styles of Scientific Reasoning', in Rajchman, J. and West, C. (eds), *Post-analytic Philosophy* (New York: Columbia University Press, 1985), 145–65.

Herder, J.G., 'This Too a Philosophy of History for the Formation of Humanity' (1774), in *Philosophical Writings*, Forster, M.N. (ed.) (Cambridge: Cambridge University Press, 2002), 272–360.

Kant, I., *Critique of the Power of Judgment*, Guyer, P. (ed.) (Cambridge: Cambridge University Press, 2000).

———. 'Review of J.G. Herder's *Ideas for the Philosophy of the History of Humanity. Parts 1 and 2* (1785)', in *Anthropology, History and Education*, Zöller, G. and Louden, R.B. (eds) (Cambridge: Cambridge University Press, 2007), 121–42.

Knörer, E., *Entfernte Ähnlichkeiten: Zur Geschichte von Witz und ingenium* (Munich: Fink Verlag, 2007).

Lambert, J.H., *Kosmologische Briefe über die Einrichtung des Weltbaues* (1761), *Philosophische Schriften*, 10 vols (Hildesheim: Olms, 1965–2008), vol. 5.

———. *Neues Organon (oder Gedanken über die Erforschung und Beziehung des Wahren und dessen Unterscheidung vom Irrthum und Schein)* (1764), *Philosophische Schriften*, 10 vols (Hildesheim: Olms 1965–2008), vols 1 and 2.

Lepenies, W., *Das Ende der Naturgeschichte: Verzeitlichung und Enthistorisierung in der Wissenschaftsgeschichte des 18. und 19. Jahrhunderts* (Munich: Hanser, 1976).

Locke, J., *An Essay Concerning Human Understanding* (1690), Nidditch, P.H. (ed.) (Oxford: Clarendon Press, 1975).

Lovejoy, A.O., *The Great Chain of Being: A Study of the History of an Idea* (Cambridge, MA: Harvard University Press, 1936).

Metzger, S., *Die Konjektur des Organismus: Wahrscheinlichkeitsdenken und Performanz im 18. Jahrhundert* (Munich: Fink, 2002).

Müller-Wille, S., *Botanik und weltweiter Handel: Zur Begründung eines natürlichen Systems der Pflanzen durch Carl von Linné (1707–78)* (Berlin: Verlag für wissenschaftliche Bildung, 1999).

Nietzsche, F., *Human, All Too Human: A Book for Free Spirits* (1878–80) (Chicago: Charles H. Kerr & Co., 1908).

Nobis, H.M., 'Definition I', in Ritter, J. et al. (eds), *Historisches Wörterbuch der Philosophie* (Basel: Schwabe, 1971–2007), vol. 2, 31–35.

Rousseau, J.-J., *Discourse upon the Origin and Foundation of the Inequality among Mankind* (London: R. and J. Dodsley, 1761).

———. *The Collected Writings of Rousseau*, vol. 7: *Essay on the Origin of Languages and Writings Related to Music*, by Scott, J.T. (trans. and ed.) (Hanover: University Press of New England, 1998).

Rudolph, A., *Figuren der Ähnlichkeit: Johann Georg Hamanns Analogiedenken im Kontext des 18. Jahrhunderts* (Tübingen: Niemeyer, 2006).

Schiewer, G.L., *Cognitio symbolica: Lamberts semiotische Wissenschaft und ihre Diskussion bei Herder, Jean Paul und Novalis* (Tübingen: Niemeyer, 1996).

Schlegel, F., 'On the Language and Philosophy of the Indians' (1808), in *The Aesthetic and Miscellaneous Works of Friedrich von Schlegel*, trans. from the German by Millington, E.J. (London: George Bell & Sons, 1900), 425–64.

——. *On the Study of Greek Poetry* (1797), trans., ed. and with a critical introduction by Barnett, S. (Albany, NY: State University of New York Press, 2001).

Solms, F., *Disciplina aesthetica: Zur Frühgeschichte der ästhetischen Theorie bei Baumgarten und Herder* (Stuttgart: Klett-Cotta, 1990).

Steinmetz, W., '"Vergleich" – eine begriffsgeschichtliche Skizze', in Epple, A. and Erhart, W. (eds), *Die Welt beobachten: Praktiken des Vergleichens* (Frankfurt am Main: Campus, 2015), 85–134.

Toulmin, S., and Goodfield, J., *The Discovery of Time* (Chicago: University of Chicago Press, 1982).

Von Humboldt, W., 'Plan einer vergleichenden Anthropologie' (1795), in Wagner, H.-J. (ed.), *Wilhelm von Humboldt: Anthropologie und Theorie der Menschenkenntnis* (Darmstadt: Wissenschaftliche Buchgesellschaft, 2002).

Wackenroder, W.H. and Tieck, L., *Outpourings of an Art-Loving Friar* (1796), trans. from the German and with an introduction by Mornin, E. (New York: Frederick Ungar, 1975).

Willer, S., 'Die Allgemeinheit des Vergleichs. Ein komparatistisches Problem und seine Entstehung um 1800', in Eggers, M. (ed.), *Von Ähnlichkeiten und Unterschieden: Vergleich, Analogie und Klassifikation in Wissenschaft und Literatur (18./19. Jahrhundert)* (Heidelberg: Universitätsverlag Winter, 2011), 143–65.

Zittel, C., *Theatrum philosophicum: Descartes und die Rolle ästhetischer Formen in der Wissenschaft* (Berlin: Akademie Verlag, 2009).

# 2

# Comparative Practices and Their Implications

*The Case of Comparative Viewing*

Johannes Grave

## Omnipresence and Critique of Comparisons

Comparisons are fraught with an irritating tension.[1] On the one hand, their diverse forms are self-evident and ubiquitous in every sphere of life. On the other hand, there have been only halting attempts to make comparison per se an object of explicit reflection or academic study. Comparisons affect everyday practices in society, politics, the economy, culture and the sciences, but considerations about them have hitherto focused almost exclusively on particular scientific procedures and fields of application.[2] In its most elementary form, comparison seems too trivial, too self-evident to become the object of research. The applicability and suitability of particular comparisons in specific situations and contexts have been hotly debated, but what constitutes a comparison as such has seemed to require no further explanation.

Comparisons may be described as a basic form of drawing relations between objects or phenomena. At least two units of a comparison (*comparata*) are examined under a specific aspect (the *tertium comparationis*) in order to find equalities, congruences, similarities or differences.[3] The choice of the *tertium comparationis* presupposes that the *comparata* are of the same kind in at least one respect, otherwise no *tertium comparationis* could be identified. But the choice of the *tertium* also implies a certain degree of attentiveness and intentionality (in the wider philosophical sense of directedness) by the subject who draws the comparison. It is important to stress that even the most basic comparisons, although often used as a strategy to objectivize knowledge, are always linked to a subject who is situated within his or her own contexts. Comparisons can serve different purposes and may have unintended effects. The mere operation of bringing two or more *comparata* into a relationship by means of a *tertium comparationis* can open up new insights into objects and their relations with each other or help reordering already available knowledge. References to congruences or differences may also appear in very different concrete forms (e.g. as a categorial disparity, as a gradual differentiation or as an indistinguishable equality) and thus become the basis of broader, sometimes even contradictory conclusions or arguments.

Given the fact that recourse to comparison is deemed unavoidable for examining all sorts of questions,[4] the vehemence with which it has been repeatedly criticized is surprising.[5] Comparison is suspected of blocking out what is characteristic and of peculiar value in a unique individual case.[6] Another objection against the operation of comparing is that it may be used to gain mastery over previously unknown phenomena and thereby suppress their irritating strangeness. According to this view, comparisons tend to rigidify certain ways of ordering the world and, by implication, subject the objects compared to uncritical value judgements. Moreover, it is claimed that comparisons by selecting a particular aspect (the *tertium comparationis*) always deflect the view from the multifaceted qualities that can characterize an object. Finally, a fundamental critique of comparisons is often linked to situations in which something is said to be incomparable or unrelated to anything else – for instance, in theological discussions about God or in conversations about works of art.

Such far-reaching criticisms of comparison can hardly be brought into harmony with the impression that comparing is a basic and virtually unavoidable operation of thought and knowledge acquisition. Some of the problems mentioned by the critics could presumably be resolved by tracing them back to faulty logical operations on the part of those who made the comparisons. Another way of dealing with the critics' concerns would be to inquire more thoroughly into the ethics that should govern comparisons. Above all, however, the fact that comparisons have elicited such extensive, and diverse, criticism should be seen as an indication of the extent to which comparing has always been a practice situated in multifarious contexts. Among critics, a twofold intuition is particularly discernible. *First*, comparison is not a neutral, 'innocent' operation of thought, only to be corrupted by its misleading implementation on the part of an intentional subject. Comparisons can even direct the attention against the comparer's original purpose; they can narrow the view and contribute towards making constructions appear essential or natural. *Second*, comparison is not always and as a matter of principle problematic and deserving of criticism. Comparisons usually become the object of criticism when *practices* of comparing are up for discussion. And these *practices* of comparing include not only the usage of already completed comparisons for drawing conclusions, but also the various processes of executing comparisons. Therefore, the operation of comparing itself should not lurk in the background as a black box between the subject's preceding intentions and the subsequent application of the comparison's results. Rather, we should be looking at those processes and practices that are interwoven with the comparison – that in fact even constitute it in the first place.

The following thoughts focus on the question what it means to examine comparisons as practices. To this end, in a first step I will take up essential insights into the more recent theories of practice and discuss their relevance for an investigation of comparisons. The particular value of such an approach comes to the fore by looking at comparative practices that do not take place in language alone. Therefore, I choose the example of comparative viewing in connoisseurship in order to show how an examination that is guided by basic insights of theories of practice can draw attention to the momentous effects of comparison, which are often overlooked or underestimated. As an example, Goethe's comparing between some engravings and their later copies is discussed in the third and fourth sections to demonstrate how the connoisseurial practice of comparing implicitly leads to a particular, namely semiotic understanding of pictures in general. In this way, the case study indicates how practices of comparing shape and, in a certain manner, constitute what is compared.

## Doing Comparisons – from a Practical Point of View

Studying comparisons as practices requires overcoming a sham alternative between two points of focus that at first glance seem mutually exclusive. When focusing on comparative *practices*, we should neither take the perspective of action theory or methodological individualism and retrace all comparisons and their effects solely to the intentions of the acting subjects, nor should we adopt an abstract, structuralistic viewpoint and look exclusively for universally valid 'mechanisms' and rules of comparison. Rather, we should search for a 'third' way beyond the theory of action and structuralistic approaches. In this attempt, we may follow more recent considerations of practice theory, conceptualized, amongst others, by Andreas Reckwitz and Frank Hillebrandt and inspired by Pierre Bourdieu and Anthony Giddens.[7]

Practice theory focuses neither solely on the acting subjects nor exclusively on the structures in which the actions are embedded. Instead of having actions traced back to a few factors external to them, attention is directed to the practices themselves, which are understood as the proper manifestation as well as the smallest unit of the social and cultural world.[8] Practices resort to implicit, often nonverbal knowledge, to distinctions, criteria and ways of ordering phenomena, as well as to practical knowhow. They constitute, stabilize or modify this knowledge. Without continuous updating at the practical level, this informal knowledge could not be articulated or gain relevance. Practices, even purely discursive practices, cannot be considered without the physicality and corporeality of the acting subjects,[9] the material conditions of the objects or tools involved and the particular situation with all its contingencies. Practices can recall embodied, 'tacit knowledge' and may be performed as routines or habitualized behaviour, but they also shape experiences of corporeality and help inculcate a stable comportment (*habitus*). Analogously, the objects, artefacts and instruments employed in actions cannot be reduced to a purely passive instrumental function.[10] There is no complete determination of actions by them either, yet the thing-like presence and material make-up of the objects participating in the practices imply that the scope of the actions is by no means arbitrary. Putatively passive objects that open up options for action, that suggest manners of behaviour or that exclude possibilities play a substantial part in the formation of habits or routines.

Practices that claim the interest of practice theory sway between the routinized and the unpredictable. Repetitions, habits and routines are decisive in stabilizing the orders of knowledge being actualized in them. At the same time, however, a basic incalculability arises from the plurality of the factors involved in any practice.[11] Repeated actualizations of particular actions can gradually cause almost imperceptible shifts that in the end can lead to profound changes.

The programme of practice theory has been worked out most consistently to date in sociology. Attached to this comparatively recent approach has been the hope of being able to describe society or the social as a set of localized, interlocking practices rather than as a pre-existing structure. But practice theory does not only offer the possibility to determine the location of what is social in another, more suitable way. As numerous papers, above all in science studies, have demonstrated, it also proves to be a distinctly productive heuristic.[12] It permits analyses of concrete social or historical phenomena in their full complexity without running the risk of favouring, in a reductionist manner, one of the factors involved. Because practice theory also takes into account the corporeally embodied situation of the practice, it can direct our attention to the interplay between the acting subjects and their embodiments, to implicit orderings of knowledge, to participating objects and their material constraints, as well as to situations and contexts. In addition, it dissuades the analysis from prematurely neglecting 'the "incorporatedness" of knowledge and the "performativity" of action'.[13]

This approach is particularly promising for the study of comparisons, for a number of reasons. First of all, examinations inspired by practice theory permit a differentiated analysis of the *ways in which comparisons are made*. Processes that have remained hidden, as it were, inside the black box may thus come to light. The examination is no longer uniquely centred around the question of who is striving to make a comparison, for which purposes and motivated by which interests. The attention is rather tuned to a diverse bundle of factors: the practices, habits and routines, the corporeal executions and implicit orderings of knowledge, the material properties of the involved objects, as well as the processes of representation. In this way the performative character of comparisons can specifically emerge. Practices of comparing regularly require decisions when the *comparata* and aspects of comparison are chosen. They demand that some perspective be assumed in a closer definition and perception of the units to be compared. They tend to favour or even constitute categories and demand an evaluation of the relevance of congruencies and disparities. Besides the mental operation of juxtaposing the *comparata*, comparisons often involve other executions and operations as well. Consider, for instance, the practices of collecting, viewing and selecting information or, more generally, the bodily activities involved in the examination of any given units of a comparison. Consider the processes in the technical manipulation of data (for example, through the use of computers) or the practices of notation and representation (for instance, in highly standardized tables).[14] An analysis inspired by practice theory sharpens the sensibility towards the potential relevance of all these factors and uncovers the microdynamisms that always go along with practices of comparison. These microdynamisms, in turn, are an essential reason why we should attribute to comparisons the capability of triggering larger changes and developments beyond their own executions.

The performative moment of comparisons is exemplarily demonstrated in the basic tendency of the *tertium comparationis* to constitute, essentialize and naturalize categories. Any judiciously selected aspect of comparison presupposes comparability – i.e. the fact that both phenomena are of the same kind in at least one respect – which implies the assumption that the chosen aspect is relevant for all the units to be compared. Already at this level, attributions are made that remain mostly unquestioned, although often based on very broad preconceptions. These attributions frequently become self-evident and quasi-'natural' precisely because they prove to be productive in the comparison. It is hardly coincidental that Ludwig Wittgenstein chose comparison as an example to explain the naturalizing effects of such mental or linguistic operations: 'One predicates of the thing what lies in the mode of representation. We take the possibility of the comparison, which impresses us, as the perception of a highly general state of affairs.'[15] Similar processes can also be observed in the choice and constitution of the *comparata*.[16] Whenever entities or groupings are specifically formed in order to serve as units of a comparison, they seem to be validated by a successful performance of the comparison and thereby gain the outlook of self-evident 'facts'. We may therefore safely conclude that practices of comparison are to a considerable degree involved in, or even responsible for, the emergence of social and cultural entities.

Studies based on practice theory are suited to evince not only the performativity, but also the *situatedness* of comparative operations. All comparisons presuppose directed attentiveness, and that is why they are indeed hardly conceivable outside the contexts in which they are conducted. There are continuous interactions going on between the contextual situation and the process of comparing. The practice of making a comparison relies on orderings of knowledge, horizons of meaning and practical skills, but at the same time, it can transmit into these contexts previously unknown distinctions and allocations as well as new 'tangible' routines. Studies inspired by practice theory can stimulate the development of denser descriptions of this situatedness of comparisons.

Yet another essential aspect of comparisons brought to light by such an approach is the negotiation processes that occur when comparers are dealing with obstacles to comparing.[17] Thus, whenever someone claims that certain units are incommensurable or noncommensurable, a sufficient degree of shared characteristics appears to be lacking for comparisons to be carried out. Noncommensurability is asserted when a meaningful aspect of comparison cannot be established between two units. In the extreme case, this leads to the assertion that an object is incomparable or even unique. By contrast, incommensurabilities are claimed when many units are indeed being compared under various aspects, but the similarities and differences that occur cannot be put together to form a coherent overall picture – in other words, when an overarching, complex comparison proves to be impossible to achieve.

Dealing with such obstacles is an integral component of comparison practices. It is important to point out that noncommensurabilities and incommensurabilities do not result 'naturally' from any 'objective' properties of the units subjected (without success) to a comparison. Rather, they can be traced back to the process of selecting and evaluating the perspectives taken by the comparer. They presuppose failed operations of comparison or at least suggest that operations of comparison had previously led to no satisfactory result. Hence, any assertion of noncommensurability or incommensurability relies on decisions that are part of the practice of comparing. These decisions, in turn, may trigger further actions, for instance, when a comparison obstacle becomes the topic of debate and is eventually eliminated by means of an adjustment of the *comparata* or the aspects of comparison.

A practice-theoretical approach is also well suited to investigate the *results*, or *functions*, of a comparison. Comparisons may serve the acquisition of genuinely new insights or the reordering of existing knowledge. They can be integrated into broad reasoning or understood as immediate calls for action. They may also contribute to individual orientation or elicit irritation. In all these cases an approach based on the theory of practice will highlight the situatedness of the comparison and, more particularly, the ways in which the results of comparing are often anticipated by the choice of the *comparata* or the *tertium*. Later application options are then already inherent in the actual comparison.

Finally, the theory of practice offers a particularly suitable approach to comprehending *nonverbal comparisons* in their full complexity. In fact, comparisons are not exclusively apprehensible in linguistic expressions; their examination is by no means necessarily bound to texts. Images, for example, or particular manners of conduct (mimicry, gesture, dress, etc.) can also contain comparative signals that incite observers to make a comparison. Signals of this kind are set particularly when the potential objects of comparison are placed ostensibly next to each other and a similarity or sameness becomes obvious that affords the basis for its choice as a *tertium comparationis*. On this basis, the comparing subject can determine aspects of comparison and identify similarities or differences. Such cases are good examples of comparisons that have a specific corporeal or material anchoring and are actualized in practices.

All the aforementioned aspects – the performative executions and the situatedness of comparisons, the ways of dealing with comparison obstacles and results, the specific features of verbal and nonverbal comparisons – are moments of comparison that are often overlooked. By contrast, the initial assumption that comparisons should be understood as practices helps us to become aware of the numerous and unavoidable (although often not consciously sought) decisions and actions included in the execution of a comparison. What needs to be analysed, then, are the multifarious practices constituting comparing: the processes of collection, perception and selection of objects or pieces of information, the actual comparative examination of the *comparata*, the techniques of notation, processing of data and evaluation of comparisons, the practices of representation and, last but not least, the impulses to action derived from comparisons. With regard to all these practices, their specific corporeal and material anchoring deserves particular attention. In this way it is possible to describe how practices of comparing resort not just to discourses but also to implicit orders of knowledge and 'tacit knowledge', which they can stabilize, modify or challenge through practical actualization. Starting from observing the microdynamisms at work in individual comparative practices, we may eventually proceed towards a better understanding of the more comprehensive dynamics stimulated by comparisons drawn within the fields of social, political, economic or cultural affairs. This research perspective is based on the assumption that small comparative practices can lead to profound changes, above all when individual practices are regularized in diverse *habitus*, in material, medial or technical devices (*dispositifs*), as well as in institutionalized routines or rules (as defined by Anthony Giddens).[18] Thus, the study of small comparative practices will be of particular importance for understanding historical change at large, for instance, the emergence of social structures or ways of ordering the world. A first step towards examining such effects is a comparatively modest shift of accent: the focus should no longer be 'comparison', but the 'doing' of comparisons. This will enable us to better understand not only how we observe and explore this world but also how we change it. Comparing emerges neither as an entirely controlled and reflective act of subjects nor as the subliminal or abysmal work of systems of language or representation, but as a corporeally embodied and materially situated practice.

## The Semiotic Shadow of Comparative Viewing: The Case of Goethe

For the academic discipline of art history, which was institutionalized in the nineteenth century, comparative viewing (*vergleichendes Sehen*) became a central, indeed, an identity-forming method early on.[19] The field primarily defined itself by its range of subject matter: the artefacts conceived as art in painting, sculpture, print making and architecture, along with the artistic crafts. However, a reference to comparative viewing could serve to lay claim to an independence of method against other historically hermeneutic disciplines. Over the course of the nineteenth century, the comparative method seemed to have become 'almost the sovereign in science', as Adolf von Harnack remarked in 1907,[20] yet art history excelled within the comparative disciplines by virtue of its competence in visual phenomena.

Therefore, it is hardly coincidental that in the preliminary remarks to a very successful, frequently reprinted, introduction to the history of art, Heinrich Dilly spoke of a 'disciplinary imperative of comparative viewing'.[21] Similarly, in a recently published primer, Sergiusz Michalski characterized art history as 'a historically informed discipline of comparative viewing'.[22] This pivotal role of comparing also seems to warrant the scientific credentials of art history, because at least to a certain degree, the comparative gaze can be intersubjectively transmitted, learned and inculcated. The comparison of works of art can serve very different purposes: stylistic dependencies and differences can be exhibited, originals can be distinguished from copies, or quotes, allusions and influences can be displayed.

While the merits of visual comparison seem evident, its problematic implications are almost totally neglected. They only come to the fore when we understand comparative viewing as a specific practice. On a very basic level, comparisons of pictures, or other works of art, produce important effects by decisively influencing the bodily movement and sensorial perception of the beholder, by restricting the temporality of viewing and by determining the physical distance that the body of the recipient must assume to the objects. This is where the effective implications of comparison become most powerful in art history. Due to these rather trivial effects, comparative practices substantially influence the ways in which art historians usually understand the nature of pictures and the way in which they function. The thesis I would like to explicate in the following is that comparative viewing promotes an understanding of pictures as systems of signs and hence leads to an underestimation of those qualities of pictures that defy semiotic approaches. More specifically, comparative viewing may very well have had a hitherto overlooked share in the unique success of iconology in the professional discourse of art history.

In order to develop my thesis, I choose an example from the antecedents of academic art history. How comparison can contribute to apprehending pictures as systems of signs is already observable with Johann Wolfgang Goethe. Goethe's example is particularly interesting as it indicates the importance of comparative practices already in this early stage of a discourse that later should become the academic discipline of art history. Goethe's intense occupation with the graphic arts over a period of many years made constant recourse to comparative viewing.[23] In 1780, when his print collection was just beginning, he enthusiastically sought to acquire expertise in connoisseurial viewing, which included comparison in particular. Later Goethe incorporated the key method of comparative viewing into a form of looking at art analogous to his morphological nature studies.[24]

Among the texts in which Goethe explicitly compared images, a review that appeared in 1789 in the journal *Teutscher Merkur* deserves special notice.[25] The complicated title – *On Christ and the Twelve Apostles, engraved after Raphael by Marcantonio and copied by Prof. Langer in Düsseldorf*[6] – already suggests that Goethe felt faced with an intricate task. The occasion and actual subject of the review were copperplate engravings by Johann Peter Langer (Figure 2.1). Langer's prints reproduced engravings by Marcantonio Raimondi (Figure 2.2), which, in turn, were related to frescoes partly attributed to Raphael in the Church of SS. Vincenzo e Anastasio alle Tre Fontane in Rome.[27] Goethe may well have agreed to review Langer's series of prints because he had seen those frescoes himself in December 1787. But a central aim of his review must have been to compare Raimondi's prints with Langer's in critical detail. In accordance with the conventions followed by such reviews, the reader could expect an answer to the question of whether Langer's copper engravings would be a worthwhile purchase.

However, the far longer first part of Goethe's text ignores this question entirely. The affiliation Raphael–Raimondi–Langer is mentioned in passing in the introduction, but instead of differentiating the works of those three artists, Goethe blurs the temporal, medial and stylistic differences between them, with the result that their works form a kind of trinitarian unity. Goethe's strategy of elision ultimately becomes visible at the linguistic level when he relates the personal and demonstrative pronouns in a purposefully ambiguous way. After cursorily mentioning 'Raphael's masterpieces', Raimondi's series of copperplates and Langer's copies, he continues:

> The task of properly presenting a luminary teacher with his twelve first and principal disciples, who clung to his every word and very presence, and whose simple walks in life were mostly crowned by a martyr's death, *he* met with such a simplicity, multifariousness, cordiality, and such a rich understanding of art, that we can deem *these* sheets as one of the finest monuments of *his* fortunate existence.[28]

Whereas the pronoun 'he' refers to Raimondi and Langer or, most likely, to Raphael himself, 'these sheets' cannot refer to the originals attributed to Raphael, but only to the series of prints by Raimondi or Langer. However, the 'fortunate existence' mentioned at the end of the quote, to which the 'sheets' attest, clearly refers to Raphael's life. The strategy behind this multiple signification is obvious: Goethe shifts the three different cycles so closely together that he can easily speak about Raphael's 'masterpieces' with Langer's prints before his eyes.

Consequently, as he walks through the series of figurative depictions, Goethe foregoes making any distinction between Raimondi's sheets, Langer's prints and the frescoes in SS. Vincenzo e Anastasio.[29] Figure by figure, each is succinctly characterized, with the analysis concentrating less on the attributes of the apostles than on the differing draperies of their robes. The philologist Ernst Osterkamp

**Figure 2.1** Johann Peter Langer, Saint Thomas, after Marcantonio Raimondi, c. 1789, engraving, 20.9 × 13.6 cm, Weimar, Klassik Stiftung Weimar, Goethe-Nationalmuseum, Credit: Klassik Stiftung Weimar, GNM (Schuchardt I, p. 63, no. 589/5).

**Figure 2.2** Marcantonio Raimondi, Saint Thomas, c. 1520, engraving, 21.1 × 14 cm, Amsterdam, Rijksmuseum, Credit: Rijksmuseum, Amsterdam.

has examined Goethe's basic descriptive method in a detailed study, pointing out that the text almost entirely ignores the religious context in order to concentrate instead on a statuary conception of the figures with their characterizing 'significant folds.' In this way, Osterkamp was able to show that Goethe's kind of fold-philology relates back to descriptions of antique works of art by Johann Joachim Winckelmann.[30]

Experts and print enthusiasts were only given their due in the final paragraphs of the essay, where Goethe adds a critical acknowledgement of Langer's copies. It seems as if the perspective has radically changed. Raphael's figurative creations are no longer at the centre of attention; now it is the accuracy of Langer's reproductions. Goethe's gaze is now directed to the 'contours' (*Conture*) as he compliments the elaboration of 'light and shade' and assesses the effect of the 'light-gray paper':

> These sheets thus indisputably grant a notion of the value of the originals with their intent of invention, postures, draping of the folds, character of the hair, and the faces, and we may surely say that no lover of the arts should fail to procure these *Langer* copies, even in the rare case that he owned the originals; as even then, these copies offer much food for thought as a good translation.[31]

The largely positive total impression is slightly constrained in Goethe's further argumentation when he points out deviations in the details of individual examples and variations in the copyist's precision. Yet even without these specifics, Goethe's recommendation to make the purchase is more provocative than it might initially seem. A glimpse into contemporary manuals for print collectors – William Gilpin's *An Essay upon Prints* (1768), Johann Caspar Füssli's *Raisonirendes Verzeichniß der vornehmsten Kupferstecher und ihrer Werke* (1771) or Michael Huber's *Handbuch für Kunstliebhaber* (1796–1808) – leaves no doubt that an owner of original prints would be ill-advised to acquire later copies.[32] Accordingly, anyone in possession of an original should not clutter his portfolio with more derivatives.

Goethe's suggestion that Langer's engravings might be able to sharpen the appreciation of the original in the same way 'as any good translation' probably irritated contemporary readers more than reassuring them. The drawing of comparisons between graphic reproductions and literary translations was prevalent in eighteenth-century discourse on prints and had even become a *topos* in the relevant literature.[33] Yet, Goethe's usage of it went against the established understanding. Reproductions of paintings or sculptures were mentioned to accord fair recognition of the transfer, especially considering that the engraver had to reproduce an image under entirely different material and medial conditions. Langer's project, however, did not have those difficulties to contend with. His reproductions of Raimondi's engravings were rather characterizable as copies, or at best as facsimiles, but not as translations.

There are some arguments in favour of Goethe having consciously and purposefully gone against established conventions among collectors with his review.

At least, in the final paragraphs of his text, he needed to justify his recommendation of a purchase, as well as the unusual adaptation of the *topos* of a reproduction print as a 'translation', by taking a critical look at the details of Langer's prints. It is notable that his gaze centred on the folds even in his criticism:

> Since all the figures are clothed, and the greatest artistic value lies in harmonious robes fitting each character in every posture: obviously the blossoming height of these works gets lost if the copier does not everywhere treat the folds most delicately. Not only the main folds of the originals are masterfully conceived, but from the sharpest and shortest strokes up to the broadest taperings, everything is considered and each part is expressed according to its character by the most sensible of burins.[34]

If Goethe therefore pursues the 'various shadings, small depressions, elevations, edges, breaks, [and] seams'[35] in order to check how they are completed by Langer's copies, it is not without reason that the burin's graphical marks and the represented folds would merge into indistinguishability. Goethe's postulate that 'everything be considered' down to the slightest detail attaches a specific meaning to each trace, each dash:

> In the originals there is not a fold to which we do not dare to grant full legitimacy; none that would not be followed down to its last nuance, even in the fainter prints which we have before us. This is not always the case with the copies.[36]

By pointing out the weak spots of Langer's engravings, Goethe demonstrates where the special merit of the copies lies for an owner of originals. A comparison of the two series brings awareness not only of the differences lending occasion for a critique of the reproductions, but also of the essential qualities of Raimondi's original engravings. Conscious juxtapositioning of the two series of engravings permits a sharpening of the perception that does not stop at a differentiation between original and copy, but also ought to promote a proper basic understanding of the originals. Thus, Goethe exposes a precondition of his interpretative analyses of folds in the first, longer part of his article: comparison against the copies sharpens his insight into the significance of the folds in Raimondi's engravings and thus smooths the way to characterizing the figures from their draping robes. By comparing the smallest details, Goethe was able to understand them as significant motifs.

By placing his focus on apparently marginal details and making such a differentiating comparison of these sheets, Goethe radicalized practices in the engagement with prints that other experts exercised less consistently and reflectively, yet much more as a matter of course. It is possible that while he was working on his review, Goethe had a particular model in mind: Johann Heinrich Merck, a close friend of his, especially prior to his trip to Italy.[37] Merck wrote regular contributions for Wieland's *Teutscher Merkur*, and more than a few dealt with questions involving print collecting. In several articles he emphasized the importance of practising the gaze and sharpening the eye by systematic comparative viewing.[38] A review that he published in 1787, likewise in *Teutscher Merkur*, two years before Goethe's, to comment on 'some of the most deceptive copies of Dürer's engravings',[39] is an exemplary illustration of how expert discourse about genuineness and quality could proceed almost seamlessly with the attribution of meaning to the minutest of graphic details. Merck's mission to provide new and better criteria for the identification of fakes motivated him to look beyond signatures and the laterally correct impression of a print to an abundance of details. Wanting to communicate his findings to other experts and collectors, he had to attach names to significant details. Under these circumstances, it no longer sufficed just to speak of lines, their courses and lengths; Merck had to mention depicted objects. Upon reading his considerations with particular attention to this identifying task, it becomes apparent that Merck's search for deviations became an avenue for incursive interpretational issues. For example, he repeatedly refers to physiognomic details and their false renditions in the 'deceptive copies', such as the way the corners of the mouth were drawn, or whether the eyes were closed or half-open, or how the eyebrows were shaped.[40] In passages that Merck wanted to formulate particularly plastically, it becomes clear how apparently trivial details, when falsely copied, could acquire significance. About the depiction of the child in Dürer's engraving *Madonna by the Wall* (1514), for instance, he writes: 'In the new reprint ... the lower eyelid on the left is fully shaded and the temple muscle and brow muscle are indicated so strongly that the child is entirely grimacing and seems to have stomach ache.'[41] The linking of two approaches, comparative viewing and the conceptual fixing of observed discrepancies, made it possible to read graphical traces that, at first glance, might seem inconspicuous as symptoms that would affect the interpretation of the representation.

## Implications of Comparison

In performing his comparisons, Goethe was merely carrying on a tendency to assign significance to details that also existed elsewhere in the discourse among experts and amateurs. Even so, it would be wrong to explain this tendency as a more or less contingent historical phenomenon of the eighteenth century. In fact, close attention to details was a widespread practice in the context of comparative viewing – at least among connoisseurs.

Generally speaking, comparative viewing implies a perceptual process with reference to two or more objects that is coordinated by the aim of comparing. In the case of connoisseurs, the search for disparities or for similarities serves specific purposes: to determine the artist, to differentiate an original from a copy or to distinguish different states of a print. If, however, one analyses more closely the ways in which connoisseurs direct and coordinate their gaze in the process of comparative viewing, one can discover how this specific form of perception does not just consist in such explicit functions, but impels the beholder towards a semiotic interpretation of an image and of individual pictorial elements.

Comparisons of pictures imply the isolation of individual phenomena out of their context, because without the establishment of clearly delimited units, it is impossible to ascertain what is being compared to what. Often elements in the image first become determined by this definition of units, which permits congruencies and discrepancies to be identified. But if lines, hatches or other traces are understood as distinct units within a medium for conveying meaning, then they attain a decisive property that makes them comparable to signifiers.[42] Each element of a signification can only derive its value by difference from other elements of the system, hence signs function only as units delimited by other signs. Therefore, conversely, the distinction of differing elements in an image is a first step towards comprehending these elements as signs. The definition of such units provides at least one necessary precondition for a semiotic conceptualization of the image. Particularly if the depiction as a whole represents some physical object, it thus seems to be only consistent to understand a trace grasped as an individual unit as a sign carrying meaning or an element of differentiating significance.[43]

A century after Goethe's labours on his print review, this tendency of comparative viewing would be demonstrated by one of the most reputable connoisseurs, Giovanni Morelli, in a particularly exaggerated form (Figure 2.3). In his *Kunstkritische Studien über italienische Malerei* (1890–93), Morelli depicted lengthy series of hands or ears to exemplify the individual styles of each painter. Here, comparison has dissected the representation into individual pictorial signs.[44]

The tendency towards a semiotic conception of the units forming the basis of the comparison is intensified further when two images are juxtaposed. This conditions the perception of visual traces and markings, as well as their interrelations, to a substantial degree. Viewers concentrating on only one picture can get caught up in their attempt to reconstruct individual traces, without even consciously steering the perceptual process fully. But the constantly alternating glances of comparative viewing prevent such absorption of the eye. Thus, the comparison ignores a potential by which lineaments, for instance, could resist full interpretation as signs. The very effort of wringing clear meaning out of each graphic trace or mark can entangle the viewer of a single picture so much in those traces that the eye is distracted away from the depiction itself to the pictorial means. The more exactly and near-sightedly the viewer follows individual lines, the more blurred their context becomes, until in the end he or she is confronted by an abstract web of visual traces. Something that originally drew attention as a fold, for instance, then appears as an opaque line that assumes a visual weight of its own. Late paintings by Titian, or Rembrandt's etchings, play with this possibility, just as many impressionistic paintings do. By contrast, perceptual processes such as these are eliminated in the functionalized comparative viewing of connoisseurs because the gaze is then subjected to the external regulation of alternating glances. As it follows a definite intention, the comparison process must be largely subjected to the viewer's control.

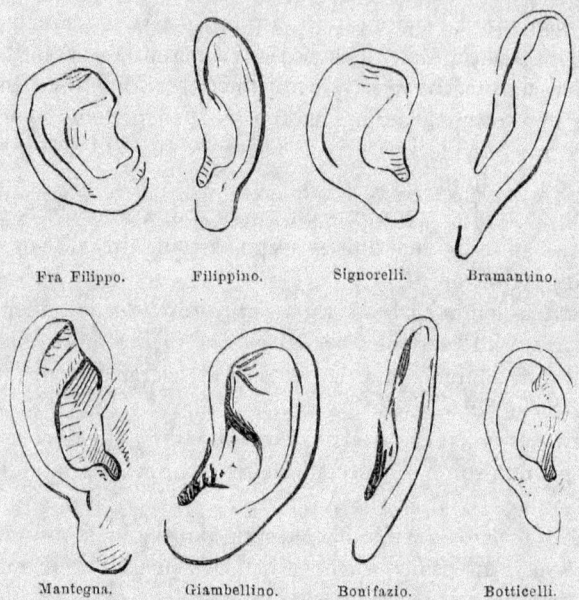

**Figure 2.3** Ivan Lermolieff (i.e. Giovanni Morelli), *Kunstkritische Studien über italienische Malerei*, vol. 1 (Leipzig: Brockhaus, 1890), 99, Credit: Heidelberg University Library, C 7012–20::1, p. 99. – CC-BY-SA 3.0.

Moreover, by subdividing the fabric of graphic traces and marks into an arrangement of distinct units, the expert comparison limits the opportunities of interrelating the different dashes, spots, points, surfaces or intervals. The comparing viewer is forced to privilege specific traces over their contexts, even though those traces themselves would permit infinite options of referencing and relationing. This preliminary decision eliminates the constitutive indefiniteness peculiar to every image in favour of an unequivocal assignment of meaning; as a consequence, it becomes more difficult to resist attempts at interpreting pictures, or other works of art, in an exhaustive, semiotic manner.[45]

Comparative viewing additionally gives the process of perception a rigid rhythm. This limits to a substantial degree the possibility of different temporal experiences during the perception.[46] The eye must move regularly between the distinct units in order to be able to assess the congruencies and discrepancies. This kind of comparison prohibits other experiences of time which could be evoked in the process of discerning the image. Dashes and hatches, for example, often refer to the time of their creation; in a way, a resonance of the time that elapsed as the line was being drawn seems to be preserved. Of course, the viewer cannot re-enact this time straightforwardly, as the inference made from the drawn line to the drawing act always takes place afterwards and in another measure of time. Nonetheless, although the viewer cannot go back to the origin, the moment of the tracing of the line, he or she is inevitably involved in retrospection and re-enactment.[47] The peculiar ability of the graphical trace to evoke the thought of its emergence and simultaneously to evade reactualization of it is obscured in comparative viewing. Then, any observation of a line in detail is arrested at the latest when the eye moves on to the comparison object, so as not to endanger the comparability.

The sketched implications of comparative viewing suggest that the operation of comparison tends to deflect the view from those pictorial phenomena that could disturb a semiotic understanding of the image. At the same time, comparison generates those distinct units that can operate as signifiers in the interpretation of the picture. The tendency to apprehend elements of a picture and graphical traces as signs thus proves to be a suggestive, perhaps almost unavoidable implication of comparative viewing. However, pictures cannot be exhaustively conceived as a fabric of stable graphic units. In the process of reception, those units are rather in a constant state of flow; indeed, they are continually being generated anew, sundered from each other and regrouped in constellations. Traces, dashes, hatches, etc. – to borrow a formulation by James Elkins – distinguish themselves by an 'ontological instability'[48] and by their intermediate position 'between linguistic sign and painterly babble'.[49]

Goethe's comparison between Langer's and Raimondi's engravings exemplarily illustrates how comparative viewing as employed by connoisseurs is unable to take into regard the instability of graphic traces mentioned by Elkins. By conditioning the eye, comparative viewing encouraged, in Goethe's case, a semiotic understanding and interpretation of images. Closer analysis of the comparative process has shown that this latent transformation of the image into a sign-like structured visual field did not happen by chance. An unexpected proximity to pictorial semiotics thus accompanies the method of comparative seeing like a shadow. It is not a conscious component of the method itself, but can be strongly stimulated by comparison.

## Critique of Comparative Viewing

The example of Goethe's review gives occasion to question the close, if not identity-forming connection between the discipline of art history and the practice of comparative viewing. As we have seen, comparisons can contribute to a latent promotion of semiotic 'readings' of images. By the extraction of distinct graphical units and coordination of motions of the eye, pictorial comparisons favour a perception that charges graphical traces with signifying meaning. Of course, this does not characterize comparative viewing in general, or more specifically comparison as a method employed in art history. However, what our case study has shown is that a genuine critique of comparative viewing is an urgent task. Such a critique should involve an examination of the conditions that make this form of observation possible, and it should also point out the potentials and achievements, as well as the limits, of comparative viewing.

Such a fundamental critique of visual comparison necessarily exceeds the bounds of the field of historical studies and demands theoretical clarification. It must raise elementary questions about perception and epistemology: How do the acts of looking and comparing, the sensorial perception and the act of insight by reason, meet? Although an exemplary case study cannot completely resolve this problem, a closer reading of Goethe's print review does point to aspects that could well be of particular relevance to a theory of comparative viewing. Above all, Goethe's case has demonstrated that the application of comparative viewing as a method not only follows more or less obvious, and conscious, intentions, but also implies far-reaching preliminary decisions that as a rule are left unconsidered.

If the practice of comparative viewing is understood in this sense, particular dimensions of images or works of art could only emerge when a comparison has failed. Only when sight leads comparison to limits do phenomena of indeterminacy or overdeterminacy become ascertainable. The fact that comparative viewing has its limitations certainly does not fundamentally draw it into question. It would be misleading to search for the phantom of an innocent and purified vision. Comparison flanked by other forms of perception, which is adapted to knowledge about its limitations, may undoubtedly contribute towards a substantial sharpening of the eye. But more acute looking is always subject to the inherent risk of flipping over into overlooking.

**Johannes Grave** is Professor of Art History at Friedrich Schiller University Jena and editor of the journal *Zeitschrift für Kunstgeschichte*. He has published numerous works on Caspar David Friedrich, Giovanni Bellini, and Johann Wolfgang Goethe as a collector of prints and drawings as well as on theoretical questions of viewing works of art.

# Notes

1. Earlier versions of parts of this chapter have been published in German: J. Grave, 'Der semiotische Schatten des vergleichenden Sehens: Zu Goethes Falten-Philologie', in L. Bader, M. Gaier and F. Wolf (eds), *Vergleichendes Sehen* (Munich: Fink, 2010), 273–91; J. Grave, 'Vergleichen als Praxis: Vorüberlegungen zu einer praxistheoretisch orientierten Untersuchung von Vergleichen', in A. Epple and W. Erhart (eds), *Die Welt beobachten. Praktiken des Vergleichens* (Frankfurt on the Main: Campus, 2015), 135–59. For the translation of this chapter I thank Ann M. Hentschel.
2. See G. Jucquois, *La méthode comparative dans les sciences de l'homme* (Louvain-la-Neuve: Peeters, 1989); G. Jucquois and C. Vielle (eds), *Le comparatisme dans les sciences de l'homme : Approches pluridisciplinaires* (Brussels: De Boeck, 2000); M. Eggers (ed.), *Von Ähnlichkeiten und Unterschieden: Vergleich, Analogie und Klassifikation in Wissenschaft und Literatur (18./19. Jahrhundert)* (Heidelberg: Winter, 2011); M. Eggers, *Vergleichendes Erkennen: Zur Wissenschaftsgeschichte und Epistemologie des Vergleichs und zur Genealogie der Komparatistik* (Heidelberg: Winter, 2016).
3. See G. Schenk, 'Vergleich', in H.J. Sandkühler (ed.), *Europäische Enzyklopädie zu Philosophie und Wissenschaften* (Hamburg: Meiner, 1990), vol. 4, 698–701; I. Max, 'Vergleich', in H. J. Sandkühler (ed.), *Enzyklopädie Philosophie* (Hamburg: Meiner, 2010), vol. 3, 2880–82.
4. See M. Schießl, 'Untersuchungen über die Ideenassociation und ihren Einfluß auf den Erkenntnisakt', *Zeitschrift für Philosophie und philosophische Kritik. Neue Folge* 61 (1872), 247–82 at 257: 'Thinking is nothing else than comparing.'
5. See W.J.T. Mitchell, 'Why Comparisons are Odious', *World Literature Today* 70(2) (1996), 321–24; A. Dorschel, 'Einwände gegen das Vergleichen. Ein Versuch, sie zu beantworten', *Philosophisches Jahrbuch* 113 (2006), 177–85; A. Mauz and H. von Sass, 'Vergleiche verstehen. Einleitende Vorwegnahmen', in A. Mauz and H. von Sass (eds), *Hermeneutik des Vergleichs: Strukturen, Anwendungen und Grenzen komparativer Verfahren* (Würzburg: Königshausen & Neumann, 2011), 1–21, esp. 1–4; S. Kierkegaard, *Upbuilding Discourses in Various Spirits*, H.V. Hong (ed. and trans.) (Princeton: Princeton University Press, 1978), 146: 'all comparison is damaging, indeed, it is evil'.
6. See P. Geimer, 'Vergleichendes Sehen oder Gleichheit aus Versehen? Analogien und Differenz in kunsthistorischen Bildvergleichen', in Bader, Gaier and Wolf (eds), *Vergleichendes Sehen*, 45–69, at 65: 'Comparisons absorb the particular.'
7. See A. Reckwitz, 'Toward a Theory of Social Practices: A Development in Culturalist Theorizing', *European Journal of Social Theory* 5(2) (2002), 243–63; A. Reckwitz, 'Grundelemente einer Theorie sozialer Praktiken: Eine sozialtheoretische Perspektive', *Zeitschrift für Soziologie* 32 (2003), 282–301; A. Reckwitz, 'Auf dem Weg zu einer kultursoziologischen Analytik zwischen Praxeologie und Poststrukturalismus', in M. Wohlrab-Sahr (ed.), *Kultursoziologie: Paradigmen – Methoden – Fragestellungen* (Wiesbaden:

Verlag für Sozialwissenschaften, 2010), 179–205; F. Hillebrandt, 'Praxistheorie', in G. Kneer and M. Schroer (eds), *Handbuch Soziologische Theorien* (Wiesbaden: Verlag für Sozialwissenschaften, 2009), 368–94; F. Hillebrandt, *Soziologische Praxistheorien: Eine Einführung* (Wiesbaden: Verlag für Sozialwissenschaften, 2014). For a more critical view on practice theory, see G. Bongaerts, 'Soziale Praxis und Verhalten: Überlegungen zum Practice Turn in Social Theory', *Zeitschrift für Soziologie* 36 (2007), 246–60.

8. See T.R. Schatzki, 'Introduction. Practice Theory', in T.R. Schatzki, K. Knorr-Cetina and E. von Savigny (eds), *The Practice Turn in Contemporary Theory* (London: Routledge, 2001), 1–14, at 10.
9. On the differentiation between physicality ('Körperlichkeit') and corporeality ('Leiblichkeit'), see R. Gugutzer, *Soziologie des Körpers* (Bielefeld: Transcript, 2015).
10. On the status of objects in actions and practices, see B. Latour, *Reassembling the Social: An Introduction to Actor-Network-Theory* (Oxford: Oxford University Press, 2005). In this respect, even marginal and accessory elements as *parerga* and framing devices can be relevant; see J. Grave, C. Holm, V. Kobi and C. van Eck, 'The Agency of Display: Objects, Framing and Parerga. Introductory Thoughts', in J. Grave, C. Holm, V. Kobi and C. van Eck (eds), *The Agency of Display: Objects, Framings and Parerga* (Dresden: Sandstein: 2018), 7–19.
11. See Reckwitz, 'Grundelemente einer Theorie sozialer Praxis', 284 and 294–95.
12. See K. Knorr-Cetina, *The Manufacture of Knowledge: An Essay on the Constructivist and Contextual Nature of Science* (Oxford: Pergamon Press, 1981); K. Knorr-Cetina, *Epistemic Cultures: How the Sciences Make Knowledge* (Cambridge, MA: Harvard University Press, 1999); H.-J. Rheinberger, *Experimentalsysteme und epistemische Dinge: Eine Geschichte der Proteinsynthese im Reagenzglas* (Göttingen: Wallstein, 2002).
13. Reckwitz, 'Grundelemente einer Theorie sozialer Praxis', 290.
14. On numerical comparisons, see B. Heintz, 'Numerische Differenz: Überlegungen zu einer Soziologie des (quantitativen) Vergleichs', *Zeitschrift für Soziologie* 39 (2010), 162–81.
15. L. Wittgenstein, *Philosophische Untersuchungen: Philosophical Investigations*, P.M.S. Hacker and J. Schulte (eds) (Oxford: Wiley, 2009), 50: 'Man prädiziert von der Sache, was in der Darstellungsweise liegt. Die Möglichkeit des Vergleichs, die uns beeindruckt, nehmen wir für die Wahrnehmung einer höchst allgemeinen Sachlage' (§ 104).
16. See J. Matthes, 'The Operation Called "Vergleichen"', in J. Matthes (ed.), *Zwischen den Kulturen? Die Sozialwissenschaften vor dem Problem des Kulturvergleichs* (Göttingen: Schwartz, 1992), 75–99.
17. I would like to thank Martin Carrier, Bielefeld, for sharing his ideas on incommensurability and noncommensurability.
18. See A. Giddens, *The Constitution of Society: Outline of the Theory of Structuration* (Berkeley: University of California Press, 1984), 16–25.
19. See Bader, Gaier and Wolf (eds), *Vergleichendes Sehen*.
20. A. von Harnack, 'Gedanken über Wissenschaft und Leben', in *Aus Wissenschaft und Leben*, vol. 1 (Gießen: Töpelmann, 1911), 3–9.
21. H. Dilly, 'Einleitung', in H. Belting et al. (eds), *Kunstgeschichte: Eine Einführung* (Berlin: Reimer, 1986), 7–16, at 12.
22. S. Michalski, *Einführung in die Kunstgeschichte* (Darmstadt: Wissenschaftliche Buchgesellschaft, 2015), 149.
23. On Goethe as a collector of prints and drawings, see J. Grave, *Der 'ideale Kunstkörper': Johann Wolfgang Goethe als Sammler von Druckgraphiken und Zeichnungen* (Göttingen:

Vandenhoeck & Ruprecht, 2006); J. Grave, 'Ideal and History: Johann Wolfgang Goethe's Collection of Prints and Drawings', *Artibus et historiae* 53 (2006), 175–86; J. Grave, 'Goethes Kunstsammlungen und die künstlerische Ausstattung des Goethehauses', in A. Beyer and E. Osterkamp (eds), *Goethe-Handbuch. Supplemente, Band III: Kunst* (Stuttgart: Metzler, 2011), 46–83.

24. See Grave, *Der 'ideale Kunstkörper'*; and J. Grave and J. Maatsch, 'Das Allgemeine im Anschaulichen: Morphologische Reihen in Goethes Sammlungen', in T. Valk (ed.), *Heikle Balancen: Die Weimarer Klassik im Prozess der Moderne* (Göttingen: Wallstein, 2014), 287–310.
25. J.W. Goethe, 'Über Christus und die zwölf Apostel', in *Italien und Weimar, 1786– 1790 (Sämtliche Werke nach Epochen seines Schaffens: Münchner Ausgabe*, K. Richter (ed.), vol. 3.2) (Munich: Hanser, 1990), 275–79. On this text, see also E. Osterkamp, 'Bedeutende Falten: Goethes Winckelmann-Rezeption am Beispiel seiner Beschreibung von Marcantonio Raimondis Apostelzyklus', in T.W. Gaehtgens (ed.), *Johann Joachim Winckelmann. 1717–1768* (Hamburg: Meiner, 1986), 265–88; E. Osterkamp, *Im Buchstabenbilde: Studien zum Verfahren Goethescher Bildbeschreibungen* (Stuttgart: Metzler, 1991), 54–71; and S. Schulze (ed.), *Goethe und die Kunst* (Ostfildern: Hatje-Cantz, 1994), 77–81.
26. The full German title reads as follows: Über Christus und die zwölf Apostel, nach Raphael von Mark-Anton gestochen, und von Herrn Prof. Langer in Düsseldorf kopiert.
27. Today Raimondi's engravings are considered as copies after prints by Marco Dente, which probably reproduce drawings by Raphael; see C. Höper, W. Brückle and U. Felbinger, *Raffael und die Folgen: Das Kunstwerk im Zeitalter seiner graphischen Reproduzierbarkeit* (Ostfildern-Ruit: Hatje Cantz, 2001), 172, no. A 26.
28. Goethe, 'Über Christus und die zwölf Apostel', 275 (emphasis added): 'Die Aufgabe, einen verklärten Lehrer, mit seinen zwölf ersten und vornehmsten Schülern, welche ganz an seinen Worten und an seinem Dasein hingen, und größtenteils ihren einfachen Wandel, mit einem Märtyrer Tode krönten, gebührend vorzustellen, hat *er* mit einer solchen Einfalt, Mannigfaltigkeit, Herzlichkeit, und mit so einem reichen Kunstverständnis aufgelöst, daß wir *diese* Blätter für eins der schönsten Monumente *seines* glücklichen Daseins halten können.' Unless otherwise noted, all translations of quotations are by Ann M. Hentschel.
29. Goethe quite consistently included these paragraphs in the report on his visit to SS. Vincenzo e Anastasio when he wrote his *Italian Journey* in 1829: see J.W. Goethe, *Italienische Reise (Sämtliche Werke nach Epochen seines Schaffens: Münchner Ausgabe*, vol. 15) (Munich: Hanser, 1992), 533–38.
30. See Osterkamp, *Im Buchstabenbilde*, 62–64.
31. Goethe, 'Über Christus und die zwölf Apostel', 278: 'Diese Blätter gewähren also unstreitig einen Begriff von dem Wert der Originale in Absicht auf Erfindung, Stellung, Wurf der Falten, Charakter der Haare und der Gesichter, und wir dürfen wohl sagen, daß kein Liebhaber der Künste versäumen sollte, sich diese *Langerischen* Kopien anzuschaffen, selbst in dem seltenen Falle wenn er die Originale besäße; denn auch alsdann würden ihm diese Kopien, wie eine gute Übersetzung noch manchen Stoff zum Nachdenken geben.'
32. See [W. Gilpin], *An Essay upon Prints* (London: Robson, 1768), 243–44; [W. Gilpin], *Abhandlung von Kupferstichen, worinn die allgemeinen Grundsätze von den Regeln der Malerey, in so weit sie die Kupferstiche betreffen, abgehandelt ... Aus dem Englischen übersetzt* [by J.J. Volkmann] (Frankfurt am Main: Dodsley, 1768), 191–92; J.C. Füssli,

*Raisonirendes Verzeichniß der vornehmsten Kupferstecher und ihrer Werke: Zum Gebrauche der Sammler und Liebhaber* (Zurich: Orell, Geßner, Füeßlin u. Comp., 1771), 65–66; M. Huber, *Handbuch für Kunstliebhaber und Sammler über die vornehmsten Kupferstecher und ihre Werke: Vom Anfange dieser Kunst bis auf gegenwärtige Zeit. Chronologisch und nach Schulen geordnet*, 9 vols (Zurich: Orell, Geßner, Füßli, 1796–1808), vol. 1, 71–72.

33. See V. Meyer, 'Gravure d'interprétation ou de reproduction? Invention, traduction et copie: Réalités historiques et techniques', *Travaux de l'Institut d'histoire d'Histoire de l'Art de l'Université de Lyon* 12 (1989), 41–46; C. Karpinski, 'The Print in Thrall to its Original: A Historiographic Perspective', in K. Preciado (ed.), *Retaining the Original: Multiple Originals, Copies, and Reproductions* (Washington, DC: National Gallery of Art, 1989), 101–9, esp. 106; S. le Men, 'Printmaking as Metaphor for Translation: Philippe Burty and the Gazette des Beaux-Arts in the Second Empire', in M.R. Orwicz (ed.), *Art Criticism and its Institutions in Nineteenth-Century France* (Manchester: Manchester University Press, 1994), 88–108; N. Gramaccini, *Theorie der französischen Druckgraphik im 18. Jahrhundert: Eine Quellenanthologie* (Bern: Lang, 1997), 100; C. Rümelin, 'Stichtheorie und Graphikverständnis im 18. Jahrhundert', *Artibus et historiae* 44 (2001), 187–200, esp. 187–88; S. Bann, 'Der Reproduktionsstich als Übersetzung', *Vorträge aus dem Warburg-Haus* 6 (2002), 41–76. Goethe must have known this commonplace; see Gilpin, *Abhandlung von Kupferstichen*, 192; Füssli, *Raisonirendes Verzeichniß*, 65.

34. Goethe, 'Über Christus und die zwölf Apostel', 278–79: 'Da alle Figuren bekleidet sind, und der größte Kunstwert in den harmonischen, zu jedem Charakter, zu jeder Stellung passenden Gewändern liegt: so geht freilich die höchste Blüte dieser Werke verloren wenn der Kopierende nicht überall die Falten auf das zarteste behandelt. Nicht allein die Hauptfalten der Originale sind meisterhaft gedacht, sondern von den schärfsten und kleinsten Brüchen, bis zu den breitesten Verflächungen ist alles überlegt, und mit dem verständigsten Grabstichel jeder Teil nach seiner Eigenschaft ausgedruckt.'

35. Ibid., 279.

36. Ibid.: 'In den Originalen ist keine Falte, von der wir uns nicht Rechenschaft zu geben getrauen; keine, die nicht, selbst in den schwächern Abdrücken welche wir vor uns haben, bis zu ihrer letzten Abstufung zu verfolgen wäre. Bei den Kopien ist das nicht immer der Fall.'

37. On Merck's importance for the intensified interest in the graphic arts in Weimar, see M. Bertsch, 'Johann Heinrich Merck und die Anfänge der Graphiksammlung von Herzog Carl August', in M. Bertsch and J. Grave (eds), *Räume der Kunst: Blicke auf Goethes Sammlungen* (Göttingen: Vandenhoeck & Ruprecht, 2005), 47–75; Grave, *Der 'ideale Kunstkörper'*, 58–74; M. Bertsch and J. Grave, '"Deine Albrecht Dürer sind nunmehr schön geordnet": Lavaters Dürer-Sammlung in Goethes Händen', in B. Schubiger (ed.), *Sammeln und Sammlungen im 18. Jahrhundert in der Schweiz* (Genf: Slatkine, 2007), 291–313.

38. See J.H. Merck, 'Aus einem Schreiben an den H. über die Frage: wie eine Kupferstichsammlung anzulegen sey?', *Der Teutsche Merkur*, 1778, vol. 2, 170–75; J. H. Merck, 'Einige Rettungen für das Andenken Albrecht Dürers gegen die Sage der Kunst-Literatur', *Der Teutsche Merkur*, 1780, vol. 3, 3–14. On Merck's essays on Dürer see J. Białostocki, *Dürer and His Critics 1500–1971: Chapters in the History of Ideas* (Baden-Baden: Koerner, 1986), 147–160; and A. Grieger, '"Sie freuen sich über das, was sie verstehen": Kriterien bürgerlicher Kunstanschauung in der zweiten Hälfte des 18. Jahrhunderts am Beispiel Johann Heinrich Mercks', *Lenz-Jahrbuch. Sturm-und-Drang-Studien* 3 (1993), 163–82.

39. J.H. Merck, 'Bemerkungen über einige der betrüglichsten Copien von den Kupferstichen Albrecht Dürers', *Der Teutsche Merkur*, 1787, vol. 2, 158–66.
40. See ibid., 162–63.
41. Ibid., 160.
42. See U. Eco, *Zeichen: Einführung in einen Begriff und seine Geschichte* (Frankfurt am Main: Suhrkamp, 1977), 167; U. Eco, *Semiotik: Entwurf einer Theorie der Zeichen* (Munich: Fink, 1987), 76.
43. This does not imply that a semiotics of the image necessarily presupposes distinct and invariant semiotic units that serve as basic elements for pictorial compositions. See W. Nöth, *Handbuch der Semiotik*, 2nd revised edn (Stuttgart: Metzler, 2000), 477–80; G. Sonesson, 'Die Semiotik des Bildes: Zum Forschungsstand am Anfang der 90er Jahre', *Zeitschrift für Semiotik* 15 (1993), 127–60, esp. 142–45; O.R. Scholz, *Bild, Darstellung, Zeichen: Philosophische Theorien bildlicher Darstellung*, 2nd revised edn (Frankfurt am Main: Klostermann, 2004), 102–36.
44. See Ivan Lermolieff [i.e. Giovanni Morelli], *Kunstkritische Studien über italienische Malerei*, 3 vols (Leipzig: Brockhaus, 1890–93).
45. See G. Boehm, *Wie Bilder Sinn erzeugen: Die Macht des Zeigens* (Berlin: Berlin University Press, 2007), 199–212.
46. On the temporality of perceiving pictures, see J. Grave, 'Der Akt des Bildbetrachtens: Überlegungen zur rezeptionsästhetischen Temporalität des Bildes', in M. Gamper and H. Hühn (eds), *Zeit der Darstellung: Ästhetische Eigenzeiten in Kunst, Literatur und Wissenschaft* (Hannover: Wehrhahn, 2014), 51–71.
47. See J. Grave, 'Zeichnung ohne Zug: Über das Unzeichnerische in der deutschen Kunst um 1800', *Zeitschrift für Ästhetik und allgemeine Kunstwissenschaft* 53(2) (2008), 233–60.
48. J. Elkins, 'Marks, Traces, "Traits", Contours, "Orli", and "Splendores": Nonsemiotic Elements in Pictures', *Critical Inquiry* 21 (1995), 822–60, at 841.
49. Ibid., 824.

# Bibliography

Bader, L., Gaier, M. and Wolf, F. (eds), *Vergleichendes Sehen* (Munich: Fink, 2010).
Bann, S., 'Der Reproduktionsstich als Übersetzung', *Vorträge aus dem Warburg-Haus* 6 (2002), 41–76.
Bertsch, M., 'Johann Heinrich Merck und die Anfänge der Graphiksammlung von Herzog Carl August', in Bertsch, M. and Grave, J. (eds), *Räume der Kunst: Blicke auf Goethes Sammlungen* (Göttingen: Vandenhoeck & Ruprecht, 2005), 47–75.
Bertsch, M., and Grave, J., '"Deine Albrecht Dürer sind nunmehr schön geordnet": Lavaters Dürer-Sammlung in Goethes Händen', in Schubiger, B. (ed.), *Sammeln und Sammlungen im 18. Jahrhundert in der Schweiz* (Genf: Slatkine, 2007), 291–313.
Białostocki, J., *Dürer and His Critics 1500–1971: Chapters in the History of Ideas* (Baden-Baden: Koerner, 1986).
Boehm, G., *Wie Bilder Sinn erzeugen: Die Macht des Zeigens* (Berlin: Berlin University Press, 2007).
Bongaerts, G., 'Soziale Praxis und Verhalten: Überlegungen zum Practice Turn in Social Theory', *Zeitschrift für Soziologie* 36 (2007), 246–60.

Dilly, H., 'Einleitung', in Belting, H. et al. (eds), *Kunstgeschichte: Eine Einführung* (Berlin: Reimer, 1986), 7–16.
Dorschel, A., 'Einwände gegen das Vergleichen. Ein Versuch, sie zu beantworten', *Philosophisches Jahrbuch* 113 (2006), 177–85.
Eco, U., *Zeichen: Einführung in einen Begriff und seine Geschichte* (Frankfurt am Main: Suhrkamp, 1977).
———. *Semiotik: Entwurf einer Theorie der Zeichen* (Munich: Fink, 1987).
Eggers, M. (ed.), *Von Ähnlichkeiten und Unterschieden: Vergleich, Analogie und Klassifikation in Wissenschaft und Literatur (18./19. Jahrhundert)* (Heidelberg: Winter, 2011).
Eggers, M., *Vergleichendes Erkennen: Zur Wissenschaftsgeschichte und Epistemologie des Vergleichs und zur Genealogie der Komparatistik* (Heidelberg: Winter, 2016).
Elkins, J., 'Marks, Traces, "Traits", Contours, "Orli", and "Splendores": Nonsemiotic Elements in Pictures', *Critical Inquiry* 21 (1995), 822–60.
Füssli, J.C., *Raisonirendes Verzeichniß der vornehmsten Kupferstecher und ihrer Werke: Zum Gebrauche der Sammler und Liebhaber* (Zurich: Orell, Geßner, Füeßlin u. Comp., 1771).
Geimer, P., 'Vergleichendes Sehen oder Gleichheit aus Versehen? Analogien und Differenz in kunsthistorischen Bildvergleichen', in Bader, L., Gaier, M. and Wolf, F. (eds), *Vergleichendes Sehen* (Munich: Fink, 2010), 45–69.
Giddens, A., *The Constitution of Society: Outline of the Theory of Structuration* (Berkeley: University of California Press, 1984).
[Gilpin, W.], *Abhandlung von Kupferstichen, worinn die allgemeinen Grundsätze von den Regeln der Malerey, in so weit sie die Kupferstiche betreffen, abgehandelt ... Aus dem Englischen übersetzt* [by Volkmann, J.J.] (Frankfurt am Main: Dodsley, 1768).
[Gilpin, W.], *An Essay upon Prints* (London: Robson, 1768).
Goethe, J.W., 'Über Christus und die zwölf Apostel', in *Italien und Weimar, 1786–1790* (*Sämtliche Werke nach Epochen seines Schaffens. Münchner Ausgabe*, Richter, K. (ed.), vol. 3.2) (Munich: Hanser, 1990), 275–79.
———. *Italienische Reise* (*Sämtliche Werke nach Epochen seines Schaffens: Münchner Ausgabe*, Richter, K. (ed.), vol. 15) (Munich: Hanser, 1992).
Gramaccini, N., *Theorie der französischen Druckgraphik im 18. Jahrhundert: Eine Quellenanthologie* (Bern: Lang, 1997).
Grave, J., *Der 'ideale Kunstkörper': Johann Wolfgang Goethe als Sammler von Druckgraphiken und Zeichnungen* (Göttingen: Vandenhoeck & Ruprecht, 2006).
———. 'Ideal and History: Johann Wolfgang Goethe's Collection of Prints and Drawings', *Artibus et historiae* 53 (2006), 175–86.
———. 'Zeichnung ohne Zug: Über das Unzeichnerische in der deutschen Kunst um 1800', *Zeitschrift für Ästhetik und allgemeine Kunstwissenschaft* 53(2) (2008), 233–60.
———. 'Der semiotische Schatten des vergleichenden Sehens: Zu Goethes Falten-Philologie', in Bader, L., Gaier, M. and Wolf, F. (eds), *Vergleichendes Sehen* (Munich: Fink, 2010), 273–91.
———. 'Goethes Kunstsammlungen und die künstlerische Ausstattung des Goethehauses', in Beyer, A. and Osterkamp, E. (eds), *Goethe-Handbuch. Supplemente, Band III: Kunst* (Stuttgart: Metzler, 2011), 46–83.
———. 'Der Akt des Bildbetrachtens: Überlegungen zur rezeptionsästhetischen Temporalität des Bildes', in Gamper, M. and Hühn, H. (eds), *Zeit der Darstellung: Ästhetische Eigenzeiten in Kunst, Literatur und Wissenschaft* (Hannover: Wehrhahn, 2014), 51–71.

——. 'Vergleichen als Praxis: Vorüberlegungen zu einer praxistheoretisch orientierten Untersuchung von Vergleichen', in Epple, A. and Erhart, W. (eds), *Die Welt beobachten. Praktiken des Vergleichens* (Frankfurt am Main: Campus, 2015), 135–59.

Grave, J., and Maatsch, J., 'Das Allgemeine im Anschaulichen: Morphologische Reihen in Goethes Sammlungen', in Valk, T. (ed.), *Heikle Balancen: Die Weimarer Klassik im Prozess der Moderne* (Göttingen: Wallstein, 2014), 287–310.

Grave, J. et al., 'The Agency of Display: Objects, Framing and Parerga. Introductory Thoughts', in Grave, J. et al. (eds), *The Agency of Display: Objects, Framings and Parerga* (Dresden: Sandstein: 2018), 7–19.

Grieger, A., '"Sie freuen sich über das, was sie verstehen": Kriterien bürgerlicher Kunstanschauung in der zweiten Hälfte des 18. Jahrhunderts am Beispiel Johann Heinrich Mercks', *Lenz-Jahrbuch. Sturm-und-Drang-Studien* 3 (1993), 163–82.

Gugutzer, R., *Soziologie des Körpers* (Bielefeld: Transcript, 2015).

Harnack, A. von, 'Gedanken über Wissenschaft und Leben', in *Aus Wissenschaft und Leben*, vol. 1 (Gießen: Töpelmann, 1911), 3–9.

Heintz, B., 'Numerische Differenz. Überlegungen zu einer Soziologie des (quantitativen) Vergleichs', *Zeitschrift für Soziologie* 39 (2010), 162–81.

Hillebrandt, F., 'Praxistheorie', in Kneer, G. and Schroer, M. (eds), *Handbuch Soziologische Theorien* (Wiesbaden: Verlag für Sozialwissenschaften, 2009), 368–94.

——. *Soziologische Praxistheorien: Eine Einführung* (Wiesbaden: Verlag für Sozialwissenschaften, 2014).

Höper, C., Brückle, W. and Felbinger, U., *Raffael und die Folgen: Das Kunstwerk im Zeitalter seiner graphischen Reproduzierbarkeit* (Ostfildern-Ruit: Hatje Cantz, 2001).

Huber, M., *Handbuch für Kunstliebhaber und Sammler über die vornehmsten Kupferstecher und ihre Werke: Vom Anfange dieser Kunst bis auf gegenwärtige Zeit. Chronologisch und nach Schulen geordnet*, 9 vols (Zurich: Orell, Geßner, Füßli, 1796–1808), vol. 1.

Jucquois, G., *La méthode comparative dans les sciences de l'homme* (Louvain-la-Neuve: Peeters, 1989).

Jucquois, G., and Vielle, C. (eds), *Le comparatisme dans les sciences de l'homme : Approches pluridisciplinaires* (Brussels: De Boeck, 2000).

Karpinski, C., 'The Print in Thrall to its Original: A Historiographic Perspective', in Preciado, K. (ed.), *Retaining the Original: Multiple Originals, Copies, and Reproductions* (Washington, DC: National Gallery of Art, 1989), 101–9.

Kierkegaard, S., *Upbuilding Discourses in Various Spirits*, Hong, H.V. (ed. and trans.) (Princeton: Princeton University Press, 1978).

Knorr-Cetina, K., *The Manufacture of Knowledge: An Essay on the Constructivist and Contextual Nature of Science* (Oxford: Pergamon Press, 1981).

——. *Epistemic Cultures: How the Sciences Make Knowledge* (Cambridge, MA: Harvard University Press, 1999).

Latour, B., *Reassembling the Social: An Introduction to Actor-Network-Theory* (Oxford: Oxford University Press, 2005).

Le Men, S., 'Printmaking as Metaphor for Translation: Philippe Burty and the Gazette des Beaux-Arts in the Second Empire', in Orwicz, M.R. (ed.), *Art Criticism and its Institutions in Nineteenth-Century France* (Manchester: Manchester University Press, 1994), 88–108.

Lermolieff, I. [i.e. Morelli, G.], *Kunstkritische Studien über italienische Malerei*, 3 vols (Leipzig: Brockhaus, 1890–93).

Matthes, J., 'The Operation Called "Vergleichen"', in Matthes, J. (ed.), *Zwischen den Kulturen? Die Sozialwissenschaften vor dem Problem des Kulturvergleichs* (Göttingen: Schwartz, 1992), 75–99.

Mauz, A., and von Sass, H., 'Vergleiche verstehen. Einleitende Vorwegnahmen', in Mauz, A. and von Sass, H. (eds), *Hermeneutik des Vergleichs: Strukturen, Anwendungen und Grenzen komparativer Verfahren* (Würzburg: Königshausen & Neumann, 2011), 1–21.

Max, I., 'Vergleich', in Sandkühler, H.J. (ed.), *Enzyklopädie Philosophie* (Hamburg: Meiner, 2010), vol. 3, 2880–82.

Merck, J.H., 'Aus einem Schreiben an den H. über die Frage: wie eine Kupferstichsammlung anzulegen sey?', *Der Teutsche Merkur*, 1778, vol. 2, 170–75.

———. 'Einige Rettungen für das Andenken Albrecht Dürers gegen die Sage der Kunst-Literatur', *Der Teutsche Merkur*, 1780, vol. 3, 3–14.

———. 'Bemerkungen über einige der betrüglichsten Copien von den Kupferstichen Albrecht Dürers', *Der Teutsche Merkur*, 1787, vol. 2, 158–66.

Meyer, V., 'Gravure d'interprétation ou de reproduction? Invention, traduction et copie: Réalités historiques et techniques', *Travaux de l'Institut d'histoire d'Histoire de l'Art de l'Université de Lyon* 12 (1989), 41–46.

Michalski, S., *Einführung in die Kunstgeschichte* (Darmstadt: Wissenschaftliche Buchgesellschaft, 2015).

Mitchell, W.J.T., 'Why Comparisons are Odious', *World Literature Today* 70(2) (1996), 321–4.

Nöth, W., *Handbuch der Semiotik*, 2nd revised edn (Stuttgart: Metzler, 2000).

Osterkamp, E., 'Bedeutende Falten: Goethes Winckelmann-Rezeption am Beispiel seiner Beschreibung von Marcantonio Raimondis Apostelzyklus', in Gaehtgens, T.W. (ed.), *Johann Joachim Winckelmann. 1717–1768* (Hamburg: Meiner, 1986), 265–88.

———. *Im Buchstabenbilde: Studien zum Verfahren Goethescher Bildbeschreibungen* (Stuttgart: Metzler, 1991).

Reckwitz, A., 'Toward a Theory of Social Practices: A Development in Culturalist Theorizing', *European Journal of Social Theory* 5(2) (2002), 243–63.

———. 'Grundelemente einer Theorie sozialer Praktiken: Eine sozialtheoretische Perspektive', *Zeitschrift für Soziologie* 32 (2003), 282–301.

———. 'Auf dem Weg zu einer kultursoziologischen Analytik zwischen Praxeologie und Poststrukturalismus', in Wohlrab-Sahr, M. (ed.), *Kultursoziologie: Paradigmen – Methoden – Fragestellungen* (Wiesbaden: Verlag für Sozialwissenschaften, 2010), 179–205.

Rheinberger, H.-J., *Experimentalsysteme und epistemische Dinge: Eine Geschichte der Proteinsynthese im Reagenzglas* (Göttingen: Wallstein, 2002).

Rümelin, C., 'Stichtheorie und Graphikverständnis im 18. Jahrhundert', *Artibus et historiae* 44 (2001), 187–200.

Schatzki, T.R., 'Introduction: Practice Theory', in Schatzki, T.R., Knorr-Cetina, K. and von Savigny, E. (eds), *The Practice Turn in Contemporary Theory* (London: Routledge, 2001), 1–14.

Schenk, G., 'Vergleich', in Sandkühler, H.J. (ed.), *Europäische Enzyklopädie zu Philosophie und Wissenschaften* (Hamburg: Meiner, 1990), vol. 4, 698–701.

Schießl, M., 'Untersuchungen über die Ideenassociation und ihren Einfluß auf den Erkenntnisakt', *Zeitschrift für Philosophie und philosophische Kritik. Neue Folge* 61 (1872), 247–82.

Scholz, O.R., *Bild, Darstellung, Zeichen: Philosophische Theorien bildlicher Darstellung*, 2nd revised edn (Frankfurt am Main: Klostermann, 2004).

Schulze, S. (ed.), *Goethe und die Kunst* (Ostfildern: Hatje-Cantz, 1994).
Sonesson, G., 'Die Semiotik des Bildes: Zum Forschungsstand am Anfang der 90er Jahre', *Zeitschrift für Semiotik* 15 (1993), 127–60.
Wittgenstein, L., *Philosophische Untersuchungen: Philosophical Investigations*, Hacker, P.M.S. and Schulte, J. (eds) (Oxford: Wiley, 2009).

# 3

# Above/Below, Better/Worse or Simply Different?

*Metamorphoses of Social Comparison, 1600–1900*

Willibald Steinmetz

## Introduction

Social comparisons – comparisons with others to evaluate ourselves – are a ubiquitous and apparently timeless practice.[1] If we can believe Thomas Hobbes, they are not only an anthropological constant but also socially disruptive. In his *Leviathan* of 1651, he maintains 'that men are continually in competition for Honour and Dignity ... and consequently amongst men ariseth on that ground, Envy and Hatred, and finally Warre.' And he adds that 'man, whose Joy consisteth in comparing himselfe with other men, can relish nothing but what is eminent'.[2] When human beings compare themselves with others, they do so in a competitive mood and with a short time horizon. According to Hobbes, this attitude distinguishes them from more socially predisposed animals – the bees are his example – who cooperate for the common weal without being forced to do so. By contrast, the competitive comparisons among humans are driven by, and generate, strong emotions. There may be brief moments of joy, to be sure, but envy, hatred and war will follow all the more certainly. For Hobbes, the way out of this malaise is of course an almighty sovereign who is called to curb the dynamism of envious comparisons by issuing and enforcing an order of ranks.[3] The sovereign for his part is, by the way, a category of its own. No power on earth can be compared to him (or her) as Hobbes declares on the upper edge of the

*Leviathan*'s famous title engraving, quoting from the book Job 41:24: 'Non est potestas Super Terram quae comparetur ei.'[4]

If social comparisons may be considered an anthropological constant, warnings against their evil consequences for social integration and the self equally abound from Hobbes' times up to current debates on the use and misuse of social media. It requires only a brief internet search to come across dozens of webpages devoted to giving advice on how to cope with all sorts of negative feelings that result from comparing ourselves with others, whether through Facebook, Twitter or otherwise. A website called *mediarethink* features a story of a recent study among 600 German students encountering primarily invidious emotions when following others on social media.[5] Another website called *Erica finds...* comments on Theodore Roosevelt's putative dictum 'Comparison is the Thief of Joy' and gives useful hints taken from various other webpages.[6] One of the recommendations referred to is as follows:

> When you're tempted to compare yourself to others, stave off the comparing by feeling your way into your dream. Rather than comparing, imagine. Imagine yourself feeling the way you want to feel – successful, brilliant, artistically free, earthy, healthy, connected. That's it. You're not making yourself *less than* or *more than* anyone else – you're simply giving yourself permission to want what *you* want. (Emphasis added)

Another piece of advice to be found at *Erica finds...* reads:

> – Recognize what your 'hot button' comparison items are (looks, bodies, houses, careers, families, money, etc.).
> – Stop reading the messages that don't build you up. Remove them from your daily life. Unfriend, unfollow, do what you need to do to avoid the temptation to obsessively compare.
> – Find people to follow, things to watch and blogs to read that inspire you, leave you feeling good and help you become a better version of YOU.

The message is clear: instead of comparing yourself with others and experiencing frequent deceptions or illusory joy when finding out that you are 'less than' or 'more than' anyone else, the only standard against which to measure yourself should be your own (former) self and your own wishes for the future. The implication is that 'YOU' are fundamentally different and do not need others, or their alleged achievements, to account for yourself.

Social comparisons in general, then, may be a pervasive and timeless practice, but it is important to note that they can exist in more than one shape. Besides the nowadays much-lamented competitive comparisons with others, which for the purposes of this chapter I will call 'better/worse comparisons', there is another variant that gives priority to individual difference. In a brief formula I will name the latter type the assertion of being 'simply different'. To these two variants a third one should be added: comparisons across legally or conventionally fixed barriers of rank, estate or class. In this chapter's terminology they will be called 'above/below comparisons'. The aim of this chapter is to flesh out all three types of social comparison with empirical examples taken from a variety of source materials (encyclopaedias, novels, visual images, moralistic literature, treatises on social order, etc.) and to formulate hypotheses on their respective trajectories in historical time.

It is tempting to assign a particular historical period and a certain type of society to each of the three variants of social comparison and thereby arrange them in a linear narrative. In such a narrative, the above/below comparisons would prima facie belong to a premodern world with sharp boundaries between estates, ranks or classes. Ideally, comparisons between lord and peasant, master and servant, noble and roturier, or burgher of a city and member of the clergy would not only be illegitimate, but almost inconceivable in a society based on a hierarchy of privileges in which each group is supposed to be almost a species of its own. In practice, however, there is plenty of evidence that such comparisons, whether upwards, downwards or sideways, did indeed happen quite often and were deplored ever more frequently from the seventeenth century onwards.

Moving forwards in our hypothetical narrative, the better/worse comparisons would clearly be associated with a modern, market-based society with equal opportunities, at least in principle, for all individuals. Whether that society is conceived in classical liberal fashion as a stratified yet permeable superimposition of classes or in systems-theoretical terms as an assemblage of functional systems is of secondary importance in our context, for the essential condition here is that individuals should be free to choose between, and hence compare, various ways of life and roads to happiness in relation to their own, more or less favourably evaluated situation.

It is slightly more difficult to attribute a certain historical period and type of society to the third variant of social comparison: the assertion of being simply different. Yet there is a strong presumption that self-assertions of this kind must have come to the fore at around the same time as the better/worse comparisons, because even more than these, they are based on a notion of free and self-determining individuals, if not an elaborate doctrine of individualism. Although the academic debate on the genealogy of an individualistic conception of the self is far from concluded, most specialists agree that only scarce evidence can be found for such an idea, as well as the corresponding practices, before the eighteenth century.[7]

On the whole, the linear narrative sketched here seems fairly plausible in a very long-term perspective that would comprise the Middle Ages and include the twenty-first century. In this chapter, however, I will concentrate on a shorter, yet still long, transitional period reaching from the early seventeenth to the end of the nineteenth centuries. It will be argued that this period, especially from the later eighteenth century onwards, was characterized not so much by a chronological succession as by a continuous interaction side by side, or reaction against each other, of all three types of social comparison: above/below, better/worse and simply different. All three variants competed, as it were, with regard to their validity and scope of application. While there is a lot to suggest that above/below comparisons have been in decline along with the dissolution of privilege since the late eighteenth century, they may indeed resurface at any time, even today, as long as there are a sufficient number of people around who interpret the society they live in as one in which barriers between the higher and the lower classes appear so rigid as to amount to an impermeable hierarchy. Being above all an everyday practice, social comparisons pay little attention to macrohistorical narratives or sociological models; in the first place, they are attempts by individuals or small groups to position themselves against significant others in concrete situations.

## Above/Below Comparisons: Symptoms of an *Ancien Régime* in Crisis

Complaints about comparisons cutting across the boundaries of ranks or estates proliferate in Western Europe from the mid seventeenth century onwards. French dictionaries and encyclopaedias of the time, diligently collating set phrases, proverbs and quotes from literary sources, can serve as a valuable guide to the worries evoked by illicit above/below comparisons. Thus, the article 'Comparaison' in the *Dictionnaire de l'Académie Française* (1694) contains the following sample of sentences:

> *do not compare this man with such an eminent person* ... When someone wants to compare persons or things that are extremely disproportionate one says ironically *what a comparison. here's a nice comparison.* A proverb says that *All comparisons are odious* to indicate that it is dangerous to compare two persons because one of them might be offended.[8]

Social comparisons in general, and comparisons between persons of inferior and superior rank in particular, are 'odious' because they violate our sense of proportion and may cause offence. Moreover, what lurks behind such comparisons and makes them a positive danger for the established order is a pretence to equality. The egalitarian aspiration is subtly registered in the second edition of Furetière's *Dictionnaire Universel* (1727):

> Comparison is sometimes assumed to mean Equality, resemblance. ... In that sense one says that *comparing* someone with someone else is pretending to be equal to him [or her]; wishing to treat him [or her] like a peer.[9]

While these examples in the French dictionaries reflect a view in which social comparisons from below upwards were a major source of irritation, one may also find abundant criticism of comparisons in the opposite direction, from top to bottom. Late seventeenth and early eighteenth-century French moralistic literature and satires are full of dismissive remarks on downwards social comparison. Time and again, the moralists are concerned about the exaggerated pride and condescension to be found in the higher ranks towards those further down the hierarchy. Jean de La Bruyère's *Caractères* (1688–94), a collection of short pieces on the social mores of the time, provides telling examples. In the twenty-third piece of his chapter on 'Society and Conversation', La Bruyère castigates a typical attitude of thoughtless and inappropriate complacency shown by a well-to-do person of higher rank who is causing a feeling of debasement in his less well-situated interlocutor by boasting about his magnificent meals, his treasures, revenues, furniture and general luck in life:

> There is good talk, easy talk, just talk and appropriate talk. It is a sin against the latter to bluster about a magnificent meal one has given in front of people who are forced to save their bread, to entertain a man who has neither an income nor a domicile about one's own riches, revenues or furnitures; in other words to talk about one's own happiness in front of those who are miserable: that kind of conversation is too strong for them, and the comparison between their own condition and yours is odious for them.[10]

Whereas upwards social comparisons are more often exposed to ridicule – think of Molière's *Le Bourgeois Gentilhomme* (1670) – implicit downwards comparisons of the kind described by La Bruyère are reprobated as effectively harmful; they are 'odious' for persons of low rank and small means who are thereby compulsorily reminded of their relative misery. Without questioning the legitimacy of a hierarchical order, La Bruyère even draws near a position of advocating a kind of compensatory equality between the different conditions in society, 'a sort of compensation between good and bad that would establish equality between them'.[11] From here it is just a short step away to openly taking sides with the 'people' against the 'grands' – at least as far as public morality and behaviour are concerned. In the twenty-fifth piece of his chapter on 'Les Grands', La Bruyère indeed comes to that conclusion: 'If I had to choose I wouldn't hesitate: I want to be of the people.'[12] With such an attitude, La Bruyère was not exceptional among French moralists. In France as well as elsewhere in late seventeenth and early eighteenth-century Europe, moralistic literature was an important site for actively contending with, and not just writing about, social comparisons. In the process, this literature contributed significantly to a sense of crisis that increasingly beset those who, in principle, still embraced the existing order of the *ancien régime*.

For long periods in medieval and early modern history, the preferred way in which the defenders of the established social order sought to preserve it was the issuing of positive laws and regulations prescribing rules of precedence at solemn public occasions as well as codes of dress and luxury display in everyday life. Scholars have brought to light several thousands of such regulations issued by sovereign rulers or city authorities in Continental Europe and re-enacted time and again up to the late eighteenth century.[13] In England, by contrast, such regulations fell into disuse much earlier, the last monarch attempting to enforce them with some vigour being Henry VIII. By the time of the Tudor and Stuart monarchs, it was generally common practice for men and women appearing in

English courtrooms to refer to outward signs of material wealth, often expressed in a bare monetary figure (forty shillings and ten pounds being seen as critical thresholds), when asked to account for themselves.[14] As Alexandra Shephard has shown, this practice affected people in all walks of life and nothing objectionable was found in it.

Things were different on the European continent, where it was still considered indecorous, if not a sign of disrespect for rank and privilege, to define one's own social position in purely pecuniary terms. Yet, while in principle there was hardly anyone who doubted the legitimacy of distinctions by rank or estate, Continental Europeans deployed much energy and talent in blurring these distinctions in practice. Thus, they invented myriad ways to circumvent dress codes and sumptuary laws, for example, by displaying hitherto unregulated signs of material wealth (high tower buildings, coaches, exotic food, etc.) or by making use of ever new fashion items (golden shoe buckles, fur collars, embroideries, etc.) that were impossible to police by the authorities.[15] By the late sixteenth century, contemporary observers were well aware of the futility of enforcing dress and luxury regulations. Michel de Montaigne knew that it would be in vain when he appealed in his essay on sumptuary laws (first published in 1580) to the French king that he should renounce all external marks of grandeur, thus setting an example of public virtue for the court and society at large. Even more unrealistic was his proposal for a law that would only allow the 'courtisanes' to walk around in crimson dress and only the male 'ruffians' to wear golden finger rings and 'delicate robes'. Montaigne's idea that such a law might put a halt to envious comparisons and inaugurate a negative spiral of shame and blame was well devised, but obviously utopian.[16]

By the early eighteenth century, the authorities increasingly despaired about their inability to contain the dynamism of fashion waves and the underlying desire of outbidding each other that threatened any fixed order of estates. Thomas Weller, who studied conflicts of rank in the German city of Leipzig, describes the predicament in which the city rulers found themselves when they were forced to keep pace with fashion novelties. Time and again, they had to 'redefine the relation between the signifiers and the signified' to make sure that the distinctions between the estates could still be recognized – a 'hopeless enterprise' in the long run. The 'legibility of the social sign system' became increasingly precarious.[17] A similar mechanism of growing complexity also undermined all attempts to regulate the order of precedence in the everyday life of the city. In 1740, the senior clerk responsible for drawing up new rules for Leipzig declared himself incapable of doing so because the local customs of giving precedence differed infinitely depending on place or situation. There were now different habits, he wrote, 'for horse riding, walking, sitting, or standing, in the church, the city council, or public gatherings, for addressing others, speaking, or writing'.[18]

Faced with the unending circumvention and progressive erosion of official dress and precedence rules, members of the noblesse and urban patriciates had to look for other means to mark their superiority over the lower orders and the *nouveaux riches*. A promising route for them to take was the continuous refinement of manners, gestures and body postures. Unlike luxury or fashion items, good manners, delicate gestures and elegant postures could never be had with money alone; they required above all a certain sense of tact, a feeling for aesthetic proportions and a sound knowledge of how to behave properly – qualities only to be acquired by good breeding, eventually supported by instruction through governesses and private tutors (so money was still an advantage). How one should imagine – and realize in practice – such a process of refinement was described in printed conduct books, but also in visual images. An example for the latter can be seen in Gerard de Lairesse's *Groot Schilderboek*, a manual for prospective painters, first published in Dutch in 1707, soon translated into German (1728/1730) and English (1738), and re-edited several times.[19] A tripartite plate in de Lairesse's book, explained in much detail by the author, illustrates body postures, gestures and manners of persons of different rank in similar situations (see Figure 3.1). Subsection one of the plate shows more or less elegant ways of holding a glass, subsection two deals with mannerly and unmannerly ways of how to eat, and subsection three presents different body postures of persons listening to an interlocutor in a conversation. Here, the two boorish male figures on the right and the female figure on the left are clearly marked as inferior through their grotesquely crooked bodies and clumsy movements, whereas the female figure at the centre represents the ideal of restrained gracefulness; compared to her, de Lairesse explains, the upright female figure to her left, although in outward appearance belonging to the same rank, stands in an unfavourable contrast because she has both her hands resting on the hips, thrusts out her chin and shows a rather 'gawping mouth'.[20]

It should be noted that the social comparisons suggested by de Lairesse's tripartite plate exhibit a fair amount of ambivalence. On the one hand, they still confirm traditional distinctions by rank and estate: those figures that represent peasants while eating or listening are in all respects – manners, postures as well as dress – sharply distanced from the figures that represent persons of higher rank. The above/below comparisons here serve to reinforce the existing social order. On the other hand, the contrast between the two female figures in the centre of subsection three already approaches a better/worse comparison. Their dress marks the two figures as equal by rank, and their only distinguishing features are personal qualities that can (and should) be acquired through individual exertion. Here, de Lairesse's comparison is designed to stimulate emulation of the behaviour presented as the 'better' one.

A similar ambivalence may be discerned in seventeenth and eighteenth-century conduct books addressed to persons of higher rank, often described as 'gentlemen', 'honnêtes hommes' or 'cavaliers'. The use of these denominations already tends to dissolve the boundaries between different estates, yet the terms still rest on an implicit understanding that people below a certain line, such as peasants and manual workers, may never count as gentlemen (or gentlewomen); the principle of a hierarchical society is still accepted.[21] For the imagined readers, those who are expected to come within the circle of gentlemen (and gentlewomen), the conduct books recommend a philosophical attitude towards purely external marks of distinction such as honorific titles or seating orders at festive dinners. While the readers are taught to respect those external marks as a matter of courtesy, they are at the same time urged to strive for inner values and qualities that are deemed essential for social harmony and personal happiness.

**Figure 3.1** Gerard de Lairesse, Body postures, gestures and manners of persons of different rank in similar situations, tripartite plate in Gerard de Lairesse, *Groot Schilderboek* (Amsterdam: Hendrick Desbordes, 1712), between pages 54 and 55. © SUB Göttingen: 8ART PLAST VIII, 225.

This line of argument is followed, for example, in Julius Bernhard von Rohr's *Ceremoniel-Wissenschafft der Privat-Personen* (1728), a guidebook addressed to 'young German cavaliers'.[22] Mocking himself about the craving for honorific titles ('Titul-Sucht'), the author traces the reasons for this silly pursuit to the erroneous belief that persons of higher rank or predicate would also be blessed with a higher degree of happiness ('Glückseligkeit'). However, true happiness, von Rohr says, does not reside in titles and predicates, and therefore everyone might as well be happy remaining in the place given to him (or her) by God.[23] On the surface, von Rohr's admonition can be read as an affirmation of the traditional order of estates, but the thrust of his argument points in another direction: towards a society in which persons of different rank or estate should measure themselves, and their own merits, according to one and the same ideal.[24] In Rohr's case, that common ideal is 'Glückseligkeit', a moral category that means not just happiness in a material sense, but above all the forming of a virtuous character leading to harmony with oneself as well as with one's fellow beings in society.

To resume, by the early decades of the eighteenth century, the critique of above/below comparisons often went along with a cautious move towards better/worse comparisons. Even if authors like La Bruyère, de Lairesse or von Rohr were far from repudiating the principles of rank, hierarchy and privilege, they in fact helped to undermine them when they suggested that people from all walks of life, especially gentlemen, should emulate others who excelled through their fine behaviour, their moral virtues or any valuable pursuits that led to happiness.

## Varieties of Better/Worse Comparisons: Contending with the Measures of Merit

As we have seen, proposals to emulate others rested on the assumption that well-educated human beings were, if not equal, at least equally capable of bettering themselves and in that sense equivalent, though belonging to different social conditions. An idea of moral *equivalency* was thus the minimum requirement for an unfolding of better/worse comparisons. However, these comparisons could still happen in a mental framework that recognized clear above/below distinctions. More far-reaching claims to legal, political and social *equality* were grafted onto the idea of equivalency as enlightened and revolutionary demands progressed in the later eighteenth century. Once human beings were accepted as equals in principle, there was hardly any room left for above/below comparisons. The most obvious way to distinguish oneself was now to become 'better than' or 'less good than' anyone else. Individual merit and value replaced traditional or attributed rank as the major criterion for social comparison.

Even so, what constituted the ideal to be pursued, the model to be emulated and the best practice to be realized remained a contested issue. The ideal could be a fixed absolute standard (of graceful behaviour, beauty, morality, happiness, etc.) or a moving target. If it was a fixed standard, one had to choose an abstract model or a concrete person that in common opinion represented the ideal and emulate it to reach perfection. But if it was a moving target, a neverending and open-ended competition became the dominant mode of social comparison. Social comparisons were in that case temporalized. This implied that others who, for the time being, seemed to be more advanced than oneself were taken as measures to evaluate oneself, only to be replaced again by still others as soon as relative positions had changed. In addition, an exchange of exemplary persons as models could also happen when new standards or best practices imposed themselves in the sphere of life in question – for whatever reason. Like social comparisons in general, then, better/worse comparisons appeared in more than one shape.

It is perhaps no surprise that the more competitive type of better/worse comparison gained currency first in Britain (including its American colonies), where a full-blown market society took hold earlier than in most other parts of Europe.[25] A graphic example is provided by one of several print series produced by William Hogarth in the middle decades of the eighteenth century, the series *Industry and Idleness* (1747). Apparently for commercial reasons, the series appeared in the form of inexpensive engravings only. There are no painted originals as for his earlier series *A Harlot's Progress* (1731) and *Marriage à la Mode* (1743). And unlike these and most other print series by Hogarth (except his well-known double image *Beer Street and Gin Lane*, 1751), *Industry and Idleness* is consistently arranged as a sequence of corresponding double images, or two-part single images, that invite comparisons. Like a narrative, the double and two-part images present the parallel life trajectories of two protagonists: an idle and an industrious apprentice. For the viewer, it is almost impossible not to compare; the structure of the series enforces a comparative gaze, the message of the narrative is completely unambiguous and the images themselves contain little that distracts from the moral message conveyed through the comparison. This lack of ambiguity is probably the reason why art historian Werner Busch has dismissed *Industry and Idleness* as the most uninspiring of Hogarth's series from an artistic point of view and refrained from commenting on it.[26] In our context, however, it is precisely its unambiguousness that makes *Industry and Idleness* worthwhile to describe.[27]

Both protagonists are presented starting under the same condition, hence with equal opportunities, in the first two-part image (Plate 1): here they appear as fellow apprentices in a master weaver's workshop (Figure 3.2). Both end their careers at the opposite ends of the social spectrum, as told in the last pair of corresponding images: In Plate 11, the idle ex-apprentice is being pulled in a miserable cart to Tyburn, London's execution site, accompanied by a priest, while in Plate 12, the industrious ex-apprentice is being driven through the city in a splendid coach amidst cheering crowds after having been sworn in as Lord Mayor of London.[28] Inbetween, the diverging life stories of the two protagonists are unfolded in consecutive pairs of images – exhibiting the progressive moral and social downfall of the idle, and the rise of the industrious apprentice. The parallel story culminates in the second two-part image of the series (Plate 10), which shows their second personal encounter, now before the London

Court of Aldermen where the idle ex-apprentice appears at the bar as a criminal and is judged by none other than his ex-colleague, the industrious apprentice, now one of London's Aldermen and obviously despairing when recognizing his former fellow.

A closer look at the initial two-part image reveals that the career of the two protagonists appears predestined early on (see Figure 3.2). Beyond the obvious contrast between the industrious apprentice being diligently at work and the idle leaning against a wooden pillar, half-asleep from a pot of beer still visible on the top of his loom, many details in the image itself and around the outer edges of the frame presage their destinies. In the case of the idle apprentice, the master is looking angrily towards him with a raised stick, ready to beat him; a shredded and almost illegible copy of the *Prentice's Guide* is lying on the floor; a page of Daniel Defoe's *Moll Flanders* (a story of an orphan child who ends as a prostitute and criminal) is pinned at the wooden pillar; and at the outer edge of the frame, a whip, shackles and a rope are symbolizing his future as a convicted criminal. By contrast, in the case of the industrious apprentice, one can see a well-kept copy of the *Prentice's Guide* neatly displayed in front of his loom, a page from the life story of Richard Whittington, a benevolent and influential London Lord Mayor in the late Middle Ages, pegged against the wall behind him, and at the outer

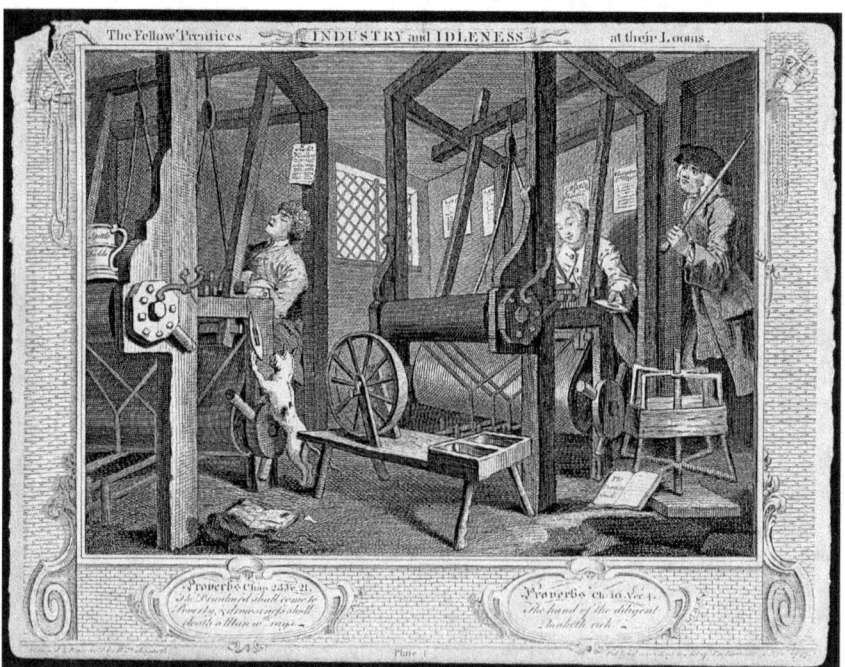

**Figure 3.2** William Hogarth, *Industry and Idleness* (1747), plate no. 1: The Fellow 'Prentices at their Looms, https://wellcomecollection.org/works/e38v27wt, Credit: Wellcome Collection CC BY.

edge of the frame a sword, ceremonial mace and chain of office pointing to his end of career as Lord Mayor. Finally, to drive home the message, two citations from the Book of Proverbs are placed in the space underneath the frame, below the idle apprentice: 'The Drunkard shall come to Poverty, & drowsiness shall cloath a Man wth rags'; and below the industrious apprentice: 'The hand of the diligent maketh rich.'

Moral, religious and economic virtues appear closely intertwined in Hogarth's *Industry and Idleness*. Together, they define a standard of behaviour that leads to moral wellbeing and social prestige as well as material wealth and political power. The print series is ostentatiously arranged as a comparison, yet it is the *viewer* who is invited, almost compelled, to carry out the comparison, whereas the two main figures themselves, as presented by Hogarth, actually do *not* enter into a competitive comparison among themselves. The industrious apprentice follows his own chosen course, emulating ideal figures he has got to know in history books (the story of Whittington) or manuals for his job (the *Prentice's Guide*). The comparative gaze of the viewer turns particularly to the idle apprentice who does *not* do what he *should* do in the eyes of the critical beholder, namely follow the example of, and hence compare himself with, his industrious fellow apprentice. Hogarth's series is of a didactic, even performative character: it is the *viewer* who is forced to practise, and eventually internalize, a new kind of competitive social comparison that is not (yet) realized by the protagonists as presented in the images themselves.

Another example of better/worse comparisons elicited through visual images and to be performed by the viewer is the print series *Natürliche und affectirte Handlungen des Lebens* (*Natural and Affected Forms of Conduct in Life*) by the Polish-German engraver and illustrator Daniel Chodowiecki (1726–1801). The series consists of twelve pairs of images that were published for the first time in 1779–80 in the form of monthly engravings in the *Göttinger Taschen Calender*, an almanac with a circulation of several thousand copies and edited by the moralist Georg Christoph Lichtenberg.[29] The almanac for 1780 also contained an explanation of the engravings by Lichtenberg.[30] Each pair of Chodowiecki's corresponding images contrasts a 'natural' with an 'affected' form of conduct by presenting one or several persons, male or female, engaged in the same pursuit that is identified in the captions using German and French terms: instruction of children, conversation, prayer, promenade, greeting, dancing, sentiment (in a landscape), tastefulness (through dress and gestures), connoisseurship of artworks, walking in bad weather and horseriding in a riding arena. One of the pairs (January–February 1780) illustrates the subject of the whole series by contrasting 'Nature' and 'Affectation', represented respectively by a scantily clad, barefooted, antique-looking, unpretentiously walking male-female couple facing each other ('Nature'), and another couple dressed and coiffed in an exuberantly rich baroque style, posing pretentiously and facing the viewer as if fishing for compliments from him or her ('Affectation').[31] This as well as some other double images (most notably instruction, conversation, salutation and tastefulness) are unmistakably critical of an excessively pompous aristocratic style that was already outdated by the 1780s, even within the higher European aristocracy itself. Therefore, it seems to me that it would be an oversimplification to interpret the whole series, as has sometimes been insinuated, as a glorification of a new, 'bourgeois' simplicity against a corrupt and decadent 'aristocratic' behaviour.[32] Moreover, the majority of the double images do *not* evoke any significant contrast between bourgeois and aristocrats as social groups (prayer, promenade, dancing, sentiment, connoisseurship, bad weather, horseriding). The persons whose behaviour is compared here are marked by their dress as socially equal, and the point of the comparison is uniquely the behaviour itself.

For example, both corresponding images on connoisseurship show a couple of male figures in front of an artwork, a statue representing the goddess Pomona, and in both images the men are dressed almost identically, the rapier worn by one of them identifying them as nobles (see Figures 3.3 and 3.4). Here, the comparison to be drawn by the viewer is clearly not one between two different estates and a form of conduct identified as 'aristocratic' or 'bourgeois', but one between a more or less appropriate way of appreciating artworks generally – irrespective

**Figure 3.3** Daniel Chodowiecki, *Natural and Affected Forms of Conduct in Life*, 2nd series, no. 7: Connoisseurship of Art, in *Goettinger Taschen Calender vom Jahr 1780* (Göttingen: Joh. Chr. Dieterich, 1780), digitized copy Universitätsbibliothek Bielefeld, http://ds.ub.uni-bielefeld.de/viewer/image/2235093_005/67. Credit: Universitätsbibliothek Bielefeld.

**Figure 3.4** Daniel Chodowiecki, *Natural and Affected Forms of Conduct in Life*, 2nd series, no. 8: Connoisseurship of Art, in *Goettinger Taschen Calender vom Jahr 1780* (Göttingen: Joh. Chr. Dieterich, 1780), digitized copy Universitätsbibliothek Bielefeld, http://ds.ub.uni-bielefeld.de/viewer/image/2235093_005/73. Credit: Universitätsbibliothek Bielefeld.

of the social background of the persons involved. What Chodowiecki seems to prefer and ranges as 'natural' is a silent, almost reverent contemplation of artworks as a whole, and what he criticizes as 'affected' is a fervently gesticulating and loquacious form of discussing art in which the connoisseurs try to outbid each other in salient remarks on details such as, in the words of Lichtenberg, the 'pleat of linnen marble', the 'smoothness of a grape' or the 'smell of a flower turned into stone'.[33]

Unlike Hogarth's series *Industry and Idleness*, Chodowiecki's engravings and Lichtenberg's comments do not contain any allusion, not even indirect references, to competition as a model to follow. Equally absent is any positive evaluation of economic virtues or an appreciation of material wealth, social prestige or political power as goals worth pursuing. The situations presented by Chodowiecki, and the better/worse comparisons suggested by his engravings, are not about outperforming others in the accumulation of merits, achievements or economic output, but only about emulating an ideal standard of behaviour defined by Chodowiecki as 'natural' in opposition to 'affected'.

Although it would be rash to generalize on the basis of only two examples, we may formulate as a hypothesis – further to be tested – that by the mid to late eighteenth century, better/worse comparisons had begun to unfold in various shapes. Judging on the basis of our examples, it seems that they were still slow to embrace a restless competition for economic success, money, material goods, prestige or power – in short, the market model – as their dominant underlying rationale. While in Hogarth's Britain this pattern was already clearly discernible, elsewhere the form of temporalized social comparisons with moving targets as yardsticks and an imperative of unending re-adjustments to keep pace with, or surpass, the progress of others was not yet fully established.

## ... Or Simply Different? Preserving Individuality in a World of Better/Worse Comparisons

In conjunction with a perceived increase of better/worse comparisons, criticism of those comparisons also grew from the mid eighteenth century onwards. Indeed, one may hypothesize that the most outspoken descriptions of competitive better/worse comparisons were actually brought forward by their critics, not by the early defenders of capitalist values. One prominent argument used by the critics was the assertion that individuals were unique and, in the last resort, incomparable. For that reason, the critics argued, individuals had to take nothing but their own potential as a yardstick for improvement, while they should disregard the supposed achievements of others or, worse still, the coveted (or feared) *evaluations* of others. In this chapter's shorthand terminology, these criticisms amounted to asserting that individuals were 'simply different'.

Quests for 'genius' and 'originality' in the sphere of the arts were only one – perhaps the most remarkable – manifestation of that assertion.[34] Another prominent site in which uniqueness was emphasized were late eighteenth and early nineteenth-century discourses on romantic love.[35] The same applied to debates on education and self-formation – *Bildung* in German. Strictly speaking, any openly proclaimed postulate of one's own (or someone else's) absolute uniqueness and incomparability is of an intrinsically paradoxical nature, for in order to raise such a claim, one has to rely on previous comparisons with others, be they implicit or explicit. What is more, the very act of saying that one is 'incomparable' is in fact nothing other than a specific form of social comparison.[36] This is probably the major reason why the assertion of being simply different very often appears closely intertwined with rejections of better/worse comparisons.

A *locus classicus* for the simultaneous emergence of claims to individuality and vehement criticisms of better/worse comparisons is Jean-Jacques Rousseau's *Émile, ou de l'éducation* (1762), a key text for reformers of education and self-formation in late eighteenth and early nineteenth-century Europe. It is here that Rousseau elaborates his well-known distinction between a good natured *amour de soi*, which only cares for oneself and one's own true needs, and its harmful counterpart, the *amour propre*, 'that feeds itself by comparisons, is never satisfied nor can ever be satisfied'. Thus, Rousseau says, 'what makes a human being essentially good is to have small needs and to compare oneself as little as possible with others.'[37] According to Rousseau, thus was the condition of man in the original state of nature as imagined by him. However, he goes on, once enlightenment set in, people learned to choose, to develop preferences and to see themselves in the eyes of others in order to be preferred by them. Social comparison became a habit: 'one cannot love without having assessed, and one cannot prefer without having compared ... To be loved, one has to make oneself lovable; to be preferred, one has to make oneself more lovable than someone else ... That's where the first regards towards our fellow humans came from, that's where the first comparisons with them set in; that's where emulation, rivalry and jealousy had their origin'.[38]

Up to a certain point then, comparisons with others are inevitable for Rousseau, unless one could imagine humans to live as monads. Love, and the desire to be loved, propels competitive better/worse comparisons. And these comparisons again, as well as the powerful emotions generated by them, also produce the social inequalities that are typical for human societies in their civilized state, as Rousseau had already demonstrated a few years earlier in his *Discours sur l'inégalité* (1755).[39] The intriguing (and at that time exceptional) point of Rousseau's discussion of better/worse comparisons is that he does not content himself with deploring them, as so many others have done until today, but accepts them as a social force to reckon with, a force whose detrimental effects may perhaps be attenuated, but no longer completely eliminated.

As Rousseau's *Émile* is a novel dealing with education, a *Bildungsroman*, in which the author slips into the role of the tutor, he has to point out ways and means to make sure that the passions incited by the inevitable comparisons are at least not harmful for the protégé himself, as well as for others. Rousseau's first concern in this context is that Émile, while comparing himself with others, should never lose sight of feeling his own self-worth first. Comparisons with others, even competitive ones, whether with living persons or famous historical figures (Rousseau recommends Plutarch's *Parallel Lives* as reading), are innocuous as long as the young protégé does not thereby forget who he is, as long as he does not wish to be somebody else: 'but should it happen in the course of these parallels that only once he preferred to be someone else, be it even Socrates or Cato, everything is lost; he who once begins to turn himself into a stranger to himself will soon enough forget completely who he is'.[40] In modern terms, Rousseau's philosophy of self-formation could be condensed in a conception of 'identity' that rejects any reference to peer groups or role models, but relies exclusively on the idea of an 'authentic' self to be developed in the first place through introspection.

This is the therapeutic remedy Rousseau applied to himself in his *Confessions*, completed by 1769–70 and first published posthumously in 1782. In the Preface and first paragraphs of the *Confessions*, he unashamedly claims uniqueness for himself and combines this postulate with the bold contention that the work that he is going to present to the readers will also be unique because of its true authenticity and that it would therefore never find an imitator:

> 1. I start an enterprise that is unprecedented and will have no imitator. I want to show to my fellow-humans a man as truly created by nature, and that man is myself. 2. Only myself. I feel into my heart and I know mankind. I am not made like anyone I have seen; I dare to believe that I am not made like anyone else who exists; if I am not better [than all others], then at least I am different.[41]

'If I am not better [than all others], then at least I am different.' There is no shorter formulation for the displacement of better/worse comparisons by a conscious policy of 'being simply different'. At the same time, it is hard to believe that Rousseau was not fully aware of the paradoxical nature of his enterprise – to claim absolute uniqueness for himself on the one hand, but to praise his own work as 'a prime piece of comparison for the study of mankind' on the other hand.[42]

Even assertions of incomparability may give rise to new comparisons – and thus start a new cycle of efforts to outdo each other, this time with 'authenticity', 'originality', 'genius', 'eccentricity' or 'individuality' as the prizes to strive for and the criteria for evaluating better or worse performance. Is it possible to be more authentic, original or eccentric than past masters like Rousseau? Is it possible to top the genius of Beethoven? Many philosophers, artists, poets and musicians in the nineteenth and twentieth centuries thought so, or at least they tried hard to prove it. Assertions of uniqueness, for sure, were no effective antidote against the dynamism of competitive comparisons.

Another famous author who wrote his autobiography about one hundred years later than Rousseau and whose account of his childhood and youth in some respects sounds like a distant echo of Rousseau's *Émile* was John Stuart Mill.

Written around 1860 and published in 1873, the year of his death, Mill's autobiography as well as his best-known political work *On Liberty* (1859) may be cited as proof that, since Rousseau, the appeal – and even pathos – of making individuality and originality for oneself a programme, in Mill's case a personal as well as *political* programme, had not disappeared. A key passage in Mill's autobiography exposes the fundamental dilemma of a person who is taught, and indeed eager, not to compare himself with others, yet cannot avoid doing so. The person who taught the young Mill was his father, James Mill. He assumed the same role in reality that Rousseau had assigned to himself with respect to his fictional protégé Émile, the role of a tutor for all aspects of life and a dominant, if not exclusive, reference point.

It seems as if James Mill had taken to heart some of the lessons in Rousseau's *Émile*. For he kept his son, as John Stuart Mill recalls in his autobiography, 'with extreme vigilance, out of the way of hearing myself praised, or of being led to make self-flattering comparisons between myself and others'. Father James would accept only one 'standard of comparison' for his son, and that 'was not what other people did, but what a man could and ought to do'.[43] If James Mill was successful in shielding his son from comparisons with others that might awaken his *amour propre*, he could not blank out competitive comparisons completely, for his educational strategy in fact resulted in creating in his son a feeling of relative backwardness towards him, the ever-present and omniscient father. In John Stuart Mill's words:

> I neither estimated myself highly or lowly: I did not estimate myself at all. If I thought anything about myself, it was that I was rather backward in my studies, since I always found myself so, in comparison with what my father expected from me.[44]

The word 'backwards' indicates that John Stuart Mill gave the perceived comparative gap between himself and his father a temporal dimension: he had to catch up and, if possible, surpass his role model. As he recollects in the following chapters of his *Autobiography*, it took him many years – and a severe personal crisis – to step out of his father's shadow and develop his own personality; in other words, to escape the mode of better/worse comparison and replace it with the assertion of being different.

In his most popular work of political philosophy, *On Liberty* (1859), John Stuart Mill praised his own, painfully achieved attitude in life, using the terms 'individuality', 'originality' and 'eccentricity' almost interchangeably, and elevated it to a political creed – individualism. The third chapter of *On Liberty* ('Of Individuality, as One of the Elements of Well-Being') is devoted to that theme, and it is striking to see how Mill reproduces for society at large a configuration of temporalized comparison that is similar to the one he had experienced himself in his childhood towards his father. For Mill, originality, individuality and eccentricity must be guaranteed secure spaces in society, because according to him only persons who have developed a great amount of originality are able to 'commence new practices and set the example of more enlightened conduct and better taste and sense in human life' – in other words, make sure that there is any 'improvement' for society as a whole. If it is the role of the original and eccentric persons who will always be only 'few persons, in comparison with the whole of mankind' to set the pace, then the task Mill assigns to the many, the average men, is to follow their example: 'The honour and glory of the average man is that he is capable of following that initiative; that he can respond internally to wise and noble things, and be led to them with his eyes open.'[45]

What Mill, along with many other liberals of his age, feared most was an opposite tendency he saw at work in his own times, the tendency of the masses to 'make everyone conform' to their average standard.[46] The widest possible creative freedom for the few (the original and eccentric) and emulation of their example for the many ('average man') – that was the distribution of tasks Mill stood up for in his political works. With that elitist figure of thought, Mill was able to accommodate assertions of being 'simply different' (for the few) in a world of competitive and temporalized better/worse comparisons (for the many). The idea that individuality might be a legitimate programme for all human beings to pursue, that there might even be such a thing as a human right to be 'different' in whatever capacity, although conceiveable in principle, was still far from Mill's own concerns. In that respect, he was a typical exponent of high Victorian morale.

## Three Types of Social Comparison in one Dialogue: A Literary Example

In the same year when John Stuart Mill published *On Liberty*, in 1859, an up-till-then moderately successful Russian author, Ivan Goncharov, published his second novel that caused a sensation in Russia and whose title figure *Oblomov* even gave rise to a social-political concept of its own: *Oblomovshchina* (Oblomovism).[47] The character of Oblomov, and the concept formed on his model, stood for the paralysing inertia that Russian elites saw in their own country. It was a product of the critical years after the defeat in the Crimean War and the great reforms of Alexander II that started in 1861 with the most difficult of all reforms, the liberation of the peasants. Goncharov's novel was a literary success because it contended with the great themes of those years, a widely perceived Russian backwardness and inability to move, yet did so by creating a likeable character with whom many Russians could identify, Oblomov – also named Ilya Ilyitch.

A member of the small Russian gentry and owner of a village of 300 souls, Oblomov spends most of his time, night or day, sitting, dozing, walking around, clothed only with a dressing gown, in his slightly rundown flat in St Petersburg. Occasionally he receives visitors, but for days and weeks he remains alone at home with his only servant, Zakhar. Oblomov is a born procrastinator who tends to defer annoying tasks such as writing an urgent letter to his village eldest to remind him of overdue rent payments to the next day and then again to the next and so on. Very often it is Zakhar, the servant, who has to remind his master to do his duties, usually to no effect.

In one of these typical situations, Zakhar tries to exhort Oblomov that he should finally react to a request by the flat's landlord to move house because the landlord wished to carry out much-needed repairs. Of course, the mere thought of being obliged to move causes Oblomov to lament his fate and accuse Zakhar of having mentioned such an impossibility, whereupon Zakhar replies that 'other people are no worse than us, and if they move, it's possible for us too'.[48] This unsuspecting remark by Zakhar, containing an implicit comparison with 'other people', gives rise to a long dialogue, full of misunderstandings and irony, about what it means to compare and how one should, or should not, compare. In the book the dialogue comprises almost ten pages. For the purposes of the argument here, it is necessary to present longer than usual quotations of select passages, interspersed with short comments that 'translate' what is being said into this chapter's shorthand language, in order to convey the subtle insinuations with which Zakhar and Oblomov spur on each other in that dialogue. Zakhar's casual remark deeply upsets Oblomov:

> 'What? What?' Oblomov asked in surprise, rising from his armchair ... 'Other people are no worse!' Oblomov repeated in dismay. 'So that's what you've been leading up to! Now I shall know that I am the same as "other people" to you!'
>
> Oblomov bowed to Zakhar ironically, and looked highly offended.
>
> 'Good Lord, sir, I never said that you were the same as anyone else, did I?' ...
>
> Oblomov could not compose himself for a long time; he lay down, got up, paced the room, and again lay down. In Zakhar's attempt to reduce him to the level of *other people* he saw a violation of his rights to Zakhar's exclusive preference of his own master. He tried to grasp the whole meaning of that comparison and analyze what *the others* were and what he was, and to what an extent a parallel between him and other people was justified and how gravely Zakhar had insulted him.[49]

In this chapter's terminology: Oblomov complains of an illicit equation of himself with 'other people' by Zakhar, a comparison that crossed the established barriers between above and below and expressed disrespect for him, the master. Oblomov sends Zakhar out, calls him in again, and a long interchange follows in which Oblomov tries to confront Zakhar, still ignorant of his misdemeanour, with what he has done:

> [Zakhar:] 'How have I grieved you, sir?' he asked, almost in tears.
>
> 'How?' Oblomov repeated. 'Why, did it occur to you to think what *other people* are?' ...

'What are *other people*?' Oblomov went on. 'They are people who do not mind cleaning their boots and dressing themselves, and though they sometimes look like gentlemen, it's all a put-up show; ...'

'There are many Germans who are like that,' Zakhar said gloomily.

'No doubt, there are! And I? What do you think? Am I *another*?'

'You're quite another, sir,' Zakhar said piteously, still at a loss to know what his master was driving at.[50]

To escape the awkward situation, Zakhar tries to appease Oblomov by saying that he is 'quite another' – not only compared to the Germans,[51] but indeed to anyone else. In the immediate context, Zakhar's reply is above all an avowal of respect, an assertion that the master, at least for him, the servant, is unique and incomparable. In the context of a hierarchical order of estates, Zakhar's assertion could be interpreted as a denial of comparability between members of different estates. But in the multicultural context of nineteenth-century St Petersburg, it could also be understood to allude to a more modern concept of individuality that stresses the uniqueness of individuals in general. The interchange goes on for a while, when Oblomov again sends Zakhar away with the words: 'I hope ... you've understood your misdemeanour and that you won't ever again compare your master to "other people"!'[52] Zakhar having finally left the room, Oblomov indulges in a long inner monologue, deeply worried about the meaning and portent of the comparisons made so far:

He became absorbed in a comparison of himself with those 'others'. He thought and thought, and presently an idea quite different from the one he had been expounding to Zakhar was formed in his mind. He had to admit that another would have managed to write all the letters ... that another would have moved to a new flat, carried out the plan, gone to the country ...

'Why, I, too, could have done it,' he reflected ... 'The "others",' he added a further characteristic of those other people, 'never wear a dressing-gown' – here he yawned – 'they hardly ever sleep, they enjoy life, they go everywhere, see everything, are interested in everything ... And I – I am not like them!' he added sadly and sank into deep thought ...

It was one of the most clear-sighted and courageous moments of Oblomov's life. Oh, how dreadful he felt when there arose in his mind a clear and vivid idea of human destiny and the purpose of a man's life, and when he compared this purpose with his own life ... It grieved and hurt him to think that he was undeveloped, that his spiritual forces had stopped growing, that some dead weight hampered him; he bitterly envied those whose lives were rich and full, while he felt as though a heavy stone had been thrown on to the narrow and pitiful path of his existence.[53]

Thus, Oblomov's musings lead him to reinterpret the meaning he had given to Zakhar's comparison of himself with 'others' earlier on. In fact, he now has to admit to himself that compared to others he is less active, less purposeful, less well educated, arrested in his development – in other words, backwards. His thoughts carry him on into a series of temporalized and envious better/worse comparisons with others whom he perceives as in many respects better than himself.

The dialogue as a whole and especially the last-quoted explicit reflections on temporalized comparisons are a key passage in Goncharov's novel. It is here that *Oblomov* becomes a parable for the state of Russia as a whole in the mid nineteenth century. Whether for individuals, nations or other collective entities, the mode of competitive and temporalized better/worse comparisons became a dominant figure of thought in mid nineteenth-century Europe, from Victorian England to Tsarist Russia.

## Conceptualization and Historicization of Social Comparisons around 1900

Towards the end of the nineteenth century, social comparison as a practice that pervaded all walks of life was increasingly theorized and historicized. Sociologists, economists and moral philosophers made attempts to identify different types of social comparison and speculated about their historical trajectories and cultural specificities. A particular point of their enquiries was whether the modern industrial age in which they lived had exacerbated certain features of social comparison or even brought forth completely new forms. It is perhaps no accident that the most elaborate of these reflections appeared in the United States and Wilhelmine Germany, countries that in the decades around 1900 saw an extremely dynamic economic growth and where the consequences of that growth – sharpening of social cleavages, restless and nerve-breaking competition, and disruption of traditional communities – were acutely experienced and often lamented.

Perhaps the best-known contributions to the modern theory of social comparison are Thorstein Veblen's concepts of 'conspicuous consumption' and its counterpart 'invidious comparison'. Both are developed at length in *The Theory of the Leisure Class* (1899). For Veblen, invidious comparisons as such are nothing new. They can be observed among primitive hordes as well as in the complex modern societies of his own time. What has changed are the criteria and scope of the comparisons. The decisive shift for him was the consolidation of private property as a basis for both public esteem of a person and his or her own self-respect.[54] Although Veblen does not fix that shift to any precise date, it is clear that what he has in mind are above all the modern commercial and industrial societies, particularly in the Anglo-American world, from the eighteenth century onwards. Since then, he says, extravagance – conspicuous consumption – brings prestige, whereas parsimony no longer counts as merit in the eyes of others. Even though Veblen admits that other criteria may still be of use in the comparative evaluation of persons, they all tend to be encompassed by one single criterion, material wealth and more particularly its abstract unit of measurement, money:

> A standard of life would still be possible which should admit of invidious comparison in other respects than that of opulence; as, for instance, a comparison in various directions in the manifestation of moral, physical, intellectual or aesthetic force. Comparison in all these directions is in vogue to-day, and the comparison made in these respects is commonly so inextricably bound up with pecuniary comparison as to be scarcely distinguishable from the latter.[55]

In some of his earlier writings, in which he anticipated many insights of the *Theory of the Leisure Class*, Veblen used somewhat more drastic terms to describe what for him distinguished social comparisons in the modern industrialist and consumerist age from earlier forms. Thus, in an essay on *Some Neglected Points in the Theory of Socialism* (1891), he declared 'the system of free competition', not just the consolidation of private property, to be a major driving force for what he then termed 'economic emulation' and held it responsible for 'cutting off other forms of emulation from the chance of efficiently ministering to the craving for a good fame'.[56] Besides the narrowing down of 'the scope of emulation to this one line',[57] he also pointed to another specificity of invidious comparisons in modern times of Darwinistic competition, namely the supplanting of substance by appearance: 'Under modern conditions the struggle for existence has, in a very appreciable degree, been transformed into a struggle to keep up appearances.'[58] It is not the absolute degree of wealth or poverty, measurable through statistical indicators, that is decisive for stirring up envious comparisons, but the relative appearance of wealth in relation to one's immediate neighbour: 'It is a striving to be, and more immediately to be thought to be, better than one's neighbor.'[59] Until today, 'Keeping up with the Joneses' and 'Keeping up Appearances' have remained condensed formulae to resume the practices of social comparison as experienced, often painfully, sometimes with a good sense of humour, by average people in America as well as in Britain.[60]

The same mechanism that guided comparisons in the sphere of consumption also applied to the sphere of production. Workers too, Veblen observed in an essay on 'The Instinct of Workmanship and the Irksomeness of Labor' (1898), were now measured – and compared one another – by their 'visible achievement' rather than by the 'servicability' of their conduct: 'It becomes the proximate end of effort to put forth *evidence* of power, rather than to achieve an impersonal end for its own sake, simply as an item of human use.'[61] The visible, and if possible quantifiable, appearance of success became more important than the use value of the produced things or services themselves for comparing people's achievement. From here, it is only a short step to our present-day experience of ubiquitous rankings and ratings.[62] In contrast to modern industrial societies, the criterion for success was different in archaic societies. The crucial point there, Veblen explains, was the capability to fight against wild beasts or nature: 'Exploit becomes the conventional ground of invidious comparison between individuals, and repute comes to rest on prowess.' In such a condition, regular manual labour in the modern sense was of less value and hence less esteemed – something to be done by women or slaves.[63]

In late Wilhelmine Germany, reflections on social comparison in some instances took a less analytical and more polemical and moralizing twist. There was a tendency to attribute certain types of social comparison not just to stages of historical development, as had been done by Veblen, but also to alleged specific characters of nations, races or social groups. An example is Werner Sombart's small book on the *Bourgeois* (1913), in which he identifies the extreme practices of measuring success of any kind, economic and noneconomic, in purely monetary terms with contemporary America.[64] In the same book, Sombart also speculates about differences between so-called *Heldenvölker* (peoples of heroes) and *Händlervölker* (peoples of traders), the latter being characterized by a subordination of all spheres of life under an economic ratio of bookkeeping. As one might expect, Sombart ranges the Jews among the *Händlervölker*, along with the Scots and the Florentines. However, curiously enough, he ranges the English together with the Germans, the Venetians, the Genoese and – going further back in time – the Romans, the Normans, the Langobards, the Saxons and the Franks among the *Heldenvölker*, at least as far as the early stages of adventurous capitalism in England were concerned.[65] Only two years later, in the context of war polemic, the English would become for Sombart the negative prototype of a trader people.[66]

In his book on the *Bourgeois*, Sombart constructs yet another, related pair of opposites, this time associated with particular social groups or types rather than with entire nations or peoples. It is the opposition between a 'seigneurial' social type who is characterized by a courageous, unconventional lifestyle, high artistic feeling and generous magnificence on the one hand, and a 'bourgeois' type whose puritan thriftiness, industry and frugality lead him to subject all creative and heroic feelings (in himself and others) to his quantifying logic of bookkeeping on the other hand.[67] Apparently, Sombart's 'seigneurial' type was partially inspired by Friedrich Nietzsche's ideal of a new aristocracy that combined nonconformity with ruthlessness, while for some character features of his 'bourgeois' type, notably his penchant for *ressentiment*, Sombart referred explicitly to the moral philosopher Max Scheler (1874–1928).[68] Shortly before Sombart's *Bourgeois*, Scheler had published a long essay on 'Ressentiment' (1912)[69] and, like Scheler, Sombart suspected that deep in their hearts, the 'bourgeois' were profoundly envious at the 'seigneurial' types and their lifestyle – a feeling that in turn resulted in *ressentiment* and an even stronger willingness of the bourgeois to make everyone conform to their own humble virtues of parsimony and frugality.

Max Scheler again reviewed Sombart's *Bourgeois* in 1914 (a typical example of a citation cartel). In that review, Scheler incorporated Sombart's opposite social types in his own theory of *ressentiment*, which was at the same time (and that makes it important in our context) a theory of social comparison. For Scheler, the 'bourgeois' type, being of 'inferior vitality' (*minderwertigen Vitaltyps*), was one who anxiously and invidiously compared himself with others, whereas the 'seigneurial' type, being sure of his 'self-worth' (*Selbstwertgefühl*), could generously afford not to compare:

> Where the latter [the seigneurial type] behaves liberally and generously, the former [the bourgeois type] compares and wants to outperform. *His* rule will lead to a system of unbounded competition and an idea of progress in which only being better than a compared entity (a human being or a phase of life or history) counts as valuable.[70]

Scheler here associates the 'bourgeois' better/worse comparisons with limitless competition and a progressive attitude, and sees their scope extending not just to other humans as individuals, but also to their lifecycles and historical epochs in general.

Scheler's own treatise on *Ressentiment*, republished in an enlarged version in 1915, is grounded on more detailed social-psychological and political observations that define comparisons driven by resentment as a very peculiar variety of social comparison.[71] According to Scheler, the feeling of resentment is basically fuelled by an 'experience of powerlessness' (*Ohnmachtserlebnis*) coupled with an 'impulse for revenge' (*Racheimpuls*) that imperiously demands the 'levelling' (*Gleichstellung*) of the person feeling injured and the person who has (unconsciously) inflicted the injury. The resentment is exacerbated when *in fact* the power gap between the injured and the person inflicting the injury remains as it has been, and when the injured *knows and feels* that he (or she) can nowhere reach, let alone level, the person who injured him (or her).[72] Lifting his thoughts to a political level, Scheler then argues that resentment is driven to extremes in a 'society like ours' where 'approximately equal political and other rights' are publicly recognized, while the factual gaps in power, wealth and education continue – in other words, a society where 'everyone has the "right" to compare oneself with everyone else, yet "cannot be compared" to him (or her) in fact'. In that case, Scheler says, the 'structure of society' itself gives birth to a massive charge of resentment.[73] A similar figure of thought applies to envy as a driving force of resentment. Envy is strongest when the goods or values one desires are, by their nature, unattainable yet at the same time are located 'within the sphere of comparison in which we move while comparing us with others'.[74] In a further turn of his argument, Scheler also tries to reconcile his resentment theory with Georg Simmel's distinction between nobleness (*Vornehmheit*) and baseness or commonness (*Gemeinheit*). For Scheler, the 'noble' attitude consists in never even entering into a comparative measuring of one's own self-worth; the noble's consciousness of his own self-worth is in that sense 'naïve, unreflected', and can for that reason not be described as 'pride' (*Stolz*), which is a reflected attitude of someone who has already lost his original, naïve self-consciousness. By contrast, the 'base' or 'common' attitude realizes itself only in and through comparison with others. The 'common man' (*der Gemeine*) experiences his self only in relation to others whose worth he ranges as 'higher' or 'lower', 'more' or 'less' than his own. In short: 'The noble experiences worth *before* comparison, the common man only *by* and *through* comparison.'[75]

To resume, the social figuration of resentment, described by Scheler, combines all three variants of social comparison discussed in this chapter in a peculiar way. The 'noble' social type – an ideal type more than a real one – is habitually beyond any comparison and does not even think of comparing himself or herself with others, and that is why he or she can also avoid the paradox inherent in any open incomparability claim; he or she is 'simply different'. The 'common' man or woman experiences a feeling of debasement as a result of the very existence of the noble and is habitually enmeshed in endless better/worse comparisons to regain and raise his or her own self-esteem. At the same time, the 'common' man or woman knows that he or she can never cross the wide distance that separates him or her from the noble, and yet cannot avoid the comparison with the noble – an above/below comparison in a world of supposed equality.

## Conclusion

In a medium-range and long-range historical perspective, practices of social comparison are far more diversified than one might assume when focussing on its nowadays most conspicuous form, the ranking or rating of ourselves and others in quantitative or qualitative terms. This chapter's rough classification into comparisons based on an 'above/below', 'better/worse' or 'simply different' form of distinguishing ourselves from others has helped to identify historical conditions under which one, several or all of these varieties were performed and critically observed. In the period examined here – the centuries between 1600 and 1900 – all three basic forms of social comparison could be shown to have had some relevance, although the 'better/worse' and 'simply different' variants only came to the fore from the mid eighteenth century onwards. Since then, all three basic comparison types have coexisted and may be re-enacted at any time, even if frictions between temporalized and competitive better/worse comparisons on the one hand, and claims to be simply different on the other hand, have clearly become a dominant feature in our modern lifeworld.

The chapter has also demonstrated that critical observers – authors like La Bruyère, Rousseau or Veblen – were often most attentive in dissecting the wide variety of *emotions* driving social comparisons or generated by social comparisons. It would need an investigation of its own to systematize these observations. Visual images should be included in such a discussion because they, as has been shown in our brief comments on de Lairesse, Hogarth and Chodowiecki, can be powerful *agents* in promoting or discrediting certain forms of (social) comparison by forcing the viewers to actually perform those comparisons while looking.

Finally, our enquiry into the varieties of social comparison between individuals and small groups has revealed a limited number of basic figures of argument that could also be applied, and are indeed continuously applied, to comparisons between larger collective entities such as peoples, nations, races, classes or civilizations. In literary works such as Goncharov's *Oblomov*, the different levels of application – from individual figures up to nations at large – can be fused into one parabolic narrative, or a dialogue, or an assemblage of metaphors. However, the use of such literary techniques is not limited to novelists. Authors who claim to write as analytical ('scientific') observers, as we have seen in the case of Sombart and Scheler, may also use analogies or projections to argue that comparisons among individuals function in ways similar to those among nations, classes or civilizations.

**Willibald Steinmetz** is Professor of Modern and Contemporary Political History at Bielefeld University. He has published widely on political languages, parliamentary rhetoric and the use of sociopolitical concepts. His current research interests include the history of comparison as a practice in modern and contemporary history. Among his publications in English are three edited collections of essays: *Political Languages in the Age of Extremes* (2nd edn, 2012); *Writing Political History Today* (2013); and *Conceptual History in the European Space* (coedited with M. Freeden and J. Fernández-Sebastián, Berghahn Books, 2017).

# Notes

1. A starting point for contemporary discussions on social comparison is L. Festinger, 'A Theory of Social Comparison Processes', *Human Relations* 7 (1954), 117–40. For a historical overview from Rousseau to recent theories see F. Nullmeier, *Politische Theorie des Sozialstaats* (Frankfurt: Campus Verlag, 2000), and F. Nullmeier, 'Politische Theorie des Komparativs: Soziale Vergleiche und gerechte Gesellschaft', *Mittelweg 36* 25(2) (2016), 56–73.
2. T. Hobbes, *Leviathan* (1651), C.B. Macpherson (ed.) (Harmondsworth: Penguin, 1968), 225–26.
3. See ibid., 235–36.
4. Ibid., 71.
5. *Mediarethink*, Social Comparison Theory, 3 October 2014, retrieved 14 March 2019 from https://mediarethink.wordpress.com/tag/social-comparison-theory; the study referred to is H. Krasnova et al., 'Envy on Facebook: A Hidden Threat to Users' Life Satisfaction?' (Paper presented at the 11th Conference on Wirtschaftsinformatik, Leipzig, 2013), retrieved 14 March 2019 from https://ktwop.files.wordpress.com/2013/01/facebook-envy.pdf.
6. The following quotes can be found at *Erica Finds…*, retrieved 14 March 2019 from http://ericafinds.com/2012/08/comparison-is-the-thief-of-joy-a-few-finds-to-grow-on. I have been unable to locate the source for the dictum attributed to Theodore Roosevelt.
7. For a recent synthesis on the intellectual history of the self, see J. Seigel, *The Idea of the Self: Thought and Experience in Western Europe since the Seventeenth Century* (Cambridge: Cambridge University Press, 2005); on ideas and practices of the self, see A. Corbin, 'Le

secret de l'individu', in P. Ariès and G. Duby (eds), *Histoire de la vie privée*, vol. 4: *De la Révolution à la Grande Guerre* (Paris: Le Seuil, 1987), 419–501.
8. *Dictionnaire de l'Académie Françoise*, vol. 1 (Paris: Jean Baptiste Coignard, 1694), 219 (art. 'Comparaison'): '*ne faites point entrer cet homme-là en comparaison avec un si grand personnage* … Quand quelqu'un veut comparer des personnes ou des choses extrememement disproportionnées, on dit par ironie *Quelle comparaison. voilà une belle comparaison* … On dit prov.[erbialement] que *Toutes comparaisons sont odieuses,* pour marquer, qu'il est dangereux de comparer deux personnes ensemble, parce que l'une des deux pourroit s'en offenser'. Unless otherwise indicated, all translations are my own.
9. A. Furetière, *Dictionnaire Universel: Contenant généralement tous les mots François, tant vieux que modernes, et les termes des sciences et des arts*, 2nd edn, vol. 1 (La Haye: Pierre Husson et al., 1727), n.p. (art. 'Comparaison'): 'Comparaison, se prend quelquefois pour, Égalité; ressemblance. … En ce sens on dit, Faire *comparaison* avec quelqu'un; c'est-à-dire, pretendre s'égaler à lui; le vouloir traitter de pair à compagnon.'
10. J. de La Bruyère, *Les Caractères, ou les mœurs de ce siècle* (1688–94), R. Pignarre (ed.) (Paris: Garnier-Flammarion, 1965), 155: 'Il y a parler bien, parler aisément, parler juste, parler à propos. C'est pécher contre ce dernier genre que de s'étendre sur un repas magnifique que l'on vient de faire, devant des gens qui sont réduits à épargner leur pain; … d'entretenir de ses richesses, de ses revenus et de ses ameublements un homme qui n'a ni rentes ni domicile; en un mot, de parler de son bonheur devant des misérables: cette conversation est trop forte pour eux, et la comparaison qu'ils font alors de leur état au vôtre est odieuse.'
11. Ibid., 227 (piece no. 5 of the chapter on 'Les Grands'): 'une espèce de compensation de bien et de mal, qui établirait entre elles l'égalité'.
12. Ibid., 232: 'Faut-il opter? Je ne balance pas: je veux être peuple.'
13. On dress codes, see N. Bulst, 'Kleidung als sozialer Konfliktstoff: Probleme kleidergesetzlicher Normierung im sozialen Gefüge', *Saeculum* 44 (1993), 32–46; M. Dinges, 'Von der "Lesbarkeit der Welt" zum universalisierten Wandel durch individuelle Strategien: Die soziale Funktion der Kleidung in der höfischen Gesellschaft', *Saeculum* 44 (1993), 90–122. On rules of precedence, see T. Weller, *Theatrum Praecedentiae: Zeremonieller Rang und gesellschaftliche Ordnung in der frühneuzeitlichen Stadt. Leipzig 1500–1800* (Darmstadt: Wissenschaftliche Buchgesellschaft, 2006). More generally on conflicts of rank in early modern Europe, see B. Stollberg-Rilinger, 'Logik und Semantik des Ranges in der Frühen Neuzeit', in R. Jessen (ed.), *Konkurrenz in der Geschichte. Praktiken – Werte – Institutionalisierungen* (Frankfurt: Campus Verlag, 2014), 197–227. For a long-term study on sumptuary regulations ranging from antiquity to the contemporary age, see C.J. Berry, *The Idea of Luxury: A Conceptual and Historical Investigation* (Cambridge: Cambridge University Press, 1994).
14. See A. Shepard, *Accounting for Oneself: Worth, Status and the Social Order in Early Modern England* (Oxford: Oxford University Press, 2015).
15. Examples in Dinges, 'Von der "Lesbarkeit der Welt"'; see also P. Burke, 'Conspicuous Consumption in Seventeenth-Century Italy', in *The Historical Anthropology of Early Modern Italy: Essays on Perception and Communication* (Cambridge: Cambridge University Press, 1987), 132–49.
16. M. de Montaigne, *Essais*, Book I, Chapter 43 ('Des Lois Somptuaires'), Œuvres complètes, R. Barral (ed.) (Paris: Le Seuil, 1967), 121–2.
17. Weller, *Theatrum Praecedentiae*, 110.
18. Quoted in ibid., 39.

19. G. de Lairesse, *Het Groet Schilderboek* (Amsterdam: Willem de Coup, 1707); I used another edition of 1712, available in digitized form: G. de Lairesse, *Groot Schilderboek* (Amsterdam: Hendrick Desbordes, 1712), retrieved 14 March 2019 from http://resolver.sub.uni-goettingen.de/purl?PPN655983945; G. de Lairesse, *Des Herrn Gerhard de Lairesse, Welt-belobten Kunst-Mahlers, Grosses Mahler-Buch*, 2 vols (Nürnberg: Weigel, 1728/30); G. de Lairesse, *The Art of Painting, in all its branches methodically demonstrated by discourses and plates*, J.F. Fritsch (trans.) (London: printed for the author, 1738).
20. De Lairesse, *Groot Schilderboek* (1712), 55 (the plate is between pages 54 and 55). See also the interpretation of the plate and de Lairesse's explanations (based on the German edition) by W. Busch, *Das sentimentalische Bild: Die Krise der Kunst im 18. Jahrhundert und die Geburt der Moderne* (Munich: C.H. Beck, 1993), 317–20.
21. On conduct books and related literary genres addressed to gentlemen and ladies, see J. Carré (ed.), *The Crisis of Courtesy: Studies in the Conduct Book in Britain, 1600–1900* (Leiden: Brill, 1994); and A. Bryson, *From Courtesy to Civility: Changing Codes of Conduct in Early Modern England* (Oxford: Oxford University Press, 1998). For changes in the scope and meaning of the French concept *honnête homme* from the late seventeenth to the early nineteenth centuries, see A. Höfer and R. Reichardt, 'Honnête homme, Honnêteté, Honnêtes gens', in R. Reichardt and E. Schmitt (eds), *Handbuch politisch-sozialer Grundbegriffe in Frankreich 1680–1820*, vol. 7, Munich: Oldenbourg, 1986), 8–73.
22. J.B. von Rohr, *Einleitung zur Ceremoniel-Wissenschafft der Privat-Personen, welche ... von einem jungen Teutschen Cavalier in Obacht zu nehmen* (Berlin: Rüdiger, 1728); a digitized, fully searchable version is available at the Deutsches Textarchiv (DTA), retrieved 14 March 2019 from http://www.deutschestextarchiv.de/book/show/rohr_einleitung_1728.
23. Ibid., 78.
24. See also the interpretation by Busch, *Das sentimentalische Bild*, 316–17.
25. See C. Eisenberg, *The Rise of Market Society in England, 1066–1800* (New York: Berghahn Books, 2013).
26. Busch, *Das sentimentalische Bild*, 247. In this verdict, Busch follows the German moralist Georg Christoph Lichtenberg (1742–99), who commented extensively on Hogarth's engravings and paintings, including *Industry and Idleness*; see W. Promies (ed.), *Lichtenbergs Hogarth: Die Kalender-Erklärungen von Georg Christoph Lichtenberg mit den Nachstichen von Ernst Ludwig Riepenhausen zu den Kupferstich-Tafeln von William Hogarth* (Munich: Hanser Verlag, 1999), 200–31, at 200: 'bleiben sie hinter den meisten Werken dieses Künstlers etwas zurück' ('fall short compared to most other works by this artist').
27. For a more detailed analysis, see P. Wagner, 'Hogarth's Industry and Idleness: Subversive Lessons on Conduct', in Carré (ed.), *Crisis of Courtesy*, 51–65.
28. In his comment, first published in 1791–92, G.C. Lichtenberg remarks that in Germany such a spectacular social advancement would be unthinkable for a journeyman: Promies (ed.), *Lichtenbergs Hogarth*, 200–1: 'Those who learn a craft in Germany may eventually very well be hanged with eclat, but rarely their industriousness is rewarded with a corresponding eclat ... In England however it is not uncommon that the son of a weaver or brewer excels in the House of Commons and his grandson or great-grandson in the House of Lords.'
29. *Goettinger Taschen Calender vom Jahr 1779* (Göttingen: Joh. Chr. Dieterich, 1779); a digitized copy is available at the Bayrische Staatsbibliothek (retrieved 14 March 2019 from http://reader.digitale-sammlungen.de/de/fs1/object/display/bsb10861349_00001.html); *Goettinger Taschen Calender vom Jahr 1780* (Göttingen: Joh. Chr. Dieterich, 1780); a

digitized copy is available at Universitätsbibliothek Bielefeld (retrieved 14 March 2019 from http://ds.ub.uni-bielefeld.de/viewer/image/2235093_005/1).

30. [G.C. Lichtenberg], 'Erklärung der Monats-Kupfer', in *Goettinger Taschen Calender vom Jahr 1780*, 127–41. Engravings and explanations have been edited jointly: R. Focke (ed.), *Chodowiecki und Lichtenberg* (Leipzig: Dieterich'sche Verlagsbuchhandlung, 1901); a digitized copy is available at the Universitätsbibliothek Weimar (retrieved 14 March 2019 from https://digitalesammlungen.uni-weimar.de/viewer/resolver?urn=urn:nbn:de:gbv:wim2-g-615100).

31. Unfortunately, the pages for February 1780 with the engraving called 'Affectation' are missing in the digitized version of Universitätsbibliothek Bielefeld, but see Focke (ed.), *Chodowiecki und Lichtenberg*, vii.

32. For this line of argument, with some reservations, see M. Ehler, *Daniel Nikolaus Chodowiecki: 'Le petit maître' als großer Illustrator* (Berlin: Lukas Verlag, 2003), 118–25; however, see the more subtle interpretation by Busch, *Das sentimentalische Bild*, 310.

33. [Lichtenberg], 'Erklärung der Monats-Kupfer', 138. On this pair and the tension between the images and Lichtenberg's explanation, see also Busch, *Das sentimentalische Bild*, 324–26.

34. For debates on 'genius' in various fields, see D.M. McMahon, *Divine Fury: A History of Genius* (New York: Basic Books, 2013); see also J.E. Chaplin and D.M. McMahon (eds), *Genealogies of Genius* (Basingstoke: Palgrave Macmillan, 2016). On ideas of 'genius' in Germany, see J. Schmidt, *Die Geschichte des Genie-Gedankens in der deutschen Literatur, Philosophie und Politik, 1750–1945*, 3rd edn, 2 vols (Heidelberg: Winter, 2004).

35. See N. Luhmann, *Liebe als Passion: Zur Codierung von Intimität* (Frankfurt am Main: Suhrkamp, 1982).

36. Luhmann, *Liebe als Passion*, 154: 'Anyone who emphasizes his or her own incomparability by that very act compares him- or herself [with others].'

37. J.-J. Rousseau, *Émile, ou de l'éducation* (1762), Œuvres complètes, B. Gagnebin (ed.), vol. 4 (Paris: Éditions de la Pléiade, 1969), 239–877, ast 493.

38. Ibid., 493–94.

39. J.-J. Rousseau, *Discours sur l'origine et les fondemens de l'inégalité parmi les hommes* (1755), Œuvres complètes, B. Gagnebin (ed.), vol. 3 (Paris: Éditions de la Pléiade, 1964), 109–194, esp. 165–66, 169–70, 188–89.

40. Rousseau, *Émile*, 535; the discussion of Plutarch in ibid., 530–31.

41. J.-J. Rousseau, *Les Confessions* (1782), Œuvres complètes, B. Gagnebin (ed.), vol. 1 (Paris: Éditions de la Pléiade, 1959), 1–656, at 5: '1. Je forme une entreprise qui n'eut jamais d'éxemple, et dont l'exécution n'aura point d'imitateur. Je veux montrer à mes semblables un homme dans toute la vérité de la nature; et cet homme, ce sera moi. 2. Moi seul. Je sens mon coeur et je connois les hommes. Je ne suis fait comme aucun de ceux que j'ai vus; j'ose croire n'être fait comme aucun de ceux qui existent. Si je ne vaux pas mieux, au moins je suis autre.'

42. Ibid., 3.

43. J.S. Mill, *Autobiography* (1873), J.M. Robson (ed.) (Harmondsworth: Penguin, 1989), 45–46.

44. Ibid., 46.

45. J.S. Mill, *On Liberty* (1859), G. Himmelfarb (ed.) (Harmondsworth: Penguin, 1982), 129 and 131.

46. Ibid., 135.

47. I used two English translations; both are rather free translations and do not always exactly render the Russian wording, which however is essential here. Therefore, with the kind help of Kirill Postoutenko, I checked the translations against the original and changed the wording where necessary. I. Goncharov, *Oblomov*, N. Duddington (trans.), introduction by E. Rhys (London: J.M. Dent & Sons, no year [1932]); I. Goncharov, *Oblomov*, trans. and with an introduction by D. Magarshack (Harmondsworth: Penguin, 1967).
48. Goncharov, *Oblomov*, 85 (transl. Duddington) and 93 (transl. Magershack); slightly changed by me.
49. Ibid., 85–86 (transl. Duddington), 93 (transl. Magershack); slightly changed by me.
50. Ibid., 88–89 (transl. Duddington), 96 (transl. Magershack); slightly changed by me.
51. On Germans in nineteenth-century Russia, see H.-H. Dreßler (ed.), *Russen über Deutsche: russische Zeugnisse aus dem Zarenreich* (Berlin: Westkreuz Verlag, 2012).
52. Goncharov, *Oblomov*, 91 (trans. Duddington), 98 (trans. by Magershack, unchanged here).
53. Ibid., 93 (trans. Duddington for the last sentence), 100–1 (trans. Magershack for the rest).
54. T. Veblen, *The Theory of the Leisure Class: An Economic Study of Institutions* (New York: Macmillan Company, 1912), 27–29 and 31–32.
55. Ibid., 97.
56. T. Veblen, 'Some Neglected Points in the Theory of Socialism' (1891), in C. Camic and G.M. Hodgson (eds), *Essential Writings of Thorstein Veblen* (London: Routledge, 2011), 64–76, at 69.
57. Ibid.
58. Ibid., 71.
59. Ibid., 67.
60. For the United States, see S.J. Matt, *Keeping up with the Joneses: Envy in American Consumer Society, 1890–1930* (Philadelphia: University of Pennsylvania Press, 2003); and with a focus on prestige claims at work and in everyday life, see the classic study by C. Wright Mills, *White Collar: The American Middle Classes* (Oxford: Oxford University Press, 1951), esp. 239–58 (Chapter 11, 'The Status Panic', at 257: 'fetishism of appearance'). The prime reference for Britain is of course the BBC Television sitcom *Keeping Up Appearances* (5 series, 1990–95) with Patricia Routledge, alias Hyacinth Bucket, who insists that her last name is pronounced 'Bouquet', in the lead role; see also O. James, *Britain on the Couch: Why We're Unhappier Compared with 1950 Despite Being Richer* (London: Century, 1997).
61. T. Veblen, 'The Instinct of Workmanship and the Irksomeness of Labor' (1898), in Camic and Hodgson (eds), *Essential Writings*, 158–68, at 167 (emphasis added).
62. See the chapters by Wendy Espeland and Bettina Heintz in this volume.
63. Veblen, 'Instinct of Workmanship', 166.
64. W. Sombart, *Der Bourgeois: Zur Geistesgeschichte des modernen Wirtschaftsmenschen* (1913) (Reinbek: Rowohlt, 1988), 172.
65. Ibid., 103–4 (on the Scots), and 208–9.
66. W. Sombart, *Händler und Helden: Patriotische Besinnungen* (Munich: Duncker & Humblot, 1915).
67. Sombart, *Bourgeois*, 250–51 and 327–28.
68. Ibid., 327–28.

69. M. Scheler, 'Über Ressentiment und moralisches Werturteil: Ein Beitrag zur Pathologie der Kultur', *Zeitschrift für Pathopsychologie* 1(2–3) (1912), also published separately: M. Scheler, *Über Ressentiment und moralisches Werturteil* (Leipzig: Engelmann, 1912).
70. M. Scheler, 'Der Bourgeois', *Die Weißen Blätter* 1(6) (February 1914); in a slightly revised version again published 1915, and in that form in M. Scheler, *Gesammelte Werke*, vol. 3: *Vom Umsturz der Werte: Abhandlungen und Aufsätze*, 4th edn (Bern: Francke Verlag, 1955), 343–61, at 356–57; the German text of the indented quote is: 'Wo jener gönnt und leben läßt, da vergleicht dieser und will übertreffen. *Seine* Herrschaft wird zum System schrankenloser Konkurrenz führen und zum Fortschrittsgedanken, in denen nur das *Mehr*sein über einen Vergleichsfall (Mensch oder Lebens- oder Geschichtsphase) *hinaus* als Wert überhaupt empfunden wird.'
71. M. Scheler, 'Das Ressentiment im Aufbau der Moralen' (1915), in *Gesammelte Werke*, vol. 3, 33–147.
72. Ibid., 38–43.
73. Ibid. 43.
74. Ibid., 45.
75. Ibid., 46–47.

# Bibliography

Berry, C.J., *The Idea of Luxury: A Conceptual and Historical Investigation* (Cambridge: Cambridge University Press, 1994).
Bryson, A., *From Courtesy to Civility: Changing Codes of Conduct in Early Modern England* (Oxford: Oxford University Press, 1998).
Bulst, N., 'Kleidung als sozialer Konfliktstoff: Probleme kleidergesetzlicher Normierung im sozialen Gefüge', *Saeculum* 44 (1993), 32–46.
Burke, P., 'Conspicuous Consumption in Seventeenth-Century Italy', in *The Historical Anthropology of Early Modern Italy: Essays on Perception and Communication* (Cambridge: Cambridge University Press, 1987), 132–49.
Busch, W., *Das sentimentalische Bild: Die Krise der Kunst im 18. Jahrhundert und die Geburt der Moderne* (Munich: C.H. Beck, 1993).
Carré, J. (ed.), *The Crisis of Courtesy: Studies in the Conduct Book in Britain, 1600–1900* (Leiden: Brill, 1994).
Chaplin, J.E., and McMahon, D.M. (eds), *Genealogies of Genius* (Basingstoke: Palgrave Macmillan, 2016).
Corbin, A., 'Le secret de l'individu', in Ariès, P. and Duby, G. (eds), *Histoire de la vie privée*, vol. 4: *De la Révolution à la Grande Guerre* (Paris: Le Seuil, 1987), 419–501.
De la Bruyère, J., *Les Caractères, ou les mœurs de ce siècle* (1688–94), Pignarre, R. (ed.) (Paris: Garnier-Flammarion, 1965).
De Lairesse, G., *Het Groet Schilderboek* (Amsterdam: Willem de Coup, 1707).
———. *Groot Schilderboek* (Amsterdam: Hendrick Desbordes, 1712).
———. *Des Herrn Gerhard de Lairesse, Welt-belobten Kunst-Mahlers, Grosses Mahler-Buch*, 2 vols (Nürnberg: Weigel, 1728/30).
———. *The Art of Painting, in all its branches methodically demonstrated by discourses and plates*, Fritsch, J.F. (trans.) (London: printed for the author, 1738).
*Dictionnaire de l'Académie Françoise*, vol. 1 (Paris: Jean Baptiste Coignard, 1694).

Dinges, M., 'Von der "Lesbarkeit der Welt" zum universalisierten Wandel durch individuelle Strategien: Die soziale Funktion der Kleidung in der höfischen Gesellschaft', *Saeculum* 44 (1993), 90–122.

Dreßler, H.-H. (ed.), *Russen über Deutsche: russische Zeugnisse aus dem Zarenreich* (Berlin: Westkreuz Verlag, 2012).

Ehler, M., *Daniel Nikolaus Chodowiecki: 'Le petit maître' als großer Illustrator* (Berlin: Lukas Verlag, 2003).

Eisenberg, C., *The Rise of Market Society in England, 1066–1800* (New York: Berghahn Books, 2013).

Festinger, L., 'A Theory of Social Comparison Processes', *Human Relations* 7 (1954), 117–40.

Focke, R. (ed.), *Chodowiecki und Lichtenberg* (Leipzig: Dieterich'sche Verlagsbuchhandlung, 1901).

Furetière, A., *Dictionnaire Universel: Contenant généralement tous les mots François, tant vieux que modernes, et les termes des sciences et des arts*, 2nd edn, vol. 1 (La Haye: Pierre Husson et al., 1727).

*Goettinger Taschen Calender vom Jahr 1779* (Göttingen: Joh. Chr. Dieterich, 1779).

*Goettinger Taschen Calender vom Jahr 1780* (Göttingen: Joh. Chr. Dieterich, 1780).

Goncharov, I., *Oblomov*, Duddington, N. (trans.), introduction by Rhys, E. (London: J.M. Dent & Sons, no year [1932]).

———. *Oblomov*, trans. and with an introduction by Magarshack, D. (Harmondsworth: Penguin, 1967).

Hobbes, T., *Leviathan* (1651), Macpherson, C.B. (ed.) (Harmondsworth: Penguin, 1968).

Höfer, A., and Reichardt, R., 'Honnête homme, Honnêteté, Honnêtes gens', in Reichardt, R. and Schmitt, E. (eds), *Handbuch politisch-sozialer Grundbegriffe in Frankreich 1680–1820*, vol. 7 (Munich: Oldenbourg, 1986), 8–73.

James, O., *Britain on the Couch: Why We're Unhappier Compared with 1950 Despite Being Richer* (London: Century, 1997).

Krasnova, H. et al., 'Envy on Facebook: A Hidden Threat to Users' Life Satisfaction?' (Paper presented at the 11th Conference on Wirtschaftsinformatik, Leipzig, 2013), retrieved 14 March 2019 from https://ktwop.files.wordpress.com/2013/01/facebook-envy.pdf.

[Lichtenberg, G.C.] 'Erklärung der Monats-Kupfer', in *Goettinger Taschen Calender vom Jahr 1780* (Göttingen: Joh. Chr. Dieterich, 1780), 127–41.

Luhmann, N., *Liebe als Passion: Zur Codierung von Intimität* (Frankfurt am Main: Suhrkamp, 1982).

Matt, S.J., *Keeping up with the Joneses: Envy in American Consumer Society, 1890–1930* (Philadelphia: University of Pennsylvania Press, 2003).

McMahon, D.M., *Divine Fury: A History of Genius* (New York: Basic Books, 2013).

Mediarethink, *Social Comparison Theory*, 3 October 2014, retrieved 14 March 2019 from https://mediarethink.wordpress.com/tag/social-comparison-theory.

Mill, J.S., *On Liberty* (1859), Himmelfarb, G. (ed.) (Harmondsworth: Penguin, 1982).

———. *Autobiography* (1873), Robson, J.M. (ed.) (Harmondsworth: Penguin, 1989).

Montaigne, M. de, *Essais*, Œuvres complètes, Barral, R. (ed.) (Paris: Le Seuil, 1967), 20–449.

Nullmeier, F., *Politische Theorie des Sozialstaats* (Frankfurt: Campus Verlag, 2000).

———. 'Politische Theorie des Komparativs: Soziale Vergleiche und gerechte Gesellschaft', *Mittelweg 36* 25(2) (2016), 56–73.

Promies, W. (ed.), *Lichtenbergs Hogarth: Die Kalender-Erklärungen von Georg Christoph Lichtenberg mit den Nachstichen von Ernst Ludwig Riepenhausen zu den Kupferstich-Tafeln von William Hogarth* (Munich: Hanser Verlag, 1999).

Rohr, J.B. von, *Einleitung zur Ceremoniel-Wissenschafft der Privat-Personen, welche ... von einem jungen Teutschen Cavalier in Obacht zu nehmen* (Berlin: Rüdiger, 1728).

Rousseau, J.-J., *Les Confessions* (1782), Œuvres complètes, Gagnebin, B. (ed.), vol. 1 (Paris: Éditions de la Pléiade, 1959), 1–656.

———. *Discours sur l'origine et les fondemens de l'inégalité parmi les hommes* (1755), Œuvres complètes, Gagnebin, B. (ed.), vol. 3 (Paris: Éditions de la Pléiade, 1964), 109–94.

———. *Émile, ou de l'éducation* (1762), Œuvres complètes, Gagnebin, B. (ed.), vol. 4 (Paris: Éditions de la Pléiade, 1969), 239–877.

Scheler, M., 'Über Ressentiment und moralisches Werturteil: Ein Beitrag zur Pathologie der Kultur', *Zeitschrift für Pathopsychologie* 1, no. 2–3 (1912), also published separately: Scheler, M., *Über Ressentiment und moralisches Werturteil* (Leipzig: Engelmann, 1912).

———. 'Der Bourgeois', *Die Weißen Blätter* 1(6) (February 1914), revised version: Scheler, M., 'Der Bourgeois' (1915), in *Gesammelte Werke*, vol. 3: *Vom Umsturz der Werte: Abhandlungen und Aufsätze*, 4th edn (Bern: Francke Verlag, 1955), 343–61.

———. 'Das Ressentiment im Aufbau der Moralen' (1915), in *Gesammelte Werke*, vol. 3: *Vom Umsturz der Werte: Abhandlungen und Aufsätze*, 4th edn (Bern: Francke Verlag, 1955), 33–147.

Schmidt, J., *Die Geschichte des Genie-Gedankens in der deutschen Literatur, Philosophie und Politik, 1750–1945*, 3rd edn, 2 vols (Heidelberg: Winter, 2004).

Seigel, J., *The Idea of the Self: Thought and Experience in Western Europe since the Seventeenth Century* (Cambridge: Cambridge University Press, 2005).

Shepard, A., *Accounting for Oneself: Worth, Status and the Social Order in Early Modern England* (Oxford: Oxford University Press, 2015).

Sombart, W., *Händler und Helden: Patriotische Besinnungen* (Munich: Duncker & Humblot, 1915).

———. *Der Bourgeois: Zur Geistesgeschichte des modernen Wirtschaftsmenschen* (1913) (Reinbek: Rowohlt, 1988).

Stollberg-Rilinger, B., 'Logik und Semantik des Ranges in der Frühen Neuzeit', in Jessen, R. (ed.), *Konkurrenz in der Geschichte. Praktiken – Werte – Institutionalisierungen* (Frankfurt: Campus Verlag, 2014), 197–227.

Veblen, T., *The Theory of the Leisure Class: An Economic Study of Institutions* (New York: Macmillan Company, 1912).

———. 'The Instinct of Workmanship and the Irksomeness of Labor' (1898), in Camic, C. and Hodgson, G. M. (eds), *Essential Writings of Thorstein Veblen* (London: Routledge, 2011), 158–68.

———. 'Some Neglected Points in the Theory of Socialism' (1891), in Camic, C. and Hodgson, G. M. (eds), *Essential Writings of Thorstein Veblen* (London: Routledge, 2011), 64–76.

Wagner, P., 'Hogarth's Industry and Idleness: Subversive Lessons on Conduct', in Carré, J. (ed.), *The Crisis of Courtesy: Studies in the Conduct Book in Britain, 1600–1900* (Leiden: Brill, 1994), 51–65.

Weller, T., *Theatrum Praecedentiae: Zeremonieller Rang und gesellschaftliche Ordnung in der frühneuzeitlichen Stadt. Leipzig 1500–1800* (Darmstadt: Wissenschaftliche Buchgesellschaft, 2006).

Wright Mills, C., *White Collar: The American Middle Classes* (Oxford: Oxford University Press, 1951).

# 4

# Empowering Comparisons?

## *The Making of Republics in the Early Modern Period*

### Lars Behrisch

What was a 'republic' in the early modern period and was there any such clearly definable thing as 'republican' thinking?[1] These questions are among the most contested issues of early modern political and intellectual history.[2] There was a vast spectrum of contemporary usage: at one end of it, the term 'republic' could denote any form of polity – all the way from Jean Bodin's absolutist *République* to the Swiss Confederacy. Whatever polity the term was thus describing, it was always used in the affirmative, setting the specific 'republic' apart from other, supposedly worse forms of government. At the other end of the spectrum, in a more restricted sense, the term 'republic' denoted government without a monarchical head. This meaning became more frequent from the seventeenth century onwards, but it was not exclusive until at least the end of the eighteenth century.[3] To use the term *only* in this restricted sense is a possible choice, but one that needs to acknowledge its analytical and semi-anachronistic nature. The longstanding, highly sophisticated debate about the nature of early modern 'republics' and 'republicanism' has, unfortunately, suffered from the lack of clarity of the term (and of its definition) – different scholars tend to speak of different things.[4]

The focus of the present chapter is on the actual emergence of monarchless government, i.e. of 'republics' narrowly defined; from here onwards, the term will be used in this narrower sense. The use of the term 'emergence' in this context points to an underlying question: did such government, in the early modern period, come about rather accidentally as the result of political upheavals or was it actively aspired to? Were republics 'made' in the sense of being desired and planned or were they 'made' as politicians and revolutionaries were struggling to re-adjust government in times of crisis?

The present volume's perspective on 'comparison' is promising if one wants to study the emergence of early modern republics from a new angle. Specialist scholars have pointed out, for individual instances of political upheaval, the parallels drawn by protagonists with the situation in other states (and here we will draw heavily on their findings). But the fact that such comparisons were common to most, if not all, such moments has not yet been accounted for, nor – as a consequence – have the different forms of these comparisons been compared. The chapter will do this, and by doing so it will approach those moments of political upheaval from a new, as yet unexplored vantage point.

The comparisons primarily discussed here are with existing, contemporary republics. Venice and Switzerland were on hand from the outset of the early modern period. With the Dutch Revolt, the Netherlands became the most prominent example, only temporarily eclipsed by the English Commonwealth. All of them were referred to as models – or countermodels – by protagonists elsewhere in moments of political upheaval, so as to embolden and, potentially, legitimize and empower themselves. It remains to be seen to what extent this happened and what exactly people felt empowered to do by making these comparisons – or whether they were, on the contrary, dissuaded by them.

Comparisons with existing republics were of course only part of a wider frame of references available to political protagonists. More prominent, generally speaking, were references to the legal and political traditions of one's own state. Treatises on political theory tended to rely heavily on the examples from antiquity. All kinds of references could be combined to render a political argument as convincing as possible, especially in times of major political crisis. During those times, too, contemporary examples seem to have taken on increased relevance, also because now a wider public wanted and needed to be addressed. This became most crucial when political crisis escalated into civil war, as militias and their leaders needed very concrete justifications and goals: this end could potentially be served by straightforward and accessible comparisons with contemporary states featuring (apparently) similar conditions.

A number of more specific questions can be asked when such comparisons are studied. Most basically, we can ask which kind of foreign examples were adduced and how they were used: what was their intended purpose and can we say anything about their actual mobilizing potential? A further question addresses the veracity of the comparisons. While they were necessarily based on fragmentary knowledge, were shaped by ingrained modes of perception and were interpreted through the lens of concrete experiences, we can ask to what extent they were consciously distorted or consciously selective. If it is true that references to contemporary states could be relevant for political or military mobilization, the temptation to manipulate them might have been great. Finally, what kind of comparisons was considered plausible in a given context? Did those who made them differentiate between different elements that could be compared to increase their plausibility?

The cases chosen comprise all the eminent instances of an at least temporary establishment of republican government: the Dutch Revolt in the late sixteenth century, the English Revolution in the mid seventeenth century and the American Revolution in the late eighteenth century. This is not the only possible selection; other, less 'successful' political upheavals such as the Bohemian rebellion[5] could have been included – as is, in fact, the *Fronde* in mid seventeenth-century France. The French Revolution, on the other hand, is considered only during its first months, i.e. some two years before the notion of creating a republic came to the fore. However, this happened already outside the parameters of early modern politics, within the modern type of a political nation created during the first months of revolution. During the initial period considered here, the main object of comparison was not a republic (although the new United States also played a role), but the constitutional monarchy of Britain – an object of comparison that was nevertheless contested and soon discarded. The French revolutionaries' debates over the usefulness of the British model are a valuable addition to the picture and are therefore included in the sample.

## The Dutch Revolt

Shortly after the 'Pacification of Ghent' in 1576, the last attempt by the seventeen provinces of the Netherlands to join ranks in resistance against their overlord, the Spanish King Philip II, suggestions were made to turn this alliance into an independent republic after the Swiss model:[6] 'Why could we not, in these states, achieve the liberty that the Swiss are enjoying?'[7] The analogy was endorsed by Marnix van Sint-Aldegonde, closest associate of rebel leader William of Orange.[8] Even a new word was forged to designate the plan of imitating the Swiss – namely, to 'canton' (*kantonnieren, se cantonner*).[9] The potential of the analogy was picked up abroad too: English commentators, among others, envisaged the possibility of a government 'after the manner of the Swiss'.[10]

As more than one Dutchman saw it, the similarity between Switzerland and the Netherlands was twofold. First, the Netherlands consisted of diverse, self-organized and independent-minded provinces, just like the Swiss cantons (it could be added that they were even *more* multi-confessional). At the same time, the Swiss diet or *Tagsatzung* coordinating the otherwise autonomous cantons could be juxtaposed with the *Staten Generaal* (Estates General), the gathering of delegates from the provincial estates. Second, a foreign monarch – and in both cases a Habsburg – disregarded the political and legal traditions of the provinces. To resist such royal encroachments, 'a special union of the Netherlands, similar to the Helvetic constitution'[11] seemed both legitimate and feasible. A firm step in this direction was taken by the northern provinces when they founded the defensive Union of Utrecht in 1579.[12]

Such a union seemed feasible because of yet another parallel: the geographical complexities both of Switzerland (mountains) and of the Netherlands (water) –

and especially of the core northern provinces of Holland and Zeeland – favoured local defenders over intruders. This judgement was in fact vindicated by the course of the war from the 1570s to the 1590s.

However, behind the apparent similarities, there loomed possibly unsurmountable differences that, in the eyes of some observers, forbade any such comparison and made it unwise to follow the Swiss example. Unsurmountable, first of all, in quite a literal sense: the Alps were, arguably, more of a barrier to intruders than the sea and the waterways; the Netherlands were thus more exposed than Switzerland – but also more exposed than Venice – to invading armies.[13] Moreover, the Swiss had a strong military tradition and were, in contrast to the Dutch, disciplined, uncorrupted and hardworking; while they loved liberty more than riches, the Dutch had become spoiled, effeminate and corrupt, not least so because of bad foreign (i.e. French) influence.[14] On a more sober note, pamphleteers considered factionalism and the divergent interests of the individual provinces to be massive obstacles to revolt, as well as the existence of a nobility – again in contrast to Switzerland.[15]

As a result of such a sceptical analysis, 'the state of the one [Switzerland] will be the ruin of the other'.[16] After Philip II of Spain had finally been declared deposed in 1581 by the northern provinces, this argument was used by those who urgently advocated the search for a new foreign prince; the frightening Spanish military advances of the past years added to their plea. Such an option was generally favoured during the 1580s and led to the choice, first, of the brother of the French king, the Duc d'Anjou, and then of the Earl of Leicester. Both choices, however, met with very limited success, not least because neither was willing to cooperate with the provinces on a par, as they had promised. Already the failure of Anjou had led one author to reject the need for a foreign prince, and consequently also all the arguments against aligning the Netherlands along Swiss lines.[17] In the late 1580s, the (eventually seven) northern 'United' provinces took matters into their own hands and became, by default, a *Republiek*.[18]

The reference to Switzerland had worked on a local level too, where it was compounded by yet another element: militant Calvinism. This at least was the case in the Flemish metropolis of Ghent that in 1577 was turned into a rigidly Calvinist city-state.[19] Its erstwhile leader, Jan van Hembyze, was accused by his opponents of reducing the Flemish to 'Swiss manners',[20] while he himself praised them for 'cantonning themselves in the Swiss mode, that is in turning themselves into confederate cantons'.[21] One of the first and most outspoken proponents of the Dutch-Swiss comparison, a German Calvinist, set out to show that Ghent was set on the right path.[22] And when Hembyze was forced to leave town in 1579 – not least because of his intransigent Calvinism in a city that was still overwhelmingly Catholic – he declared that 'all he had wanted to do was to turn Ghent into an invincible and thriving commercial city like Geneva'.[23] Whilst the political and economic aspects are at the forefront of this apology, it is obvious that Geneva also served as a pedigree for Hembyze's all-but-theocratic regime (an aspect that at this moment he might have been reluctant to stress). In the same context, Hembyze claimed that he had studied the constitutions of all ancient and contemporary republics.[24] Thus, in his own thinking as well as (arguably) in that of the citizenry he was addressing,[25] the decisive point of reference was not an abstract ideal, but a concrete manifestation – one that could be found in a contemporary, and co-religious, city.

To sum up, there was a discourse running through the decisive years of the Dutch Revolt, taking the independence and the political constitution of the Swiss Confederacy as a positive example.[26] Although we can certainly grasp only the tip of the iceberg of this discourse, there is evidence suggesting that it was mooted not only in tracts and pamphlets but also in mansions and taverns, on board ships and in army camps. As such, it was doubtless influential in strengthening the self-confidence and legitimacy of the Estates General (or from the 1580s, its northern 'rump') to represent and ultimately lead the Netherlands into independence, as no compromise could be found with the king. While the comparison with Switzerland was not in any obvious way distorted, there *was* the counterargument that the seemingly straightforward comparison was misleading and that the Netherlands was too different to warrant any confidence that the attempt to become an independent republic might be similarly successful. However, events showed that the comparison was indeed valid enough to pass the test.

## The English Revolution

We might expect a similar constellation in 1649, at the onset of the republican phase of the English Revolution, with the Dutch Revolt now serving as an important and possibly catalytic pedigree. After all, the Dutch republic had not only ultimately defeated the Spanish Empire, but in the process had become one of the most powerful, prosperous and culturally radiant states of Europe. However, this expectation turns out to be wrong: whilst resistance to the king that led to the Civil War in 1642 did to some extent draw on the legacy of the Dutch Revolt,[27] the legitimation to govern without a king, as well as the confidence of being able to do so, were firmly and de facto exclusively based on English legal and political traditions, with Parliament at their core – while references to models abroad were all but absent.

Seemingly the first robust reference to the republican Netherlands, and possibly the only one before the regicide, appears just after the end of the (first) Civil War in a 'Leveller' tract from the summer of 1646, entitled 'A remonstrance of many thousand citizens'.[28] This was an important piece as, to all appearances, it for the first time called openly for the abolition of monarchy, combined with a claim for full sovereignty of the people.[29] The Netherlands come up somewhat obliquely in the context of criticism of Parliament's practices of military conscription: the New Model Army impressed infantry like 'galley-slave[s] in Turkey or A[l]giere'. By contrast, 'the Hollanders, our provident neighbours, have no such cruelties, esteeming nothing more unjust or unreasonable; yet they want no men'. This leads to a more general exhortation: 'If ye would in many things follow their good example and make this nation a state free from the oppression of kings', the people would gladly follow Parliament's lead.[30]

There were only few such voices aiming at a republican, kingless constitution before the regicide in January 1649[31] and it seems that, much like the Netherlands, the English Commonwealth was 'a republic by default'.[32] Republican practice and convictions followed the regicide rather than vice versa, and they were to remain wavering and not clear-cut. On a terminological level, the indigenous 'Commonwealth' and 'Free State'[33] were preferred over 'Republic'.[34] The Commons decided, in principle, to abolish the monarchy (and the House of Lords) in the first week of February, but they did so properly only in the second half of March, more than one-and-a-half months after the execution of the king. In a lengthy legitimation of their acts, they referred – albeit not too prominently – to the example of other 'free states', both past and present. 'Herein the Parliament received Encouragement, by their Observation of the Blessing of God upon other States': not only Rome and Venice, but also 'Switzerland, and other free States, exceed those who are not so, in Riches, Freedom, Peace, and all Happiness' – and above all 'our Neighbours in the United Provinces, since their Change of Government, have wonderfully increased in Wealth, Freedom, Trade, and Strength, both by Sea and Land'.[35]

However, to the dismay of the young republic, their neighbours did not endorse this comparison. The Dutch declined offers for a union and were largely hostile to the Commonwealth. Many Dutch had hedged political (and religious) sympathies for the cause of Parliament during the 1640s, remembering their own past struggles. But the regicide made public opinion in the Netherlands side with the Stuart cause,[36] regardless of the political and religious alignments at home[37] and in spite of the fact that the country was to enter its first 'stadholderless period' – its first truly republican era – in 1650. The enmity was sealed when the two countries went to war over their commercial rivalry – calling forth, among other things, English bitterness about 'the Hollanders['] ingratitude' for the 'former kindnesse received from England' – i.e. support for their revolt – and 'their base requitall now, being so effascinated [and] foolishly charm'd with the magicall spells of monarchy, to subvert their owne fundamentall principles [and] engage in a warre against England, to the ruine of her ... liberties'.[38]

Against this background, it is also not surprising that there was relatively little contemporary reflection on the political similarities of the two states. James Harrington and other republican theorists sometimes referred to the Netherlands – albeit taking some issue with their federal, and thus divisive, character – but for most contemporaries, the two states had very little in common beyond the sheer absence of a king. The Dutch, in fact, saw in Cromwell's Protectorate a resurrection of monarchy in its worst, tyrannical form. Conversely and ironically, the Stuart Restoration of 1660, which was initially much hailed in the Netherlands, yet soon turned out not only to worsen Anglo–Dutch relations but also to strengthen the Orangist (Stadholder) position, might have contributed to making republican positions in the Netherlands more explicit than ever before.[39] Even now, though, references to the English republican experience and also to English republican authors remained all but absent, due to the lasting catastrophic image of the Commonwealth and the Protectorate.[40]

All taken together, it seems obvious only in retrospect that the English Commonwealth and the Dutch republic should have found much common ground, or indeed taken relevant cues from each other. Similarly to the Dutch Revolt – but already much less prominently – resistance against a 'tyrannical' king could be buttressed by the memory of an earlier historical example. However, the regicide and the ensuing kingless constitution were based on purely indigenous legal and political arguments, especially such as pertained to parliamentary sovereignty.[41] In spite of the strong political, commercial, religious and cultural connections with the Netherlands and the corresponding knowledge of that country's political setup – or rather *because* of it – the Dutch example did not (or only very marginally) complement England's own history and polity in the task of constructing and legitimizing the Commonwealth. Parliament had been a central element of political authority for centuries; during the 1640s, it became, in practice as in theory, the only one and did not need, or could possibly only be weakened by, the juxtaposition with such a comparatively makeshift and uneasily composite governing body as the Dutch Estates General. If the English were 'insular', it was thus not so much a 'conspicuous fail[ure] to … consider whether there might be working models of republicanism abroad',[42] but a consequence of the fundamental differences between their own political traditions, institutions and discourses, and those of others – whether they had a monarch or not.

## The *Fronde* and *Ormée*

In contrast to both the positive endorsement of the Swiss model in the Dutch Revolt and the little interest shown in the Dutch model during the English Revolution, the *Fronde* that took place in France at the same time presents yet a third type: an explicit rejection of a potential comparison. In the *Fronde* various protagonists – from urban craftsmen and magistrates through *parlements* (high courts of justice) to highest aristocrats – fought against Cardinal Mazarin, first minister of the regent queen mother Anna of Austria. They were nonetheless firm royalists and claimed to fight not against, but for the minor Louis XIV. Much the same could be said, of course, for the English parliamentarians who, in the first instance, fought not against kingship or the Stuart dynasty, but against the perceived abuse of royal power at the hands of Charles I. However, the latter's execution only months after the *Fronde* had begun was to drive the rebels in both countries in opposite directions: towards kingless government in England and towards an even more assertive royalism in France. Here, all the various rebel groups, from princes of the blood all the way down to urban craftsmen, not only condemned the regicide in London but also rejected various polemical attempts to associate them with English political developments as vehemently as, to all appearances, genuinely.⁴³

The English comparison was in fact so vehemently and genuinely rejected that when, in early 1651, Mazarin dared to draw too close a parallel between English revolutionaries and the *Frondeurs*, this was catalytic for them to overcome their disagreements, join ranks for the first time and drive him into exile.⁴⁴ One writer stressed that the *parlement* of Paris was the very opposite of the English Parliament – namely, the most loyal and obedient servant to its king. Consequently, it could also 'not condone the foundation of the Roman republic, let alone those republics which in more recent times had appeared in Switzerland, Holland, and England'.⁴⁵ Thus, it seems that the *Frondeurs*, by comparing themselves with their neighbours, became *less* rather than *more* revolutionary. The comparison discouraged them more than it encouraged them from derogating the monarchy.⁴⁶

Against this thoroughly conservative background, some *Frondeurs* could use the English example as a warning against their opponent Mazarin: if *he* were to continue his lawless rule, comparable to that of Charles I prior to the Civil War, some people might end up 'follow[ing] the unfortunate example of England and … declare that all the royal authority resided in the Parlement'.⁴⁷ This warning, however, did not frighten Mazarin and his entourage; if anything, such a prospect frightened the *Fronde* leaders themselves and made them back away from appealing to more popular support.

They need not have been frightened. Not only among rebellious *parlementaires* and high aristocrats, but also among urban rebels, there was no aspiration to modify the French political system, let alone take England as an example. This is testified in the most striking way by the so-called *Ormée* of Bordeaux – named after the elm trees (*ormes*) overshadowing the insurgents' meeting place at the edge of town – the most radical urban revolt in the context of the *Fronde*. Between the summer of 1652 and the summer of 1653, Bordeaux was ruled by self-constituted citizen councils, supported by urban militias, who had ousted the traditional authorities, i.e. the governor, magistrate and local *parlement*. But what did they aspire to? Nothing more in fact than a fairer share of the citizenry – essentially the urban elite of merchants, lawyers and guild masters – in the running of urban affairs and, concomitantly, more transparent urban finances.⁴⁸ It was the traditional call for more autonomy and the well-known catalogue of urban grievances spelled out all across Western and Central Europe during the early modern period. At most, here was a city republic in the making. But no more than in any other early modern urban revolt was there an aspiration to transfer broader participation in politics beyond the city walls, let alone to encroach on the monarchy as an overarching political institution – an institution that was seen as the traditional safeguard of the city's autonomy too.

In the spring of 1653, in union with the Prince of Conti, royal cousin and figurehead of the aristocratic *Fronde* next to his brother, the Grand Condé, the *Ormistes* sought an alliance with England to withstand the onslaught of Mazarin's army and fleet. In this context, there was some talk of 'republican' tendencies.[49] But their very limited extent became clear when the English, in place of the desired military support,[50] provided an entirely undesired French version of the Levellers' 1649 'Agreement of the free people of England'.[51] *This* kind of antimonarchical republicanism was to find 'absolutely no echo' in Bordeaux.[52] If members of the Commonwealth had thought their new political notions to be exportable, they were clearly mistaken.

## The American Revolution

In the context of the American Revolution, references especially to the Dutch republic were legion, flanked by those to Switzerland and Venice. They strongly supported the notion that a kingless state, even of some size and of composite structure, was viable and indeed desirable. Countering current allegations of the internal and external bellicosity of republics, Thomas Paine asserted in early 1776, on the eve of independence: 'The republics of Europe are all (and we may say always) in peace. Holland and Swisserland are without wars, foreign or domestic.'[53] This was far from the truth – and possibly deliberately so – but American patriots seem to have endorsed such arguments.

A decade later, in the constitutional debate, references to contemporary states, particularly to republics, were at least as relevant as those to antiquity. However, more often than not, their respective shortcomings made both of them instances of what to avoid rather than what to emulate.[54] At the same time, the American situation was increasingly perceived to be unique – in terms of its challenges as well as opportunities. Benjamin Franklin stated in the Philadelphia Convention that 'we have gone back to ancient history for models of Government, and examined the different forms of those Republics which [carried] the seeds of their own dissolution ... And we have viewed Modern States all round Europe, but find none of their Constitutions suitable to our circumstances'.[55]

When Alexander Hamilton and James Madison defended the draft constitution in the series of articles known as *The Federalist*, they repeatedly compared their own situation with the Netherlands, Switzerland and Venice, as well as with the semi-republican, elective monarchies of Poland and the Holy Roman Empire.[56] Whilst the Netherlands and Switzerland in particular remained positive examples of the viability of a kingless state, their defects pointed towards a better, if not the ideal republic. The central issue was the degree of union: should America, judging by the experience of those existing republics, become a *federal* state rather than remaining just a *confederate* state? Such of course was the intention of the Constitution, and *The Federalist* sought to buttress it. If the colonies were to remain separate entities, its authors argued, they might end up in war with each other – for, contrary to Paine's assertion, republics were *not* inherently peaceful.[57] They also rebuffed his view that existing republican 'confederacies' were internally stable; on the contrary, they were highly unstable and therefore also potential prey to neighbours. The pitiable case of Poland had only just testified to this logic.[58]

As for Switzerland, it functioned only because it was very different from all other republics – including America – particularly in terms of its geography and its relative homogeneity. And yet, even Switzerland had proven to be fragile in the face of major challenges, such as the religious divide. Consequently, 'so far as the peculiarity of their case will admit of comparison with that of the United States, it serves to confirm the principle … to be established': namely, that a mere Confederation is not a viable state.[59] This principle was heavily contested by the 'Anti-Federalists', who, in turn, invoked the Swiss as a *positive* example for their cause.[60]

An entire article of *The Federalist* is devoted to the Netherlands – the most impressive example of a republic during the previous centuries but also one that, after the recent 'Patriot' troubles and the victory of the Stadholder-cum-Prussian arms, looked much like a failed one.[61] *The Federalist* sketches the finely tuned equilibrium between centralization and decentralization in this 'celebrated … confederacy, as delineated on parchment'.[62] But what came of it? 'Imbecility in the government; discord among the provinces; foreign influence and indignities; a precarious existence in peace, and peculiar calamities from war.' Having further corroborated this view with observations on Dutch politics, Madison concludes: 'I make no apology for having dwelt so long on the contemplation of these federal precedents [as] experience [i.e. comparison] is the oracle of truth.'[63] For years, he had in fact spent enormous time and energy learning as much as he could about 'ancient and modern Federal Republics'.[64]

In hindsight, some 'Founding Fathers' were to refer to the Netherlands as an encouraging example.[65] However, the example was the Dutch Revolt, not the political constitution of the Netherlands. To the extent that the Fathers' memory was correct, the comparison possibly had a similarly encouraging effect as it had had in England during the 1640s. The crucial difference was that Americans felt encouraged to establish a republic outright rather than just to resist their king. As opposed to previous centuries, the concept of a kingless state, whether going by the name of 'republic' or not,[66] was present and virulent. From 1776, and *a fortiori* from 1783, the question was not *if* such a state should be established, but *what kind* of such a state. In the debate, existing 'republics' – three kingless states, but also elective monarchies and sometimes even Britain – served as important roadsigns. The road taken went well beyond previous examples, avoiding the weaknesses of all existing republics and establishing a new kind of state altogether.

## The French Revolution

Finally, back to France. In at least two ways, its revolution can be said to have been prompted by Britain. First, in the long run, the desperate competition with the smaller but more powerful – because much more efficient – neighbour overstretched the capacities of the (highly inefficient) monarchy and thus led to its collapse. Second, most contemporaries reflecting on this issue were aware of the institutional and constitutional superiority of Britain and, in various mixtures of Anglophobia, Anglophilia and Anglomania, wondered how France could copy the example or at least parts of it. The British Parliament took central stage, of course, securing taxation, public credit and efficient administration as well as guaranteeing the permanent representation of the political nation.

References to the British constitution were widespread but often ambiguous. Characteristic of the tendency to use it as a model but, at the same time, to rebuff direct imitation are the writings of the Abbé Sieyès.[67] In his influential *Qu'est-ce que le Tiers État?*, published on the eve of the Revolution in early 1789, he discussed – and at once dismissed – various suggestions to imitate the British Parliament. The situation was too different, Sieyès insisted, to warrant any direct transfers: 'How could you, with such different material, erect the same political edifice in France as in England?'[68] The French aristocracy, in particular, was much more hierarchical than the British, both vis-à-vis the rest of society and within itself. This ingrained social hierarchy had to disappear *before* any representative constitution à l'anglaise could possibly be established. On the other hand, once these hierarchies were levelled, a second chamber such as the Lords became superfluous.[69] The nation was to be represented by one chamber – one *Chambre des communes*, as Sieyès and others called it, nevertheless, for want of an alternative political and semantic pedigree.[70]

Sieyès discussed this lack of an indigenous political and semantic tradition of national representation, and the corresponding habit of using Britain as a model, in a further chapter entitled 'Que l'esprit d'imitation n'est pas propre à nous bien conduire' – the spirit of imitation is not a good guide for us.[71] The French would not rely so much on British examples, Sieyès complained, if they had a better knowledge of politics. At the same time, the British constitution was not only unsuited for France, it was also a crude, 'exotic', irrational product of chance and historical accidents.[72] It was wrong to ascribe Britain's advantages to its political institutions: the absence of a large army, an enviable privilege of an island state, was the key for the preservation of liberty there. This observation should discredit all attempts at simply copying Britain, i.e. 'the mania', as Sieyès put it, 'of imitating our neighbours'.[73] Instead of looking across the Channel and to the past, France should consider its own present situation, draw on more recent political and social theory, and become itself a model for other nations.[74]

The central figure of such recent theory, for Sieyès and others, was Rousseau. While Sieyès, unlike others, did not follow Rousseau's doctrinaire statements against the concept of representation, he *did* follow his insistence on unitary, indivisible national sovereignty. Therefore, while he was to become the foremost defender of the National Assembly's exclusive claim to expressing the 'general will' (as opposed to forms of direct democracy), he was also to become one of the foremost spokesmen against a bicameral legislature and a royal veto.[75] He and all others who rejected these two elements of shared (legislative) sovereignty dismissed the British model, featuring both, as deficient and, measured by their notion of theoretical consistency, inconsistent and irrational.[76] Defenders of mixed legislative sovereignty, on the other hand, praised the British model as proven by long experience to prevent any kind of 'despotism' – royal, oligarchic or popular.[77]

The antagonism between these two visions was to unfold only after 17 June, when the Third Estate declared itself, together with any members from the other two Estates wishing to join them, the *Assemblée Nationale*. Up to this point, reference to British Parliament was an overwhelmingly positive, if not an empowering one: from the beginning of the meetings of the Estates General in early May, the Third Estate had liked to call itself '[Chambre des] communes (de France)' – and even on 17 June, commentators often referred to it as 'les communes'.[78] The deputy Duquesnoy complained, not unlike Sieyès, that the assembly was obsessed with a 'ridiculous and childish imitation of the English':[79] The deputies frequently used neologisms such as 'l'honorable membre', 'motion' and 'amendement', testifying to their close acquaintance with English parliamentary practice and, once again, to the need to borrow its language. And together with the name and the language, it seems, the Third Estate espoused its very spirit and self-confidence. The comparison with the neighbour and the example of its Parliament that had haunted French political reflection for a century was thus an important element in making such a thing as a national assembly conceivable in the first place, and in fixing its existence in June 1789.

However, from now on, the cleavages mentioned above came to the fore.[80] As Keith Michael Baker has shown, reference to Britain – and, still on an opposite side at this point, reference to the United States – first became controversial in the debates on the nature of the future constitution: was it to be a demiurgic creation of an entirely new polity, discarding all the debris of the old, or was it to be the remodelling and reframing of the existing one? Advocates of the first, more radical approach extolled the American example, rejecting the British polity with much the same principled rigour as Sieyès had done;[81] advocates of the second, conservative approach referred to the British pedigree, while cautiously opposing the American parallel as suited for a virgin society, but not for a centuries-old society and polity like France.[82] This more abstract antagonism was soon complemented, if not exactly reproduced, by the more concrete one mentioned above, pitching defenders and opponents of mixed legislative sovereignty against each other. With the victory of the latter in early September, the British model was essentially discarded.[83] And discarded it was, as one commentator put it, echoing Sieyès, 'as a reproach to human reason'.[84]

## Conclusion

On the previous pages, we encountered five different types of comparison with other states in phases of massive political upheaval during the early modern period. First, when the Dutch rebelled against their Spanish overlord, they referred to the Swiss example in order to embolden themselves in their fight and even to envisage a state without a king. No doubt because this line of comparison was so potent, more than one author opposed to such a radical outcome felt obliged to explicitly reject the potential parallels on the grounds of the two countries' very different geographical and cultural conditions. In England half a century later, there were references to the Dutch Revolt and the Dutch republic, endorsing the parallel. They were, however, few and far between, hardly instrumental in emboldening Roundheads and soon discouraged by Dutch enmity to the Commonwealth. In the contemporaneous *Fronde* in France, by contrast, protagonists keenly rejected any resemblance to English revolutionaries – the comparison was made by their enemies in order to discredit them as disloyal to the king. And when the Commonwealth tried to inject republican thought into the most radical setting of the rebellion, the *Ormée* in Bordeaux, seeking military support from England, this attempt was entirely ignored. American revolutionaries evoked the Dutch Revolt, but their constitution was founded at least as much on a thorough criticism of all hitherto-existing republics as on their positive appraisal. Finally, in the early phase of the French Revolution, the example of British parliamentarianism was as vital as it was forcefully rejected by all-out revolutionaries who insisted on erecting a new polity from scratch and also by many who disdained the idea of owing any of their heroic achievements to the arch-enemy.

There are thus as many varieties of (non)comparison as cases studied, and it is more than likely that other moments of political upheaval or change – like, for example, the Bohemian revolt – would present us with yet more varieties. At this point of research, it would therefore make little sense to try and set up some kind of systematic typology. Instead, two further reflections will be broached. First, to what extent did the comparisons in the cases discussed influence their outcome and do we have to add yet another dimension to the already inextricably complex set of causal elements for rebellions and revolutions in the early modern period? The evidence assembled here suggests otherwise: references to successful revolts in other contemporary states could act in support, but they were probably never decisive in facilitating outcomes, let alone in causing revolt in the first place.[85] Only for the Dutch Revolt, the case might be made for a very substantial, if not in certain contexts even crucial impact of the Swiss example on the self-confidence and perseverance of the rebels (as stated, the British parliamentary model was of massive importance in 1789, but this concerns only the early, still monarchical phase of the French Revolution). Thus, only for the Netherlands does the concept of 'empowering comparison' make sense to the full extent of its potential meaning.

Finally, what can the comparisons tell us about the concept and reality of 'republics' in the early modern period? All the cases studied here – and thus, arguably, the most eminent cases of the erection of republican government during that time – suggest quite strongly that there was no clear concept of republican (kingless) government, let alone a general desire for it. On the contrary, all the emboldening comparisons with Switzerland notwithstanding, the Dutch tried very hard to find a new prince.[86] The English Commonwealth, to all appearances a default republic too, is conspicuous by a near-absence of references to its Dutch neighbour. On neither side of the Channel was there a feeling that the two had more in common than not. Dutch republicans of the time were eager, primarily, to dissociate themselves from the act of regicide – not to mention *Frondeurs* of all shades, rejecting comparison with the English Parliament outright. Likewise, the first two years of the French Revolution saw very little ambition to depose the king, although constitutional monarchists, in their majority, took pride in outdoing the British example in terms of their legislative's rights. And even in the most obviously republican rebellion of the early modern period, the American Revolution, opposition to monarchy as such was not the prime mover and was late to be fully endorsed.[87] Monarchy was no realistic option once independence had been achieved, but when it came to establishing a national constitution, comparison was still not biased in favour of existing kingless states, as they were mostly seen as negative examples.

These findings corroborate an increasing scholarly minimalism concerning 'republicanism' in the early modern period and underscore the notion that earlier historiography was often guided by modernist conceptions of an all but necessary trend, long before the nineteenth century, towards the establishment of republican regimes. They also underscore – as an underlying reason for the quasi-absence of an overarching republican mindset – what has long been argued for individual contexts, but rarely as yet for the early modern period in general: political institutions and legitimations were highly conservative – in the literal sense of the word – and, accordingly, highly parochial. Dutch towns, Provincial Estates and Estates General (as their respective emanations) were hell-bent on preserving *their* rights and prerogatives, not on establishing a regime à la suisse. Much the same can be said about the English Parliament, the Paris *parlement*, the 'respectable' citizens of Bordeaux as well as – *mutatis mutandis* – the settlers in the American colonies. They were rebels for a cause: their own. They did not fight for wider political emancipation, nor did they, in the first place, rebel against their king, even if that was the consequence (a consequence acknowledged, so much is conceded, more quickly in the eighteenth century than in the sixteenth). And therefore they rarely compared themselves emphatically to states without a king. Such a comparison could be emboldening and potentially empowering – but it was always embarrassing.

**Lars Behrisch** is Assistant Professor of Early Modern Political History at the University of Utrecht. He has published on crime and crime control in sixteenth-century cities, on church and religion in early modern Europe and Russia, and on the role of statistics in politics in eighteenth-century France and Germany. His monograph on this last topic is *Die Berechnung der Glückseligkeit: Statistik und Politik in Deutschland und Frankreich im späten Ancien Régime*

(2016). Currently he is preparing a book on the roots of democracy in early modern Europe.

## Notes

1. The author would like to thank Leonhard Horowski, René Koekkoek and Lina Weber for their help and advice.
2. It is therefore impossible to offer any overview of the literature at this point. For recent contributions and reflections, see U. Weeber, *Republiken als Blaupause: Venedig, die Niederlande und die Eidgenossenschaft im Reformdiskurs der Frühaufklärung* (Berlin: De Gruyter Oldenbourg, 2016); R. von Friedeburg, 'Republic and Republicanism', in H. Scott (ed.), *The Oxford Handbook of Early Modern European History, 1350–1750*, vol. 2 (Oxford: Oxford University Press, 2015), 538–58; B. Worden, 'Liberty for Export: "Republicanism" in England, 1500–1800', in G. Mahlberg and D. Wiemann (eds), *European Contexts for English Republicanism* (London: Taylor & Francis, 2013), 13–32; W. Nippel, 'Klassischer Republikanismus in der frühen Neuzeit. Kritische Nachfragen', in U. Niggemann and K. Ruffing (eds), *Antike als Modell in Nordamerika? Konstruktion und Verargumentierung 1763–1809* (Munich: Oldenbourg, 2011), 23–34; R. Hammersley, *The English Republican Tradition and Eighteenth-Century France: Between the Ancients and the Moderns* (Manchester: Manchester University Press, 2010); T. Maissen, *Die Geburt der Republic: Staatsverständnis und Repräsentation in der frühneuzeitlichen Eidgenossenschaft* (Göttingen: Vandenhoeck & Ruprecht, 2008).
3. Witness, among others, the Polish *Rzespospolita*. In the American constitutional debate, Britain could still pass as a 'republic' (see the section entitled 'The American Revolution' below).
4. To name but a few important examples, John Pocock leans towards a broad conception (including monarchical government), Quentin Skinner towards a somewhat more narrow and analytical one, Blair Worden wants to reserve the term to explicit theories of kingless government and Rachel Hammersley elaborates on the distinction between types of 'ancient', 'early modern' and 'modern republicanism', existing alongside each other throughout most of the period.
5. For contemporary comparisons with the Netherlands in this particular context, see G. Mortimer, *The Origins of the Thirty Years War and the Revolt in Bohemia, 1618* (London: Palgrave Macmillan, 2015), 166.
6. References to Switzerland are documented in L. Delfos, *Die Anfänge der Utrechter Union 1577–1587: Ein Beitrag zur Geschichte der niederländischen Erhebung, insbesondere zu deren Verfassungsgeschichte* (Berlin: Verlag Dr. Emil Ebering, 1941); A.A. van Schelven, *De staatsvorm van het Zwitserse Eedgenootschap den Nederlanden ter navolging aanbevolen* (Brussels: Éditions universitaires, 1947); M. van Gelderen, *The Political Thought of the Dutch Revolt* (Cambridge: Cambridge University Press, 1992), 171–91. See also M. van Gelderen, 'Turning Swiss? Discord in Dutch Debates', in A. Holenstein, T. Maissen and M. Prak (eds), *The Republican Alternative: The Netherlands and Switzerland Compared* (Amsterdam: Amsterdam University Press, 2008), 151–69, esp. 156–58; O. Mörke, 'Der "schwache" Staat als Erfolgsrezept? Die niederländische Republik und die Schweizer Eidgenossenschaft', in W. Buchholz and S. Kroll (eds), *Quantität und Struktur: Festschrift für Kersten Krüger zum 60. Geburtstag* (Rostock: Universität Rostock, 1999), 45–62, esp.

51–54; N. Mout, 'Ideales Muster oder erfundene Eigenart. Republikanische Theorien während des niederländischen Aufstands', in H.G. Koenigsberger (ed.), *Republiken und Republikanismus im Europa der frühen Neuzeit* (Munich: Oldenbourg, 1988), 169–94, esp. 174–75 and 178–80.

7. 'Pourquoi ne pourrions[-nous] parvenir en ces pays à la liberté de laquelle joyssent les Suysses?' (1577 or earlier), quoted by van Schelven, *Staatsvorm*, 749 and Delfos, *Anfänge*, 23.
8. 'Que les provinces se liguassent ensemble et formassent des cantons comme en Suisse' (1578), quoted by van Schelven, *Staatsvorm*, 748. See also Delfos, *Anfänge*, 50, for a similar pronouncement made in 1577. William of Orange seems to have endorsed the slogan at this time too (ibid., 41).
9. Van Schelven, *Staatsvorm*, 749; Delfos, *Anfänge*, 46. While the French *canton* for the original German *Ort* or *Stand* was not in use in the German-speaking parts of Switzerland before the seventeenth century, it had already gained currency in Western Europe.
10. State Papers (1583), quoted by Delfos, *Anfänge*, 227; the analogy had already been mooted in England as well as in Germany by 1576 (ibid., 41 note***).
11. 'Een besonder unie van Nederlandt, der Helvetischen ordinantie gelick' (1578), quoted by Delfos, *Anfänge*, 89.
12. The Union was signed by Holland, Zeeland, Utrecht, Guelders and Groningen (only the countryside – the town joined later); Friesland and Overijssel followed, thus forming the seven northern provinces.
13. *Waerschouwinghe aen alle goede inghesetenen vanden Nerderlanden* ... (1583); see van Gelderen, *Political Thought*, 174–75.
14. *Emanuel-Erneste: Dialogue de deux personnages sur l'Estat du Pais Bas* (Gerard Prouninck van Deventer, 1580); see van Schelven, *Staatsvorm*, 750–51; and van Gelderen, *Political Thought*, 171–73.
15. This was indeed an obstacle to political unison in the Southern Netherlands, where the nobility was both stronger and more internally divided than in the North.
16. *Emanuel-Erneste: Dialogue*, quoted by van Gelderen, *Political Thought*, 171.
17. *Discours verclaerende wat forme ende manier van regieringhe dat die Nederlanden voor die alderbeste ende zekerste tot desen tyden aenstellen mochten* (1583); see van Gelderen, *Political Thought*, 189–91; and van Schelven, *Staatsvorm*, 751–52.
18. While not usually part of the official designation of the new state, the term was nevertheless used – and also in a comparative context. See van Schelven, *Staatsvorm*, 751 (example from 1580); Delfos, *Anfänge*, 227, 240 (examples from 1583).
19. Similar, if less militant, Calvinist regimes were established in the other major Flemish and Brabantine cities. Ghent also led their way in joining the Union of Utrecht in 1579, but was (again like them) conquered by the Duke of Parma in 1584. See A. Despretz, 'De instauratie der Gentse Calvinistische Republiek (1577–1579)', *Handelingen der Maatschappij voor Geschiedenis en Oudheidkunde te Gent* 17 (1963), 119–229; A.-L. van Bruaene, 'A Breakdown of Civic Community? Civic Traditions, Voluntary Associations and the Ghent Calvinist Regime (1577–84)', in N. Eckstein and N. Terpstra (eds), *Sociability and its Discontents: Civil Society, Social Capital, and Their Alternatives in Late Medieval and Early Modern Europe* (Turnhout: Brepols, 2009), 273–91.
20. '... op de Zwitsersche manieren Vlaenderen zocht te bringhen', quoted by Delfos, *Anfänge*, 118.
21. Quoted in ibid.

22. *Le vray patriot aux bons patriots* (Peter Beutterich, 1578); see van Gelderen, *Political Thought*, 187–88; and van Schelven, *Staatsvorm*, 754–55. The author knew Switzerland and might well have been the most important broker of the Swiss comparison (ibid., 755). On the label *patriot* that gained enormous currency in the wake of the Pacification of Ghent, see A. Duke, 'In Defence of the Common Fatherland. Patriotism and Liberty in the Low Countries, 1555–1576', in R. Stein and J. Pollmann (eds), *Networks, Regions and Nations: Shaping Identities in the Low Countries, 1300–1650* (Leiden: Brill, 2010), 217–39.
23. '… dat in alles zyn voornemen was geweest van Ghendt te maken een onverwinnelijke, en bloeiende koopstad, gelijk Geneve' (1579), quoted by Despretz, 'Instauratie', 161; see also van Bruaene, 'Breakdown', 284–85 (there are different versions of the exact wording; on the original sources, see Despretz, 'Instauratie', 124–26).
24. Van Bruaene, 'Breakdown', 285; Delfos, *Anfänge*, 118.
25. He spoke in front of the assembled captains of the civic guard (van Bruaene, 'Breakdown', 285).
26. Apparently, only in one writing the example of Switzerland (and Venice) was used in a truly negative way (i.e. beyond doubting the sheer comparability with the Netherlands): in the *Vriendelick Vertooch … wat middelen dese bedruckte Landen te wercke moghen legghen tot haerlieder conservatie …* (1583), the author pointed to discord and corruption in Switzerland and to oligarchy and repression in Venice in order to discourage any attempts to follow their examples (see van Gelderen, *Political Thought*, 178). – The (positive) comparison with Venice became fashionable in the seventeenth century; see E.O.G. Haitsma Mulier, *The Myth of Venice and Dutch Republican Thought in the Seventeenth Century* (Assen: Van Gorcum, 1980) (for the sixteenth century, see 57).
27. This also holds for the Scottish and Irish rebellions of 1639 and 1641; see H. Dunthorne, *Britain and the Dutch Revolt 1560–1700* (Cambridge: Cambridge University Press, 2013), xiv, 189–91.
28. [R. Overton and W. Walwyn], 'A remonstrance of many thousand citizens and other freeborn people of England to their House of Commons … how they [the Commons] have discharged their duties to the universality of the people, their sovereign lord, from whom their power and strength is derived' (7 July 1646), in A. Sharp (ed.), *The English Levellers* (Cambridge: Cambridge University Press, 1998), 33–53.
29. Ibid., 33–34 and passim. See S. Barber, *Regicide and Republicanism: Politics and Ethics in the English Revolution, 1646–1659* (Edinburgh: Edinburgh University Press, 1998), 42–44 (and 41 for another tract, written a few months later, explicitly recommending a 'republic'); B. Worden, 'Republicanism, Regicide and Republic: The English Experience', in M. van Gelderen and Q. Skinner (eds), *Republicanism and Constitutionalism in Early Modern Europe: A Shared European Heritage* (Cambridge: Cambridge University Press, 2002), 307–27, 318–20, who stresses the Levellers' contribution to the concept of kingless government, but also notes that they were not necessarily, and not always, antimonarchical.
30. [Overton and Walwyn], 'A remonstrance', 47–48. The example of the Netherlands had already been adduced by coauthor William Walwyn earlier that year in the context of religious toleration (W. Walwyn, 'Toleration Justified and Persecution Condemned' (29 January1646), in Sharp, *Levellers*, 9–30, at 16).
31. B. Worden, *The Rump Parliament 1648–1653* (Cambridge: Cambridge University Press, 1974), 36–37, 50; Worden, 'Republicanism', 319; Barber, *Regicide and Republicanism*, Chapters 1–3.

32. B. Worden, *The English Civil Wars 1640–1660* (London: Weidenfeld & Nicolson, 2009), 104; similarly already Worden, *Rump Parliament*, 172–73. Worden's insistence on the improvised and unassertive nature of the republican experiment is generally endorsed; see Barber, *Regicide and Republicanism*, 3, who also argues that 'there was no necessary connection between regicide and republicanism'. However, this view has not gone unchallenged; see S. Kelsey, *Inventing a Republic: The Political Culture of the English Commonwealth, 1649–1653* (Manchester: Manchester University Press, 1997).
33. Both were officially (but not for the first time) stated in the 'Act declaring England to be a Commonwealth' (19 May 1649), in S.R. Gardiner (ed.), *The Constitutional Documents of the Puritan Revolution 1625–1660*, 3rd edn (Oxford: Clarendon Press, 1906), 388. See also Worden, *Rump Parliament*, 173; Worden, 'Republicanism', esp. 323, n.10.
34. It was first used prominently on 22 February 1649 in the 'Engagement taken by the members of the Council of State' (constituted nine days earlier) 'concerning the settling of the government of this nation for the future in way of a Republic, without King or House of Lords' (Gardiner, *Constitutional Documents*, 384).
35. 'A Declaration of the Parliament of England, Expressing the Grounds of Their Late Proceedings, and of Setling [sic] the Present Government in the Way of a Free State' (22 March 1649), in J.L. Malcolm (ed.), *The Struggle for Sovereignty: Seventeenth-Century English Political Tracts*, vol. 1 (Indianapolis: Liberty Fund, 1999), 369–90, at 381. The comparison had been made before (but again after the regicide), notably by John Milton (see Dunthorne, *Britain and the Dutch Revolt*, 193; for another instance, see Barber, *Regicide and Republicanism*, 134). Praise for the Netherlands and its political setup – without direct political ramifications for England – of course had a longer pedigree; see Dunthorne, *Britain and the Dutch Revolt*, 200–2; J. Scott, *Commonwealth Principles: Republican Writing of the English Revolution* (Cambridge: Cambridge University Press, 2004), 135, 235–36.
36. And thus in line (on this question) with Stadholder William II who had supported Charles I, had married his daughter and (until his death of smallpox in 1650) protected his son, the future Charles II, who was exiled in The Hague.
37. H.J. Helmers, *The Royalist Republic: Literature, Politics, and Religion in the Anglo-Dutch Public Sphere, 1639–1660* (Cambridge: Cambridge University Press, 2015). In any case, political and religious alignments crisscrossed as – in a direct inversion of the English situation – the 'republican' (States', regents') faction in the Netherlands was *less*, the 'royalist' (Orangist) faction *more* rigidly Calvinist.
38. *Brandy-wine, in the Hollanders ingratitude...*, anonymous pamphlet published in London in 1652. See also G. Rommelse, 'Negative Mirror Images in Anglo-Dutch Relations, 1650–1674', in L. Jensen (ed.), *The Roots of Nationalism: National Identity Formation in Early Modern Europe, 1600–1815* (Amsterdam: Amsterdam University Press, 2016), 199–216.
39. Notably in the works of Pieter de la Court. The causality seems somewhat overstressed by Helmers, *The Royalist Republic*, 264. See also W.R.E. Velema, '"That a Republic is Better than a Monarchy": Anti-monarchism in Early Modern Dutch Political Thought', in van Gelderen and Skinner (eds), *Republicanism*, 9–25; H. Schilling, 'Dutch Republicanism in its Historical Context', in H. Schilling (ed.), *Religion, Political Culture and the Emergence of Early Modern Society* (Leiden: Brill, 1992), 413–27.
40. H.W. Blom, 'Popularizing Government: Democratic Tendencies in Anglo-Dutch Republicanism', in Mahlberg and Wiemann (eds), *European Contexts*, 121–35, shows that

de la Court drew on Harrington (if not openly so); however, the latter had been highly critical of both the Rump Parliament and of the Protectorate.
41. As argued especially by B. Worden (see footnotes above) and by A. Cromartie, *The Constitutionalist Revolution: An Essay on the History of England, 1450–1642* (Cambridge: Cambridge University Press, 2006).
42. I. Roy, 'The English Republic, 1649–1660: The View from the Town Hall', in Koenigsberger (ed.), *Republiken und Republikanismus*, 213–36, at 224 ('insularity'; similarly see Worden, 'Liberty for Export', 20).
43. P.A. Knachel, *England and the Fronde: The Impact of the English Civil War and Revolution on France* (Ithaca: Cornell University Press, 1967), Chapter 4; C. Jouhaud, *Mazarinades: la Fronde des mots* (Paris: Aubier, 1985), Chapter 6.
44. Knachel, *England and the Fronde*, 84–85.
45. *Les souhaits de la France* (1649), quoted in Knachel, *England and the Fronde*, 93. Especially in the last two cases, the religious dimension was a further reason for taking distance.
46. Similarly, see Knachel, *England and the Fronde*, 106: 'The English example aborted rather than stimulated the growth of republican sentiment among most Frondeurs.'
47. Quoted in Knachel, *England and the Fronde*, 103, n.71 (1649). See also ibid., 27, n.21.
48. W. Beik, *Urban Protest in Seventeenth-Century France: The Culture of Retribution* (Cambridge: Cambridge University Press, 1997), 229, 238–49.
49. There was also talk of Huguenot involvement (Beik, *Urban Protest*, 242; Knachel, *England and the Fronde*, 197–98). The *Ormistes* had been said to strive for a 'République' (and even a 'gouvernement démocratique') in a highly tendentious pamphlet printed in Paris in 1652, whereas another Parisian pamphlet with different intentions stressed in 1653: 'Ils aiment le Roy autant que le peut faire le plus fidèle sujet du royaume' ['They love the King as much as the most faithful subject of the kingdom'] (and they represented the urban elite). Quoted after Jouhaud, *Mazarinades*, 187–88, 190–91, who gives an intriguing account of the various uses that the *Frondeurs* in Paris made of the comparison with Bordeaux.
50. There had been some half-hearted military and logistical support in 1652.
51. 'Les principes, fondement et gouvernement d'une république' (probably 1653), in E. Vernon and P. Baker, 'Les principes, fondement et gouvernement d'une république: The French Agreement of the People', in *The Agreements of the People, the Levellers, and the Constitutional Crisis of the English Revolution* (London: Palgrave Macmillan, 2012), 262–66. The (shortened) translation was commissioned by Edward Sexby, an army Leveller – he had participated in the Putney debates – who had been sent to Bordeaux, with the backing of the Council of State, as early as 1651 (ibid., 262; Sharp (ed.), *The English Levellers*, 211). The document thus starts (the rough French has led to speculation about the translator): 'Que la suprême authorité de France … pour [i.e. par] lesquels [i.e. laquelle] nous voulons estre gouvernés, sera et résidera sy après en une représentation du peuple consistant en nombre de personnes aux choix desquelles, selon le droict naturel, tous hommes de l'âge de vingt et un ans; ou plus haut, n'estant serviteurs ou vivant d'aumosne …, auront voix et seront cappables d'eslire ceux qui feront la représentative [!]'. This was an almost literal translation of the first passage – after the preamble that is left out in the French version – of 'An agreement of the free people of England, tendered as a peace-offering to this distressed nation …' (1 May 1649), in Sharp (ed.), *The English Levellers*, 168–78, at 170. For the differences between the texts, see Vernon and Baker, 'Les principes', 262.

52. 'Mais il n'y a rencontré absolument aucun écho' ; Jouhaud, *Mazarinades*, 162. Similarly, see Beik, *Urban Protest*, 247; Vernon and Baker, 'Les principes', 262.
53. T. Paine, 'Common Sense' (1776), in *Rights of Man, Common Sense and Other Political Writings* (Oxford: Oxford University Press, 2008) 1–59, at 31; similarly, see ibid., 11.
54. W. Nippel, *Ancient and Modern Democracy: Two Concepts of Liberty?* (Cambridge: Cambridge University Press, 2016), 118–19, 121–22. As for the ancient polities, John Adams (who probably knew most of them; ibid., 126) held that their lack of 'checks and balances' made the Greek city-states less valuable models than the contemporary Netherlands, Venice or Bern *with* such mechanisms (ibid., 125). Rome, on the other hand, was the prime example of the self-destruction of a republic (ibid., 121).
55. Quoted after ibid., 119 note 3 (28 June 1787).
56. After the Netherlands, Germany was mentioned most often, followed by Poland and then (equally often) Switzerland and Venice. In most cases, they were mentioned in the same context and in various combinations with references to antiquity: G.W. Carey and J. McClellan (eds), *The Federalist. By Alexander Hamilton, John Jay, and James Madison: The Gideon Edition* (Indianapolis: Liberty Fund, 2001).
57. *The Federalist*, no. 6 (1787) (Hamilton), 24. T. Paine, 'Rights of Man' (1791) (in *Rights of Man*, 89–197, at 196) continued to insist on the peacefulness of republics – with curious reference to 'the republican principles of peace and domestic prosperity' occurring in France since the Revolution.
58. *The Federalist*, no. 19 (1787) (Madison), 94 (previous pages: Germany).
59. Ibid., 94.
60. As they did with the Netherlands too. See J.W. Schulte Nordholt, 'The Example of the Dutch Republic for American Federalism', *Bijdragen en Mededelingen betreffende de Geschiedenis der Nederlanden* 94 (1979), 437–49, at 443, 448. They rejected of course the (intermittently) quasi-monarchical Stadholder, while the federalists were in different minds about him (ibid., 445–47); see also Nippel, *Ancient and Modern Democracy*, 122.
61. Probably against the background of the Patriot revolt, Paine had also changed his mind on the matter (T. Paine, 'American Crisis XIII' (1783), in *Rights of Man*, 72–82, at 76): 'Their disjointed condition exposes them to numerous intrigues ... the almost impossibility of bringing their measures to a decision ... is to them, and would be to us, a source of endless misfortune.'
62. *The Federalist*, no. 20 (1787) (Madison), 96 (also the following quote). See again *The Federalist*, no. 54 (1788) (Madison), 285 on the difference between the proposed U.S. legislature and that of the Netherlands.
63. *The Federalist*, no. 20 (1787), 99.
64. On his repeated request, Thomas Jefferson had sent him some 200 books on the subject from Paris (Schulte Nordholt, 'Example of the Dutch Republic', 443; quote ibid.). The texts on the Netherlands offered overwhelmingly positive judgments (ibid., 444–45), but Madison 'was evidently not in the least impressed by them' (445).
65. W.W. Mijnhardt, 'The Limits of Present-Day Historiography of Republicanism', *De Achttiende Eeuw* 37 (2005), 75–89, at 86. There has been speculation about the role of the *Plakkaat van Verlatinge* (1581) and the Union of Utrecht (1579) as models for, respectively, the Declaration of Independence and the Articles of Confederation, but there is no evidence for a direct impact and there are fundamental differences – such as the declaration of kingless government rather than the deposition of a specific king, and the insistence on individual rather than corporate rights. See ibid., 85–88; Schulte Nordholt, 'Example of the Dutch Republic', 441–42.

66. In his discussion of the term 'republic' (*The Federalist*, no. 39 (1788), 194), Madison pointed out that it was used for a variety of states (including Britain) that had little in common, not even always kingless government (while his own definition seems applicable properly only to the United States).
67. For his obvious and repeated – but never avowed – loans from James Harrington on such important issues as (among others) regular deputy rotation and the departmental division of the territory, see Hammersley, *English Republican Tradition*, 164–65.
68. 'Comment voulez-vous avec des matériaux si dissemblables construire en France le même édifice politique qu'en Angleterre?' E.J. Sieyès, *Qu'est-ce que le Tiers État*? (Paris: Flammarion, 1988), Chapter IV, § VI ('On propose d'imiter la constitution anglaise'), 109.
69. Ibid., 109–11. In Britain it was superfluous but harmless: 'une institution gothique et ridicule en même temps' (ibid., 107, note 1). See also ibid.: 'Il n'y a en Angleterre qu'un seul ordre, la nation' (There is only one estate in England, the nation); ibid., 110: 'chez nos voisins tous les intérêts de la nation sont réunis dans la Chambre des communes' (In our neighbouring country all interests of the nation are united in the House of Commons).
70. Ibid., 106 and passim.
71. Sieyès, *Qu'est-ce que le Tiers État*, Chapter IV, § VII.
72. Ibid., 114–15, 119 ('cette constitution exotique').
73. '… la nation anglaise … est donc la seule qui puisse être libre sans une bonne constitution. Cette pensée devrait suffire pour nous dégoûter de la manie d'imiter nos voisins'; ibid., 118.
74. 'Élevons-nous tout d'un coup à l'ambition de vouloir nous-mêmes servir d'exemple aux nations' (ibid., 118); see also ibid., 119: 'La véritable science de l'état de société ne date pas de loin. Les hommes ont construit longtemps des chaumières avant d'être en état d'élever des palais.' (The true science of society is not very old. For a long time mankind has built cottages before being able to erect palaces.)
75. K.M. Baker, 'Representation Redefined', in *Inventing the French Revolution* (Cambridge: Cambridge University Press) 224–51, esp. 244–46; K.M. Baker, 'Fixing the French Constitution', in ibid., 252–305, esp. 295–97. Sieyès stood rather alone in his opposition to *both* an absolute and a suspensive veto (also favoured by many on the left as a means to appeal to direct popular arbitration; see ibid., esp. 289–91).
76. See ibid., esp. 266, 274, 279, 286, 296.
77. Ibid., esp. 262, 269, 273, 277–78, 281.
78. L. Hunt, 'The "National Assembly"', in K.M. Baker (ed.), *The French Revolution and the Creation of Modern Political Culture, Vol. 1: The Political Culture of the Old Regime* (Oxford: Pergamon, 1987), 403–15, at 412.
79. 'Une imitation ridicule et puérile de l'anglais règne dans l'Assemblée.' Quoted after ibid., 411.
80. Already shortly after 17 June, it was alleged that 'the leading members were little disposed to borrow any thing from England' (after Hammersley, *English Republican Tradition*, 156).
81. For positive references to America, see Baker, 'Fixing the French Constitution', 262, 265–66, 269.
82. For such disqualification of the American example, see ibid., 262, 265, 276.
83. As was the American, featuring a suspensive veto but also a bicameral legislature. The latter was rejected in France on 9 September, the absolute royal veto two days later. For the

continuing relevance of the British model for Mirabeau and his group, see Hammersley, *English Republican Tradition*, 155–56, 174–75.
84. Quoted after ibid., 156 (this was a sarcastic remark against such a posture).
85. In his magisterial study on the impact of references to antiquity on political thought and practice, Wilfried Nippel comes to very similar conclusions (Nippel, *Ancient and Modern Democracy*).
86. The same was the case in Bohemia fifty years later, in spite of – or rather because of – the comparison with the Netherlands; see Mortimer, *Origins of the Thirty Years War*, 166.
87. See the (possibly somewhat overstated) account by E. Nelson, *The Royalist Revolution: Monarchy and the American Founding* (Cambridge, MA: Belknap Press, 2014). The first to vigorously and prominently declare against monarchy in America was the British émigré Thomas Paine.

## Bibliography

Baker, K.M., 'Fixing the French Constitution', in *Inventing the French Revolution* (Cambridge: Cambridge University Press, 1990), 252–305.
———. 'Representation Redefined', in *Inventing the French Revolution* (Cambridge: Cambridge University Press, 1990), 224–51.
Barber, S., *Regicide and Republicanism: Politics and Ethics in the English Revolution, 1646–1659* (Edinburgh: Edinburgh University Press, 1998).
Beik, W., *Urban Protest in Seventeenth-Century France: The Culture of Retribution* (Cambridge: Cambridge University Press, 1997).
Blom, H.W., 'Popularizing Government: Democratic Tendencies in Anglo-Dutch Republicanism', in Mahlberg, G. and Wiemann, D. (eds), *European Contexts for English Republicanism* (London: Taylor & Francis, 2013), 121–35.
Carey, G.W., and McClellan, J. (eds), *The Federalist. By Alexander Hamilton, John Jay, and James Madison: The Gideon Edition* (Indianapolis: Liberty Fund, 2001).
Cromartie, A., *The Constitutionalist Revolution: An Essay on the History of England, 1450–1642* (Cambridge: Cambridge University Press, 2006).
Delfos, L., *Die Anfänge der Utrechter Union 1577–1587: Ein Beitrag zur Geschichte der niederländischen Erhebung, insbesondere zu deren Verfassungsgeschichte* (Berlin: Verlag Dr. Emil Ebering, 1941).
Despretz, A., 'De instauratie der Gentse Calvinistische Republiek (1577–1579)', *Handelingen der Maatschappij voor Geschiedenis en Oudheidkunde te Gent* 17 (1963), 119–229.
Duke, A., 'In Defence of the Common Fatherland. Patriotism and Liberty in the Low Countries, 1555–1576', in Stein, R. and Pollmann, J. (eds), *Networks, Regions and Nations: Shaping Identities in the Low Countries, 1300–1650* (Leiden: Brill, 2010), 217–39.
Dunthorne, H., *Britain and the Dutch Revolt 1560–1700* (Cambridge: Cambridge University Press, 2013).
Friedeburg, R. von, 'Republic and Republicanism', in Scott, H. (ed.), *The Oxford Handbook of Early Modern European History, 1350–1750*, vol. 2 (Oxford: Oxford University Press, 2015), 538–58.
Gardiner, S.R. (ed.), *The Constitutional Documents of the Puritan Revolution 1625–1660*, 3rd edn (Oxford: Clarendon Press, 1906).Haitsma Mulier, E.O.G., *The Myth of Venice and Dutch Republican Thought in the Seventeenth Century* (Assen: Van Gorcum, 1980).

Hammersley, R., *The English Republican Tradition and Eighteenth-Century France: Between the Ancients and the Moderns* (Manchester: Manchester University Press, 2010).
Helmers, H.J., *The Royalist Republic: Literature, Politics, and Religion in the Anglo-Dutch Public Sphere, 1639–1660* (Cambridge: Cambridge University Press, 2015).
Hunt, L., 'The "National Assembly"', in Baker, K.M. (ed.), *The French Revolution and the Creation of Modern Political Culture*, vol. 1: *The Political Culture of the Old Regime* (Oxford: Pergamon, 1987), 403–15.
Jouhaud, C., *Mazarinades: la Fronde des mots* (Paris: Aubier, 1985).
Kelsey, S., *Inventing a Republic: The Political Culture of the English Commonwealth, 1649–1653* (Manchester: Manchester University Press, 1997).
Knachel, P.A., *England and the Fronde: The Impact of the English Civil War and Revolution on France* (Ithaca: Cornell University Press, 1967).
Maissen, T., *Die Geburt der Republic: Staatsverständnis und Repräsentation in der frühneuzeitlichen Eidgenossenschaft* (Göttingen: Vandenhoeck & Ruprecht, 2008).
Malcolm, J.L. (ed.), *The Struggle for Sovereignty: Seventeenth-Century English Political Tracts*, vol. 1 (Indianapolis: Liberty Fund, 1999).
Mijnhardt, W.W., 'The Limits of Present-Day Historiography of Republicanism', *De Achttiende Eeuw* 37 (2005), 75–89.
Mörke, O., 'Der "schwache" Staat als Erfolgsrezept? Die niederländische Republik und die Schweizer Eidgenossenschaft', in Buchholz, W. and Kroll, S. (eds), *Quantität und Struktur. Festschrift für Kersten Krüger zum 60. Geburtstag* (Rostock: Universität Rostock, 1999), 45–62.
Mortimer, G., *The Origins of the Thirty Years War and the Revolt in Bohemia, 1618* (London: Palgrave Macmillan, 2015).
Mout, N., 'Ideales Muster oder erfundene Eigenart. Republikanische Theorien während des niederländischen Aufstands', in Koenigsberger, H.G. (ed.), *Republiken und Republikanismus im Europa der frühen Neuzeit* (Munich: Oldenbourg, 1988), 169–94.
Nelson, E., *The Royalist Revolution: Monarchy and the American Founding* (Cambridge, MA: Belknap Press, 2014).
Nippel, W., 'Klassischer Republikanismus in der frühen Neuzeit. Kritische Nachfragen', in Niggemann, U. and Ruffing, K. (eds), *Antike als Modell in Nordamerika? Konstruktion und Verargumentierung 1763–1809* (Munich: Oldenbourg, 2011), 23–34.
———. *Ancient and Modern Democracy: Two Concepts of Liberty?* (Cambridge: Cambridge University Press, 2016).
[Overton, R., and Walwyn, W.], 'A remonstrance of many thousand citizens and other freeborn people of England to their House of Commons … how they [the Commons] have discharged their duties to the universality of the people, their sovereign lord, from whom their power and strength is derived' (7 July 1646), in Sharp, A. (ed.), *The English Levellers* (Cambridge: Cambridge University Press, 1998), 33–53.
Paine, T., *Rights of Man, Common Sense and Other Political Writings* (Oxford: Oxford University Press, 2008).
Rommelse, G., 'Negative Mirror Images in Anglo-Dutch Relations, 1650–1674', in Jensen, L. (ed.), *The Roots of Nationalism: National Identity Formation in Early Modern Europe, 1600–1815* (Amsterdam: Amsterdam University Press, 2016), 199–216.
Roy, I., 'The English Republic, 1649–1660: The View from the Town Hall', in Koenigsberger, H.G. (ed.), *Republiken und Republikanismus im Europa der frühen Neuzeit* (Munich: Oldenbourg, 1988), 213–36.

Schilling, H., 'Dutch Republicanism in its Historical Context', in Schilling, H. (ed.), *Religion, Political Culture and the Emergence of Early Modern Society* (Leiden: Brill, 1992), 413–27.

Schulte Nordholt, J.W., 'The Example of the Dutch Republic for American Federalism', *Bijdragen en Mededelingen betreffende de Geschiedenis der Nederlanden* 94 (1979), 437–49.

Scott, J., *Commonwealth Principles: Republican Writing of the English Revolution* (Cambridge: Cambridge University Press, 2004).

Sharp, A. (ed.), *The English Levellers* (Cambridge: Cambridge University Press, 1998).

Sieyès, E.J., *Qu'est-ce que le Tiers État?* (Paris: Flammarion, 1988).

Van Bruaene, A.-L., 'A Breakdown of Civic Community? Civic Traditions, Voluntary Associations and the Ghent Calvinist Regime (1577–84)', in Eckstein, N. and Terpstra, N. (eds), *Sociability and its Discontents: Civil Society, Social Capital, and Their Alternatives in Late Medieval and Early Modern Europe* (Turnhout: Brepols, 2009), 273–91.

Van Gelderen, M., *The Political Thought of the Dutch Revolt* (Cambridge: Cambridge University Press, 1992).

———. 'Turning Swiss? Discord in Dutch Debates', in Holenstein, A., Maissen, T. and Prak, M. (eds), *The Republican Alternative: The Netherlands and Switzerland Compared* (Amsterdam: Amsterdam University Press, 2008), 151–69.

Van Schelven, A.A., *De staatsvorm van het Zwitserse Eedgenootschap den Nederlanden ter navolging aanbevolen* (Brussels: Éditions universitaires, 1947).

Velema, W.R.E., '"That a Republic is Better than a Monarchy": Anti-monarchism in Early Modern Dutch Political Thought', in van Gelderen, M. and Skinner, Q. (eds), *Republicanism and Constitutionalism in Early Modern Europe: A Shared European Heritage* (Cambridge: Cambridge University Press, 2002), 9–25.

Vernon, E., and Baker, P., 'Les principes, fondement et gouvernement d'une république: The French Agreement of the People', in *The Agreements of the People, the Levellers, and the Constitutional Crisis of the English Revolution* (London: Palgrave Macmillan, 2012), 262–66.

Weeber, U., *Republiken als Blaupause: Venedig, die Niederlande und die Eidgenossenschaft im Reformdiskurs der Frühaufklärung* (Berlin: De Gruyter Oldenbourg, 2016).

Worden, B., *The Rump Parliament 1648–1653* (Cambridge: Cambridge University Press, 1974).

———. 'Republicanism, Regicide and Republic: The English Experience', in van Gelderen, M. and Skinner, Q. (eds), *Republicanism and Constitutionalism in Early Modern Europe: A Shared European Heritage* (Cambridge: Cambridge University Press, 2002), 307–27.

———. *The English Civil Wars 1640–1660* (London: Weidenfeld & Nicolson, 2009).

———. 'Liberty for Export: "Republicanism" in England, 1500–1800', in Mahlberg, G. and Wiemann, D. (eds), *European Contexts for English Republicanism* (London: Taylor & Francis, 2013), 13–32.

# 5
# Comparing Europe and the Americas
*The Dispute of the New World between the Sixteenth and Nineteenth Centuries*

Angelika Epple

The 500-year history of relations between Europe and America all started with the sighting of a flock of birds. Passing birds, Christopher Columbus writes in his log, led him to change course towards the southwest.[1] If he had carried on sailing further to the north, he and his completely exhausted crew might never have reached the far more distant coast of Florida. But, on 12 October 1492, he landed on the small island of Guanahaní in the Bahamas. Columbus had a peaceful encounter with the inhabitants, named the island San Salvador (holy saviour), before soon sailing on to Hispaniola, the island that is now home to the two crisis-ridden states of Haiti and the Dominican Republic. Columbus was not aware that he had reached a previously unknown continent.

Although the history of these relations started with the sighting of a flock of birds, the ways in which Europeans responded to contact with the flora and fauna, the native inhabitants, or the climate of the Americas were soon to be determined lastingly by other activities than just an impartial sighting. Even just a short time after Columbus' arrival, the practice of comparing shaped the relationship between Europe and America. The fundamental importance of comparing found a significant verbal expression in a name given to the continent that persisted until the end of the nineteenth century. Scarcely 'discovered', the continent was labelled the 'New World'. Without being questioned, this was a comparison with the 'Old World'.

In recent decades, postcolonial and alterity studies have fuelled important debates across the humanities. In the vein of Edward Said, Homi Bhabha and

Gayatri Chakravorty Spivak, their main interests have been the dichotomous relationship between Europe and its colonized 'other', as well as the often hidden agenda of *othering*.[2] In the following, I wish to show how we can go one step further and gain new insights into the history of the colonizing self and the colonialized other. Instead of analysing the strategies of *othering* in the writings of scholars over the last 500 years, I will analyse the practices of comparing carried out by scholars when writing about Europe and America. This will cast the relationship between the self and the colonized other in a new light. Instead of a dichotomous relation between the 'Old' and the 'New World', we can see how scholars negotiated different shades of similarity and difference. We are then prepared to better understand a complex, asymmetrical and multilayered history of the relationship between the self and the colonized other told by scholars on both sides of the Atlantic.

I will start by introducing the debate on the New World since the sixteenth century. With this as my background, I will develop a theoretical argument in favour of studying the 'doing' of comparisons as a new research agenda. Then, I will test these ideas on an empirical example: the historical (re)construction of the units of comparison known as 'America' and 'Europe' within what became known as the 'dispute of the New World'[3] in the second half of the eighteenth century. I will conclude by summarizing the results of my analyses.

## The Debate over the 'New World' and Changes in the Practices of Comparing

The history of the conquest of the Americas, the slave trade, the plantation economy, and the exchange of goods and knowledge all led Europe and America to become entangled with each other. They influenced each other reciprocally in terms of not only (identity) politics and economics but also in terms of culture.[4] This increasingly close entanglement was both accompanied and driven by a discourse aiming to determine how the 'old' and the 'new' related to each other. Comparisons became highly significant in this endeavour. This did not just apply to discursive practices: mountains, flora and fauna were measured; species and genera were distinguished; and animals and plants were dissected, analysed, weighed and laid side by side for comparison.

Even as early as the *Controversia de Valladolid* (1550/1551) between Las Casas and Sepúlveda over the enslavement of the 'Indios', it became clear that the relationship between the two worlds was an issue that continuously had to be clarified anew. This applied predominantly but not exclusively to European authors. In 1609, for example, the Peruvian Inca Garcilaso took part in the discussion with a history of the Incas.[5]

In the seventeenth century, the discussion over the New World was flanked by the so-called quarrel of the Ancients and the Moderns (*Querelle des anciens et des modernes*). Initially in France, but then also in England and Germany, the *Querelle* represented an attempt to assert the independence of the modern age compared to antiquity. When Charles Perrault stressed that there was no injustice in comparing contemporary times with the 'Augustan Age', what he was doing was stressing that these units of comparison were of equal value. This is already evident in the way he entitled his work *Parallels of the Ancient and the Modern*.[6] The two discussions over the 'New' and the 'Old' world and the 'modern' or 'ancient' age did not have to conflict; indeed, both arguments could overlap and reinforce one other.[7] The comparison between European antiquity and the postclassic (600–1521) American cultures played a recurring role in the debates over the cultural achievements of the Americans or their purported cultural inferiority.

When it came to the eighteenth century, leading philosophers of the Enlightenment such as Hume, Montesquieu, Abbé Raynal and Diderot all contributed to the debate over how to define the relationship between Europe and the Americas, its inhabitants, its flora and fauna, and its geology. Buffon's *Natural History*, in which he used the Americas to illustrate his degeneration theory,[8] fuelled the controversy that finally culminated in the 'dispute of the New World'.[9] The Dutch academic Cornelis de Pauw was at the centre of this debate. He took an even more radical approach to Buffon's degeneration theory and related it exclusively to the Americas.[10] Although now almost completely forgotten, de Pauw was considered to be the leading expert on the Americas for many years because of his learnedness and his convincing style of argument. However, like Buffon, de Pauw never left Europe. Nonetheless, many agreed with his pronouncements. For example, Georg Friedrich Wilhelm Hegel adopted de Pauw's views and paraphrased his contemptuous pronouncements on the inferiority of non-White races.[11]

However, there were also critics. Numerous academics rejected de Pauw, drawing a markedly more positive picture of the Americas. Examples are the Mexican historian Clavijero, the Benedictine Antoine-Joseph Pernetry, who accompanied Louis-Antoine de Bougainville on his journeys to America, and Alexander von Humboldt.[12] Most of the work of these authors was empirical and based on their own experience or investigations. Thomas Jefferson and other Founding Fathers of the United States also defended themselves vehemently against Buffon.[13] Over the centuries, the discourse was linked to the issue of how to either justify enslavement or demand its abolition. At the end of the eighteenth century, Jefferson's rejoinder to Buffon also addressed the question regarding which was the better form of government.

In 1830, one of the first Afro-American writers, David Walker, took up these comparisons, giving them a completely different focus.[14] He countered Jefferson the slave-owner's argument on why Americans and Europeans were equal by applying the same argument to the unequal treatment of Blacks by Whites. Even in the nineteenth century, the dispute did not subside. A final example of the long-term impact of the traditional practices of comparison as well as the ability to recontextualize them is the essay 'Nuestra America' (1891).

In this powerfully eloquent essay, José Martí, a Cuban who spent many years in exile in the United States, constructed a vision of America that liberated it from either European or U.S.-American appropriation. Martí made the farsighted historical-political demand for the American people that 'our Greece must take priority to the Greece that is not ours; we need it more'.[15] 'Our Greece' in his wording referred to Incan antiquity.

Over the centuries and depending on the standpoint of the actors making the comparisons, it is not only the evaluation of Europe compared to the Americas that has changed and inverted repeatedly. Beyond the semantic surface of the essays, something has also changed on a deeper text level: the ways in which actors do their comparing. In order to recognize the full extent of this change, we need to look beyond the semantics of comparisons and focus on the practices of comparing: the *doing of comparisons*.

## The Analysis of Practices of Comparing as a New Research Agenda

The ever-changing practices of comparing Europe and the Americas performed by a whole range of different actors offer a telling illustration of the potential of this comprehensive new approach. However, any call for a new research agenda must go beyond just one empirical case study. Generally speaking, the analysis of practices of comparing proposes a new foundation for research on both, alterity (or its postcolonial shifts) and on entangled (connected, shared, transcultural or transnational) history.

After the pioneering work of Tzvetan Todorov and Sidney Mintz in the early 1980s, research on the history of European–American relations focused on the handling of alterity and on the multitude of entangled relations.[16] Studies of alterity delivered controversial discussions over the relationship between the perception of the other and of the self along with the construction of the own in light of the other. Their postcolonial variants – studies on *othering, orientalism* or *occidentalism* – focused on superimpositions, amalgamations, hybridizations or *mestizaje* in order to present them in conceptually differentiated ways.[17] Scholars of entangled history addressed colonial power relations, the close relationship between European consumption habits, the colonial system, the slave trade and the emergence of capitalism from the plantation economy.

In the approach presented here, it is neither the dichotomous relations of alterity nor entangled history but the *doing of comparisons* that forms the starting point for analysis. Although these approaches have much in common, they also differ clearly. Like earlier research on the perception of the other and the self, the analysis of comparisons also focuses on the construction of relations. And, like entangled history, it also addresses the interactions between different actors and the formation of new, hybrid types of action. Nonetheless, it takes a different approach to these issues.

Research on *othering* takes alterity as its starting point. Research on practices of comparing, in contrast, starts by examining the construction of the units of comparison and the dynamics of complex relations. This shift of perspective makes it possible to discern highly differentiated nuances of commonalities, similarities, idiosyncrasies and differences. By making comparisons, actors can process alterity issues and place the other in a dichotomous relationship to the self ('we' versus 'them'). However, actors are under no obligation to do this. They can also focus on equality or similarity in one regard and on differences in another regard, or they can compare third parties with another ('these' in comparison to 'those').

The history of comparisons can also be understood as a further development of entangled history. Entangled history bases its analyses on the entities that become entangled. Frequently, however, the entanglement concept itself remains underdetermined.[18] The analysis of doing comparisons is interested in how the units of comparison are constructed and in the social or historical dynamics these comparisons provoke.

However, this change of outlook is not just an expression of a change in research interest; it is in fact based on two fundamental shifts in theory. First, the analysis of practices of comparing shifts the focus from a binary to a more complex relationship. When people compare something with something else, they always imply a criterion that enables them to place differences and similarities in a comparative relation. This criterion, in respect to which entities are being compared, is the *tertium comparationis*. Comparing transforms the relationship between (at least) two entities into a triadic relation. This is what makes the entities that are being compared into what can be called the *comparata*. Hence, the *comparata* do not exist in any way by themselves, but only within their comparative relationship to at least one other *comparatum* and a *tertium*. An analysis of the practices of comparing focuses on the negotiation of similarities and differences between *comparata* in relation to a *tertium*. It does not concentrate merely on dichotomously formed entities or on the self via the circuitous route of the other, nor is it content with studying the perception of the self and the other, nor is it limited to explore the many-layered relation between identity and alterity. The analysis of comparisons is thus not an analysis of relationships between two clearly demarcated entities such as the relationship between Europe and America; rather, it is interested in studying how Europe and America are each 'put into a relation' with the other – that is, how they are placed in a comparative relationship and thus constructed as *comparata* in the first place.

Overcoming the analyses of binary relations between two entities is associated with another theoretical shift. When analysing the *practices* of comparing, the actor positioned within a historical context becomes the mainstay of what constitutes the relationship. It is the actor who places the *comparata* in a relation. Therefore, practice theory leads to a reformulation of the presumably dichotomous relationship between the self and the other. Instead of analysing a binary relation, the new research agenda leads to an analysis of a tetradic relation: an *actor* compares at least two *comparata* in terms of at least one *tertium*. Even if an actor is performing an individual action when comparing, and it is logical and analytically necessary to retain the concept of action, the focus of interest in practice theory is not on the individual act as such.[19] Instead, practice theory assumes a reciprocal relationship of mutual dependence between action and practice: individual actions are integrated into socially shared practices based on socially shared routines, action patterns and repetitions of individual actions. Of course, it goes without saying that a literal repetition of the same individual action is impossible due to the time index of acting alone. In this sense, a repetition is always an alteration.

Let me sum up so far: single actors perform individual actions when they compare. However, they do this with the aid of socially shared practices. Therefore, drawing on practice theory, the focus of the analysis is on what actors are *doing* when they compare.

Comparing begins with an assumption that the two *comparata* are in some way similar. Otherwise, they cannot be compared. This is even the case when an actor postulates the incomparability of two entities. Hence, although postulating that incomparability is based on comparability might be a logical contradiction, it is not a praxeological contradiction. An actor has to assume a similarity between two *comparata* in one aspect before he or she can state with any justification that the *comparata* are not similar in any way.[20] Put differently, a person doing comparisons looks for an appropriate *tertium* that will function as a spotlight when placing the specific *comparata* into a relationship. Certain properties assigned to the *comparata* then come to the fore, whereas others become masked or remain in the shadows. Hence, it is not the objects or *comparata* that do the comparison, but the actors. One who compares presents the *comparata* in a certain light. Hence, comparing can hardly ever be neutral. It is integrated into situational contexts in which the given power relations or the given epistemic system encourage certain comparisons while discouraging others. These theoretical considerations, in all their brevity, will have to suffice in order to show that countless actions of different kinds are linked to doing comparisons.

In contrast to research on comparisons, alterity research and studies on *othering* have managed without the *tertium comparationis*.[21] When studying how the self had been placed in relation to the other, they focused on the way in which difference was addressed. In the approach being developed here, the focus is on the practices of comparing, that is, on the *doing of comparisons*, and not just on the perception of otherness or alterity or the construction of difference. The new research agenda makes it possible to overcome thinking in fixed dichotomies by gaining new insights into how actors have negotiated shades of similarity and difference in different situational contexts. The ascertainment of differences can then be recognized as *one* possible consequence of making comparisons. Nonetheless, other consequences are also conceivable: a comparison can, for example, also lead to the recognition – with reference to a selected *tertium* – of complete agreement between two *comparata*. Hence, depending on the outcome, making comparisons can have completely different effects and consequences.

This is why the analysis of practices of comparing also goes beyond alterity research by focusing not only on the construction of the *comparata* but also on the effects and outcomes of the comparative relationing. Comparing is an activity that does not take place in a vacuum. It is performed by actors and is always integrated into the *politics of comparisons*[22] – into the given power relations. It does not proceed from the properties of the objects themselves; rather, it is tied to places and actors and therefore neither neutral nor objective. The effects and outcomes of comparing can become very powerful and lead to the stabilization of existing orders, the naturalization of differences and similarities or the emergence of social dynamics of change. The wrangling over the specific *comparata* and *tertia*, how the practice of making comparisons changes or differs – both historically and depending on the location of the actor – can be traced particularly impressively in the 'dispute of the New World'.

## Constructing the *Comparata* of 'America' and 'Europe'

When *making comparisons*, it is necessary to construct appropriate *comparata* and *tertia*. What makes the 'dispute of the New World' such an interesting case study with which to address this construction process is that one can draw on scholars from an exceptionally broad range of backgrounds who have been analysing the writings of both their predecessors and their contemporaries over many centuries. This permits insights into the ways in which making comparisons has changed. Hence, large parts of this case study concentrate on an exemplary analysis of discursive practices of comparing. Nonetheless, this should not be allowed to hide the fact that discursive practices of comparing are frequently an expression of earlier nondiscursive practices of comparing – or even serve as a trigger for ones to come. This dispute would have been inconceivable without the increasing interest in comparative practices such as correlating statistics, weighing and measuring. From the eighteenth century onwards, comparisons based on numbers gained ever more importance.[23]

In 1767, when Cornelis de Pauw was compiling his *Recherches* in Berlin, he was able to draw on an extensive literature. Hence, *making comparisons* between 'America' and 'Europe' and thereby the construction of these two *comparata* already had a long history. In the following, I will present selected stages in this history that de Pauw draws on repeatedly in his analyses.[24]

The two descriptions of the continent – as either a 'New World' or as 'America' – trace back to Amerigo Vespucci from Florence. Only a few years after Columbus, he was commissioned by the King of Portugal to cross the Atlantic and sail down the east coast of what is now Brazil. Vespucci's detailed travel report survives only in its Latin translation. However, for many centuries, its title remained a familiar expression: *mundus novus*.[25] This depiction as a 'New World',

Vespucci's reports on cannibalism and on the sexual practices of the natives, and his detailed accounts of the climate, flora and fauna became strongly rooted in the European mind. Indeed, it was to honour Amerigo Vespucci that the German cartographer Martin Waldseemüller chose to name this world region America in 1507.

Both designations of the continent as either 'America' or the 'New World' place it in an asymmetric relation to 'Europe', but they do this in different ways. Whereas the name 'America' honours the European 'discoverers' and colonizers, thereby underlining the asymmetry with the claims of power politics, the designation 'New World' places the continent in a comparative relation to the old. The Eurocentric perspective on the continent and the power-political claim this implies are also inscribed in the second designation as 'mundus novus'. It was European authors who prescribed what was to be understood by 'old', what was to be viewed in comparison as 'new' and how the relationship between the two was to be evaluated. Whereas the object being discussed was marked as 'new', the position of the speaker remained either implicit or unmarked.[26] One early reflection on the labelling of America as the 'New World' came from José de Acosta, who spent sixteen years living in Peru and Mexico. In the preface to his *Historia Natural y Moral de las Indias* published in 1590, he addresses his readers directly:

> So, as although this new World be not new, but old, in respect of the much which hath beene written thereof; yet this historie may, in some sort, be held for new, for it is partly historicall and partly philosophicall, as well for that they are the workes of nature as of free will, which are the deeds and customes of men.[27]

'New', according to how he saw the world, could not be applied to the term 'nature' because nature was not subject to any history. Accordingly, only history could be labelled 'new', insofar as it is precisely not nature and deals with the deeds and customs of human beings. He refers only to a very specific, to a limited newness ('in some sort') in order to be able to classify it within an unchangeable spiritual order. This transforms the new into a (previously unknown) manifestation of the old. Nonetheless, at the same time, he talks about a 'free will' that people pursue in their deeds and customs. Acosta's essay switches between a history of nature and a history of life and customs that enables both the need for the Christian mission and the lack of faith in the indigenous population to appear as something new.[28] Particularly in Volumes v–vii, in which he addresses the history of life and customs, Acosta also becomes involved in a debate going back to the *Controversia de Valladolid* (1550/1551) over the category of slaves or barbarians to which the 'Indians' should be assigned. Aristotle's distinction between natural slaves and enslaved prisoners of war was an important starting point for both Las Casas and Acosta.[29] The title of Chapter 1 in Acosta's sixth book explicitly addresses those who maintain that the 'Indians' are natural slaves: 'That they erre in their opinion, which hold the Indians to want iudgement.' Because how to deal with the 'Indians' was still controversial, Acosta was unable to simply apply either the classification developed by Las Casas or the distinction between different types of slaves in the tradition handed down from Greek antiquity. Hence, comparisons were unavoidable. After harshly judging those showing a lack of respect towards the 'Indians', he compares the errors of the 'Indians' with those of the Greek philosophers. He refers repeatedly to Aristotle's and Plato's writings, but also to the *naturalis historia* of Pliny the Elder. He is confident that both the Greeks and the Romans would have highly approved of the laws of the Incas and the Mexicans.[30] His method, which is typical for the genre of *historias* and schooled in the rules of Greek rhetoric, remains consistent: the seemingly new (errors of the 'Indians') of the New World is transferred to the previously already known (errors of the Greeks and Romans). The ambivalences regarding the relationship between 'old' and 'new' show how difficult it was for the Jesuits to reconcile the relationship of the Europeans to the Americans with the Christian doctrine of salvation and the European traditions of antiquity. Comparisons could help here to find out how to nonetheless justify the unity of divine creation despite the evident deviations.

It is informative to compare this way of comparing with the practices of comparing in an essay published only a few years later. In 1609, the Peruvian Gómez Suárez de Figueroa wrote a history of the Incas that reveals a completely different approach to the historical situation. As the son of a Peruvian aristocrat and a Spanish colonial officer, he grew up in the capital of the Incas, the Peruvian city of Cuzco. At the age of twenty-one, he travelled to Spain to claim his inheritance after the death of his father. Although baptized as a Christian, he gave himself the pseudonym of 'el Inca Garcilaso'. In strictly legal terms, he was not entitled to call himself an 'Inca' because Incan inheritance is patrilineal. In his *Comentarios Reales de los Incas*, he drew on the oral lore of his childhood to present Cuzco to the Europeans as an *other* Rome and one of equally high status.[31] This is a unique document permitting valuable insights into Incan culture. Like the Jesuit Acosta, it was important for him to show that there is only the one divine world: 'there is but one world, and although we call it the Old World and the New World, this is because the latter has been discovered anew for ourselves, and not because there are two of them, but because they are all one'.[32]

He backs this 'one world' claim with analogies comparing the history of the Incas with that of the Spanish. It is conspicuous that he expressly wishes to avoid explicit comparisons between Europe and America: 'toda comparación es odiosa' (every comparison is odious).[33] In contrast to José Acosta's closed Christian worldview, Garcilaso's writings reveal the manipulative power of comparisons. The search for appropriate *tertia* generates, forms and manipulates the *comparata*. Garcilaso's *comentarios* rejected this manipulation. Although Inca Garcilaso was opposed to comparisons, his text works with implicit and sometimes also explicit comparisons such as that between pre-Incan and Greek or Roman idolatry.[34] Not only Cornelis de Pauw but also José Martí would take up these comparisons.

During the sixteenth and seventeenth centuries, the New World was a topic for which a high level of attention and comparably strong book sales could always be anticipated. The European competition for colonies, increasingly professional book printing skills and the so-called 'Leyenda Negra' (Black Legend)[35] fuelled the interest in Spanish atrocities while also encouraging popular accounts of monstrosities and heathen customs among the so-called 'Indians' as well as both fabricated and actual travel reports.

With the Age of Enlightenment,[36] the discussion gathered momentum again and developed a new dimension within the context of the 'invention of human rights'[37] and abolitionism. Whereas José de Acosta or Inca Garcilaso in the sixteenth and seventeenth centuries wanted to use comparisons to transform the differences between the inhabitants of Europe and America into a divinely based unity, the interest was now in either creating an order in the first place or justifying it with the help of comparisons. Encyclopaedists and dedicated abolitionists such as Abbé Raynal and Cornelis de Pauw applied an aspect of comparison that had not played any role in the Christian forerunner to the debate of the New World: comparing makes it possible to grade both differences and similarities and rank them in hierarchies. The different *tertia* in respect to which comparisons were carried out could then have overlapping evaluations or could point in different directions. This potential was exploited particularly by European academics who, following the publication of Montesquieu's book *De L'Esprit de Lois* (1748), worked on relating the social constitution, religion and customs to specific aspects of the meteorological climate.[38] A bit more or a bit less moisture, heat or cold could be used to classify certain world regions as being more similar in one respect and as more different in another. In order to translate these different outcomes of comparisons into an evaluative hierarchy, it was necessary to take the *tertia* with regard to which the *comparata* were constructed, compare these with each other and weight them appropriately.[39] Hence, the authors of these complicated layers of comparisons repeatedly reappraised them in relation to different intentions.

Frequently, however, this second stage of processing – which could be called a second-order comparison (see below) – was not mentioned specifically and was hidden behind generalizing statements that represented the outcome of a detailed process of comparing. This was particularly the case for text genres such as the popular encyclopaedias and dictionaries. These mostly presented 'Europe' and 'America' as 'asymmetric counter-concepts'.[40] Then, differences regarding the Americas were emphasized, whereas similarities, in contrast, were left in the background. For example, in his article 'America', the Scottish apothecary and editor of the *Encyclopaedia Britannica*, James Tytler, wrote between 1778 and 1784: 'Between the New World and the Old there are several very striking differences, but the most remarkable is the general predominance of cold throughout the whole of America.' Tytler does not spell out the comparison of the numerous differences. Instead, he hides them behind this second-order comparison – a comparison of (comparison-based) differences: 'the most remarkable ... difference'. Together with a further argument, he uses this to derive his evaluation of America:

> Another particularity in the climate of America is the excessive moisture in general. In some places, indeed, in the western coast, rain is not known; but in all other parts the moistness of the climate is as remarkable as the cold; and this moisture undoubtedly contributes to render America in general very unhealthy.[41]

Although he has to admit that there are exceptions, the grading of the differences is eclipsed by his generalizing statement that the combination of cold and moisture make America very unhealthy.

Cornelis de Pauw, who had written the corresponding article in the French encyclopaedia under the heading 'Amérique'[42] one or two years earlier, came to very similar conclusions, and Tytler may even have drawn on these for his own entry. However, David Hume had already come to similar conclusions in 1748 when he wrote that America was as a whole colder.[43] Although, like de Pauw and Raynal a few years later, Hume also criticized slavery, his beliefs about 'Negroes' were in no way less conclusive:

> I am apt to suspect the Negroes, and in general all other species of men, to be naturally inferior to the whites ... no ingenious manufactures amongst them, no arts, no sciences. On the other hand, the most rude and barbarous of the whites, such as the ancient Germans, the present Tartars, have still something eminent about them, in their valour, form of government, or some other particular. Such a uniform and constant difference could not happen, in so many countries and ages, if nature had not made an original distinction between these breeds of men.[44]

Even though Hume was not talking exclusively about those 'Negroes' who had been brought to the Americas here, the text also shows how gradings of difference were used to naturalize the contrast between Black and White races. The uniformly constructed Blacks are contrasted with the diversely constructed Whites who, even as White barbarians (the Germans), still always reveal something particular. De Pauw argued in an even more differentiated way in his *Recherches Philosophique sur les Americains*, published in 1768 while he was living in Berlin.[45]

De Pauw wrote his *Recherches* in 1767 while attending the court of Frederick the Great. He integrated all the descriptions of the Americas available to him from the previous 300 years. Acosta and Garcilaso were only the start. De Pauw took up the common stereotypes that had formed during this long period and questioned their rational soundness. He used stories about giants from Patagonia or miracle reports of missionaries as proof of the need to question the credibility of eyewitness reports in general. He positioned himself, in contrast, as a philosophically trained scholar who wanted to separate the wheat from the chaff, the imagined from the rational, and the false from the true. He considered the best method for doing this was comparing. The first lines of his preface already underlined his scholarly claim:

> Which naturalist of Antiquity had ever suspected that a planet would have two such different hemispheres, of which one would be overcome, subjected, and devoured by the

other as soon as it was discovered after centuries of being concealed by the night and the abyss of the times?[46]

This short quote shows the complexity of his comparisons: de Pauw constructed the 'such different hemispheres' of Europe and America as being fundamentally different – at first glance.[47] A second look, however, shows that this difference is eclipsed almost completely by another comparison. The quote reveals a historical depth accompanied by a complicated demarcation from antiquity that addresses the *querelle*: de Pauw introduces 'Antiquity' as an important benchmark and identifies himself with the Antique tradition and against the 'such different hemispheres'. As previous examples have already shown, Greek antiquity was an important criterion for determining the difference between Europe and the Americas. Whereas Greek antiquity becomes the marker of difference in the proven manner, de Pauw simultaneously emphasizes the limited imagination of the naturalists of antiquity. Hence, alterity does not describe the relationship to antiquity appropriately. Regarding the significance of naturalists – one could extend this to say the significance of science – the epochs are similar. However, regarding imagination or empirical knowledge, they are different. The communality becomes clear through the shared difference compared to the Dark Ages ('night and the abyss of the times') that makes not only the Age of Enlightenment but also antiquity shine even more brightly. Whereas the difference between the two hemispheres was taken as known and not treated further, a much greater difference now emerges between the lines: a difference compared to slavery and the brutal actions of the Spanish ('subjected, and devoured'). With the help of comparisons, de Pauw works out similarities with antiquity while simultaneously denying participation to Spain. Hence, neither the Americas nor Spain are part of the world region Europe and the Age of Enlightenment. What starts with a contrasting comparison between the two hemispheres and a criticism of the limited imagination of the natural scientists of antiquity ends up with a picture of a world in which a degenerate part of Europe has assimilated the degenerate Americas. Spain had thereby increased its distance from the project of the Enlightenment. Slavery, colonialism, subjection and assimilation become a difference within Europe.

Hence, compared to his predecessors Acosta and Garcilaso, de Pauw treats unity and difference completely differently.[48] He does not assume that this unity is given. Instead, comparisons reveal a hidden ordering of the world. De Pauw first separates self into both self and other ('two such different hemispheres'). Then he constructs similarities and differences in the self (antiquity versus own present day). In a third step, he uses a detour over antiquity to identify one part of Europe as different. Spain thus becomes the different one that has assimilated America. America marks a difference within Europe.

So far, this interpretation of de Pauw's writings is still in line with alterity studies. However, by going beyond the dichotomous order of the self and the other, an analysis of the practices of comparing shows how similarities and differences can mutually overlap. One sign of the argument based on grading similarity and difference is when de Pauw literally talks about shades: shades of skin colour. In the second part of his *Recherches*, he addresses the differences among the Americans, focusing particularly on the 'Eskimos', the 'Blasards', the 'Patagonians', the 'Panamanians', the 'white negroes of Orang-Outang', the 'Hermaphrodites' of Florida and others.[49] The inhabitants of the New World come off markedly worse compared to inhabitants of the same climate zones in other world regions. The difference between Blacks and Whites, for example, is markedly secondary to the difference compared to the people of the New World. He writes that although there is an important difference between Whites and Blacks, this difference can disappear: former white Jews who had fled to Africa and never mixed with other people were also Black nowadays.[50] If one were to have made such an attempt with a Black in a White country, one would have seen that this person's descendants would at some point have become White:

> If one were to classify humankind into types just according to colour, it would be necessary to conclude that if the Negro were to constitute a special type through being Black, then the olive-coloured and brown would also constitute a class through not being White. Furthermore, the Spaniards and the Swedes are among themselves two different kinds of people. And hence with too many classifications, with too many proofs, nothing would be proven or an absurdity would be proven.[51]

In this quote, shades of skin colour lead to a negative conclusion: it is not the colour of the skin but the climate that is decisive. Because of the great moisture in the Americas, there are also no Blacks there. This names a further important reference in the text: to a theory of the humours. In the first volume of the *Recherches*, de Pauw had already emphasized that due to the lack of heat, American men with their 'short rods' are not only vindictive and as quickly offended as women in Europe, but are also less resilient. He uses analogies to conclude that as women are able to breastfeed their children through being more moist and phlegmatic, the moist and cold climate has led to an error of nature in American men: 'Hence, the lack of heat led to the production of milk in American men.'[52] The moisture was linked to the unhealthy climate and the proliferation of insects and snakes, and it was underscored with a misogynistic subtext. More and more new comparisons lead to even more new comparisons. Indeed, the complete text of the *Recherches* consists almost exclusively of the greatest variety of kinds of comparison.

What nowadays seems no less curious than the legends that de Pauw criticized so strongly in his *Recherches* met with much approval towards the end of the eighteenth century. It may well be that the essential ideas here also flowed into a joint work by a team of authors (who initially published autonomously) that would also gain great popularity: the *Histoire des deux Indes*.[53] The main author is considered to be Abbé Raynal, but a large proportion of the text was also written by others, and particularly by Denis Diderot. This traced – in contrast to the comparison between the New World and the Old World – the economic and colonial relations of Europe both in the Far East and in the Americas. Although the work was strongly influenced by Montesquieu, it deviates in one decisive point: it does not explain the end of slavery in Europe through the rise of Christianity, but through an increase in trade. The main objection is not, for example, to climate theory and its consequences when explaining human customs, but to Christianity. The proof is given by complex comparisons over historical variants of slavery that had spread and persisted not only in antiquity but also in regions shaped by Christianity. Hence, religion cannot prevent slavery.[54]

Against the background of these writings, the form of the less differentiated *othering*, as found pre-eminently in the dictionaries, can be viewed as the outcome of markedly more complex, earlier practices of comparing. The tediously developed main premise of the two-volume *Recherches* can be found in a very simplified form in the encyclopaedia entry. In *Amérique*, de Pauw concluded that it was amazing to see that in 1492, the development of the human intellect in America was 3,000 years behind that in Europe. Even today, there was no American tribe (*peuplade*) that was free and wanted to develop its intellect.[55] Alongside the simplification of complex comparisons in the dictionary, it can also be seen that regardless of the genre, the judgement on slavery and the degeneration premise went hand in hand in the aforementioned writings of Hume, Raynal, Diderot and de Pauw. Before finally summarizing the findings, it is necessary to briefly sketch the further development of the debate.

Unlike Tytler, Raynal or Diderot, not all the subsequent contributors to the 'dispute of the New World' agreed with the arguments of de Pauw. The Mexican author Fray Servando Teresa de Mier Noriega y Guerra, for example, took up de Pauw's comparative approach, but applied it to a European country. Major passages of his *Memoirs* are similar to de Pauw's description of the Americas, but they address conditions in Spain. Like de Pauw and other Enlighteners, he drew on the rich reservoir of comparison-based anti-Spanish stereotypes that had been circulating in Europe since the sixteenth century.[56] In Fray de Mier, this is used to characterize a part of the Old World as a backward or even degenerated region.

Francisco Javier Clavijero also rejected both de Pauw's and Raynal's arguments, though he did this in another way. The native Mexican, son of a Creole mother and a Spanish father, claimed a greater closeness to the facts in the introduction to his ten-volume work. In contrast to the aforementioned and numerous other European colleagues, he was familiar with not only the numerous books written by Spanish and Mexican historians, but also the surviving pictorial sources from pre-Hispanic Mexico. He pointed out that it was simply false to claim that there were no remains of Aztec history.[57] His final volume concludes with nine *dissertations* that read as a devastating criticism of Buffon and de Pauw. He disproves not only the purported lack of cultural achievements but also the negative descriptions of the climate, the animals, the plainness of the fruits and vegetation, and so forth. His main weapon in this is comparing. When de Pauw claims that the original variety of plants is smaller, then Clavijero questions this with counterexamples: '[T]hat if America had no wheat, Europe had no maiz, which is not less useful or wholesome; if America had not pomegranates, lemons, &c. it has them now: but Europe never had, has, nor can have, chirimoyas, aguacates, musas, chicozapotes, &c.'[58]

The American Founding Fathers also reacted vehemently to the degeneration premise – above all, Thomas Jefferson in his *Comparative View of the Quadrupeds of Europe and of America* from 1787.[59] Handwritten documents confirm Jefferson's prior research. He surveyed 'elks, mooses, caribous, and other quadrupeds', recorded them in tables and organized these tables so that a numerical comparison would quickly reveal to any observer how far Buffon and, as a consequence, de Pauw had been mistaken.[60] Not only Jefferson but also Benjamin Franklin, George Washington and Alexander Hamilton were among those who objected vehemently to the degeneration premise.[61] It was these comparisons, used to refute criticism of the Americas, that were fundamental for the development of a self-concept of the Americas as a world region dominated by the United States.[62]

However, the slave owner Jefferson nonetheless adopted from Buffon and de Pauw the idea that comparisons could be used to differentiate human characteristics and could be transformed into a discriminatory classification. It was not the climate that was decisive here:

> Comparing them [Blacks and Whites] by their faculties of memory, reason, and imagination, it appears to me, that in memory they [Blacks] are equal to the whites; in reason much inferior, as I think one [Black] could scarcely be found capable of tracing and comprehending the investigations of Euclid and that in imagination they are dull, tasteless, and anomalous … In music they are more generally gifted than the whites with accurate ears for tune and time … Whether they will be equal to the composition of a more extensive run of melody, or of complicated harmony, is yet to be proved. Misery is often the parent of the most affecting touches in poetry. – Among the blacks is misery enough, God knows, but no poetry.[63]

The classification – an outcome of prior comparisons – proceeds accordingly along the 'colour line'. What is notable in these arguments is how Jefferson uses the antiquity of the Old World – addressed through Euclid in the quote – to mark this differentiation. Blacks had neither the intellectual ability to understand Euclid's work nor possessed the taste for it, and they were also unable to develop it. It is not surprising that this argument, which links up structurally with the main arguments of the European Enlighteners, also did not remain uncontested in the United States – even when it initially succeeded in asserting itself.[64]

There were also individuals such as Alexander von Humboldt or Wolfgang von Goethe who criticized the degeneration premise until far into the nineteenth century. They sought commonalities in the differences between the world regions regarding, for example, geological issues or the structure and development of plants. They avoided dichotomous classifications. Even though coming from a completely different direction, Goethe expressed this in his drawing *Die neue und die alte Welt bildlich vergleichend* (*The New and the Old World Compared in Pictures*). The depiction of the American Andes together with the European mountain chains, which also included, alongside the Alps, the volcano Pico del Teide on Tenerife in northern Africa, illustrated his search for a universally valid geological principle. Alexander von Humboldt expressed his claim to be impartial through exuberant empirical comparative studies that were also mostly of a nondiscursive nature. As a glance at his famous *Chimborazo* sketch shows, he was unable to restrain his observations and findings in either written or pictorial form. The labelling of the flora and fauna as well as the additional written comparisons and explanations in the tables following the picture sprawl beyond all limits. Only comparisons of the tertia, i.e. second order comparisons, would have made the comparisons manageable. However, they would have led to hierarchic rankings, and that was something he avoided, just like Inca Garcilaso before him.[65]

This is not the place to give a detailed account of how the making and remaking of the two *comparata*, the 'Old' and the 'New World', developed over the course of the nineteenth and twentieth centuries. Nonetheless, this much can be stated in advance of other studies: at the end of the nineteenth century, the Cuban José Martí – completely in the tradition of Garcilaso – called for a Latin American politics of memory that would not have to fear comparison with either the United States or Europe. He replaced European antiquity with Inca culture as Latin American antiquity.[66] However, his practices of comparing also failed to become hegemonic in the American discussions of the nineteenth and twentieth centuries.

The labelling of the two American continents as the 'New World' became narrower over the course of the nineteenth century, rather like the term 'America' became restricted increasingly to the northern continent and, more specifically, to the United States. With Jefferson and the intervention of other Founding Fathers, there arose a way of talking in the self-description of the United States, as well as in the way it was described by others, that the French America traveller Alexis de Tocqueville in the nineteenth century grasped as making it 'exceptional'.[67] That the determination of exceptionality can be confirmed only in comparison to a commonplace shows the longevity and transformation of the practices of comparing between the 'Old' and the 'New World'.

Antonín Dvořák's symphony *From the New World* written in the United States designated two things at the end of the nineteenth century: the North American state and the land of the future. He premiered his music in this land of the future before travelling back to the old Europe of the past. This temporal reinterpretation shook up the interpretations of the world based on de Pauw's classification of the Americas as a world region of regression and degeneration that had found such widespread acceptance within Europe. This shake-up continues to resonate today in some expressions of anti-Americanism.

## Dispute of the New World Revisited: Summary Conclusions

For Antonello Gerbi, the 'dispute of the New World' began with Buffon's *Natural History*. Although earlier chroniclers of American nature such as Acosta had pointed to its differences and unique features compared to European flora and fauna, it was Buffon who first systematized these differences and subordinated them under an all-encompassing premise. Proceeding from climate theory and a dynamic concept of nature, he was convinced that he was able to confirm the general immaturity or even inferiority of American nature.[68] However, if we only look at how this discourse has been shaped by differences and *othering*, we fail to understand that difference and similarity were at work simultaneously.

A cursory analysis of the practices of comparing since the sixteenth century makes it necessary to reformulate the change in dealing with the New World. When comparing, actors draw up not only *comparata* (i.e. that which they compare) but also *tertia* (i.e. that in respect to which they make their comparisons). Although specific topics of comparison formed during the *dispute*, and these persisted up to the end of the nineteenth century, they were applied in completely different ways. Prominent topics were comparisons of climate (moisture, warmth); of the sizes of animals, plants and mountains; of the role of European antiquity, religion and customs; of the level of art, culture and sciences; and of physique, disease and sexuality or the relationship between the sexes. Alongside continuously recurring topics of comparison, one can also perceive a change in the practices of comparing over this long period of time: the increasing differentiation of practices of comparing, in which the grading of similarities and differences became all the more important, made it necessary to carry out second-order comparisons. This was the only way to bring into a hierarchy the *tertia* in respect to which comparisons were being shaped. However, the accompanying evaluations were criticized frequently, thereby repeatedly provoking new comparisons.

In his *Natural History*, José de Acosta compared the Americans and the Europeans in terms of their religious behaviour or their status as heathens, Christians or heretics. As different as the outcomes of these comparisons could be, they nonetheless never cast doubt on the existence of a unity behind this difference. This unity did not need to be found; it was given. Comparing could then come to an end and be restrained. This changed over the following centuries. Hume, Raynal, Diderot, and de Pauw mostly addressed the different relations between nature and human beings and their effects on cultural accomplishments. What they compared was distinctive features regarding the status of development. The results of comparing were placed in a reciprocal causal relationship by applying climate theory. Whereas Buffon viewed degeneration only as the expression of a natural development, it led de Pauw to deduce from this the degeneration premise as a history of decline. This had a powerful impact in Europe.

The American reactions to this premise transformed its content. However, they also linked up with the practices of comparing used by the European Enlighteners. Although vehemently rejecting the climate-related theory of degeneration, Jefferson nonetheless used it to derive a comparison-based classification of differently gifted peoples. This can be seen as not just the precursor of a biologically based race theory, because comparing was also assigned the potential to gain an understanding of the natural order of the world. Whereas in Acosta, comparing was brought to an end against the background of a divine unity, comparisons now took on a completely different function: they should first make it possible to grasp the natural order. This launched a scarcely stoppable dynamic process: comparisons continuously provoked further comparisons that could be rejected or confirmed only by further, better, more appropriate comparisons. Comparisons were now attributed with delivering a truth effect going beyond the authenticity of eyewitness reports. This was a reaction to the loss of trust in the many fabulous reports from the 'New World'. In the Age of Enlightenment, tales of giants or other monstrosities were no longer convincing. De Pauw had – like other academics of his time – raised the method of comparison to the scientific method (*recherches philosophique*) per se.

From Acosta to José Martí, the two *comparata* 'America' and 'Europe' were always shaped by an asymmetry that was not necessarily accompanied by explicit evaluations. Mostly, however, evaluations were already rolled into one with the drawing-up of the specific *tertia* and *comparata*. An individual such as David Hume, who places 'the most barbarous Whites' higher than 'Negroes' no longer has to put his evaluation specifically into words. Comparing is always a wrangling over which practices of comparing assert themselves, are adopted, reinterpreted and recognized, and, in this sense, become hegemonic.

Within the scholarly discourse of the Enlightenment, some practices of comparing could become hegemonic; others were rejected. Although both Acosta and Garcilaso were taken as references, Cuzco was not viewed as another Rome, but – as emerged from the French translation of the original – as a second Rome, inferior to the first.[69]

In contrast, the geographical composition of the Old World was not defined unequivocally. Western Europe and Ancient Greece were held to be fixed parts. However, whether Africa, Asia or also Eastern and South European regions belonged to the 'Old World' was controversial for many authors. James Tytler or Cornelis de Pauw included Asia, Europe and Africa in the 'Old World' when it came to geography. In contrast, when it came to culture, the 'Old World' fell apart, leaving mostly only a small core. For these Enlighteners, it did not include Spain.

If the intention was to present 'Europe' and 'America' as being as different as possible, then contradictions and opposites within the 'Americas' along with those in various national cultures within 'Europe' had to be hidden behind the uniformly constructed *comparata*. In this way, communalities could be eclipsed by differences, and the stereotype of alterity could be consolidated. However, *othering* is only the result of a more complex way of relating two entities to one another.

Even when the internal differences between the *comparata* could be concealed within dichotomized contrasts, it was important for European and American writers since the eighteenth century to work out different shades of similarity and difference through comparisons. Authors who wished to produce hierarchizations and evaluations had to weight the gradings of both difference and similarity. This weighting required second-order comparisons: a comparison of the *tertia* in relation to which the comparisons were shaped. In the late nineteenth century and during the twentieth century in both the 'Old' and the 'New World', 'race' became one of the most powerful *tertia*. What made the comparisons carried out in the 'dispute of the New World' so powerful was their ability to naturalize the gradings of difference.

**Angelika Epple** is Professor of Modern European and Global History at Bielefeld University. She is also the director of Bielefeld's Collaborative Research Centre *Practices of Comparing. Ordering and Changing the World*. She has worked on comparative historiography and on the asymmetries, transfers and intertwinements between economic and political actors at both the global and local levels. Her recent publications include 'Calling for a Practice Turn in Global History. 'Practices as Drivers of Globalization/s', *History & Theory* 57 (2018); and *Die Welt beobachten: Praktiken des Vergleichens* (2015, coedited with Walter Erhart).

# Notes

1. Columbus's log, entry for 14 September. Humboldt already stressed how significant this flock of birds was for the course of history that led to South America coming under the influence of Spain. This passage in Columbus's log has been interpreted repeatedly. See, e.g., O. Ette, *Literatur in Bewegung: Raum und Dynamik grenzüberschreitenden Erzählens in Europa und Amerika* (Göttingen: Velbrück Wissenschaft, 2001), 85.
2. The literature on this is abundant. For short definitions, see the entries on 'the other' and 'othering' in B. Ashcroft, G. Griffiths and H. Tiffin (eds), *Post-colonial Studies: The Key Concepts*, 2nd edn (New York: Routledge, 2007), 154–58. For an early adaptation in Latin American studies, see F. Coronil, 'Beyond Occidentalism: Toward Nonimperial Geohistorical Categories', *Cultural Anthropology* 11 (1996), 55–87. This led to journals being founded that were devoted to alterity research, including several ones in Latin America (see, e.g., http://corpusarchivos.revues.org).
3. This phrase has gained a fixed place in the international discussion since it was coined by Antonello Gerbi in the book he originally published in Italian in 1955. See A. Gerbi, *Dispute of the New World: The History of a Polemic, 1750–1900* (Pittsburgh: University of Pittsburgh Press, 1973).
4. Guillaume Thomas François Raynal provided a very similar description of the initial historical situation in his introduction to the *Histoire des deux Indes* (1780) that he wrote together with other authors. See the English translation: G.T.F. Raynal, *A philosophical and political history of the settlements and trade of the Europeans in the East and West Indies*, 2nd edn, 6 vols (London: A. Strahan, 1798), vol. 1, 1–2.

5. I. Garcilaso de la Vega, *Primera Parte de los Commentarios Reales que Tratan del Origen de los Yncas, Reyes, que fueron del Peru, de su Idolatria, Leyes y gouierno en paz y en guerra: sus vidas y conquistas, y de todo lo que fue aquel Imperio y su Republica, antes de que los Españoles passaran a el* (Lisbon: Pedro Crasbeeck, 1609); *Historia general del Perú: trata el descubrimiento del, y como lo ganaron los Españoles. Guerras civiles que huvo entre Picarros, y Almagros, sobre la partija de la tierra. Castigo y levantamiento de tiranos; y otros sucessos particulares que en la Historia se contienen* (Córdoba: Viuda de Andrés Barrera, 1616).
6. C. Perrault, *Parallèle des anciens et des modernes en ce qui regarde les arts et les sciences* (Paris: Jean Baptiste Coignard, 1693).
7. It was Hans-Jürgen Lüsebrink who drew attention to the overlapping of the two discourses, particularly also in Clavijero. See H.-J. Lüsebrink, 'De L'usage de la comparaison dans les écrits des Jésuites sur les Amériques', in M.A. Bernier, C. Donato and H.-J. Lüsebrink (eds), *Jesuit Accounts of the Colonial Americas: Intercultural Transfers, Intellectual Disputes, and Textualities* (Toronto: University of Toronto Press, 2014), 418–36.
8. G.-L. Leclerc de Buffon, *Buffon's Natural History (Histoire Naturelle)* (London: H.D. Symonds, 1797).
9. Vicente Bernaschina, Tobias Kraft and Anne Kraume have processed important aspects of the *dispute* in their collection of essays and sources, and provided access to some of the texts. However, they limit themselves to what they call the 'Berlin debate', thereby giving voice to predominantly European authors. See V. Bernaschina, T. Kraft and A. Kraume (eds), *Globalisierung in Zeiten der Aufklärung: Texte und Kontexte zur 'Berliner Debatte' um die Neue Welt (17./18. Jh.)*, 2 vols (Frankfurt am Main: Peter Lang Verlag, 2015).
10. C. de Pauw, *Recherches philosophiques sur les Américains, ou Mémoires intéressants pour servir à l'Histoire de l'Espèce humaine*, 3 vols (Berlin: Chez Georges Jacques Decker, Imp. du Roi, 1768–69); C. de Pauw, 'Amérique', in D. Diderot and J.B. le Rond d'Alembert (eds), *Supplément à l'Encyclopédie ou Dictionnaire raisonné des sciences, des arts et des métiers* (Amsterdam: M.M. Rey, 1776–77), 343–62.
11. G.W.F. Hegel, 'Geographical Basis of History', in *Lectures on the Philosophy of World History* (Kitchener, Ontario: Batoche Books 2001), 96–120, at 99. German edition: G.W.F. Hegel, 'Geographische Grundlagen der Weltgeschichte', in *Vorlesungen über die Philosophie der Geschichte* (Berlin: Duncker & Humblot, 1848), 98–113, at 101.
12. F.J. Clavijero, *History of Mexico*, 2 vols (London: J. Johnson, 1807), vol. 1, 7. On Pernety, see C. Martínez, 'Usos del pasado y confiabilidad de las fuentes: Antoine-Joseph Pernety y la disputa sobre la naturaleza de América en el siglo XVIII', *Corpus* 5(2) (2015). Retrieved 5 March 2019 from https://journals.openedition.org/corpusarchivos/1449. On Pernety, de Pauw, and Humboldt, see O. Ette, 'Die "Berliner Debatte" um die Neue Welt: Globalisierung aus der Perspektive der europäischen Aufklärung', in Bernaschina et al. (eds), *Globalisierung in Zeiten der Aufklärung*, vol. 1, 27–55.
13. T. Jefferson, *Notes on the State of Virginia* (London: John Stockdale, 1787).
14. D. Walker, *Walker's Appeal, in four articles* (Boston: D. Walker, 1830).
15. 'Nuestra Grecia es preferible a la Grecia que no es nuestra. Nos es más necesaria.' J. Martí, 'Nuestra America', *Revista Ilustrada*, 1 January 1891. In his meticulous interpretation of Martí's *Nuestra America*, Ottmar Ette talks about Martí bringing the debate to an end with his essay. See O. Ette, 'José Martís America oder Wege zu einem amerikanischen Humanismus', in D. Röseberg (ed.), *El arte de crear memoria: Festschrift zum 80. Geburtstag von Hans-Otto Dill* (Berlin: Trafo-Wissenschafts-Verlag, 2015), 75–98.
16. T. Todorov, *The Conquest of America and the Question of the Other* (New York: Harper Perennial, 1992 [1982]); S. Mintz, *Sweetness and Power* (New York: Viking Press, 1985).

17. Following on from the classic studies of Homi Bhabha, Edward Said and Gayatri Chakravorty Spivak, there is now an impressive body of literature on this set of topics. Examples are W. Mignolo, *The Idea of Latin America* (Malden, MA: Wiley-Blackwell, 2005); A. Epple, O. Kaltmeier and U. Lindner (eds), journal issue: 'Entangled Histories: Reflecting on Concepts of Coloniality and Postcoloniality', *Comparativ* 21(1) (2011); R. Stam and E. Shohat, *Race in Translation: Culture Wars around the Postcolonial Atlantic* (New York: New York University Press, 2012); J. Laviña and M. Zeuske (eds), *The Second Slavery: Mass Slaveries and Modernity in the Americas and in the Atlantic Basin* (Zürich: LIT Verlag, 2014).
18. 'Circulation', 'flows', 'mestizaje' and similar terms offer a metaphorical description of the entanglements between entities that are then frequently defined no further. However, this results in the terms losing their explanatory power. See, for a more detailed account, A. Epple, 'Lokalität und die Dimensionen des Globalen: Eine Frage der Relationen', *Historische Anthropologie* 21 (2013), 4–25. This is where research on doing comparisons comes in and studies, among other things, how units are generated as *comparata*.
19. For Theodore Schatzki, this is why the smallest unit of analysis is the practice and not the act. Giddens, in contrast, turns away from the action concept because he rejects the justification of actions through intentionality. See A. Giddens, *The Constitution of Society: Outline of the Theory of Structuration* (Cambridge: Polity, 1984); T.R. Schatzki, K. Knorr-Cetina and E. Savigny (eds), *The Practice Turn in Contemporary Theory* (London: Routledge, 2001). Nonetheless, this leads both authors into different types of contradictions.
20. Hence, as Bettina Heintz claims, the similarity assumption can be distinguished analytically from the construction of a way of comparing. See B. Heintz, '"Wir leben im Zeitalter der Vergleichung": Perspektiven einer Soziologie des Vergleichs', *Zeitschrift für Soziologie* 45 (2016), 305–23. However, in praxeological terms, the similarity assumption can be conceived as the prior construction of a way of comparing that consolidates into a categorization.
21. This is particularly notable in the studies on 'othering'. A classic example is the two volume-collection of works by numerous prominent authors such as Homi K. Bhabha, Gayatri Chakravorty Spivak or Edward W. Said: F. Barker et al. (eds), *Europe and its Others*, 2 vols (Colchester: University of Essex, 1985). This collected work has also provided the title for more recent books such as P. Gifford and T. Hauswedell (eds), *Europe and its Others: Essays on Interperception and Identity* (Frankfurt am Main: Peter Lang 2010).
22. Z. Longxi, 'Crossroads, Distant Killing, and Translation: On the Ethics and Politics of Comparison', in R. Felski and S. Stanford Friedman (eds), *Comparison: Theories, Approaches, Uses* (Baltimore: Johns Hopkins University Press, 2013), 46–63.
23. On the significance for society of comparing with numbers, see e.g. B. Heintz, 'Numerische Differenz: Überlegungen zu einer Soziologie des (quantitativen) Vergleichs', *Zeitschrift für Soziologie* 39 (2010), 162–81; W. Espeland and M. Sauder, 'Rankings and Reactivity: How Public Measures Recreate Social Worlds', *American Journal of Sociology* 113 (2007), 1–40. From a historical perspective, see L. Behrisch, *Die Berechnung der Glückseligkeit: Statistik und Politik in Deutschland und Frankreich im späten Ancien Régime* (Ostfildern: Thorbecke Verlag, 2016).
24. De Pauw's *Recherches* is full of intertextual references that would be impossible to address in entirety within this article. Therefore, only a few, particularly influential positions can be presented here. This would have been far more difficult without the informative collection of sources in Bernaschina et al. (eds), *Globalisierung in Zeiten der Aufklärung*.

25. The questionable nature of the history of this travel report already prompted a literary analysis from Stefan Zweig: S. Zweig, *Amerigo: Die Geschichte eines historischen Irrtums* (Frankfurt am Main: Fischer Verlag, 1989 [1944]).
26. Referring to Bernhard Waldenfels, Peter Strohschneider points out how terms that introduce differences mark that *which* they differentiate while leaving that *from which* they are differentiated unmarked. See P. Strohschneider, 'Fremde in der Vormoderne. Über Negierbarkeitsverluste und Unbekanntheitsgewinne', in A. Becker (ed.), *Alterität als Leitkonzept für historisches Interpretieren* (Berlin: Akad.-Verl., 2012), 387–416, at 391. One can only agree with this. Reformulated in praxeological terms, this can be understood as indicating that actors are situated historically and that any comparison that also includes the self of the actor literally leads to bias.
27. J. de Acosta, *The natural & moral history of the Indies*, 2 vols (London: Hakluyt Society, 1880 [1604]), vol. 1 (book I-III), XXV. Spanish original: 'Asi que aunque el mundo nuevo ya no es nuevo sino viejo, segun hay mucho dicho, y escripto del, todavia me parece que en alguna manera se podra tener esta Historia por nueva, por ser juntamente Historia, y en parte Philosophia, y por ser no solo las obras de naturaleza, sino tambien de las del libre albedrío, que son los hechos y costumbres de hombres', quoted in Bernaschina et al. (eds), *Globalisierung in Zeiten der Aufklärung*, vol. 2, 20.
28. P. Validvia Orozco, 'Hypotheken des Wissens: José de Acosta und die Naturgeschichte', in Bernaschina et al. (eds), *Globalisierung in Zeiten der Aufklärung*, vol. 1, 79–97, at 81. The Third Council of Lima 1582–83, the history of which he documents in his work, proclaimed that Christianization had to be accompanied by a just treatment of the natives. In addition, it should not be carried out exclusively in Spanish. The result was a catechism in three languages – Spanish, Quechua and Aymara – that remain the three major languages of Peru up to the present day.
29. Aristotle distinguished between natural slaves and those who had been enslaved through becoming prisoners of war. Las Casas, in contrast, distinguished four kinds of barbarian, and Acosta drew on his argument. See W. Reinhard, 'Universale Xenophobie: Die Konstruktion des Anderen in der Geschichte', in Bernaschina et al. (eds), *Globalisierung in Zeiten der Aufklärung*, vol. 1, 125–40, especially 132–33.
30. See de Acosta, *The natural and moral history*, vol. 1, 390–91.
31. Garcilaso, *Commentarios Reales*, Proemio al lector, vol. 1, 15. For interesting reading, see V. Bernaschina, '"Toda comparación es odiosa" oder die Weltengeschichten der Menschheit: El Inca Garcilaso und die französischen Übertragungen der *comentarios reales*', in Bernaschina et al. (eds), *Globalisierung in Zeiten der Aufklärung*, vol. 1, 99–121.
32. Garcilaso, *Comentarios Reales*, vol. 1, 19: '… que no hay más que un mundo, y aunque llamarnos Mundo Viejo y Mundo Nuevo, es por haberse descubierto aquél nuevamente para nosotros, y no porque sean dos, sino todo uno.'
33. See ibid., 56.
34. See ibid., 39.
35. This term comes from the early twentieth century and remains controversial up to the present day. See F. Edelmayer, 'The "Leyenda Negra" and the Circulation of Anti-Catholic and Anti-Spanish Prejudices', *European History Online* (EGO), published by the Institute of European History (IEG), 29 June 2011, retrieved 5 March 2019 from http://www.ieg-ego.eu/edelmayerf-2010-en.
36. Sebastian Conrad convincingly argues why the Enlightenment should be assessed within the framework of global history; see S. Conrad, 'Enlightenment in Global History: A Historiographical Critique', *American Historical Review* 117 (2012), 999–1027. The

'Atlantic Enlightenment' (Stam and Shohat, *Race in Translation*, 1) is only a world-regional part of this broader story.
37. See L. Hunt, *Inventing Human Rights: A History* (New York, London: W. W. Norton & Company, 2008).
38. C. Montesquieu, 'Of Positive Laws', in C. Montesquieu, *The Spirit of Laws. (De L'esprit des Loix)*, 19 vols (London: J. Nourse and P. Vaillant, 1773), vol. 1, 7.
39. Even when it is conceivable that practices of comparing made a fundamental contribution to developing that which is labelled Western modernity as a *comparatum*, second-order comparing cannot be equated with second-order observation. For a historicizing of Niklas Luhmann's concept, see Gumbrecht, *Second Order Observation Historicized*; see http://www.design-in-human.de/lectures/gumbrecht.html.
40. R. Koselleck, 'The Historical-Political Semantics of Asymmetric Counterconcepts', in *Futures Past: On the Semantics of Historical Time* (New York: Columbia University Press, 2004), 155–91.
41. J. Tytler, 'America', in *Encyclopaedia Britannica, 2nd Edition (1778–1784)*, reprinted in Bernaschina et al. (eds), *Globalisierung in Zeiten der Aufklärung*, vol. 2, 229–43, at 231–32.
42. De Pauw, 'Amérique', 343–62.
43. D. Hume, 'Of National Characters', in *Essays, Moral, Political, and Literary*, 2 vols (London: Longmans, Greens and Co., 1889), vol. 1, 244–58, at 253.
44. See ibid., 252.
45. The *Recherches* was translated immediately into German; see C. de Pauw, *Philosophische Untersuchungen über die Amerikaner, oder wichtige Beyträge über die Geschichte der Menschheit* (Berlin: G.J. Decker and G.L. Winter, 1769).
46. German original: 'Welcher Naturforscher des Alterthumes hat jemals gemuthmaßet, daß ein Planete zwo so verschiedene Hemisphäre habe, davon eine von der anderen überwunden, unterjocht und verschlungen seyn würde, sobald sie nach Verlauf von Jahrhunderten, die sich in die Nacht und den Abgrund der Zeiten verhüllen, entdeckt wäre?' See de Pauw, *Philosophische Untersuchungen*, preface.
47. Vincente Bernaschina, Tobias Kraft and Anne Kraume stick to the alterity paradigm in their analysis of this debate when they assume that the emergence of the new continent implied a 'radical alterity'; Bernaschina et al. (eds), *Globalisierung in Zeiten der Aufklärung*, vol. 1, 11.
48. Even when he repeatedly refers affirmatively to Acosta (see e.g. de Pauw, *Amérique*, 182) or also Garcilaso (see e.g. ibid, 189).
49. De Pauw, *Philosophische Untersuchungen*, 103.
50. Ibid., 147.
51. Ibid., xxx.
52. Ibid., 34. This argument has a long tradition and goes back to Aristotle, who had already pointed to the phenomenon that human males can produce milk under certain conditions.
53. The full title is [G.T.F. Raynal], *Histoire philosophique et politique des établissements & du commerce des européens dans les deux Indes* (Amsterdam: n.p., 1770).
54. Raynal, *A philsophical and political history*, vol. 1, 16–17. Compare the informative interpretation of the text by A. Fraser Terjanian, *Commerce and its Discontents in Eighteenth Century French Political Thought* (Cambridge: Cambridge University Press, 2013), especially 86–89.
55. De Pauw, *Amérique*, 199.

56. Later to be called the 'Black Legend', as mentioned above.
57. Clavijero, *History of Mexico* (1807), vol. 1, 25–28.
58. F.J. Clavijero, *History of Mexico*, 3 vols (Philadelphia: Thomas Dobson, 1817), vol. 3, 189.
59. Jefferson, *Notes on the State of Virginia*, 71–72 and 77–80 (table 'A Comparative View of the Quadrupeds of Europe and of America').
60. Massachusetts Historical Society (MHS) Collections Online: Table comparing information about moose, caribou and elk, notes compiled by Thomas Jefferson. Loose memoranda for Notes on the State of Virginia [manuscript] from the Coolidge Collection of Thomas Jefferson Manuscripts, p. 32, attachment 3.
61. However, their united opposition should not detract from the differences in their arguments. See J.W. Ceaser, *Reconstructing America: The Symbol of America in Modern Thought* (New Haven: Yale University Press, 1997), 49.
62. For more details, see C.A. Fitz, 'The Hemispheric Dimensions of Early U.S. Nationalism: The War of 1812, its Aftermath, and Spanish American Independence', *Journal for American History* 102 (2015), 356–79.
63. Jefferson, *Notes on the State of Virginia*, 232–34.
64. Compare David Walker's criticisms of the Founding Fathers. As one of the oldest writings of an African American to survive, his appeal directed towards the 'colored citizens of the world' deliberately addresses an international public – an international public that was mostly imagined to be White; Walker, *Walker's Appeal*.
65. The literary device of avoiding second-order comparisons in Humboldt is flanked by both a 'rage of comparisons' and a literary device that Ottmar Ette, with reference to the term 'kühne Metapher' (bold metaphor), has called the 'bold comparison'. What seems to be incomparable is placed in a surprising combination of ideas without aiming towards the *tertium comparationis*. See O. Ette, '"… daß einem leidt tut, wie er aufgehört hat, deutsch zu sein": Alexander von Humboldt, Preußen und Amerika', in *Alexander von Humboldt im Netz (HiN). International Review for Humboldtian Studies* 3/4 (2002), retrieved 5 March 2019 from http://www.uni-potsdam.de/romanistik/hin/hin4/ette_1.htm.
66. Martí, 'Nuestra America'.
67. A. de Tocqueville, *Democracy in America. Second Part*, H. Reeve (trans.) (London: Saunders and Otley, 1840), 69: 'The position of the Americans is therefore quite exceptional, and it may be believed that no other democratic people will ever be placed in a similar one.'
68. Gerbi, *Dispute*, xvi.
69. The hierarchization as a consequence of comparison was inserted into Garcilaso's text afterwards by European interpreters. See Bernaschina, '"Toda comparación es odiosa"', 99–121, particularly 109.

# Bibliography

Ashcroft, B., Griffiths, G. and Tiffin, H. (eds), *Post-colonial Studies: The Key Concepts*, 2nd edn (New York: Routledge, 2007).
Barker, F. et al. (eds), *Europe and its Others*, 2 vols (Colchester: University of Essex, 1985).
Behrisch, L., *Die Berechnung der Glückseligkeit: Statistik und Politik in Deutschland und Frankreich im späten Ancien Régime* (Ostfildern: Thorbecke Verlag, 2016).
Bernaschina, V., '"Toda comparación es odiosa" oder die Weltengeschichten der Menschheit: El Inca Garcilaso und die französischen Übertragungen der *comentarios* reales', in

Bernaschina, V., Kraft, T. and Kraume, A. (eds), *Globalisierung in Zeiten der Aufklärung: Texte und Kontexte zur 'Berliner Debatte' um die Neue Welt (17./18. Jh.)*, 2 vols (Frankfurt am Main: Peter Lang Verlag, 2015), vol. 1, 99–121.

Bernaschina, V., Kraft, T. and Kraume, A. (eds), *Globalisierung in Zeiten der Aufklärung: Texte und Kontexte zur 'Berliner Debatte' um die Neue Welt (17./18. Jh.)*, 2 vols (Frankfurt am Main: Peter Lang Verlag, 2015).

Buffon, G.-L. Leclerc de, *Buffon's Natural History (Histoire Naturelle)* (London: H.D. Symonds, 1797).

Ceaser, J.W., *Reconstructing America: The Symbol of America in Modern Thought* (New Haven: Yale University Press, 1997).

Clavijero, F. J., *History of Mexico*, 2 vols (London: J. Johnson, 1807).

———. *History of Mexico*, 3 vols (Philadelphia: Thomas Dobson, 1817).

Conrad, S., 'Enlightenment in Global History: A Historiographical Critique', *American Historical Review* 117 (2012), 999–1027.

Coronil, F., 'Beyond Occidentalism: Toward Nonimperial Geohistorical Categories', *Cultural Anthropology* 11 (1996), 55–87.

De Acosta, J., *The natural & moral history of the Indies*, 2 vols (London: Hakluyt Society, 1880, [1604]).

De Pauw, C., *Recherches philosophiques sur les Américains, ou Mémoires intéressants pour servir à l'Histoire de l'Espèce humaine*, 3 vols (Berlin: Chez Georges Jacques Decker, Imp. du Roi, 1768–69).

———. *Philosophische Untersuchungen über die Amerikaner, oder wichtige Beyträge über die Geschichte der Menschheit* (Berlin: G.J. Decker and G.L. Winter, 1769).

———. 'Amérique', in Diderot, D. and le Rond d'Alembert, J.B. (eds), *Supplément à l'Encyclopédie ou Dictionnaire raisonné des sciences, des arts et des métiers* (Amsterdam: M.M. Rey, 1776–77), 343–62.

Edelmayer, F., 'The "Leyenda Negra" and the Circulation of Anti-Catholic and Anti-Spanish Prejudices', *European History Online* (EGO), published by the Institute of European History (IEG), 29 June 2011, retrieved 5 March 2019 from http://www.ieg-ego.eu/edelmayerf-2010-en.

Epple, A., 'Lokalität und die Dimensionen des Globalen: Eine Frage der Relationen', *Historische Anthropologie* 21 (2013), 4–25.

Epple, A., Kaltmeier, O. and Lindner, U. (eds), journal issue: 'Entangled Histories: Reflecting on Concepts of Coloniality and Postcoloniality', *Comparativ* 21(1) (2011).

Espeland, W. and Sauder, M., 'Rankings and Reactivity: How Public Measures Recreate Social Worlds', *American Journal of Sociology* 113 (2007), 1–40.

Ette, O., *Literatur in Bewegung: Raum und Dynamik grenzüberschreitenden Erzählens in Europa und Amerika* (Göttingen: Velbrück Wissenschaft, 2001).

———. '"… daß einem leidt tut, wie er aufgehört hat, deutsch zu sein": Alexander von Humboldt, Preußen und Amerika', *Alexander von Humboldt im Netz (HiN). International Review for Humboldtian Studies* 3/4 (2002), retrieved 5 March 2019 from http://www.uni-potsdam.de/romanistik/hin/hin4/ette_1.htm.

———. 'Die "Berliner Debatte" um die Neue Welt: Globalisierung aus der Perspektive der europäischen Aufklärung', in Bernaschina, V., Kraft, T. and Kraume, A. (eds), *Globalisierung in Zeiten der Aufklärung: Texte und Kontexte zur 'Berliner Debatte' um die Neue Welt (17./18. Jh.)*, 2 vols (Frankfurt am Main: Peter Lang Verlag, 2015), vol. 1, 27–55.

———. 'José Martís America oder Wege zu einem amerikanischen Humanismus', in Röseberg, D. (ed.), *El arte de crear memoria: Festschrift zum 80. Geburtstag von Hans-Otto Dill* (Berlin: Trafo-Wissenschafts-Verlag, 2015), 75–98.

Fitz, C.A., 'The Hemispheric Dimensions of Early U.S. Nationalism: The War of 1812, its Aftermath, and Spanish American Independence', *Journal for American History* 102 (2015), 356–79.

Fraser Terjanian, A., *Commerce and its Discontents in Eighteenth Century French Political Thought* (Cambridge: Cambridge University Press, 2013).

Garcilaso de la Vega, I., *Primera Parte de los Commentarios Reales que Tratan del Origen de los Yncas, Reyes, que fueron del Peru, de su Idolatria, Leyes y gouierno en paz y en guerra: sus vidas y conquistas, y de todo lo que fue aquel Imperio y su Republica, antes de que los Españoles passaran a el* (Lisbon: Pedro Crasbeeck, 1609).

———. *Historia general del Perú: trata el descubrimiento del, y como lo ganaron los Españoles. Guerras civiles que huvo entre Picarros, y Almagros, sobre la partija de la tierra. Castigo y levantamiento de tiranos; y otros sucessos particulares que en la Historia se contienen* (Córdoba: Viuda de Andrés Barrera, 1616).

Gerbi, A., *Dispute of the New World: The History of a Polemic, 1750–1900* (Pittsburgh: University of Pittsburgh Press, 1973).

Giddens, A., *The Constitution of Society: Outline of the Theory of Structuration* (Cambridge: Polity, 1984).

Gifford, P., and Hauswedell, T. (eds), *Europe and its Others: Essays on Interperception and Identity* (Frankfurt am Main: Peter Lang, 2010).

Hegel, G.W.F., *Vorlesungen über die Philosophie der Geschichte* (Berlin: Duncker & Humblot, 1848).

———. *Lectures on the Philosophy of World History* (Kitchener, Ontario: Batoche Books, 2001).

Heintz, B., 'Numerische Differenz: Überlegungen zu einer Soziologie des (quantitativen) Vergleichs', *Zeitschrift für Soziologie* 39 (2010), 162–81.

———. '"Wir leben im Zeitalter der Vergleichung": Perspektiven einer Soziologie des Vergleichs', *Zeitschrift für Soziologie* 45 (2016), 305–23.

Hume, D., 'Of National Characters', in *Essays, Moral, Political, and Literary*, 2 vols (London: Longmans, Greens and Co., 1889), vol. 1, 244–58.

Hunt, L., *Inventing Human Rights: A History* (New York: W.W. Norton & Company, 2008).

Jefferson, T., *Notes on the State of Virginia* (London: John Stockdale, 1787).

Koselleck, R., 'The Historical-Political Semantics of Asymmetric Counterconcepts', in *Futures Past: On the Semantics of Historical Time* (New York: Columbia University Press, 2004), 155–91.

Laviña, J., and Zeuske, M. (eds), *The Second Slavery: Mass Slaveries and Modernity in the Americas and in the Atlantic Basin* (Zürich: LIT Verlag, 2014).

Longxi, Z., 'Crossroads, Distant Killing, and Translation: On the Ethics and Politics of Comparison', in Felski, R. and Stanford Friedman, S. (eds), *Comparison: Theories, Approaches, Uses* (Baltimore: Johns Hopkins University Press, 2013), 46–63.

Lüsebrink, H.-J., 'De L'usage de la comparaison dans les écrits des Jésuites sur les Amériques', in Bernier, M.A., Donato, C. and Lüsebrink, H.-J. (eds), *Jesuit Accounts of the Colonial Americas: Intercultural Transfers, Intellectual Disputes, and Textualities* (Toronto: University of Toronto Press, 2014), 418–36.

Martí, J., 'Nuestra America', *Revista Ilustrada*, 1 January 1891.

Martínez, C., 'Usos del pasado y confiabilidad de las fuentes: Antoine-Joseph Pernety y la disputa sobre la naturaleza de América en el siglo XVIII', *Corpus* 5(2) (2015), retrieved 5 March 2019 from https://journals.openedition.org/corpusarchivos/1449.

Mignolo, W., *The Idea of Latin America* (Malden, MA: Wiley-Blackwell, 2005).

Mintz, S., *Sweetness and Power* (New York: Viking Press, 1985).

Montesquieu, C., *The Spirit of Laws. (De L'esprit des Loix)*, 19 vols (London: J. Nourse and P. Vaillant, 1773).

Perrault, C., *Parallèle des anciens et des modernes en ce qui regarde les arts et les sciences* (Paris: Jean Baptiste Coignard, 1693).

[Raynal, G.T.F.], *Histoire philosophique et politique des établissements & du commerce des européens dans les deux Indes* (Amsterdam: n.p., 1770).

———. *A philosophical and political history of the settlements and trade of the Europeans in the East and West Indies*, 2nd edn, 6 vols (London: A. Strahan, 1798).

Reinhard, W., 'Universale Xenophobie: Die Konstruktion des Anderen in der Geschichte', in Bernaschina, V., Kraft, T. and Kraume, A. (eds), *Globalisierung in Zeiten der Aufklärung: Texte und Kontexte zur 'Berliner Debatte' um die Neue Welt (17./18. Jh.)*, 2 vols (Frankfurt am Main: Peter Lang Verlag, 2015), vol. 1, 125–40.

Schatzki, T.R., Knorr-Cetina, K. and Savigny, E. (eds), *The Practice Turn in Contemporary Theory* (London: Routledge, 2001).

Stam, R., and Shohat, E., *Race in Translation: Culture Wars around the Postcolonial Atlantic* (New York: New York University Press, 2012).

Strohschneider, P., 'Fremde in der Vormoderne: Über Negierbarkeitsverluste und Unbekanntheitsgewinne', in Becker, A. (ed.), *Alterität als Leitkonzept für historisches Interpretieren* (Berlin: Akad.-Verl., 2012), 387–416.

Tocqueville, A. de, *Democracy in America. Second Part*, Reeve, H. (trans.) (London: Saunders and Otley, 1840).

Todorov, T., *The Conquest of America and the Question of the Other* (New York: Harper Perennial, 1992 [1982]).

Tytler, J., 'America', in *Encyclopaedia Britannica, 2nd Edition (1778–1784)*, reprinted in Bernaschina, V., Kraft, T. and Kraume, A. (eds), *Globalisierung in Zeiten der Aufklärung: Texte und Kontexte zur 'Berliner Debatte' um die Neue Welt (17./18. Jh.)*, 2 vols (Frankfurt am Main: Peter Lang Verlag, 2015), vol. 2, 229–43.

Validvia Orozco, P., 'Hypotheken des Wissens: José de Acosta und die Naturgeschichte', in Bernaschina, V., Kraft, T. and Kraume, A. (eds), *Globalisierung in Zeiten der Aufklärung: Texte und Kontexte zur 'Berliner Debatte' um die Neue Welt (17./18. Jh.)*, 2 vols (Frankfurt am Main: Peter Lang Verlag, 2015), vol. 1, 79–97.

Walker, D., *Walker's Appeal, in four articles* (Boston: D. Walker, 1830).

Zweig, S., *Amerigo: Die Geschichte eines historischen Irrtums* (Frankfurt am Main: Fischer Verlag, 1989 [1944]).

# 6

# European Colonial Empires and Victorian Imperial Exceptionalism

## Alex Middleton

Comparison has played a leading role in the scholarly study of European empires since the 1960s. Political and social scientists have spent the subsequent decades reaching across temporal and geographical boundaries to build models of 'empire' and 'imperialism',[1] while for the last thirty years students of comparative literature have been mesmerized by 'imperial' texts.[2] Historians of empire have also been impressed by the interpretative power of comparison, but their use of the tool has been more intermittent. Imperial history drew heavily on comparative approaches between the 1960s and the early 1980s, especially in accounts of competitive 'high' imperialism, in work on theories and ideologies of empire, and in imperial economic history.[3] For some years thereafter, historians became more preoccupied with specific imperial cultures (and how they were constructed, perceived and imagined), leaving less space for the imperial structures (constitutions, coercion, diplomacy, trade) that had more readily lent themselves to comparative study. But since the turn of the twenty-first century – thanks not least to the rise of new global and transnational histories, which emphasize connection and circulation – the comparative study of empires has been comprehensively revitalized, as historians have realized its potential to cast light on a series of fresh problems.[4]

Meta-level comparisons remain central to this more recent scholarship. But they are now complemented by an interest in how historical actors themselves used comparison as a rhetorical, political and intellectual tool.[5] Historians of imperial political ideas and argument have started to investigate, in an increasingly concerted way, how inter- and intra-imperial comparisons helped to shape (or at least to rationalize) the worldviews and actions of those involved with empires at all levels: from policy-makers and traders, to 'ordinary' subjects and resistance movements. Some of this writing has dealt with the already well-established subject of European attitudes towards the empires of the ancient world.[6] The most innovative studies, however, have been those that look at the complex imagined similarities and disparities between the various modern empires, established and aspiring, as well as at more abstract questions about what made imperial comparisons plausible and useful. In this work we see imperial administrators and party politicians devising concrete imperial policies, and constructing public appeals, on the basis of comparisons with other contemporary (or recently collapsed) empires; we see groups resisting imperial rule developing imagined solidarities with other movements rejecting 'empire' in distant parts of the globe; and we see theorists, scholars and commentators base influential arguments on comparisons between imperial formations.[7]

The burgeoning literature on these themes indicates that empires have been compared by their rulers, subjects and observers for almost as long as they have existed.[8] But there are several reasons why we might expect European imperial agents and commentators to have developed a sharper comparative consciousness during the phase of modern history with which this book deals. The most obvious is that there were simply more empires around. More than half a dozen European nations embarked upon or renewed projects of transoceanic imperial enterprise in the nineteenth century – namely France, Germany, Belgium, the Netherlands, Spain, Portugal and Italy. In the 1880s and 1890s, the scramble for new colonies among these nations reached an unprecedented level of intensity, while the United States and Japan also began to expand, in rivalry with and emulation of the European powers. But it was mainly the European empires which came into direct competition with one another for territory, in Africa and in the Pacific, and which in some cases came to share borders. Increasingly, they came to face analogous problems in shaping commercial policy, managing colonization, handling resistance and structuring government. Inter-imperial comparison was further promoted by a series of technological changes: railways and steamships facilitated intercolonial travel among administrators, missionaries, engineers, travel writers, businessmen and politicians, while the telegraph and developments in the international news media accelerated the volume and velocity of transfers of information.[9] Comparisons between empires assumed new functions in the early twentieth century, thanks to the development of international bodies which brought together representatives of the different imperial powers – all with axes to grind – while rapid decolonization after the Second World War encouraged the comparative analysis of imperial decline.[10]

These are some of the wider historiographical and geopolitical contexts for the present chapter, which deals with imperial comparison in nineteenth-century Britain. Victorian imperial politics and political ideas is now a crowded field of research. Most recent work, however, focuses on arguments about the British Empire itself, or about its relationship to the Greek and Roman Empires.[11] A smaller number of studies have dealt with British thinking about the empires of China, the Ottomans and the United States.[12] Virtually none say anything about what the Victorians made of contemporary European imperial expansion, decline and rule.[13] This is despite the fact that Europe is widely acknowledged to be the most significant international context for nineteenth-century British politics. It was the subject of far more domestic attention than the Americas, or the Middle East, or indeed the British Empire.[14] Part of the explanation for historians' disinclination to examine British views of Continental empires perhaps lies in axioms about the nature of British political culture. As Susan Pedersen has suggested, modern British historians often assume that while contemporary international comparison came naturally to the Germans and the French and the Russians, '[e]xcept at rare moments and among restricted circles … it did not come naturally to the British … who were always more likely to think historically than comparatively, and to judge their political institutions against some idealized version of their own past, or against classical examples'.[15] There is unquestionably something in this, on a general cultural level. But the picture is somewhat more complex in the case of imperial ideas.

The purpose of the present chapter is to show that the Victorians took European empires seriously, and that historians of Victorian imperial thought and politics should as well. The political and intellectual significance of European empires in nineteenth-century Britain grew and changed over time: boosted by the French return to paths of imperial conquest in Algeria in 1830, it peaked amidst the global competition between colonial powers in the 1880s and 1890s. Continental empires gradually took on central roles in long-running, cyclical debates about what made imperial rule work, what made it legitimate, and what role it played in world order. They were discussed in detail in relation to strategies of imperial conquest, global geopolitics, the making of international law, the bureaucratic and constitutional structures of imperial rule, the impacts of empires on their mother countries, the principal branches of imperial policy, and the relationships between empire and nationality. At the end of the nineteenth century, they began to play crucial roles in attempts to construct wider theories of 'imperialism' and ideologies of 'anti-imperialism'. So this is a big subject. This chapter leaves aside debates about the structures of state systems and global legal orders, in which empires necessarily played significant parts, but in which comparison was not always prominent. It focuses instead on more contingent arguments about European imperial expansion and government, in which comparison came more readily to the fore, and on the ways in which those comparisons helped British commentators discern what was distinctive about Britain's own imperial projects.

Nineteenth-century European 'empires' came in a wide variety of forms, and even individual empires rarely projected a coherent image.[16] Russian imperial autocracy had only so much in common with the scattered remnants of the Dutch colonial empire in the Far East, or the multinational territorial rule of Austria. The plebiscitary despotism of the French Second Empire at home looked quite different from the militaristic French regime in North Africa, while the British perceived sharp distinctions even between France's various trans-Mediterranean possessions. There are complex questions which currently lack answers about how far the Victorians saw these entities as belonging to a common political category, why they drew the lines they did between them, and under what conditions those lines shifted. What contemporaries made of the 'territorial', autocratic Continental empires (Napoleonic France, Austria, Prussia, Russia) *as* empires is a fascinating subject.[17] The focus of this chapter, however, is on attitudes towards transoceanic colonial empires: both as a starting point and because, thanks to the fact that Britain's empire was also transoceanic and colonial, these other seaborne empires seem to have attracted comfortably the most comparison with Britain's own.

The rest of this chapter looks at two sets of issues. First, it deals with some of the structures which conditioned imperial comparison in nineteenth-century Britain: where and when we find writing on European colonial empires, and the circumstances under which politicians and political writers took an interest in them. Second, the chapter turns to the characterization of European transoceanic empires, and the comparisons contemporaries drew between them and Britain's own imperial projects. The focus is squarely on mainstream elite political debate, especially in leading periodicals, newspapers, pamphlets and published books. The chapter does not deal with various subgroups – missionaries and humanitarians, for instance, or Irish nationalists – which might be expected to have different ideas about European imperial rule. The approach taken is to paint with a broad yet tentative brush, and to try to say something about the whole period of Britain's imperial pre-eminence, between the Vienna settlement of 1815 and the Boer War at the end of the century. There are, of course, other ways of handling this topic, not least through the more detailed analysis of comparisons with individual European empires or colonies, or through the study of particularly rich single texts or groups of texts.[18]

Victorian engagement with other European colonial empires was a complex phenomenon. It responded to overlapping academic, political, commercial, historical and rhetorical imperatives; it involved the analysis (or stereotyping) of a large range of distinct and sometimes internally incoherent political projects; and it stretched across a century that saw radical transformations in the international order, the structures of domestic politics and the emphases of imperial debate, all of which impacted significantly on its discursive dynamics. What this chapter argues is that if we raise our heads above these intricacies and aim at generalization, it is possible to identify a dominant mode of comparative engagement with European colonial empires, and that this can usefully be called 'exceptionalist'. The widely (though never universally) shared presumption of British imperial distinctiveness vis-à-vis Europe rested on deep-seated convictions among the political and literary classes about the British national character and political system, and especially about the superiority of independent initiative over state direction and intervention. The latter belief remained firm, in this imperial context, even during the last decades of the century, when the potential role of the state in British society was beginning to be rethought. The dominance of this broad exceptionalist mode is strikingly consistent across the period under review, though it was articulated in a range of different ways. For most of the century, it was expressed in writing on specific European empires and colonies; but in the 1880s and 1890s, we find writers beginning to talk in terms of a 'Continental' approach to overseas empire as a counterpoint to the 'British'. European colonial comparison, then, drew on and bolstered particular claims about national and imperial identity.

## Structures of Imperial Comparison

The first questions we need to consider are where writing on other contemporary European empires in nineteenth-century Britain was to be found, what forms it took, and how much of it there was. For the purposes of introduction, this writing can be roughly divided into two broad and somewhat overlapping categories: the 'scholarly' and the 'occasional'. The first describes writing that sought to impose some sort of academic rigour upon the discussion of Continental empires. This category encompasses, first, analyses that sought to deal at a level of some abstraction with the workings of 'colonial' and/or 'imperial' institutions, commerce and social structures. These did not emerge from that peculiar segment of the 'high' intellectual life of Victorian Britain that historians of political thought have imbued with special prominence and coherence. European transoceanic empires do not appear to have seriously troubled any of the leading nineteenth-century political and social thinkers: Jeremy Bentham's *Rid Yourselves of Ultramaria* is the only (borderline) 'canonical' text that engages at length with a foreign European empire. But political economists interested in colonies and colonization had a considerable amount to say about the strategies pursued by other modern colonial empires, as did a smaller collection of writers interested in elaborating a science of colonial government.[19] Compendia of statistics relating to other European empires, most of them produced later on in the century, also appear to have found a market.[20]

Histories of European colonial empires are the second major component part of this category of 'scholarly' engagement. Again, this is not a field in which we find major contributions from the most celebrated figures in the discipline. In fact, the pickings are relatively slim in general as far as full-dress, book-length or multivolume histories of single or multiple European empires are concerned, though these begin to emerge from the presses in somewhat greater numbers towards the end of the century.[21] Few of these texts would stand up to sustained historiographical analysis. One of the most ambitious in its sweep, Walter Frewen Lord's *The Lost Empires of the Modern World* of 1897, offered accounts of the Spanish, Portuguese, Dutch and French Empires; but not atypically, the book was explicitly motivated by a desire to demonstrate the comparative superiority of the British imperial project, a polemical purpose made unambiguously clear throughout the volume.[22] There is, however, a much larger and livelier tradition of writing on the history of European colonial empires squirreled away in periodical and travel literature, usually in the form of prolegomena or pendants to accounts of more recent developments. It varies enormously in terms of quality and scope, but some of the writing is impressively sophisticated. To this can be added the extremely numerous historical accounts of the British Empire, or of individual British colonies, in which historians and reviewers were compelled to discuss the other European empires with which their own nation's had come into contact. Many of these present only basic narratives, but a significant minority include meaningful elements of analysis or comparison.

Most Victorian writing on other European empires belonged to the 'occasional' category. It was found in the world of mainstream political commentary, in newspapers, periodicals, and (especially in the first half of the nineteenth century) pamphlets. There is a huge amount of this material, and shards of political and commercial information gleaned from Continental colonial empires are to be found all over the newspaper press. But there does not seem to have been any systematic reporting of news from within the colonies of other European empires, meaning that attempts at serious critical assessment tended to be sporadic. It is not unusual even at the end of the century to find commentators assuming broad ignorance of the workings, or even of the composition, of other European colonial empires. So it does not appear as though there was any sustained, sophisticated, evolving attempt to analyse the politics of these empires in the public press – unlike with, for instance, the domestic politics of France or the United States – in the same way that 'scholarly' publication did not come close to creating a fund of erudite knowledge comparable to that available about the great empires of antiquity. We are dealing here with a political discourse of a different species.

The second issue here, then, is about the circumstances in which British political writers did engage more seriously with European colonial projects. In short, European empires attracted the most sustained attention when it appeared to contemporaries that they might have the capacity to hamper or to advance wider British interests, understood geopolitically or commercially.[23] Flurries of commentary on Continental empire-building and imperial rule almost always responded to contemporary political events which could be interpreted in this way: the publication of 'scholarly' work was rarely able to shift the dial by itself. These outbreaks of analysis were much more regular in the closing decades of the nineteenth century than earlier on, thanks to empire having become a more significant issue in domestic politics, and the 'scramble for Africa' making the subject of other European empires more pressing for Britain. Often they dealt with technical aspects of imperial diplomacy, when the territorial claims of other countries intersected with British colonies or spheres of influence. Much was written, for instance, about Dutch claims in the Far East in the first half of the century, while the niceties of African partition from the 1870s caused endless gnashing of journalistic teeth.[24] But it tended to be larger regional questions, which raised issues about Britain's empire or its diplomatic and commercial relations, that generated the most ambitious analysis and sustained comparisons. So the Latin American colonies were a focus of debate in the era of their revolutions in the 1810s and 1820s;[25] the Dutch colonies in the Eastern Archipelago came to prominence when they were returned to their original owners after the conclusion of the Napoleonic Wars in 1815, and again when 'Rajah' James Brooke's controversial enterprise in Sarawak briefly became a domestic *cause célèbre* in the late 1840s and early 1850s;[26] while the German and Belgian Empires came into focus among British commentators when they became relevant to questions about Britain's destiny in Africa in the 1880s and 1890s. The French Empire represents a partial exception to this pattern, in that after the invasion of Algeria in 1830 it consistently attracted more attention among British commentators than any other European empire. This was partly because France was the single most important European foil for Britain in public political argument; partly because Algeria, always considered France's most important possession, was close enough that numerous British politicians and writers actually visited it; partly because there were specific comparisons to be drawn between practices of rule over different species of 'Orientals' in Algeria and in India; and partly because the French presented such a heartening series of object lessons in imperial failure.[27] Even so, many of France's acquisitions later in the century, not having any obvious bearing on British interests, attracted limited attention.

Nothing has been said so far about the roles played by the colonial empires of the Continent in more formal politics, parliamentary or popular. This is because they do not appear to have mattered very much in these arenas. References to European colonial empires in Parliament were relatively rare and often took the form of unrevealing passing remarks. Much the same seems to have been true of their place in platform speeches and electoral propaganda. Partly as a result, it is difficult to detect any party-political 'Liberal' or 'Conservative' position either on specific European colonial empires, or on Continental overseas empire-building as a whole. While writers of opposed party persuasions could read sharply different lessons in the course of French domestic politics, they found only one in the failures of the French colonial empire. It seems unlikely, then, that ideas about European colonial empires were a significant motivating factor behind partisan political activity. They mattered instead as part of the wider intellectual contexts within which that activity took place. As Victorian political historians have shown so effectively in the last thirty years, however, these contexts could play decisive roles in determining political outcomes and in reshaping political orders.[28]

Finally here, it needs to be noted that the stereotypes of other empires upon which British writers leant so heavily were not all purely British either in their genesis or their deployment. In many cases they circulated throughout Europe, and were accepted to a greater or lesser degree in a number of countries. British audiences gained partial sight of this wider culture of European imperial comparison through the press. We find, for instance, reports of critical Dutch commentary on German colonialism;[29] of German commentary on Portuguese Africa ('the rule of Portugal in Africa affords a good object lesson to the newer colonial powers how not to colonize');[30] and of Bismarck comparing French and English empire-building, to the advantage of the latter (and echoing many arguments that British writers habitually made).[31]

British writers were most interested, however, not in what foreign commentators had to say about one another's empires, but in what they had to say about Britain's. These comments, as reported domestically, fell into two broad categories. The first was flattery. A German writer in the *Contemporary Review* of 1897, who can stand for many others, can be found placing England as the 'undisputed leader' in modern colonization.[32] But also widely reported were references by Continental observers both to the supposed jealousy of the British towards other nations' expansionary ambitions, and to British imperial greed and perfidy more generally.[33] These accusations were hotly denied by most British commentators who took notice of them – and, indeed, in many cases appear to have been noticed only for the purpose of refutation. Sir George Goldie remarked indignantly in the face of one such set of charges in 1894 that 'most Englishmen are completely indifferent to the fact that France has now acquired, or rather excluded from foreign interference, nearly one-third of Africa'.[34] In examining British conceptions of other European empires, then, we are dealing not with a set of constructions specific to Britain, but rather with a subset of a larger collection of European stereotypes. Moreover, we are not dealing with a situation in which British and European discourses proceeded along similar lines as a consequence of similarities in imperial experience, national cultures and intellectual heritage, but rather with patterns of written representation coming into direct contact with one another. Nineteenth-century European writers drew upon, and contributed to, patterns of imperial representation which were formed, sustained and reconfigured within dynamic transnational networks of communication. In other words, we are here only scratching the surface of a wider set of intellectual dynamics. Acknowledging these complexities, this chapter aims only to deal with how imperial stereotypes, and the comparisons they underpinned, were connected with wider schemes of political thinking and analysis in Britain.

## European Empires and British Imperial Character

The second section of this chapter explores, in broad terms, how Victorian writers portrayed other contemporary European colonial empires, and how they compared Britain's imperial project with its Continental counterparts. Most British depictions of other European colonies were at least condescending, if not explicitly critical; and nearly all direct comparisons were to Britain's advantage. Explanations for why these European imperial projects had not fulfilled their promise rested primarily on claims about the national characters and political tendencies of the nations of the Continent – which is to say, on extending arguments already made about those countries in other contexts. These explanations were bolstered by more scientific contentions about strategies of imperial expansion, the nature of a properly enlightened colonial policy and the state of the art in the practice of colonial government.

Before coming to these arguments, it needs to be emphasized that Victorian imperial exceptionalism was also underpinned by broader assumptions about the place of Britain's empire in the sweep of history and the international order. Consistently, an imperial power since the sixteenth century and possessor of comfortably the largest and most successful transoceanic empire in the nineteenth-century world, British commentators were afflicted by none of the anxiety afflicting nations entering upon colonial empire for the first time about positioning themselves relative to the older imperial powers, or about learning lessons from them.[35] Blunt statistical comparisons between the relative size and wealth of the European colonial empires were fairly rare, but where drawn pointed clearly in Britain's favour.[36] So British commentators tended to assume that Britain would represent the natural model for Continental nations seeking to build empires.[37] Furthermore, British writers rarely perceived any serious political threat to the British colonies from the Continental empires.[38] The overwhelming majority of those who wrote about other European overseas empires were sanguine about what their existence and their (potential) expansion meant for Britain's imperial position.[39] It seemed unlikely to most commentators that European rapacity could ever threaten the integrity of the British possessions, or seriously harm British commerce.[40] Many observers suggested that a larger number of European overseas colonies simply meant more hostages to fortune in any future war, or that they represented a safety valve by which aggressive energies (and military spending) might be redirected outside of Europe, helping to safeguard peaceful relations on the Continent.[41] Calls for European imperial cooperation towards greater regional or global objectives were relatively common. It was rare for political writers to express any serious desire for Britain to appropriate colonies belonging to other nations: those who did usually presented such seizures as a regrettable necessity, consequent upon other countries' political incapacity.

Looking across the nineteenth century as a whole, the most sharply drawn European imperial portraits were those of the contemporary colonial empires that seemed to touch British political and commercial interests most closely – those of France, the Netherlands and Germany. These are dealt with in turn below. Two more particular cases are not treated in the same depth. The Iberian empires, first, had a rather more distinct history as a problem in British political thought, especially in the era of revolutions and dictators between c. 1800 and 1850, when the uncertain political fate of Latin America bore strongly on how they were characterized. Across the century, the Spanish were frequently described as the most intolerant and illiberal of all the European imperial powers; Portugal was charged with having lazily neglected splendid opportunities to develop its colonies over the course of centuries.[42] The reassertion of Spanish and Portuguese imperialism in Africa later in the century provided an occasion for renewed critical comment of a similar order, and both projects were fitted into the wider critique of 'Continental' empire which emerged towards the end of the century.[43] The other more specific case, also not dealt with in detail here, is that of the Congo Free State under King Leopold of Belgium. This transformation of this project into a humanitarian *cause célèbre* at the very end of the nineteenth century, a subject on which there is already a large literature, made the colony stand out in Britain as a political and intellectual problem of a different order.

Among the Victorians, the most extensively discussed and clearly characterized European colonial empire was that of France. Thanks to the apparently parlous state of French Canada in the eighteenth century, the French had already acquired a bad reputation as colonizers by the time of Waterloo; but it was with the invasion of Algeria in 1830 that the critique of their imperial efforts took on a more clearly defined form.[44] British writers were very generally convinced that the French were both temperamentally and politically incapable of colonizing.[45] They lacked the capacity for hard work, sacrifice and self-reliance that the founding of colonies required: war and not colonization was their genius.[46] Even leading scholarly authorities like J.R. Seeley were prepared to endorse the commonplace that the French possessed 'a deficiency of genuine colonising power'.[47] The instability of France's domestic government, which had profound knock-on effects overseas, made the development of the French colonies immensely difficult.[48] But this was only part of the problem, because the policy they sought to pursue in their empire was thoroughly ill-conceived, always turning out 'fitful and weak'.[49] A misguided taste for centralization and a harmful desire for political symmetry were thought, across the century, to be the radical flaws in the French system.[50] A worrying consequence of all this was that the French colonies consistently drained vast sums of money from the mother country, never coming close to being self-sustaining. They might serve as a useful safety valve for French militarism, but they were otherwise a financial, political and social abyss.

Dutch colonial rule was rather different. The Netherlands was widely seen to stand apart from the more unpleasant tendencies of Continental political and social life – having in some ways more in common with Britain – but the Dutch were not rated as colonizers. Their empire was not such an unmitigated failure as that of France, since it seemed at least to make itself pay. But it was seen to be dominated by a narrow, exclusive, commercial spirit, and by unrestrained rapacity, which left no room for the more uplifting elements of imperial rule.[51] British commentators pitied the inhabitants of the colonies being returned by Britain to the Dutch after their occupation during the Napoleonic Wars.[52] Similar negative assessments permeated writing about the Dutch in the 1840s, seeming to reflect an anxiety to differentiate Britain from the errors of another once-hegemonic, commercially driven, seafaring empire. The Dutch had achieved power in the Eastern seas, British writers asserted, by 'totally unscrupulous methods', a 'cruel and selfish policy' or simply by 'inhumanity'.[53] They were without a vision for the region, possessing 'neither the power nor the disposition to look beyond the interests of their present paltry monopolies'.[54] They were more concerned with petty boundary claims than the advancement of their subjects.[55] Ultimately, claimed one writer in 1850, 'the Dutch have illustrated by their policy a principle of conquest the very reverse of ours'.[56] There was less interest in Dutch colonial rule after the middle of the century, when it had ceased to be so relevant to British imperial and commercial interests; but when it did come up for discussion, the picture had become little more prepossessing. Charles Dilke, for instance, can be found dilating in his celebrated *Greater Britain* of 1868 on the 'plunder, slavery, and famine' that invariably followed in the wake of the Dutch system of imperial government.[57]

Reflection on German colonization dwelt almost as much on the contexts in which it was pursued as on the character of the nation it involved and the systems it sought to institute. It was clear that the Germans, as a people, *did* know how to colonize, possessing many of the required national qualities that the French so conspicuously lacked. This had been demonstrated beyond doubt in America and elsewhere.[58] They had, however, entered the game on their own account too late. By the 1880s, there were no attractive territories for settler colonization left on the globe.[59] It was difficult, moreover, to imagine the tropical colonies Germany had founded becoming entities of any national importance: empire appeared for the Germans to be a 'hobby', rather than a serious political project.[60] One commentator approvingly cited the 'epigrammatic comparison that England has both colonists and colonies, Germany colonists but no colonies, and France colonies but no colonists'.[61] Germany's violent and disrespectful handling of native races, however, also attracted extensive critical comment.[62] German colonization was a subject of particularly sustained interest among proponents of Imperial Federation, who worried that the British Empire was not popular enough among the British public, and who were intrigued that the German Empire seemed to have greater mass appeal.[63]

The explicit identification of a 'Continental' approach to colonial empire appears to have been mainly a phenomenon of the closing decades of the Victorian era. Certainly this was because there were more, and more assertive, European empires around to be fitted into the category. It also seems to have been, in part, a result of the fact that the settler colonies assumed such primacy in British discourse about empire from the 1870s onwards: the new emphasis placed on a category of colony almost exclusive to Britain helping to sharpen divisions with the Continent. But the stereotype of 'Continental' empire-building drew on arguments made about colonial projects of all kinds across the century, and added little that was new. Continental empires were disappointingly prone to adopting mistaken protective commercial systems, and had little genius for trade.[64] With the (significant) exception of the Dutch, financial management was an Achilles' heel: nobody else could make colonies viable.[65] Continental systems of colonial government also shared certain features. In particular – and in line with assumptions about the defining features of domestic administration on the Continent itself – they tended to be dominated at least by bureaucracy, and very often by militarism.[66] The German colonist, like most others, was 'overridden by officialdom'.⁶⁷ These tendencies frequently led to corruption, brutality, and immorality among colonial officials.⁶⁸ Another shared characteristic of other European colonial empires, indeed, was a capacity for inhumanity towards natives which British officials did not possess – although the worst rumours of 'wholesale and monstrous cruelties', from the Congo Free State, went beyond what most were capable of.⁶⁹

Specific comparisons were drawn between British practices and each element of this political demonology. But comparison with the 'Continental' empires was also used to teach larger lessons about what made the British Empire what it was. Comparison was used, in particular, to underline the peculiar gifts of the British as a people in the founding, peopling and governing (or self-governing) of (mainly) settler colonies, and to highlight the advantages of the state leaving those colonies well alone. It was widely argued that the founding of successful colonies was a natural and inevitable part of Britain's historical development; the nation had 'drifted' into possession of the parts of the world best suited for colonization.⁷⁰ The Continental nations, by contrast, pursued colonies out of vanity, or a futile desire to seize the spirit of the age. Sharp contrasts were drawn between the way in which republican France had been seized by 'the lust of empire', where Britain's colonial development had been guided rather by 'the spirit of genuine colonial enterprise';⁷¹ Germany's search after colonies was 'no part of her national history'.⁷² A passage from an article by Charles de Thierry in the *New Review* of 1897 elegantly epitomizes thinking on this theme at the end of the century:

> In these days Colonies are either exotic or a natural development. To the former class belong the Colonies of Continental Europe; to the latter the Colonies of England. In the one case sickly dependencies are born of, and sustained by, the brilliant policy of the Home Government. In the other States grow and flourish by means of forces generated within themselves. France and Germany have Colonies because they are resolved that Colonies they will have; England has Colonies because she cannot help herself. That is to say, Continental statesmanship encourages the growth of Empire, Downing Street restrains it ... the difference is that between national destiny working through the spontaneous efforts of individuals, and national vanity working through a government.⁷³

The use of 'Colonies of Continental Europe' as an imperial category dates the analysis; but the threads of its argument, as expressed more specifically in earlier decades with regard to individual European colonies, permeate the whole century. With Britain, as another writer put it, 'private enterprise has taken the lead and Government activity has followed, while with others the process has generally been the reverse'.⁷⁴ Continentals might think that empires were to be founded on the genius of statesmen and diplomats, but the British knew better.⁷⁵ Comparison with these contemporary competitors both demonstrated to the British that their empire was exceptional, and helped them to construct an interpretation of why that was.

Not every British assessment of the other European colonial empires was unrelentingly critical, or placed Britain as the unambiguous leader in imperial expansion and rule. There were certain foreign possessions that tended to attract more positive assessments. Many British commentators saw Tunis, for instance, as a more hopeful prospect for France at the end of the century, and as offering potentially useful hints about the structuring of protectorates.[76] As this suggests, some writers – especially boosters and propagandists of other empires – did argue that the British might be able to learn something from comparisons with their competitors.[77] The Boer War seems to have increased the appetite for this kind of practical comparison: several writers suggested that Kitchener might look at the German Empire as a model for how to resettle South Africa.[78] But most Continental comparisons deployed as a means of highlighting British imperial shortcomings took the form of suggestions that Britain had descended to the level of the inferior European empires. Critics of James Brooke suggested that he had 'substituted the approved worthless system of Holland for the approved rational and beneficial system of England … and [that] his coercion has been of an infinitely more reckless and ruthless character than that of the Dutch'.[79] Schemes of self-government for Britain's settler colonies that seemed to reserve too much power to central authority were damned as 'Algerian'.[80] Threaded through Victorian writing on the British Empire is a sense that colonial rule on the Continental model was a pathology, which misguided British imperial servants or statesmen might conceivably fall into emulating, and which needed to be resisted. So these rhetorical comparisons contributed further to a sense of Britain's imperial exceptionalism. They belong to that enormously powerful strand of 'anti-imperialism' in Victorian Britain, in which the issue was not the illegitimacy of empire as a political form, but Britain's failure to live up to its supposedly matchless potential as a colonizing and ruling power.[81]

## Conclusion

This chapter has sought to stake out a subject rather than to exhaust it. Its main aim has been to show that there is an intellectual and political history to be written of Victorian engagement with the empires of Continental Europe. But it has also made some suggestions, all tentative, about the structures which conditioned British political writers' engagement with contemporary European colonial projects, the characterization of those projects, and the principal lessons taught by comparison between British and European overseas imperial rule.

Most mainstream public writers who compared the British and European colonial empires did so to the clear advantage of the former. They found a variety of reasons for doing so, and a range of explanations for Britain's comparative imperial success: the most common seems to have been that Britain's imperial projects were defined by, and rendered fruitful by, the energies of the people rather than the interventions of government. So they extended the critique of Continental over-government (and in some cases arbitrary rule and/or militarism), which is such a conspicuous feature of the Victorian intellectual landscape, to the colonial sphere – and in doing so helped to obscure the fact that many British colonies were just as centralized as were their European counterparts.[82] The general argumentative and analytic thrust of these European imperial comparisons appears to have been remarkably stable across the nineteenth century. But there is clearly much more to say about how the transformation of the British political order in the 1870s and 1880s – with the onset of 'high' imperialism, the emergence of empire as a front-rank domestic political issue, the rethinking of the virtues of statism and the end of Liberal political dominance – affected engagement with European imperial expansion and rule. It may be that these preliminary impressions require correction.

Enough has been said, however, to indicate that historians need to integrate the Continental empires into our picture of Victorian imperial thought. The existing historiography gives the European imperial world only sideways glances, but Victorian engagement with that world clearly helped to shape attitudes towards fundamental issues about the nature of empire, colonization and imperial government, and to frame anti-imperial critiques. We need to understand how this worked, not least by charting the relative imaginative significance of European empires against the ancient and American variants. In the process, we are likely to have to rethink the relations between the 'imperial' and 'foreign' dimensions of Victorian public politics, not to mention the role of attitudes towards the past, in a more far-reaching way.

**Alex Middleton** is the M.G. Brock Junior Research Fellow at Corpus Christi College, Oxford. His work focuses on nineteenth-century British political and intellectual history, and particularly on debates over imperial government, expansion and decline. He is finishing a book on British Politics and Imperial Government, 1828–1857, and is in the early stages of new projects on Victorian attitudes towards European empires of all kinds – territorial and transoceanic, contemporary and historic – and on Latin America in British political thought, c. 1800–50.

## Notes

1. Influential examples include: M.W. Doyle, *Empires* (Ithaca: Cornell University Press, 1996); J. Osterhammel, *Colonialism: A Theoretical Overview* (Princeton: M. Wiener, 1997); M. Hardt and A. Negri, *Empire* (Cambridge, MA: Harvard University Press, 2000); and R. Kiely, *Rethinking Imperialism* (Basingstoke: Palgrave Macmillan, 2010). For a survey of recent developments see J. Pitts, 'Political Theory of Empire and Imperialism', *Annual Review of Political Science* 13 (2010), 211–35.
2. Most famously E. Said's *Orientalism* (New York: Pantheon Books, 1978) and *Culture and Imperialism* (London: Chatto & Windus, 1993). More recent examples include J. Hart, *Comparing Empires: European Colonialism from Portuguese Expansion to the Spanish-American War* (New York: Palgrave Macmillan, 2003); P. Kerslake, *Science Fiction and*

*Empire* (Liverpool: Liverpool University Press, 2007); and Y. Siddiqi, *Anxieties of Empire and the Fiction of Intrigue* (New York: Columbia University Press, 2008).
3. See e.g. A.P. Thornton, *Doctrines of Imperialism* (New York: John Wiley & Sons, 1965); D.K. Fieldhouse, *The Colonial Empires: A Comparative Survey from the Eighteenth Century* (London: Weidenfeld & Nicolson, 1966); W. Baumgart, *Imperialism: The Idea and Reality of British and French Colonial Expansion, 1880–1914* (Oxford: Oxford University Press, 1982); V.G. Kiernan, *European Empires from Conquest to Collapse, 1815–1960* (Leicester: Leicester University Press, 1982); A. Pagden, *Lords of All the World: Ideologies of Empire in Spain, Britain and France, c. 1500–c. 1800* (New Haven: Yale University Press, 1995).
4. On the new global history, see J. Belich et al. (eds), *The Prospect of Global History* (Oxford: Oxford University Press, 2016); R. Drayton and D. Motadel, 'Discussion: The Futures of Global History', *Journal of Global History* 13 (2018), 1–21. Key contributions to, and summaries of, this renaissance of comparative analysis in imperial history include: J. Leonhard and U. von Hirschhausen (eds), *Comparing Empires: Encounters and Transfers in the Long Nineteenth Century* (Göttingen: Vandenhoeck and Ruprecht, 2010); M. Fitzpatrick (ed.), *Liberal Imperialism in Europe* (Basingstoke: Palgrave Macmillan, 2012); B. Porter, *Empire and Superempire: Britain, America and the World* (New Haven: Yale University Press, 2006); J. Burbank and F. Cooper, *Empires in World History: Power and the Politics of Difference* (Princeton: Princeton University Press, 2010); the review article by A. Morrison, 'The Pleasures and Pitfalls of Colonial Comparisons', *Kritika: Explorations in Russian and Eurasian History* 13 (2012), 919–36; J. Pitts, *A Turn to Empire: the Rise of Imperial Liberalism in Britain and France* (Princeton: Princeton University Press, 2005); J. Darwin, *After Tamerlane: The Global History of Empire since 1405* (London: Allen Lane, 2007); B. Sèbe, *Heroic Imperialists in Africa: The Promotion of British and French Colonial Heroes, 1870–1939* (Manchester: Manchester University Press, 2013); J.M. MacKenzie, *European Empires and the People: Popular Responses to Imperialism in France, Britain, the Netherlands, Belgium, Germany and Italy* (Manchester: Manchester University Press, 2011); P.A. Kramer, 'Power and Connection: Imperial Histories of the United States in the World', *American Historical Review* 116 (2011), 1348–91; R. Ross, 'Legal Communications and Imperial Governance: British North America and Spanish America Compared', in C. Tomlins and M. Grossberg (eds), *The Cambridge History of Law in America, Volume 1: Early America, 1580–1815* (Cambridge, 2008), 104–43.
5. Key methodological statements include A.L. Stoler, 'Tense and Tender Ties: The Politics of Comparison in North American History and (Post) Colonial Studies', *Journal of American History* 88 (2001), 829–65; A.L. Stoler and C. McGranahan, 'Introduction: Refiguring Imperial Terrains', in A.L. Stoler, C. McGranahan and P.C. Perdue (eds), *Imperial Formations* (Santa Fe: School of American Research Press, 2007), 3–47, at 4–5 and 13–15.
6. On the ancient empires, see, recently, K. Kumar, 'Greece and Rome in the British Empire: Contrasting Role Models', *Journal of British Studies* 51 (2012), 76–101; C. Hagerman, *Britain's Imperial Muse: The Classics, Imperialism, and the Indian Empire, 1784–1914* (Basingstoke: Palgrave Macmillan, 2013).
7. For a sense of the range of this now large literature, see V. Dimier, *Le Gouvernement des Colonies: Regards Croisés Franco-Brittaniques* (Brussels: Éditions de l'Université Libre de Bruxelles, 2004); B. Naranch and G. Eley, *German Colonialism in a Global Age* (Durham, NC: Duke University Press, 2014); C.S. Maier, *Among Empires: American Ascendency and its Predecessors* (Cambridge, MA: Harvard University Press, 2006); A. Morrison, 'Russian Rule in Turkestan and the Example of British India, c. 1860–1917', *Slavonic and East*

*European Review* 84 (2006), 666–707; G. Paquette, 'Views from the South: Images of Britain and its Empire in Portuguese and Spanish Political Discourse, c. 1740–1810', in S. Reinert and P. Røge (eds), *Political Economy and Empire* (London: Palgrave Macmillan, 2013), 76–104; S. Mizutani, 'Anti-colonialism and the Contested Politics of Comparison: Rabindranath Tagore, Rash Behari Bose and Japanese Colonialism in Korea in the Interwar Period', *Journal of Colonialism and Colonial History* 16(1) (2015), n.p.; I. Tyrrell and J. Sexton (eds), *Empire's Twin: U.S. Anti-imperialism from the Founding Era to the Age of Terrorism* (Ithaca: Cornell University Press, 2015); T. Mason Roberts, 'The Role of French Algeria in American Expansion during the Early Republic', *Journal of the Western Society for French History* 43 (2015), 153–64; and very recently M. Thomas and R. Toye, *Arguing about Empire: Imperial Rhetoric in Britain and France, 1882–1956* (Oxford: Oxford University Press, 2017); and P. Bernhard, 'Colonial Crossovers: Nazi Germany and its Entanglements with Other Empires', *Journal of Global History* 12 (2017), 206–27. All this work is closely connected with an even more expansive literature dealing with inter- (and intra-) imperial networks, connections, and circuits: see e.g. V. Barth and R. Cvetkovski, *Imperial Co-operation and Transfer: Empires and Encounters, 1870–1930* (London: Bloomsbury, 2015).

8. D. Armitage, *The Ideological Origins of the British Empire* (Cambridge: Cambridge University Press, 2000); J.H. Elliott, *Empires of the Atlantic World: Britain and Spain in America, 1492–1830* (New Haven: Yale University Press, 2006); S. Muthu (ed.), *Empire and Modern Political Thought* (Cambridge: Cambridge University Press, 2012); A. Pagden, *The Burdens of Empire. 1539 to the Present* (Oxford: Oxford University Press, 2015); R. Bourke, *Empire and Revolution: The Political Life of Edmund Burke* (Princeton: Princeton University Press, 2015), Chapter 4.

9. For an argument about how these changes were imagined, see D. Bell, 'Dissolving Distance: Technology, Space, and Empire in British Political Thought, 1770–1900', *Journal of Modern History* 77 (2005), 523–62; and on international news, see A. Asseraf, 'La société coloniale face à l'actualité internationale : diffusion, contrôle, usages (1881–1899)', *Revue d'histoire moderne et contemporaine* 63 (2016), 110–32.

10. S. Pedersen, *The Guardians: The League of Nations and the Crisis of Empire* (Oxford: Oxford University Press, 2015); A.R. Forclaz, *Humanitarian Imperialism: The Politics of Anti-slavery Activism, 1880–1940* (Oxford: Oxford University Press, 2015); M.C. Thomas, 'A Path Not Taken? British Perspectives on French Colonial Violence after 1945', in L.J. Butler and S. Stockwell (eds), *The Wind of Change: Harold Macmillan and British Decolonization* (Basingstoke: Palgrave Macmillan, 2013), 140–58; M.C. Thomas and R. Toye, *Rhetorics of Empire: Languages of Colonial Conflict after 1900* (Manchester: Manchester University Press, 2017). See also K. Barkey and M. von Hagen, *After Empire: Multiethnic Societies and Nation-Building: The Soviet Union and the Russian, Ottoman, and Habsburg Empires* (Boulder: Westview Press, 1997).

11. For the state of the field, see D. Bell, *Reordering the World: Essays on Liberalism and Empire* (Princeton: Princeton University Press, 2016), Chapters 1–2 and 4.

12. R.G. Forman, *China and the Victorian Imagination: Empires Entwined* (Cambridge: Cambridge University Press, 2013); J.P. Parry, 'Disraeli, the East, and Religion: *Tancred* in Context', *English Historical Review* 132 (2017), 570–604; D. Bell, 'From Ancient to Modern in Victorian Imperial Thought', *Historical Journal* 49 (2006), 735–59.

13. That is, beyond the high-political sphere of imperial diplomacy. A few relevant articles deal with wider patterns of thought in the early decades of the century: notably P.J. Marshall, 'British Assessments of the Dutch in Asia in the Age of Raffles', *Itinerario*

12 (1988), 1–16; G. Paquette, 'The Intellectual Context of British Recognition of the South American Republics, c. 1800–1830', *Journal of Transatlantic Studies* 2 (2004), 75–95. From a different angle and on the eighteenth century, see S. Conway, '"Founded in Lasting Interests: British Projects for European Imperial Collaboration in the Age of the American Revolution', *International History Review* 37 (2015), 22–40.
14. B. Porter, '"Bureau and Barrack": Early Victorian Attitudes towards the Continent', *Victorian Studies* 27 (1984), 407–33; J. Parry, *The Politics of Patriotism: English Liberalism, National Identity, and Europe, 1830–1886* (Cambridge: Cambridge University Press, 2006). See also L. Tabili, 'A Homogenous Society? Britain's Internal "Others", 1800–Present', in C. Hall and S.O. Rose (eds), *At Home with the Empire: Metropolitan Culture and the Imperial World* (Cambridge: Cambridge University Press, 2006), 53–76, at 59–62.
15. S. Pedersen, 'What is Political History Now?', in D. Cannadine (ed.), *What is History Now?* (Basingstoke: Palgrave Macmillan, 2005), 36–56, at 47. See also M. Bentley, 'The British State and its Historiography', in W. Blockmans and J.-P. Benet (eds), *Visions sur le développement des états européens : theories et historiographies de l'état modern* (Rome: École française de Rome), 153–68.
16. For some early thoughts on this problem, see the classic work by R. Koebner and H.D. Schmidt, *Imperialism: The Story and Significance of a Political Word, 1840–1960* (Cambridge: Cambridge University Press, 1964).
17. For starting points, see S. Semmel, *Napoleon and the British* (New Haven: Yale University Press, 2004); P. Mandler, *The English National Character: The History of an Idea from Edmund Burke to Tony Blair* (Cambridge: Cambridge University Press, 2006), 61–62.
18. I have employed the former strategy elsewhere, in A. Middleton, 'French Algeria in British Imperial Thought, 1830–1870', *Journal of Colonialism and Colonial History* 16(1) (2015), n.p.
19. H. Merivale, *Lectures on Colonization and Colonies*, 2 vols (London: Longman, Orme, Brown, Green, and Longmans, 1841), and see also e.g. 'Colonial Policy: Mr. Huskisson's Colonial Trade Bill, 1828', *Monthly Magazine* 5 (1828), 259–74; G.C. Lewis, *An Essay on the Government of Dependencies* (London: John Murray, 1841); J.A. Roebuck, *The Colonies of England: A Plan for the Government of Some Portion of our Colonial Dependencies* (London: John W. Parker, 1849); R.M. Martin, *Colonial Policy of the British Empire: Part I. Government* (London: Gilbert and Rivington, 1837). On the prevalence of this kind of material, see M. Proudman, 'The Most Important History: The *American Historical Review* and Our English Past', *Journal of the Historical Society* 6(2) (2006), 177–211, at 185; and on the subject of nineteenth-century 'political science' more generally, see S. Collini, D. Winch and J. Burrow, *That Noble Science of Politics: A Study in Nineteenth-Century Intellectual History* (Cambridge: Cambridge University Press, 1983).
20. E.g. Sir R.W. Rawson, *British and Foreign Colonies* (London: Edward Stanford, 1884); J. Bonwick, *French Colonies and Their Resources* (London: Street & Co., 1886); and, earlier on, J. Macgregor, *Holland and the Dutch Colonies* (London: Whittaker and Co., 1848).
21. E.g. C.B. Norman, *Colonial France* (London: W.H. Allen & Co., 1886); A. D'Orsey, *Portuguese Discoveries, Dependencies, and Missions in Asia and Africa* (London: W.H. Allen & Co., 1893); R.G. Watson, *Spanish and Portuguese South America during the Colonial Period*, 2 vols (London: Trübner & Co., 1884). For an earlier, bitterly anti-imperial text, see W. Howitt, *Colonization and Christianity: A Popular History of the Treatment of the Natives by the Europeans in all their Colonies* (London: Longman, Orme, Brown, Green, & Longmans, 1838).

22. W.F. Lord, *The Lost Empires of the Modern World: Essays in Imperial History* (London: Richard Bentley and Son, 1897). See also 'Lost Empires', *The Academy* 1333 (1897), 422; W.F. Lord, *England and France in the Mediterranean, 1660–1830* (London: Sampson Low, Marston and Company, 1901). Comparable schoolbook accounts can also be found: see e.g. E.J. Payne, *History of European Colonies* (London: Macmillan and Co., 1877).
23. See e.g. 'The Colonies of Germany', *Chamber's Journal* 14(715) (1897), 590–92, at 590.
24. S.P. Oliver, *Madagascar as a French Colony* (unknown publisher, 1896); F.W. Chesson, 'The Dispute between England and Portugal', *St. James's Magazine* 13 (1874), 492–501; 'The Portuguese in Africa', *Anti-slavery Reporter* 3 (1883), 107; L. Cordeiro, *Portugal and the Congo: A Statement* (London: Edward Stanford, 1883).
25. 'Spain and Her Colonies', *Quarterly Review* 17 (1817), 530–62; 'Southey's History of Brazil', *Critical Review* 5 (1817), 327–48; 'Spanish America', *British Review, and London Critical Journal* 13 (1819), 150–95. For the context, see M. Brown and G. Paquette (eds), *Connections after Colonialism: Europe and Latin America in the 1820s* (Tuscaloosa: University of Alabama Press, 2013).
26. A. Middleton, 'Rajah Brooke and the Victorians', *Historical Journal* 53 (2010), 381–400.
27. Middleton, 'French Algeria'.
28. Still the best demonstrations of this point remain J.P. Parry, *Democracy and Religion: Gladstone and the Liberal Party, 1867–1875* (Cambridge: Cambridge University Press, 1986), and B. Hilton, *The Age of Atonement: The Influence of Evangelicalism on Social and Economic Thought, 1795–1865* (Oxford: Oxford University Press, 1988).
29. J.L. Bashford, 'German Colonies and Naval Power', *Fortnightly Review* 72 (1902), 622–36, at 626.
30. O. Lenz, 'A German View of Portuguese Africa', *Review of Reviews* 1 (1890), 295.
31. 'The Colonial Policy of Germany', letter to *The Economist*, 12 July 1884, 844. Cf. 'The Colonial Policy of Germany', *The Economist*, 28 June 1884, 775–76.
32. Baron [E.C.] von der Brüggen, 'The Colonial Movement in Germany', *Contemporary Review* 47 (1885), 40–50, at 40. See also 'A French Tribute to Our African Empire', *Review of Reviews*, November 1898, 476; and for an earlier example, see F. von Raumer, *Italien: Beiträge zur Kenntnis dieses Landes*, 2 vols (Leipzig: F.M. Brockhaus, 1840), vol. 2, 265–66, as brought to domestic notice in *The Athenaeum*, 1 August 1840, 609.
33. Bashford, 'German Colonies and Naval Power', 622–23; P. de Coubertin, 'England and France', *Fortnightly Review* 69 (1901), 1013–21, at 1016; 'Lost Empires', *The Academy* 1333 (1897), 422; C. De Thierry, 'Colonial Empires', *New Review* 17 (1897), 151–62, at 153.
34. Sir G.T. Goldie, *French Ambitions in Africa* (1894; reprinted from the *Asiatic Quarterly Review*), 10.
35. See e.g. F. Bösch, '"Are We a Cruel Nation?" Colonial Practices, Perceptions, and Scandals', in D. Geppert and R. Gerwarth (eds), *Wilhelmine Germany and Edwardian Britain: Essays on Cultural Affinity* (Oxford: Oxford University Press, 2008), 115–40.
36. See e.g. the unambiguous graphic provided in C.B. Norman, 'The Colonies of France', *Nineteenth Century* 15 (1884), 873–96, at 895–96.
37. R.D. Melville, 'Aspects of Empire and Colonisation', *Westminster Review* 150 (1898), 363–76, at 365; H. Birchenough, 'The Expansion of Germany', *Nineteenth Century* 43 (1898), 182–91, at 185; L. Stephen (ed.), *Letters of John Richard Green* (London: Macmillan and Co., 1901), 348.
38. Such threats tended, in any case, to focus attention on the British colonies threatened rather than the empires doing the threatening: see Parry, *Politics of Patriotism*, 3. There

was more anxiety about imperial defence towards the end of the century: see e.g. Norman, *Colonial France*, v; J.C. Rickett, 'Liberalism and Empire', *Contemporary Review* 74 (1898), 290–96, at 292–93.
39. E.g. G. Baden-Powell on German colonialism: 'It is the legitimate overflow of a nation, and it is conducted on enlightened and unselfish principles': 'The Expansion of Germany', *Nineteenth Century* 16 (1884), 869–78, at 876. See also 'The Colonial Policy of Germany', *Saturday Review* 58(1497) (1884), 6–7.
40. Though some suggested that the Germans might want to occupy part of South Africa: C.E. Dawkins, 'The German Abroad', *National Review* 5 (1885), 259–67, at 265. On the ambitions of French officers and the French 'colonial party' to chase the British from their African territories, see also Goldie, *French Ambitions in Africa*, 4.
41. Birchenough, 'The Expansion of Germany', 188; Goldie, *French Ambitions in Africa*, 10; 'The European Powers in West Africa', *Edinburgh Review* 188 (1898), 465–93, at 489–90.
42. 'The Insurrection in Cuba', *Examiner* 3316 (1871), 823; Melville, 'Aspects of Empire and Colonisation', 371. See also *The Athenaeum*, 25 December 1847, 1317. For earlier views, see G. Paquette, 'The Image of Imperial Spain in British Political Thought, 1750–1800', *Bulletin of Spanish Studies* 81 (2004), 187–214.
43. 'Portugal's Aggressions and England's Duty', *Fortnightly Review* 47 (1890), 136–48, at 147–48; J.E.C. Bodley, 'The Portuguese in East Africa', *Blackwood's Edinburgh Magazine* 146 (1888), 142–58, at 143; 'Treatment of Natives in Portuguese Africa', *Anti-slavery Reporter* 20 (1900), 161–63.
44. See Middleton, 'French Algeria'. For French criticism of the Algerian project, see J.E. Sessions, *By Sword and Plow: France and the Conquest of Algeria* (Ithaca: Cornell University Press, 2011).
45. Norman, 'The Colonies of France'.
46. J. Adye, 'The Colonial Weakness of France', *Nineteenth Century* 45 (1899), 55–66, at 60.
47. J.R. Seeley, *The Expansion of England: Two Courses of Lectures* (London: Macmillan and Co., 1904 edn), 148.
48. Geffcken, 'The Colonial Policy of France', *New Review* 6 (1892), 723–31, at 729; 'The Colonial Policy of France', *Edinburgh Review* 177 (1893), 354–88, at 376.
49. 'The Colonial Policy of France', *The Economist*, 28 October 1882, 1330–31.
50. 'The Colonial Policy of France', *Edinburgh Review*, 381–83.
51. 'Present Situation and Future Prospects of the Dutch Colonies in the East', *Oriental Herald and Journal of General Literature* 11 (1826), 85–90; 'A Statistical Account of the Cape of Good Hope', *Oriental Herald and Journal of General Literature* 23 (1829), 379–91.
52. 'They know that the British government put an end to the cruel rapaciousness of public servants, and broke the yoke of their tyrannical chiefs; that it no longer permitted their blood and sweat to be farmed out to Chinese taskmasters, nor drafted them off, manacled in slave ships, to perish under arms amid the miasmata of the capital. They know that their former masters did and permitted all this, together with other cruelties revolting to humanity': 'Raffles' History of Java', *British Review, and London Critical Journal* 11 (1818), 61–87, 84.
53. [A. Knox], 'Dutch Diplomacy and Indian Piracy', *Edinburgh Review* 96 (1852), 54–95, at 58, 60, 72.
54. *Chambers' Edinburgh Journal* 116 (1846), 180.
55. [H. St. John], 'English and Dutch in the Indian Archipelago', *Tait's Edinburgh Magazine* 16 (1849), 1–8, at 6.

56. 'Rajah Brooke and Borneo', *Chambers' Papers for the People* 5 (1850), 16. See also James Brooke's diaries, as extracted at length in Captain R. Mundy, *Narrative of events in Borneo and Celebes, Down to the Occupation of Labuan*, 2 vols (London: John Murray, 1848), passim. However, hopes for cooperation were entertained in some quarters: e.g. J.B. Jukes, *Narrative of the Surveying Voyage of H.M.S. Fly*, 2 vols (London: T. & W. Boone, 1847), vol. 2, 229–30.
57. C.W. Dilke, *Greater Britain: A Record of Travel in English-Speaking Countries during 1866 and 1867*, 3rd edn (London: Macmillan and Co., 1869), 515–16. However, the Dutch did find one rather unexpected admirer of their colonizing achievements in South Africa in J.A. Froude: J.A. Froude, *Oceana, or England and her Colonies* (London: Longmans, Green, and Co., 1886), 37. Some credit was also given to the reformed government of Java later in the century: e.g. R.S. Gundry, 'British North Borneo, or Sabah', *Contemporary Review* 41 (1882), 768–87, at 786; [R. Alcock], 'North Borneo', *Edinburgh Review* 156 (1882), 137–70, at 167.
58. Dawkins, 'The German Abroad', 259. It was nonetheless widely argued that what good qualities German settlers possessed were but a pale imitation of the ideal British type: e.g. 'The Colonial Policy of Germany', *Saturday Review*, 6.
59. Bashford, 'German Colonies and Naval Power', 624; Dawkins, 'The German Abroad', 265.
60. 'The Hobby of an Empire', *The Speaker* 16 (16 October 1897), 423–24.
61. Baden-Powell, 'The Expansion of Germany', 874.
62. E.g. 'German Policy in Central Africa', *New Review* 16 (1897), 223–40, at 226–27. On this issue, see F. Bösch, *Öffentliche Geheimnisse: Skandale, Politik und Medien in Deutschland und Großbritannien 1880–1914* (Munich: Oldenbourg Verlag, 2009), Chapter 4.
63. Bashford, 'German Colonies and Naval Power', 622. On this theme, see S.J. Potter, 'Jingoism, Public Opinion, and the New Imperialism', *Media History* 20 (2014), 34–50.
64. 'German Annexation', *Saturday Review* 59(1523) (1885), 7–8, at 7.
65. Bashford, 'German Colonies and Naval Power', 625; 'The Germans as Colonisers', *The Speaker* 13 (21 March 1896), 307–9; 'The Colonial Policy of France', *The Economist*, 30 May 1896, 691–2.
66. Porter, 'Bureau and Barrack'; and see e.g. Bashford, 'German Colonies and Naval Power', 626.
67. Birchenough, 'The Expansion of Germany', 186.
68. 'The Germans as Colonisers', 307–9; C.W. Dilke, 'Civilisation in Africa', *Cosmopolis* 3 (1896), 18–35, at 23–24; E.D. Morel, 'The Congo State and the Bahr-el-ghazal', *Nineteenth Century* 50 (1901), 202–13, at 202.
69. H.R. Fox Bourne, 'The Congo Crisis', *Fortnightly Review* 70 (1901), 294–306, at 302–4.
70. J.S. Keltie, 'British Interests in Africa', *Contemporary Review* 54 (1888), 115–25, at 119.
71. Baden-Powell, 'The Expansion of Germany', 875.
72. Bashford, 'German Colonies and Naval Power', 624.
73. De Thierry, 'Colonial Empires', 152. De Thierry had French heritage, but was very much an Englishman. See also on these themes *The Times*, 2 January 1885, 9.
74. 'Europe in Africa', *London Quarterly Review* 25 (1896), 205–32, at 220.
75. De Thierry, 'Colonial Empires', 161; Sir G. Grey, *German Colonisation: A Review of the Samoan Situation* (1889), 10–11.
76. 'The Colonial Policy of France', *Edinburgh Review*, 377–79.
77. D.C. Boulger, *The Congo State, or the Growth of Civilisation in Central Africa* (London: W. Thacker and Co., 1898); D.C. Boulger, 'The Congo State and its Critics', *Fortnightly*

Review 65 (1899), 433–34; 'Colonial Politics', *The Athenaeum* 3703 (1898), 526–27; and see H.M. Stanley's frustrated comparison between the practicality of the Belgian colonial project and short-sighted English attitudes paraphrased in J. Heartfield, *The British and Foreign Anti-slavery Society, 1838–1956* (London: Hurst & Company, 2016), 322–23.
78. H. Reade, 'Empire – as Made in Germany', *Westminster Review* 158 (1902), 42–49.
79. *Daily News*, 24 January 1850, 4.
80. Middleton, 'French Algeria'.
81. G. Martin, '"Anti-imperialism" in the Mid-nineteenth Century and the Nature of the British Empire, 1820–70', in R. Hyam and G. Martin (eds), *Reappraisals in British Imperial History* (London: Macmillan, 1975), 88–120; M. Matikkala, *Empire and Imperial Ambition: Liberty, Englishness and Anti-imperialism in Late Victorian Britain* (London: I.B. Tauris, 2011); G. Claeys, *Imperial Sceptics: British Critics of Empire, 1850–1920* (Cambridge: Cambridge University Press, 2010); for a wider European perspective on anti-colonial arguments and attitudes, see B. Stuchtey, *Die europäische Expansion und ihre Feinde: Kolonialismuskritik vom 18. bis in das 20. Jahrhundert* (Munich: Oldenbourg Verlag, 2010).
82. On the bearing of that critique on ideas about British character, see Parry, *Politics of Patriotism*, 16–20.

# Bibliography

Adye, J., 'The Colonial Weakness of France', *Nineteenth Century* 45 (1899), 55–66.
[Alcock, R.], 'North Borneo', *Edinburgh Review* 156 (1882), 137–70.
Armitage, D., *The Ideological Origins of the British Empire* (Cambridge: Cambridge University Press, 2000).
Asseraf, A., 'La société coloniale face à l'actualité internationale : diffusion, contrôle, usages (1881–1899)', *Revue d'histoire moderne et contemporaine* 63 (2016), 110–32.
Baden-Powell, G., 'The Expansion of Germany', *Nineteenth Century* 16 (1884), 869–78.
Barkey, K., and von Hagen, M., *After Empire. Multiethnic Societies and Nation-Building: The Soviet Union and the Russian, Ottoman, and Habsburg Empires* (Boulder: Westview Press, 1997).
Barth, V., and Cvetkovski, R., *Imperial Co-operation and Transfer: Empires and Encounters, 1870–1930* (London: Bloomsbury, 2015).
Bashford, J.L., 'German Colonies and Naval Power', *Fortnightly Review* 72 (1902), 622–36.
Baumgart, W., *Imperialism: The Idea and Reality of British and French Colonial Expansion, 1880–1914* (Oxford: Oxford University Press, 1982).
Belich, J. et al. (eds), *The Prospect of Global History* (Oxford: Oxford University Press, 2016).
Bell, D., 'Dissolving Distance: Technology, Space, and Empire in British Political Thought, 1770–1900', *Journal of Modern History* 77 (2005), 523–62.
———. 'From Ancient to Modern in Victorian Imperial Thought', *Historical Journal* 49 (2006), 735–59.
———. *Reordering the World: Essays on Liberalism and Empire* (Princeton: Princeton University Press, 2016).
Bentley, M., 'The British State and its Historiography', in Blockmans, W. and Benet, J.-P. (eds), *Visions sur le développement des états européens : theories et historiographies de l'état modern* (Rome: École française de Rome), 153–68.

Bernhard, P., 'Colonial Crossovers: Nazi Germany and its Entanglements with Other Empires', *Journal of Global History* 12 (2017), 206–27.
Birchenough, H., 'The Expansion of Germany', *Nineteenth Century* 43 (1898), 182–91.
Bodley, J.E.C., 'The Portuguese in East Africa', *Blackwood's Edinburgh Magazine* 146 (1888), 142–58.
Bonwick, J., *French Colonies and Their Resources* (London: Street & Co., 1886).
Bösch, F., '"Are We a Cruel Nation?" Colonial Practices, Perceptions, and Scandals', in Geppert, D. and Gerwarth, R. (eds), *Wilhelmine Germany and Edwardian Britain: Essays on Cultural Affinity* (Oxford: Oxford University Press, 2008), 115–40.
———. *Öffentliche Geheimnisse: Skandale, Politik und Medien in Deutschland und Großbritannien 1880–1914* (Munich: Oldenbourg Verlag, 2009).
Boulger, D.C., *The Congo State, or the Growth of Civilisation in Central Africa* (London: W. Thacker and Co., 1898).
———. 'The Congo State and its Critics', *Fortnightly Review* 65 (1899), 433–34.
Bourke, R., *Empire and Revolution: The Political Life of Edmund Burke* (Princeton: Princeton University Press, 2015).
Brown, M., and Paquette, G. (eds), *Connections after Colonialism: Europe and Latin America in the 1820s* (Tuscaloosa: University of Alabama Press, 2013).
Burbank, J., and Cooper, F., *Empires in World History: Power and the Politics of Difference* (Princeton: Princeton University Press, 2010).
Chesson, F.W., 'The Dispute between England and Portugal', *St. James's Magazine* 13 (1874), 492–501.
Claeys, G., *Imperial Sceptics: British Critics of Empire, 1850–1920* (Cambridge: Cambridge University Press, 2010).
Collini, S., Winch, D. and Burrow, J., *That Noble Science of Politics: A Study in Nineteenth-Century Intellectual History* (Cambridge: Cambridge University Press, 1983).
'Colonial Policy: Mr. Huskisson's Colonial Trade Bill, 1828', *Monthly Magazine* 5 (1828), 259–74.
'The Colonial Policy of France', *The Economist*, 28 October 1882, 1330–31.
'The Colonial Policy of France', *The Economist*, 30 May 1896, 691–92.
'The Colonial Policy of France', *Edinburgh Review* 177 (1893), 354–88.
'The Colonial Policy of Germany', *The Economist*, 28 June 1884, 775–76.
'The Colonial Policy of Germany', letter to *The Economist*, 12 July 1884, 844.
'The Colonial Policy of Germany', *Saturday Review* 58, no. 1497 (1884), 6–7. 'Colonial Politics', *Athenaeum* 3703 (1898), 526–27.
'The Colonies of Germany', *Chamber's Journal* 14(715) (1897), 590–92.
Conway, S., '"Founded in Lasting Interests: British Projects for European Imperial Collaboration in the Age of the American Revolution', *International History Review* 37 (2015), 22–40.
Cordeiro, L., *Portugal and the Congo: A Statement* (London: Edward Stanford, 1883).
D'Orsey, A., *Portuguese Discoveries, Dependencies, and Missions in Asia and Africa* (London: W.H. Allen & Co., 1893).
Darwin, J., *After Tamerlane: The Global History of Empire since 1405* (London: Allen Lane, 2007).
Dawkins, C.E., 'The German Abroad', *National Review* 5 (1885), 259–67.
De Coubertin, P., 'England and France', *Fortnightly Review* 69 (1901), 1013–21.
De Thierry, C., 'Colonial Empires', *New Review* 17 (1897), 151–62.

Dilke, C.W., *Greater Britain: A Record of Travel in English-Speaking Countries during 1866 and 1867*, 3rd edn (London: Macmillan and Co., 1869).

———. 'Civilisation in Africa', *Cosmopolis* 3 (1896), 18–35.

Dimier, V., *Le Gouvernement des Colonies: Regards Croisés Franco-Brittaniques* (Brussels: Éditions de l'Université Libre de Bruxelles, 2004).

Doyle, M.W., *Empires* (Ithaca: Cornell University Press, 1996).

Drayton, R., and Motadel, D., 'Discussion: The Futures of Global History', *Journal of Global History* 13 (2018), 1–21.

Elliott, J.H., *Empires of the Atlantic World: Britain and Spain in America, 1492–1830* (New Haven: Yale University Press, 2006).

'Europe in Africa', *London Quarterly Review* 25 (1896), 205–32.

'The European Powers in West Africa', *Edinburgh Review* 188 (1898), 465–93.

Fieldhouse, D.K., *The Colonial Empires: A Comparative Survey from the Eighteenth Century* (London: Weidenfeld & Nicolson, 1966).

Fitzpatrick, M. (ed.), *Liberal Imperialism in Europe* (Basingstoke: Palgrave Macmillan, 2012).

Forclaz, A.R., *Humanitarian Imperialism: The Politics of Anti-slavery Activism, 1880–1940* (Oxford: Oxford University Press, 2015).

Forman, R.G., *China and the Victorian Imagination: Empires Entwined* (Cambridge: Cambridge University Press, 2013).

Fox Bourne, H.R., 'The Congo Crisis', *Fortnightly Review* 70 (1901), 294–306.

'A French Tribute to Our African Empire', *Review of Reviews*, November 1898, 476.

Froude, J.A., *Oceana, or England and her Colonies* (London: Longmans, Green, and Co., 1886).

Geffcken, 'The Colonial Policy of France', *New Review* 6 (1892), 723–31.

'German Annexation', *Saturday Review* 59(1523) (1885), 7–8.

'German Policy in Central Africa', *New Review* 16 (1897), 223–40.

'The Germans as Colonisers', *The Speaker* 13 (21 March 1896), 307–9.

Goldie, G.T., *French Ambitions in Africa* (publisher unknown, 1894; reprinted from the *Asiatic Quarterly Review*).

Grey, Sir G., *German Colonisation: A Review of the Samoan Situation* (1889).

Gundry, R.S., 'British North Borneo, or Sabah', *Contemporary Review* 41 (1882), 768–87.

Hagerman, C., *Britain's Imperial Muse: The Classics, Imperialism, and the Indian Empire, 1784–1914* (Basingstoke: Palgrave Macmillan, 2013).

Hardt, M., and Negri, A., *Empire* (Cambridge, MA: Harvard University Press, 2000).

Hart, J., *Comparing Empires: European Colonialism from Portuguese Expansion to the Spanish-American War* (New York: Palgrave Macmillan, 2003).

Heartfield, J., *The British and Foreign Anti-slavery Society, 1838–1956* (London: Hurst & Company, 2016).

Hilton, B., *The Age of Atonement: The Influence of Evangelicalism on Social and Economic Thought, 1795–1865* (Oxford: Oxford University Press, 1988).

'The Hobby of an Empire', *The Speaker* 16 (16 Oct. 1897), 423–4.

Howitt, W., *Colonization and Christianity: A Popular History of the Treatment of the Natives by the Europeans in all their Colonies* (London: Longman, Orme, Brown, Green, & Longmans, 1838).

'The Insurrection in Cuba', *Examiner* 3316 (1871), 823.

[John, H. St.], 'English and Dutch in the Indian Archipelago', *Tait's Edinburgh Magazine* 16 (1849), 1–8.

Jukes, J.B., *Narrative of the Surveying Voyage of H.M.S. Fly*, 2 vols (London: T. & W. Boone, 1847).

Keltie, J.S., 'British Interests in Africa', *Contemporary Review* 54 (1888), 115–25.
Kerslake, P., *Science Fiction and Empire* (Liverpool: Liverpool University Press, 2007).
Kiely, R., *Rethinking Imperialism* (Basingstoke: Palgrave Macmillan, 2010).
Kiernan, V.G., *European Empires from Conquest to Collapse, 1815–1960* (Leicester: Leicester University Press, 1982).
[Knox, A.], 'Dutch Diplomacy and Indian Piracy', *Edinburgh Review* 96 (1852), 54–95.
Koebner, R., and Schmidt, H.D., *Imperialism: The Story and Significance of a Political Word, 1840–1960* (Cambridge: Cambridge University Press, 1964).
Kramer, P.A., 'Power and Connection: Imperial Histories of the United States in the World', *American Historical Review* 116 (2011), 1348–91.
Kumar, K., 'Greece and Rome in the British Empire: Contrasting Role Models', *Journal of British Studies* 51 (2012), 76–101.
Lenz, O., 'A German View of Portuguese Africa', *Review of Reviews* 1 (1890), 295.
Leonhard, J., and von Hirschhausen, U. (eds), *Comparing Empires: Encounters and Transfers in the Long Nineteenth Century* (Göttingen: Vandenhoeck and Ruprecht, 2010).
Lewis, G.C., *An Essay on the Government of Dependencies* (London: John Murray, 1841).
Lord, W.F., *The Lost Empires of the Modern World: Essays in Imperial History* (London: Richard Bentley and Son, 1897).
———. *England and France in the Mediterranean, 1660–1830* (London: Sampson Low, Marston and Company, 1901).
'Lost Empires', *The Academy* 1333 (1897), 422.
Macgregor, J., *Holland and the Dutch Colonies* (London: Whittaker and Co., 1848).
MacKenzie, J.M., *European Empires and the People: Popular Responses to Imperialism in France, Britain, the Netherlands, Belgium, Germany and Italy* (Manchester: Manchester University Press, 2011).
Maier, C.S., *Among Empires: American Ascendency and its Predecessors* (Cambridge, MA: Harvard University Press, 2006).
Mandler, P., *The English National Character: The History of an Idea from Edmund Burke to Tony Blair* (Cambridge: Cambridge University Press, 2006).
Marshall, P.J., 'British Assessments of the Dutch in Asia in the Age of Raffles', *Itinerario* 12 (1988), 1–16.
Martin, G., '"Anti-imperialism" in the Mid-nineteenth Century and the Nature of the British Empire, 1820–70', in Hyam, R. and Martin, G. (eds), *Reappraisals in British Imperial History* (London: Macmillan, 1975), 88–120.
Martin, R.M., *Colonial Policy of the British Empire: Part I. Government* (London: Gilbert and Rivington, 1837).
Mason Roberts, T., 'The Role of French Algeria in American Expansion during the Early Republic', *Journal of the Western Society for French History* 43 (2015), 153–64.
Matikkala, M., *Empire and Imperial Ambition: Liberty, Englishness and Anti-imperialism in Late Victorian Britain* (London: I.B. Tauris, 2011).
Melville, R.D., 'Aspects of Empire and Colonisation', *Westminster Review* 150 (1898), 363–76.
Merivale, H., *Lectures on Colonization and Colonies*, 2 vols (London: Longman, Orme, Brown, Green, and Longmans, 1841).
Middleton, A., 'Rajah Brooke and the Victorians', *Historical Journal* 53 (2010), 381–400.
———. 'French Algeria in British Imperial Thought, 1830–1870', *Journal of Colonialism and Colonial History* 16(1) (2015), n.p.

Mizutani, S., 'Anti-colonialism and the Contested Politics of Comparison: Rabindranath Tagore, Rash Behari Bose and Japanese Colonialism in Korea in the Inter-war Period', *Journal of Colonialism and Colonial History* 16(1) (2015), n.p.

Morel, E.D., 'The Congo State and the Bahr-el-ghazal', *Nineteenth Century* 50 (1901), 202–13.

Morrison, A., 'Russian Rule in Turkestan and the Example of British India, c. 1860–1917', *Slavonic and East European Review* 84 (2006), 666–707.

———. 'The Pleasures and Pitfalls of Colonial Comparisons', *Kritika: Explorations in Russian and Eurasian History* 13 (2012), 919–36.

Mundy, R., *Narrative of Events in Borneo and Celebes, Down to the Occupation of Labuan*, 2 vols (London: John Murray, 1848).

Muthu, S. (ed.), *Empire and Modern Political Thought* (Cambridge: Cambridge University Press, 2012).

Naranch, B., and Eley, G., *German Colonialism in a Global Age* (Durham, NC: Duke University Press, 2014).

Norman, C.B., 'The Colonies of France', *Nineteenth Century* 15 (1884), 873–96.

———. *Colonial France* (London: W.H. Allen & Co., 1886).

Oliver, S.P., *Madagascar as a French Colony* (unknown publisher, 1896).

Osterhammel, J., *Colonialism: A Theoretical Overview* (Princeton: M. Wiener, 1997).

Pagden, A., *Lords of All the World: Ideologies of Empire in Spain, Britain and France, c. 1500–c. 1800* (New Haven: Yale University Press, 1995).

———. *The Burdens of Empire. 1539 to the Present* (Oxford: Oxford University Press, 2015).

Paquette, G., 'The Image of Imperial Spain in British Political Thought, 1750–1800', *Bulletin of Spanish Studies* 81 (2004), 187–214.

———. 'The Intellectual Context of British Recognition of the South American Republics, c. 1800–1830', *Journal of Transatlantic Studies* 2 (2004), 75–95.

———. 'Views from the South: Images of Britain and its Empire in Portuguese and Spanish Political Discourse, c. 1740–1810', in Reinert, S. and Røge, P. (eds), *Political Economy and Empire* (London: Palgrave Macmillan, 2013), 76–104.

Parry, J.P., *Democracy and Religion: Gladstone and the Liberal Party, 1867–1875* (Cambridge: Cambridge University Press, 1986).

———. *The Politics of Patriotism: English Liberalism, National Identity, and Europe, 1830–1886* (Cambridge: Cambridge University Press, 2006).

———. 'Disraeli, the East, and Religion: *Tancred* in Context', *English Historical Review* 132 (2017), 570–604.

Payne, E.J., *History of European Colonies* (London: Macmillan and Co., 1877).

Pedersen, S., 'What is Political History Now?', in Cannadine, D. (ed.), *What is History Now?* (Basingstoke: Palgrave Macmillan, 2005), 36–56.

———. *The Guardians: The League of Nations and the Crisis of Empire* (Oxford: Oxford University Press, 2015).

Pitts, J., *A Turn to Empire: The Rise of Imperial Liberalism in Britain and France* (Princeton: Princeton University Press, 2005).

———. 'Political Theory of Empire and Imperialism', *Annual Review of Political Science* 13 (2010), 211–35.

Porter, B., '"Bureau and Barrack": Early Victorian Attitudes towards the Continent', *Victorian Studies* 27 (1984), 407–33.

———. *Empire and Superempire: Britain, America and the World* (New Haven: Yale University Press, 2006).

'Portugal's Aggressions and England's Duty', *Fortnightly Review* 47 (1890), 136–48.

'The Portuguese in Africa', *Anti-slavery Reporter* 3 (1883), 107.
Potter, S.J., 'Jingoism, Public Opinion, and the New Imperialism', *Media History* 20 (2014), 34–50.
'Present Situation and Future Prospects of the Dutch Colonies in the East', *Oriental Herald and Journal of General Literature* 11 (1826), 85–90.
Proudman, M., 'The Most Important History: The *American Historical Review* and Our English Past', *Journal of the Historical Society* 6(2) (2006), 177–211.
'Raffles' History of Java', *British Review, and London Critical Journal* 11 (1818), 61–87.
'Rajah Brooke and Borneo', *Chambers' Papers for the People* 5 (1850), 16.
Raumer, F. von, *Italien: Beiträge zur Kenntnis dieses Landes*, 2 vols (Leipzig: F.M. Brockhaus, 1840).
Rawson, Sir R. W., *British and Foreign Colonies* (London: Edward Stanford, 1884).
Reade, H., 'Empire – as Made in Germany', *Westminster Review* 158 (1902), 42–9.
Rickett, J.C., 'Liberalism and Empire', *Contemporary Review* 74 (1898), 290–96.
Roebuck, J.A., *The Colonies of England: A Plan for the Government of Some Portion of our Colonial Dependencies* (London: John W. Parker, 1849).
Ross, R., 'Legal Communications and Imperial Governance: British North America and Spanish America Compared', in Tomlins, C. and Grossberg, M. (eds), *The Cambridge History of Law in America, Volume 1: Early America, 1580–1815* (Cambridge, 2008), 104–43.
Said, E., *Orientalism* (New York: Pantheon Books, 1978).
———. *Culture and Imperialism* (London: Chatto & Windus, 1993).
Sèbe, B., *Heroic Imperialists in Africa: The Promotion of British and French Colonial Heroes, 1870–1939* (Manchester: Manchester University Press, 2013).
Seeley, J.R., *The Expansion of England: Two Courses of Lectures* (London: Macmillan and Co., 1904).
Semmel, S., *Napoleon and the British* (New Haven: Yale University Press, 2004).
Sessions, J.E., *By Sword and Plow: France and the Conquest of Algeria* (Ithaca: Cornell University Press, 2011).
Siddiqi, Y., *Anxieties of Empire and the Fiction of Intrigue* (New York: Columbia University Press, 2008).
'Southey's History of Brazil', *Critical Review* 5 (1817), 327–48.
'Spain and Her Colonies', *Quarterly Review* 17 (1817), 530–62.
'Spanish America', *British Review, and London Critical Journal* 13 (1819), 150–95.
'A Statistical Account of the Cape of Good Hope', *Oriental Herald and Journal of General Literature* 23 (1829), 379–91.
Stephen, L. (ed.), *Letters of John Richard Green* (London: Macmillan and Co., 1901).
Stoler, A.L., 'Tense and Tender Ties: The Politics of Comparison in North American History and (Post) Colonial Studies', *Journal of American History* 88 (2001), 829–65.
Stoler, A.L., and McGranahan, C., 'Introduction: Refiguring Imperial Terrains', in Stoler, A.L., McGranahan, C. and Perdue, P.C. (eds), *Imperial Formations* (Santa Fe: School of American Research Press, 2007), 3–47.
Stuchtey, B., *Die europäische Expansion und ihre Feinde: Kolonialismuskritik vom 18. bis in das 20. Jahrhundert* (Munich: Oldenbourg Verlag, 2010).
Tabili, L., 'A Homogenous Society? Britain's Internal "Others", 1800–Present', in Hall, C. and Rose, S.O. (eds), *At Home with the Empire: Metropolitan Culture and the Imperial World* (Cambridge: Cambridge University Press, 2006), 53–76.

Thomas, M.C., 'A Path Not Taken? British Perspectives on French Colonial Violence after 1945', in Butler, L.J. and Stockwell, S. (eds), *The Wind of Change: Harold Macmillan and British Decolonization* (Basingstoke: Palgrave Macmillan, 2013), 140–58.

Thomas, M.C., and Toye, R., *Arguing about Empire: Imperial Rhetoric in Britain and France, 1882–1956* (Oxford: Oxford University Press, 2017).

———. *Rhetorics of Empire: Languages of Colonial Conflict after 1900* (Manchester: Manchester University Press, 2017).

Thornton, A.P., *Doctrines of Imperialism* (New York: John Wiley & Sons, 1965).

'Treatment of Natives in Portuguese Africa', *Anti-slavery Reporter* 20 (1900), 161–63.

Tyrrell, I., and Sexton, J. (eds), *Empire's Twin: U.S. Anti-imperialism from the Founding Era to the Age of Terrorism* (Ithaca: Cornell University Press, 2015).

Von der Brüggen, Baron [E.C.], 'The Colonial Movement in Germany', *Contemporary Review* 47 (1885), 40–50.

Watson, R.G., *Spanish and Portuguese South America during the Colonial Period*, 2 vols (London: Trübner & Co., 1884).

# 7
# Comparison and the Welfare State in Modern Europe, c. 1880–1945

Julia Moses

Comparisons seem second-nature in contemporary analyses of social policy, let alone of the values upon which it is predicated. One can, for example, pick up almost any daily newspaper or a magazine and find an article like a recent cover feature in *The Economist* that asks 'How to Make a Good Teacher'. The piece correlates teacher training with students' educational attainment across various countries, highlighting Finland and Singapore as models that should be emulated elsewhere. The author suggests that 'the use of memorisation or pupil-led learning was common among laggards', while '"cognitive activation" strategies' accounted for pupils' success, and that success could be measured statistically.[1] The article in *The Economist* draws on a recent Organisation for Economic Co-operation and Development (OECD) report, amongst a range of other qualitative and statistical research. The OECD has played a key role over the last forty years in shaping discussions about what constitutes 'good' social policy around the world, largely by producing ample statistical comparisons of its member states.[2] Many of these comparisons focus on social expenditure, which has been a key metric used in sociological research on the welfare state such as Peter Flora's influential *Growth to Limits* from 1986.[3] For example, the OECD's 2014 report on social expenditure declared that members spent, on average, 22 per cent of gross domestic product (GDP) on social provisions. By far the most generous country in this regard was France, which contrasted most sharply with Mexico, whose 'laggard' position is nicely illustrated at the end of an OECD graph.[4]

Meanwhile, comparison has also been a hallmark of rigorous historical, sociological and political studies of the welfare state. We can think here of Gøsta

Esping-Andersen's classic typology on the relationship between social policy and forms of capitalism, as well as earlier work by Gaston Rimlinger and others that highlighted causal connections between industrialization and the origins of large-scale, centralized social provision.[5] Some, like Hugh Heclo, have sought to connect welfare state developments across national borders by comparing processes of policy learning, while others such as Kathleen Thelen have compared welfare states in order to uncover the role of institutions in path dependency.[6] More recently, social-scientific comparisons have attempted to derive new typologies that take better account of the role of religion in shaping social policy and the diverse nature of economies across Europe.[7] Historians such as Peter Baldwin and Susan Pedersen have also used comparisons to uncover the complex political landscape, including the role of interest groups, in shaping social provision.[8] Other scholars like Daniel Béland and Klaus Petersen have teased out the implicit role of comparison that has been part of the long conceptual history of 'welfare' and 'social policy' that saw these concepts transfer (often uneasily) across national and institutional borders.[9]

This chapter goes back to the arguments made in the nineteenth and early twentieth centuries by those involved in the creation of Europe's modern welfare states in order to shed light on broader processes of comparison involving social provision. I shall focus on the comparisons made at international conferences involving policy experts and in broader political debate in Britain, Germany and Italy as each country enacted its early social security legislation. As we shall see, national comparisons served as a form of political argument to push for one's own policy proposals, in part, by tapping anxieties about national backwardness or aspirations to maintain national traditions. At the same time, comparison in this context also provided a powerful means to encourage new international standards, for example, in the creation of actuarial tables used for social insurance and in workplace health and safety practices. The development of the social sciences, with their visual and statistical representations and emphasis on scientific, objective and replicable methods, played a key role in shaping the welfare state in Britain, Germany and Italy, as elsewhere, informing assumptions about what constituted 'good' and 'bad' social policy.

The stories told here about social policy were derived from social-scientific comparisons that seemed to suggest in neutral and verifiable terms what was 'modern', 'civilized' or 'advanced'. By highlighting the relevance of stories and language, I build on work by Andrew Abbott and others who have called for the investigation of narrative in sociological processes such as comparison. 'If there is any one idea central to historical ways of thinking', Abbott argues, 'it is that the order of things makes a difference, that reality occurs not as time-bounded snapshots within which "causes" affect one another ... but as stories, cascades of events.'[10] The stories I trace are twofold. On an empirical level, I chart narratives told by historical actors when comparing the development of their social policies with those of other countries or 'civilizations'. On a conceptual level, I offer a story about past perceptions of history, modernization and national difference in order to shed light on the later role of comparison in studies of the welfare state in modern Europe. I suggest that these narratives prove so powerful because of the biopolitical nature of social policy: it relates to both economy and society, in principle, helping to create educated, healthy and productive citizens who contribute to explicitly national economies so they function optimally.[11]

My argument follows in three steps. First, I tease out the heritage of nineteenth-century comparisons for post-1945 analyses about the welfare state. The second section dives into the nineteenth-century example of workplace accidents as a means to explore the function of comparison in the creation of early welfare states. The case of accidents at work is particularly relevant here, as it was generally the first social-security policy that many countries adopted, so an initial and obvious point of reference for comparisons. However, it was also intimately linked to the workings of the economy and the law, both of which were seen by contemporaries to be nationally specific. In this section, I focus on comparisons made at international conferences on workplace accidents and social insurance. Finally, I examine the function of comparisons about social welfare within domestic policy debates at the turn of the twentieth century.

## Modernity and Genealogies of the Social Sciences

The welfare state has been a central preoccupation of the social sciences since the end of the Second World War. To be sure, new social programmes such as the National Health Service (NHS), the U.S. New Deal and pension reforms across Continental Europe played a role. So too did growing interests in modernization within the context of the early Cold War, which has been illustrated in work by David Engerman and others.[12] At a time when the Soviet Union offered a viable alternative model for social welfare, comparative analysis of the welfare state became crucial. However, the comparative fetish of the late 1950s had much deeper roots. Already in 1843, John Stuart Mill outlined his rationale for two methods of comparison: the 'method of agreement', that is, searching for similarities, and the 'method of difference'.[13] The assumption was that comparison could help to explain causation while taking account of the complexity of society. Like the natural sciences, the social sciences of the nineteenth century would need to identify a rigorous and replicable method, and comparison was one means to this end.[14] But the nineteenth-century heritage of comparison in the social sciences has not only been an interest in causation and scientific method; it has also been the assumption that comparisons can reveal degrees of modernity. We can see this line of thinking, for example, in Émile Durkheim's analysis of 'primitive' religion or the 'elementary forms of religious life', with the assumption that religion in some societies is 'modern' or 'civilized'. This kind of thinking is also evident in legal and anthropological work from the second half of the nineteenth century. For example, Henry Sumner Maine's *Ancient Law* argued that law gradually shifted from an emphasis on status, as was the case under 'tribal custom', or, again, in 'primitive times', to an emphasis on contract.[15]

The basic assumption behind comparison in these early social-scientific analyses was that modernity is universal. Eventually, all societies will get there, even if they do so in slightly different ways and at different points in time. Its universality makes modernity an ideal basis for comparative analysis: it is a constant that stabilizes comparisons between two diverse things. In addition, modernity in nineteenth-century social-scientific tracts is characterized by several common traits, including: territorial, sovereign states; economic development denoted by open markets mixed with specific forms of taxation; education and related technological development; and democratization and secularization as additional, though not necessarily universal, aspects. Max Weber's *Economy and Society* (1922) perhaps best encapsulates this thinking.[16]

This social-scientific heritage has proved transformative for research on social policy. We can think, for example, of early studies that emphasized the welfare state as an outgrowth of modernization. Richard Titmuss' work comes to mind here, but perhaps most influential in this regard has been T.H. Marshall's 1949 Cambridge lectures on *Citizenship and Social Class*, which outlined a linear progression of rights in societies. While the eighteenth century saw the rise of civil rights, characterized by negative freedoms such as the right to hold property or free speech, the nineteenth century witnessed the emergence of mass political rights. The twentieth century was the culmination of this transition and witnessed a shift towards positive freedoms and an emphasis on social rights. In theory, this transition ran in lockstep with technological and economic development, from the invention of Watt's steam engine to the 'great transformation' of modern capitalism that Karl Polanyi described and Marshall drew upon.[17] Marshall's model was not only one of universal progress towards welfare states; it seemed to have universal appeal, and his essay was translated into numerous languages and continues to be translated and reissued today. For Marshall, 'modern' social policy could be measured on a clear yardstick; it erased inequality. Accordingly, some countries (and the assumption in this essay was that social policy was run through national legislation, not local government or philanthropy) were ahead of the game. By the 1960s, he decried Britain as 'dithering' in its social legislation, while Germany – despite military collapse in 1945, political division between East and West and a bombing war that had left much of the country obliterated – was miles ahead.[18]

Over time, social-scientific comparisons, whether explicit or implicit, of the welfare state began to shift focus from an emphasis on universal modernization to an emphasis on diversity. By the 1980s, vast comparative studies like the work of Peter Flora and Arnold J. Heidenheimer began to tally social expenditure across over sixty countries,[19] while others like Gøsta Esping-Andersen and Francis Castles attempted to create different typologies of welfare states.[20] Some scholars like Philip Manow and Sheila Orloff began grappling with new causal factors, such as religion and gender norms, in the development of welfare states.[21] Others, like Theda Skocpol and Jacob Hacker, began emphasizing new causal mechanisms such as the role of interest groups and institutional path dependency.[22] Despite its emphasis on diverse factors and outcomes, this research nonetheless continues to draw on the heritage of comparative analysis in the social sciences in the nineteenth century that sought to chart the growth of social programmes that would improve standards of living. Assumptions about modernity also remain implicit in this work, even if they reveal various paths towards healthier and wealthier lives.

## Comparison and Norm Setting

The post-1945 zeal for the comparison of welfare states, the term itself a neologism that took off at this time,[23] drew on a nineteenth-century consensus that comparing social policy made sense. Not only were Durkheim and other social scientists engaged in the comparison game, but vast numbers of midlevel bureaucrats, physicians, engineers and others who were involved in creating and administering early social legislation did the same. Social reformers throughout the nineteenth century looked across national borders to solve problems ranging from public health to saving for old age, and innovative new policies like Britain's introduction of a national factory inspectorate in 1833 or Germany's social insurance system from 1883 attracted swathes of observers across the globe and proved particularly influential in considerations about workplace accidents.

Ideas about social problems and potential solutions diffused easily in the nineteenth century, even if they were not always taken up in the same way on the ground. Comparing these different options proved an important means to choose *different* social policies.[24] Paradoxically, these ideas also contributed to a general consensus about *universal, international norms* of what social policy – and, implicit in these discussions, the state – should, in theory, do. In this sense, the comparison of social policy always implied two possible outcomes: differentiation and coming together. Accordingly, contemporaries measured their country's (or municipalities', as Pierre-Yves Saunier and others have shown) social legislation against that elsewhere as a means to gauge whether it was on the appropriate track.[25] The International Congresses on Accidents at Work offer an ideal prism into how comparisons were formed and used in these expert circles. The organization was an outgrowth of a broader boom in international associations focused on social issues, ranging from prison reform to education, which often met parallel to world's fairs, which also included pavilions focused on social issues. For example, the 1900 *Exposition Internationale* in Paris featured a number of national exhibits that illustrated successes with social insurance or innovations in public hygiene or workplace safety.

In 1889, the International Congress on Accidents at Work (ICAW) met for the first time, spearheading much of this broader circulatory movement.[26] Its founding marked a sea change for the transnational circulation – and comparison –

of ideas about social policy. The group's first meeting was held in Paris when the city was hosting an *Exposition universelle* in honour of the centenary of the French Revolution. The French Ministry of Commerce, Industry and Colonies spearheaded the meeting, and most of the membership of the organizing committee and conference participants were French. The organizing committee set out a single, broad goal: to 'study questions on the nature of workplace accidents'.[27] The Permanent Committee claimed that all 'civilized nations' would come together in a form of 'social solidarity' to combat the accident problem and related issues. The emphasis on being civilized here denoted a complex of assumptions, ranging from humanitarianism and compassion, on the one hand, to modernity and progressiveness, on the other. Ideas about civilization were also linked to the organization's aim to be scientific, rational and neutral. In a later circular, the Committee claimed that the congress would aim to be 'scientific and absolutely independent'.[28] To this end, congress members included a range of experts drawn from across the globe, including the Chief Factory Inspector from Britain and the Spanish Chief Forestry Engineer, and covering various professions, from career bureaucrats to engineers, actuaries and physicians. Most conference delegates came from across Europe, as far as Norway, Portugal and Romania, and some came from as far as Canada. The General Consul of Brazil for Belgium also attended on behalf of his country.[29] The United States gradually began to take a stronger role in the congress and had planned to hold the first extra-European meeting on American soil, and states further afield, from Guatemala to China, regularly began sending local consuls to ICAW meetings.

Following the first meeting in Paris, the group met every two to three years and maintained a Permanent International Committee in Paris. Between 1889 and 1912, it held eleven congresses. The Permanent Committee regularly published a *Bulletin* with articles on parliamentary bills, recently adopted laws and national accident statistics that proved crucial for comparisons made within various national contexts as well as those made at the congresses. The articles appeared in their original language as long as they were in French, German, Italian or English. Members of the congress, including governmental administrators based in statistical departments, ministries of commerce and social insurance offices, received copies of the *Bulletin*.[30] All of these activities enabled policy-makers to draw comparisons about legislation around the world, partly because they facilitated a consensus about the nature of the problems at hand.

In fact, there was a great deal of agreement within the group about most questions related to workplace accidents and especially about those that were perceived to be most 'neutral' due to their ostensibly scientific and objective nature. Collecting statistics, devising strategies for preventing accidents and defining the general problem of accidents and all its constituent elements – workplace risk, issues of negligence and malingering – were never contentious matters within the group. The lack of disagreement surrounding definitions is all the more surprising in light of the fact that member states of the organization held vastly different understandings of some of these concepts, and, not least, understandings of liability, which was already noted in an extensive report to the first congress in 1889. Moreover, different legal understandings of 'occupational risk', fault, *force majeure* – known in the English context as 'Acts of God' – and 'accidents' proved difficult to translate across cultures, let alone from language to language.[31] The fact that defining the basic tenets underlying accidents and risk and agreeing on preventive measures involved the insights of seemingly apolitical experts such as actuaries, engineers, lawyers and physicians may have played a role in easing translation and coming to a consensus within the network. In this light, it was already possible at the end of its first meeting, in 1889, for members of the congress to reach an agreement over the most essential aspect of the accident problem: the legal concept of *risque professionnel* – that certain risks are inherent to certain kinds of jobs and that, as a consequence, workers injured due to those risks should receive compensation from their employers. In a similar vein, participants at the first congress concluded that accident statistics should be collected along 'uniform principles'. They argued that the 'nature and duration' of injuries should be taken into consideration and suggested sending a form to national governments for this purpose.[32] The group passed a formal resolution that states should compile annual statistics on workplace accidents, including occupational illnesses, and that they should use as a model the form of the Germany's Imperial Accident Insurance Office, which was founded following the adoption of Germany's accident insurance law in 1884.[33]

Members of the German government viewed the congress' advocacy of its statistical form as a victory.[34] High-level officials, including the Secretary of the Interior and the head of the Imperial Insurance Office, sought to advocate abroad what they saw as Germany's national model for dealing with workplace accidents. However, accident statistics were not what they were most concerned to propagandize. Instead, they sought to show policy experts around the world that *social insurance* was the optimal solution to workplace accidents. For the German government, like others, the meetings of the congresses on accidents at work provided an opportunity to encourage other states to adopt its own policy solutions. The example of the international congresses on accidents at work therefore reveals how international expert communities could be sites of competition and contestation where national comparisons were employed for various reasons. In this case, Germany attempted to diffuse its policy model largely due to concerns that social insurance was an economic burden that other states, too, should bear.[35]

From the late 1880s until the outbreak of the First World War, the German government commissioned numerous posters, pamphlets and books on German social insurance for international exhibitions and congresses like this in order to help others compare Germany's system with their own.[36] Advocating Germany's system of social insurance at meetings of the congress became all the more important after other countries began introducing less comprehensive legislation for the compensation of workplace accidents. Thus, for example, trumping the British and French models of social legislation that were on display at the 1900 *Exposition Universelle*, which ran parallel to the 1900 accidents at work congress, was an aim of the administration in Berlin.[37] However, many members of the accident congresses were sceptical about the so-called 'German model', and the roots of this scepticism went back to the origins of this organization. As Oscar Lindner, the French President of the predominantly French Permanent Committee, put it at the first congress, Germany's approach was 'authoritarian' in nature.[38]

When it came to deciding how to treat the problem of workplace accidents, there was a noticeable split amongst conference delegates between what some at the time called the 'Anglo-Saxon', 'Germanic' and 'Latin' elements of the association.[39] Tensions around competing models of social legislation on accidents were finally resolved at the 1908 meeting of the congress. At this session, members resolved that a compulsory, yet minimal, level of compensation was the best remedy for workplace accidents. However, they did not agree on social insurance, let alone through a corporatist arrangement like Germany's.[40] In the context of these meetings, comparisons facilitated the agreement of some basic standards in social provision. Yet, it was clear to participants that approving a single model of welfare – whether Germany's social insurance or another option – was impossible given the specific needs of different countries, let alone widespread biases against the national provenance of certain policies. Nonetheless, members of the ICAW repeatedly drew on German, British and French examples above others, indicating that only some kinds of policies were worth comparing at all. It was this assumption that would infuse national discussions about social policies from abroad.

## Comparison as a Political Argument

Comparisons of different social policies not only permeated international expert arenas like the international congresses on accidents at work, but they were also central to local, regional and national political discussions. In these fora, comparisons took on a related function. They became a kind of political argument that could be used to lobby for specific policies based on the tacit agreement that certain kinds of policies were 'modern' or 'advanced' and therefore worthy of adopting. Drawing on social-scientific research proved especially potent here, as it seemed to validate objectively how specific social legislation improved living standards, birth rates and other aspects of wellbeing. Ideas about national specificity also coursed through these discussions, but they worked in conjunction with claims about falling behind or racing ahead of international norms in social policy. The general consensus was that social policy was 'good', but it could take different forms. Nonetheless, as in discussions at the International Congresses on Accidents at Work, some sort of agreement was reached about what constituted 'good'. It was predicated on the idea that there was a frontrunner in social legislation, and that was Germany. To be sure, however, not everyone agreed that this particular frontrunner was a model worth emulating – even if it was worth debating.

Why did Germany's social legislation prove so compelling to contemporary observers? Within just decades of national unification, a comprehensive network of policies had been constructed, including social insurance policies for sickness (1883), accidents (1884) and old age and disability (1889). Indeed, this early period of social legislation in Germany helped to contribute to a 'myth' of national specialness surrounding the German social state, a 'myth' that was upheld both within the Wilhelmine discussions about welfare policy and in the considerations of foreign observers at the time.[41] Thus, for example, German labour exchanges attracted attention from Lloyd George and others in Britain, while Germany's system of social insurance found an admirer in the American Frederic Howe.[42] As the first country to adopt a comprehensive system of social legislation, in Germany, state building and nation building were intimately connected. As a consequence, the German government touted its social insurance abroad as a hallmark of progress, while Germans at home often shared a sense that the state of their social policy signified Germany's place on the global stage.

Although its national system of social insurance did not apply to all citizens, discussions about social politics were extensive in Imperial Germany. Social insurance was targeted primarily at male urban workers, and many of those brought into the new web of national social legislation were disgruntled with its relatively stingy benefits and coarse means to overcoming employer–worker animosities. Yet its significance extended far beyond the several million people who were directly involved in social insurance schemes or factories now subject to national regulations.[43] It was widely seen as a means of social integration, and government propaganda to this effect contributed to the sense that social insurance helped to forge a national community bound together by a protective state.[44] This understanding of national community through social policy was based on a consensus that was often articulated in terms of being a 'Kulturstaat', or cultured state.[45] The notions *Kultur* and *Zivilisation* served as frames through which social legislation was viewed in Germany, and they informed how policy ideas from abroad were compared. They proved especially poignant within these discussions due to Germany's status as a relatively young nation state. *Kultur* and *Zivilisation* commanded a wide consensus that crossed party lines and would hold even into the First World War.[46] Tellingly, the references to *Kultur* and *Zivilisation* that shaped German discussions about welfare during this period never drew a distinction between the two concepts.[47] The German discussion of social policy only distinguished between *Kulturstaaten* and *zivilisierte Staaten*, or 'cultured states' and 'civilized states', on the one hand, and non-'cultured' or 'civilized states', on the other. Since Germany seemed to be a *Kulturstaat*, only the policy ideas of other 'cultured' or 'civilized' states would do. Similarly, it was crucial within these public debates to be able to claim that Germany was 'far ahead of other *Kulturstaaten*' in the area of welfare policy.[48] The reference to *Kultur* or *Zivilisation* was so widespread about social legislation that the connotation of who or what possessed *Kultur* status was often implicit.[49]

Foremost, in the context of social policy, *Kultur*, and its synonymous *Zivilisation*, came to refer to the positive aspects of progress. This progress might be modernity itself, heralded by new technologies that would improve the 'standard of life'[50] about which many parliamentarians were concerned. It might also be a form of progress in combating the negative aspects of modernity, such as the sharp disparities in living standards that became apparent as squalid rental barracks began to litter the urban landscape in the last quarter of the nineteenth century.[51] It is noteworthy that the term 'standard of life' cited in these discussions was itself an English import, indicating that German notions of *Kultur* were also influenced from abroad. Although there was widespread agreement about the connection between being 'civilized' and maintaining a good 'standard of life', parliamentarians did not always agree on how to achieve the latter. As August Reichensperger, a representative from the Catholic Centre Party, argued, 'the so-called English standard of life is no absolute, firm size, but rather an extremely relative concept'. In the case of Germany, he claimed, the 'standard of life' should be achieved through social legislation aimed at workers. Otherwise, Germany might fall to the level of 'Russia or Ireland or other non-European states'.[52] Countries that did not maintain a certain 'standard of life' were not only 'non-European', they were also non-*Kulturstaaten*: states that should not be emulated.

The list of *Kulturstaaten* cited in German political discussions of social policy remained relatively constant between the 1880s and the First World War. In this context, being economically 'developed' and having a healthy population were at the root of being 'cultured' or 'civilized'. Thus, England, 'one of the most developed *Kulturnationen*', headed the list. On the other hand, Russia, and 'other non-European countries', which maintained a low 'standard of life', stood alongside Ireland at the opposite end of the ranking.[53] However, the level of economic development alone was not the sole characteristic of a *Kulturstaat*. An underlying yet unspoken theme of *Kultur* was that it was a characteristic of Western European peoples and their colonial offshoots. In this way, considerations of *Kulturstaaten* in German discussions about welfare policy reflected broader European trends dating from the post-Napoleonic period, when Europe was 'Europeanized' through the creation of a 'unifying grid of civilization, against which all other cultures could be measured and classified'. A key feature in this grid was a presumed East/West divide of the European cultural map, with nominally Eastern European states often viewed by self-described Western Europeans as economically and, generally but not always, culturally backward.[54] Thus, Russia would never be a candidate amongst the more civilized states.[55] Likewise, while Japan might be praised for its public health initiatives, it too would never stand amongst the *Kulturstaaten* during this period. Paranoiac fear of Japanese competition, alongside underlying racism, also contributed to this impression.[56]

However, throughout these debates, race did not play a key role in determining understandings of civilization. Instead, as both Ezequiel Adamovsky and Bernard Porter have indicated for nineteenth-century France and Britain,

'Western European' notions of 'the other' were largely founded on predominantly middle-class social and cultural values whereby foreign groups were judged primarily according to 'the "stages" of progress they had reached, rather than as species'. This value system predominated even after racial language became widespread in Western European discussions from the late nineteenth century.[57] It was therefore likely that politicians in Imperial Germany, as in Britain and Italy, entirely neglected contemporaneous South American social policy developments because the policies themselves were latecomers from socioeconomic and political systems that were viewed to be less developed than those in Western Europe. As the discussions about social policy evolved, a clear and explicit line of reference to *Kulturstaaten* emerged amongst the parties. For Social Democrats, conservatives and National Liberals, *Kulturstaaten* were those countries that had implemented some form of social legislation. Centre Party representatives, who held a more ambivalent attitude towards both central state intervention and public welfare initiatives, vacillated on this view but often agreed. In this light, England, Scotland, France, Austria, Switzerland, the Netherlands, Sweden, Norway, Denmark, New Zealand, Australia and a handful of American states joined the ranks. By this standard, Germany was not only a *Kulturstaat*, but it had also achieved an 'enormous *Kulturwerk*' through the implementation of social insurance.[58] The combination of a certain level of economic advancement with an ostensibly just social contract thus seemed to underscore *Kultur*. In public political debates about social policy, then, there was a clear assumption guiding comparisons. Policies were ranked according to whether they stemmed from a country that was perceived as 'modern'. The specific semantics of risk and the details of regulations for workplace accidents, as for other social policies, were less important and did not transfer easily from the domain of transnational expert networks such as the International Congresses on Accidents at Work.

Nonetheless, these discussions coincided with the existence of the congresses and related associations and meetings, from the 1880s and into the First World War. Moreover, the assumptions behind what constituted 'civilized' social policy were implicit and widely shared in Germany as well as in Italy and Britain. In Germany, these kinds of comparisons became particularly prominent from the 1890s, as pride in the novelty of Germany's national insurance policies began to wane.[59] For Social Democrats and conservatives, who were keen for Germany to take on further social provisions, international comparisons – however translated and mediated – could serve as a tool to gain policy objectives at home.[60] The Social Democrat Wilhelm Liebknecht, for example, claimed that Germany must follow other 'Kulturstaaten' by addressing unemployment. How it did so was not a matter of 'local, nor national appearances'; instead, he argued, it was a matter of 'international appearances'. These comparisons were made in Germany not so much to address workplace accidents – though references to safety legislation abroad were frequent – but rather to deal with other social problems. Since Germany had been the first country to enact a social insurance law for accidents, there was a general consensus that this policy was a frontrunner and the model for *other* countries to adopt.

Over time, a surprising amount of cross-party approval emerged for the expansion of Germany's social legislation to new areas, and comparisons with provisions in other countries proved to be key here. Parliamentary consensus now indicated that the 'modern' state was an interventionist one. Social Democrats and conservatives even began rallying together with left liberals in favour of policy ideas transmitted from abroad. Social Democrats were particularly active in this regard, calling for greater regulation of work hours, the introduction of a minimum wage and the establishment of a national unemployment insurance scheme. They looked to Britain and France as examples of states that had already introduced the ten-hour workday for women and children in the mid nineteenth century. Moreover, argued one Social Democrat, Switzerland, Austria and 'even Russia' had adopted similar measures. The invocation of an allegedly 'uncivilized' state as a model for reform cast into sharp relief Germany's lack of progressive legislation.[61]

This emphasis on 'culture' and 'civilization' – a discourse outlined in detail by Fritz Stern – was especially widespread in Germany.[62] But the assumptions behind this language were part of a broader global discourse about modernity and social legislation that comparisons helped to fuel. For example, in Britain, social reformers like the Webbs and Lloyd George agonized over the prospect of falling behind what they saw as the innovative labour exchanges in Belgium (the Ghent system), old-age pensions in New Zealand, which were a particular source of anxiety and wonder given their colonial provenance, and, of course, Germany's social insurance system.[63] Moreover, comparisons in Britain, as in Germany, were by no means a device solely used by social reformers when proposing policy change at home. British trade unionists and daily newspapers constantly referred to new social policies abroad, and especially in Germany, in order to argue for what they saw as the most appropriate proposals for Britain. And in the press, as amongst social reformers and trade unionists, comparisons offered a dual function because they supported arguments both *for* and *against* change. In fact, to many observers, it seemed that Britain was so different from Germany (and from most of continental Europe) – in terms of its politics, economy and, of course, legal system – that continental social legislation simply could not translate across the Channel, even if that legislation stemmed, in principle, from 'civilized' countries.

As in Germany, an idea of national specificity – within a broader framework of modernity or 'civilization' – was key in these considerations. For example, British advocates of friendly societies invoked a trope of respectability, based on 'self-reliance' and 'manfulness' as particularly 'English' characteristics that a German-style social insurance scheme would tarnish.[64] The *Daily News* helped synthesize these views when it sent out a questionnaire on social insurance to the heads of trade unions. The majority argued that workplace safety should be prioritized, yet it could not be ensured by requiring employers to buy accident insurance. The survey concluded that most unionists were against a 'German-style compulsory insurance scheme'.[65]

Even Joseph Chamberlain, who had initially sought to emulate Germany's accident insurance law in Britain, ultimately concluded that the policy would be 'objectionable to English people'.[66] Germany's social insurance system seemed to go too far in addressing what was essentially a legal and technical issue within the common law: how to compensate workers for accidents. As Colonial Secretary, Chamberlain helped provide the Home Office with alternative policy models, collecting reports on liability systems throughout the empire, from Australia to Canada, in 1896. Chamberlain, like many observers in Britain at the time, recognized that colonial practices might be more meaningful for Britain. British colonies shared the same common law legal heritage, meaning that the problem with workplace accidents could be solved in similar ways throughout the empire.[67] The white-settler colonies of Australia, New Zealand, Canada and South Africa also seemed to resemble Britain culturally and administratively, which led civil servants like Chamberlain to examine colonial social policy time and time again from the 1880s. The Workmen's Compensation Act of 1897 that resulted from these discussions reflected these concerns about British particularity: its common law, heritage of classical liberalism, and tradition of friendly societies and other voluntarist arrangements could provide care for the injured and their families better than a centralized, compulsory and state-run insurance system ever could.

As in Britain, in Italy, debates about compensating workplace accidents went on for almost two decades before an accident insurance law was enacted in 1898. Throughout these discussions, comparisons with legislation in other countries proved decisive. In 1883, Italy took a first step towards introducing social insurance by setting up a National Accident Insurance Fund to encourage citizens to take up insurance voluntarily. Its creator, the liberal politician and economist Luigi Luzzatti, argued that Italy should 'be spared the cyclopean proposals for compulsory insurance for sickness, accidents and the disability of old age, which, in Germany, have tried to solve social problems with the same method of blind military discipline with which a powerful standing army would be organized'.[68] Luzzatti's dismissal of German's accident insurance was part of an entrenched debate about the purpose of the state that had raged in Italian legal, political and economic communities since the 1870s.[69] In this context, German social legislation seemed to epitomize exactly what Italy should avoid. The moderate conservative lawyer Antonio Salandra was amongst Luzzatti's sparring partners in these debates. Nonetheless, echoing critics in Britain and across the border in France,[70] he agreed with Luzzatti that German accident insurance was a product of 'state socialism' of the worst kind. For Salandra, compulsory accident insurance served as an example that 'the best of foreign scientific production is not always diffused'; rather, 'imports [are like] a vogue that favours certain doctrines, certain writers, certain countries'.[71] According to this line of thinking, it would be best for Italy to avoid modish forms of governance and continue its liberal course. Despite Luzzatti's and Salandra's critique of German social legislation, it was clear to both, as to many other legislators and social reformers on the peninsula, that Germany was a natural point of reference, as were Britain and France. Each country's legislation and informal policy initiatives, such as the use of friendly societies to ease the negative consequences of work, was studied closely in the Ministry of Agriculture, Commerce and Industry, with special reports commissioned on topics such as Germany's accident insurance system.[72]

In Italy, as in Britain and Germany, comparisons were drawn against a grid of countries according to their presumed international status in terms of social policy. In turn, this schema was informed by assumptions about national levels of social, economic and political development. The composition of the grid shared some similarities across national borders: for Italians, Germans and Britons, social policy from Western Europe and Britain's white settler colonies seemed particularly advanced. Comparisons with legislation from these regions pointed to possible policies to emulate, but they also sparked anxieties about falling behind in a presumed international competition in social progress. By contrast, comparisons with regions at the bottom of the chart comforted national pride or helped encourage policy reform at home. In any case, comparisons proved a vital tool in political arguments about policy decisions because they confirmed ideas about national difference. Comparisons were based on the assumption that social policies around the world shared a common end goal: to be modern or advanced and, in theory, improve population health, economic growth and social relations. However, there were different paths to get there. In the context of the late nineteenth century, when the creation of European social states went hand in hand with the creation of nation states, those paths were understood as nationally specific.

## Conclusions: We All Compare

The emphasis on national difference was particularly potent in comparisons of welfare at the turn of the twentieth century. However, the assumption upon which it was based – about the relationship between social policy and modernity, and the objective and verifiable nature of that relationship – could, to a certain extent, be found in some of the social-scientific research on, and popular discourse about, the welfare state after 1945, and it continues to inform how we discuss the 'welfare state' today. We all compare, as Peter Baldwin argues in an essay on comparison as an historical method, even if social-scientific scholarship has long since cast off agreement about the pursuit of objectivity, and a concomitant understanding about what constitutes 'modernity'.[73] Of course, it is not just scholars who compare; there is a sociological aspect to comparison and there is a politics of comparison. Comparison is a means through which individuals make sense of their own society by telling stories about themselves and others. The welfare state, and social policy more broadly, is a natural object of comparison because of its connection to aspirations to be 'modern', 'developed' and 'advanced', on the one hand, and to anxieties about population health and economic competition, on the other.

Social science has been integral to this history of comparison and the welfare state. The history of the social sciences is intertwined with the history of modern social policy, going back to the nineteenth century and continuing up to the present day. They served as a tool to study similarities and differences between policies at home but also across national borders, and their theoretical and quantitative methods enabled social scientists to make what appeared to be neutral arguments about 'good' and 'bad' policies. The normative basis of social-scientific comparisons can be seen in some of the arguments made by social reformers and in the discussions at international expert conferences at the turn of the twentieth century. In turn, normative assumptions within social-scientific accounts often informed and intermingled with broader political discussions about social policy at the time.

The example of the European welfare state thus reveals the paradoxical nature of comparison as an exercise. As we see in the case of accidents at work, comparisons contributed to understandings of national difference. However, they also created discourses about (and policy proposals on) international standards. In the context of the welfare state, comparisons held the potential to be both unifying and divisive. Moreover, comparisons – aided by the tools of the social sciences – made implicitly emotive languages of 'frontrunners' and 'laggards' seem objective, scientific and universal, thereby legitimating political arguments about specific policies.

**Julia Moses** is Reader in Modern History at the University of Sheffield and Marie Curie Fellow in Sociology at the University of Göttingen, where she is completing her book *Civilizing Marriage: Family, Nation and State in the German Empire*. She is the author of *The First Modern Risk: Workplace Accidents and the Origins of European Social States* (2018) and editor of *Marriage, Law and Modernity: Global Histories* (2017) and *The Impact of Ideas on Legal Development* (with Michael Lobban, 2012).

## Notes

1. 'Teaching the Teachers', *The Economist*, 11–17 June 2016, 23–25, at 24.
2. M. Leimgruber, 'The Embattled Standard-Bearer of Social Insurance and its Challenger: The ILO, the OECD, and the "Crisis of the Welfare State", 1975–1985', in S. Kott and J. Droux (eds), *Globalizing Social Rights: The ILO and Beyond* (Basingstoke: Palgrave Macmillan, 2013), 293–309.
3. P. Flora, *Growth to Limits: The Western European Welfare States since World War II* (Berlin: De Gruyter, 1986).
4. 'Social Expenditure Update: Social Spending is Falling in Some Countries, But in Many Others it Remains at Historically High Levels', OECD: Directorate for Employment, Labour and Social Affairs, *Insights from the OECD Social Expenditure Database (SOCX)*,

November 2014, retrieved 11 March 2019 from https://www.oecd.org/els/soc/OECD2014-Social-Expenditure-Update-Nov2014-8pages.pdf.

5. G. Esping-Anderson, *The Three Worlds of Welfare Capitalism* (Oxford: Polity Press, 1990); G.V. Rimlinger, *Welfare Policy and Industrialization in Europe, America, and Russia* (New York: Wiley, 1971).
6. H. Heclo, *Modern Social Politics in Britain and Sweden: From Relief to Income Maintenance* (New Haven: Yale University Press, 1974); K.A. Thelen, *How Institutions Evolve: The Political Economy of Skills in Germany, Britain, the United States, and Japan*, Cambridge Studies in Comparative Politics (Cambridge: Cambridge University Press, 2004).
7. K.J. Morgan, *Working Mothers and the Welfare State: Religion and the Politics of Work-Family Policies in Western Europe and the United States* (Stanford: Stanford University Press, 2006); M. Ferrera, and M. Rhodes, *Recasting European Welfare States* (Ilford: Frank Cass, 2000).
8. P. Baldwin, *The Politics of Social Solidarity: Class Bases of the European Welfare State, 1875–1975* (Cambridge: Cambridge University Press, 1990); S. Pedersen, *Family, Dependence, and the Origins of the Welfare State: Britain and France, 1914–1945* (Cambridge: Cambridge University Press, 1993). These are two of the most influential comparative historical works, though numerous other examples exist, such as (amongst others): G.A. Ritter, *Social Welfare in Germany and Britain: Origins and Development* (Leamington Spa: Berg, 1986); A. de Swaan, *In Care of the State: Health Care, Education and Welfare in Europe and the USA in the Modern Era* (New York: Oxford University Press, 1988); E.P. Hennock, *The Origin of the Welfare State in England and Germany, 1850–1914* (Cambridge: Cambridge University Press, 2007). See also, for example, the comparative remarks within S. Kott, *Sozialstaat und Gesellschaft: das deutsche Kaiserreich in Europa* (Göttingen: Vandenhoeck & Ruprecht, 2014).
9. D. Béland and K. Petersen (eds), *Analysing Social Policy Concepts and Language: Comparative and Transnational Perspectives* (Bristol: Policy Press, 2014).
10. A. Abbott, 'History and Sociology: The Lost Synthesis', *Social Science History* 15 (1991), 201–38.
11. M. Foucault, *The Birth of Biopolitics: Lectures at the Collège de France, 1978–79*, M. Senellart (ed.), G. Burchell (trans.) (Basingstoke: Palgrave Macmillan, 2008).
12. D.C. Engerman, *Modernization from the Other Shore: American Intellectuals and the Romance of Russian Development* (Cambridge, MA: Harvard University Press, 2003). See also D. Harrison, *The Sociology of Modernization and Development* (London: Routledge, 1988).
13. J.S. Mill, *A System of Logic: Ratiocinative and Inductive: Being a Connected View of Principles of Evidence and the Methods of Scientific Investigation*, 2 vols (London: John W. Parker, 1843), vol. 1, 450–79.
14. M. Dogan, 'Strategies in Comparative Sociology', *Comparative Sociology* 1 (2002), 63–92. On the broader background, see M. Lange, *Comparative Historical Methods* (Thousand Oaks, CA: Sage, 2013); J. Mahoney and D. Ruschemeyer (eds), *Comparative Historical Analysis in the Social Sciences* (Cambridge: Cambridge University Press, 2003), especially Chapter 3: E. Amenta, 'What We Know about the Development of Social Policy: Comparative and Historical Research in Comparative and Historical Perspective', at 91–130.
15. É. Durkheim, *Les formes élémentaires de la vie religieuse : le système totémique en Australie* (1912; Paris: Presses Universitaires de France, 1960); H. Sumner Maine, *Ancient Law: Its Connection with the Early History of Society and its Relation to Modern Ideas* (London: John

Murray, 1861). On the context of late nineteenth-century comparisons, see J. Burrow and S. Collini, 'The Clue to the Maze: The Appeal of the Comparative Method', in D. Winch, J. Burrow and S. Collini (eds), *That Noble Science of Politics: A Study in Nineteenth-Century Intellectual History* (Cambridge University Press: Cambridge, 1983), 207–46.
16. M. Weber, *Economy and Society: An Outline of Interpretive Sociology*, G. Roth and C. Wittrich (eds), 2 vols (Berkeley: University of California Press, 2013 [1922]). Although modernization is but one of several paradigms that has occupied comparative sociological research, it relates in various ways to the others: D.E. Apter, 'Comparative Sociology: Some Paradigms and Their Movements', in C. Calhoun et al. (eds), *The SAGE Handbook of Sociology* (Thousand Oaks, CA: Sage, 2005), 103–28.
17. T.H. Marshall and T. Bottomore, *Citizenship and Social Class* (1950; London: Pluto Classics, 1992).
18. J. Moses, 'Social Citizenship and Social Rights in an Age of Extremes: T. H. Marshall's Social Philosophy in the *longue durée*', *Modern Intellectual History* 16 (1) (2019), 155–84.
19. P. Flora and A.J. Heidenheimer (eds), *The Development of Welfare States in Europe and America* (New Brunswick, NJ: Transaction, 1981).
20. F.G. Castles, *Families of Nations: Patterns of Public Policy in Western Democracies* (Dartmouth, NH: Aldershot, 1993); Esping-Anderson, *Three Worlds*.
21. K. van Kersbergen and P. Manow (eds.), *Religion, Class Coalitions, and Welfare States* (Cambridge: Cambridge University Press, 2009); A. Orloff, 'Gender in the Welfare State', *Annual Review of Sociology* 22 (1996), 51–78.
22. T. Skocpol, *Protecting Soldiers and Mothers: The Political Origins of Social Policy in the United States* (Cambridge, MA: Belknap Press, 1992); J.S. Hacker, *The Divided Welfare State: The Battle over Public and Private Social Benefits in the United States* (Cambridge: Cambridge University Press, 2002).
23. On the term, see D. Béland and K. Petersen, 'Introduction: Social Policy Concepts and Language', in Béland and Petersen (eds), *Analysing Social Policy Concepts and Language*, 1–12, at 1. See also the chapter by Daniel Wincott in the volume: 'Original and Imitated or Elusive and Limited? Towards a Genealogy of the Welfare State in Britain', at 127–41.
24. Diffusion, as Francis Galton noted early on, makes the comparison of outcomes tricky because it obfuscates causation, but it also helps actors to compare options. See M.H. Ross and E. Homer, 'Galton's Problem in Cross-national Research', *World Politics* 29 (1976), 1–28.
25. P.-Y. Saunier, 'Circulations, connexions et espaces transnationaux', *Genèses* 57 (2004), 110–26.
26. Some of this analysis of the ICAW builds on my earlier work: J. Moses, 'Policy Communities and Exchanges across Borders: The Case of Workplace Accidents at the Turn of the Twentieth Century', in D. Rodogno et al. (eds), *Shaping the Transnational Sphere: Experts, Networks and Issues from the 1840s to the 1930s* (Oxford: Berghahn Books, 2014), 60–81.
27. É. Gruner (ed.), *Exposition universelle internationale de 1889 : Congrès international des accidents du travail*, vol. 2: *Comptes Rendus des séances et visite du congrès* (Paris: Librarie Polytechnique Baudrie et Cie, 1890), 7, 11–13, 19.
28. *Congrès international des accidents du travail et des assurance sociales, troisième session, Milan, 1–6 octobre 1894*, vol. 1: *Rapports presentés ...* (Milan: Impr. H. Reggiani, 1894–5), 8–10.
29. Ibid., 1–3.

30. Secretary of the Permanent Committee to the President of the Imperial Insurance Office, 13 June 1900, Bundesarchiv Berlin Lichterfelde (BArch): unnumbered: 110527: R89 (Imperial Insurance Office).
31. C. Dejace, 'La responsabilité des accidents du travail et le risque professionnel', in Gruner (ed.), *Exposition universelle*, 2, 194–6.
32. Ibid., 21.
33. Copy of the resolutions from the 1894 meeting of the ICAW: BArch: Fl. 100–1, Box 100645, R1501, Imperial Ministry of the Interior Papers.
34. Ibid.
35. 11th Session of the Permanent Committee of the Volkswirthschaftsrath, 24 March 1882, 296–7, 300, Geheimes Staatsarchiv Preußischer Kulturbesitz (GStAPK): Fl. 168–73, Box 11031, I. H.A. Rep. 84a, Prussian Ministry of Trade Papers; Committee of the Fabrik-Arbeiter-Unterstützungs-Kasse of Lüdenscheid to the Minister of the Interior, 2 February 1881: BArch Fl. 37–38, Box 100393, R1501, Ministry of the Interior Papers; Chancellor Hohenlohe-Schillingsfürst to Secretary of the Interior Boetticher, 25 July 1895, BArch: Fl. 27–29, Box 101098, R1501, Imperial Ministry of the Interior Papers; Head of the Imperial Accident Insurance Office to the Secretary of the Interior, 31 October 1894, BArch: Fl. 92–95, Box 100645, R1501, Imperial Ministry of the Interior Papers.
36. For example, G.A. Klein, *Die Arbeiterversicherung des Deutschen Reichs* (Berlin: Reichsdruckerei, 1904).
37. President of the Imperial Insurance Office to the Secretary of the Interior, 30 March 1899, BArch: Fl. 7–10, Box 101093, R1501, Imperial Ministry of the Interior Papers.
38. Gruner, *Exposition universelle*, 2, 12.
39. British Envoy to the Swiss Confederation to the Secretary of State for the Home Office, 28 September 1891, National Archives of the UK (NA): Fl. 5, Box 9841: B11058, Series 45, HO, Home Office Papers.
40. For example, Petition of the Employees of the *Allgemeiner Deutscher Versicherungs-Verein* in Stuttgart (Reichstag petition no. 44), BArch: Fl. 1–2, Box 331, R101, *Reichstag* Papers.
41. S. Kott, 'Der Sozialstaat', in E. François and H. Schulze (eds), *Deutsche Erinnerungsorte*, 3rd edn (Munich: C.H. Beck, 2001), vol. 2, 485–501.
42. F.C. Howe, *Socialized Germany* (New York: Charles Scribner's Sons, 1915), especially vi–vii, 1–8. See also, for example, W.H. Dawson, *Social Insurance in Germany 1883–1911: Its History, Operation, Results and a Comparison with the National Insurance ACT, 1911* (London: Unwin, 1912); D.T. Rodgers, *Atlantic Crossings: Social Politics in a Progressive Age* (Cambridge, MA: Belknap Press, 1998); E.P. Hennock, *English Social Reform and German Precedents: The Case of Social Insurance, 1880–1914* (Oxford: Oxford University Press, 1987).
43. On average, more than 40% of employed Germans were covered by some form of social insurance on the eve of the First World War.
44. H.-P. Ullmann, 'Industrielle Interessen und die Entstehung der deutschen Sozialversicherung', *Historische Zeitschrift* 229 (1979), 574–610.
45. The following discussion builds on J. Moses, *The First Modern Risk: Workplace Accidents and the Origins of European Social States* (Cambridge: Cambridge University Press, 2018), Chapter 2.
46. *Stenographische Berichte des deutschen Reichstags* (SBDR) 12 January 1893, vol. 128, 430; 25 May 1900, vol. 169, 5764; 29 February 1908, vol. 231, 3502; 19 March 1915, vol. 306, 67.

47. In contrast to contemporaneous distinctions outlined in discourses of 'cultural pessimism'. See J. Fisch, 'Zivilisation, Kultur', in O. Brunner et al. (eds), *Geschichtliche Grundbegriffe: Historisches Lexikon zur politisch-sozialen Sprache in Deutschland* (Stuttgart: Klett-Cotta, 1992), vol. 7, 688–792.
48. SBDR, 25 May 1900, vol. 202, 5764.
49. SBDR 1 February 1906, vol. 215, 959; 5 December 1913, vol. 291, 6211; 22 May 1916, vol. 307, 1198.
50. The 'Standard of Life', rather than the 'Standard of Living', was the term quoted in English by a variety of parliamentary representatives when referring to this notion.
51. SBDR, 23 April 1896, vol. 145, 1871; 6 February 1906, vol. 215, 1049; 15 February 1912, vol. 283, 46.
52. SBDR, 30 March 1889, vol. 106, 1135; see also 14 January 1893, vol. 127, 494.
53. SBDR, 30 March 1889, vol. 106, 1144; 4 April 1889, vol. 106, 1261.
54. S.J. Woolf, 'The Construction of a European World-View in the Revolutionary-Napoleonic Years', *Past and Present* 137 (1992), 72–101, at 89; E. Adamovsky, 'Euro-orientalism and the Making of the Concept of Eastern Europe in France, 1810–80', *Journal of Modern History* 77 (2005), 591–628.
55. SBDR, 22 April 1896, vol. 145, 1866; 1 February 1906, vol. 215, 959; 8 May 1911, vol. 266, 6483.
56. SBDR, 30 November 1908, vol. 233, 5837; 28. April 1914, vol. 294, 8307.
57. Adamovsky, 'Euro-orientalism', 591, 613, 617–18; B. Porter, *The Absent-Minded Imperialists: Empire, Society and Culture in Britain* (Oxford: Oxford University Press, 2004), 185–86, 308–10, quoted at 78.
58. SBDR 22 April 1896, vol. 145, 1866; SBDR, 1 March 1905, vol. 202, 4888; 8 May 1911, vol. 266, 6483.
59. See, for example, SBDR 22 April 1896, vol. 145, 1866; see also: SBDR, 13 January 1892, vol. 118, 3601.
60. SBDR, 13 December 1897, vol. 159, 173; 8 Jun. 1899, vol. 167, 2416.
61. SBDR, 3 February 1906, vol. 215, 991; 28 January 1913, vol. 287, 3320–1; 13 January 1892, vol. 118, 3608; 9 February 1906, vol. 215, 1160.
62. F. Stern, *The Politics of Cultural Despair: A Study in the Rise of the Germanic Ideology* (Berkeley: University of California Press, 1974).
63. Hennock, *English Social Reform*; E. Rogers, '"A Most Imperial Contribution": New Zealand and the Old Age Pensions Debate in Britain, 1882–1912', *Journal of Global History* 9, no. 2 (2014), 189–207.
64. 'Compensation for Accidents', *Oddfellows Magazine* 29 (January 1898), 11–12, at 11. See P. Thane, 'The Working Class and State "Welfare in Britain, 1880–1914', *Historical Journal* 27 (1984), 877–900; T. Alborn, 'Senses of Belonging: The Politics of Working-Class Insurance in Britain, 1880–1914', *Journal of Modern History* 73 (2001), 561–602.
65. 'Labour's Death Roll: Employers' Liability versus Insurance: A Trades Union Plebiscite: What the Leaders of a Million Workmen Say', *Daily News*, 8 February 1897.
66. 4 *Hansard* vol. 48 (3 May 1897), 1467; E.H.H. Green, *The Crisis of Conservatism: The Politics, Economics and Ideology of the British Conservative Party, 1880–1914* (London: Routledge, 1995), 128–30.
67. R.D. to Kenelm Digby, 13 August 1896, NA: Fl. Unnumbered, Box 9867. B13816H, Series 45, HO, Home Office Papers; Edward Wingfield to Kenelm Digby, 13 August 1896, NA: Fl. Unnumbered, Box 9867. B13816H, Series 45, HO, Home Office Papers.

68. L. Luzzatti, 'La Cassa nazionale di assicurazione per gli infortuni degli operai sul lavoro', *Nuova antologia*, 3rd series, 21 (May 1889), 312ff, at 328.
69. V. Sellin, *Die Anfänge staatlicher Sozialreform* (Stuttgart: Clett-Kotta, 1971), Chapter 1.
70. A. Mitchell, *The Divided Path: The German Influence on Social Reform in France after 1870* (Chapel Hill: University of North Carolina Press, 1991), 14–15, 310.
71. A. Salandra, 'Un caso del socialismo di stato: lo stato assicuratore', *Nuova Antologia*, 2nd series, 27 (1 June 1881), 444–79, at 445.
72. U. Mazzola, 'L'assicurazione degli operai nella scienza e nella legislazione germanica', *Annali del credito e della previdenza* 14 (1885).
73. P. Baldwin, 'Comparing and Generalizing: Why All History is Comparative, Yet No History is Sociology', in D. Cohen and M. O'Connor (eds), *Comparison and History: Europe in Cross-national Perspective* (New York: Routledge, 2004), 1–22, at 6.

# Bibliography

Abbott, A., 'History and Sociology: The Lost Synthesis', *Social Science History* 15 (1991), 201–38.
Adamovsky, E., 'Euro-orientalism and the Making of the Concept of Eastern Europe in France, 1810–80', *Journal of Modern History* 77 (2005), 591–628.
Alborn, T., 'Senses of Belonging: The Politics of Working-Class Insurance in Britain, 1880–1914', *Journal of Modern History* 73 (2001), 561–602.
Amenta, E., 'What We Know about the Development of Social Policy: Comparative and Historical Research in Comparative and Historical Perspective', in Mahoney, J. and Ruschemeyer, D. (eds), *Comparative Historical Analysis in the Social Sciences* (Cambridge: Cambridge University Press, 2003), 91–130.
Apter, D.E., 'Comparative Sociology: Some Paradigms and Their Movements', in Calhoun, C. et al. (eds), *The SAGE Handbook of Sociology* (Thousand Oaks, CA: Sage, 2005), 103–28.
Baldwin, P., *The Politics of Social Solidarity: Class Bases of the European Welfare State, 1875–1975* (Cambridge: Cambridge University Press, 1990).
———. 'Comparing and Generalizing: Why All History is Comparative, Yet No History is Sociology', in Cohen, D. and O'Connor, M. (eds), *Comparison and History: Europe in Cross-National Perspective* (New York: Routledge, 2004), 1–22.
Béland, D., and Petersen, K., 'Introduction: Social Policy Concepts and Language', in Béland, D. and Petersen, K. (eds), *Analysing Social Policy Concepts and Language: Comparative and Transnational Perspectives* (Bristol: Policy Press, 2014), 1–12.
Béland, D., and Petersen, K. (eds), *Analysing Social Policy Concepts and Language: Comparative and Transnational Perspectives* (Bristol: Policy Press, 2014).
Burrow, J., and Collini, S., 'The Clue to the Maze: The Appeal of the Comparative Method', in Winch, D., Burrow, J. and Collini, S. (eds), *That Noble Science of Politics: A Study in Nineteenth-Century Intellectual History* (Cambridge University Press: Cambridge, 1983), 207–46.
Castles, F.G., *Families of Nations: Patterns of Public Policy in Western Democracies* (Dartmouth, NH: Aldershot, 1993).
'Compensation for Accidents', *Oddfellows Magazine* 29 (January 1898), 11–12.
*Congrès international des accidents du travail et des assurance sociales, troisième session, Milan, 1–6 octobre 1894*, vol. 1: *Rapports presentés*... (Milan: Impr. H. Reggiani, 1894–95).

Dawson, W.H., *Social Insurance in Germany 1883–1911: Its History, Operation, Results and a Comparison with the National Insurance Act, 1911* (London: Unwin, 1912).
De Swaan, A., *In Care of the State: Health Care, Education and Welfare in Europe and the USA in the Modern Era* (New York: Oxford University Press, 1988).
Dejace, C., 'La responsabilité des accidents du travail et le risque professionnel', in Gruner, É. (ed.), *Exposition universelle internationale de 1889: Congrès international des accidents du travail*, vol. 2: *Comptes Rendus des séances et visite du congrès* (Paris: Librarie Polytechnique Baudrie et Cie, 1890), 194–96.
Dogan, M., 'Strategies in Comparative Sociology', *Comparative Sociology* 1 (2002), 63–92.
Durkheim, É., *Les formes eléméntaires de la vie religieuse: le système totémique en Australie* (1912; Paris: Presses Universitaires de France, 1960).
Engerman, D.C., *Modernization from the Other Shore: American Intellectuals and the Romance of Russian Development* (Cambridge, MA: Harvard University Press, 2003).
Esping-Anderson, G., *The Three Worlds of Welfare Capitalism* (Oxford: Polity Press, 1990).
Ferrera, M., and Rhodes, M., *Recasting European Welfare States* (Ilford: Frank Cass, 2000).
Fisch, J., 'Zivilisation, Kultur', in Brunner, O. et al. (eds), *Geschichtliche Grundbegriffe: Historisches Lexikon zur politisch-sozialen Sprache in Deutschland*, vol. 7 (Stuttgart: Klett-Cotta, 1992), 688–792.
Flora, P., *Growth to Limits: The Western European Welfare States since World War II* (Berlin: De Gruyter, 1986).
Flora, P., and Heidenheimer, A.J. (eds), *The Development of Welfare States in Europe and America* (New Brunswick, NJ: Transaction, 1981).
Foucault, M., *The Birth of Biopolitics: Lectures at the Collège de France, 1978–79*, Senellart, M. (ed.), Burchell, G. (trans.) (Basingstoke: Palgrave Macmillan, 2008).
Green, E.H.H., *The Crisis of Conservatism: The Politics, Economics and Ideology of the British Conservative Party, 1880–1914* (London: Routledge, 1995).
Gruner, É. (ed.), *Exposition universelle internationale de 1889: Congrès international des accidents du travail*, vol. 2: *Comptes Rendus des séances et visite du congrès* (Paris: Librarie Polytechnique Baudrie et Cie, 1890).
Hacker, J.S., *The Divided Welfare State: The Battle over Public and Private Social Benefits in the United States* (Cambridge: Cambridge University Press, 2002).
*Hansard's Parliamentary Debates, Fourth Series*, vol. 48 (1897).
Harrison, D., *The Sociology of Modernization and Development* (London: Routledge, 1988).
Heclo, H., *Modern Social Politics in Britain and Sweden: From Relief to Income Maintenance* (New Haven: Yale University Press, 1974).
Hennock, E.P., *English Social Reform and German Precedents: The Case of Social Insurance, 1880–1914* (Oxford: Oxford University Press, 1987).
———. *The Origin of the Welfare State in England and Germany, 1850–1914* (Cambridge: Cambridge University Press, 2007).
Howe, F.C., *Socialized Germany* (New York: Charles Scribner's Sons, 1915).
Klein, G.A., *Die Arbeiterversicherung des Deutschen Reichs* (Berlin: Reichsdruckerei, 1904).
Kott, S., 'Der Sozialstaat', in François, E. and Schulze, H. (eds), *Deutsche Erinnerungsorte*, 3rd edn (Munich: C.H. Beck, 2001), vol. 2, 485–501.
———. *Sozialstaat und Gesellschaft: das deutsche Kaiserreich in Europa* (Göttingen: Vandenhoeck & Ruprecht, 2014).
'Labour's Death Roll: Employers' Liability versus Insurance: A Trades Union Plebiscite: What the Leaders of a Million Workmen Say', *Daily News*, 8 February 1897.
Lange, M., *Comparative Historical Methods* (Thousand Oaks, CA: Sage, 2013).

Leimgruber, M., 'The Embattled Standard-Bearer of Social Insurance and its Challenger: The ILO, the OECD, and the "Crisis of the Welfare State", 1975–1985', in Kott, S. and Droux, J. (eds), *Globalizing Social Rights: The ILO and Beyond* (Basingstoke: Palgrave Macmillan, 2013), 293–309.

Mahoney, J., and Ruschemeyer, D. (eds), *Comparative Historical Analysis in the Social Sciences* (Cambridge: Cambridge University Press, 2003).

Marshall, T.H., and Bottomore, T., *Citizenship and Social Class* (1950; London: Pluto Classics, 1992).

Mazzola, U., 'L'assicurazione degli operai nella scienza e nella legislazione germanica', *Annali del credito e della previdenza* 14 (1885).

Mill, J.S., *A System of Logic: Ratiocinative and Inductive: Being a Connected View of Principles of Evidence and the Methods of Scientific Investigation*, 2 vols (London: John W. Parker, 1843).

Mitchell, A., *The Divided Path: The German Influence on Social Reform in France after 1870* (Chapel Hill: University of North Carolina Press, 1991).

Morgan, K.J., *Working Mothers and the Welfare State: Religion and the Politics of Work-Family Policies in Western Europe and the United States* (Stanford: Stanford University Press, 2006).

Moses, J., 'Policy Communities and Exchanges across Borders: The Case of Workplace Accidents at the Turn of the Twentieth Century', in Rodogno, D. et al. (eds), *Shaping the Transnational Sphere: Experts, Networks and Issues from the 1840s to the 1930s* (Oxford: Berghahn Books, 2014), 60–81.

———. 'Social Citizenship and Social Rights in an Age of Extremes: T.H. Marshall's Social Philosophy in the *longue durée*', *Modern Intellectual History* 16 (1) (2019), 155–84.

———. *The First Modern Risk: Workplace Accidents and the Origins of European Social States* (Cambridge: Cambridge University Press, 2018).

Orloff, A., 'Gender in the Welfare State', *Annual Review of Sociology* 22 (1996), 51–78.

Pedersen, S., *Family, Dependence, and the Origins of the Welfare State: Britain and France, 1914–1945* (Cambridge: Cambridge University Press, 1993).

Porter, B., *The Absent-Minded Imperialists: Empire, Society and Culture in Britain* (Oxford: Oxford University Press, 2004).

Rimlinger, G.V., *Welfare Policy and Industrialization in Europe, America, and Russia* (New York: Wiley, 1971).

Ritter, G.A., *Social Welfare in Germany and Britain: Origins and Development* (Leamington Spa: Berg, 1986).

Rodgers, D.T., *Atlantic Crossings: Social Politics in a Progressive Age* (Cambridge, MA: Belknap Press, 1998).

Rogers, E., '"A Most Imperial Contribution": New Zealand and the Old Age Pensions Debate in Britain, 1882–1912', *Journal of Global History* 9(2) (2014), 189–207.

Ross, M.H., and Homer, E., 'Galton's Problem in Cross-national Research', *World Politics* 29 (1976), 1–28.

Salandra, A., 'Un caso del socialismo di stato: lo stato assicuratore', *Nuova Antologia*, 2nd series, 27 (1 June 1881), 444–79.

Saunier, P.-Y., 'Circulations, connexions et espaces transnationaux', *Genèses* 57 (2004), 110–26.

Sellin, V., *Die Anfänge staatlicher Sozialreform* (Stuttgart: Clett-Kotta, 1971).

Skocpol, T., *Protecting Soldiers and Mothers: The Political Origins of Social Policy in the United States* (Cambridge, MA: Belknap Press, 1992).

'Social Expenditure Update: Social Spending is Falling in Some Countries, But in Many Others it Remains at Historically High Levels', OECD: Directorate for Employment, Labour and

Social Affairs, *Insights from the OECD Social Expenditure Database (SOCX)*, November 2014, retrieved 11 March 2019 from https://www.oecd.org/els/soc/OECD2014-Social-Expenditure-Update-Nov2014-8pages.pdf.

*Stenographische Berichte des deutschen Reichstags*, vol. 106-307 (1889–1916).

Stern, F., *The Politics of Cultural Despair: A Study in the Rise of the Germanic Ideology* (Berkeley: University of California Press, 1974).

Sumner Maine, H., *Ancient Law: Its Connection with the Early History of Society and its Relation to Modern Ideas* (London: John Murray, 1861).

'Teaching the Teachers', *The Economist*, 11–17 June 2016, 23–25.

Thane, P., 'The Working Class and State "Welfare" in Britain, 1880–1914', *Historical Journal* 27 (1984), 877–900.

Thelen, K.A., *How Institutions Evolve: The Political Economy of Skills in Germany, Britain, the United States, and Japan*, Cambridge Studies in Comparative Politics (Cambridge: Cambridge University Press, 2004).

Ullmann, H.-P., 'Industrielle Interessen und die Entstehung der deutschen Sozialversicherung', *Historische Zeitschrift* 229 (1979), 574–610.

Van Kersbergen, K., and Manow, P. (eds.), *Religion, Class Coalitions, and Welfare States* (Cambridge: Cambridge University Press, 2009).

Weber, M., *Economy and Society: An Outline of Interpretive Sociology*, Roth, G. and Wittrich, C. (eds), 2 vols (Berkeley: University of California Press, 2013 [1922]).

Wincott, D., 'Original and Imitated or Elusive and Limited? Towards a Genealogy of the Welfare State in Britain', in Béland, D. and Petersen, K. (eds), *Analysing Social Policy Concepts and Language: Comparative and Transnational Perspectives* (Bristol: Policy Press, 2014), 127–41.

Woolf, S.J., 'The Construction of a European World-View in the Revolutionary-Napoleonic Years', *Past and Present* 137 (1992), 72–101.

# 8

# Comparison, Rivalry and Competition under Neoliberalism and State Socialism

## David Priestland

> Sometimes people confuse socialist emulation (*sorevnovanie*) with competition (*konkurenstiia*). This is a big mistake. Socialist emulation and competition represent two completely different principles.
>
> The principle of competition is: the defeat and death of some, the victory and domination of others.
>
> The principle of socialist emulation is: comradely help to the laggards by the leaders in order to achieve a general advance.
>
> This explains the unprecedented production enthusiasm, which has seized the millions of the worker masses, something which competition could not have achieved.[1]
>
> —I.V. Stalin, 1929

In this introduction to E. Mikulina's 1929 pamphlet, *Emulation of the Masses*, Iosif Stalin gave his imprimatur to the new 'socialist emulation' movement, which developed into the 'Stakhanovism' of the mid 1930s and became the model for similar movements across the socialist world as long as it lasted.[2] In doing so, he sought to promote a form of labour organization that avoided the evils of capitalist 'competition' and yet harnessed some of the incentives that capitalism used to ensure high productivity.

The etymological root of the Russian word *sorevnovanie* is 'envy' (*revnost*), and it is best translated as 'emulation' – a term that includes a strong element of 'imitation' and means the desire to imitate somebody and either match or surpass them. So while 'emulation' includes a process of comparison and indeed elements of rivalry (a meaning that was stronger in the past), in current usage it differs from 'competition' when it comes to what is done once the rivalrous comparison has been made. In a 'competition', the goal is to defeat the comparator; it is never enough to match them. The emulator in contrast always imitates the comparator, and 'mere' equality is an option. For Stalin and his allies, therefore, workers' collectives would improve their productivity by comparing themselves with other collectives and 'emulating' the successful ones for the greater good; this is not far from the currently fashionable concept of 'benchmarking' according to 'best practice' (though Stalin's claim that this process would inspire 'production enthusiasm' as well as technical improvements is not common in contemporary management thinking).[3]

The case of 'socialist emulation', and Stalin's eagerness to distinguish this 'good' 'socialist' form of economic comparison from a 'bad' capitalist one, raises important questions about the relationship between comparison and competition, on the one hand, and their connections with states and markets, and the ideologies of left and the pro-market right, on the other. In contemporary political debate, the increasing power of formalized comparisons – such as league tables – as well as the comparisons at an individual level encouraged by advertising and consumerism is commonly associated with the importance of competitiveness and the influence of markets and market liberalism (or 'neoliberalism') since the 1970s. Indeed, 'neoliberalism' is defined by many scholars as an ideology that has market-style competition at its core and involves a strong role for the state in extending that competition to all areas of life.[4] However, as the Stalinist case shows, states committed to nonmarket modernization projects have also encouraged comparison within the economic sphere. Indeed, in a recent *cause célèbre* in Britain, Craig Brandist, a Professor of Cultural Theory and Intellectual History at Sheffield University with expertise in Soviet history, drew attention to the parallels between state socialism and higher education under late capitalism in an article he wrote for the *Times Higher Literary Supplement* entitled 'A Very Stalinist Management Model', which included the 'spread of proxy metrics, the target culture, competition between institutions, the erosion of the autonomy of academic research and professional priorities and imported productivity mechanisms such as performance management regimes'.[5] Extraordinarily, the University of Sheffield's administration seemed keen to justify the parallel with Stalinism when it threatened to discipline him for making these criticisms in public, and it took months of effort with the help of lawyers and his trade union to ensure that no action was taken.

So why should Stalinist 'emulation' have similarities with neoliberal 'competition'? Clearly, if one sees neoliberalism primarily as the consequence of a turn towards an unconstrained form of capitalism and capitalist class rule since the 1970s, it is difficult to explain these parallels.[6] The Foucaultian approach to neoliberalism is more helpful, as it gives a role to states and 'governmentality' in encouraging competition, for Foucault related (albeit vaguely) neoliberal competition to the concepts of 'governmentality' or 'biopolitics', which states use to organize their populations, to 'ensure, sustain, and multiply life, to put this life in order'.[7] Not only are competitive markets created, but individuals are encouraged to internalize competitiveness and become 'entrepreneurs of the self'. Yet why should these forms of governmentality have any resonance in the Stalinist USSR? Foucault's own analysis of neoliberalism located these approaches to the self in various forms of twentieth-century economic liberalism, with their roots in the liberal governmentalities of the eighteenth century; these were clearly not as influential in the Soviet Union.[8]

In this chapter I shall try to address these questions by arguing that we need to think about the politics of market competition in a broader context than is normal, situating it both within and outside the context of markets and economic liberalism. But at the same time, we need to make distinctions between different forms of market competition. And an analysis of these debates across a wide range of historical periods and societies not only helps us to situate state-socialist competition and market competition within a comparative context, but also serves broader purposes: to understand more fully the issues at stake in both political and economic debates about market competition; and to provide a novel approach to the thorny and controversial concept of 'neoliberalism', allowing us to make crucial distinctions between different neoliberal conceptions of competition.

I shall first argue that the general question of competition, emulation and rivalry has been a central one for many centuries in both market and nonmarket societies because they have been seen as having benefits as well as costs – benefits in terms of dynamism (whether aristocratic 'courage' or market 'innovation'), and costs in terms of discord and feelings of dissatisfaction among those who feel themselves to be unsuccessful. However, once industry and commerce rather than agriculture began to become important foundations of wealth, both for individuals and states, market competition became more acceptable and even valuable. Not only did it establish market prices, hence enabling the powerful distributional and coordinating mechanisms established by markets, but it also established the disciplines and incentives that helped to encourage wealth creation and consumption, and could be used by states to control subjects and citizens as part of new forms of governmentality. Hence, the wholesale rejection of all forms of competition and economic comparison became increasingly marginal, even among critics of capitalism.

Second, I shall argue that the conventional conceptual framework that sees the distinction between 'state' and 'market' as the main one, and regards the 'neoliberal' competition that became so important from the 1980s as simply an extreme form of market competition obscures the important differences between liberal forms of competition, including those advocated by neoliberals themselves. Rather, it is more helpful to identify a number of distinct forms of competition related to different social ethoses, which are in turn connected to the values of particular social groups engaged in the search for power and ideological hegemony.[9] In particular, I argue that we need to distinguish between three conceptions of competition: one associated with the ethos of small merchants and businesspeople involved in trade; the second with warrior aristocrats, or their successors, the Schumpeterian 'entrepreneurs'; and the third with officials and technocrats who were involved in regulating or overseeing competition. These models of competition were defended in both market and nonmarket systems, and also justified the power of distinct groups within the society concerned.

The chapter will identify debates over the value of these different models of competition, and the desirability of competition itself, in four very different eras: first, the seventeenth and eighteenth centuries, when the issue of social comparison lay at the centre of disagreements over the moral implications of the emerging 'commercial society'; second, from the 1860s to the First World War, when debates over the role of markets became framed in scientific rather than moral terms; third, the period from the financial crisis of 1929 to the mid twentieth century, when economic liberals were on the defensive, but both they and socialists sought to reconcile competition with economies now dominated by states; and, fourth, the period from the 1970s onwards, when market competition became increasingly hegemonic and acceptable to both left and right.

## Competition, Comparison and the Emergence of 'Commercial Society'

The English word 'competition', from the Latin 'competitio' or 'seeking with', became specifically associated with economic issues in the mid eighteenth century, though it could refer to a number of forms of rivalry before then. The word included a number of concepts that are an important source of the ambiguity in its meaning. Central was the tension between a 'togetherness' element and a conflictual one. For it implies a commonality between participants' goals and acceptance of rules – in contrast to war, and early usage had no conflictual element at all – something that can be seen more clearly in the similar term 'concurrentia' ('running with'), which is both the origin of the English word 'concurrence' ('agreement') and the German *Konkurrenz* ('competition') and thence the Russian *konkurentsiia*. But both aspects are evident in the definition provided in Dr Johnson's *Dictionary* of 1755 – 'The action of endeavouring to gain what another endeavours to gain at the same time' – and have been central to the concept since then.[10]

Competition and rivalry have been present in various forms in most societies, as have efforts to control them, and the extent to which they are valued or condemned has varied. Before the modern era, aristocratic warrior codes of rivalry, violence and lavish display were often seen as enabling the manifestation of virtues such as 'courage' and 'heroism', whereas the very different type of competitive behaviour common among merchants – the competition with consumers and other merchants for advantage by buying cheap and selling dear – was generally seen as less acceptable. So, in medieval European societies, efforts were made by clerical guardians of law and morality to contain both forms of competition to different degrees. They certainly denounced aristocratic 'pride' (*superbia*) and tried to limit violence to particular periods of the week or year, or channelled it into sacred 'crusades' under their control.[11] But merchant competition was normally treated with more disapproval. The 'scholastic' moralists did not outlaw competitive market behaviour completely, instead insisting that it be subject to moral rules,[12] but they still saw it as a product of 'greed' – both offending God by overvaluing the material over the spiritual and harming other people (on the assumption that economic competition was inevitably zero-sum and excessive wealth for some was always at the expense of others). Merchant communities were therefore stigmatized, while consumerism – the desire for greater status through the acquisition of consumer goods – was condemned as 'envy' as it breached the rigid, hierarchical social imaginary. Such hostility to commerce was common in agrarian societies dominated by landowner aristocracies across the globe and was reflected in official social hierarchies; merchants tended to occupy a position below both warriors and clerics, and in East Asia they were placed below peasants as well.

Yet by the seventeenth century, the relative status of aristocratic and mercantile forms of competition was changing, especially in northwestern Europe, where states were becoming more successful in taming their warrior aristocracies and were also more reliant on trade and merchant wealth. Thomas Hobbes' *Leviathan* (1651) reflected this development when he called for a strong sovereign to curb 'competition of riches, honour, command, or other power' – vices that were particularly associated with warrior aristocracies, but which he believed were natural to all men – and which 'inclineth to contention, enmity, and war'; instead, the sovereign had to create prosperity by establishing security for property.[13]

However, more common than Hobbes' vision in the seventeenth century was a combination of aristocratic and mercantile versions of competition in 'mercantilism': the primary economic competitor was now the nation, which used monopolistic trading companies afforced by military power to seize markets from other powers; this strategy seemed to make sense at a time of sharp commercial rivalry between Holland, England and France. As Sir Josiah Child explained clearly in 1681: 'Wealth and power consists in Comparisons … England may be said to be rich or strong, as our strength or Riches bears a proportion with our Neighbouring Nations, French, Dutch, &c, and consequently whatever weakens or depopulates them, enricheth and strengtheneth England.'[14]

However, the reaction against this monopolistic mercantilist order from the end of the seventeenth century developed into a fully fledged defence of merchant competition as an alternative to the aristocratic, warrior form.[15] And by the mid eighteenth century, the ways of life encouraged by the market – whether that of the trader or the consumer – were being defended as an alternative to and remedy for the evils of violent aristocratic rivalry, as well as nationalist mercantilist competition.

Much of the justification for markets was based on the argument that self-interested competition promoted the wellbeing of everybody through the efficient allocation of resources – most influentially expressed in Adam Smith's notion of the market's 'invisible hand'. However, Smith and other defenders of markets also argued that trade would create a new kind of person. They would in part be imbued with the virtues traditionally associated with merchants, what we might call the 'bourgeois' virtues of self-discipline and expertise (real and solid professional abilities, joined to prudent, just, firm and temperate conduct).[16] But they would also involve a form of 'sociability', as David Hume put it.[17] Trade might involve comparison and competition, but it was a type of competition that required negotiation, understanding of one's interlocutor and a common goal; it was the 'togetherness' element in the word '*com*petition' that was being stressed rather than the rivalrous element. For Smith, trade was not only natural (an innate 'propensity to truck, barter, and exchange one thing for another'), but it also encouraged a natural 'sympathy' with others, which countered feelings of envy and resentment.[18] He combined this defence of trade with a more common argument at the time – that competition in the market encouraged a flexible, gentle, 'doux' behaviour, in contrast to the aggressive competition for honour and glory between warrior aristocrats, and hence trade would promote peace.[19] As Montesquieu put it in *The Spirit of the Laws*: 'It is almost a general rule that wherever we find agreeable (*doux*) manners there is commerce. And wherever there is commerce, there we meet with agreeable manners.'[20]

Such optimistic views of trade and commerce were naturally rejected by conservative defenders of traditional hierarchy, but a more powerful and influential criticism came from a more egalitarian position, in the work of Rousseau, which laid the foundations for many future socialist critiques. For Rousseau, the commercial person only appeared to be engaging in 'civilized', *doux* sociability; in fact, they were as competitive as anybody, but hid their 'jealousy' under 'the mask of goodwill'. The fact that they did not have coercive power forced the commercial person to engage in stratagems to 'interest them in his situation, and to make them find, either in reality or in appearance, their advantage in labouring for his'. It was this that rendered 'him false and artificial with some, imperious and unfeeling with others, and lays him under a necessity of deceiving all those for whom he has occasion, when he cannot terrify them, and does not find it for his interest to serve them in reality'. The commercial person was therefore fundamentally inauthentic, as he 'must for his advantage show himself to be one thing, while in reality he is another. To be and to appear to be, became two things entirely different'.[21]

Hence, for Rousseau, all forms of competition had to be limited as far as possible, not just aristocratic ones. And, indeed, the principle underpinning competition – comparison – had to be limited too, for it rendered people slaves to the opinions of others and created dissatisfaction, preventing people from achieving virtue.[22] Rousseau had a number of solutions to these problems: one was to abandon commercial society completely, even if that was at the expense of wealth;

another was to establish a programme of moral education that discouraged any forms of competition. Thus, Émile, his exemplary pupil, is allowed to run in races as a small child, but 'once he has begun to be able to reason', there would 'never be any comparisons with other children, no rivals, no competitors, not even in running'.[23]

Rousseau's critique had a major impact on the debate over commercial society and Adam Smith's *Theory of Moral Sentiments* sought to deal with what he regarded as a serious challenge to his defence of commerce. He accepted many aspects of Rousseau's argument: the commercial person did indeed strive to 'acquire talents superior to all his competitors', while at the same time in his search for employment, 'he makes his court to all mankind; he serves those whom he hates, and is obsequious to those whom he despises'.[24] This person, who spent his time seeking approval by presenting himself as virtuous to others rather than acting in a truly virtuous way, could not be happy. And like Rousseau, Smith believed that the market could not create authentic and virtuous people by itself. However, unlike Rousseau, he insisted that commercial society was compatible with virtue if supplemented by the sort of education in virtue advocated by the stoics.[25] Hence, ultimately Smith's defence of the market was a limited one. He refused to argue that the 'sympathy' generated by commercial society was sufficient to overcome the disadvantages brought by markets that Rousseau had identified; there had to be a powerful educational sphere, as well as a political sphere, where the classical virtues reigned and commercial values were absent, in order to balance and control the market.

## The Scientization of the Debate: Neoclassicism and Marxism

As the influence of market competition on politics and economics grew, it became more common to defend markets in a more unconditional way than Smith had ever done. This can be seen in the evangelical views of markets as a divinely ordained system to reward and punish, common among British elites in the 1830s and 1840s as they established the foundations of the British-dominated global 'free trade'.[26] But it is also evident in the later 'neoclassical' political economists who sought to lay the foundations of a 'scientific' and mathematical economics later in the century. The 'marginalism' which William Stanley Jevons pioneered, founded as it was on the view that the value of goods lay in the subjective perceptions of their utility by consumers competing in the market, and that the economy was centred on establishing an equilibrium between supply and demand, was a conscious departure from the classical economics of Smith, which also located value partly in the objective cost of production, including the contribution of labour. By making the participant in competitive markets the source of value and the centre of the economy rather than the labourer, marginalist economics undermined a socialist politics, while claiming to underpin a 'democracy' of ordinary consumers and traders. As the economist Ludwig von Mises put it in 1944, 'the capitalist system of production is an economic democracy in which every penny gives a right to vote. The consumers are the sovereign people'.[27]

At the same time, the English marginalists in particular sought to overcome Smith's anxieties about the moral and psychological effects of competition and comparison by developing his 'invisible hand' into a utilitarian and mechanistic view of the economy. Jevons in particular saw the economy in a highly abstract way, as a machine that could balance the preferences of each self-interested, competitive individual in a perfect equilibrium – a view of the world that he applied to the individual as well. As he wrote in his journal in 1855, 'a man's mind and character may be likened to a complicated piece of machinery moved by steam … just as the machine may turn out the most beautiful work from the rudest material, so is the man, under the influence of his guiding passions capable of the noblest, the most disinterested & the greatest actions'.[28]

The year 1871, which marked the appearance of Jevons' *The Theory of Political Economy* (as well as the major text of the other founder of the marginalist school, Carl Menger, the *Principles of Economics*), also saw the publication of Karl Marx's *The Civil War in France*, his encomium to the recently defeated Paris Commune, which for the first time gave Marx international fame as the 'red terror doctor', just as Europe was about to enter a long depression that helped the development of the working-class socialist movement. But Jevons and Marx had more in common than contemporaneity. Just as Jevons sought to replace Adam Smith's moral discourses about citizen virtue with a scientistic economics, so Marx moved from 'philosophy' to 'science': from an older philosophical critique of capitalism founded on the objection to 'alienation' – an argument that shared features with Rousseau's condemnation of the commercial people's inauthenticity and enslavement to external measures of worth – to the search for scientifically rational forms of production that avoided 'exploitation'.

In contrast to liberal economists, Marx saw monopoly rather than competition as the more normal condition of capitalism, but he had always been a strong critic of capitalist competition – unlike socialists such as Proudhon, who saw competition between small producers as the solution to capitalist monopoly. In response to Proudhon, Marx did not condemn 'industrial emulation', the object of which was the 'product'; rather, he objected to 'competition', which he defined as 'emulation for profit', for there could be no place for profit under socialism.[29] He also feared the effect that competition had on working-class solidarity, for '[c]ompetition makes individuals, not only the bourgeois but still more so the workers, mutually hostile'.[30]

Even so, rather than condemning all economic inequalities and the comparisons they produced outright, Marx was willing to make some compromise with the principles of liberal economics, accepting that some market disciplines were needed to incentivize workers to work until the productive forces could support the ideal society. As he explained in the *Critique of the Gotha Programme* of 1875, in the 'first phase of communist society', people would need to be paid according to how much they worked, because the new society would still be 'stamped with the birthmarks of the old society from whose womb it emerges'. This economy would therefore not be a competitive market economy, but it would still involve a version of 'bourgeois right' and inequality, for some were superior to others physically and mentally, and the collective would allocate wages according to those unequal endowments. Only when 'productive capacities' had increased and people had been transformed so that 'labour has become not only a means of life but life's prime want' would the fully communist principle 'From each according to his ability, to each according to his needs!' be feasible. Any attempt, Marx insisted, to introduce fully communist principles prematurely amounted to 'vulgar socialism'.[31]

As Marx implied, some socialists still supported the Rousseauian hostility to any form of inequality and comparison, and one of them was the anarchist communist Petr Kropotkin. Kropotkin, like Marx, sought to root his proposals in science – in his case in an evolutionary biology which, in contrast with Social Darwinism, insisted humans like other animal species were naturally cooperative and not competitive. Yet his objection to Marx's efforts to combine collectivized property with payment according to the labour expended was not far from the Rousseauian one: the comparisons involved would lead to divisions and envy. For as soon as this kind of 'labour-cheque' system was introduced:

> you will minutely debate the share you are going to take in the creation of new machinery, in the digging of new mines. You will carefully weigh what part of the new produce belongs to you. You will count your minutes of work, and you will take care that a minute of your neighbours cannot buy more than yours.[32]

Before the 1930s, or even 1945, socialist economics was a major threat to liberal *laissez-faire* ideas, but so was a mercantilism adapted for the industrial age – a militaristic and imperialistic view of economic competition that gathered steam from the late 1870s with the depression and consequent challenges to free trade, and reached its apogee in the 1930s.[33] But if these nationalist conceptions of economic competition can be seen as a 'collectivized' version of the warrior aristocratic rivalry of old, economists linked with the Austrian School were developing a combination of the aristocratic conception with the new individualistic methodology of liberal economics. In contrast with marginalist theorists like Jevons, they rejected the concepts of market equilibrium and rational *homines economici*. Economic agents were not rational actors operating in conditions of perfect information, who passively responded to pre-existing conditions of supply and demand, and constantly calculated the benefits and disadvantages of each market transaction, ultimately leading to the ideal balance between everybody's interests. Rather, markets were often in disequilibrium, in part because tastes and production possibilities were changing. Hence, only bold and imaginative 'entrepreneurs', engaging in rivalrous competition with each other, would enable these dynamic markets to achieve new equilibria by bravely seeking new opportunities and employing new business methods.[34] It was therefore not the mass of rational economic actors but a special type of person – the entrepreneur – who was the main source of value. As Ludwig von Mises explained, disagreeing both with the marginalists' emphasis on the consumer, and Adam Smith's emphasis on land, capital and labour:

> The driving force of the market process is provided neither by the consumers nor by the owners of the means of productions – land, capital goods, and labour – but by the promoting and speculating entrepreneurs ... Profit-seeking speculation is the driving force of the market as it is the driving force of production.[35]

This view of markets was often closely related to a politically conservative and elitist agenda, identifying the ideal dynamic entrepreneur explicitly with the warrior aristocrat type of old operating in new market circumstances. As Friedrich von Wieser, one of the first generation of Austrian School economists and Friedrich von Hayek's teacher, explained: the world was divided into leaders and led, and the quality of leaders, and their willingness to compete as entrepreneurs, was crucial to capitalism's dynamism. The problem with the capitalism of his own time, he argued in 1914, was the rarity of 'entrepreneurs' with their 'strong personalities ... audacious technological innovators, organizers with an acute knowledge of human nature, visionary bankers, rash speculators, rulers of trusts conquering the world'.[36]

But it was Wieser's pupil, Joseph Schumpeter, who placed the remodelled aristocratic warrior at the centre of his theory of market competition. As he famously wrote of entrepreneurs' motivations in 1912:

> there is the dream and the will to found a private kingdom, usually, though not necessarily, also a dynasty. The modern world really does not know any such positions, but what may be attained by industrial or commercial success is still the nearest approach to medieval lordship possible to modern man ... Then there is the will to conquer: the impulse to fight, to prove oneself superior to others, to succeed for the sake, not of the fruits of success, but of the success itself. From this aspect, economic action becomes akin to sport.[37]

## Competition Tamed: The Crisis of Liberal Economics

Long before the financial crisis of 1929, Schumpeter, like Wieser, was pessimistic about the ability of his ideal entrepreneurial form of market competition to survive, and while he generally did not think that capitalism itself was under threat, he did believe the form of competitive capitalism he thought meaningful and creative was.[38] For unlike Marx, he did not see the *instability* of markets as the main danger, but an excessive *stability* and resulting loss of dynamism, brought about by a Weberian process of rationalization and bureaucratization, as big firms gradually edged out the small and medium-sized enterprises, and while it was possible for entrepreneurs to join big firms and change their culture, he believed that they were often fields of bureaucratic routine rather than entrepreneurialism.[39]

Yet the collapse of the experiment in a liberal global capitalism led by international banks and presided over by Washington in the 1920s seemed to bear out the Marxist rather than the Schumpeterian critics, and severely damaged the reputation of liberalism, capitalism and market competition itself. This led to a scepticism in the feasibility and desirability of an economic system founded on individual competition across the political spectrum. For challengers to liberalism from the radical right, competition was now located at the national level and was seen in quasi-aristocratic militaristic terms, as a violent Social Darwinist competition between races or an inevitable competition between states for resources or *Lebensraum*. Meanwhile, the radical left was emboldened in its wholesale rejection of market competition. Many liberals also lost faith in the market's ability to operate without serious constraints. Yet this did not mean the complete eclipse of individual competition; politicians and theorists of all persuasions still regarded it as an essential aspect of economic organization, even if it had to be organized by powerful states.

This was certainly the case with the main alternative to market liberalism – the command economy established by the Stalinists from 1928. The Stalinists did make serious attempts to find alternatives to market competition, but they did not go so far as endorsing the Rousseauian objection to all forms of economic comparison. In part this was because they saw their state as undeveloped and vulnerable at a time of violent national and imperial competition, and it was imperative to 'catch up and overtake (*dognat' i peregnat'*)' the West. And even under the less confrontational Khrushchev, who sought to downplay military competition, the Soviets saw their objective as an economic form of 'peaceful competition (*sorevnovanie*)' between systems 'for the purpose of satisfying man's needs in the best possible way'.[40] However, the Bolsheviks also found some form of individual comparative or competitive motivation essential if they were to remake their citizens as disciplined and productive participants in a modern industrial economy. It is in this context that the 'socialist emulation (*sorevnovanie*)' should be seen.

Lenin had first introduced the idea in the months after the revolution, when he was optimistic about creating a new form of socialist economic organization that could combine efficient industrial management and coordination with popular democratic participation in administration. He saw 'emulation', which he was careful to distinguish from capitalist 'competition (*konkurentsiia*)', as a way of allowing workers to experiment with these new forms of management and then to emulate the most successful.[41] But he associated the concept directly with the issue of labour motivation and productivity later when he identified the 'communist *subbotniki*' – weekends when workers worked voluntarily out of enthusiasm for the socialist cause – as forms of socialist emulation.[42]

'Socialist emulation' as a way of promoting these new forms of labour motivation became much more influential in the early years of the first five-year plan (1928–32), when Lenin's 1917 article was published and was used to justify a new 'socialist' work incentive system that relied on 'democratic' mobilization rather than market competition or top-down discipline imposed by managers. The first five-year plan was conceived of as a tool of economic growth to promote breakneck industrialization and collectivization, but higher levels of production were also seen as inextricably linked with a 'great break' (*velikii perelom*), or leap to a more 'socialist', 'proletarian' system. In practice, this included tolerating 'wage egalitarianism', or the reduction of wage differentials between managers, skilled and unskilled workers; promoting 'workers' democracy' within the factory by establishing 'production conferences' in which workers were encouraged to make suggestions for improvements and technical experts were expected to take them seriously; and campaigns of 'criticism and self-criticism', in which workers were encouraged to criticize the 'sceptical', 'rightist' attitudes towards the plan allegedly common among managers and technicians (some of whom were foreign or of 'bourgeois origin'). Such changes in the 'style of leadership', Stalin and his allies claimed, would increase 'workers' activism' (*aktivnost*), 'enthusiasm' for work and the socialist project, and strengthen their feeling that they were 'masters of the country' (*chuvstvo khoziaina*).[43] 'Socialist emulation' was therefore seen as a central method of establishing these new relations between workers and the regime: 'democratic' relations would operate within these 'production collectives' or 'shock brigades' (*udarnye brigady*), individual competition and managerial authoritarianism alike would be discouraged, and groups of workers would engage in friendly 'emulation' with others, copying productive techniques, 'voluntarily' setting themselves high work targets and seeking to match or surpass collectives elsewhere, hence ultimately 'fulfilling and overfulfilling' the plan.[44]

In practice, there was a 'democratic' participatory element to these campaigns; as Viktor Kravchenko, the editor of a factory newspaper at the time, recalled, as long as the worker-critic remained 'within the party line', 'considerable freedom of speech' was possible, especially if the targets were managers or lesser officials.[45] But there were also strong quasi-military elements to this 'socialist' system of incentives; 'socialist competition' could be remarkably close to a military mobilization, with strong resonances of the heroic warrior form of competition: workers were encouraged to become 'labour heroes', to fight on the 'economic front' and to win labour 'honour (*pocheta*)'. As Stalin put it in 1930, the Soviet style of production transformed 'labour from the shameful and heavy burden which it was thought to be previously, into a matter of *honour*, a matter of *glory*, a matter of *valour* and *heroism*. Nothing like this exists or could exist in capitalist countries'.[46]

However, the era of 'proletarian democracy' was a short-lived one, and as the hugely overambitious plan ran into trouble, the leadership came to believe that socialist emulation was leading to disorder because it undermined the power of managers and gave too much power to workers to organize work and set targets. In place of these 'socialist' incentives, the leadership increasingly adopted more conventional methods: individual material incentives and top-down discipline. In 1931, Stalin signalled the beginning of what many Bolsheviks saw as a 'retreat' from socialism in his famous 'six conditions' speech: wage egalitarianism was denounced; hierarchical 'one-man management' was restored; and technical specialists were given authority.[47] In the 1930s, managerial and technocratic authority had the most important place in the economic system, but there was also an effort to ensure that material incentives played a role, together with slightly more emphasis on consumer goods and, implicitly, the consumer desire, aspiration and comparisons that would make the higher wages worth earning.[48] Consumerism became more important from the 1950s under post-Stalin leaders, though efforts were always made to stress the collective, as opposed to individual, benefits of consumption and prevent people falling 'prey to capitalist decadence and commodity fetishism'.[49]

Even so, 'socialist emulation' survived and spread throughout the socialist world, though it was now reconciled with more hierarchical and technocratic forms of management: state officials managed an economic system based in part on material incentives, while using comparisons between enterprises to promote 'rational' improvements to economic units and encouraging harder work by giving selected workers status and other benefits as model workers.[50] Workers were now seen less as 'labour heroes', applying their revolutionary zeal to economic activity and challenging management, than as 'people who have mastered technology' (*tekhnika*), working according to established organizational structures, as well as for money and consumer goods, and thus implicitly influenced by individual competition and comparison.

However, socialist emulation always contained within it a tension between the collectivist, voluntarist and mobilizatory, and the individualistic, hierarchical and technocratic. This is most evident in the Stakhanovite Movement of 1935, named after the Donbas miner Aleksei Stakhanov. Stressing the role of individual heroic Stakhanovites and hailed as a new form of socialist emulation that would combine the need for individual (as opposed to collective) incentives with socialist enthusiasm, it was used by radical mobilizers and technocrats within the Stalinist leadership and bureaucracy to further very different agendas, some undermining managers and others supporting them, and disputes over the goals of the movement helped to fuel the 'Great Terror' of 1937–38.[51] These conflicts can be also seen in several other state-socialist countries and especially in China during the Great Leap Forward of the late 1950s.[52]

If communist states were moving from radical mobilization to a combination of technocratic controls on the one hand and individual competition and material incentives on the other, defenders of liberal capitalism were also reaching a compromise between state and market power, though they were moving from the opposite ideological pole and their vision of the economy was very different. The Ordoliberals – a group of economists associated with the University of Freiburg – were learning from the experience of the collapse of support for markets and the liberal politics that underpinned it in the Weimar era, and its contribution to the rise of Nazism. The lesson they absorbed was that if individual competition was to be saved from statist fascisms or communisms, it had to be controlled by strong, interventionist, pro-market states. Competition, they argued, was needed for economic efficiency and also to promote an ethos of self-discipline and responsibility, and in this they agreed with conventional economic liberals. However, the *laissez-faire* liberal assumption that market competition without nonmarket controls would create a peaceful, cohesive society – whether based on self-interest or 'sympathy' – was false, for it created concentrations of economic power, and hence social resentment from workers, and more generally it caused contention between different sections of society. As Wilhelm Röpke put it:

> We do not demand more from competition than it can give. It is a means of establishing order and exercising control in the narrow sphere of a market economy based on the division of labour, but not a principle on which the whole society can be built ... If competition is not to have the effect of a social explosive and is at the same time not to degenerate, its premise will be a correspondingly sound political and moral framework.[53]

The solution was a type of 'third way' between socialism and *laissez-faire* involving a powerful 'Rechtsstaat' (law-based state) above all particularistic interests, which would establish a powerful legal framework to control monopolies, prevent concentrations of market power to the detriment of small business and workers, and enforce a 'standard of business ethics'. However, more than that, it would pursue a policy of moral and cultural transformation to change the mentality of citizens.[54] For *pace* Adam Smith, there was no natural propensity to 'truck' and trade that could be recruited to underpin a peaceful form of competition. Rather, left to its own devices, industrialization brought a 'natural tendency to proletarianization'[55] – a homogenization, rootlessness and dissatisfaction with the monotony of work, which was the real cause of social discontent, and which was only exacerbated by the 'dependency' encouraged by welfare states. Some Ordoliberals therefore defended a moral role for the state, designed to instil the right entrepreneurial, competitive spirit in the 'degenerated' and 'proletarianized' masses by, for instance, giving ordinary people the opportunity to have property, buy shares or have a share in the profits.[56] The state would thus forge competitive citizens with, as Röpke explained, 'self-discipline, a sense of justice, honesty, fairness, chivalry, moderation, public spirit, respect for human dignity, firm ethical norms – all of these are things which people must possess before they go to market and compete with each other'.[57] In some ways, these were similar to the modest small businessperson idealized by Smith or Weber, though the term 'chivalry' also suggests a more Schumpeterian vision of entrepreneurship, and there are certainly elitist, aristocratic elements to Ordoliberal thought (as Röpke put it, there was a need for a 'sufficient number of such aristocrats of public spirit' made up of unprejudiced and disinterested 'businessmen, farmers, and bankers' to achieve Ordoliberal goals).[58]

Not all pro-market economists and thinkers in the 1940s and 1950s accepted the moral role that the Ordoliberals were willing to grant the state; others, including Friedrich von Hayek, emphasized the role of law and institutions.[59] But many economic liberals agreed that a 'renovation of liberalism' was required, as the American journalist Walter Lippmann put it, a third way between state planning and *laissez-faire* that accepted a significant role for the state in creating the conditions for and defending capitalism.[60] This position came to be termed 'neoliberalism' on the suggestion of one of the participants at the 'Walter Lippmann Colloquium' held in Paris in 1938 (an alternative to other possibilities, such as 'liberalism of the left', 'positive liberalism' and 'social liberalism'), and it was this approach to liberalism, propagated through the international group of liberal economists, the Mont Pèlerin Society, that came to be influential in economic liberal circles in the postwar years.[61]

A version of this form of economic liberalism also had an influence on policy-makers in Germany, and the 'Social Market Economy', as the Ordoliberals described their ideal system, was formally advocated by Ludwig Erhard's Christian Democrats after the Second World War. However, in practice, German governments were much more welfarist and redistributive than Ordoliberal theorists' hostility to welfare dependency might suggest (and indeed many economists associated with Ordoliberalism accepted a significant degree of welfare spending).[62] For like many other governments in the wealthy West after the Second World War, learning the lessons of the 1920s and 1930s produced a rather different 'third way' between *laissez-faire* and socialism to Ordoliberalism: Keynesianianism and welfarism. Christian Democratic, Social Democratic and American 'New Deal Liberal' ideologies did not just call on the state to establish legal regulation of competition to and promote an entrepreneurial spirit, but also established extensive welfare states as well as (in some countries) presiding over corporatist bargains between capital and labour to sustain high employment. Competition was similarly constrained, though by no means eliminated, at the international level: ideas of liberal (and communist) universalism, a reaction against the radical nationalisms of the interwar era, and a transposition of competition to the supranational level of ideological blocs all contributed to this. Though governments often still relied on implicitly competitive ideologies of national development – whether the national 'reconstruction' efforts of Germany and Japan or the developmental projects in postcolonial and communist states – such economic nationalism was much more constrained than it had been before.

## The Return of Market Optimism: The Search for Corporate and National Competitiveness

If economic liberalism was eclipsed in the 1940s and 1950s, and the rather marginal 'neoliberalisms' that did survive shared an acceptance of the need for strong states to create and defend the conditions of a competitive market of small entrepreneurs, from the late 1970s, market competition underwent a serious rehabilitation. Just as the crisis of competitive markets founded on individualistic competition in the 1920s precipitated the turn to statism, so opposition to the extension of welfare states from the 1960s and the crisis of Keynesianism in the 1970s precipitated a loss of faith in state involvement in the economy and society more generally. Indeed, the charges levelled against the state's absence of market competition echoed those against market competition from the 1930s: they were based first on social justice grounds – statist and welfarist systems reallocated resources to 'lazy' workers and welfare recipients – and second on the grounds of effective governance. It became common not only on the neoliberal right, but also more broadly, to make the Ordoliberal argument that the main problem was the 'overburdened state' and that states were undergoing a crisis of 'ungovernability' because their interventionism and activism had made them hostages to particularistic social interests.[63] It followed that they had to withdraw from day-to-day interventions in the economy and insulate themselves from social interests; they might have to restore order after socialist-inspired chaos using harsh methods (hence the support of some neoliberals for Pinochet's mixture of authoritarianism and markets),[64] while relying largely on market disciplines to ensure morality and social order.

This, of course, had much in common with the ordoliberal position in the 1940s, but it was a more antistatist form of neoliberalism that gained ideological hegemony in the 1970s and 1980s, with its roots in a mistrust of the state common in the United States ('statophobia' as Foucault called it); this contrasted with the Ordoliberals' quasi-Hegelian faith in the state as potential embodiment of progress, standing above all particularistic interests. One of the earliest signs of this shift to a greater scepticism of the state and optimism about the efficacy of individualistic market competition can be seen in the thinking of the second-generation members of the Chicago School from the 1950s – George Stigler, Aaron Director and especially its most public figure Milton Friedman – a development that was to cause tensions within the Mont Pèlerin Society with those, like Hayek, who had seen their project as a genuine 'third way' between *laissez-faire* and socialism.[65]

In many ways, Friedman and his Chicago allies were returning to the market optimism of the era of Jevons and the nineteenth-century utilitarian marginalists; as Friedman wrote:

> The closest approach that the United States has had to true free enterprise capitalism was in the nineteenth century ... it was a period when the motto on the Statue of Liberty meant what it said ... It was a period in which the ordinary man experienced the greatest rise in his standard of life that was probably ever experienced in a comparable period in any country at any time.[66]

Ordoliberal anxieties about the socially 'explosive' effects of unfettered markets were replaced with an optimistic faith in the invisible hand, coordinating individual self-interest. And at the same time, Friedman used a more moralistic language about the ability of markets to encourage the bourgeois virtues of self-reliance, one that Hayek generally avoided. For him, capitalism tended 'to develop an atmosphere which is more favourable to the development on the one hand of a higher moral climate of responsibility and on the other to greater achievements in every realm of human activity.'[67]

However, Friedman and his Chicago associates recognized that the world had changed since Adam Smith: in the modern world of complex technology and capital-intensive firms and powerful states, modelling the economy as the interaction between self-interested competitive individuals as the early neoclassical economists had done was unrealistic. They realized that the state had to have some limited role in promoting market competition, but they found their ideal market actor in the manager of the large corporation rather than in either the legalistic state official or in the small businessperson.

Relying on the ideas of Ronald Coase and his theory of the efficiency advantages of locating some activities within firms rather than outside them in competitive markets, the Chicago economists argued, *contra* the Ordoliberals, that large monopolistic organizations could create efficiencies that competition between many small firms could not. It was still argued that market competition would create efficiency and that firms had to be efficient, but the concept of competition was reinterpreted in order to take account of the overall efficiency, in aggregate, of any given arrangement. The solution, then, was to deregulate the 'anti-trust', antimonopoly legislation that had prevailed in the United States and instead trust economists, or lawyer-economists, to judge whether breaking up the monopoly might be more efficient than preserving it. Henceforth corporate managers, not the invisible hand of the market or state officials, would manage competition, with pro-market economists and lawyers judging whether the outcome promoted the greatest degree of efficiency.[68] Understandably, this position was very popular among the American corporations that funded the pro-market thinktanks which became so influential in the 1970s and 1980s.

There was of course no reason in principle why these expert judgements of competitive efficiency could not be applied to bureaucracies in the state as well as the private sector, and neoliberals, unlike classical liberals such as Smith, argued that there was no need to separate an economic from a political sphere; as the utilitarians of the nineteenth century assumed, economic principles of rational entrepreneurship could be applied to all spheres of life, as could efforts to achieve maximum levels of efficiency. The Public Choice school of administration was most explicit in analysing state officials not as public servants above all interests, but as the self-interested actors of neoclassical economic theory.[69] Therefore, the best way to manage the state was not through hierarchical bureaucracies, which only allowed state officials to pursue their selfish sectional interests without any constraint, leading to conservatism and inefficiency.

Rather, decision-making had to be decentralized and competition encouraged between a mixture of public and private service providers, regulated transparently by auditors. It was this approach that in turn laid the foundations for 'New Public Management' – a project developed first in some municipal governments in the United States and in the United Kingdom under Margaret Thatcher –

which sought to bring private-sector management mechanisms to the public sector in order to make it cheaper and more efficient.[70] These often included the decentralization of management to 'executive agencies', the contracting-out of services to private providers, the setting of targets and performance indicators, and in some cases performance-related pay.[71] It is here that we can find the origins of the management of higher education that Craig Brandist complained about, and the reasons for comparison with Stalinist industrial policy are also evident. Both Stalinist 'socialist emulation' and New Public Management systems are dependent on quasi-markets, in which state-employed officials monitor competitions between individuals, units in an organization and state institutions through league tables and targets, incentivizing winners and punishing losers through various financial rewards and punishments.

There was much, then, that was reminiscent of the Ordoliberal vision in these neoliberal public-sector reforms of the 1980s and 1990s: state organizations were to preside over a quasi-market system designed to encourage competitiveness in order to promote the 'bourgeois virtues' of self-disciplined and efficient behaviour amongst large numbers of individuals within them. But in the private sector, the Chicago School vision of deregulated, competitive markets dominated by *large* firms was more dominant, especially among governments of the right, such as those of Ronald Reagan and Margaret Thatcher. And meanwhile, at the level of the individual self, it seemed that the neoliberal project of inculcating competitive values was having some success, especially among the middle classes. The 'entrepreneur of the self', identified by Foucault in 1979, devoted himself or herself to improving their human capital through 'investing' in themselves and their education, transforming themselves into effective market agents. Elements of this figure, especially the emphasis on salesmanship and 'marketability', were very close to the commercial person discussed by Rousseau and Adam Smith in the mid eighteenth century.

Yet, the 1980s and 1990s also saw another version of neoliberal competition emerge, with strong Schumpeterian influences. Schumpeter, like Coase and his Chicago successors, had seen large, monopolistic firms as the very likely outcome of capitalism. However, unlike them, he looked not to technocratic managers and economists ensuring maximum efficiency as a way of managing them, but to creative, dynamic 'entrepreneurs'; they might be rare within these firms, but they could in principle operate and create dynamism within them.[72] And at a time when corporate profits in the United States were being squeezed by costs and foreign competition, Schumpeter's notion of a new, quasi-aristocratic and heroic class of elite business people proved to be attractive.

This vision of competition was popularized by a theorist of management 'strategy' (a field itself owing something to military studies), the Harvard Business School management theorist Michael Porter, whose extraordinarily influential *Competitive Strategy* (1980) presented a very different world from that of the Chicago School. Business was not a field in which managers and economists scientifically assessed the relationship between competition and efficiency; it was a dangerous world of 'threats' from competitors, in which businesses had to adapt or die. The most important of Porter's 'five forces' to which businesses had to respond was 'industry rivalry', to which four other 'forces' contributed: first, two 'threats', both from new entrants to the market and from new technologies; and, second, increased 'bargaining power' from both customers and suppliers.[73] Porter then identified three strategies to deal with these threats: the first, 'cost minimization', accorded with the Chicago School efficiency agenda, but the second, 'differentiation' or 'diversification' and the third, 'niche-targeting', involved a more Schumpeterian agenda of innovation in response to changes in the market environment and the behaviour of rivals.[74] These were clearly tasks that only a special group of insightful strategists, able to understand the market and predict new opportunities, could fulfil, and it is no surprise that these ideas legitimized the emergence of 'heroic' CEOs at a time when the 'shareholder value' movement was seeking to replace old managers with new 'dynamic' figures who would increase profitability.[75] This was a new, winner-takes-all world in which, as Jack Welch, the star CEO of General Electric from 1981, famously said, you should either 'be number one or number two' or get out of the market, for only the strong survived.[76]

Michael Porter was also instrumental in extending these ideas of competitiveness from firms to nations. In his 1990 work *The Competitive Advantage of Nations*, he explained how activist political leaders, in alliance with businesspeople, could improve the competitiveness of states, criticizing the passivity of neoclassical approaches which assumed that 'comparative advantage' largely depended on differential resource or 'factor' endowments. 'Competitive advantage', for Porter, also included 'firms' structure, strategy and rivalry', 'related and supporting industries' (or particularly successful clusters of industries), as well as demand conditions, and these were foundations for success that could be improved upon. Innovation was an especially important part of the strategy for advanced economies, though he accepted that it had to build on pre-existing factor endowments and efficiency.[77]

The concept of national competitiveness became enormously influential among political leaders across the world. Reagan established a Commission on Industrial Competitiveness in 1983, which Porter was appointed to, and in the 1980s and 1990s, many politicians found the concept useful as they struggled to position their states within the newly emerging liberal world order – one that echoed that of the mid 1920s with its American leadership and stress on the importance of private finance, but which went much further in its promotion of global trade and interconnected production chains. Soon, a whole industry of competitiveness consultants provided advice for politicians, while global competitiveness league tables, combining both quantitative and survey evidence, provided benchmarks by which leaders could measure their policies. Indeed, Porter himself joined Klaus Schwab, the organizer of the World Economic Forum with its annual Davos meetings, in overseeing the compilation of the 'Global Competitiveness Report' first published in 1979.[78] And in 1990, the political scientist Philip Cerny went so far as to identify a fundamental change in the nature of the state, from the 'welfare state' to the 'competition state',[79] which now saw its goal as 'flexible response to competitive conditions in a range of diversified and rapidly evolving international marketplaces, i.e. the pursuit of "competitive advantage" as distinct from "comparative advantage"'.[80]

Cerny accepted that 'competition' states could take different forms, and pursuing national competitiveness could involve a more developmental strategy, determined to make its national industries suitable for international competition, or a more *laissez-faire* strategy to attract investment by making one's domestic economy as friendly to mobile global capital as possible (including by climbing up competitiveness rankings). And these strategies were related to two different visions of international 'competition' that underpin the post-1970s global market order: one founded on a form of peaceful mercantilism (the type which Porter himself had in mind); and the other closer to the eighteenth-century vision of a trade- and finance-friendly *doux commerce*. It was the latter that came to dominate policy in the course of the 1990s as both trade and the scale of investment by global banks expanded, and the appeal of integration into global markets grew.

## Conclusion

Financial crises – initially outside the West in 1997–98 and then at the centre of the global market economy in 2007–8 – have cast serious doubts on the appeal of those global markets, and the less controlled versions of market competition that have been so dominant since the late 1970s have been questioned. Some of the criticisms have come from supporters of statist developmentalism, particularly in East Asia, or of a revival of Keynesian Social Democratic ideas of limits to the market. But others have championed post-1960s 'postmaterialist' values of authenticity, self-fulfilment and environmental awareness as part of a more radical quasi-Rousseauian critique of not just market competition, but of all competition and, indeed, the comparisons between individuals underlying it. For instance, recent critiques of Facebook for causing mass feelings of inadequacy and even depression have focused on its encouragement of 'social comparison' – a feature that the Silicon Valley titan Peter Thiel, its major initial investor, remembers was the reason he invested in it in the first place, for as a student of the French anthropologist René Girard, he understood how susceptible naturally 'mimetic' human beings were to competitive comparisons with others.[81]

As this account of debates on competition have shown, such critiques are not new and tend to occur after major crises that can be attributed to competitive liberal markets – whether the food crises of 1846–48 or the depressions following 1873 and 1929. Yet it is unclear how far this disillusionment with market competition will go. Since industry and commerce have played a more important role in the economy than agriculture, market competition has been seen as a central part of life, not just for generating wealth for individuals and states, but also as a means by which states and employers discipline subordinates in order to make them orderly and productive citizens.

The debate over competition and the comparisons underlying it has therefore continued throughout the period, but the perceived benefits of competition – in terms of governmentality and incentives, as well as economic efficiency – have increasingly been seen to outweigh their disadvantages, namely the conflicts and feelings of inadequacy that they can generate. Hence, the Rousseauian critique has become less influential than it once was in the eighteenth century when Adam Smith felt it necessary to respond to it. And at the same time, it may well be that market liberal projects, with their focus on creating the 'entrepreneurial self', have internalized competitive values more effectively and amongst a larger group of the population than ever before.

Yet, as has been seen, it is not helpful to see the debate as a simple one between supporters and opponents of market competition; ideas and models of competition assume very different ethical frameworks, and it is most likely that we will see changes in the balance of these varieties of market competition rather than the victory or demise of competition as an organizing political and economic principle. The aftermath of the financial crises, and the consequent loss of faith in the equitable nature of global markets, has not seen major challenges to market competition per se. Rather, it has led to the erosion of ideas of competition founded on notions of *doux commerce* and spontaneous market orders, which became more influential in the 1990s, and their replacement with more elitist, nationalistic or regulated forms of market competition; this can take the form of zero-sum neomercantilist competition presided over by 'warrior' political leaders, or more technocratic, developmental neomercantilism.

Which of these approaches is likely to become dominant ultimately is difficult to judge, as we are in the midst of the crisis of a decaying market-optimistic order. But what previous crises do suggest is that we are only at the beginning of an era of ideological polarization on a number of issues and that the question of markets and market competition will continue to lie at the centre of these conflicts.

**David Priestland** is Professor of Modern History at the University of Oxford. His main fields of interest are the history of the Soviet Union and the comparative study of communist, postcommunist and neoliberal ideologies and practices. His major publications include: *Stalinism and the Politics of Mobilization: Ideas, Power, and Terror in Interwar Russia* (2007); *The Red Flag: Communism and the Making of the Modern World* (2010); and *Merchant, Soldier, Sage: A New History of Power* (2012).

# Notes

1. I.V. Stalin, *Sochineniia*, vol. 12 (Moscow: Gosudarstvennoe izdatel′stvo politicheskoi literatury, 1949), 108–11.
2. E. Mikulina, *Sorevnovavie mass* (Moscow: Partiinoe izdatel'stvo, 1929).
3. A. Kouzmin et al., 'Benchmarking and Performance Measurement in Public Sectors: Towards Learning for Agency Effectiveness', *International Journal of Public Sector Management* 12(2–3) (1999), 121–44.
4. W. Davies, *The Limits of Neoliberalism: Authority, Sovereignty and the Logic of Competition* (London: Sage, 2014).
5. This quotation comes from the follow-up article: C. Brandist, 'The Risks of Soviet-Style Managerialism in UK Universities', *Times Higher Education Supplement* (*THES*), 5 May 2016; see also C. Brandist, 'A Very Stalinist Management Model', *THES*, 29 May 2014.
6. D. Harvey, *A Brief History of Neoliberalism* (Oxford: Oxford University Press, 2005).
7. M. Foucault and R. Hurley, *The History of Sexuality. Volume 1: The Will to Knowledge* (Harmondsworth: Penguin, 1990), 138.
8. M. Foucault, *The Birth of Biopolitics: Lectures at the Collège de France, 1978–79*, M. Senellart and G. Burchell (trans.) (Basingstoke: Palgrave Macmillan, 2008), esp. Lecture Four, 31 January 1979.
9. For the defence and use of a framework relating ethoses to social groups and analysing them historically, see D. Priestland, *Merchant, Soldier, Sage: A New History of Power* (London: Allen Lane, 2012), especially 263–68.
10. K. Dennis, 'Competition in the History of Economic Thought', D.Phil. thesis (Oxford: Oxford University, 1975), 4–7.
11. G. Duby, *The Three Orders: Feudal Society Imagined*, A. Goldhammer (trans.) (Chicago: University of Chicago Press, 1982), 7–13.
12. A. Roncaglia, *The Wealth of Ideas: A History of Economic Thought* (Cambridge: Cambridge University Press, 2001), 31–40.
13. T. Hobbes, *Leviathan*, J.C.A. Gaskin (ed.) (Oxford: Oxford University Press, 1998), 66, 166.
14. Quoted in Dennis, 'Competition', 32.
15. Dennis, 'Competition', 40–3.
16. A. Smith, *The Glasgow Edition of the Works and Correspondence of Adam Smith*, vol. 1: *The Theory of Moral Sentiments*, D.D. Raphael, and A.L. Macfie (eds) (Oxford: Oxford University Press, 2014), 63.
17. L. Dickey, 'Doux-Commerce and Humanitarian Values: Free Trade, Sociability and Universal Benevolence in Eighteenth-Century Thinking', *Grotiana* 22(1) (2001), 279–88.
18. R. Debes, 'Adam Smith and the Sympathetic Imagination', in R. Hanley (ed.), *Adam Smith: His Life, Thought and Legacy* (Princeton: Princeton University Press, 2016), 198–201; J.W. Danford, 'Adam Smith, Equality, and the Wealth of Sympathy', *American Journal of Political Science* 24(4) (1980), 674–95.
19. A.O. Hirschman, *The Passions and the Interests: Political Arguments for Capitalism before its Triumph*, 20th anniversary edn (Princeton: Princeton University Press, 1997).
20. Baron de Montesquieu, *The Spirit of the Laws*, T. Nugent (trans.) (London: George Bell, 1902), 354.

21. Rousseau, 'Second Discourse', quoted in R. Hanley, 'Commerce and Corruption: Rousseau's Diagnosis and Adam Smith's Cure', *European Journal of Political Theory* 7(2) (2008), 137–58, at 140.
22. Hanley, 'Commerce and Corruption'.
23. J.-J. Rousseau, Émile; Éducation, Morale, Botanique, B. Gagnebin and M. Raymond (ed.), *Oeuvres complètes*, vol. 4 (Paris: Gallimard, 1969), 453–54, cited in M. McLendon, 'Rousseau, Amour Propre, and Intellectual Celebrity', *Journal of Politics* 71(2) (2009), 506–19, at 517.
24. Smith, *The Theory of Moral Sentiments*, 181.
25. For this argument, see Hanley, 'Commerce and Corruption', 144–48.
26. B. Hilton, *The Age of Atonement: The Influence of Evangelicalism on Social and Economic Thought, 1795–1865* (Oxford: Clarendon, 2001); M. Berg, 'Progress and Providence', *Early Nineteenth-Century Political Economy* 5 (1990), 365–75.
27. L. von Mises, *Bureaucracy* (Liberty Fund, 2007), 17, retrieved 13 March 2019 from http://oll.libertyfund.org/titles/1891. For the marginalist challenge to economics, see C. Robin, 'Wealth and the Intellectuals: Nietzsche, Hayek and the Austrian School of Economics', in R. Leeson (ed.), *Hayek: A Collaborative Biography: Part 5, Hayek's Great Society of Free Men, Archival Insights into the Evolution of Economics* (Basingstoke: Palgrave Macmillan, 2014), 118–24.
28. S. Bostaph, 'Jevons' Antipodean Interlude: The Question of Early Influences, with a Rejoinder by M.V. White and a Reply by Bostaph', *History of Political Economy* 21(4) (1989), 601–23, at 607.
29. K. Marx, *The Poverty of Philosophy* (New York: Cosimo Classics, 2008), 158–59.
30. K. Marx, *The German Ideology*, quoted in I. Deutscher, 'Socialist Competition', *Foreign Affairs* 30(3) (1952), retrieved 13 March 2019 from https://www.marxists.org/archive/deutscher/1952/socialist-competition.htm.
31. K. Marx, *Critique of the Gotha Programme* (1875), retrieved 13 March 2019 from https://www.marxists.org/archive/marx/works/1875/gotha/ch01.htm.
32. P.A. Kropotkin, *The Conquest of Bread* (London: Penguin Classics, 2015), Chapter 13.
33. C. Torp, 'The Coalition of "Rye and Iron" under the Pressure of Globalization: A Reinterpretation of Germany's Political Economy before 1914', *Central European History* 43(3) (2010), 401–27.
34. See I. Kirzner, 'Entrepreneurial Discovery and the Competitive Market Process: An Austrian Approach', *Journal of Economic Literature* 35(1) (1997), 60–85.
35. L. von Mises, *Human Action* (New Haven: Yale University Press, 1949), 325–26.
36. F. Wieser, *Social Economics* (1914), quoted in J.-J. Gislain, 'Les origines de l'entrepreneur schumpétérien', *Revue Interventions économiques* 46 (2012), 26, retrieved 13 March 2019 from https://journals.openedition.org/interventionseconomiques/1481.
37. J.A. Schumpeter, *Fundamentals of Economic Development* (Cambridge, MA: Harvard University Press, 1912), 93.
38. J. Osterhammel, 'Varieties of Social Economics: Joseph A. Schumpeter and Max Weber', in W. Mommsen and J. Osterhammel (eds), *Max Weber and His Contemporaries* (London: Allen & Unwin, 1987), 106–20, at 116–18.
39. Osterhammel, 'Varieties'.
40. N.S. Khrushchev, 'On Peaceful Coexistence', *Foreign Affairs*, October 1959, retrieved 13 March 2019 from https://www.cvce.eu/content/publication/1997/10/13/a231db94-ad9e-430c-8b61-12354f373ffc/publishable_en.pdf.
41. V.I. Lenin, 'Kak organizovat' sorevnovanie', *Pravda* 17 (20 January 1929).

42. Deutscher, 'Socialist Competition'.
43. Stalin, *Sochineniia*, vol. 12, 37.
44. L.H. Siegelbaum, 'Production Collectives and Communes and the "Imperatives" of Soviet Industrialization, 1929–1931', *Slavic Review* 45(1) (1986), 64–85; H. Kuromiya, *Stalin's Industrial Revolution: Politics and Workers, 1928–1932* (Cambridge: Cambridge University Press, 1988).
45. V. Kravchenko, *I Chose Freedom: The Personal and Political Life of a Soviet Official* (London: Robert Hale, 1947); Kuromiya, *Stalin's Industrial Revolution*, Chapters 2 and 3.
46. Stalin, *Sochineniia*, vol. 12, 315.
47. Ibid., vol. 13, 51–80.
48. On Stalinist 'consumerism', see J. Grunow, *Caviar with Champagne: Common Luxury and the Ideals of the Good Life in Stalin's Russia* (Oxford: Berg, 2003).
49. Cited in P. Betts, *Within Walls: Private Life in the German Democratic Republic* (Oxford: Oxford University Press, 2010), 134; P. Bren and M. Neuburger, *Communism Unwrapped: Consumption in Cold War Eastern Europe* (New York: Oxford University Press, 2012), 9.
50. L.H. Siegelbaum, *Stakhanovism and the Politics of Productivity in the USSR, 1935–1941* (Cambridge: Cambridge University Press, 1988), 264–67, 277–93; D. Priestland, *Stalinism and the Politics of Mobilization: Ideas, Power, and Terror in Inter-War Russia* (Oxford: Oxford University Press, 2007); D.A. Kaple, *Dream of a Red Factory: The Legacy of High Stalinism in China* (Oxford: Oxford University Press, 1994), 49–52, 98–99.
51. Priestland, *Stalinism*, 313–15; Siegelbaum, *Stakhanovism*, Chapter 3.
52. R. MacFarquhar, *The Origins of the Cultural Revolution, vol. 3: The Coming of the Cataclysm, 1961–1966* (New York: Columbia University Press, 1999), Chapters 1–4.
53. W. Röpke, *The Social Crisis of Our Time* (New Brunswick, NJ: Transaction, 2009), 181.
54. Ibid., 181.
55. Ibid., 218.
56. W. Bonefeld, 'Freedom and the Strong State: On German Ordoliberalism', *New Political Economy* 17(5) (2012), 633–56, at 644.
57. Röpke, quoted in Bonefeld, 'Freedom and the Strong State', 645.
58. Röpke, quoted in Bonefeld, 'Freedom and the Strong State', 650.
59. For the early debates between supporters of moral-culturalist and legalistic approaches to neoliberalism, see Q. Slobodian, *Globalists: The End of Empire and the Birth of Neoliberalism* (Cambridge, MA: Harvard University Press, 2018), 81–85. On legalistic approaches, see B. Jackson, 'Freedom, the Common Good, and the Rule of Law: Lippmann and Hayek on Economic Planning', *Journal of the History of Ideas* 73 (2012), 49–68.
60. On Lippmann's ideas, see Jackson, 'Freedom', 49–52.
61. 'Le Colloque Walter Lippmann', in S. Audier (ed.), *Le Colloque Lippmann: Aux Origines du 'néo-libéralisme'* (Paris: Le Bord de l'Eau, 2012), 487.
62. See, for instance, B. Caldwell, *The Collected Works of F.A. Hayek*, vol. 2: *The Road to Serfdom: Text and Documents: The Definitive Edition* (New York: Routledge, 2014), Chapter 9.
63. R. Rose, *Challenge to Governance: Studies in Overloaded Polities* (London: Sage, 1980).
64. J. Meadowcroft and W. Ruger, 'Hayek, Friedman, and Buchanan: On Public Life, Chile, and the Relationship between Liberty and Democracy', *Review of Political Economy* 26(3) (2014), 358–67.
65. A. Burgin, *The Great Persuasion: Reinventing Free Markets since the Depression* (Cambridge, MA: Harvard University Press, 2012), Chapter 5.
66. Quoted in ibid, 177.

67. Friedman, cited in ibid. 189.
68. For the roots of these ideas in the Chicago School, see Davies' important *The Limits of Neoliberalism*, Chapter 3.
69. J.M. Buchanan and R. Tollison, *Theory of Public Choice: Political Applications of Economics* (Ann Arbor: University of Michigan Press, 1972).
70. A. Dunsire, 'Administrative Theory in the 1980s: A Viewpoint', *Public Administration* 73 (1995), 17–40. For other influences on New Public Management, see G. Gruening, 'Origin and Theoretical Basis of New Public Management', *International Public Management Journal* 4(1) (2001), 1–25.
71. C. Pollitt and G. Bouckaert, *Public Management Reform: A Comparative Analysis: New Public Management, Governance, and the Neo-Weberian State*, 3rd edn (Oxford: Oxford University Press, 2011); J.-E. Lane, *New Public Management* (London: Routledge, 2000).
72. For the influence of Schumpeterian ideas in this period, see Davies, *The Limits of Neoliberalism*, 113–14.
73. M.E. Porter, *The Competitive Advantage of Nations* (London: Macmillan, 1990), Chapter 1.
74. Ibid., Chapter 2. For the influence of Porter, see Davies, *The Limits of Neoliberalism*, 124–27.
75. M. Sullivan, *Contests for Corporate Control: Corporate Governance and Economic Performance in the United States and Germany* (Oxford: Oxford University Press, 2000), Chapter 5.
76. R. Slater, *Jack Welch on Leadership* (New York: McGraw-Hill Professional, 2004), 31.
77. Porter, *The Competitive Advantage of Nations*.
78. T. Fougner, 'Neoliberal Governance of States: The Role of Competitiveness Indexing and Country Benchmarking', *Millennium – Journal of International Studies* 37(2) (2008), 303–26, at 312–14.
79. P. Cerny, *The Changing Architecture of Politics: Structure, Agency, and the Future of the State* (London: Sage, 1990).
80. P. Cerny, 'Paradoxes of the Competition State: The Dynamics of Political Globalization', *Government and Opposition* 32(2) (1997), 225.
81. 'New Study Links Facebook to Depression: But Now We Actually Understand Why', *Forbes*, 8 April 2015; Q. Hardy, 'René Girard, French Theorist of the Social Sciences, Dies at 91', *New York Times*, 10 November 2015; see also Willibald Steinmetz's chapter in this volume.

# Bibliography

Audier, S. (ed.), *Le Colloque Lippmann: Aux Origines du 'néo-libéralisme'* (Paris: Le Bord de l'Eau, 2012).

Berg, M., 'Progress and Providence', *Early Nineteenth-Century Political Economy* 5 (1990), 365–75.

Betts, P., *Within Walls: Private Life in the German Democratic Republic* (Oxford: Oxford University Press, 2010).

Bonefeld, W., 'Freedom and the Strong State: On German Ordoliberalism', *New Political Economy* 17(5) (2012), 633–56.

Bostaph, S., 'Jevons' Antipodean Interlude: The Question of Early Influences, with a Rejoinder by M.V. White and a Reply by Bostaph', *History of Political Economy* 21(4) (1989), 601–23.

Brandist, C., 'A Very Stalinist Management Model', *Times Higher Education Supplement*, 29 May 2014.

———. 'The Risks of Soviet-Style Managerialism in UK Universities', *Times Higher Education Supplement*, 5 May 2016.

Bren, P., and Neuburger, M., *Communism Unwrapped: Consumption in Cold War Eastern Europe* (New York: Oxford University Press, 2012).

Buchanan, J.M., and Tollison, R., *Theory of Public Choice: Political Applications of Economics* (Ann Arbor: University of Michigan Press, 1972).

Burgin, A., *The Great Persuasion: Reinventing Free Markets since the Depression* (Cambridge, MA: Harvard University Press, 2012).

Caldwell, B., *The Collected Works of F.A. Hayek*, vol. 2: *The Road to Serfdom: Text and Documents: The Definitive Edition* (New York: Routledge, 2014).

Cerny, P.G., *The Changing Architecture of Politics: Structure, Agency, and the Future of the State* (London: Sage, 1990).

———. 'Paradoxes of the Competition State: The Dynamics of Political Globalization', *Government and Opposition* 32(2) (1997), 251–74.

Danford, J.W., 'Adam Smith, Equality, and the Wealth of Sympathy', *American Journal of Political Science* 24(4) (1980), 674–95.

Davies, W., *The Limits of Neoliberalism: Authority, Sovereignty and the Logic of Competition* (London: Sage, 2014).

Debes, R., 'Adam Smith and the Sympathetic Imagination', in Hanley, R. (ed.), *Adam Smith: His Life, Thought and Legacy* (Princeton: Princeton University Press, 2016), 198–201.

Dennis, K., 'Competition in the History of Economic Thought', D.Phil. thesis (Oxford: Oxford University, 1975).

Deutscher, I., 'Socialist Competition', *Foreign Affairs* 30(3) (1952), retrieved 12 March 2019 from https://www.marxists.org/archive/deutscher/1952/socialist-competition.htm.

Dickey, L., 'Doux-Commerce and Humanitarian Values: Free Trade, Sociability and Universal Benevolence in Eighteenth-Century Thinking', *Grotiana* 22(1) (2001), 279–88.

Duby, G., *The Three Orders: Feudal Society Imagined*, Goldhammer, A. (trans.) (Chicago: University of Chicago Press, 1982).

Dunsire, A., 'Administrative Theory in the 1980s: A Viewpoint', *Public Administration* 73 (1995), 17–40.

Foucault, M., *The Birth of Biopolitics: Lectures at the Collège de France, 1978–79*, Senellart, M. and Burchell, G. (trans.) (Basingstoke: Palgrave Macmillan, 2008).

Foucault, M., and Hurley, R., *The History of Sexuality*, vol. 1: *The Will to Knowledge* (Harmondsworth: Penguin, 1990).

Fougner, T., 'Neoliberal Governance of States: The Role of Competitiveness Indexing and Country Benchmarking', *Millennium – Journal of International Studies* 37(2) (2008), 303–26.

Gislain, J.-J., 'Les origines de l'entrepreneur schumpétérien', *Revue Interventions économiques* 46 (2012), retrieved 13 March 2019 from https://journals.openedition.org/interventionseconomiques/1481.

Gruening, G., 'Origin and Theoretical Basis of New Public Management', *International Public Management Journal* 4(1) (2001), 1–25.

Grunow, J., *Caviar with Champagne: Common Luxury and the Ideals of the Good Life in Stalin's Russia* (Oxford: Berg, 2003).

Hanley, R., 'Commerce and Corruption: Rousseau's Diagnosis and Adam Smith's Cure', *European Journal of Political Theory* 7(2) (2008), 137–58.

Hardy, Q., 'René Girard, French Theorist of the Social Sciences, Dies at 91', *New York Times*, 10 November 2015.

Harvey, D., *A Brief History of Neoliberalism*, (Oxford: Oxford University Press, 2005).

Hilton, B., *The Age of Atonement: The Influence of Evangelicalism on Social and Economic Thought, 1795–1865* (Oxford: Clarendon, 2001).

Hirschman, A.O., *The Passions and the Interests: Political Arguments for Capitalism before Its Triumph*, 20th anniversary edn (Princeton: Princeton University Press, 1997).

Hobbes, T., *Leviathan*, Gaskin, J.C.A. (ed.) (Oxford: Oxford University Press, 1998).

Jackson, B., 'Freedom, the Common Good, and the Rule of Law: Lippmann and Hayek on Economic Planning', *Journal of the History of Ideas* 73 (2012), 49–68.

Kaple, D.A., *Dream of a Red Factory: The Legacy of High Stalinism in China* (Oxford: Oxford University Press, 1994).

Khrushchev, N.S., 'On Peaceful Coexistence', *Foreign Affairs*, October 1959, retrieved 13 March 2019 from https://www.cvce.eu/content/publication/1997/10/13/a231db94-ad9e-430c-8b61-12354f373ffc/publishable_en.pdf.

Kirzner, I., 'Entrepreneurial Discovery and the Competitive Market Process: An Austrian Approach', *Journal of Economic Literature* 35(1) (1997), 60–85.

Kouzmin, A. et al., 'Benchmarking and Performance Measurement in Public Sectors: Towards Learning for Agency Effectiveness', *International Journal of Public Sector Management* 12(2–3) (1999), 121–44.

Kravchenko, V., *I Chose Freedom: The Personal and Political Life of a Soviet Official* (London: Robert Hale, 1947).

Kropotkin, P.A., *The Conquest of Bread* (London: Penguin Classics, 2015).

Kuromiya, H., *Stalin's Industrial Revolution: Politics and Workers, 1928–1932* (Cambridge: Cambridge University Press, 1988).

Lane, J.-E., *New Public Management* (London: Routledge, 2000).

Lenin, V.I., 'Kak organizovat' sorevnovanie', *Pravda* 17 (20 January 1929).

MacFarquhar, R., *The Origins of the Cultural Revolution*, vol. 3: *The Coming of the Cataclysm, 1961–1966* (New York: Columbia University Press, 1999).

Marx, K., *Critique of the Gotha Programme* (1875), retrieved 13 March 2019 from https://www.marxists.org/archive/marx/works/1875/gotha/ch01.htm.

———. *The Poverty of Philosophy* (New York: Cosimo Classics, 2008).

McLendon, M., 'Rousseau, Amour Propre, and Intellectual Celebrity', *Journal of Politics* 71(2) (2009), 506–19.

Meadowcroft, J., and Ruger, W., 'Hayek, Friedman, and Buchanan: On Public Life, Chile, and the Relationship between Liberty and Democracy', *Review of Political Economy* 26(3) (2014), 358–67.

Mikulina, E., *Sorevnovavie mass* (Moscow: Partiinoe izdatel'stvo, 1929).

Mises, L. von, *Human Action* (New Haven: Yale University Press, 1949).

———. *Bureaucracy* (Liberty Fund, 2007), 17, retrieved 13 March 2019 from http://oll.libertyfund.org/titles/1891.

Montesquieu, Baron de, *The Spirit of the Laws*, Nugent, T. (trans.) (London: George Bell, 1902).

'New Study Links Facebook to Depression: But Now We Actually Understand Why', *Forbes*, 8 April 2015.
Osterhammel, J., 'Varieties of Social Economics: Joseph A. Schumpeter and Max Weber', in Mommsen, W. and Osterhammel, J. (eds), *Max Weber and His Contemporaries* (London: Allen & Unwin, 1987), 106–20.
Pollitt, C., and Bouckaert, G., *Public Management Reform: A Comparative Analysis: New Public Management, Governance, and the Neo-Weberian State*, 3rd edn (Oxford: Oxford University Press, 2011).
Porter, M.E., *The Competitive Advantage of Nations* (London: Macmillan, 1990).
Priestland, D., *Stalinism and the Politics of Mobilization: Ideas, Power, and Terror in Inter-War Russia* (Oxford: Oxford University Press, 2007).
———. *Merchant, Soldier, Sage: A New History of Power* (London: Allen Lane, 2012).
Robin, C., 'Wealth and the Intellectuals: Nietzsche, Hayek and the Austrian School of Economics', in Leeson, R. (ed.), *Hayek: A Collaborative Biography: Part 5, Hayek's Great Society of Free Men, Archival Insights into the Evolution of Economics* (Basingstoke: Palgrave Macmillan, 2014), 118–24.
Roncaglia, A., *The Wealth of Ideas: A History of Economic Thought* (Cambridge: Cambridge University Press, 2001).
Röpke, W., *The Social Crisis of Our Time* (New Brunswick, NJ: Transaction, 2009).
Rose, R., *Challenge to Governance: Studies in Overloaded Polities* (London: Sage, 1980).
Rousseau, J.-J., Émile; Éducation, Morale, Botanique, Gagnebin, B. and Raymond, M. (eds), Œuvres completes, vol. 4 (Paris: Gallimard, 1969).
Schumpeter, J. A., *Fundamentals of Economic Development* (Cambridge, MA: Harvard University Press, 1912).
Siegelbaum, L.H., 'Production Collectives and Communes and the "Imperatives" of Soviet Industrialization, 1929–1931', *Slavic Review* 45(1) (1986), 64–85.
———. *Stakhanovism and the Politics of Productivity in the USSR, 1935–1941* (Cambridge: Cambridge University Press, 1988).
Slater, R., *Jack Welch on Leadership* (New York: McGraw-Hill Professional, 2004).
Slobodian, Q., *Globalists: The End of Empire and the Birth of Neoliberalism* (Cambridge, MA: Harvard University Press, 2018).
Smith, A., *The Glasgow Edition of the Works and Correspondence of Adam Smith*, vol. 1: *The Theory of Moral Sentiments*, Raphael, D.D. and Macfie, A.L. (eds) (Oxford: Oxford University Press, 2014).
Stalin, I.V., *Sochineniia*, vol. 12 (Moscow: Gosudarstvennoe izdatel'stvo politicheskoi literatury, 1949).
Sullivan, M., *Contests for Corporate Control: Corporate Governance and Economic Performance in the United States and Germany* (Oxford: Oxford University Press, 2000).
Torp, C., 'The Coalition of "Rye and Iron" under the Pressure of Globalization: A Reinterpretation of Germany's Political Economy before 1914', *Central European History* 43(3) (2010), 401–27.

# 9

# Comparing Economic Activities on a Global Level in the 1920s and 1930s

*Motives and Consequences*

Martin Bemmann

## Introduction

'The soul of statistics is comparison' and a single number does not explain anything. Many authors of statistical textbooks or articles have made these or similar statements.[1] Indeed, statistical tables and graphs promise to provide information on different phenomena as seen in relation to each other or in their development over time. It frequently happens that diachronic and synchronic dimensions are even presented together so as to make statistics a prototypical tool for comparisons across time and space. However, a prerequisite for this is that the aspects that statistics compare have been made comparable before. Statisticians have to agree on actually comparable units and they have to define categories and *tertia comparationis* that allow the creation of meaningful relations between the units. The development and establishment of statistics are therefore adequate topics for a history of comparisons.[2]

The emergence of statistical reasoning is a relatively recent phenomenon, tightly linked to, and of vital relevance for, a variety of developments that characterize modernity, such as the advance of market-based economies and a scientific worldview, the democratization and functional differentiation of societies, imperial expansions and decolonization processes. Originating in the natural sciences, statistical reasoning became a standard approach in the social sciences, including economics, during the nineteenth century. At the same time, state administrations and private organizations increasingly generated, diffused and applied quantitative knowledge.[3] Both scientific curiosity and administrative needs made statistics 'the most important tool for the constant self-monitoring of society', as Jürgen Osterhammel has pointed out recently.[4]

In this chapter I focus on a hitherto neglected aspect of these developments – the emergence of a new form of international economic statistics after the First World War. Historians have convincingly argued that the years around 1870 marked the beginning of an 'Age of Economic Measurement' and that especially the crisis-ridden decades between the two world wars were crucial for the refinement of modern economic statistics. However, most authors who dealt with these issues have concentrated on the development of statistical methods in a purely scientific sense or on the expansion of official statistical institutions in individual countries. In these contexts, the increasing application of statistical methods to describe and analyse economic activities and the utilization of quantitative information by decision-makers in specific countries have received considerable attention.[5] By contrast, there are few studies available so far on how and why economists and statisticians managed to aggregate *comparable* quantitative data on production, (foreign) trade, prices and consumption in different countries, world regions and the world at large – in short, how and why *international* economic statistics were established.[6]

In this chapter I argue that although the history of international economic statistics can be traced back at least to the mid nineteenth century, the period from the 1920s to the 1940s witnessed the emergence of a *new form* that I propose to call 'world economic statistics'.[7] By using this term, I draw on a similar proposal made by the Swiss economist Alois Vladimir Furlan in 1914, a proposal that was hardly discussed at the time.[8] 'World economic statistics' differed from an older form of international economic statistics regarding their producers, their contents, their appearance, their publication frequency and their geographical focus, and they resembled much more our current approaches to describe and analyse global economic processes. Whereas until the early twentieth century most international economic statistics were compilations of already published, often outdated and hardly comparable country related information, 'world economic statistics' promised to enable a permanent, reliable and comprehensive comparison of up-to-date economic data on production, trade, prices and consumption from different countries.

It is not difficult to understand why after the First World War and especially in the 1930s – a period in which states massively expanded their activities in the fields of economic, financial and social policy[9] – politicians and state officials were keen to get the most reliable, comprehensive and current information on economic and social aspects of their own countries. Without such information, the expanded administrative action would have been impossible. But why did state authorities and companies additionally invest considerable financial, intellectual and institutional resources in an international statistical infrastructure?

Why did they reckon it important to compare the 'economic activities' of different countries with each other? And why did they think that they needed indices of 'world economic production' or 'world trade'?

In the following I argue that in the 1920s and 1930s, politicians, government officials and businessmen were driven by three major motives. Their aspiration to fabricate comparative world economic statistics came, first, from a straightforward 'desire to know', that is, a strong need for information gathering, second, from a wish to secure political influence on decision-making in international bodies and, third, from an ambition to take part in the shaping of national identities and prestige. All three motives can be seen as reactions to the manifold economic and political crises and hostilities of the 1920s and 1930s. The comparative statistical efforts reflect the observation that during those years, nation states increasingly became an ideal form of state organization and that these states wanted to compete with each other on a global scale. However, in order to enable this competition with statistical means, it was mandatory that border-crossing and global networks and infrastructures were established and that the participating actors cooperated with each other. This last remark corresponds with a recent observation by Glenda Sluga. Both nationalism and internationalism, she claims, did not stand in opposition to each other, but were closely entwined 'ways of thinking about the self and society, about the borders (and point) of political communities and government, and about liberty and equality'.[10] Or, to put it differently, fragmentation (of states, economies and societies) and globalization (of networks, concepts and techniques) were two sides of the same coin whose close relationship with each other should be further analysed.[11]

This chapter starts with a brief historical outline of how the new 'world economic statistics' emerged during the 1920s and 1930s. I will then proceed to discuss the three motives that I see as the main driving forces behind that emergence. In the concluding section, I will reflect on the ways in which the emerging permanent statistical monitoring of international economic processes might have influenced the 'worldviews' and political actions of those who used, or were observed by, those statistics.

## International and 'World Economic Statistics'

International economic statistics in a modern sense have been produced and published since the nineteenth century. State offices, private bodies, economists, statisticians and a growing number of international organizations began to collect and publish quantitative information on a growing variety of aspects. There was thus no lack of international economic statistics at the beginning of the twentieth century.[12] Often, however, the numbers presented in these statistics differed or even contradicted each other – they were simply not comparable. In order to overcome this cacophony, statisticians had already striven for an international standardization of statistical methods from the mid nineteenth century onwards.[13] Some of them had even campaigned for the establishment of an international statistical office – for example, the head of the German statistical office, Richard van der Borght in 1908.[14] Yet, before 1914, their efforts met with little success, which was mainly due to three fundamental problems.[15]

First, those who conducted statistical surveys were organized differently, had different objectives and applied different surveying and displaying methods. Since they compiled information for specific purposes, any change in their methods and terms would have jeopardized the usability of their older statistics. Second, international standardization was hampered by the reluctance and even resistance of national authorities and private bodies to let international actors interfere with their internal affairs. The willingness to apply international agreements on a national level hardly existed. Third, and most importantly, the complexity and the variety of economic and social reality as well as the dynamics of economic processes made the international standardization of statistical methods complicated or even impossible. In the 1930s, Franz Žižek, one of the leading German academic statisticians, distinguished 'formal' difficulties of standardization from those that he called 'material' difficulties. Whereas it would be rather easy to agree on a common standard methodology in order to overcome formal hindrances, it would remain doubtful whether what was measured by these methods in various countries could really be compared. As an example, he referred to the difficulties of comparing standards of living on an international level.[16]

Although the three problems mentioned did not vanish after the First World War, efforts to establish comparative international economic statistics and to standardize national surveying and displaying methods multiplied, intensified and, more importantly, became more successful.[17] The League of Nations' Economic and Financial Organization (EFO) quickly became one of the most important actors in this process. Its dedicated staff members established themselves in the centre of growing and border-crossing institutional and social networks of international organizations, state authorities, private associations, economists and statisticians.[18] These emerging permanent networks were crucial to find agreements on what was to be compared internationally in what way and to provide for the actual implementation of these agreements in the several countries. Furthermore, a well-working global material statistical infrastructure had to be established for enabling a permanent monitoring of economic activities internationally. This encompassed an increasing number of staff in statistical institutions of single countries and on the international level, and the establishment of permanent telegraph and telephone connections between the different contributors, as well as the application of state-of-the-art tabulating machines and punch card systems in order to process the growing mass of data.[19] Taken together, these developments revolutionized international economic statistics during the 1920s and 1930s.

This revolution became most obvious in the statistical and economic periodicals published by the EFO from 1921 onwards.[20] In at least four ways, these publications differed from most of the earlier international economic statistics:

first, they were compiled and published by a single institution according to a more or less common concept; second, they appeared regularly, more frequently and as independent periodicals; third, the EFO strove for a permanent monitoring of all the activities it considered as economically relevant; and, fourth, the geographical scope was widened, and at least in the 1930s the EFO's statisticians explicitly focused on the 'world', understood as including all independent countries and dependent territories. In 1940, the American journalist and internationalist Arthur Sweetser praised Geneva's statistical publications for their unprecedented global perspective: 'for the first time in history', he claimed, they afforded 'a perspective of the world looking down from above rather than the usual foreshortened view as seen horizontally from the window of a particular nation'.[21]

The permanent statistical monitoring of global economic processes that the EFO and its collaborators were envisioning and shaping during the 1920s and 1930s was as different from earlier international economic statistics as it resembles our own current approach to describe the global economy. Simply spoken, the new 'world economic statistics' aimed at describing and understanding international and global interconnectedness rather than just comparing single states. However, at the same time, 'world economic statistics' mandatorily required strong statistical institutions at the country level in order to collect data according to the same concept. Consequently, it was not only the 'world economy' that was shaped by statistical means,[22] but also distinguishable economic entities that could be compared to each other.

The emerging 'world economic statistics' required material infrastructure as well as social and institutional networks that evinced an urge to become global. Prior to the First World War, neither the infrastructures nor the networks of experts and statistical institutions had been developed far enough. Their planning, establishment and enlargement between the 1920s and 1940s meant that actors in many countries of the world – not only in Europe and North America, but also in Asia, Africa and South America – made considerable financial, intellectual and institutional investments that they had been unwilling to make before 1914.

## Motives

The most obvious purpose of international statistics was to satisfy a simple 'desire to know'. This was to be achieved by the provision of reliable information on foreign countries on a comparable basis for civil servants, politicians and businessmen. For decades, many national governments had already conducted statistical surveys concerning foreign countries and, most importantly, foreign trade. The statistical offices of some countries had even begun to publish separate chapters in their national statistical yearbooks or monographic studies that provided a compilation of related information.[23] These services, though, were as laborious as they were expensive. The American Department of Commerce, for instance, was supposed to have spent more than $200,000 a year for such a survey in the mid 1920s (which would correspond to about one per cent of the Department of Commerce's proposed budget for 1923/24).[24] More importantly, the data received and analysed by the responsible statisticians hardly allowed for comparisons due to the different surveying and displaying methods applied in the countries under observation. This lack of comparability made judgements on specific issues quite difficult or impossible.[25] The situation was similar in the case of private businesses. Internationally active companies had always been dependent on well-working networks of informants who also had compiled and sent statistical overviews of respective national and commodity markets.[26]

After the First World War, the demand for comprehensive, reliable, permanent and comparable statistical information on international economic processes increased significantly. '[A]ll statesmen', the renowned Swiss academic and internationalist William E. Rappard told the delegates of an international statistical conference in 1928, were 'aware that good economic statistics are an essential condition for good economic policy'.[27] Indeed, in order to discuss and determine tariffs and other measures to control foreign trade, civil servants and politicians needed a certain level of knowledge of foreign trade volumes and flows. Moreover, they required a reliable and understandable overview of the financial and economic situation in other countries when they participated and negotiated at international conferences, of which those taking place in Brussels (1920), Genoa (1922), Geneva (1927) and London (1933) were only the biggest and best known. Last but not least, the growing international division of labour and the emergence of global markets for a number of commodities made reliable and up-to-date information on national and international economic processes an indispensable precondition for economic planning.[28] Private companies, in turn, had to cope with an increasing de-Europeanization of trade, with the emergence of new markets and producers in South America, Africa and Asia, and with a trend towards international cartelization.[29] In fact, many of those who advocated the establishment of comparative international economic statistics justified their demand based on the needs of private businesses.[30] The new quest for international statistics naturally increased costs for those who required them, costs that could have been diminished if there had been a central international, independent and impartial statistical office – which did not exist.

As a consequence, even governments of countries with a huge and differentiated statistical machinery like Great Britain and Germany supported the efforts of the League of Nations and other bodies to establish a border- and continent-crossing statistical infrastructure as well as endeavours to standardize statistical methods at the international level. As early as 1920, for instance, Alfred W. Flux, the head of the British Board of Trade's Statistical Department, endorsed a proposal to establish a statistical section within the League of Nations. According to him, his Canadian colleague Robert H. Coats and the American Royal Meeker, head of the statistics branch of the International Labour Organization, this would be a 'step now imperatively needed to unify and standardise international statistics'.[31]

Although this step was never taken due to the resistance of several states (including Britain)[32] and a refusal of that proposal by the League's second Assembly in 1921,[33] the British government discontinued its regular annual publication of economic statistics of foreign countries that it had started in the nineteenth century. Its series of annual statistical abstracts had been, as an official history of the Board of Trade claimed, 'superseded by the monthly and annual publications of the League of Nations'.[34] In 1928, the British and the German governments – as well as twenty-four others – signed an International Convention Relating to Economic Statistics in Geneva.[35] Government officials in London and Berlin hoped that this convention would help to provide comparable economic information on foreign countries. As the German government let the Reichstag know in 1932, this information would be of 'great importance in international deliberations [and] negotiations of trade agreements'.[36] Although Germany never ratified the convention and although the country withdrew from the League in 1933, thereby ending the official cooperation with Geneva, its statistical bureau continued a certain exchange of information. It even initiated a change of surveying methods in its trade statistics in order to provide comparable data for a special publication series on international trade that the EFO started in 1936 as a consequence of the convention of 1928.[37]

Similar reasoning can be found on the side of private businesses. The League of Nations' archives in Geneva contain a huge number of letters and enquiries from companies and business associations of all continents, illustrating their active examination and utilization of the League's statistical publications.[38] Accordingly, in 1928, during the conference at which state delegates agreed on the already-mentioned convention on economic statistics, the official British delegate and President of the Association of British Chambers of Commerce, George A. Mitchell, claimed that he as a businessman 'strongly believed in the value of statistics to commerce and industry' and that a 'want of knowledge of what was happening in other countries' could expose a businessman 'to heavy capital losses'.[39] In 1934, Sir Harry Lindsay, Trade Commissioner of India in London, claimed in front of members of the Royal Statistical Society that 'the ordinary business man ... is growing more and more interested not merely in the improvement of his own national statistics, but also in those of other countries with which, as a producer for his own or foreign markets, he may happen to be in competition'.[40] And shortly before the beginning of the Second World War, participants of the tenth conference of the International Chamber of Commerce (ICC), a global organization of business associations, 'automatically' took the League's economic publications 'as the authoritative source of information', as an observer wrote. According to him, many of the attending businessmen also expressed the wish 'that whatever happened to the League it was imperative that the Intelligence Service should continue'.[41] It is no surprise, then, that the ICC as well as other private organizations at the national and international levels were very active to assist the League of Nations and other bodies in order to establish a permanent statistical monitoring of as many countries as possible.[42]

The second motive mentioned above, the wish to influence political decision-making in international bodies, revealed a somewhat technocratic vision of politics among the officials involved. The aim was to use economic statistics as a basis for rankings of states with the intention of facilitating political decisions or even making them in some cases superfluous. For this purpose, the comparability of data was paramount, and it was assumed that all states had a vital interest in presenting information comparable to that of others. One example was the question of how the individual countries' financial contributions to international organizations should be determined.[43] Another example was the utilization of a ranking of states based on economic statistics in order to determine the members of the executive organ of the International Labour Organization (ILO), its Governing Body. From 1919 onwards, this determination was a 'matter of great political importance', as a League official underlined in 1920.[44] This example reveals the extent to which state governments became increasingly interested after the First World War in investing in their statistical machinery and establishing permanent international statistical monitoring.

The ILO was established in 1919 and its statutes were part of the Versailles Peace Treaty.[45] According to its Article 393, the ILO's Governing Body was supposed to comprise twenty-four members. Being part of this body was not only a matter of prestige, but of practical political influence, as its task was to control the work of the International Labour Office in Geneva, the ILO's permanent secretariat. Consequently, the determination of the Governing Body's members was always a source of argument.[46] According to Article 393 of the Versailles Peace Treaty, half of the twenty-four seats were supposed to be filled by elected delegates from workers' and employers' organizations. 'Of the twelve persons representing the Governments', the article reads, 'eight shall be nominated by the Members which are of the chief industrial importance.' The remaining four delegates were to be elected from all other member states.[47]

However, the article suggested no criteria as to how to determine 'industrial importance'; it simply referred related disputes to the League's Council. But when the organizing committee of the first International Labour Conference met in the summer of 1919, the League's Council did not yet exist. Therefore, the committee had to decide on a list of the eight countries by itself in order to enable the election of delegates for the remaining four seats. It agreed on seven statistical criteria on which data were gathered from a number of countries: (1) Total Industrial Population; (2) Proportion of the Industrial Population to the Total Population; (3) Total Horse-Power in Industry (including hydraulic and steam-power, but not locomotives and ships); (4) Horse-Power per Head of the Population; (5) Total Length of Railway Lines; (6) Length of Railway Lines per Thousand Square Miles; and (7) Size of Mercantile Marine.[48] Accordingly, a list was prepared including, in the order of importance, the United States, Britain, France, Italy, Belgium, Japan, Switzerland and Spain. If Germany were allowed to accede to the ILO, Spain was supposed to leave the group.[49] Unsurprisingly, complaints were soon raised against the selection of this group composed mainly of European countries. Before the beginning of the International Labour Conference in October 1919, the governments of Poland, Sweden, Canada and India all submitted protests.[50] The fact that the criteria on which the organizing committee had based its decision remained rather obscure made things worse. During the conference itself, the president of the organizing committee, Arthur Fontaine, even refused 'to examine fully the reasons which inspired the action of the committee'.[51]

Nevertheless, the Governing Body was elected in November 1919 by the International Labour Conference and the ILO officially came into being. Since delegates of most of the complaining countries were elected on to the Governing Body, they withdrew their protests. Only India maintained its complaint and the country's delegates even refused to take part in the voting.[52] Although the ILO and the League's secretariat attempted to appease Delhi, India pushed its claim during the subsequent months. In the spring of 1920, the country submitted an official protest to the League.[53] Therefore, in August 1920, the League's Council had to put the question on its agenda and when its related resolution did not support Delhi's case, India made it an object for a debate at the League's first Assembly, taking place in November and December 1920.[54] Within the framework of the ILO and the League, this was the last possible step in the escalation of a political dispute.

The dispute points to the fact that none of the actors involved was able to find a definite solution to the question as to which countries actually were the eight states of 'chief industrial importance'. Due to the differences in the economic organization and performance between the countries, their respective industrial significances appeared to be not comparable at all.[55] Solving the problem therefore seemed impossible by means of 'purely statistical and economic grounds', as one League official put it in 1920.[56] For him, as for the complaining Indian government, the matter was clearly a political, not a technocratic, question. In a statement written for the League's first Assembly, the Indian government maintained that it was 'perfectly clear' that the organizing committee of the International Labour Conference had 'made no attempt to classify countries with reference to their actual industrial importance'. During the Assembly itself, the delegate for India, William Meyer, added that 'surely, it is not more difficult to come to a conclusion as to what are the most important industrial Powers of the world than to specify what are the Great Powers with reference to other matters'.[57]

Nonetheless, in 1919, the organizing committee of the International Labour Conference had indeed produced a comparison of statistical data and a ranking of concerned states. And even if the chosen criteria were later criticized by the complaining states as well as by an expert committee set up in spring 1921 by the ILO and the League's secretariat, the very same committee recommended the further use of the ranking method. It only suggested slightly altering one of the criteria and applying the most current statistical data in order to guarantee a fair result. And it also advised further developing statistical coverage on a comparative basis, especially with regard to national income which the committee perceived as the most appropriate criterion.[58] The whole incident can be interpreted as an attempt to depoliticize a highly problematic issue that obviously would be raised again in the future, something that happened several times before the Second World War. However, what the later complainants questioned was never the ranking method as such, but the criteria and the reliability of the statistical data applied. Accordingly, the political issue was never again put on to the agenda of the League's Council since it had become a technical issue that was mainly referred to statisticians and economists.

The third motive mentioned above, the ambition to invest into the establishment of 'world economic statistics' in order to enhance national identity and prestige, was of a more general nature and seems to have been of particular importance for representatives of relatively 'young' and 'developing' countries. It is well known that statistics contributed to the emergence of nation states during the nineteenth and twentieth centuries.[59] For reasons of prestige and visibility on the international and global stage, an important part of national identity, statistical data also had to be comparable to that of other countries. Hence, the adoption of at least certain international methodological standards became imperative. Seen from this perspective, it is no surprise that relatively 'young' nation states and even some dependent countries had an interest in adjusting their statistical systems to international standards and becoming part of the emerging global statistical infrastructure, even if this required considerable financial investments. Three examples support this argument.

When in the summer of 1919 the members of the organizing committee of the International Labour Conference drafted the list of the eight countries of 'chief industrial importance', they explicitly omitted to include Czechoslovakia and Poland in their deliberations. The committee argued that these 'States have still to establish their position' in an economic and a political sense and that they lacked reliable statistics.[60] Therefore, it is not surprising that the governments of the successor states in East Central Europe, which actually had to establish statistical bureaus more or less from scratch, supported a resolution of the conference in Genoa in 1922, asking for the international standardization of statistical methods.[61] They thereby helped to initiate extensive and long-lasting deliberations on that topic to which the EFO contributed significantly and of which the conference on economic statistics in 1928 was just the most visible event.[62] During the 1920s and 1930s, government authorities of several states and territories sent enquiries to the League asking for international guidelines for the establishment or a revision of their domestic statistics.[63]

A second example is the participation of the Indian government in the international statistical conference of 1928. Answering to the official invitation which the League of Nations had sent in April of that year and which had also asked for comments on the proposed agenda, the government in Delhi replied with a rather short telegram that it did not 'desire to be represented at the Conference' and that it would 'have no observation to make on the Agenda'. The India Office in London was bewildered by this attitude. It considered sending an expert of the British government on behalf of India, since the economic importance of that country was regarded as too great as not to be represented at the conference. When the India Office asked the Indian government to reconsider its decision, the Delhi government agreed to send the head of its Commercial Intelligence and Statistics Department, David B. Meek.[64] From Meek's perspective, this proved to be a most important step. In his conference report, he underlined that in Geneva he had 'found an unexpected state of ignorance among many delegates regarding India's economic development and a surprisingly low estimate of her international importance'. These 'wrong impressions', he continued, could 'be only gradually corrected', amongst other things, 'by the extended collection and publication of the statistical information which [would] place India in her true International perspective'. 'The modern tendency', he concluded, 'is toward closer touch in international affairs, and the days when a country could remain in isolation profitably appear to have passed.'[65] And in fact, India signed and ratified the Convention in the summer of 1931, 'willing to contribute her statistics on some agreed and reciprocal basis for conversion to international standards for international consumption'.[66]

A last example refers to China. From 1921 onwards, the EFO published a *Monthly Bulletin of Statistics*. During the 1920s, China was barely visible in this 'collection … of indices illustrating commercial and industrial movements'[67] in an increasing number of countries;[68] only an index of wholesale prices in Shanghai referred to the country. This unsatisfactory state of reporting on China began to change after the establishment of the National Government in Nanjing in 1928 and with the implementation of a relatively intense technical cooperation of that government with the League of Nations during the 1930s.[69] In June 1930, China's National Tariff Commission asked the country's Maritime Customs Service to introduce a monthly coverage on foreign trade instead of the quarterly returns delivered up to that point. Having such monthly returns, the National Tariff Commission explained, would make China's international position more visible as well as enabling it 'to participate in the International Convention relating to Economic Statistics'. To this end, Chinese statisticians were despatched to Japan and Great Britain in order to become accustomed with modern statistical methods. In addition, tabulating machines and a punch card system had to be installed and applied in China's Customs Service.[70]

Due to these necessary preparations, it took more than a year until China could present monthly returns of its foreign trade[71] and only from December 1932 onwards was the information regularly published in the *Monthly Bulletin*.

## Conclusion

During the 1920s and 1930s, a revolution occurred in the compilation, presentation and utilization of international economic statistics. Various state and nonstate actors from politics, administration, science and private businesses established border-crossing material, institutional and social networks in the framework of a potentially global statistical infrastructure and sought ways to standardize surveying and displaying methods as much as possible. Their efforts were deemed necessary in order to establish a permanent monitoring of international economic processes and to 'show the economic position and development in the world as a whole and in different countries on a comparable basis', as the 1928 convention on economic statistics put it.[72] Furthermore, the build-up of an international statistical infrastructure and the standardization attempts of the interwar period were crucial preconditions for the surprisingly fast rise of more refined instruments after 1945. In the aftermath of the Second World War, techniques of national accounting such as gross domestic product and other internationally standardized economic indicators quickly became the most important instruments and points of reference for policy measures. The statistical knowledge and instruments elaborated in the years after the First World War thus had a long-lasting impact on how people looked at, and thought of, the 'world economy'.

But why is it that 'world economic statistics' in the sense described only came into its own during the 1920s and 1930s, a time of increasing international conflicts, economic crises and hostilities, and not *before* the First World War, an era often referred to as the 'first globalization'? To be sure, already at that time, statisticians and economists had been willing to cooperate internationally and there had been claims for an international statistical office and a standardization of statistical methods. What changed with the First World War, however, was that national actors were increasingly willing to invest the necessary financial, intellectual and institutional resources in the establishment of an international statistical infrastructure. Of course, the three motives discussed in this chapter were not the only factors driving the process; purely scientific or professional interests were also involved. Thus, economists who were interested in studying global economic interdependencies were willing to cooperate with other scholars, institutions and authorities to supply, receive and analyse data. Similarly, many of the mushrooming international organizations and expert groups could legitimate their very existence by dedicating themselves to data collection and standardization.[73] I highlighted the three motives, though, because without the cooperation of state governments, companies and business organizations, any attempt to establish more than a compilation of heterogeneous statistics would have been fruitless. It was mainly their increased interest in comparing economic activities and markets that enabled the emergence of 'world economic statistics'.

Finally, a few words may be in order here on the consequences brought about by the emergence of the new 'world economic statistics' in the interwar period. The general growth of information and the possibility of depoliticizing international disputes by statistical means, discussed above, were clearly among the more visible consequences. Less obvious, but perhaps even more important, were some other effects. A growing consciousness about global interdependencies is one of them. Recently, Jürgen Osterhammel characterized the Wall Street Crash of 1929 as 'the first economic event [in world history] of truly global weight', affecting producers and consumers on all continents within a few months.[74] However, before the 'world economy' could disintegrate in front of the global public in the early 1930s, it had to be determined and observed statistically in a reliable and permanent way. Whereas there surely had been earlier global economic crises, none of them had been described as broadly in a geographical sense, as differentiated and as up to date as the Great Depression. Without the new statistical instruments, this would not have been possible.

At the same time, the establishment of 'world economic statistics' not only shaped what we nowadays know as the 'world economy'.[75] Due to the necessity to provide comparable data for the purpose of describing the 'world economy', economic activities in *individual* countries too became more and more comparable to each other. In the 1920s and 1930s, data gathering still remained restricted to several aspects such as industrial production, foreign trade and the finances of individual countries. It was not yet possible, perhaps not even conceivable, to compare national economies as whole entities with each other in the way that became common after the Second World War.[76] However, as I have indicated by the examples from Eastern Europe, India and China, 'world economic statistics' could, and would, already be used to strengthen national identities and enhance national prestige, and this, one might argue, contributed to the emergence of the notion of 'national economies'.[77]

To conclude, it seems reasonable to argue that those who, in the 1920s and 1930s, invested scarce resources in the establishment of an international statistical infrastructure and set out to compare economic activities within their own country with those of others, as well as with those of an imagined 'world economy', were mostly driven by motives of a 'nationalist' nature. One of their objectives, if not the most pertinent one, was certainly to help their own national governments, authorities or businesses to compete more successfully in an increasingly uncertain world. At the same time, the consequences of these endeavours appeared to be long-lasting border- and continent-crossing infrastructures as well as potentially global methodological perspectives and approaches to observe, understand and influence economic processes.

**Martin Bemmann** is a lecturer at the Department of History of the University of Freiburg. His research interests cover the history of economic knowledge and globalization as well as the relationship between the economy and ecology. He published a monograph on the emergence of forest damages as an environmental problem in twentieth-century Germany (*Beschädigte Vegetation und sterbender Wald: Zur Entstehung eines Umweltproblems in Deutschland, 1893–1970*, 2012) and coedited essay collections on the relevance of ignorance within the management of ecosystems and on the emergence of ecological modernization concepts since the 1970s. He is currently preparing a monograph on the establishment of international economic statistics.

# Notes

1. See, for example, F. Zahn, 'Statistik', in L. Elster, A. Weber and F. Wieser (eds), *Handwörterbuch der Staatswissenschaften*, 4th ed., vol. 7 (Jena: Fischer, 1926), 869–972, 937. I would like to thank Willibald Steinmetz, Michel Abeßer and Johannes Becker for their thorough reading of and their helpful comments on earlier versions of this text.
2. A. Epple and W. Erhart (eds), *Die Welt beobachten: Praktiken des Vergleichens* (Frankfurt am Main: Campus, 2015).
3. For an introduction into the history of statistics and statistical reasoning, see A. Desrosières, *The Politics of Large Numbers: A History of Statistical Reasoning* (Cambridge, MA: Harvard University Press, 1998); T. Porter, *The Rise of Statistical Thinking* (Princeton: Princeton University Press, 1986); T. Porter, *Trust in Numbers: The Pursuit of Objectivity in Science and Public Life* (Princeton: Princeton University Press, 1995); L. Behrisch, *Die Berechnung der Glückseligkeit: Statistik und Politik in Deutschland und Frankreich im späten Ancien Régime* (Ostfildern: Thorbecke Verlag, 2016).
4. J. Osterhammel, *The Transformation of the World: A Global History of the Nineteenth Century* (Princeton: Princeton University Press, 2014), 26.
5. M.S. Morgan, *The History of Econometric Ideas* (Cambridge: Cambridge University Press, 1990); J.L. Klein and M.S. Morgan (eds), *The Age of Economic Measurement* (Durham, NC: Duke University Press, 2001); J.A. Tooze, *Statistics and the German State, 1900–1945: The Making of Modern Economic Knowledge* (Cambridge: Cambridge University Press, 2001); T. Stapleford, *The Cost of Living in America. A Political History of Economic Statistics, 1880–2000* (Cambridge: Cambridge University Press, 2009); H. Maas and M.S. Morgan (eds), *Observing the Economy. Historical Perspectives* (Durham, NC: Duke University Press, 2012); W.A. Friedman, *Fortune Tellers: The Story of America's First Economic Forecasters* (Princeton: Princeton University Press, 2014).
6. This desideratum mainly concerns the history of international economic statistics in the nineteenth and early twentieth centuries. See, however, D. Kévonian, 'La légitimation par l'expertise: Le Bureau International du Travail et la statistique internationale', *Les cahiers Irice* 2 (2008), 81–106; R. Cussó, 'L'activité statistique de l'Organisation économique et financière de la Société des Nations: Un nouveau lien entre pouvoir et quantification', *Histoire & Mesure* 27 (2012), 107–36; Q. Slobodian, 'How to See the World Economy: Statistics, Maps, and Schumpeter's Camera in the First Age of Globalization', *Journal of Global History* 10 (2015), 307–32; A. Ribi Forclaz, 'Agriculture, American Expertise, and the Quest for Global Data: Leon Estabrook and First World Agricultural Census, 1930', *Journal of Global History* 16 (2016), 44–65; M. Bemmann, 'Das Chaos beseitigen: Die internationale Standardisierung forst- und holzwirtschaftlicher Statistiken in den 1920er und 1930er Jahren und der *Völkerbund*', *Economic History Yearbook* 57 (2016), 545–87. The research situation is better for the second part of the twentieth century because the surprisingly quick career of national accounting and the concept of the 'Gross Domestic Product' after 1945 attracted much attention in recent years: L. Fioramonti, *Gross Domestic Problem: The Politics behind the World's Most Powerful Number* (London: Zed Books, 2013); P. Lepenies, *The Power of a Single Number: A Political History of GDP* (New York: Columbia University Press, 2016); E. Mahsood, *The Great Invention: The Story of GDP and the Making of and Unmaking of the Modern World* (New York: Pegasus, 2016); D. Philipsen, *The Little Big Number: How GDP Came to Rule the World and What to Do about it* (Princeton: Princeton University Press, 2015); M. Schmelzer, *The Hegemony of Growth:*

*The OECD and the Making of the Economic Growth Paradigm* (Cambridge: Cambridge University Press, 2016); D. Speich Chassé, *Die Erfindung des Bruttosozialprodukts: Globale Ungleichheit in der Wissensgeschichte der Ökonomie* (Göttingen: Vandenhoeck & Ruprecht, 2013). On the United Nations' statistical activity, see also M. Ward, *Quantifying the World: UN Ideas and Statistics* (Bloomington: Indiana University Press, 2004).

7. For an elaboration of this argument, see M. Bemmann, 'Internationale und Weltwirtschaftsstatistik: Beobachtungen, Überlegungen und Thesen zur Genese internationaler Wirtschaftsstatistik in den 1920er und 1930er Jahren', in S. Haas, M.C. Schneider and N. Bilo (eds), *Die Zählung der Welt: Kulturgeschichte der Statistik vom 18. bis 20. Jahrhundert* (Stuttgart: Steiner, 2019), 195–217.
8. A.V. Furlan, 'Weltwirtschaftsstatistik', *Weltwirtschaftliches Archiv* 4 (1914), 295–340; see also J. Breuer, *Die Methoden der Handelsstatistik* (Paderborn: Schöningh, 1920), 1–2.
9. D. Aldcroft, *From Versailles to Wall Street, 1919–1929* (Berkeley: University of California Press, 1977); C.P. Kindleberger, *The World in Depression 1929–1939* (Berkeley: University of California Press, 1973); K.K. Patel, *The New Deal: A Global History* (Princeton: Princeton University Press, 2016).
10. G. Sluga, *Internationalism in the Age of Nationalism* (Philadelphia: University of Pennsylvania Press, 2013), 150; see also P. Clavin and G. Sluga (eds), *Internationalisms: A Twentieth-Century History* (Oxford: Oxford University Press, 2017).
11. I. Clark, *Globalization and Fragmentation: International Relations in the Twentieth Century* (Oxford: Oxford University Press, 1997); A. Epple, *Globalisierung/en*, Version 1.0, *Docupedia-Zeitgeschichte*, 11 June 2012, retrieved 13 March 2019 from https://www.docupedia.de/zg/Globalisierung; J. Osterhammel, 'Globalizations', in J.H. Bentley (ed.) *The Oxford Handbook of World History* (Oxford: Oxford University Press, 2011), 89–104; R. Robertson, 'Glokalisierung: Homogenität und Heterogenität in Raum und Zeit', in U. Beck (ed.), *Perspektiven der Weltgesellschaft* (Frankfurt am Main: Suhrkamp, 1998), 192–220; B. Barth, S. Gänger and N.P. Petersson, 'Einleitung: Globalisierung und Globalgeschichten', in B. Barth, S. Gänger and N.P. Petersson (eds), *Globalgeschichten: Bestandsaufnahme und Perspektiven* (Frankfurt am Main: Campus, 2014), 7–18.
12. See, for instance, United Kingdom Board of Trade, *Statistical Abstract for the Principal Foreign Countries* (London, 1874); United States Department of Commerce and Labor, 'Commercial and Financial Statistics of the Principal Countries of the World', *Statistical Abstract of the United States* 30 (1907), 729–51 (and the following years); Metallgesellschaft, *Statistische Zusammenstellungen über Blei, Kupfer, Zink und Zinn von der Metallgesellschaft Frankfurt am Main* (Frankfurt am Main: Metallgesellschaft, 1892); *The Statesman's Yearbook* (London: Macmillan, 1864); F.X. Neumann, 'Übersichten über Produktion, Welthandel und Verkehrsmittel', *Geographisches Jahrbuch* 3 (1870), 420–81 (and the following years); F.X. von Neumann-Spallart, *Uebersichten über Produktion, Verkehr und Handel in der Weltwirthschaft* (Stuttgart: Meier, 1878); M.G. Mulhall, *The Dictionary of Statistics* (London: Routledge, 1892); Conseil International pour l'Exploration de la Mer, *Bulletin Statistique des Pêches Maritimes des Pays du Nord de l'Europe* (Copenhagen: Høst, 1903/4); International Federation of Master Cotton Spinners and Manufacturers Association, *Statistics of Consumption of Cotton and Stocks of Cotton in Spinners Hands* (Manchester, 1908/9); Institut International d'Agriculture, *Annuaire International de Statistique Agricole* (Rome, 1910/12).
13. N. Randeraad, *States and Statistics in the Nineteenth Century: Europe by Numbers* (Manchester: Manchester University Press, 2010); H. Genzmer, *Die Bestrebungen zur Schaffung eines international-einheitlichen Zolltarifschemas* (Münster: Baader, 1929), 3–6.

14. R. van der Borght, 'Fondation d'un Office International de Statistique', *Bulletin de l'Institut International de Statistique* 18 (1909), vol. 1, 568–90.
15. For the following paragraph, see Bemmann, 'Internationale und Weltwirtschaftsstatistik'.
16. F. Žižek, Review of F. Zahn, *50 années de l'Institut International de Statistique* (Munich, 1934), *Weltwirtschaftliches Archiv* 42 (1935), 251*–259*; see also F. Žižek, 'Der statistische Vergleich', *Allgemeines Statistisches Archiv* 21 (1931), 525–50.
17. If not specified otherwise, this and the next paragraph are based on preliminary results of my research project.
18. For EFO's statistical activities, see A. Loveday, 'Geneva as a Centre of Economic Information', *INDEX* 9 (1934), 195–209; C.K. Nichols, 'The Statistical Work of the League of Nations in Economic, Financial and Related Fields', *Journal of the American Statistical Association* 37 (1942), 336–42; T. Griffin, 'The League of Nations and the Conference of European Statisticians', in C. Malaguerra (ed.), *50 Years of the Conference of European Statisticians* (Geneva, 2003), 7–24; Kévonian, 'La légitimation'; Cussó, 'L'activité statistique'; Bemmann, 'Das Chaos beseitigen'.
19. See J.A. Tooze, 'Die Vermessung der Welt: Ansätze zu einer Kulturgeschichte der Wirtschaftsstatistik', in H. Berghoff and J. Vogel (eds), *Wirtschaftsgeschichte als Kulturgeschichte: Dimensionen eines Perspektivenwechsels* (Frankfurt am Main: Campus, 2004), 325–51, at 342–43.
20. The most important publications were the *Monthly Bulletin of Statistics* (1921), the *International Statistical Year-Book* (1927), *Memorandum on Balances of Payments and Foreign Trade Balances* (1924), *Memorandum on Production and Trade* (1927) and *World Economic Survey* (1932). For an overview, see M.H. Hill, *The Economic and Financial Organization of the League of Nations: A Survey of Twenty-Five Years' Experience* (Washington, DC: Carnegie Endowment for International Peace, 1945), 98–102.
21. A. Sweetser, 'The Non-political Achievements of the League', *Foreign Affairs* 19 (1940), 179–92, at 183.
22. For related debates in the late nineteenth and early twentieth centuries, see Slobodian, 'How to See'.
23. See, e.g., United Kingdom Board of Trade, *Statistical Abstract for the Principal Foreign Countries* (London, 1874); United Kingdom Board of Trade, *Accounts Relating to the Trade and Commerce of Certain Foreign Countries and British Countries Overseas* (London, 1901); International sections in: Kaiserliches Statistisches Amt, *Statistisches Jahrbuch für das Deutsche Reich*, 1903; United States Bureau of Statistics, *Statistical Abstracts of the United States*, 1902.
24. Letter from Arthur Sweetser to Arthur Salter, 13 June 1924, League of Nations' Archives, Geneva (hereinafter LoNA), 10/36897/36897; *Message of the President of the United States Transmitting the Budget for the Service of the Fiscal Year Ending June 30, 1924* (Washington DC, 1922), 249–320.
25. See for related criticism, e.g., P. Hermberg, 'Über Handelsstatistik', *Weltwirtschaftliches Archiv* 16 (1920/21), 306–16; A.W. Flux, 'International Statistical Comparisons', *Journal of the Royal Statistical Society* 86 (1923), 297–331; C. Lewis, *The International Accounts: A Constructive Criticism of Methods Used in Stating the Results of International Trade, Service, and Financial Operations* (London: George Allen & Unwin, 1927), 7–8, 74–92, 109–29; D.C.M Platt, *Mickey Mouse Numbers in World History* (Basingstoke: Macmillan, 1989), 26–30.
26. S. Beckert, *King Cotton: Eine Globalgeschichte des Kapitalismus* (Munich: Beck, 2014), 218–20; Bemmann, 'Das Chaos beseitigen', 567–8.

27. League of Nations, *Proceedings of the International Conference Relating to Economic Statistics* (Geneva, 1929), 27.
28. Aldcroft, *From Versailles*; Kindleberger, *The World in Depression*; Patel, *The New Deal*.
29. C. Dejung and N.P. Petersson (eds), *The Foundations of Worldwide Economic Integration: Power, Institutions, and Global Markets, 1850–1930* (Cambridge: Cambridge University Press, 2013); J. Fear, 'Cartels', in G. Jones and J. Zeitlin (eds), *The Oxford Handbook of Business History* (Oxford: Oxford University Press, 2008), 268–92; H. Schröter, 'Cartelization and Decartelization in Europe, 1870–1995: Rise and Decline of an Economic Institution', *Journal of European Economic History* 25 (1996), 129–53.
30. For instance, Flux, 'International Statistical Comparisons', 300–1.
31. League of Nations, *International Statistical Commission: Report by M. Lucien March*, League Document E.F.S. 74, 22, in British Library, India Office Records (hereinafter BL IOR), IOR/L/E/7/1223, File 1196.
32. While principally endorsing Flux's demand, the British cabinet refused to back it because of its budgetary restraints at that time: Letter from Thomas Jones, Acting Secretary to the Cabinet, to the League's Secretary-General, 25 August 1921, The National Archives, Kew (hereinafter TNA), T 161/36/4 (partly reproduced in the League Documents A.12(3).1921, in BL IOR, IOR/L/E/7/1223, File 1196).
33. League of Nations, *The Records of the Second Assembly: Meetings of the Committees* (Geneva, 1921), 230–32; League of Nations, *The Records of the Second Assembly: Plenary Meetings* (Geneva, 1921), 459. For the statements of several states on the above-mentioned proposal, see League of Nations, *Organisation of International Statistics: Memorandum by the Secretary-General* and Addendums, League Documents A.12.1921 and A.12(1).1921–A.12(6).1921, in BL IOR, IOR/L/E/7/1223, File 1196.
34. H. Llewellyn Smith, *The Board of Trade* (London: Putnam, 1928), 214.
35. League of Nations, *International Conference Relating to Economic Statistics: International Convention – Protocol – Final Act of the Conference* (Geneva, 1928).
36. Draft Law on the International Convention Relating to Economic Statistics, Fifth Legislative Period of the Reichstag, Drucksache No. 1460, 27 April 1932 (Berlin 1932), 112; for the similar attitude of the British government, see the notes on an 'Interdepartmental Conference on Economic Statistics' on 9 October, 1928, TNA, BT 70/18/S664/28.
37. 'Confidential Report of a Visit to the Statistisches Reichsamt, Berlin', by Gerhard Fürst, Secretary of the League's *Committee of Statistical Experts*, 8 January 1935, Archives of Nuffield College, Oxford University, Papers of Alexander Loveday, Box 9. The special publication series was League of Nations, *International Trade in Certain Raw Materials and Foodstuffs by Countries of Origin and Consumption* (Geneva, 1936–39).
38. See, for instance, LoNA, 10/59240/25480; 10B/13283/10942; 10B/15413/1219; 10B/18929/1095.
39. League of Nations, *Proceedings of the International Conference*, 30–31.
40. H.A.F. Lindsay, 'India's Trade and Imperial Statistics, Past, Present, and Future', *Journal of the Royal Statistical Society* 97 (1934), 399–422, at 403.
41. Anonymous and confidential 'Report on the Tenth Congress of the International Chamber of Commerce at Copenhagen – June 1939', Archives of Nuffield College, Oxford University, Papers of Alexander Loveday, Box 13, 3.
42. See for related efforts of the ICC: G. Olivetti, 'Internationale Industriestatistiken', *Internationale Wirtschaft* 1(1) (1929), 21–25; for the case of the timber industry, see Bemmann, 'Das Chaos beseitigen'.

43. Schmelzer, *Hegemony*, 94; for the discussions on the determination of the state's contributions to the League of Nations, see H. Ames, *Financial Administration and Apportionment of Expenses* (Geneva: League of Nations, 1924), 22–42; L.G. Marcantonato, *L'administration financière de la Société des Nations* (Paris: Éditions a Pedone, 1938).
44. Memorandum of E.M.H. Lloyd, 16 March 1920, LoNA, 15/3293/245.
45. A. Alcock, *History of the International Labour Organisation* (London: Macmillan, 1971); J. van Daele (ed.), *Histories: Essays on the International Labour Organization and its Impact on the World during the Twentieth Century* (Bern: Peter Lang, 2010); S. Kott and J. Droux (eds), *Globalizing Social Rights: The International Labour Organization and Beyond* (Basingstoke: Palgrave Macmillan, 2013).
46. For more recent debates on this issue, see E. Osieke, *Constitutional Law and Practice in the International Labour Organization* (Dordrecht: Nijhoff, 1985), 103–7.
47. 'Conditions of Peace: Summary', in *Verhandlungen der verfassunggebenden Deutschen Nationalversammlung*, vol. 337: *Anlagen zu den stenographischen Berichten* (Berlin: Julius Sittenfeld, 1920), 242–43, quote at 243.
48. Note by Arthur Fontaine, former head of the Organising Committee for the Washington Conference, 14 March 1922, in *Minutes of the Twelfth Session of the Governing Body of the ILO, Rome, April 1922*, 102, retrieved 13 March 2019 from http://www.ilo.org/public/libdoc/ilo/P/09601/09601%281922-12%29.pdf.
49. Circular letter of the organizing committee, 20 August 1919, LoNA, 15/1151/245.
50. Memorandum of Arthur Fontaine, 8 October 1919, 2, LoNA, 15/1710/245.
51. League of Nations, *International Labour Conference: First Annual Meeting, October 29, 1919–November 29, 1919* (Washington DC, 1920), 13.
52. Ibid., 131.
53. *Memorandum on the Claim of India to Be Included among the Eight States of Chief Industrial Importance*, March 1920, LoNA 15/3826/245.
54. 'Procès-Verbal of the Eighth Session of the Council of the League of Nations', San Sebastian, 30 July–5 August 1920, *Official Journal of the League of Nations* 1 (1920), 304–45, 321–24; League of Nations, *The Records of the First Assembly. Meetings of the Committees* (Geneva, 1920), 120, 205–14; League of Nations, *The Records of the First Assembly: Plenary Meetings* (Geneva, 1920), 551–5.
55. See, for example, the Memorandum of Arthur Fontaine, 8 October 1919, 3–4, LoNA, 15/1710/245.
56. Memorandum of Edward M.H. Lloyd, 16 March 1920, LoNA 15/3293/245; similar observations of the Japanese delegate to the ILO, Shunzo Yoshisaka, in a Memorandum of 22 May 1922, LoNA, 15/21001/245.
57. Note by the Indian Delegation. Assembly Document No. 226, LoNA, 15/9154/245; League of Nations, *The Records… Plenary Meetings*, 553.
58. 'Report of the Committee Appointed to Consider the Criteria to Be Adopted in the Selection of the Eight States of Chief Industrial Importance', 31 May 1922, *Official Journal of the League of Nations* 3 (1922), 1343–74.
59. See, for instance, J.D. Hansen, *Mapping the Germans: Statistical Science, Cartography and the Visualization of the German Nation, 1848–1914* (Oxford: Oxford University Press, 2015); D. Speich Chassé, 'Nation', in C. Dejung, M. Dommann and D. Speich Chassé (eds), *Auf der Suche nach der Ökonomie: Historische Annäherungen* (Tübingen: Mohr Siebeck, 2014), 207–33; J.A. Tooze, 'Imagining National Economies: National and International Economic Statistics, 1900–1950', in G. Cubitt (ed.), *Imagining Nations* (Manchester: Manchester University Press, 1998), 212–28.

60. Memorandum of Arthur Fontaine, 8 October 1919, 5 (quote), LoNA, 15/1710/245; League of Nations, *International Labour Conference ... 1919*, 14.
61. Minutes of the 8th Meeting of the First Sub-Committee of the Third Committee (Economic) of the Genoa Conference, 26 April 1922, TNA, CAB 31/9, 254–72, at 256–62; 'Report of the League's Provisional Economic and Financial Committee on its 5th Session', 8–10 June 1922, *Official Journal of the League of Nations* 3 (1922), 990–94, at 992; for the historical relevance of the Genoa conference, see C. Fink, *The Genoa Conference: European Diplomacy, 1921–1922* (Chapel Hill: University of North Carolina Press, 1984).
62. See W. E. Rappard, 'Zum internationalen Abkommen über Wirtschaftsstatistik vom 14. Dezember 1928', *Weltwirtschaftliches Archiv* 30 (1929), 95–111; M. Huber, 'Le Comité d'Experts Statisticiens de la Société des Nations', *Revue de l'Institut International de Statistique* 7 (1939), 117–37; see also Bemmann, 'Das Chaos beseitigen'.
63. Letter from W.W. Cumberland, Peruvian government, to Eric Drummond, the League's Secretary-General, 25 September 1922, LoNA 10/24450/24450; speech of the Portuguese delegate to the International Conference Relating to Economic Statistics in 1928: League of Nations, *Proceedings of the International Conference*, 45; correspondence with and notes on a visit of the head of the statistical authority of British Malaya to the League of Nations in 1932 in LoNA, 10B/39638/1219 and TNA, BT 70/35/S1201/32; see also the similar enquiry of Fiji's Comptroller of the Customs to the British Colonial Office in TNA, CO 852/292/2.
64. Copy of the telegram of 13 June 1928, as well as further related correspondence and documents in: BL IOR, IOR/L/E/9/259.
65. D.B. Meek, *Report of the Representative of India at the International Conference Relating to Economic Statistics, Geneva 1928* (Calcutta, 1929), in: BL IOR, IOR/L/E/9/259.
66. Lindsay, 'India's Trade', 403.
67. League of Nations, *Monthly Bulletin of Statistics* 2 (7) (1920/21), 3.
68. For the increasing number of reporting countries, see Bemmann, 'Internationale und Weltwirtschaftsstatistik'.
69. See J. Osterhammel, '"Technical Cooperation" between the League of Nations and China', *Modern Asian Studies* 13(4) (1979), 661–80; R. Meienberger, 'China and the League of Nations', in UN Library/Graduate Institute for International Studies (eds), *The League of Nations in Retrospect: Proceedings of a Symposium* (Berlin: De Gruyter, 1983), 313–18; M. Zanasi, 'Exporting Development: The League of Nations and Republican China', *Comparative Studies in Society and History* 49 (2007), 143–69.
70. The Maritime Customs, *Documents Illustrative of the Origin, Development, and Activities of the Chinese Customs Service*, vol. IV: *Inspector General's Circulars, 1924 to 1931* (Shanghai, 1939), 494–506, quote at 494 (I would like to thank Yin Lin for the translation of the annexed Chinese documents); see F. Otte, 'Commercial Statistics in China', *Chinese Economic Journal* 1 (1933), 241–57, at 244–50.
71. Collected from October 1931 onwards and probably published for the first time in *Tong ji yue bo/Statistical Monthly* 2 (March/April 1932), 65–73.
72. League of Nations, *International Conference*, 2.
73. Bemmann, 'Internationale und Weltwirtschaftsstatistik'.
74. Osterhammel, *The Transformation*, 54.
75. It was not before the 1920s that the terms 'world economy' and 'économie mondiale' were widely used by English and French-speaking observers. Before the First World War, only Germans used a corresponding term (*Weltwirtschaft*); Slobodian, 'How to See', 308.

For a conceptual history of the German term, see H. Pohl, *Aufbruch der Weltwirtschaft: Geschichte der Weltwirtschaft von der Mitte des 19. Jahrhunderts bis zum Ersten Weltkrieg* (Stuttgart: Steiner, 1989), 9–25.
76. On the emergence of the concept of a distinguishable social entity called 'the economy', see T. Mitchell, 'Fixing the Economy', *Cultural Studies* 12 (1998), 82–101; T. Mitchell, 'The Work of Economics: How a Discipline Makes its World', *European Journal of Sociology* 46 (2005), 297–320; M.S. Morgan, 'Economics', in T.M. Porter and D. Ross (eds), *The Cambridge History of Science*, vol. 7: *Modern Social Sciences* (Cambridge: Cambridge University Press, 2003), 275–305; M. Emmison, '"The Economy": Its Emergence in Media Discourse', in H. Davis and P. Walton (eds), *Language, Image, Media* (Oxford: Blackwell, 1983), 139–55.
77. See more generally on this nexus Tooze, 'Imagining National Economies'.

# Bibliography

Alcock, A., *History of the International Labour Organisation* (Basingstoke: Macmillan, 1971).

Aldcroft, D., *From Versailles to Wall Street, 1919–1929* (Berkeley: University of California Press, 1977).

Ames, H., *Financial Administration and Apportionment of Expenses* (Geneva: The League of Nations, 1924).

Barth, B., Gänger, S. and Petersson, N.P., 'Einleitung: Globalisierung und Globalgeschichten', in Barth, B., Gänger, S. and Petersson, N.P. (eds), *Globalgeschichten: Bestandsaufnahme und Perspektiven* (Frankfurt am Main: Campus, 2014), 7–18.

Beckert, S., *King Cotton: Eine Globalgeschichte des Kapitalismus* (Munich: Beck, 2014).

Behrisch, L., *Die Berechnung der Glückseligkeit: Statistik und Politik in Deutschland und Frankreich im späten Ancien Régime* (Ostfildern: Thorbecke Verlag, 2016).

Bemmann, M., 'Das Chaos beseitigen: Die internationale Standardisierung forst- und holzwirtschaftlicher Statistiken in den 1920er und 1930er Jahren und der *Völkerbund*', *Economic History Yearbook* 57 (2016), 545–87.

———. 'Internationale und Weltwirtschaftsstatistik: Beobachtungen, Überlegungen und Thesen zur Genese internationaler Wirtschaftsstatistik in den 1920er und 1930er Jahren', in Haas, S., Schneider, M.C. and Bilo, N. (eds), *Die Zählung der Welt: Kulturgeschichte der Statistik vom 18. bis 20. Jahrhundert* (Stuttgart: Steiner, 2019), 195–217.

Breuer, J., *Die Methoden der Handelsstatistik* (Paderborn: Schöningh, 1920).

Clark, I., *Globalization and Fragmentation: International Relations in the Twentieth Century* (Oxford: Oxford University Press, 1997).

Clavin, P., and Sluga, G. (eds), *Internationalisms: A Twentieth-Century History* (Oxford: Oxford University Press, 2017).

Conseil International pour l'Exploration de la Mer, *Bulletin Statistique des Pêches Maritimes des Pays du Nord de l'Europe* (Copenhagen: Høst, 1903/4).

Cussó, R., 'L'activité statistique de l'Organisation économique et financière de la Société des Nations: Un nouveau lien entre pouvoir et quantification', *Histoire & Mesure* 27 (2012), 107–36.

Dejung, C., and Petersson, N.P. (eds), *The Foundations of Worldwide Economic Integration: Power, Institutions, and Global Markets, 1850–1930* (Cambridge: Cambridge University Press, 2013).

Desrosières, A., *The Politics of Large Numbers: A History of Statistical Reasoning* (Cambridge, MA: Harvard University Press, 1998).
Emmison, M., '"The Economy": Its Emergence in Media Discourse', in Davis, H. and Walton, P. (eds), *Language, Image, Media* (Oxford: Blackwell, 1983), 139–55.
Epple, A., *Globalisierung/en*, Version 1.0, *Docupedia-Zeitgeschichte*, 11 June 2012. Retrieved 13 March 2019 from https://www.docupedia.de/zg/Globalisierung.
Epple, A., and Erhart, W. (eds), *Die Welt beobachten: Praktiken des Vergleichens* (Frankfurt am Main: Campus, 2015).
Fear, J., 'Cartels', in Jones, G. and Zeitlin, J. (eds), *The Oxford Handbook of Business History* (Oxford: Oxford University Press, 2008).
Fink, C., *The Genoa Conference: European Diplomacy, 1921–1922* (Chapel Hill: University of North Carolina Press, 1984).
Fioramonti, L., *Gross Domestic Problem: The Politics behind the World's Most Powerful Number* (London: Zed Books, 2013).
Flux, A.W., 'International Statistical Comparisons', *Journal of the Royal Statistical Society* 86 (1923), 297–331.
Friedman, W.A., *Fortune Tellers: The Story of America's First Economic Forecasters* (Princeton: Princeton University Press, 2014).
Furlan, A.V., 'Weltwirtschaftsstatistik', *Weltwirtschaftliches Archiv* 4 (1914), 295–340.
Genzmer, H., *Die Bestrebungen zur Schaffung eines international-einheitlichen Zolltarifschemas* (Münster: Baader, 1929).
Griffin, T., 'The League of Nations and the Conference of European Statisticians', in Malaguerra, C. (ed.), *50 Years of the Conference of European Statisticians* (Geneva, 2003), 7–24.
Hansen, J.D., *Mapping the Germans: Statistical Science, Cartography and the Visualization of the German Nation, 1848–1914* (Oxford: Oxford University Press, 2015).
Hermberg, P., 'Über Handelsstatistik', *Weltwirtschaftliches Archiv* 16 (1920/21), 306–16.
Hill, M.H., *The Economic and Financial Organization of the League of Nations: A Survey of Twenty-Five Years' Experience* (Washington, DC: Carnegie Endowment for International Peace, 1945).
Huber, M., 'Le Comité d'Experts Statisticiens de la Société des Nations', *Revue de l'Institut International de Statistique* 7 (1939), 117–37.
Institut International d'Agriculture, *Annuaire International de Statistique Agricole* (Rome, 1910/12).
International Federation of Master Cotton Spinners and Manufacturers Association, *Statistics of Consumption of Cotton and Stocks of Cotton in Spinners Hands* (Manchester, 1908/9).
Kévonian, D., 'La légitimation par l'expertise: Le Bureau International du Travail et la statistique internationale', *Les cahiers Irice* 2 (2008), 81–106.
Kindleberger, C.P., *The World in Depression 1929–1939* (Berkeley: University of California Press, 1973).
Klein, J.L., and Morgan, M.S. (eds), *The Age of Economic Measurement* (Durham, NC: Duke University Press, 2001).
Kott, S., and Droux, J. (eds), *Globalizing Social Rights: The International Labour Organization and Beyond* (Basingstoke: Palgrave Macmillan, 2013).
League of Nations, *International Labour Conference: First Annual Meeting, October 29, 1919–November 29, 1919* (Washington: Government Printing Office, 1920).
———. *The Records of the First Assembly: Plenary Meetings* (Geneva, 1920).
———. *The Records of the First Assembly: Meetings of the Committees* (Geneva, 1920).

———. *Monthly Bulletin of Statistics* 2 (7) (1920/21).

———. *The Records of the Second Assembly: Plenary Meetings* (Geneva, 1921).

———. *The Records of the Second Assembly: Meetings of the Committees* (Geneva, 1921).

———. *International Conference Relating to Economic Statistics: International Convention – Protocol – Final Act of the Conference* (Geneva, 1928).

———. *Proceedings of the International Conference Relating to Economic Statistics* (Geneva, 1929).

———. *International Trade in Certain Raw Materials and Foodstuffs by Countries of Origin and Consumption* (Geneva, 1936–39).

Lepenies, P., *The Power of a Single Number: A Political History of GDP* (New York: Columbia University Press, 2016).

Lewis, C., *The International Accounts: A Constructive Criticism of Methods Used in Stating the Results of International Trade, Service, and Financial Operations* (London: George Allen & Unwin, 1927).

Lindsay, H.A.F., 'India's Trade and Imperial Statistics, Past, Present, and Future', *Journal of the Royal Statistical Society* 97 (1934), 399–422.

Llewellyn Smith, H., *The Board of Trade* (London: Putnam, 1928).

Loveday, A., 'Geneva as a Centre of Economic Information', *INDEX* 9 (1934), 195–209.

Maas, H., and Morgan, M.S. (eds), *Observing the Economy. Historical Perspectives* (Durham, NC: Duke University Press, 2012).

Mahsood, E., *The Great Invention: The Story of GDP and the Making of and Unmaking of the Modern World* (New York: Pegasus, 2016).

Marcantonato, L.G., *L'administration financière de la Société des Nations* (Paris: Éditions a Pedone, 1938).

Maritime Customs, *Documents Illustrative of the Origin, Development, and Activities of the Chinese Customs Service*, vol. IV: *Inspector General's Circulars, 1924 to 1931* (Shanghai, 1939).

Meienberger, R., 'China and the League of Nations', in UN Library/Graduate Institute for International Studies (eds), *The League of Nations in Retrospect: Proceedings of a Symposium* (Berlin: De Gruyter, 1983), 313–18.

Metallgesellschaft, *Statistische Zusammenstellungen über Blei, Kupfer, Zink und Zinn von der Metallgesellschaft Frankfurt am Main* (Frankfurt am Main: Metallgesellschaft, 1892).

*Minutes of the Twelfth Session of the Governing Body of the ILO, Rome, April 1922*, retrieved 13 March 2019 from http://www.ilo.org/public/libdoc/ilo/P/09601/09601%281922-12%29.pdf.

Mitchell, T., 'Fixing the Economy', *Cultural Studies* 12 (1998), 82–101.

———. 'The Work of Economics: How a Discipline Makes its World', *European Journal of Sociology* 46 (2005), 297–320.

Morgan, M.S., *The History of Econometric Ideas* (Cambridge: Cambridge University Press, 1990).

———. 'Economics', in Porter, T.M. and Ross, D. (eds), *The Cambridge History of Science*, vol. 7: *Modern Social Sciences* (Cambridge: Cambridge University Press, 2003), 275–305.

Mulhall, M.G., *The Dictionary of Statistics* (London: Routledge, 1892ff.).

Neumann, F.X., 'Übersichten über Produktion, Welthandel und Verkehrsmittel', *Geographisches Jahrbuch* 3 (1870), 420–81.

Neumann-Spallart, F.X. von, *Uebersichten über Produktion, Verkehr und Handel in der Weltwirthschaft* (Stuttgart: Meier, 1878).

Nichols, C.K., 'The Statistical Work of the League of Nations in Economic, Financial and Related Fields', *Journal of the American Statistical Association* 37 (1942), 336–42.

Olivetti, G., 'Internationale Industriestatistiken', *Internationale Wirtschaft* 1(1) (1929), 21–25.
Osieke, E., *Constitutional Law and Practice in the International Labour Organization* (Dordrecht: Nijhoff, 1985).
Osterhammel, J., '"Technical Cooperation" between the League of Nations and China', *Modern Asian Studies* 13(4) (1979), 661–80.
———. 'Globalizations', in Bentley, J.H. (ed.) *The Oxford Handbook of World History* (Oxford: Oxford University Press, 2011), 89–104.
———. *The Transformation of the World: A Global History of the Nineteenth Century* (Princeton: Princeton University Press, 2014).
Otte, F., 'Commercial Statistics in China', *Chinese Economic Journal* 1 (1933), 241–57.
Patel, K.K., *The New Deal: A Global History* (Princeton: Princeton University Press, 2016).
Philipsen, D., *The Little Big Number: How GDP Came to Rule the World and What to Do about it* (Princeton: Princeton University Press, 2015).
Platt, D.C.M., *Mickey Mouse Numbers in World History* (Basingstoke: Macmillan, 1989).
Pohl, H., *Aufbruch der Weltwirtschaft: Geschichte der Weltwirtschaft von der Mitte des 19. Jahrhunderts bis zum Ersten Weltkrieg* (Stuttgart: Steiner, 1989).
Porter, T., *The Rise of Statistical Thinking* (Princeton: Princeton University Press, 1986).
———. *Trust in Numbers: The Pursuit of Objectivity in Science and Public Life* (Princeton: Princeton University Press, 1995).
'Procès-Verbal of the Eighth Session of the Council of the League of Nations', San Sebastian, 30 July–5 August 1920, *Official Journal of the League of Nations* 1 (1920), 304–45.
Randeraad, N., *States and Statistics in the Nineteenth Century: Europe by Numbers* (Manchester: Manchester University Press, 2010).
Rappard, W.E., 'Zum internationalen Abkommen über Wirtschaftsstatistik vom 14. Dezember 1928', *Weltwirtschaftliches Archiv* 30 (1929), 95–111.
'Report of the Committee Appointed to Consider the Criteria to Be Adopted in the Selection of the Eight States of Chief Industrial Importance', 31 May 1922, *Official Journal of the League of Nations* 3 (1922), 1343–74.
'Report of the League's Provisional Economic and Financial Committee on its 5th Session', 8–10 June 1922, *Official Journal of the League of Nations* 3 (1922), 990–94.
Ribi Forclaz, A., 'Agriculture, American Expertise, and the Quest for Global Data: Leon Estabrook and First World Agricultural Census, 1930', *Journal of Global History* 16 (2016), 44–65.
Robertson, R., 'Glokalisierung: Homogenität und Heterogenität in Raum und Zeit', in Beck, U. (ed.), *Perspektiven der Weltgesellschaft* (Frankfurt am Main: Suhrkamp, 1998), 192–220.
Schmelzer, M., *The Hegemony of Growth: The OECD and the Making of the Economic Growth Paradigm* (Cambridge: Cambridge University Press, 2016).
Schröter, H., 'Cartelization and Decartelization in Europe, 1870–1995: Rise and Decline of an Economic Institution', *Journal of European Economic History* 25 (1996), 129–53.
Slobodian, Q., 'How to See the World Economy: Statistics, Maps, and Schumpeter's Camera in the First Age of Globalization', *Journal of Global History* 10 (2015), 307–32.
Sluga, G., *Internationalism in the Age of Nationalism* (Philadelphia: University of Pennsylvania Press, 2013).
Speich Chassé, D., *Die Erfindung des Bruttosozialprodukts: Globale Ungleichheit in der Wissensgeschichte der Ökonomie* (Göttingen: Vandenhoeck & Ruprecht, 2013).
———. 'Nation', in Dejung, C., Dommann, M. and Speich Chassé, D. (eds), *Auf der Suche nach der Ökonomie: Historische Annäherungen* (Tübingen: Mohr Siebeck, 2014), 207–33.

Stapleford, T., *The Cost of Living in America: A Political History of Economic Statistics, 1880–2000* (Cambridge: Cambridge University Press, 2009).
*The Statesman's Yearbook* (London: Macmillan, 1864ff.).
Sweetser, A., 'The Non-political Achievements of the League', *Foreign Affairs* 19 (1940), 179–92.
*Tong ji yue bo/Statistical Monthly* 2 (March/April 1932).
Tooze, J.A., 'Imagining National Economies: National and International Economic Statistics, 1900–1950', in Cubitt, G. (ed.), *Imagining Nations* (Manchester: Manchester University Press, 1998), 212–28.
———. *Statistics and the German State, 1900–1945: The Making of Modern Economic Knowledge* (Cambridge: Cambridge University Press, 2001).
———. 'Die Vermessung der Welt: Ansätze zu einer Kulturgeschichte der Wirtschaftsstatistik', in Berghoff, H. and Vogel, J. (eds), *Wirtschaftsgeschichte als Kulturgeschichte: Dimensionen eines Perspektivenwechsels* (Frankfurt am Main: Campus, 2004), 325–51.
United Kingdom Board of Trade, *Statistical Abstract for the Principal Foreign Countries* (London, 1874).
United States Department of Commerce and Labor, 'Commercial and Financial Statistics of the Principal Countries of the World', *Statistical Abstract of the United States* 30 (1907), 729–51.
Van Daele, J. (ed.), *ILO Histories: Essays on the International Labour Organization and its Impact on the World during the Twentieth Century* (Bern: Peter Lang, 2010).
Van der Borght, R., 'Fondation d'un Office International de Statistique', *Bulletin de l'Institut International de Statistique* 18 (1909), vol. 1, 568–90.
*Verhandlungen der verfassunggebenden Deutschen Nationalversammlung*, vol. 337: *Anlagen zu den stenographischen Berichten* (Berlin: Julius Sittenfeld, 1920).
Ward, M., *Quantifying the World. UN Ideas and Statistics* (Bloomington: Indiana University Press, 2004).
Zahn, F., 'Statistik', in Elster, L., Weber, A. and Wieser, F. (eds), *Handwörterbuch der Staatswissenschaften*, 4th edn, vol. 7 (Jena: Fischer, 1926), 869–972.
Zanasi, M., 'Exporting Development: The League of Nations and Republican China', *Comparative Studies in Society and History* 49 (2007), 143–69.
Žižek, F., 'Der statistische Vergleich', *Allgemeines Statistisches Archiv* 21 (1931), 525–50.
———. Review of F. Zahn, *50 années de l'Institut International de Statistique* (Munich, 1934), *Weltwirtschaftliches Archiv* 42 (1935), 251*–259*.

# 10
# In Search of a Global Centre of Calculation
## *The Washington Statistical Conferences of 1947*

Daniel Speich Chassé

**Introduction**

This chapter highlights the institutional and epistemological conditions of the possibility of global statistical ventures. The focus lies on the Statistical Conferences that were held in Washington, DC in September 1947, where the question of global statistical comparison was a key issue. The Washington Conferences have so far been largely ignored by scholars in global history and in the history of international organizations.[1] Some global historians have stressed the importance of making the world comparatively readable when studying the nineteenth century.[2] But surprisingly, global historical scholarship for the twentieth century, when this task effectively took shape, remains almost silent with respect to the impact of comparative statistics.[3]

Global political communication today seems intrinsically connected to comparative statistics of all kinds. Large numerical apparatuses have been set in place after the Second World War that allow for the comparison of different nations' performance in health and fertility, life expectancy, education, social security, agricultural and urban development, poverty, industrial production, external trade and many more respects. One might think of the System of National Accounts that was issued by the Organisation for European Economic Co-operation (OEEC) and the United Nations (UN) in the early 1950s,[4] or of the Human

Development Reports of the 1990s, or of the numerical monitoring of the UN Millennium Development Goals that was followed by an even more encompassing apparatus in order to monitor some Sustainable Development Goals as of 2015.[5]

Comparative economic statistics were very important in turning the whole world into something readable. According to the German philosopher Hans Blumenberg, the phenomenal world is not openly accessible to modern knowledge production. It is not lying out there ready to be read, but must be processed in order to become so.[6] This means that as historians, we can reconstruct the composition of whole sets of practices that were necessary in order to subject complicated phenomena to governance. Such a task has two dimensions: first, it must be asked which institutional dynamics were connected to the quest of political centres of power to gather information; and, second, the epistemic problems of creating homogeneous and methodologically sound databases need to be put under scrutiny. Studying the institutional and the epistemic history of comparative world statistics is a prerequisite for global enquiries and an interesting topic in its own right.

Some stages in this more general process shall be clarified by focusing on the International Statistical Conferences hosted by the International Statistical Institute (ISI), the U.S. government and the UN in Washington, DC in 1947. The guiding question in the first section of this chapter is to what extent a global statistical centre of calculation emerged with the advent of a new social formation that sociologists have termed a 'world society'. Scholars like Theodore Porter, Alain Desrosières and Bruno Latour have highlighted the importance of specific 'centres of calculation'[7] that institutionally and epistemically controlled the production of comparative numbers. But when taking the impact of numerical statistics in the post-1945 world order into view, such a centre is conspicuously absent. The second section looks at international institutional innovation in the years immediately after the Second World War. In 1947, statistical experts from all corners of the world convened in Washington, DC in order to create one single numerical worldview. They faced a great task of creating new organizations that to a certain degree surpassed their capacity and most certainly promoted the idea that there should be the position of one global centre of power and calculation that no existing international body or national government, including those of the United States and the Soviet Union, were able to fill. The concluding section focuses on the epistemic problems by taking an exemplary look at macroeconomic statistics. For the first generation of post-1945 economic statisticians, data were not simply to be collected like pebbles on the beach, but they considered their figures to be the effects of macroeconomic theory and controversially debated theoretical issues. These objections notwithstanding, macroeconomic statistics gained considerable importance in the international culture of political communication over the twentieth century.[8]

Existing scholarship on the cultural history of politics has so far largely focused on the national level. While research in the knowledge-power nexus is burgeoning,[9] studies in international diplomatic history tend to ignore the dimension of knowledge.[10] This chapter, in contrast, shows the evolution of historically new modes of knowledge and expertise that today are constantly being used to legitimate political power while presenting themselves as being apolitical, worldly, real or simply 'objective'. The issued numbers do not stem from one centre of power. How can this empirical finding be explained? Taking statistics into view and focusing on the great task of appropriating social difference globally into political communication through numerical comparison might help in terms of strengthening a new research agenda.

## Historical Roots of the Quest for a Global 'Centre of Calculation'

According to Wendy Espeland, social-scientific quantification is 'a peculiar modern ontology, in which the real easily becomes coextensive with what is measurable'.[11] But the use of numbers as a basis for societal communication has a complicated history. Bettina Heintz posits that numbers generate objectivity and offer a kind of generalized language that objectifies social difference. According to her, an assumed political neutrality makes numbers especially well-suited for communication on political cleavages and difference in a comparative move.[12] As Willibald Steinmetz has shown, making social conditions suitable to comparison is a highly improbable thing that seems to be less reflected the more it is being applied.[13] We can thus consider numerical comparison on a global scale to be a historically new phenomenon that is closely connected to the communicative appropriation of difference.

The global trust in the objectivity of numbers is the result of a process that took roughly 200 years. I wish to focus on two main features: the globality of numbers and their assumedly apolitical nature. It is quite astonishing to see that over a long period in the history of statistics, numbers were not at all seen as apolitical, but rather as a tool to strengthen political power. Moreover, their use was decidedly nonglobal, but was connected to the numerical representation of a single nation as opposed to the rest of the world.

Starting in the late eighteenth century, comparative statistics propelled understandings of society and of 'the economy' as mechanical devices that would deliver certain results if run correctly. As early as 1804, the German scholar August Ludwig Schlözer defined 'Statistik' as putting systematically gathered numbers under the eye of the sovereign in order for him to compare different phenomena on an assumedly rational basis and to take advantage of these differences in the perfection of rule over royal possessions. Schlözer specifically named statistics of the territory, of the people and of the resulting economic potential.[14] Following Schlözer, the predominant political concern of modernity, the building of nations, could never have been imagined collectively without the compilation of sound – and comparative – numerical data. During the German 'Vormärz', several philosophers designed the project of unifying a heterogeneous landscape of sometimes very small political communities into one single entity, a nation state based on liberal political thought. Schlözer's 'Statistik' gained strength as authors like Ludwig Heinrich von Jakob, Bruno Hildebrand and Friedrich List started to speak of a specifically German 'Nationalökonomie', a national economy, the characteristics of which were to be made visible through numbers.[15] This project was decidedly set against the British imperial space of free trade. For German statisticians, the French revolutionary experience of centrally gathering information worked as a template. Inventing the meter, setting standard measures and depicting all local instances in one unified form was seen as a mode of creating power.

The historiography of statistics has intensely focused on this power-knowledge nexus at the national level. As Alain Desrosières and others have shown,[16] late eighteenth-century philosophical conceptions of the state produced a specific demand for statistical knowledge, which then helped the new conceptions of the state to materialize. Desrosières borrowed from Abbé Sieyès the term 'adunation' to name the process of unifying the manifold systems of reference to the nation. The category of the nation was one of the foremost effects of statistics, and numbers have helped strengthening national institutions. Recent historical studies of the United Kingdom, Germany and the United States have substantiated the connection.[17] Theodore Porter argued convincingly how the trust in numbers helped in objectifying central issues of the state's purposes.[18] With respect to France, Bruno Latour analysed the cascade of inscriptions through which scientific expertise creates a 'centre of calculation', which politically was also a centre of national power.[19]

But what about the international realm that unfolded in the twentieth century? The Washington Conferences and the many statistical apparatuses that built upon them have not given rise to one global centre of power. No world government emerged post-1945, despite the fact that we constantly envision the world as a whole through comparative statistics. Existing analyses of the power-knowledge nexus at the national level cannot easily be generalized to the global polity because of constraints in the history of international organizations.

Several candidates have fruitlessly competed in becoming global numerical centres. The first institutions confronted with such a geographically wide task were the European empires. With the notable exception of the Chinese, other non-Western imperial powers conspicuously refrained from gathering numbers.[20] Portuguese and Spanish administrators documented first experiences.[21] The British government used statistics namely for the census when, in the 1860s, it took over control in India from the private East India Company after the Sepoy uprising of 1857.[22] But during late colonial rule, and especially after 1945, one can observe a specific mismatch between the way in which London or Paris ruled domestic lands and the technologies that were applied by the same governmental centres to the Overseas Territories.[23] Beginning in the 1920s, at least the British organized regular conferences of colonial statisticians to find ways of standardizing the epistemic procedures.[24] But sources show that these experts were largely overwhelmed by all the differences in social organization that were reported to them from the periphery. Apart from the racial prejudice that made them fundamentally separate Whites and non-Whites, their effort to build up stable categories did not lead to any substantial results and the quality of their numerical fact-finding remained poor.

The second group of institutions that started to take global differences into view were single-issue-meetings of experts in telecommunications, railroad management, meteorology and time measurement.[25] In the interwar period, the League of Nations formed an institutional environment for solving many questions of international standardization.[26] Most specifically, the International Labour Organization (ILO) created a conference of labour statisticians who started to convene regularly and exchange local experiences.[27] A new group of internationalists emerged from this connection who proposed 'technocratic internationalism'[28] as a solution to the persistent unreadability of the world. The League of Nations reacted to the advent of technical experts who seemed to take over competence in international politics from the diplomats. In the late 1930s, the Australian Stanley Bruce was commissioned with a report concerning a thorough reform of the organization in order to make it less political, more technical and more statistics-based.[29]

The third source for the global process that I envision here stems from the scholarly internationalism that unfolded in the second half of the nineteenth century. In the 1850s, a world conference of statisticians took place that subsequently evolved into the important International Statistical Institute (ISI). Acknowledging the growing need for international standards, scholars like the Frenchman Jacques Bertillon used the ISI as a vehicle to press ahead with, for example, an 'International Categorisation of the Human Lethal Diseases and Reasons of Death' that is still in use today (known as the ICD). The ILO followed this move in standardization with an International Standard Industrial Classification (ISIC), which is also still in use, that was designed to make the conditions of labour in different industrial branches comparable. The history of the ISI as an academic institution is well documented in the sources, but has remained under-researched by scholars of global history.[30]

Some of its members observed a change in global political communication that took place in the middle decades of the twentieth century quite closely and started to voice the quest for a global centre of statistical calculation. Arnold Schwarz of the Swiss Statistical Bureau, for example, bemoaned the absence of a stable framework for global economic statistics in 1943. In his view, no sound internationally comparable data were available, although highly demanded.[31] When the British Royal Statistical Society met in the same year in order to discuss problems of the emerging postwar order, Ernest C. Snow made the quest for a global statistical centre the core of his presidential address.[32] In 1946, the statistically minded political scientist Earl Latham summarized ongoing efforts in standardizing international statistics in a contribution to the *Journal of the American Statistical Association* under the heading of 'One Statistical World'. He found that as yet, no unified language of numbers existed in order to describe all social instances on the planet in a truly comparative form.[33]

These experts thought that the world could be made a better place if statisticians were allowed more influence and could make their quest for a coherent statistical worldview better heard. But they underestimated the contests over political power that came to the fore when different institutions and bodies in world politics tried to create one single global centre of calculation.

## International Organizational Innovation: The Washington Conferences on Statistics in 1947

The totalitarian movements of the interwar period and the catastrophe of the Second World War were major challenges to the statisticians' global quest. Seen from the perspective of the ISI, these instances brutally disrupted the traditional scholarly internationalism by giving rise to chauvinist superiority claims over different national scientific styles and by imposing severe travel restrictions. Concurrently, the waging of a 'total war' forced all combatant parties to include the gathering and the processing of information into their respective arsenals of weaponry.[34] Informational warfare led to important computational innovations. On the side of those nations that joined forces with the United States as of 1942, the young historian Walt W. Rostow worked for intelligence on defining German bomb targets, while the British mathematician Alan Turing broke the enemy's secret code. And the Australian officer Robert 'Jacko' Jackson set up a 'Middle East Supply Centre' in 1940 that drew on new methods of informational management to feed people on the Arabian peninsula despite the blockage of all ports. Except for Turing, whose accomplishments remained unrecognized for decades, these men became heroes in post-1945 world history. Rostow made modernization theory useful for American foreign policy, Turing made important contributions to developing the computer and Jackson became a mastermind of international organization.[35] The members of the ISI always thought that statistics were important, but never reckoned with such a great boost in their field. What used to be an exclusive armchair science for well-established scholars turned into a key issue of global politics. Most importantly, the Allied Forces gave rise to the United Nations Organization at the founding conference in San Francisco in 1945 and thereby institutionalized the possibility of a world government (but not such an operational government itself).

It is interesting to see how the ISI reacted to this organizational challenge. In 1935, distinguished members of the American Statistical Association convinced the U.S.Congress to host a gathering of the ISI on the occasion of its own centenary jubilee for 1939. But the board of the ISI had already decided to hold the 1939 conference in Prague, the Czechoslovakian capital. Unfortunately, the participants had to leave after only one day because Nazi Germany occupied Prague in September 1939 and war broke out.[36] The crème de la crème of international statistics rushed home under difficult circumstances and only met again in 1947 in Washington, DC.

Following the account by Stuart A. Rice, who was the President of the ISI during these difficult years, the organizing of the 1947 Washington meeting was a sheer nightmare.[37] In a retrospective view, he declared: 'The International Statistical Conferences provided a new and unfamiliar form of international statistical consultation. There were no precedents for the reduction of the particular international events composing the conferences into an inclusive whole. It is amusing to recall that this lack of precedents threatened to produce nervous breakdowns among experts on protocol.'[38]

In 1945, members of the American Statistical Association in cooperation with the newly founded Inter-American Statistical Institute got the green light from the U.S. Congress to organize a venue in 1947. This latter body had been set up under Stuart A. Rice's leadership in around 1943 and envisioned among other projects the computation of a continental census of the Americas. Because of difficulties in travel, institutional synergies were sought and the organizers requested subsidies from the U.S. government to enable foreign representatives to come to Washington. Other scholarly initiatives profited from the occasion. The foundation meetings of an International Conference on Public Opinion Research and of an International Biometric Society were set shortly before the Washington meeting in Williamstown and Woods Hole respectively, both in Massachusetts, so that the participants could then easily head south towards Washington. Older bodies such as the Econometric Society (founded in 1930) and the International Union for the Scientific Study of Population Problems (founded in 1928) joined in and also adjusted the timing of their conference agendas. The statistically minded economists envisioned the founding of a new International Association for Research in Income and Wealth at the event. According to protocol, it seemed clear that U.S. President Harry Truman would be the official host of a convention of a series of mainly private associations. But the scale of the event quickly surpassed the organizational experience of the ISI. Because of the rising importance that the Truman Administration assigned to global statistics, the ISI lost control over its twenty-fifth assembly.

A further irritating challenge to Stuart A. Rice was the founding of an Economic and Social Council within the UN system, where a new global statistical office was established.[39] Things became even more complicated when the United Nations Statistical and Population Commissions decided to organize a World Statistical Congress by its own on the same date and at the same location, and set its regular sessions at Lake Success immediately prior to it. The Food and Agricultural Organization (FAO) and the World Bank followed up by also rescheduling their calendars, while the ILO moved its first post-war Conference of Labour Statisticians in the spring of 1947 from Geneva to Montreal, which motivated several statisticians from Asia and Europe to remain in the United States for the Washington meeting in September. The conference threatened to turn into a UN function, which would officially have to be hosted by the acting

UN Secretary-General Trygve Lie. To keep matters operational, a rather heterogeneous Joint Arrangements Committee resulted that consisted of representatives of the scholarly associations, some UN officials and the chief of the International Conferences Division of the U.S. Department of State. U.S. Secretary of Commerce Averell Harriman made generous funding available, while IBM and other private U.S. enterprises offered sponsoring, and a hospitality committee was created to arrange for side-events and receptions. As a name for the event, the plural form seemed appropriate so that the meeting finally became known as the 'International Statistical Conferences'. But it actually remained unclear whether it was a scholarly convention of independent experts, a U.S. or a UN event.

The official opening ceremony took place on Monday 8 September 1947 at 2.30 pm. with Willard L. Thorp in the chair. This was a wise choice as Thorpe wore many hats. He was the President of the American Statistical Association, an official of the United Nations Economic and Social Council and also an Assistant Secretary of State for Economic Affairs, and could therefore also act as a representative of the U.S. government. Due to the many bodies involved, word of mouth had spread and applications for registration to the event exploded in numbers. A restriction for U.S. citizens had to be introduced on the basis that no more domestic than international participants would be accredited. In the end, 324 statisticians (and spouses) from 55 nations plus 294 experts from the United States registered in Washington during 6 to 18 September 1947 in order to discuss statistical issues. In terms of the number of participants, this was probably the biggest event ever held in the history of statistics to that date, and in terms of the origin of the participants, it was also the most global. Participants included, for example, Mr Thorstein Thorsteinson from the Icelandic statistical office as well as Mr and Mrs Rafaeil Alberto Zuniga, who took part on behalf of a Costa Rican private enterprise, Mr Julius Wyler, a professor of economics and statistics at the University of Geneva, Switzerland, or Mr P.C. Mahalanobis, the Secretary of the Indian Statistical Institute in Calcutta, who was accompanied by his wife. Other participants were Mr Ismail Raafat, a controller at the Statistical Department in Cairo, Mr H.M. Stoker, Assistant Director of Census and Statistics in Pretoria, South Africa, and Mr Kuo-Pao King, a director of the accounting department of the Central Bank of China in Shanghai.[40]

The UN Secretary-General Trygve Lie had the honour of holding the first welcome address. As all participants were well aware of the organizational novelty of the occasion, their speeches were full of pathos and a rhetoric of newness. They also constitute rich written sources for a historian of statistics and numerical comparison. Lie said:

> We cannot cure our troubles unless we know in the first place what those troubles are. Likewise we cannot achieve international understanding, which is the basis of advancement, unless the peoples of the world are given the facts about each other. Nations are now too large, economic affairs are now too complicated and too highly interrelated, for us to rely upon the accounts of returned travellers for our information on economic and

> social progress. We are much farther upon our course than we were in the days of Marco Polo and of Captain Cook. There is no substitute for facts, for clear and systematically organized facts. They alone can be relied upon to measure resources and potentialities for progress and to direct policies and actions designed to achieve the objectives of all civilized peoples ... Secondly, the statistics must be carefully organized. By this I mean that they must be comparable from time to time and from place to place. This problem of comparability is especially acute when we deal with the interrelated problems of many countries of vastly different characteristics. Difficult as the problem of comparability is, it must be solved. Unless it is solved, we shall be seriously handicapped in studying and dealing with problems on an international scale ... It is shocking to realize that no statistics worthy of the name exist for probably half of the world's peoples. No one knows exactly how many people there are, how they make their living, or the characteristics of their social, economic, and political institutions.[41]

Lie was a Norwegian social democrat who was well aware of the usefulness of statistics in governing social difference. His aim was to expand the Norwegian experience of rational rule to a global scale. Moreover, he decidedly held to 'facts' as a basis in political practice as opposed to ideology or simple lies. And finally, he used the occasion to substantiate the global horizon of his organization that in his view necessarily included the poor regions of the Global South. This address is an important testimony to the unconditional belief in the powers of reason that informed the first generation of UN officials in their technocratic stance. They had experienced the malfunction of political deliberation after the global economic crisis broke out in 1929. And they put high hopes for a brighter future in statistics as an art of rationally executing political power.

The address by Lie also bears witness of a specifically global political thought. If statistics were 'carefully organized', i.e. if scholars could agree upon categories and methodological procedures, they might be able to bring global differences and the complexities of social life onto the desks of informed administrators and could thus help in substantiating empirically the new vision of the world as one. But Lie also reminded his audience of the severe problems connected to the establishment of such comparative worldviews and he scandalized the lack of evidence and information specifically concerning nonsovereign territories under colonial rule.

Following Trygve Lie, Averell Harriman greeted the participants in the name of the U.S. government by presenting a letter from Harry Truman in which the President stated:

> We look to the leaders of the world's statistical profession who are here assembled to strengthen and improve existing standards respecting official statistics, their international compilation and use. As a contribution on our part we shall continue to make the official statistics of the United States as adequate and readily available as possible.[42]

This is an early formulation of some contents of Truman's famous Point Four address in which he offered to the world the opening of the U.S. store of technical expertise in order to improve the living conditions of all the world's inhabitants. The promise was innovative if measured against the secrecy of intelligence that had been crucial during the Second World War.

Then the acting ISI President Walter F. Willcox responded to these speeches on behalf of his fellow presidents Stuart A. Rice (who was at this point of his career at the Inter-American Statistical Institute), Jan Tinbergen (Econometric Society), Adolphe Landry (International Union for the Scientific Investigation of Population Problems) and Simon Kuznets (International Association for Research in Income and Wealth).

At 4.30 pm, all speakers and their audience moved to the White House, where the U.S. government offered a reception and a garden party. During the following ten days, a plethora of panels was offered. One can only speculate about the content of all the informal talks that were held individually among the participants. On Thursday 18 September at 7.30 pm, the International Statistical Conferences were closed at an official farewell dinner given by the Joint Arrangements Committee. The following day, interested participants could join a visit to the U.S. Bureau of the Census, the National Office of Vital Statistics and the Permanent Office of the Inter-American Statistical Institute or get an impression of the Social Security Administration in Baltimore, Maryland.[43] The hospitality committee had done a fine job.

The twenty-fifth convention of the ISI in Washington, DC in 1947 grew into a new landscape of global statistics that was populated by some old and many new competing institutions. The UN used the audience successfully in order to present its services and prospects.[44] Some UN officials made quite far-reaching statements and boldly claimed leadership for their organization in front of the assembled international statistical community. The former Chief Statistician of Canada, Herbert Marshall, who acted as the chair of the UN Statistical Commissions during their first three regular sessions in 1947 and 1948, took the practices of private business administration as a benchmark for the UN:

> If no wise corporation nowadays would attempt to conduct its affairs by guess or by rule of thumb, how much more must governments, with their greater range of operations, depend upon comprehensive statistical data of high quality to assist them in making policies? World War II demonstrated the indispensability of a thoroughly developed statistical organization as a basis for the controls necessary to wage total war. Now this postwar period presents a further challenge to national governments of the United Nations. There is required an international organization of statistics of a scope and quality hitherto unattained.[45]

These were high standards. William R. Leonard, the person who helped building up the UN Statistical Office under the auspices of Herbert Marshall and who directed the agency from 1948 until 1962, clearly saw that statistics, in the first place, were connected to national centres of power and that the UN statisticians' role was to standardize procedures through compromise rather than through prescriptive imposition:

> With any one country ... there exist possibilities of arbitration and resources of authority which are not available to the United Nations or to other international organizations now in existence. Problems facing international agencies in improving comparability of statistics must be solved through compromise ... Now, if ever, is the time and here is the opportunity for coordinated action by all countries to make statistics comparable from country to country, and thus to achieve through statistics a truly universal medium of communication.[46]

Leonard was well aware of the weakness of his UN body. In order to run the world as if it were a business corporation, he assigned the authorship of the eventually emerging statistical world picture to the governments of the individual member states. But when he found himself at the Washington Conferences in the privileged position of talking to chief statisticians from all corners of the world, he did not fall short in creating a vision. Shared standards in a universal community of statisticians should create homogeneity. The UN offered technical aid to all those governments that could not comply for different reasons.

For the ISI, the future looked less bright. It tried to retain authority by systematically collecting the protocols of all panels, conventions and debates, and eventually published the proceedings of the conferences in six volumes. But even this task turned out to be troublesome, as Stuart A. Rice recalled.[47] Lack of funding, technical problems in communication and a shortage of paper accompanied the ISI when it decided to print the volumes in Calcutta, while copyediting was done in New York and Mexico City. The distribution and the marketing of the proceedings were further challenges.

It was quite evident that the ISI could no longer sustain the role it had acquired internationally as a 'semi-official' issuer of statistical standards. If not even the UN was believed to have the power of forcing national statistical authorities to comply with international standards, such institutional powers lay way beyond the possibilities of a scholarly association, irrespective of the sometimes very high reputation its members enjoyed in their individual countries. Rice reacted by defining new statutes for the ISI:

> The Institute as an organization is now confronting forms of competition to which it was not subjected during the earlier years of its life ... The creation of official international statistical agencies leaves open to the Institute a scientific and voluntary role in international statistics as distinguished from an official role ... The institute can no longer regard itself as a semi-official organization, collecting international statistics for government use, drafting conventions and the like.[48]

Acknowledging the rise of new state-funded statistical authorities, Rice felt that his free association of scholars had to rejuvenate itself and to focus more clearly on its academic role. No follow-ups of Bertillon's successful International Classification of Deaths (ICD) seemed plausible. Rice was an optimistic character and envisioned new tasks and a new identity for the ISI. He simply rejoiced in the fact that statistics had started to become a ubiquitous governmental tool, but as it turned out, he was overconfident that his organization would profit from this move:

> On every hand there is a new dependence upon statistics and statisticians. The organizational competition which the Institute must face on every hand is itself an evidence of the vitality and growth of our professional field. There is a crying need for world leadership in this field; and no existing unofficial organization occupies so favourable a position to seize that leadership as does the Institute.[49]

Unfortunately for Rice, the ISI fell into relative oblivion. The leadership that he envisioned was carefully distributed to a range of other organizations, but never materialized into one single centre and certainly did not settle with the ISI.

## Epistemic Problems in Creating Comparative Economic Numbers

One important reason why the ISI lost control over international statistics during the middle decades of the twentieth century was the fact that politicians started to use numerical findings in international diplomacy irrespective of the epistemic value that statistical scholars assigned to them. Up to this point, the professors of the ISI had been convinced that it was their task to create adequate numerical representations of social reality that could then inform public debate. This sender-receiver model was now turned upside down. The science-policy nexus changed, and scholars in statistics increasingly saw themselves confronted with a demand for their findings that they could no longer control. This was the case in global agricultural policy, with respect to population problems, education and other fields.[50] I have shown elsewhere that in the domain of economic growth and development, the use of numbers certainly was driven by political demand and not by academic supply.[51]

Ernest C. Snow, the President of the British Royal Statistical Society, sensed the shift in the science-policy nexus on the global level in 1944 when he declared to his fellow statisticians that the compilation of national incomes 'has now become a matter of practical importance as a result of the recent decision of the United Nations Relief and Rehabilitation Administration [UNRRA] conference at Atlantic City to asses nations on the basis of estimates of their national income'.[52] Already in the League of Nations, the question of how to define the budgetary shares of the member states had been an issue, and national income totals were seen as a possible basis. However, the statistical practice of income accounting was not yet well established.[53] Not all governments provided such figures and those that did followed different procedures.

Towards the end of the 1930s, the British statistician Colin Clark set out as a private scholar to collect all available data and to compile it in a truly global framework. His 1940 publication on *The Conditions of Economic Progress*[54] for the first time listed all territories of the world – be they sovereign nation states or dependent territories – in a unified frame of macroeconomic reference. This was a tremendous empirical task of compiling all sorts of published material and it included the paramount theoretical achievement of creating a standard framework. Among other innovations, Clark suggested an 'international unit' to compare economic life across continents without having to struggle with currency exchange rates. It was based on the analysis of average purchasing power for the years 1925 to 1934.

Clark's book was vitriolically criticized by fellow economists for its weak empirical basis and for its speculative nature. But despite this fact, and despite the fact that few of his data were officially sanctioned by respective state authorities, his compilation still came to heavily influence international state action and political communication. The book established a comparative worldview that had long been sought. It basically showed that the majority of people on planet earth lived under dire economic constraints. Clark used maths. He divided, for example, the assumed total Chinese economic activity by an estimated population figure and assigned to China an annual average national income per capita of under 200 international units – as compared to 1,000 units for the United States, Argentina or Switzerland.[55] International organizations such as the UNRRA or the FAO immediately referred to this set of numbers. The UN used gross domestic product (GDP) as of 1945 in order to define each member state's share to the budget of the organization.

Economic statisticians were shocked. When the members of the Econometric Society debated the international comparability of economic statistics at their Washington meeting in 1947, Richard Stone and Simon Kuznets, the two doyens of the profession, found it important to criticize Colin Clark's work (who sat – by the way – in the audience). They both emphasized the epistemic uselessness of making national accounts a basis for international comparisons. They ridiculed a worldview that their academic colleague had put forward in 1940 and, at the same time, they realized that it had started to gain ground in international politics.[56] Richard Stone said: 'Why do we want to compare the United States with, say, China or India? What possible interest is there in it? Everybody knows that one country is, in economic terms, very rich and another country very poor.'[57]

In addition, Simon Kuznets dwelled on the U.S.–China comparison. He translated Clark's figure of below 200 international units per capita and year into 40 U.S. Dollars and contrasted this piece of information with American everyday economic life. His aim was to reconnect the abstract speak with local experiences, because in his view, economics were about locality:

> If we ask, could people live in the United States during 1925–34 for several years on an income substantially below $40 per capita, the answer would be 'yes', if they were sufficiently wealthy to have lots of provisions to sell, sufficiently lucky to have rich relations, or sufficiently bold to rob other people. The one-third to one-half of the pre-industrial population of the world would scarcely be in that position; all would be dead by now.[58]

For Simon Kuznets, it was quite clear that economic statisticians first had to define what economic activities were before they could reasonably start to count. And when trying to set up an international comparative framework, they needed to reflect more deeply upon local differences than Colin Clark had done. Quite obviously the figure given in Clark's compilation on China did not adequately represent Chinese economic reality. Adequate definitions, in Kuznets' view, necessarily remained local in terms of historical time and geography.

Earlier, Kuznets had struggled hard to calculate a GDP for the United States since the late 1920s.[59] In order to attain reliable standards for depicting U.S. economic life, he had strongly engaged in the U.S. Conference on Research in Income and Wealth (CRIW). Local instances in, say, Florida or Michigan, were to be reported in a bottom-up process. For Kuznets, turning such a venture into a global effort was an epistemic challenge. He made use of the Washington Conferences to found an International Association for Research in Income and Wealth (IARIW), which he envisioned as a global forum of debate about what 'economic life' meant in different corners of the world and how these instances could be accumulated into one numerical framework. He also cofounded a new academic journal called *Economic Development and Cultural Change*, in which he published a monograph-length series of articles on the problem.[60]

But world history stood against such a careful procedure. In global politics, the quest for one comparative framework was much stronger than the interest in local difference. The 'Emergence of Globalism'[61] demanded global forms of communication, and economic statistics had that potential. As one economist at the Washington Conferences observed with respect to the compilation of data to compare GDP:

> These figures have been produced and people use them. They will continue to be produced, and people will continue to use them. If we were starting afresh, I would have a great deal of sympathy with what has been said about not using a single figure, and not even producing one. But the way the thing stands now is that in every governmental problem where a multiplicity of regions or countries is involved, national-income figures are used ... And every international organization that has been formed has used national-income statistics in one way or another. Therefore, I think the statistician cannot bury his head in the sand in this matter. He should know the practical politicians will use his results and probably will misuse them. And therefore I do believe that it is imperative to make the best single figure that is possible and to use a few very simple rules for its application.[62]

Economists were unhappy with the way things went in the immediate postwar years, but they also saw their discipline potentially rising in political importance. The misuse of national income data and its usefulness in making the world a better place stood against each other.

## Conclusion

Following the Washington Conferences of 1947, experts struggled for a long time to establish a stable numerical framework according to which the economic performance of as many nations as possible could be compared. A whole range of academic institutions and research projects were involved in this major task. Kuznets' British adversary Richard Stone raced ahead and compiled an internationally normative 'System of National Accounts' (SNA) by virtue of the UN statistical organs, the Organisation for European Economic Co-operation (OEEC) and the Department of Applied Economics at his host university in Cambridge in the United Kingdom. This book of rules, first issued in the early 1950s, has since been revised many times and has become the unquestioned source of standards in computing global GDPs and derived comparative macroeconomic data. It set the economic conditions of industrialized countries as a template for monitoring developing nations. The SNA became an authoritative instance for comparing national economies in the era of imperial decline. And much to the unease of Kuznets, it took as a theoretical basis the macroeconomic analysis of John Maynard Keynes, thereby working secretly as a conveyor for the global spread of Keynesian economic policy.[63] In 1968, the United Nations Statistical Division in cooperation with the World Bank and the Ford Foundation decided to regularly fund research at the University of Pennsylvania in order to standardize international wealth statistics and to create a coherent statistical view of the whole globe. The result was the so-called Penn World Tables. One major issue in their composition was how to make different economic realities internationally comparable. This task became known as the 'International Comparison Program'.[64] By 2016, it involved 199 countries and produced comparable price and volume measures for GDPs and its component expenditures. The project encompassed the perfection of so-called 'Purchasing Power Parities' (PPP) according to which monetary values for basic expenditures from a broad range of different social realities can be inserted into one statistical calculus.

Over a period of several decades, the initial debates at the Washington Conferences resulted in the availability of big databases. Comparative figures are available online from sources like the University of Pennsylvania, the University of Groningen, the University of Toronto and the University of California at Davis. The World Bank and the International Monetary Fund base their actions on such data, as do almost all national governments, and they form an unquestioned basis for social-scientific research and political deliberation on a global scale.[65] One could consider them being centres of calculation, but they seem strangely detached from the political centres of global power.

**Daniel Speich Chassé** is Professor of Modern History at the University of Lucerne, Switzerland. His research focuses on the evolution of global political communication since 1800. His recent publications include a monograph on the invention of the gross national product (*Die Erfindung des Bruttosozialprodukts:*

*Globale Ungleichheit in der Wissensgeschichte der* Ökonomie, 2013) and numerous articles and coedited books on the establishment of global statistics and standards, among them 'The Roots of the Millennium Development Goals: A Framework for Studying the History of Global Statistics', *Historical Social Research* 41 (2016).

## Notes

1. Comprehensive volumes do not specifically highlight the event. See M. Mazower, *Governing the World: The History of an Idea* (New York: Penguin, 2012).
2. J. Osterhammel, *Die Verwandlung der Welt: Eine Geschichte des 19. Jahrhunderts* (Munich: C.H. Beck, 2009), 57–62.
3. The exception is a volume of the UN Intellectual History Project: M. Ward, *Quantifying the World: UN Ideas and Statistics* (Bloomington: Indiana University Press, 2004); for the interwar period, see Chapter 9 by M. Bemmann in this volume.
4. D. Speich, 'The Use of Global Abstractions: National Income Accounting in the Period of Imperial Decline', *Journal of Global History* 6(1) (2011), 7–28.
5. D. Speich Chassé, 'The Roots of the Millennium Development Goals: A Framework for Studying the History of Global Statistics', *Historical Social Research* 41 (2016), 218–37.
6. H. Blumenberg, *Die Lesbarkeit der Welt* (Frankfurt am Main: Suhrkamp, 1981).
7. The term 'centre of calculation' is borrowed from B. Latour, *Science in Action: How to Follow Scientists and Engineers through Society* (Cambridge, MA: Harvard University Press, 1987). See also B. Latour, 'Drawing Things Together', in M. Lynch and S. Woolgar (eds), *Representation in Scientific Practice* (Cambridge, MA: MIT Press, 1990), 19–68. The idea can also be found in T.M. Porter, *Trust in Numbers: The Pursuit of Objectivity in Science and Public Life* (Princeton: Princeton University Press, 1995) and A. Desrosières, *La politique des grands nombres : Histoire de la raison statistique* (Paris: Editions La Découverte, 1993).
8. For the underlying idea of framing politics as a communicative process, see W. Steinmetz and H.-G. Haupt, 'The Political as Communicative Space in History: The Bielefeld Approach', in W. Steinmetz, I. Gilcher-Holtey and H.-G. Haupt (eds), *Writing Political History Today* (Frankfurt am Main: Campus, 2013), 11–33.
9. One important trigger in the German academia was the seminal paper by L. Raphael, 'Die Verwissenschaftlichung des Sozialen als methodische und konzeptionelle Herausforderung für eine Sozialgeschichte des 20. Jahrhunderts', *Geschichte und Gesellschaft* 22 (1996), 165–93.
10. A recent textbook in German contains surprisingly few references to statistics. See J. Dülffer and W. Loth (eds), *Dimensionen internationaler Geschichte* (Munich: Oldenbourg, 2012).
11. W. Espeland and M. Stevens, 'A Sociology of Quantification', *European Journal of Sociology* 49 (2008), 401–36, at 432.
12. B. Heintz, 'Numerische Differenz: Überlegungen zu einer Soziologie des (quantitativen) Vergleichs', *Zeitschrift für Soziologie* 39 (2010), 162–81.
13. W. Steinmetz, '"Vergleich" – eine begriffsgeschichtliche Skizze', in A. Epple and W. Erhart (eds), *Die Welt beobachten: Praktiken des Vergleichens* (Frankfurt am Main: Campus, 2015), 85–134.

14. A.L. Schlözer, *Theorie der Statistik: Nebst Ideen über das Studium der Politik überhaupt* (Göttingen: Vandenhoek & Ruprecht, 1804).
15. L.H. Jakob, *Grundsätze der National-Oekonomie oder National-Wirthschaftslehre* (Halle: Ruffsche Verlagshandlung, 1805); B. Hildebrand, *Die Nationalökonomie der Gegenwart und Zukunft* (Frankfurt am Main: Literarische Anstalt (J. Rütten), 1848); F. List, *Das nationale System der politischen Oekonomie* (Stuttgart: Cotta, 1841). See also D. Speich Chassé, 'Nation', in C. Dejung, M. Dommann and D. Speich Chassé (eds), *Auf der Suche nach der Ökonomie: Historische Annäherungen* (Tübingen: Mohr Siebeck, 2014), 207–34.
16. Desrosières, *La politique*; M. Sandl, *Ökonomie des Raumes: Der kameralwissenschaftliche Entwurf der Staatswirtschaft im 18. Jahrhundert* (Cologne: Böhlau, 1999); L. Behrisch, *Die Berechnung der Glückseligkeit: Statistik und Politik in Deutschland und Frankreich im späten Ancien Régime* (Ostfildern: Thorbecke, 2016).
17. See K. Brückweh, *Menschen zählen: Wissensproduktion durch britische Volkszählungen und Umfragen vom 19. Jahrhundert bis ins digitale Zeitalter* (Berlin: De Gruyter Oldenbourg, 2015); J.A. Tooze, *Statistics and the German State, 1900–1945: The Making of Modern Economic Knowledge* (Cambridge: Cambridge University Press, 2001); E. Didier, *En quoi consiste l'Amérique? Les statistiques, le New Deal et la démocratie* (Paris: La Découverte, 2009).
18. Porter, *Trust in Numbers*.
19. Latour, 'Drawing Things'.
20. J. Burbank and F. Cooper, *Empires in World History: Power and the Politics of Difference* (Princeton: Princeton University Press, 2010).
21. A. Brendecke, *Imperium und Empirie: Funktionen des Wissens in der spanischen Kolonialherrschaft* (Cologne: Böhlau, 2009).
22. C.A. Bayly, *Empire and Information: Intelligence Gathering and Social Communication in India 1780–1870* (Cambridge: Cambridge University Press, 1996).
23. Speich Chassé, 'Roots'.
24. J.-G. Prévost and J.-P. Beaud, *Statistics, Public Debate and the State, 1800–1945: A Social, Political and Intellectual History of Numbers* (London: Pickering & Chatto, 2012).
25. R. Wenzlhuemer, *Connecting the Nineteenth-Century World: The Telegraph and Globalization* (Cambridge: Cambridge University Press, 2013); V. Ogle, *The Global Transformation of Time 1870–1950* (Cambridge, MA: Harvard University Press, 2015).
26. See Martin Bemmann's chapter in this volume.
27. The serial sources of this body have not been studied systematically yet. On the ILO as a global agent, see S. Kott and J. Droux (eds), *Globalizing Social Rights: The International Labour Organization and Beyond* (Basingstoke: Palgrave Macmillan, 2013).
28. The notion of a 'technocratic internationalism' is proposed in W. Kaiser and J. Schot, *Writing the Rules for Europe: Experts, Cartels, and International Organizations* (Basingstoke: Palgrave Macmillan, 2014).
29. D. Speich Chassé, 'Technical Internationalism and Economic Development at the Founding Moment of the UN System', in M. Frey, C. Unger and S. Kunkel (eds), *International Organizations and Development, 1945–1990* (Basingstoke: Palgrave Macmillan, 2014), 23–45.
30. The authoritative historical account is still J.W. Nixon, *A History of the International Statistical Institute 1885–1960* (The Hague: International Statistical Institute, 1960).
31. A. Schwarz, 'Probleme der internationalen Vergleichbarkeit der Wirtschaftsstatistik', *Weltwirtschaftliches Archiv* 57 (1943), 572–83. The same complaint is to be found in W.

Grävell, 'Die Statistik im Grosswirtschaftsraum', *Weltwirtschaftliches Archiv* 56 (1942), 457–69.
32. E.C. Snow, 'The International Comparison of Industrial Output', *Journal of the Royal Statistical Society* 107 (1944), 1–55.
33. E. Latham, 'One Statistical World', *Journal of the American Statistical Association* 41 (September 1946), 275–92.
34. On the close nexus of war and numbers, see P.N. Edwards, *The Closed World: Computers and the Politics of Discourse in Cold War America* (Cambridge, MA: MIT Press, 1996).
35. The historical importance of Rostow and Turing are well known. On Jackson, see C. Murphy, *The United Nations Development Programme: A Better Way?* (Cambridge: Cambridge University Press, 2006), 38–39.
36. A.L. Bowley, 'The International Institute of Statistics', *Journal of the Royal Statistical Society* 102 (1939), 83–85.
37. Nixon, *A History*, 45–46. Rice included an instructive account in the official documentation of the Washington Conferences. S.A. Rice, 'Introduction', in International Statistical Institute (ed.), *International Statistical Conferences, September 6–18, 1947, Washington DC, Proceedings of the International Statistical Conferences* (Calcutta: Eka Press, 1947), vol. I, 3–10.
38. Rice, 'Introduction', 3.
39. Ward, *Quantifying*, 36–40.
40. A full list can be found in International Statistical Institute (ed.), *International Statistical Conferences, September 6–18, 1947, Washington DC, Proceedings of the International Statistical Conferences* (Calcutta: Eka Press, 1947), vol. I, 39ff.
41. T. Lie, 'Address of Welcome', in W.J. Bruce (ed.), *International Statistical Conferences, September 6–18, 1947, Washington DC, Proceedings of the International Statistical Conferences* (Calcutta: Eka Press, 1947), vol. II, 3.
42. H. Truman, 'To Participants', in International Statistical Institute (ed.), *International Statistical Conferences*, vol. I, 1–2, at 1.
43. International Statistical Institute (ed.), *International Statistical Conferences*, vol. I, 95.
44. On the early UN statistical organization, see the account by its first administrator H. Campion, 'International Statistics', *Journal of the Royal Statistical Society, Series A* 112 (1949), 105–43.
45. H. Marshall, 'The Role of the UN Statistical Commission', in Bruce (ed.), *International Statistical Conferences*, vol. II, 23–33, at 23.
46. W.R. Leonard, 'Development of International Comparability of Statistics', in Bruce (ed.), *International Statistical Conferences*), vol. II, 202–14, at 211 and 212.
47. Rice, 'Introduction', 8.
48. Rice quoted in Nixon, *A History*, 45–46.
49. Rice quoted in ibid., 46.
50. On global agricultural statistics, see A. Ribi Forclaz, 'Agriculture, American Expertise, and the Quest for Global Data: Leon Estabrook and the First World Agricultural Census of 1930', *Journal of Global History* 11 (2016), 44–65. Population and educational issues were addressed by the United Nations Educational, Scientific and Cultural Organization (UNESCO). Only in labour statistics could the ILO uphold expert ownership on numbers because of the tripartite structure of this organization.
51. Speich, 'The Use'; D. Speich Chassé, *Die Erfindung des Bruttosozialprodukts: Globale Ungleichheit in der Wissensgeschichte der Ökonomie* (Göttingen: Vandenhoeck & Ruprecht, 2013).

52. Snow, *The International Comparison*, 1.
53. P. Studenski, *The Income of Nations: Theory, Measurement, Analysis Past and Present. A Study in Applied Economics and Statistics* (New York: New York University Press, 1958). See also the ongoing work by Martin Bemmann.
54. C. Clark, *The Conditions of Economic Progress* (London: Macmillan, 1940).
55. Speich Chassé, *Erfindung*, 44–47.
56. Clark, *Conditions*.
57. R. Stone cited in M. Gilbert et al. (eds), 'The Measurement of National Wealth: Report of the Washington Meeting', *Econometrica* 17 (1949), 255–72, at 259.
58. S. Kuznets, 'National Income and Industrial Structure', *Econometrica* 17 (1949), 205–41, at 205.
59. S. Kuznets, 'National Income', in E.R.A. Seligman (ed.), *Encyclopedia of the Social Sciences* (New York: Macmillan, 1933), 205–24.
60. S. Kuznets, 'International Differences in Income Levels: Reflections on Their Causes', *Economic Development and Cultural Change* 2(1) (1953), 3–26. The following article series was entitled 'Quantitative Aspects of Economic Growth of Nations'. Its last chapter appeared in 1964.
61. O. Rosenboim, *The Emergence of Globalism: Visions of World Order in Britain and the United States, 1939–1950* (Princeton: Princeton University Press, 2017).
62. A. Smithies cited in Gilbert, 'The Measurement', 270.
63. J.K. Galbraith, 'The National Accounts: Arrival and Impact', in US Department of Commerce (ed.), *Reflections of America: Commemorating the Statistical Abstract Centennial* (Washington, DC: Department of Commerce, 1980), 75–80.
64. I.B. Kravis, Z. Kenessey, A. Heston and R. Summers, *A System of International Comparisons of Gross Product and Purchasing Power* (Baltimore: Johns Hopkins University Press, 1975).
65. http://www.rug.nl/research/ggdc/data/penn-world-table, accessed 8 January 2015, and the 'World Development Indicators', retrieved 13 March 2019 from http://data.worldbank.org/data-catalog/world-development-indicators.

# Bibliography

Bayly, C.A., *Empire and Information: Intelligence Gathering and Social Communication in India 1780–1870* (Cambridge: Cambridge University Press, 1996).

Behrisch, L., *Die Berechnung der Glückseligkeit: Statistik und Politik in Deutschland und Frankreich im späten Ancien Régime* (Ostfildern: Thorbecke, 2016).

Blumenberg, H., *Die Lesbarkeit der Welt* (Frankfurt am Main: Suhrkamp, 1981).

Bowley, A.L., 'The International Institute of Statistics', *Journal of the Royal Statistical Society* 102 (1939), 83–85.

Brendecke, A., *Imperium und Empirie: Funktionen des Wissens in der spanischen Kolonialherrschaft* (Cologne: Böhlau, 2009).

Brückweh, K., *Menschen zählen: Wissensproduktion durch britische Volkszählungen und Umfragen vom 19. Jahrhundert bis ins digitale Zeitalter* (Berlin: De Gruyter Oldenbourg, 2015).

Burbank, J., and Cooper, F., *Empires in World History: Power and the Politics of Difference* (Princeton: Princeton University Press, 2010).

Campion, H., 'International Statistics', *Journal of the Royal Statistical Society, Series A* 112 (1949), 105–43.

Clark, C., *The Conditions of Economic Progress* (London: Macmillan, 1940).
Desrosières, A., *La politique des grands nombres : Histoire de la raison statistique* (Paris: Editions La Découverte, 1993).
Didier, E., *En quoi consiste l'Amérique? Les statistiques, le New Deal et la démocratie* (Paris: La Découverte, 2009).
Dülffer, J., and Loth, W. (eds), *Dimensionen internationaler Geschichte* (Munich: Oldenbourg, 2012).
Edwards, P.N., *The Closed World: Computers and the Politics of Discourse in Cold War America* (Cambridge, MA: MIT Press, 1996).
Espeland, W., and Stevens, M., 'A Sociology of Quantification', *European Journal of Sociology* 49 (2008), 401–36.
Galbraith, J.K., 'The National Accounts: Arrival and Impact', in US Department of Commerce (ed.), *Reflections of America: Commemorating the Statistical Abstract Centennial* (Washington, DC: Department of Commerce, 1980), 75–80.
Gilbert, M. et al. (eds), 'The Measurement of National Wealth: Report of the Washington Meeting', *Econometrica* 17 (1949), 255–72.
Grävell, W., 'Die Statistik im Grosswirtschaftsraum', *Weltwirtschaftliches Archiv* 56 (1942), 457–69.
Heintz, B., 'Numerische Differenz: Überlegungen zu einer Soziologie des (quantitativen) Vergleichs', *Zeitschrift für Soziologie* 39 (2010), 162–81.
Hildebrand, B., *Die Nationalökonomie der Gegenwart und Zukunft* (Frankfurt am Main: Literarische Anstalt (J. Rütten), 1848).
International Statistical Institute (ed.), *International Statistical Conferences, September 6–18, 1947, Washington DC, Proceedings of the International Statistical Conferences* (Calcutta: Eka Press, 1947), vol. I.
Jakob, L.H., *Grundsätze der National-Oekonomie oder National-Wirthschaftslehre* (Halle: Ruffsche Verlagshandlung, 1805).
Kaiser, W., and Schot, J., *Writing the Rules for Europe: Experts, Cartels, and International Organizations* (Basingstoke: Palgrave Macmillan, 2014).
Kott, S., and Droux, J. (eds), *Globalizing Social Rights: The International Labour Organization and Beyond* (Basingstoke: Palgrave Macmillan, 2013).
Kravis, I.B. et al., *A System of International Comparisons of Gross Product and Purchasing Power* (Baltimore: Johns Hopkins University Press, 1975).
Kuznets, S., 'National Income', in Seligman, E.R.A. (ed.), *Encyclopedia of the Social Sciences* (New York: Macmillan, 1933), 205–24.
———. 'National Income and Industrial Structure', *Econometrica* 17 (1949), 205–41.
———. 'International Differences in Income Levels: Reflections on Their Causes', *Economic Development and Cultural Change* 2(1) (1953), 3–26.
Latham, E., 'One Statistical World', *Journal of the American Statistical Association* 41 (September 1946), 275–92.
Latour, B., *Science in Action: How to Follow Scientists and Engineers through Society* (Cambridge, MA: Harvard University Press, 1987).
———. 'Drawing Things Together', in Lynch, M. and Woolgar, S. (eds), *Representation in Scientific Practice* (Cambridge, MA: MIT Press, 1990), 19–68.
Leonard, W.R., 'Development of International Comparabality of Statistics', in Bruce, W.J. (ed.), *International Statistical Conferences, September 6–18, 1947, Washington DC, Proceedings of the International Statistical Conferences* (Calcutta: Eka Press, 1947), vol. II, 202–14.

Lie, T., 'Address of Welcome', in Bruce, W.J. (ed.), *International Statistical Conferences, September 6–18, 1947, Washington DC, Proceedings of the International Statistical Conferences* (Calcutta: Eka Press, 1947), vol. II, 3.

List, F., *Das nationale System der politischen Oekonomie* (Stuttgart: Cotta, 1841).

Marshall, H., 'The Role of the UN Statistical Commission', in Bruce, W.J. (ed.), *International Statistical Conferences, September 6–18, 1947, Washington DC, Proceedings of the International Statistical Conferences* (Calcutta: Eka Press 1947), vol. II, 23–33.

Mazower, M., *Governing the World: The History of an Idea* (New York: Penguin, 2012).

Murphy, C., *The United Nations Development Programme: A Better Way?* (Cambridge: Cambridge University Press, 2006).

Nixon, J.W., *A History of the International Statistical Institute 1885–1960* (The Hague: International Statistical Institute, 1960).

Ogle, V., *The Global Transformation of Time 1870–1950* (Cambridge, MA: Harvard University Press, 2015).

Osterhammel, J., *Die Verwandlung der Welt: Eine Geschichte des 19. Jahrhunderts* (Munich: C.H. Beck, 2009).

Porter, T.M., *Trust in Numbers: The Pursuit of Objectivity in Science and Public Life* (Princeton: Princeton University Press, 1995).

Prévost, J.-G., and Beaud, J.-P., *Statistics, Public Debate and the State, 1800–1945: A Social, Political and Intellectual History of Numbers* (London: Pickering & Chatto, 2012).

Raphael, L., 'Die Verwissenschaftlichung des Sozialen als methodische und konzeptionelle Herausforderung für eine Sozialgeschichte des 20. Jahrhunderts', *Geschichte und Gesellschaft* 22 (1996), 165–93.

Ribi Forclaz, A., 'Agriculture, American Expertise, and the Quest for Global Data: Leon Estabrook and the First World Agricultural Census of 1930', *Journal of Global History* 11 (2016), 44–65.

Rice, S.A., 'Introduction', in International Statistical Institute (ed.), *International Statistical Conferences, September 6–18, 1947, Washington DC, Proceedings of the International Statistical Conferences* (Calcutta: Eka Press, 1947), vol. I, 3–10.

Rosenboim, O., *The Emergence of Globalism: Visions of World Order in Britain and the United States, 1939–1950* (Princeton: Princeton University Press, 2017).

Sandl, M., *Ökonomie des Raumes: Der kameralwissenschaftliche Entwurf der Staatswirtschaft im 18. Jahrhundert* (Cologne: Böhlau, 1999).

Schlözer, A.L., *Theorie der Statistik: Nebst Ideen* über *das Studium der Politik* überhaupt (Göttingen: Vandenhoek & Ruprecht, 1804).

Schwarz, A., 'Probleme der internationalen Vergleichbarkeit der Wirtschaftsstatistik', *Weltwirtschaftliches Archiv* 57 (1943), 572–83.

Snow, E.C., 'The International Comparison of Industrial Output', *Journal of the Royal Statistical Society* 107 (1944), 1–55.

Speich, D., 'The Use of Global Abstractions: National Income Accounting in the Period of Imperial Decline', *Journal of Global History* 6(1) (2011), 7–28.

Speich Chassé, D., *Die Erfindung des Bruttosozialprodukts: Globale Ungleichheit in der Wissensgeschichte der* Ökonomie (Göttingen: Vandenhoeck & Ruprecht, 2013).

———. 'Nation', in Dejung, C., Dommann, M. and Speich Chassé, D. (eds), *Auf der Suche nach der Ökonomie: Historische Annäherungen* (Tübingen: Mohr Siebeck, 2014), 207–34.

———. 'Technical Internationalism and Economic Development at the Founding Moment of the UN System', in Frey, M., Unger, C. and Kunkel, S. (eds), *International Organizations and Development, 1945–1990* (Basingstoke: Palgrave Macmillan, 2014), 23–45.

———. 'The Roots of the Millennium Development Goals: A Framework for Studying the History of Global Statistics', *Historical Social Research* 41 (2016), 218–37.

Steinmetz, W., '"Vergleich" – eine begriffsgeschichtliche Skizze', in Epple, A. and Erhart, W. (eds), *Die Welt beobachten: Praktiken des Vergleichens* (Frankfurt am Main: Campus, 2015), 85–134.

Steinmetz, W., and Haupt, H.-G., 'The Political as Communicative Space in History: The Bielefeld Approach', in Steinmetz, W., Gilcher-Holtey, I. and Haupt, H.-G. (eds), *Writing Political History Today* (Frankfurt am Main: Campus, 2013), 11–33.

Studenski, P., *The Income of Nations: Theory, Measurement, Analysis Past and Present. A Study in Applied Economics and Statistics* (New York: New York University Press, 1958).

Tooze, J.A., *Statistics and the German State, 1900–1945: The Making of Modern Economic Knowledge* (Cambridge: Cambridge University Press, 2001).

Truman, H., 'To Participants', in International Statistical Institute (ed.), *International Statistical Conferences, September 6–18, 1947, Washington DC, Proceedings of the International Statistical Conferences* (Calcutta: Eka Press 1947), vol. I, 1–2.

Ward, M., *Quantifying the World: UN Ideas and Statistics* (Bloomington: Indiana University Press, 2004).

Wenzlhuemer, R., *Connecting the Nineteenth-Century World: The Telegraph and Globalization* (Cambridge: Cambridge University Press, 2013).

# 11
# Formalized Comparisons

*Rankings and Status in Higher Education*

Wendy Espeland

> Wherever there is persuasion, there is rhetoric. And wherever there is 'meaning' there is persuasion.
>
> —Kenneth Burke, *A Rhetoric of Motives*

## Introduction: The Power of Form and Formal Analysis

Comparison, as this volume makes clear, is a fundamental form for organizing and understanding the social world. To paraphrase Willibald Steinmetz, our editor, comparisons are forceful.[1] What does that mean? Comparisons are generative. They produce energy, induce change – in our thinking, feeling and behaviour – and they have consequences. And they are also ubiquitous. We are mostly unaware of how fundamental comparison is in organizing our thinking and our actions. To notice differences, singularities and similarities requires comparison, as does parsing inside and outside, then and now, us and other, better and worse. Comparison is a fundamental means of organizing social life.

One way to think about comparison is that it is a form, a mode of organizing that involves including, excluding, boundaries and arrangements, foreground and background. Two important theorists have made form the centrepiece of their investigations of literary, artistic and social texts; the sociologist and philosopher Georg Simmel, and the literary and social theorist Kenneth Burke. While there is not space for a sophisticated rendering of their thinking here, some strategic borrowing is useful for my analysis and warrants some cursory comments. For each thinker, I emphasize their focus on form as a methodological choice rather than a more fully developed presentation of their broader theoretical ambitions, and the insights that devolve from that use. The investigations of each provide a strong case for the advantages of a focus on form: in establishing the preconditions and potential continuity of social life; in structuring human actions and feelings; in conveying the potential of an aesthetics of interaction; and, most importantly, in helping to disclose the dynamism of forms that are made, used in dazzling variety, and sometimes abandoned, but not without leaving their traces. I extend their thinking to demonstrate how their approaches might productively inform an understanding of quantitative forms such as rankings.

Drawing on Kant, Georg Simmel is the sociologist best known for analysing society through the lens of forms and content (as well as social types, which I will not discuss here). Unlike Kant, the central motivation of Simmel's sociology is the study of the eminence and transcendence of mutable social forms as they are made, adapted and sometimes fade away; the contents can be variable kinds of actions and meanings that lend themselves not only to analysis but also to comparison with other similar forms, and this, for Simmel, should be the project of sociology. Simmel's analyses – of forms ranging from sociability to exchange – demonstrate both the variety of contents that can be organized into enduring social forms as well as the dynamism of forms as they are moved across time and contexts. If sociability once required name cards left with butlers or visits to parlours, today it requires timely responses to text messages and a rich vocabulary of acronyms and emojis.

For Simmel, the point of 'formal analysis' was a combined geographical and aesthetic rendering of social action that, again, contra Kant, emphasized their history and mutability, as well as their transcendence. Like many foundational figures, Simmel was concerned to carve out a unique intellectual role for sociology, one that distinguished it from philosophy, history, psychology and economics. His formal analysis was his conceptual framework and his method, even if his presentation was rarely as sustained or systematic as some might prefer.[2] Akin to Weber's ideal types, forms were heuristic abstractions that do not exist in any pure state, but are always combinations of various formal characteristics, some of which are more heuristic or less 'real' than others. Where Weber's ideal types are primarily intended to capture broad historical changes, Simmel's forms reflect changes that when deployed properly often attend to more intimate areas of social life, including one's affect and cognition. But other forms capture change at even the largest scale. These, Simmel contends, are universal in human societies, such as conflict, cooperation and exchange, while others are considerably more narrow and contingent. As the philosopher and translator of Simmel, Guy Oakes, describes Simmel's theory of forms: 'All of the work for which Simmel is remembered is based on the assumption that the world as a whole and specific aspects of it become possible objects of experience and knowledge only if they are constituted by some form or forms.'[3] Quite simply, we inherit forms and process the world through them; they are human creations, made orderly by sociologists who analyse them, but most fundamentally they are what make us social beings.

Social forms are constituents and, in the right circumstances, celebrations of social life, the satisfying and often collective triumphs of using and adapting forms in productive or playful ways. Being in 'good form' is satisfying and offers recognition (although often we are not aware of this) and a roadmap for social interaction. Analogously to art (and Simmel makes many such analogies), we find the experience of being in or witnessing good form deeply fulfilling, partly because it is our means of recognizing ourselves and our mutual obligations and partly because it offers the security of a familiar script. Like Kant, Simmel sees forms as selecting from the flow of experience aspects of social life and imposing an order that makes perception, cognition and emotion possible. Forms encourage participation and reflection. Where Durkheim relies on totemic symbols to make our ties to one another tangible and expressive, Simmel elaborates and complicates Durkheim's understanding of the symbolic by incorporating *forms* into the sociologist's mix of methods: patterns or 'kinds of social action' that can be deployed by categories of people (*types*). This offers a lens on social life that enables an aesthetics of experience, as well as a conceptual symbolic framework for doing sociology. We make and inherit forms. Forms make us social. We understand society by investigating forms.

While Simmel does not make comparison the explicit object of his formal analysis, it is only just below the surface of many of the forms he analyses, being most accessible in his conception of exchange and most elaborated in his remarkable *The Philosophy of Money*. His treatise on money explores the philosophical underpinnings and empirical consequences of how value emerges, is exchanged and is transformed through the use of money. Money for Simmel (and for Marx) is the perfect tool for symbolizing comparison. But for Simmel, money is also a telling, tangible sign of that even more fundamental pattern, the relativity of social life. Following Simmel, one can see rankings as a historical, globalized and consequential *specific* symbolic form of social life, one grounded in comparison, hierarchy and exchange – of a particular form – as well as a commodity form that is consistent with his analysis of contemporary modernity, and consistent with his understanding of the tragedy and freedom of modern life.

The task of elaborating a formal analysis of social action was taken up more recently by the philosopher and literary theorist Kenneth Burke. For Burke, a form is 'an arousing and fulfillment of desires' or 'the creation of an appetite in the mind of the auditor, and the adequate satisfying of that appetite'.[4] Put another way, forms produce desires and expectations, and satisfy them. Forms prime us, tempt us and deliver on their implied promises. They channel cognition and emotion in patterned ways and sometimes deviate in relation to these patterns. These responses, Burke suggests, are often but not always preconscious or habitual emotional responses from people.[5] Forms organize our experience in ways we seldom appreciate *because* they are so fundamental. Understanding these responses is crucial for comprehending the power of form. So too is appreciating the work that is required to produce forms and the work that forms produce through abstraction and simplification.

Because of his experience as a literary critic, Burke uses that language in his method of analysis; yet, he became convinced, especially later in his career, of its value for the analysis of social life, partly due to his close relations with many sociologists, some of whom were luminaries in sociology and philosophy including Louis Wirth, Edward Shils and Talcott Parsons. Burke describes his approach as 'dramatism', due to its reliance on metaphors of the theatre (Erving Goffman's version, called dramaturgy, is better known, but Goffman's debt to Burke is fundamental and underacknowledged). Burke organizes this analysis of form as a series of key dialectical relationships in which forms are the products of action that takes place in a particular scene or location, by actors, with cultural scripts (my term, not his) guiding expectations and activity. For Burke, all forms (and concepts) simplify as there is no way to represent the world in all its fullness and flux. But it is possible to show patterns in how particular forms simplify and the effects of this. While Burke is best known for his literary criticism, he broadens his analyses to include other cultural texts, including nonliterary texts and forms of social interaction.

The power of form devolves partly from its cognitive appeal. 'Purely formal patterns', Burke says, 'can readily awaken an expectation of collaborative expectancy in us ... Once you grasp the trend of the form it invites participation, regardless of the subject matter ... in cases where a decision is still to be reached, yielding to the form prepares for assent to the matter identified with it. Thus, you are drawn to the form, not in your capacity as a partisan, but because of some "universal" appeal in it. And this attitude of assent may then be transformed to the matter which happens to be associated with it.'[6]

The forms that I will analyse here are university rankings, a specialized form of comparison and one whose use generates many other kinds of comparisons.[7] I will discuss the properties of rankings as forms and will focus on just one of the consequences that rankings have generated: how rankings have propelled law schools to amplify the logic of the marketplace in their relations with their constituents and each other. I will conclude with some observations about the value of conceiving of numerical forms, such as rankings, as forms of rhetoric.

## Rankings as a Special Kind of Form: The Formal Properties of Rankings and the Numbers that Comprise Them

Drawing on Burke, we can understand rankings as comprised of (numeric) symbols that are arranged into forms that are cognitively familiar, elicit expectations and are satisfying in their production of meaning. Numbers can be combined into an almost endless variety of forms that are continually evolving. For example, we now have sophisticated computer programs for visualizing quantitative data in aesthetically pleasing ways as graphs, networks or mappings and we offer advanced degrees in data visualization.

Numbers, even a single number, imply comparison. We cannot make sense of a number unless we understand it in relation to other numbers, whether implicit or explicit. Numbers are extraordinarily good at generating comparisons; understanding numbers as the product of and catalysts for comparison helps us to appreciate their power. Unlike ratings, rankings produce a zero-sum relationship among its objects. This means, for educational rankings, that the fates of particular universities are linked by their shared metric. Depending on a school's ranking, if any other school's ranking rises, its own ranking may drop. While many movies may be rated three stars, only one school can hold the eleventh or forty-seventh position – unless there is a tie. That rankings are relative measures matters enormously for the emotions and the competition they generate.

Another important feature of rankings is their apparent simplicity. Because numbers are so abstract, they severely edit the worlds they represent. This involves many layers of commensuration in which test scores, combined with grade averages and matriculation rates, are weighted and turned into 'selectivity', how difficult it is to be admitted to this particular school, which becomes one of many factors that comprise rankings. Making things commensurate, whether students, environmental impacts or complex organizations, is hardly a simple process, but the end results are reductions of reductions of reductions.

We have many expectations about numbers. Sometimes these have to do with the peculiar kind of quantitative authority we grant to numbers. Numbers are seen as hard, rational and objective, as displacing emotion, subjectivity and bias. Numbers, understood this way, are supposedly superior to other forms of knowledge because they are more reliable. One of the paradoxes of quantification is that we expect numbers to represent the world in clear, neutral ways at the same time as we want numbers to do things. Numbers represent and intervene, often at the same time. If we think with or act on a numerical representation, the world is different. Quantification is often motivated by a desire to persuade, about the value, merit or efficiency of some plan or person. We also use quantification to measure some property of the world. But used in this way, persuasion is still a feature of measures if we want to convince others that our measures are correct. Regardless of the motivations behind them, numbers are rhetorical in the sense that Burke defines it: they have meanings. And we have mixed reactions to numbers depending on the form we give to numbers and what we want numbers to do. We also have aesthetic expectations about numbers. They simplify messy information and create parsimony and patterns that are elegant.

## Rankings Are Familiar Forms

As Simmel explained, one feature of the durability of social forms like rankings is that they can be adapted to new circumstances and purposes, and absorb new kinds of content. We all grow up familiar with the ranking of sports teams, pop music and businesses. The first rankings of football teams, or league tables as they are called in the United Kingdom, were produced in 1892–93, just five years after the first professional English Football League was created in 1888.[8] In the United States, *Billboard* started ranking the top forty hits in popular music beginning in 1936. *Consumer Magazine* began ranking consumer products in the same year. *Fortune Magazine* began ranking the 500 largest companies in 1955. Rankings in education are thus an instance of a form with deep historical roots; Michel Foucault writes about the classifying and ranking of individual students as part of the disciplinary practices that emerged in eighteenth-century education.[9] Beginning in 2000, the Programme for International Student Assessment (PISA), part of the Organisation for Economic Co-operation and Development (OECD), began ranking countries every three years for how well their fifteen-year-old students did on standardized tests in reading, maths and science. For 2015, Singapore was top, followed by Japan and Estonia. Formerly number one, Finland still does well in the rankings, but has lost ground in recent iterations.[10] There has been a huge proliferation of rankings in recent years, which is partly explained by the success of early media rankings and by the computational power and data that are now available. Rankings organize their targets as explicit objects of comparison.[11] The point and power of rankings is hierarchy, an easily absorbed representation of status and quality.

In the United States, the first ranking of universities was published by James Cattell in 1910 in *American Men of Science*, in which he ranked schools based on how many prominent scientists were on their faculty.[12] There were a few scattered attempts to rank graduate programmes or law schools, but these efforts were primarily for academic audiences. It was only in 1983 that *U.S. News and World Reports* (USN), then a weekly news magazine, launched its widely successful and broadly emulated rankings franchise. USN began with college rankings, initially based on a simple reputational survey, but soon the magazine began publishing them annually, using a more sophisticated methodology including statistics such as grade averages and test scores into its rankings.[13]

## The Broader Context for Rankings

I do not have the space here to describe in any detail the social processes that help explain why rankings emerged when they did,[14] but their creation is linked to broad shifts in the organization of higher education. In the United States, one important change was the expansion of the opportunities for higher education. Unlike in most European countries, the cost of tuition has mostly been paid for by families. After the Second World War, veterans were granted substantial educational benefits and this led to a big increase in the numbers of less affluent men attending university. The civil rights movements of the 1960s and 1970s also increased the numbers of women and minorities who enrolled. This further solidified the idea that a university education should no longer be the privilege of the wealthy or the most talented. In order to accommodate all these new students, new universities were created and old ones expanded. Instead of going to the local university, more students applied to schools across the country. And while there have long been elite universities, as higher education became more available, the status of one's universities became more important. Where one went to school mattered more.

Along with the increase in the numbers of people going to university, two other sweeping changes were critical for the emergence of rankings. First, the neoliberal politics of the late 1970s and 1980s, especially in the United Kingdom and the United States, made universities easy targets for efforts to increase competition and incorporate business discipline into public institutions. This gave rise to a global accountability movement where accountability was nearly always defined as some sort of performance measure.[15] The research and teaching assessment exercises in the United Kingdom transformed administration and gave rise to the publication of league tables by the media. Of course, rankings required the computational power of increasingly sophisticated technology that made possible the statistics, calculations and diffusion used by rankers.

## Expectations and Desire

As Burke would suggest, rankings elicit expectations and we expect a lot from rankings. Often, they reflect a desire for order. Not understanding better and worse can undermine our sense of control, especially when the stakes of a decision are high, as they are for many young people deciding where to attend university or graduate school. Rankings help us to feel more powerful in the face of the staggering volumes of information now available to us. The abstractness of rankings, their capacity for simplifying and synthesizing disparate kinds of information, creates clarity from confusion. They make decisions seem less overwhelming and action more defensible by making them seem less arbitrary and more rational.

We also expect to be entertained by rankings. Perhaps because of a sense of wanting to feel superior to others, we enjoy rankings – unless, of course, the stakes are high. But especially if something is safely removed from us or our superiority is secure, we look to rankings as sport. Rankings provide an object for argument, a way to engage that may or may not be tinged with status anxiety.

The job of rankings is to produce standardized variation in the service of hierarchy or, put more pejoratively, inequality: in quality, merit, status, performance or whatever. Rankings produce difference among things by creating symbolic boundaries around objects.[16] One feature of the boundaries created by rankings is how we interpret the interval between ranked objects; we assume that these are equal and that the underlying metric is stable. We project onto intervals the sameness that we project onto the objects that are being measured because we want them to mark a meaningful difference. Standardized intervals are easier to understand than inconsistent ones. We assume that the objects marked by these boundaries are members of some shared classification, one that is represented by a metric. This may be a taken-for-granted sameness, the result of long-settled cultural categories, or it may be a projection of sameness that overlooks important differences.

If, for example, a magazine is ranking consumer products, the boundaries around sameness are those we consider to be similar products. We compare trucks with other trucks and their truckness is taken to be self-evident. But if we were to rank 'vehicles', comparing cars, trucks and bicycles, this may seem a less meaningful comparison. Their categorical differences would threaten the integrity of the ranking – unless, of course, we created an overarching sameness through some more encompassing and abstract definition. We could rate various vehicles for how polluting they are or how much infrastructure is required to support them. We often project onto these boundaries a durability that may be unwarranted. Some of this is an overdeveloped confidence in the use and results of scientific methods. Quantification is so bound up with reason, objectivity and the taming of emotions that we often misread its precision and are too easily assured by its results. Experts in quantification are taught to be sceptical, but being so is risky and time-consuming for those who desire confidence.

A central feature of an economics framework is that markets are ubiquitous, that one can conceptualize almost anything as a market, that price is a fundamental feature of all markets and that even if there is not an explicit price for something, standard methodical techniques permit the calculation of an implicit price. That prices render objects the same so that precise trade-offs can be made between the most disparate seeming objects is at the heart of cost-benefit analysis and, as Marx suggested, capitalism. But once forms such as cost-benefit analysis or prices that are intended to integrate dissimilar things become widely used and familiar, disparate objects can come to be seen as more alike over time.[17] We now take for granted that the value of most things can be compared and expressed as prices. Rankings, like cost-benefit ratios and prices, are products of commensuration in which difference is expressed as variation in magnitude.[18]

For example, rankings presume that universities are 'fungible', that schools of the same value can be replaced or substituted for one another. What matters most in terms of evaluating them is the equivalence in measure or units rather than other forms of difference. In other words, universities with a similar rank are interchangeable. In markets, the fungibility of goods is established via price and volume. With rankings, fungibility is produced via processes of commensuration, in which differences are transformed into units on a shared metric. Differences in quality become differences in quantity. Instead of assuming that price accurately reflects salient differences, as with most market goods, education rankings presume that rank reflects the important differences. Although rankings do not directly shape the tuition that universities charge, they do convey them as having distinct, precise, relative qualities that can be measured.

## Rankings, Classification and Cognition

Rankings simultaneously impose unity and precise differences among the objects they measure. Their shared metric unites objects as variations on the same ontological category while the intervals between numbers produce precise differences among them. This difference is what draws our attention and our investment. These are part of the expectations of form that we bring to rankings, and, depending on the audience, rankings satisfy these desires.

In contrast to numbers that are used merely to identify particular objects (for example, phone numbers or clothing sizes), the distance between numbers that are used to measure something is *the* crucial information.[19] With interval numbers, say a test score of 98 per cent, we are assuming a real or an implied shared metric that produces standardized intervals that allow us to locate the scores of individuals along some distribution. We interpret this number as not only better than 90 per cent, but eight notches better. What those notches mean, of course, depends on lots of other relationships, such as the shape of a distribution and where other thresholds are drawn – for example, the difference between the grade of an A or an A-. The calibrated, standardized and precise difference that rankings construct is a far more complex form of difference than is produced by numbers that identify.

## Commodification

At the risk of stating the obvious, it merits pointing out that media rankings literally turn educational status into commodities that are bought, sold and circulated like other commodities. And they are always fetishized. As commodities, rankings turn social relations (status, excellence, identity) into *things*: you buy rankings, in the form of newspapers or magazine issues, guidebooks, access to websites, or you can buy the products that rankings spin off – detailed information about your school or other schools, advertising in various media, consultants hired to boost rankings. Now, not all education rankings are literally commodities, in the sense that some are created by governments or international organizations. But even when rankings are not literally bought and sold, the aura of commodification surrounds them: they are understood as products, take labour to produce, turn status into a thing that circulates rather than as a complex set of social relations, and people become fixated on the thing, often at the expense of what the thing is for (or in this case, what it is trying to measure). Rankings encourage thinking of education as an 'investment' and students as 'customers'.

Moreover, rankings reinforce the idea that departments within universities are productive units, each of which contributes a specific piece of the ranking. For law schools, the number of books in a law library is directly connected to the percentage of students employed at graduation, which is linked to faculty salaries and so on. A change in one characteristic reverberates through others, demonstrating their interconnections. The admissions office is responsible for the selectivity factor that includes students' test scores and grade averages. This emphasis on precise contributions obscures the other work done by these departments, as well as the conditions that influence the production of these numbers. The 'joint fate' that rankings highlight make it easy to scapegoat departments when the numbers they produce do not improve or drop.

## Rankings and Competition

At least in the United States, universities and colleges have long understood themselves as somehow competing with other higher education institutions. Universities have competed over the number of students and the 'best' students, faculty and administrators. They have competed over resources that come from local or national government, tuition dollars, research grants, alumni or other private donations. They have competed over the cosmopolitan affiliations or the unique accomplishments of their students. And they have competed in their efforts to shape their reputations or status as these are expressed in various ways: in the accomplishments of their alumni, the diversity of their students, broadly conceived, or through awards, fellowships, research, media and sports, or to be the best in their city, region or state. What has changed in the last thirty years is the proliferation and influence of media rankings in defining and mediating competition. Rankings not only expand the scope of competition, they also become the goal of competition. In a survey of leaders in higher education from forty-one countries, Ellen Hezelkorn reports that 71 per cent want their institution to be in the top 25 per cent internationally.[20]

Rankings have shaped who universities think their competitors are. Rankings have redefined what universities have to do to be competitive. Rankings have also influenced the scope of competition (how expansive it is and which parts of the world must be attended to) and they have affected the temporality or periodization of competition (how experiences of time are organized around competition). And rankings have shaped how those who work or study in universities experience competition as members of organizations. Rankings induced changes in competition among and between schools that are too varied to offer an exhaustive account here, so what I offer is only a sampling of how they do so, focusing on a few of the broader types of changes in the nature of competition.

## The Propulsion of Categories and the Construction of Competitors

I have already argued that the spread of rankings evokes a proliferation of classifying which then produces more arenas and more characteristics over which universities compete.[21] This, of course, is deeply bound up with *whom* universities compete with. With the creation of global rankings in 2003 and the other world rankings they have spawned, one's competitors are quite literally scattered across the globe. I was recently sent the survey of schools to rank for one of the global rankers and was asked to evaluate some one hundred different universities. It is a struggle for me to render ordinal the top sociology departments in the United States. But as absurd as this global exercise seemed, these rankings now pit universities against one another on a global scale, ignorance be damned. Universities that are distinguished by some specialities (social science or humanities, i.e. the French Ecole system) or that catered to a regional population (the Siberian Federal University), or whose mission was teaching-centred (Makrary University Kampala), or who have only recently begun to expand their higher education institutions (Nigeria) now find themselves in competition with research-oriented universities around the globe, a competition they cannot win due to the types of indicators incorporated by global rankings and their efforts at specialization that are not captured in their components. Rankings, in an abstract sense, supplant localities, missions and other ties in their efforts to bind and parse universities. After an elite law school dropped two notches in the ranking, two days after it was published, the dean circulated a carefully written memo to all faculty and staff. In it he outlined why its 'rival' schools – defined by rankings – had improved a notch or two and why his school had dropped two notches.

## Rankings Define the Terms: The 'How' of Competition

If the 'who' of competition is subject to the dictates of USN or its ranking competitors, the 'how' is even more deeply implicated. As with the overarching categories used to distinguish types of undergraduate institutions, the machinery of rankings is fuelled by some well-established markers of university status, including selectivity, graduation rates and so on. While there are new categories – for example, student satisfaction as measured by the percentage of students who donate money to their university (guess which universities this favours) – there are old categories put to new uses and new distinctions. Selectivity is measured by the median scores of standardized tests among students who matriculate. Of course, these have long been important numbers in the admission decisions. But now these numbers are weighted, scored and turned into ranking factors, which creates enormous pressure on admissions personnel and students to improve their scores. High test scores become more valuable and 'merit' has increasingly come to be defined as such. Students who typically do less well on standardized tests – for law school tests, these groups include women, students of colour (except certain Asian groups), low-income students, first-generation students, older students and students from certain regions of the country – are less likely to get into the best schools as defined by rankings, and this powerfully affects their job prospects. Here are some of the kinds of things administrators and faculty are saying about the effects of wholesale efforts to raise median test scores:

> The thing [that rankings pressure] does is that it induces some constituencies – particularly the faculty – to be very anxious, to focus admissions on students with high LSAT scores. That's probably the single most pernicious consequence of the USN survey. It puts enormous pressure on law schools to become homogeneous and to all compete for the same students.[22]

Administrators say they often feel forced to make hard trade-offs, to choose between a higher median LSAT score and a more diverse student body, a decision that the rankings have made much more acute than in the past:

> What I would say is that how much people are willing to take a risk in the admissions process, or how diverse they will become, or whether a school is willing to take one more student who if you take that one student puts you at a tipping point where it changes what you're bottom quarter or your top quarter looks like, I think it does have that effect, absolutely. Yeah, I think it has [a homogenizing] effect.

In this sense, often despite deep commitments to diversifying its student body, admitting students who tend to score less well on standardized tests becomes a much 'riskier investment' in terms of the rankings. Administrators also described performing 'balancing acts' between goals that are often conflicting. As a faculty member at a first-tier school explained:

> We're making it much more difficult for those who aren't upper-middle class kids to get into law school. Because there is clearly a correlation between family income and how you do on that test – whether you can afford preparation on that test. I teach half the students in a tax class every year and I've always done a poll, which I use for pedagogic reasons, where I'm correlating family income to attitudes towards valuated tax issues like progressive rate structure. And I don't do it anymore because last year in my class there was only one person who indicated that their family income was less than $40,000. The school has always been somewhat that way, but it has been much more extreme in the last few years.

An assistant dean of student affairs at a second-tier school says:

> My perspective is that LSAT scores are very closely tied to socioeconomic factors. I know that I spent a lot of money and time preparing for the LSATs. I took the Kaplan [test-preparation] course twice before I took the exam. But I was fortunate because my parents could afford to pay for the course. So as much as there is a correlation between racial, ethnic, and socioeconomic identity, there is going to be a clear fallout there.

And efforts to boost test scores affect other parts of law schools. The work of admissions officers has shifted so that admissions in many places become more mechanical, with recruitment becoming harder:

> I had a friend who I actually trained who left [admissions] to work for a law firm because the school she was at had a formula: for every two you admit above the median you could only admit one below. They had figured out this mathematical formula and this was just last year. And a lot of people who are new to law school admissions are fairly recent

graduates and they are being hired to bolster the hiring numbers. I told one of my deans that we needed to hire someone and I was very specific about the skill set I needed, and he asked me if I thought we could hire one of our graduates because it would help bolster our [placement] numbers.

## Who Goes to University

Research on law schools shows, with quantitative and qualitative evidence, that rankings affect who is admitted to which schools.[23] Research on undergraduate institutions bears this out too. The effort to manage and maximize one's ranking results in maximizing the factors as best one can, and admissions decisions offer what seems to be a small bit of control. Another broad effect of this competition is for institutions and countries to try to manage the rankings. Schools or governments redistribute resources in ways designed to improve the rank of their institutions. So, for example, schools and countries will invest heavily in marketing as an effort to try to sway reputational measures or citation counts. Because the two most prominent global rankings, Shanghai and QS, include no measures of teaching, schools and countries with teaching missions will suffer. Citation counts, a big component of all global rankings, rely on databases that favour English-language journals, big schools and fields such as science, engineering and medicine at the expense of other fields. Some schools use rankings to restrict collaborations with other schools and which universities fellowship recipients can attend.

## Short-Term Thinking

Another aspect of the effect of the intense competition that is generated by rankings and requires more investigation is how rankings change the time horizons of institutions and leaders. Just as corporations have been adopting increasingly short-term measures of their performance (from dividends to price/earnings ratios to the share price this hour), rankings are encouraging short-term orientations as well. For example, the fact that rankings are released annually at the discretion of the rankers, and that they are released with great media fanfare, has shaped the practices inside schools, who must respond to rankings. Annual rankings produce 'news' that institutions must respond to. Universities are pressured or encouraged to adopt improving their global rank as an explicit goal and investments in resources are often expected to show improvements relatively quickly. Educators at several Chinese universities described how important improvement in rankings was to the image of China that party leaders wanted to foster. In this way, rankings encourage short-term thinking, as administrators and bureaucrats scramble to boost rankings quickly. For example, a number of countries have invested in hiring expensive, highly cited scholars to quickly boost citation rates. Other schools have managed to lure Nobel Prize or Field Medal winners with enticing deals to their institutions, prizes that are factors in the Shanghai rankings. Other countries are merging scholarly institutions as a way to improve rankings that are sensitive to size. Others 'buy' the vita of faculty with the right sort of citations as measured by a ranker. The educational benefits of these relatively 'quick-fix' responses are debatable. But efforts to address long-term goals or difficult problems may come to be seen as a costly luxury in terms of impact on rankings. One director of admissions reported:

> As far as incentives go, it was basically, 'It's your model. We are giving you the money to do it. You do it. If you don't do it, you're fired.' It's like you are a basketball coach. For admissions professionals, USN has made their jobs much more like athletic coaches – we could still have a winning season and be canned. I have colleagues right now – and I don't want to say at what school – but they brought this clown in, and I call him a clown because he violated our agreed-upon code of ethics and that is you don't make invidious comparisons to other schools.[24]

Along with producing 'news' that is widely reported inside universities and by external media, annual rankings also produce visible trends as a series of rankings can be read as a trajectory of performance over time. These trends – going up or down, doing better or worse, the status quo – can powerfully shape how institutions assess themselves and others. So at the same time as there is the speed-up of getting improving numbers each year, there are also the across-time trends that are easy to chart and easy to disseminate.

## What Excellence Is and What Universities Are For

Without belabouring the point, USN and other important rankers now powerfully define what excellence in higher education means and hence what universities are good for. Embedded within the various algorithms, whether these are directed at departments inside universities or global higher education, are assumptions about how to measure what is valuable and thus what it means to be valuable. The feedback loop between rankings and effects can be a tight one, one that is amplified because of all the places that rankings can easily go. Elsewhere we have called this mechanism reactivity, the production of consequences as a result of measuring, but it shares a family resemblance with ideas of performativity, self-fulfilling prophecies and the inevitable reflexivity of people and their institutions. The upshot is that rankings are increasingly affecting how we understand education: as an investment by consumers, as ordinal, as having status that is precise, as being in a global competition with each other – in short, as kinds of markets. Along with competition, rankings generate distrust as gaming strategies become known, as colleagues look over one another's shoulders, as incentives become linked to these numbers and as declines require scapegoats.

They also produce cynicism. As efforts to manipulate rankings factors proliferate and this gaming is made public, educators, students and the public become sceptical of the practices and values of those charged with producing the raw materials for rankings.[25]

But, overwhelmingly, as rankings change jobs, shift priorities or mediate access and resources, they generate anxiety. And if this anxiety takes a different form than the alienation of Marx's workers or the impersonality of Weber's bureaucrats, it is a feeling that both would recognize. It should not surprise us that concise and highly visible markers of status should affect how people think about themselves and each other. Rankings were born out of the old-fashioned competition of companies looking to expand their market shares with innovation, technology and marketing. They have turned status into a literal commodity, where price is one part of the value they measure, but in the odd sense that more resources spent on fewer students equals a better school. But this familiar form of competition has spawned all these new forms that are mediated by numbers and the data that make them possible. Rankers compete with ever more kinds of rankings. Students compete armed with precise measures of their worth and the worthiness of the schools they attend or aspire to. Administrators and schools compete with each other in what some have wryly noted looks like a 'quantitative death spiral'. So we have to ask: is this good for society? For education? For our students?

Rankings have produced an expanded accountability of sorts. Students now feel free to challenge deans if their school's ranking goes down. Law-makers and administrators use rankings to allocate budgets or evaluate performances of departments or deans. One can know little about a particular school, but the rankings provide an easy means of evaluating it in relation to other universities, as well as its progress over time. Yet this expanded accountability is also narrow, encompassing just the numbers included in the ranking. Other important educational goals – good teaching, diverse student bodies, humanities or artistic training – may be excluded, which may make them less relevant over time.

## Conclusion

We can understand rankings as a particular form that organizes a broad array of social life. Rankings are widely used ways of creating and representing hierarchy; they are familiar symbols of quality, status or worth and are a key means through which relativity is established. By considering the formal properties of rankings, the intervals created, their apparent precision and the relative relationships among all ranked, we can better understand their power and their impact. They are comparisons whose job is to make possible an almost endless variety of comparison – between entities and over time. The seductive quality of this form, the combination of their familiarity and the expectations that attend them, including our profound impulse to produce value and inequality and to feel we are being rational in our choices, make them appealing forms, especially in a world where the volume of information at our disposal threatens to overwhelm us. And we grant them a special form of authority because we believe that numbers are a universal language and because rankings seem to conform to the dictates of rigorous methods.

Rankings reflect and reinforce the broad international trend to infuse market values and market-like discipline into our educational systems. Educators must now keep their eye on the rankings as they make decisions about resources, hiring and even the curriculum. Rankings foster competition and a 'winner takes all' philosophy that favours the Global West over the Global South and East, threatens educational systems that support broad access over a 'star' system, and turns unlikely institutions into rivals. They also make possible competition between members or even between my numbers this year and my numbers next year. It is important that we consider carefully and comparatively how rankings and their contributions to the marketization of higher education are reshaping these fundamental institutions.

**Wendy Espeland** is Professor of Sociology at Northwestern University, Evanston, IL. Her main fields of interest are the sociology of culture, theory, the sociology of law and quantification. She has published widely on commensurative practices, media rankings and their effects, especially in higher education.

# Notes

1. See the Introduction to this volume.
2. Simmel's most concise and coherent statement of his method is found in 'How is Society Possible?' – a part of his masterwork *Sociologie* that was translated into English as an essay or fragment that was subsequently published in an early volume of the *American Journal of Sociology*. Simmel's debt to Kant is explicit in this essay: G. Simmel, 'How is Society Possible?', *American Journal of Sociology* 16(3) (1910), 372–91.
3. G. Simmel, *Essays on Interpretation in Social Science*, G. Oaks (trans. and ed.) (Toronto: Rowman & Littlefield, 1980), 8.
4. K. Burke, *Counter-statement* (Berkeley: University of California Press, 1968), 217 and 124.
5. Charles Camic's influential essay argues that 'habit' or the 'habitual' was an important conceptual component for Durkheim and Weber. C. Camic, 'The Matter of Habit', *American Journal of Sociology* 91(5) (1986), 139–87.
6. K. Burke, *A Rhetoric of Motives* (Berkeley: University of California Press, 1950), 55.
7. The research on rankings discussed here is done jointly with Michael Sauder. See W.N. Espeland and M. Sauder, *Engines of Anxiety: Academic Rankings, Reputation, and Accountability* (New York: Russell Sage Press, 2016).
8. Retrieved 13 March 2019 from http://www.rsssf.com/engpaul/FLA/1892-93.html.
9. M. Foucault. *Discipline and Punish: The Birth of the Prison* (New York: Random House, 1977), 145–46.

10. Retrieved 13 March 2019 from http://www.bbc.com/news/education-38212070.
11. M. Sauder and W.N. Espeland, 'The Discipline of Rankings: Tight Coupling and Organizational Change', *American Sociological Review* 74(1) (2009), 63–82, at 72–73.
12. D. Webster, 'Rankings of Undergraduate Education in U.S. News and World Report and Money', *Change* (March/April 1992), 19–31. As Julie Bouchard shows, the French media began publishing rankings of universities in 1976 as journalists collaborated with some educators as a means to destabilize the entrenched status of the Grandes Écoles. J. Bouchard, 'Academic Media Ranking and the Configurations of Values in Higher Education: A Sociotechnical History of a Co-production in France between the Media, State and Higher Education (1976-1989)', *Higher Education* 73(6) (2017), 947–62. This professional collaboration was initiated by education journalists. Hired in large numbers during the 1960s to cover the activism at university campuses, the more placid 1970s left them with less news to cover. Rankings offered a new venue for their expertise. It is unclear whether USN was borrowing from the French media.
13. Espeland and Sauder, *Engines of Anxiety*, 9–10; U.S. News and World Reports, 'America's Best Colleges, 1987–2017'; U.S. News and World Reports, 'America's Best Graduate Schools, 1990–2017'.
14. For possible explanations, see Bettina Heintz's remarks in Chapter 12 in this volume.
15. M.K. Power, *The Audit Explosion* (London: Demos, 1994).
16. M. Lamont and V. Molnar, 'The Study of Symbolic Boundaries', *Annual Review of Sociology* 28 (2002), 167–95.
17. See T. Porter, *Trust in Numbers*, (Princeton: University of Princeton Press, 1995) and W.N. Espeland, *The Struggle for Water* (Chicago: University of Chicago Press, 1998) for two investigations of the emergence and effects of cost-benefit analysis.
18. As Dobbin, Carruthers and Fourcade have shown, markets are seldom as pure as their abstraction into economic theory makes them out to be. Their origins reflect the legal cultures, politics and historical contexts in ways that can lead to dramatic differences that are, of course, only revealed via comparison: F. Dobbin, *Forging Industrial Policy: The United States, Britain, and France in the Railway Age* (New York: Cambridge University Press, 1994); B.G. Carruthers, *City of Capital: Politics and Markets in the English Financial Revolution* (Princeton: Princeton University Press, 1996); M. Fourcade, 'Cents and Sensibility: Economic Values and the Nature of "Nature"', *American Journal of Sociology* 116 (2011), 1721–77.
19. W. Espeland and M. Stevens, 'A Sociology of Quantification', *European Journal of Sociology* 49 (2008), 401–36.
20. E. Hazelkorn, 'Learning to Live with League Tables and Rankings: The Experiences of Institutional Leaders', *Higher Education Policy* 21(2) (2008), 193–215, at 196.
21. For their depiction of our increasingly 'ordinal' societies, see M. Fourcade and K. Healy, 'Classification Situations: Life-Chances in the Neoliberal Era', *Accounting, Organizations and Society* 38 (2013), 559–72.
22. See Espeland and Sauder, *Engines of Anxiety*, for quotations at 92 and 97–98.
23. M. Sauder and R. Lancaster, 'Do Rankings Matter? The Effects of U.S. News and World Reports on the Admission Process of Law Schools', *Law and Society Review* 40(1) (2006), 105–34; Espeland and Sauder, *Engines of Anxiety*.
24. Espeland and Sauder, *Engines of Anxiety*, 97.
25. Sauder and Espeland, 'Discipline of Rankings'.

# Bibliography

Bouchard, J., 'Academic Media Ranking and the Configurations of Values in Higher Education: A Sociotechnical History of a Co-production in France between the Media, State and Higher Education (1976–1989)', *Higher Education* 73(6) (2017), 947–62.

Burke, K., *A Rhetoric of Motives* (Berkeley: University of California Press, 1950).

———. *Counter-statement* (Berkeley: University of California Press, 1968).

Camic, C., 'The Matter of Habit', *American Journal of Sociology* 91(5) (1986), 139–87.

Carruthers, B.G., *City of Capital: Politics and Markets in the English Financial Revolution* (Princeton: Princeton University Press, 1996).

Dobbin, F., *Forging Industrial Policy: The United States, Britain, and France in the Railway Age* (New York: Cambridge University Press, 1994).

Espeland, W., *The Struggle for Water* (Chicago: University of Chicago Press, 1998).

Espeland, W., and Sauder, M., *Engines of Anxiety: Academic Rankings, Reputation, and Accountability* (New York: Russell Sage Press, 2016).

Espeland, W., and Stevens, M., 'A Sociology of Quantification', *European Journal of Sociology* 49 (2008), 401–36.

Fourcade, M., 'Cents and Sensibility: Economic Values and the Nature of "Nature"', *American Journal of Sociology* 116 (2011), 1721–77.

Fourcade, M., and Healy, K., 'Classification Situations: Life-Chances in the Neoliberal Era', *Accounting, Organizations and Society* 38 (2013), 559–72.

Hazelkorn, E., 'Learning to Live with League Tables and Rankings: The Experiences of Institutional Leaders', *Higher Education Policy* 21(2) (2008), 193–215.

Lamont, M., and Molnar, V., 'The Study of Symbolic Boundaries', *Annual Review of Sociology* 28 (2002), 167–95.

Porter, T., *Trust in Numbers*, (Princeton: University of Princeton Press, 1995).

Power, M.K., *The Audit Explosion* (London: Demos, 1994).

Sauder, M., and Espeland, W.N., 'The Discipline of Rankings: Tight Coupling and Organizational Change', *American Sociological Review* 74(1) (2009), 63–82.

Sauder, M., and Lancaster, R., 'Do Rankings Matter? The Effects of U.S. News and World Reports on the Admission Process of Law Schools', *Law and Society Review* 40(1) (2006), 105–34.

Simmel, G., 'How is Society Possible?', *American Journal of Sociology* 16(3) (1910), 372–91.

———. *Essays on Interpretation in Social Science*, Oaks, G. (trans. and ed.) (Toronto: Rowman & Littlefield, 1980).

U.S. News and World Reports, 'America's Best Colleges, 1987–2017'.

———. 'America's Best Graduate Schools, 1990–2017'.

Webster, D., 'Rankings of Undergraduate Education in U.S. News and World Report and Money', *Change* (March/April 1992), 19–31.

# 12
# Good – Better – Best

*Comparisons and the Power of Ranking Orders*

Bettina Heintz

One hundred and fifty years ago, Friedrich Nietzsche described his era as an 'age of comparison': 'It is the source of its pride – but, as is only reasonable, also of its suffering. Let us not be afraid of this suffering! Let us rather confront the task which the age sets us as boldly as we can: and then posterity will bless us for it.'[1] What Nietzsche considered a novel phenomenon has by now turned into the normal case. In our 'age of comparison', almost everybody and everything is subject to being compared and often brought into a ranking order. There is practically no social field where ratings, rankings or top lists have not become an incentive for improvement or a tool for making decisions. There are ranking orders for hospitals, enterprises and states, for artists, athletes and politicians, for movies, restaurants and holiday destinations, for buildings, services and hard disks. Thus, it seems fair to say that today we not only live in an age of comparison, but additionally in an age of superlatives: good – better – best.

Ranking orders appear in various forms. They can be displayed as rankings (e.g. university rankings), as ratings (e.g. credit ratings) or as top lists (e.g. the ten best films). And although prizes only distinguish between winners and losers, they may nonetheless be seen as a kind of ranking order, albeit a binary one.[2] But despite their diversity, they are similar in one significant point as they not only compare, but also evaluate the units compared. With ranking orders, everybody knows who or what is best and who or what performs less well. In order to find out who fares better, it suffices to compare the rank numbers or count the stars. For this reason, ranking orders are particularly suited for making decisions. Whether buying a car or selecting a wine, choosing a university or granting a loan, all these decisions require comparative information. But ranking orders are not only powerful decision devices; they are also instruments to control and enhance performance – something or somebody is always at the top and beats the others. Those at the top set up a reference model for those who perform less well.

Ranking orders are often described as *quantitative devices*, but even rankings are not always based on counting and measuring; not everything that claims to be a number is based on numbers.[3] In fact, as I will argue below, many ranking orders rest not on measurement, but on qualitative assessments – on 'connoisseurial reviews', as Grant Blank puts it (see below).[4] Instead of regarding ranking orders as numerical devices, I therefore conceive them as *comparative devices* that may, but need not, be quantified.

While prizes have a long tradition, rankings, ratings and top lists are a new phenomenon. It is true that the first rankings had already been published in the eighteenth century, but it is only since the 1980s that ranking orders have become a ubiquitous phenomenon. This raises the question why rankings, ratings and top lists have proliferated only in the last few decades and what this tells us about contemporary society.

To answer these questions, I will start with definitions. In the first section I propose a definition of comparison and show how comparisons differ from other ordering techniques such as lists, classifications, dichotomies or analogies. The second section gives a short overview of the historical development of ranking orders and their various formats. Though ranking orders are often considered as numerical instruments, I will show in the third section that quantification is neither a precise nor a selective criterion to characterize ranking orders. To conclude, I will argue that the novelty and distinctiveness of ranking orders lies in their extension to fields where quality matters more than quantity: to the sphere of the subjective, expressive and aesthetic.

## Ranking Orders as Evaluative Comparisons

In history and sociology, comparisons are usually considered as a *scientific method*, but not as a social phenomenon in its own right.[5] Yet comparing is not limited to professionals; it is an ordinary *practice*. Individuals compare each other with regard to their popularity or their education, enterprises evaluate their sales and profits in comparison to their competitors, and states observe each other according to their political influence and use these comparisons to identify strategies for future action. In addition, there exist a variety of third-party organizations that are specialized in producing and publishing comparisons: statistical offices, agencies for product testing or publishing companies that regularly issue ratings or rankings. But, despite the pervasiveness of comparisons, they have rarely been focused on in an explicit manner. There are only a handful of studies that deal with comparisons as a research subject on its own.[6]

But what are comparisons? What do we do when we compare politicians, universities or hard disks? Comparisons are, generally speaking, tools that observe entities or events according to their differences or similarities.[7] By doing so, they establish connections between units that previously may not have been considered as related. German schools are compared to schools in South Korea with regard to their results in the Programme for International Student Assessment (PISA), and a city in Switzerland may be compared to a city in Australia with respect to its quality of living. Even when there are no contacts between the schools and cities, respectively, their decisions may be affected by the mere fact of being publicly compared and related to each other.

Typical comparative statements are, for instance, 'she is taller than her brother', 'the apples and pears have the same price' or 'Max Weber is the most-quoted sociologist'. To make a comparative statement, two steps are needed. *First*, in order to compare entities, we have to regard them as *comparable*, i.e. as belonging to the same *category*. To take the example above, the compared entities have to be considered as an element of the category 'sibling', 'fruit' or 'sociologists'. Only when entities are deemed comparable does it make sense to observe them according to a comparative criterion. Whether or not different entities are regarded as belonging to the same category is not based on their inherent characteristics, but is historically contingent. Phenomena that used to be seen as lacking any commonality may later be judged as belonging to the same category (and vice versa).

*Second*, comparing requires comparative criteria – *tertia comparationis* – and procedures to assess the differences or similarities between the units regarded as comparable.[8] Thus, in order to compare and rank universities, you need comparative criteria such as scientific reputation, external funding or student-to-faculty ratio, as well as methodological procedures to determine the academic excellence of each university.

Both steps are highly interwoven, also from a processual view: comparisons may lead to the emergence of new categories and new categories may induce new kinds of comparisons. An example is the rise of the so-called 'world-class universities' as a new social category. While initially the delimitation of this subgroup of the twenty or fifty top universities had been quite arbitrary, over the years it evolved into a reality of its own, which in turn induced new kinds of comparisons. The interplay between comparison and the creation of new categories is the reason why Marion Fourcade and Kieran Healy speak of a 'duality' of comparisons and categorization or, in their terminology, of 'scores' and 'classifications': '[f]irst, tools for scoring and ranking – for measuring and comparing on a cardinal or ordinal scale – are repeatedly used to produce nominal classifications associated with judgements of essential worth ... Second, over time the nominal classes and categories we interpret as basic to social life provide the starting point for new efforts to measure, score, and rank again. Prior classifications provide the basis for new measurements and scores, and scoring systems give rise to newly classified kinds.'[9]

Fourcade and Healy are particularly interested in the interplay between quantified comparisons and nominal classifications.[10] But far from all comparisons are based on counting and/or measuring (see in greater detail below).[11] For this reason, comparison and quantification or 'commensuration' should be distinguished. The term 'commensuration' has been introduced by Wendy L. Espeland and Mitchell L. Stevens, who define it as a process that 'transforms qualities into quantities, difference into magnitude. It is a way to reduce and simplify disparate information into numbers that can easily be compared'.[12] Although commensuration certainly facilitates comparisons, it is not a constitutive feature of comparing. In order to assess the quality of research proposals, no common metric is needed.

Furthermore, distinguishing between comparison and commensuration offers a new view on the social impact of quantitative measures. Generally, the power of rankings or global indicators is explained by the use of numbers: it is the capacity of numbers to reduce complexity as well as their precise and abstract character that lies behind the social effects of quantification.[13] Complementary to this explanation, it could be argued that the mere fact of being publicly compared may matter too. By being publicly compared, whether in terms of numbers or not, the actors are subject to a continuous, and sometimes even world-wide, observation. The knowledge of being compared may induce self-disciplinary processes that are similar to the reactions evoked by numerical instruments. Public comparisons are, in other words, no less 'reactive' than quantitative instruments; they change how social actors see themselves and others (see below).[14]

Compared to other tools for ordering the world, such as lists, classifications and analogies, comparisons are more complex. While classification systems focus on distinctions, and analogies on similarities, comparisons integrate both: 'The power of comparisons consists in working out the distinctiveness or peculiarity of the *comparata* as well as their commonality, i.e. in showing what separates them and what they have in common.'[15]

*Lists* such as shopping lists or to-do lists are the simplest technique. They work in a purely additive way by gathering items solely according to some functional aspect. Besides the fact that they appear in the list, no other connection between the items is needed.

*Categorization* is a more complex technique. In contrast to mere lists, categories specify additional properties that units have to meet in order to be included in the category. In order to be classified as an apple, objects have to exhibit a specific taste, shape and texture. An object that does not fulfil these criteria – a pear or a red tennis ball, for example – would not be considered as a specimen of the category 'apple'. Thus, each categorization 'lumps' things together and 'splits' them from other things. In the words of Eviatar Zerubavel: '"Lumping" entails grouping "similar" things together in a single mental cluster. "Splitting" involves perceiving different clusters as separate from one another. Lumping enables us to perceive grape juices as similar to orange juice, and chimpanzees as similar to baboons. Splitting enables us to see grape juice as different from wine and chimpanzees as different from humans.'[16] Categories are usually not isolated from each other, but are elements of larger and often hierarchically organized *classification systems*. The category 'university', for example, is a supracategory of different types of universities (comprehensive universities, business schools, technical universities, etc.) and at the same time a subcategory of the category 'higher education institution'.

*Dichotomies* are a special case of classification systems. Unlike ordinary classification systems, they relate categories according to a strictly binary logic. The binary construction distinguishes dichotomies such as man/woman from the (nondichotomous) distinction between humans and chimpanzees. Often dichotomies are not only binary but also asymmetrical: one side is favoured at the expense of the other. This amalgamation of classification and valuation or, in Marion Fourcade's words, of 'judgement of kinds' with 'judgements of worth',[17] may even go as far as denying any similarity with the other side. This happens when the privileged side claims not only otherness but also universality. 'The non-Catholic becomes heathen or traitor; to leave the Communist party does not only mean to change party allegiance, but is rather "like leaving life, leaving mankind" (J. Kuczynski).'[18]

*Analogies* operate exactly the other way round. Instead of accentuating differences, they construe homologies between units, however disparate they may appear. And, while comparisons generate knowledge by focusing on the differences between units assumed as similar, analogies, in contrast, produce knowledge by looking for similarities between units presupposed as different. As Michel Foucault argued in his book *The Order of Things*, analogies were the privileged mode of generating knowledge until the seventeenth century. But subsequently, Foucault claimed, they lost their privileged position and made way for comparative techniques, which were now considered as the royal road to knowledge.[19]

The increasing prominence of comparisons was not limited to science. As Willibald Steinmetz has shown in his conceptual-historical analysis, the term 'comparison' became increasingly popular from the eighteenth century onwards, not only in the sciences but also in other social fields.[20] At the same time, the meaning and the use of the term changed. In German, the term *Vergleich* initially referred to mutual settlement as well as to comparison in the modern sense of discovering differences according to a comparative criterion. Since the mid eighteenth century, the two meanings have become terminologically separated. While mutual settlement was still called 'Vergleich', the term 'Vergleichung' was used for comparison in the modern sense.[21] Only by the end of the nineteenth century did 'Vergleich' become the usual term, now meaning primarily comparison. Furthermore, Steinmetz's analysis reveals three general trends in the use of the term 'comparison': first, an increasing normalization and popularization of comparative terms; second, a growing theorization and sharpening of the concept of comparison; and, third, an extension of the scope of comparisons, namely temporally (historical comparisons), geographically (comparisons of different cultures and civilizations) and functionally (performance comparisons).

Even though comparing may always have been a human practice, it is fair to assume that only since the eighteenth century comparisons became a widespread and institutionalized technique for knowledge production and decision-making. This was the century when nations and cultures began to compare themselves systematically with other nations and cultures,[22] and when comprehensive statistical data were for the first time gathered not just for taxation purposes, but for political decision-making more generally.[23] Broadly speaking, three types of comparisons can be distinguished: 'neutral' comparisons that assert differences, but without valuing them; evaluative comparisons that establish a relation of better and worse; and 'progressive' comparisons that not only evaluate nations, cultures or individuals, but also situate them on a temporal scale of steps already reached or still to be taken.

Ranking orders are a prime example for evaluative comparisons, sometimes with and sometimes without a temporal component. In contrast to neutral comparisons, ranking orders not only assert differences, but rank them according to a normative standard. This may be done explicitly in words or simply by visual means, by presenting the compared units on a scale with the best at the top, the average in the middle and the worst at the bottom. How this is done can be illustrated by contrasting a statistical table with a ranking. Thus, Figure 12.1 presents an extract of an international statistical table on gross domestic product (GDP), GDP per capita and the rate of economic growth.[24]

Obviously, the table performs a comparison: countries are compared with regard to the three indicators mentioned. But the comparison is expressed in a factual, nonevaluative language; there is no explicit hint which country performs best. This does not mean that statistical tables are value-free. The very decision to use a certain indicator (and to omit others) is already a normative decision, but the normativity is hidden. Table 12.1 shows a worldwide ranking of countries according to their GDP per capita. In contrast to the statistical table, the countries are no longer presented in an alphabetical order, but according to their respective wealth.[25]

Though the empirical basis is identical – the same indicators, the same data and the same countries – the two figures convey quite different information. Whereas the statistical table only presents differences without evaluating them (a 'neutral' comparison – see above), the ranking displays an evaluative judgement by putting the wealthiest countries at the top and the poorest at the bottom. By using this presentation, the ranking draws the attention not only to the differences between the countries, but to the question of which country performs best. Although this information is already included in the statistical table, it does not make it visible.

## The Making of Ranking Orders

Although ranking orders proliferated only in the last three decades, they are not a new phenomenon. The format was already known in the eighteenth century, but it took nearly 200 years for rankings, ratings and top lists to become an

| Region, country or area | 1985 | 1995 | 2005 | 2010 | 2012 | 2013 | 2014 | Région, pays ou zone |
|---|---|---|---|---|---|---|---|---|
| Total, countries or areas | | | | | | | | Total, tous pays ou zones |
| GDP at current prices | 13 502 356 | 30 860 249 | 47 264 846 | 65 644 956 | 74 221 881 | 76 176 342 | 78 037 088 | PIB aux prix courants |
| GDP per capita | 2 784 | 5 384 | 7 251 | 9 475 | 10 460 | 10 609 | 10 743 | PIB par habitant |
| GDP at constant prices | 26 013 322 | 34 592 400 | 47 264 846 | 52 895 088 | 55 617 816 | 56 813 235 | 58 254 247 | PIB aux prix constants |
| Growth rates (annual) | 3.7 | 2.9 | 3.6 | 4.1 | 2.2 | 2.1 | 2.5 | Taux de croissance |
| **Afghanistan** | | | | | | | | **Afghanistan** |
| GDP at current prices | 3 322 | 3 236 | 6 622 | 16 078 | 21 331 | 21 610 | 21 122 | PIB aux prix courants |
| GDP per capita | 286 | 193 | 271 | 575 | 718 | 704 | 668 | PIB par habitant |
| GDP at constant prices | 7 501 | 4 532 | 6 622 | 10 393 | 12 529 | 13 341 | 13 627 | PIB aux prix constants |
| Growth rates (annual) | 0.3 | 49.9 | 9.9 | 3.2 | 10.9 | 6.5 | 2.1 | Taux de croissance |
| **Albania** | | | | | | | | **Albanie** |
| GDP at current prices | 2 389 | 2 459 | 8 094 | 11 927 | 12 345 | 12 916 | 13 413 | PIB aux prix courants |
| GDP per capita | 805 | 792 | 2 626 | 4 110 | 4 285 | 4 480 | 4 642 | PIB par habitant |
| GDP at constant prices | 5 147 | 4 744 | 8 094 | 10 417 | 10 856 | 11 007 | 11 238 | PIB aux prix constants |
| Growth rates (annual) | 1.8 | 13.3 | 5.8 | 3.7 | 1.6 | 1.4 | 2.1 | Taux de croissance |
| **Algeria** | | | | | | | | **Algérie** |
| GDP at current prices | 57 866 | 41 971 | 103 198 | 161 207 | 209 047 | 209 704 | 213 518 | PIB aux prix courants |
| GDP per capita | 2 564 | 1 452 | 3 102 | 4 473 | 5 584 | 5 492 | 5 484 | PIB par habitant |
| GDP at constant prices | 64 280 | 67 626 | 103 198 | 116 968 | 124 452 | 127 937 | 132 799 | PIB aux prix constants |
| Growth rates (annual) | 3.7 | 3.8 | 5.9 | 3.6 | 3.4 | 2.8 | 3.8 | Taux de croissance |
| **Andorra** | | | | | | | | **Andorre** |
| GDP at current prices | 429 | 1 457 | 3 248 | 3 346 | 3 146 | 3 249 | 3 278 | PIB aux prix courants |
| GDP per capita | 9 614 | 22 825 | 39 990 | 39 639 | 39 666 | 42 807 | 45 033 | PIB par habitant |
| GDP at constant prices | 1 321 | 1 774 | 3 248 | 2 674 | 2 541 | 2 499 | 2 533 | PIB aux prix constants |
| Growth rates (annual) | 2.3 | 2.8 | 7.5 | -7.4 | -0.7 | -1.6 | 1.4 | Taux de croissance |
| **Angola** | | | | | | | | **Angola** |
| GDP at current prices | 9 125 | 6 642 | 36 971 | 83 369 | 125 430 | 142 738 | 146 676 | PIB aux prix courants |
| GDP per capita | 936 | 509 | 2 064 | 3 929 | 5 529 | 6 087 | 6 054 | PIB par habitant |
| GDP at constant prices | 18 016 | 17 679 | 36 971 | 55 286 | 60 612 | 63 165 | 66 194 | PIB aux prix constants |
| Growth rates (annual) | 3.5 | 15.0 | 15.0 | 3.6 | 7.6 | 4.2 | 4.8 | Taux de croissance |

**Figure 12.1** GDP per capita, growth rate. From *United Nations Statistical Yearbook*, 59th issue (2016), Table 10, 103 by United Nations Statistics Division, New York, © 2016 United Nations. Reprinted with the permission of the United Nations.

omnipresent reality. An early example of a ranking order was published in a field one would not expect to be a forerunner, namely in the arts.[26] In his book *Cours de peinture par principe*, published in 1708, the French painter and art critique Roger de Piles compiled a table in which fifty-six painters were evaluated according to four dimensions: composition, design, colour and expressiveness. The table – or 'balance des peintres' as he called it – differs from usual art criticism by expressing the evaluation in terms of numerals, ranging from 0 to 20 (Figure 12.2).[27] By using numerals to communicate his evaluation, de Piles conveyed the impression of an objective judgement.

During the eighteenth century, de Piles' method was imitated by several other art critics and extended to authors and actors. Contemporaries considered the tables an attempt 'to measure the merits of poets according to mathematical rules',[28] and Spoerhase and others seem to share this view.[29] Yet, in fact, these tables do not represent a quantification of aesthetical quality, but a qualitative judgement expressed in a numeral (and not in a number), similar to the marking of class essays.[30] By the end of the eighteenth century and with the growing 'cult of the genius', this kind of art judgement became more and more suspect. For the German poet Christian Friedrich Daniel Schubart, 'the genius dissolved in numbers' was 'no less disgusting as the carcass of a beautiful girl who died young'.[31] To bring poets and artworks into a comparative metric was no longer compatible with the view that each work of art has its own incomparable value.

**Table 12.1** List of countries by GDP per capita, United Nations, National Accounts Main Aggregates Database, December 2016.

| Rank | Country | US$ |
| --- | --- | --- |
| 1 | Monaco | 168,004 |
| 2 | Lichtenstein | 164,437 |
| 3 | Luxembourg | 101,835 |
| 4 | Bermuda | 99,963 |
| 5 | Switzerland | 76,609 |
| ... | ... | ... |
| 190 | Mozambique | 379 |
| 191 | Niger | 364 |
| 192 | Malawi | 294 |
| 193 | Burundi | 273 |
| 194 | Somalia | 92 |

*Source:* https://en.wikipedia.org/wiki/List_of_countries_by_GDP_(nominal)_per_capita.

Of course, art was not the only field where comparisons were made. As Lars Behrisch and Paul Slack have shown, states began to observe and compare themselves in a systematic way from the seventeenth century onwards.[32] With 'the invention of improvement' (Slack), states started to count crops, cows and souls, and these practices eventually led to the implementation of nationwide statistics in the late eighteenth century. But although states were comparing each other verbally in books, visually in maps and numerically in statistical tables, interestingly, they did not convert the information into a ranking order similar to the 'balance des peintres'.

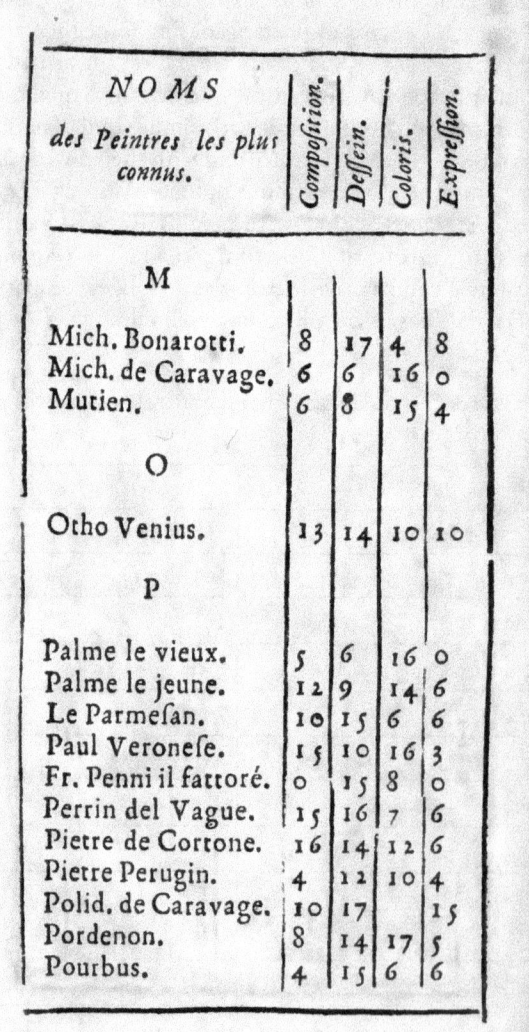

**Figure 12.2** 'Balance des peintres' (extract), Roger de Piles, *Cours de peinture par principe* (1708).

It was only towards the end of the nineteenth century that ranking orders began to appear in other social fields, but still slowly and with little long-term impact. In 1873, the Swiss botanist Alphonse de Candolle published the first international science ranking I have been able to find so far. Using the nationality of the foreign corresponding members of the three leading academies (Berlin, London and Paris) as an indicator of scientific quality, he ranked the countries according to their scientific excellence at four different times (see Figure 12.3).[33] Although he does not use numerals to mark the ranks, the list is apparently a ranking order with Switzerland at the top followed by the Netherlands, the Scandinavian countries or France, depending on the year.

The invention of the league table was a further step in the ascent of ranking orders. In sports, league tables showed up first in baseball (1876) and ten years later in football. With league tables, actual results could now be compared retrospectively and at the same time serve as a basis to derive predictions for the future.[34] In 1909, John Moody, the founder of Moody's *Credit Rating Agency*, introduced his famous triple-A system for the rating of railroad bonds which was soon extended to all kinds of credit ratings.[35] For the history of ranking orders, the significance of Moody's triple A-system lies in the fact that it introduced a marking system that is now common practice for ratings, namely designating ranks not by numerals, but by symbols such as letters, stars, points or diamonds.

At the beginning of the twentieth century, more ranking orders are to be found, but the presentation differs considerably from that of today. The information is often displayed in a visual way (see Figure 12.4 as an example) and the absence of a standardized mode of presentation indicates that the format was not yet established.[36]

**TABLEAU XII**

ORDRE DE LA VALEUR SCIENTIFIQUE D'UN MILLION D'HABITANTS DES DIVERS PAYS D'APRÈS LES MOYENNES DU TABLEAU IX [1]

| 1750 | 1789 | 1829 | 1869 |
|---|---|---|---|
| Suisse. | Suisse. | Suisse. | Suisse. |
| Hollande. | Hollande. | Suède, Norw., Danemark. | France. |
| Suède, Norw., Danemark. | Suède, Norw., Danemark. | France. | Allemagne. |
| France. | France. | Allemagne. | Angleterre. |
| Angleterre. | Espagne, Portugal. | Angleterre. | Suède, Norw., Danemark. |
| Italie. | Italie. | Hollande. | Belgique. |
| Allemagne. | Belgique. | Italie. | Hollande. |
| Espagne, Portugal. | Etats-Unis. | Belgique. | Italie. |
| Russie, Pologne. | Angleterre. | Hongrie. | Etats-Unis. |
| | Allemagne. | Espagne, Portugal. | Russie, Pologne. |
| | Russie, Pologne. | Russie, Pologne. | |
| | Hongrie. | Etats-Unis. | |

[1] Les pays qui ne sont pas sur une des colonnes n'avaient alors aucun représentant sur les listes.

**Figure 12.3** 'Le rang scientifique des nations' (1873), Alphonse de Candolle, *Histoire des Sciences et des Savants depuis deux Siècles* (Geneva: H. Georg, 1873), Table XII, 188.

At about the same time, the first university rankings were published, but they did not find much resonance outside the inner circles of university administration.[37] In the 1930s, the *Guide Michelin* introduced the three-star system to differentiate between recommended restaurants,[38] and ten years later *Billboard* published the first popular music charts.[39] But although ranking orders began to spread from the beginning of the twentieth century, they gained momentum only since the 1980s. An indicator for the proliferation of ranking orders is the increase of the term 'Ranking' in the *Google* German text corpus. While the term was practically absent before 1980, its frequency has risen exponentially since then. Today, you find ranking orders nearly everywhere, even in the sphere of intimacy. With the help of matching algorithms, 'perfect pairs' are calculated, suggesting the possibility of rational choice even in the world of love.[40]

Although ranking orders are everywhere, we know very little about them. Most studies that deal with ranking orders usually focus on one format, either on rankings or ratings or top lists or prizes. There is practically no study that takes the whole range of ranking orders into account.[41] In the following, I will refer to all four formats, conceiving them as variations of a shared basic model.[42] What are the similarities and differences between a university ranking, a credit rating, a music chart, a literary prize and an award for being the most important person of the year? As these examples show, there are a great number of highly diverse

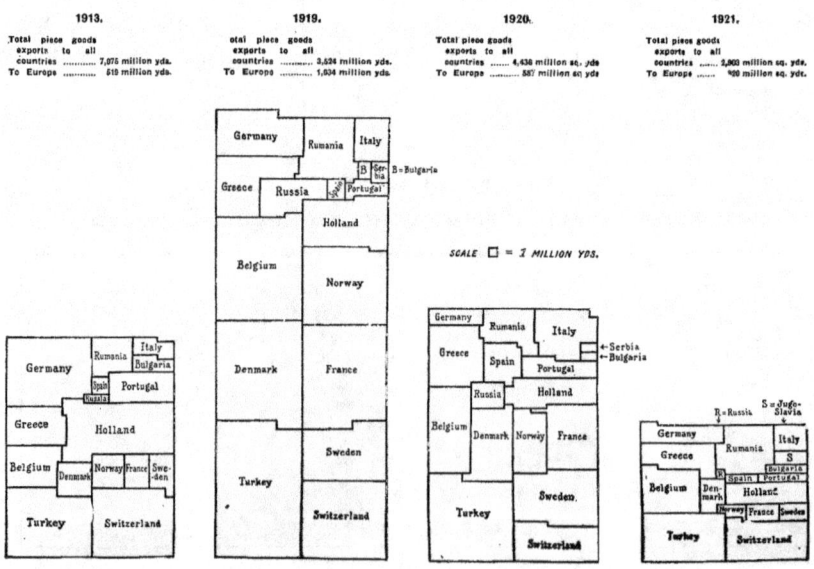

**Figure 12.4** British exports of cotton piece goods to European countries (1913 – 1919 – 1920 – 1921), R.E. Streat, 'Lancashire's Cotton Trade with Europe', *Manchester Guardian Commercial*, 15 June 1922, 165–70, at 169.

ranking orders. To bring some order into this muddle, precise demarcation criteria are needed. The most important distinctive feature is the way in which comparisons are produced. Roughly, one can distinguish between two main methods – rating and ranking procedures.

## *Ratings*

In ratings such as credit ratings or restaurant ratings, each state or restaurant is judged individually, and only afterwards compared to other states or restaurants. This means that the evaluations are *independent* of each other: the comparison comes after the evaluation. In restaurant ratings the individual reviews are only subsequently compiled, related and finally assigned to different quality classes. Ranks are usually not marked by numerals, but by other symbols such as stars, toques or letters, often supplemented by written commentaries such as degustation notes or rating reports. The sequential procedure – first the individual judgement, then the comparison – results in structural features that are typical for ratings. In contrast to rankings, the positions are not exclusive. Several states may be judged as worthy of a triple-A qualification and many restaurants may belong to the same category of two-star restaurants. And although ratings, just like rankings, create an incentive to move up in the ranking order, they are not zero-sum comparisons; the moving up of one restaurant does not imply that another has to move down.

## *Rankings*

Rankings are a different case. Unlike ratings, they are based on *direct* comparisons.[43] University rankings are a familiar example. The universities are not evaluated separately, but right from the beginning, they are directly compared to each other according to a set of standardized criteria. This is why rankings are fundamentally *relative*: the rank a university achieves depends not only on its individual performance, but also on the ranks the other universities get. If a university improves its ranking position, another will descend even if its performance remains the same or is even better than the year before.[44] For this reason, rankings are more akin to competition than ratings are: your gain is the loss of another. The competitive nature of rankings is further reinforced because rankings tend to avoid that several units share the same rank. This implies that the ranking positions are usually exclusive: one unit, one place, even if the differences are negligible. Yet, the exclusivity is not a given fact, but fabricated by drawing sharp lines between units that perform nearly identical (as an illustration, see Figure 12.5 below). By doing so, marginal and perhaps even accidental differences are presented as significant distinctions.

It should be noted that the difference between rankings and ratings is *not* that the one is based on measuring and counting and the other on qualitative judgements. Not every ranking uses quantitative data and not every rating is based on reviews. In other words, their difference lies not in their metric or non-metric character, but in the way they are *produced*. Appointment lists for university positions are a good example of this point as they combine both methods and are usually based on qualitative judgements. In a first phase, the members of the appointment committee evaluate the candidates individually without comparing them with the other applicants. The result is a rating where several candidates may share the same grade. Only in the last phase are the candidates compared directly to each other. The finally adopted appointment list is therefore a ranking that is based on a head-to-head-comparison and where the places are normally assigned exclusively. But although being a ranking, the list is usually not based on bibliometric measuring, but on a qualitative assessment of the candidates' advantages and disadvantages, at least in the social sciences and the humanities.

## Top Lists

In contrast to ratings and rankings, top lists are a hybrid format. Some top lists are based on a direct comparison (e.g. the list of the ten bestselling books) and others on a prior rating (e.g. the list of the ten best books). Apart from that, top lists work in a similar way to rankings as they assign the positions exclusively and display their evaluations in terms of a scale that pretends to be a metric scale. The special feature of a top list consists in that it explicitly restricts the range of available positions: top 10, top 100. Therefore, top lists are particularly suited to enhance the idea of permanent competition.

## Prizes

Similarly to top lists, prizes and awards are a mixed format too. Some prizes are awarded on the basis of a ranking (e.g. the Booker Prize) and others by a rating (the Oscars, for example). With their 'winner-takes-all' strategy, prizes are a special case of ranking orders. Only one or a few competitors take all — everybody else drops out.[45] Although prizes only distinguish between winners and losers, they nonetheless produce a ranking order, albeit a binary one. Robert Merton described this phenomenon as the 'Forty-first chair problem' referring to the admission to the forty seats of the *Académie Française*.[46] Only forty have the chance to be chosen; the other potential 'immortals' remain uncrowned. By drawing a sharp line between winners and losers, prizes convey the idea of an elite that differs fundamentally from all others. 'Only certain objects and individuals are "great", and, by implication ... all others are not.'[47] By translating minor differences into a huge distinction, prizes are especially suited for being used as instruments of consecration. In the increasingly complex world of cultural production, the awarding of a prize helps to recognize the truly 'good', 'true' and 'beautiful', and differentiate it from everything else.

## Governance or Seduction by Numbers?

Ranking orders, and particularly rankings, are usually seen as quantitative devices and interpreted as an indication of an ever-growing 'governance by numbers'. In the following, I will argue, first, that this assumption may be compelling at first sight, but does not hold true on closer inspection. Second, by drawing on Andrew Abbott's concept of 'fractal distinctions',[48] I will show that only a fraction of ranking orders turn out to be quantitative in a strict sense.

### *Numbers or Numerals?*

While ratings use letters or other non-numerical symbols to mark ranks, rankings and top lists designate ranks by numerals. Although these numerals are not numbers in a strong sense (see footnote 3), their very use suggests quantification. An obvious example is Parker's wine list ranging from 100 to 50 points. Although the points are assigned on the basis of a highly subjective tasting, Parker describes his scoring system as a scale 'that can *quantify* different levels of wine quality'.[49]

### *Ordinal or Metric?*

Rankings and top lists often present themselves as a metric scale, i.e. as a scale based on interval measurement. However, in fact, many rankings are ordinal scales that provide information about ordering relations (larger/smaller, better/worse), but not about quantities. The Shanghai Ranking of World Universities (see Figure 12.5) is a good example as it discloses both types of scales: the ordinal ranking scale ('World Rank') and the scores based on a metric scale ('Total Score').[50]

| World Rank | Institution | By location — All | National/Regional Rank | Total Score | Score on Alumni |
|---|---|---|---|---|---|
| 1 | Harvard University | | 1 | 100.0 | 100.0 |
| 2 | Stanford University | | 2 | 76.5 | 44.5 |
| 3 | University of Cambridge | | 1 | 70.9 | 81.4 |
| 4 | Massachusetts Institute of Technology (MIT) | | 3 | 70.4 | 68.7 |
| 5 | University of California, Berkeley | | 4 | 69.1 | 64.4 |

**Figure 12.5** Academic Ranking of World Universities 2017, Shanghai Ranking, retrieved 13 March 2019 from http://www.shanghairanking.com/arwu2017.html.

Between Harvard University ranked at the top (100 points) and Stanford University ranked second (76.5), the difference is quite large, namely 23.5 points, while the difference between the University of Cambridge (70.9) and the MIT (70.4) is only 0.5 points. But although the difference is tiny, the ranking assigns them a different rank. This shows that the usual metric interpretation of rank distances is misleading. The rank positions (1, 2, 3) only inform you *that* Harvard fares better than Stanford, and Stanford better than the MIT, but they do not give you any clue as to *how much* better they fare. For this information, you need the precise scores, which are disclosed in the Shanghai Ranking, but in many other rankings are not.

## *Judgement or Measurement?*

In his well-known book *Trust in Numbers*, Theodore M. Porter distinguishes between personal judgement and quantification. He sees quantification as a 'technology of trust' that gained momentum when personal networks dissolved and communication transcended the boundaries of local communities: 'Reliance on numbers and quantitative manipulation minimizes the need for intimate knowledge and personal trust. Quantification is well suited for communication that goes beyond the boundaries of locality and community. A highly disciplined discourse helps to produce knowledge independent of the particular people who make it.'[51] With quantification, the trustworthiness of a statement no longer depends on the credibility of the person making it, but on the supposedly impersonal and objective character of numbers. In a quite similar vein, Grant Blank distinguishes between two types of evaluative procedures that he calls 'connoisseurial reviews' and 'procedural reviews', respectively.[52] Book reviews and the reports submitted by restaurant inspectors exemplify the former, while product and service tests exemplify the latter. While connoisseurial reviews depend on the more or less subjective judgement of the reviewer, procedural reviews result from standardized measuring and testing. In the former case, the credibility of the review rests on the personal trust in the reviewer's expertise, while in the latter case, trust is impersonal and stems from the trust in the objectivity of the measurement and in the organization responsible for the test.

Both Porter and Blank draw a sharp line between judgement and quantification, and most sociologists see it the same way. However, drawing on Andrew Abbott's concept of 'fractal distinctions', I argue that the distinction between judgement and quantification is not a precise criterion to distinguish between different formats of ranking orders. Fractal distinctions are distinctions that repeat the distinction within themselves so that the distinguished parts are internally divided by the same distinction. The distinction history/sociology, for example, can be applied to both sides of the distinction by distinguishing within sociology a causal from a more narrative and interpretive strand and within history a social science approach from a microhistorical perspective.[53] In other words, the concept of fractal distinction helps to discover continuity where conventionally sharp distinctions are seen. Applying the fractal principle on ranking orders, you obtain a pattern more complex than the simple dichotomy of quantification vs. judgement (Figure 12.6).

Taking the distinction between quantification and judgement as a starting point, you can distinguish between 'quantitative' lists (A) on the one hand, and 'qualitative' lists (B) on the other. The former are based on measuring, counting and standardized procedures, while the latter are based on professional or amateur evaluations that express a personal judgement. What sounds like a clear-cut distinction is actually more permeable than it seems at first sight. Even qualitative judgements may follow highly standardized procedures, and quantitative lists may be based exclusively on quantitative data or, at least partially, on qualitative data such as expert assessments.

This permeability can be shown if you reintroduce the quantitative/qualitative distinction on the next lower level. By doing so, you will obtain four additional lists: on the *quantitative* side, lists (A1) that are produced by automatically generated numbers (e.g. Google's *PageRank* algorithm; bestseller lists based on sales figures) and lists (B1) that rely on self-collected data (e.g. product tests). On the *qualitative* side, you can distinguish between lists (A2) that rely on a large sample of reviews (e.g. consumer ratings) and lists (B2) that are based on the judgement of individual experts (e.g. wine ratings, lists of the

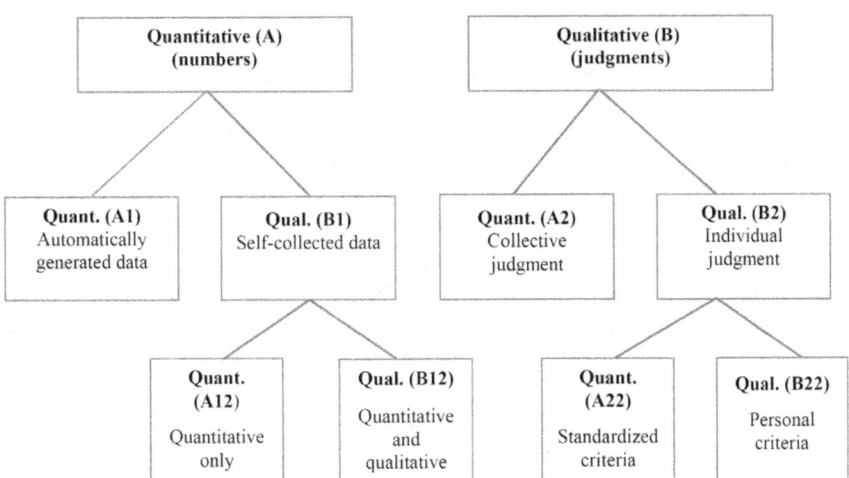

**Figure 12.6** Fractal spectrum of ranking orders © Bettina Heintz.

ten best books). Next, you reiterate this principle on the level below. Again, you obtain a more nuanced picture with a total of eight lists (not all represented in the figure). Take, for example, lists that use self-collected data (B1). Here you can distinguish between lists (A12) that rely on quantitative data only (e.g. the Shanghai university ranking) and lists (B12) that include qualitative data such as expert reviews (e.g. the World Press Freedom ranking or the Social Justice Index). Similarly, lists that rely on qualitative judgements (B2) can be differentiated into lists (A22) where the experts follow standardized procedures (e.g. voting in figure skating) and lists (B22) where the comparative criteria are not determined in advance (e.g. the Booker Prize, the *New York Times* list of the ten best books). The fractal principle could be reiterated for every side and every level, but the example may suffice to draw some conclusions.

First, quantification is neither a precise nor a selective criterion to distinguish between the four formats. It is not precise because the use of numerals and the presentation as a metric scale do not indicate whether the ranking order is *in fact* based on measuring and counting. And it is not selective because the four formats are spread over the whole spectrum. There are rankings that use quantitative data only (e.g. the Shanghai university ranking), rankings that combine quantitative and qualitative information (e.g. most city rankings) and rankings that rely solely on personal judgements (e.g. appointment lists, see above). Even prizes cannot be strictly allocated on the qualitative side. It is true that most prizes are awarded by a jury, but there are also prizes that are conferred on the basis of quantitative data, for instance, the American Music Awards.

Second, the fractal ordering sheds light on the fact that only some ranking orders are quantitative in a strict sense. This is even true for rankings and top lists that are usually interpreted as numerical devices based on measuring or counting. The fact that the numeric appearance of ranking orders is often taken at face value suggests that the *belief* in numbers has increased – but not necessarily quantification per se. Apparently, not only laypersons are prone to be seduced by numbers, but sociologists too; even if numerals do not keep their promises, the mere use of numerals seems to convey objectivity and impersonality. The seductive magic of numbers explains why, for example, the San Pellegrino list of the fifty best restaurants is deemed to be more reliable than restaurants' ratings that do not conceal the subjectivity of their evaluation. And even in the field of art, the success of artist rankings such as the *Kunstkompass* or the *artnet* ranking demonstrates that the trust in experts seems to be superseded by the trust in numbers, however fictitious they may be. This means that at least for the world of ranking orders, the assumption of an ever-growing quantification should be critically examined. It seems that the crucial point is not so much quantification itself, but rather the growing belief and trust in numbers – and that the designers of ranking orders take advantage of this (mis)understanding.

## Interpreting Ranking Orders: Concluding Remarks

In the preceding sections I analysed rankings, ratings, top lists and prizes as variants of the same basic model – the ranking order. While ranking orders are often considered as numerical tools, I have argued that they are first of all comparative devices that may, but need not, be quantified. In the first section I proposed a definition of comparison and distinguished comparisons from other techniques for reducing complexity. Using the difference between a statistical table and a ranking as an illustration, I argued that ranking orders are a special form of comparisons as they not only compare but also evaluate the units compared. After a short overview of the history of ranking orders and their various formats I then turned to the question of the quantitative character of ranking orders. Referring to Abbott's concept of 'fractal distinctions', I showed that quantification is not an accurate concept to understand ranking orders. Their special characteristic lies not in being quantitative, but in their capacity of making things comparable and in their extension to objects or achievements that used to be considered as unique and even incommensurable.

Ranking orders have invaded practically every social field. They have spread into politics, the economy and sports, but they are particularly prominent in domains where quality matters more than quantity – in the realm of the subjective, expressive and (syn)aesthetic. By transposing qualities into a standardized comparative scheme, ranking orders bring properties under their rule that previously have been defined by their unique character: the appeal of a person, the artistic quality of a painting, the taste of a wine. Restaurant ratings compare the taste, harmony and presentation of dishes that can only be judged individually by sensing and tasting them, top lists rank pianists with regard to their musical expressivity, and employees are not only compared and ranked in terms of their measurable achievements, but according to their personal qualities too.

Of course, many ranking orders still evaluate performances whose comparability or measurability is taken for granted – school performances, income or scores in tennis. Yet their most distinctive feature lies in the fact that they make performances comparable that have been considered not only as unmeasurable but also as unique and incommensurable. It is therefore no coincidence that ranking orders predominate in the sphere of cultural production and in domains where quality counts most: in art, literature and science and, more generally, in fields where the assessment of quality is based on personal judgement. How should we compare the literary quality of novels, the empathy of a therapist or the quality of a scientific publication? Of course, novels, therapists and scientific texts are constantly compared, by literary critics, patients or scientific peers, but it is an open question whether the comparison can abstain, as ranking orders do, from the complex qualities that constitute a good novel, a sensitive therapist and an innovative scientific publication.

Theodore M. Porter has shown how and why quantitative methods replaced the personal judgement of experts and were seen as the royal road to achieve objectivity, particularly in politics, the economy and the natural sciences. Ranking orders perform a similar task, but without necessarily being quantitative. Like quantification, they convey the impression of impersonality, even if they are based on highly subjective judgements. Instead of confusing ranking orders with quantification, it therefore seems more appropriate to interpret them as a kind of functional equivalent, i.e. as an alternative way to transmit objectivity. In other words, their novelty lies in the fact that they promise to tame human subjectivity and to replace it with an objective assessment, regardless of whether they are based on counting and measuring or not. It is the mere self-presentation as being quantitative and hence impersonal that gives rise to the belief that ranking orders are able to compare and evaluate the subjective, expressive and aesthetic in an objective manner.

This points to a hidden connection between the quantitative appearance of ranking orders and their dissemination to the sphere of the qualitative. The numerical presentation may function as a kind of camouflage that conceals the gap between the unique and the comparable, the subjective and the impersonal. Indeed, it is an astonishing fact that films of different quality, genres and styles are put into a common ranking scale that is assumed to represent an impersonal judgement, and it is equally astonishing that the quality of scientific texts is considered as reducible to a few standardized dimensions. The extent to which ranking orders are accepted and used as reliable 'judgment devices'[54] indicates how normalized and taken for granted they are.

This also points to the inherently paradoxical character of ranking orders. On the one hand, they fulfil the growing demand for uniqueness and distinctiveness,[55] while on the other hand, they demystify the idea of singularity by interpreting the exceptional as a gradual matter of more or less. To be a 'star', a star has to be beyond comparison, similar to the 'genius' of the eighteenth century, but she loses her shine when she is only gradually better than others. Just because the unique has become so important, instruments are needed to identify its uniqueness and make it publicly visible. But these techniques are fundamentally comparative and thus undermine the claim to be singular.[56]

By their comparative and evaluative format, ranking orders open up new modes of planning and governing, even in domains that have not been considered accessible to political control and regulation.[57] Yet, contrary to the common understanding, I assume that the regulatory use of ranking orders is not so much due to quantification, but rather to the act of comparing, regardless of whether the comparison results in a number or not. From this perspective, ranking orders can be seen as a new 'technique of governmentality' to use a Foucaultian term. The most pertinent aspect of this new technique is the substitution of the classical 'control-and-command model'[58] by a model that works basically through evaluative comparisons – benchmarks, ratings and rankings. Administrative departments are confronted with benchmarks they have to meet, theatres, hospitals and schools are monitored by comparative performance indicators, and employees can only hope for promotion if the human resources department has classified them as 'high potentials'. But the governing power of ranking orders goes much further. For ranking orders not only serve as instruments for external assessment, but as self-disciplinary devices as well. Individuals, organizations and states are not only compared and evaluated by external observers, they observe themselves in the mirror of ranking orders too. By doing so, external governing and self-governing converge: actors are trying to do what they are supposed to do, namely to perform better.

From a Foucaultian perspective, ranking orders are the intersection point between technologies of power and technologies of the self.[59] While in Jeremy Bentham's panopticon the observation was asymmetric and unilateral, with the new technologies, the observation has become both symmetrical and generalized. The asymmetrical control of panopticon-like technologies has been transformed into mutual observation. The knowledge of being publicly compared and evaluated initiates acts of self-discipline that people need not be aware of. Those who are governed tend to align themselves to the expectations set out in the ranking order. There is no longer any need for external command and control. The self-disciplinary effects are not limited to individuals, but affect corporate actors too. In order to improve their position in the ranking, universities offer merit scholarships to attract students with high test scores,[60] states include women's rights in their constitutions if gender equality becomes a global indicator,[61] and firms that are given a poor environmental rating react by reducing their emissions.[62] In other words, the knowledge of being observed evokes a behaviour that Espeland and Sauder described as 'reactivity', meaning that people react to being publicly compared and change their behaviour in the desired ways.[63]

With their focus on the best and their extension into domains that have been considered as beyond the reach of objectification, ranking orders stand for a fundamental cultural transformation. While Nietzsche described his age as an 'age of comparison', our age glorifies the superlative. In contrast to Jürgen Link's model of 'normalism',[64] where the average sets the standard, it is no longer 'l'homme moyen'[65] that serves as reference point, but the extraordinary. Deviation is no longer determined through distance from the 'normal', but through distance from the 'exceptional'. By rewarding the top position, ranking orders convey a worldview that is diametrically opposed to the 'normalistic dispositif' Jürgen Link diagnosed for the twentieth century.[66] Instead of setting the average as the standard, the excellent and exceptional has become the new norm.

**Bettina Heintz** was formerly Professor of Sociological Theory at the University of Mainz, Bielefeld University and the University of Lucerne. She has published numerous books, edited volumes and articles on the history and sociology of mathematics and the computer, global social and gender inequalities, human rights in world society, and the sociology of comparison and quantification. Among her recent publications are: 'Seen But Unnoticed: The Role of Comparisons in Economic Sociology', *Economic Sociology Newsletter* 18 (2017), 9–18 (with

Martin Bühler); and '"Wir leben im Zeitalter der Vergleichung": Perspektiven einer Soziologie des Vergleichs', *Zeitschrift für Soziologie* 45 (2016), 1–19.

## Notes

1. F. Nietzsche, *Human, All Too Human: A Book for Free Spirits*, R.J. Hollingdale (trans.), with an introduction by R. Schacht (Cambridge: Cambridge University Press, 1996), 24.
2. G. Rossman and O. Schilke, 'Close, But No Cigar: The Bimodal Rewards to Prize-Seeking', *American Sociological Review* 79 (2014), 86–108, at 104–5.
3. A terminological remark. Following W.N. Espeland and M.L. Stevens, 'A Sociology of Quantification', *European Journal of Sociology* 49 (2008), 401–36, I distinguish between *numerals* and *numbers*, i.e. between 'numbers that mark' and 'numbers that commensurate' (at 407–8). Like other symbols (e.g. letters or stars), numerals are used for designating and classifying things or people as, for example, car numbers or passport numbers do, but unlike numbers, they do not express quantitative values. This is why numerals can only capture ordinal but not metric relations. With numerals, you can assess that one thing is larger or smaller than the other, but not *how much* larger or smaller it is (see below for more details on this).
4. G. Blank, *Critics, Ratings, and Society: The Sociology of Review* (Lanham, MD: Rowman & Littlefield, 2007).
5. The understanding of comparing as a scientific method goes back to É. Durkheim, *The Rules of Sociological Method* (New York: Free Press, 1982), who considered the comparative method as the cornerstone of sociology: 'Comparative sociology is not a special branch of sociology; it is sociology itself' (at 157).
6. N. Luhmann, 'Kultur als historischer Begriff', in *Gesellschaftsstruktur und Semantik*, vol. 4 (Frankfurt am Main: Suhrkamp, 2005), 31–54; B. Heintz, '"Numerische Differenz": Überlegungen zu einer Soziologie des quantitativen Vergleichs', *Zeitschrift für Soziologie* 39 (2010), 162–81; B. Heintz, '"Wir leben im Zeitalter der Vergleichung": Perspektiven einer Soziologie des Vergleichs', *Zeitschrift für Soziologie* 45 (2016), 305–23; A. Epple and W. Erhart (eds), *Die Welt beobachten: Praktiken des Vergleichens* (Frankfurt am Main: Campus 2015).
7. Heintz, 'Vergleichung', 306–9.
8. For a historical example, see M. Bühler and B. Heintz, 'Seen But Not Noticed: The Role of Comparisons in Economic Sociology', *European Electronic Newsletter* 18 (2017), 9–18.
9. M. Fourcade and K. Healy, 'Categories All the Way Down', *Historical Social Research* 42 (2017), 286–96.
10. For a more general approach, see M. Fourcade, 'Ordinalization: Lewis A. Coser Memorial Award for Theoretical Agenda Setting 2014', *Sociological Theory* 34 (2016), 175–95. Although Fourcade uses a different terminology, her approach comes quite close to the view presented here.
11. For the difference between counting and measuring, see R. Mayntz, 'Zählen – Messen – Entscheiden: Wissen im politischen Prozess', *MPifG Discussion Paper* 17, 2017.
12. W.N. Espeland and M.L. Stevens, 'Commensuration as a Social Process', *Annual Review of Sociology* 24 (1998), 313–43, at 316.
13. See, for example, H.K. Hansen, Numerical Operations, Transparency Illusions, and the Datafictation of Governance', *European Journal of Social Theory* 18 (2015), 203–20; J.

Berten and L. Leisering, 'Social Policy by Numbers: How International Organizations Construct Global Policy Proposals', *International Journal of Social Welfare* 26 (2017), 151–67; R. Rottenburg et al. (eds), *A World of Indicators: The Making of Governmental Knowledge through Quantification* (Cambridge: Cambridge University Press, 2015).
14. See for a similar argument K. Healy, 'By the Numbers', *European Journal of Sociology* 58 (2017), 512–19.
15. C. Zelle, 'Komparatistik und *comparatio* – der Vergleich in der Vergleichenden Literaturwissenschaft: Skizze einer Bestandsaufnahme', *Komparatistik. Jahrbuch der Deutschen Gesellschaft für Allgemeine und Vergleichende Literaturwissenschaft* (2004/2005), 13–33, at 19 (my translation). 'Die Leistung des Vergleichs besteht darin, dass er sowohl die Besonderheit bzw. die Eigenart der jeweiligen Komparata, d.h. das, was sie trennt, als auch ihre Allgemeinheit, d.h. das, was sie verbindet, herausarbeitet'.
16. E. Zerubavel, 'Lumping and Splitting: Notes on Social Classification', *Sociological Forum* 11 (1996), 421–33, at 421–22.
17. Fourcade, 'Ordinalization', 179.
18. R. Koselleck, 'The Historical-Political Semantics of Asymmetric Counterconcepts, in *Futures Past: On the Semantics of Historical Time*, K. Tribe (trans.) (New York: Columbia University Press, 2004), 159–97, at 160.
19. M. Foucault, *The Order of Things: An Archaeology of Human Sciences* (New York: Pantheon Books, 1970). However, the transition was more continuous as Foucault assumes (see the chapter by Michael Eggers in this volume). In science, both methods coexisted for quite a long time, yet in the end, the trend went towards comparative techniques not only in the sciences, but also in the humanities and in the nascent social sciences, eventually leading to Émile Durkheim's famous dictum (see note 5 above).
20. W. Steinmetz, '"Vergleich" – eine begriffsgeschichtliche Skizze', in Epple and Erhart (eds), *Die Welt beobachten*, 85–134.
21. For an example, see the opening quotation by Friedrich Nietzsche.
22. J. Osterhammel, *Die Entzauberung Asiens: Europa und die asiatischen Reiche im 18. Jahrhundert* (Munich: Beck, 1998).
23. L. Behrisch, *Die Berechnung der Glückseligkeit: Statistik und Politik in Deutschland und Frankreich im Ancien Régime* (Ostfildern: Thorbecke, 2016).
24. *United Nations Statistical Yearbook*, 59th issue (2016), Table 10, 103 (extract).
25. Source: United Nations, National Accounts Main Aggregates Database, December 2016. Retrieved 14 March 2019 from https://en.wikipedia.org/wiki/List_of_countries_by_GDP_(nominal)_per_capita.
26. See for the following C. Spoerhase, 'Das Maß der Potsdamer Garde: Die ästhetische Vorgeschichte des Rankings in der europäischen Literatur- und Kunstkritik des 18. Jahrhunderts', *Jahrbuch der Deutschen Schillergesellschaft* 58 (2014), 90–126.
27. From Roger de Piles, *Cours de peinture par principe* (Paris: Jacques Estienne, 1708), n.p. (497), retrieved 14 March 2019 from https://archive.org/details/depeintureparpri00pile/page/n511.
28. C.H. Schmid, *Theorie der Poesie nach den neuesten Grundsätzen und Nachricht von den besten Dichtern nach den angenommenen Urtheilen* (Leipzig 1767), quoted in Spoerhase, 'Potsdamer Garde', 113 (my translation).
29. See e.g. V. Ginsburgh and S. Weyers, 'Evaluer l'Art. Propriétés ou Conventions?', *La Vie des Idées*, 2014, retrieved 14 March 2019 from https://laviedesidees.fr/Evaluer-l-Art-Proprietes-ou.html; A. Klawitter, 'Eine bislang übersehene, "erste Balanz der deutschen Dichter" (1772)', *Deutsche Vierteljahresschrift für Literaturwissenschaft und Geistesgeschichte*

90 (2016), 211–28. And from a critical point of view, see U. Brandes, 'Network Positions', *Methodological Innovations* 9 (2016), 1–19.
30. For the difference between numerals and numbers, see note 3 above.
31. Quoted in Spoerhase, 'Potsdamer Garde', 122–23 (my translation).
32. Behrisch, *Glückseligkeit*; P. Slack, *The Invention of Improvement: Information and Material Progress in Seventeenth-Century England* (Oxford: Oxford University Press, 2015).
33. A. de Candolle, *Histoire des Sciences et des Savants depuis deux Siècles* (Geneva: H. Georg, 1873), 188, retrieved 14 March 2019 from https://archive.org/details/histoiredesscie00candgoog/page/n203.
34. T. Werron, *Der Weltsport und sein Publikum: Zur Autonomie und Entstehung des modernen Sports* (Weilerswist: Velbrück, 2010), 292–94.
35. B.G. Carruthers, 'From Uncertainty toward Risk: The Case of Credit Ratings', *Socio-economic Review* 11 (2013), 525–51.
36. R.E. Streat, 'Lancashire's Cotton Trade with Europe', *Manchester Guardian Commercial*, 15 June 1922, 165–170, at 169. I am very grateful to Martin Bemmann, who provided me with many historical examples of rankings and ratings from the first third of the twentieth century.
37. W.N. Espeland and M. Sauder, *Engines of Anxiety: Academic Rankings, Reputation, and Accountability* (New York: Russell Sage Foundation, 2016), 9–14.
38. B.T. Christensen and J.S. Pedersen, 'Restaurant Rankings in the Culinary Field', in B. Moeran and B.T. Christensen (eds), *Exploring Creativity: Evaluative Practices in Innovation, Design, and the Arts* (Cambridge: Cambridge University Press, 2013), 235–59.
39. N. Anand and R.A. Peterson, 'When Market Information Constitutes Fields: Sensemaking of Markets in the Commercial Music Industry', *Organization Science* 11 (2000), 270–84.
40. P. Roscoe and S. Chillas, 'The State of Affairs: Critical Performativity and the Online Dating Industry', *Organization* 2 (2014), 797–820.
41. As an exception see C. Brandtner, 'Putting the World in Orders: Plurality in Organizational Evaluation', *Sociological Theory* 35 (2017), 200–27.
42. For more details, see B. Heintz, 'Vom Komparativ zum Superlativ: Eine kleine Soziologie der Rangliste', in S. Nicolae et al. (eds), *(Be)Werten: Beiträge zur sozialen Konstruktion von Wertigkeit* (Wiesbaden: Springer VS, 2019), 45–79.
43. For this difference, see also W.N. Espeland and S.E. Lom, 'Noticing Numbers: How Quantification Changes What We See and What We Don't', in M. Kornberger et al. (eds), *Making Things Valuable* (Oxford: Oxford University Press, 2015), 18–31, at 26.
44. See in more detail W.N. Espeland and M. Sauder, 'Rankings and Reactivity: How Public Measures Recreate Social Worlds', *American Journal of Sociology* 113 (2007), 1–40.
45. J.F. English, *The Economy of Prestige: Prize, Awards, and the Circulation of Cultural Value* (Cambridge, MA: Harvard University Press, 2007).
46. R.K. Merton, 'The Matthew Effect in Science', *Science* 159 (1968), 56–63, at 56.
47. M.P. Allen and N.L. Parsons, 'The Institutionalization of Fame: Achievement, Recognition, and Cultural Consecration in Baseball', *American Sociological Review* 71 (2006), 808–25, at 808.
48. A. Abbott, *Chaos of Disciplines* (Chicago: University of Chicago Press, 2001), esp. Chapter 1.
49. Retrieved 14 March 2019 from https://www.erobertparker.com/info/legend.asp (emphasis added).
50. Retrieved 14 March 2019 from http://www.shanghairanking.com/ARWU2017.html.

51. T.M. Porter, *Trust in Numbers: The Pursuit of Objectivity in Science and Public Life* (Princeton: Princeton University Press, 1995), ix.
52. Blank, *Critics*.
53. Abbott, *Chaos*, 13–15.
54. For this concept, see L. Karpik, *Valuing the Unique: The Economics of Singularities* (Princeton: Princeton University Press, 2010), Chapter 5.
55. See A. Reckwitz, *Die Gesellschaft der Singularitäten: Zum Strukturwandel der Moderne* (Frankfurt am Main: Suhrkamp, 2017).
56. For the intricate relationship between comparison and singularization, see also C.A. Heimer, 'Cases and Biographies: An Essay on Routinization and the Nature of Comparison', *Annual Review of Sociology* 27 (2001), 47–76.
57. For science, see e.g. P. Weingart, 'Nostalgia for the World without Numbers', *Soziale Welt* 66 (2015), 243–50; and for culture, see A. Styhre, 'The Economic Valuation and Commensuration of Cultural Resources: Financing and Monitoring the Swedish Culture Sector', *Valuation Studies* 1 (2013), 51–81.
58. M. Schneiberg and T. Bartley, 'Organizations, Regulation, and Economic Behavior: Regulatory Dynamics and Forms from the Nineteenth to the Twenty-First Century', *Annual Review of Law and Social Science* 4 (2008), 31–61.
59. For an overview, see e.g. U. Bröckling, S. Krasmann and T. Lemke (eds), *Governmentality: Current Issues and Future Challenges* (New York: Routledge, 2011); P. Miller and N. Rose, *Governing the Present: Administering Economic, Social and Personal Life* (Cambridge: Polity Press, 2008).
60. Espeland and Sauder, *Engines of Anxiety*, 76–79.
61. B. Heintz and A. Schnabel, 'Verfassungen als Spiegel globaler Normen: Eine quantitative Analyse der Gleichberechtigungsartikel in nationalen Verfassungen', *Kölner Zeitschrift für Soziologie und Sozialpsychologie* 58 (2006), 685–716.
62. A.K. Chatterji and M.W. Toffel, 'How Firms Respond to Being Rated', *Strategic Management Journal* 31 (2010), 917–45. Of course, the effects of ranking orders are not always as straightforward as demonstrated in these studies. For the variance of responses, see Brandtner, 'Putting the World in Orders'.
63. Espeland and Sauder, 'Rankings and Reactivity'.
64. J. Link, *Versuch über den Normalismus: Wie Normalität produziert wird* (Göttingen: Vandenhoeck & Ruprecht, 1997).
65. A. de Quetelet, *Sur l'homme et le développement de ses facultés, ou Essai de physique sociale* (Paris: Bachelet, 1835). For more details, see B. Heintz, 'Welterzeugung durch Zahlen: Modelle politischer Differenzierung in internationalen Statistiken, 1948–2010', in C. Bohn, A. Schubbach and L. Wansleben (eds), *Welterzeugung durch Bilder* (Stuttgart: Lucius & Lucius, 2012), 7–39, at 9–14.
66. Link, *Normalismus*.

# Bibliography

Abbott, A., *Chaos of Disciplines* (Chicago: University of Chicago Press, 2001).
Allen, M.P., and Parsons, N.L., 'The Institutionalization of Fame: Achievement, Recognition, and Cultural Consecration in Baseball', *American Sociological Review* 71 (2006), 808–25.

Anand, N., and Peterson, R.A., 'When Market Information Constitutes Fields: Sensemaking of Markets in the Commercial Music Industry', *Organization Science* 11 (2000), 270–84.

Behrisch, L., *Die Berechnung der Glückseligkeit: Statistik und Politik in Deutschland und Frankreich im Ancien Régime* (Ostfildern: Thorbecke, 2016).

Berten, J., and Leisering, L., 'Social Policy by Numbers: How International Organizations Construct Global Policy Proposals', *International Journal of Social Welfare* 26 (2017), 151–67.

Blank, G., *Critics, Ratings, and Society: The Sociology of Review* (Lanham, MD: Rowman & Littlefield, 2007).

Brandes, U., 'Network Positions', *Methodological Innovations* 9 (2016), 1–19.

Brandtner, C., 'Putting the World in Orders: Plurality in Organizational Evaluation', *Sociological Theory* 35 (2017), 200–27.

Bröckling, U., Krasmann, S. and Lemke, T. (eds), *Governmentality: Current Issues and Future Challenges* (New York: Routledge, 2011).

Bühler, M., and Heintz, B., 'Seen But Not Noticed: The Role of Comparisons in Economic Sociology', *European Electronic Newsletter* 18 (2017), 9–18.

Candolle, A. de, *Histoire des Sciences et des Savants depuis deux Siècles* (Geneva: H. Georg, 1873).

Carruthers, B.G., 'From Uncertainty toward Risk: The Case of Credit Ratings', *Socio-economic Review* 11 (2013), 525–51.

Chatterji, A.K., and Toffel, M.W., 'How Firms Respond to Being Rated', *Strategic Management Journal* 31 (2010), 917–45.

Christensen, B.T., and Pedersen, J.S., 'Restaurant Rankings in the Culinary Field', in Moeran, B. and Christensen, B.T. (eds), *Exploring Creativity: Evaluative Practices in Innovation, Design, and the Arts* (Cambridge: Cambridge University Press, 2013), 235–59.

Durkheim, É., *The Rules of Sociological Method* (New York: Free Press, 1982).

English, J.F., *The Economy of Prestige: Prize, Awards, and the Circulation of Cultural Value* (Cambridge, MA: Harvard University Press, 2007).

Epple, A., and Erhart, W. (eds), *Die Welt beobachten: Praktiken des Vergleichens* (Frankfurt am Main: Campus 2015).

Espeland, W.N., and Lom, S.E., 'Noticing Numbers: How Quantification Changes What We See and What We Don't', in Kornberger, M. et al. (eds), *Making Things Valuable* (Oxford: Oxford University Press, 2015), 18–31.

Espeland, W.N., and Sauder, M., 'Rankings and Reactivity: How Public Measures Recreate Social Worlds', *American Journal of Sociology* 113 (2007), 1–40.

———. *Engines of Anxiety: Academic Rankings, Reputation, and Accountability* (New York: Russell Sage Foundation, 2016).

Espeland, W.N., and Stevens, M.L., 'Commensuration as a Social Process', *Annual Review of Sociology* 24 (1998), 313–43.

———. 'A Sociology of Quantification', *European Journal of Sociology* 49 (2008), 401–36.

Foucault, M., *The Order of Things: An Archaeology of Human Sciences* (New York: Pantheon Books, 1970).

Fourcade, M., 'Ordinalization: Lewis A. Coser Memorial Award for Theoretical Agenda Setting 2014', *Sociological Theory* 34 (2016), 175–95.

Fourcade, M., and Healy, K., 'Categories All the Way Down', *Historical Social Research* 42 (2017), 286–96.

Ginsburgh, V., and Weyers, S., 'Evaluer l'Art. Propriétés ou Conventions?', *La Vie des Idées* (2014), retrieved 14 March 2019 from https://laviedesidees.fr/Evaluer-l-Art-Proprietes-ou.html.

Hansen, H.K., Numerical Operations, Transparency Illusions, and the Datafictation of Governance', *European Journal of Social Theory* 18 (2015), 203–20.

Healy, K., 'By the Numbers', *European Journal of Sociology* 58 (2017), 512–19.

Heimer, C.A., 'Cases and Biographies: An Essay on Routinization and the Nature of Comparison', *Annual Review of Sociology* 27 (2001), 47–76.

Heintz, B., '"Numerische Differenz": Überlegungen zu einer Soziologie des quantitativen Vergleichs', *Zeitschrift für Soziologie* 39 (2010), 162–81.

———. 'Welterzeugung durch Zahlen: Modelle politischer Differenzierung in internationalen Statistiken, 1948–2010', in Bohn, C., Schubbach, A. and Wansleben, L. (eds), *Welterzeugung durch Bilder* (Stuttgart: Lucius & Lucius, 2012), 7–39.

———. '"Wir leben im Zeitalter der Vergleichung": Perspektiven einer Soziologie des Vergleichs', *Zeitschrift für Soziologie* 45 (2016), 305–23.

———. 'Vom Komparativ zum Superlativ: Eine kleine Soziologie der Rangliste', in Nicolae, S. et al. (eds), *(Be)Werten: Beiträge zur sozialen Konstruktion von Wertigkeit* (Wiesbaden: Springer VS, 2019), 45–79.

Heintz, B., and Schnabel, A., 'Verfassungen als Spiegel globaler Normen: Eine quantitative Analyse der Gleichberechtigungsartikel in nationalen Verfassungen', *Kölner Zeitschrift für Soziologie und Sozialpsychologie* 58 (2006), 685–716.

Karpik, L., *Valuing the Unique: The Economics of Singularities* (Princeton: Princeton University Press, 2010).

Klawitter, A., 'Eine bislang übersehene, "erste Balanz der deutschen Dichter" (1772)', *Deutsche Vierteljahresschrift für Literaturwissenschaft und Geistesgeschichte* 90 (2016), 211–28.

Koselleck, R., 'The Historical-Political Semantics of Asymmetric Counterconcepts', in Koselleck, R., *Futures Past: On the Semantics of Historical Time*, Tribe, K. (trans.) (New York: Columbia University Press, 2004), 159–97.

Link, J., *Versuch über den Normalismus: Wie Normalität produziert wird* (Göttingen: Vandenhoeck & Ruprecht, 1997).

Luhmann, N., 'Kultur als historischer Begriff', in *Gesellschaftsstruktur und Semantik*, vol. 4 (Frankfurt am Main: Suhrkamp, 2005), 31–54.

Mayntz, R., 'Zählen – Messen – Entscheiden: Wissen im politischen Prozess', *MPifG Discussion Paper* 17, 2017.

Merton, R.K., 'The Matthew Effect in Science', *Science* 159 (1968), 56–63.

Miller, P., and Rose, N., *Governing the Present: Administering Economic, Social and Personal Life* (Cambridge: Polity Press, 2008).

Nietzsche, F., *Human, All Too Human: A Book for Free Spirits*, Hollingdale, R.J. (trans.), with an introduction by Schacht, R. (Cambridge: Cambridge University Press, 1996).

Osterhammel, J., *Die Entzauberung Asiens: Europa und die asiatischen Reiche im 18. Jahrhundert* (Munich: Beck, 1998).

Porter, T.M., *Trust in Numbers: The Pursuit of Objectivity in Science and Public Life* (Princeton: Princeton University Press, 1995).

Quetelet, A. de, *Sur l'homme et le développement de ses facultés, ou Essai de physique sociale* (Paris: Bachelet, 1835).

Reckwitz, A., *Die Gesellschaft der Singularitäten: Zum Strukturwandel der Moderne* (Frankfurt am Main: Suhrkamp, 2017).

Roscoe, P., and Chillas, S., 'The State of Affairs: Critical Performativity and the Online Dating Industry', *Organization* 2 (2014), 797–820.

Rossman, G., and Schilke, O., 'Close, But No Cigar: The Bimodal Rewards to Prize-Seeking', *American Sociological Review* 79 (2014), 86–108.

Rottenburg, R. et al. (eds), *A World of Indicators: The Making of Governmental Knowledge through Quantification* (Cambridge: Cambridge University Press, 2015).

Schneiberg, M., and Bartley, T., 'Organizations, Regulation, and Economic Behavior: Regulatory Dynamics and Forms from the Nineteenth to the Twenty-First Century', *Annual Review of Law and Social Science* 4 (2008), 31–61.

Slack, P., *The Invention of Improvement: Information and Material Progress in Seventeenth-Century England* (Oxford: Oxford University Press, 2015).

Spoerhase, C., 'Das Maß der Potsdamer Garde: Die ästhetische Vorgeschichte des Rankings in der europäischen Literatur- und Kunstkritik des 18. Jahrhunderts', *Jahrbuch der Deutschen Schillergesellschaft* 58 (2014), 90–126.

Steinmetz, W., '"Vergleich" – eine begriffsgeschichtliche Skizze', in Epple, A. and Erhart, W. (eds), *Die Welt beobachten: Praktiken des Vergleichens* (Frankfurt am Main: Campus 2015), 85–134.

Streat, R.E., 'Lancashire's Cotton Trade with Europe', *Manchester Guardian Commercial*, 15 June 1922, 165–170.

Styhre, A., 'The Economic Valuation and Commensuration of Cultural Resources: Financing and Monitoring the Swedish Culture Sector', *Valuation Studies* 1 (2013), 51–81.

*United Nations Statistical Yearbook*, 59th issue (2016).

Weingart, P., 'Nostalgia for the World without Numbers', *Soziale Welt* 66 (2015), 243–50.

Werron, T., *Der Weltsport und sein Publikum: Zur Autonomie und Entstehung des modernen Sports* (Weilerswist: Velbrück, 2010).

Zelle, C., 'Komparatistik und *comparatio* – der Vergleich in der Vergleichenden Literaturwissenschaft: Skizze einer Bestandsaufnahme', *Komparatistik. Jahrbuch der Deutschen Gesellschaft für Allgemeine und Vergleichende Literaturwissenschaft* (2004/2005), 13–33.

Zerubavel, E., 'Lumping and Splitting: Notes on Social Classification', *Sociological Forum* 11 (1996), 421–33.

# Index

Abbott, Andrew, 22, 192, 319–20, 323
abstraction, 7, 17, 35, 40, 55, 67, 88, 101, 117, 124, 168, 221, 278, 289–90, 292, 294–95, 304n18, 309
academia, 5, 20, 33–34, 41, 44, 53, 59–60, 82, 139, 146, 154, 167, 168, 215, 231, 245, 247, 270, 276–80, 281n9, 293–303, 308. *See also* education: higher *and* university
*Académie française*, 83, 318
academies of sciences, 43, 315
Acosta, José de, 144–48, 153–54, 158n29, 159n48
administration, 1, 123, 165, 174, 196, 198, 203, 215, 224, 230, 243, 252, 269, 274–75, 294, 297, 298–302, 316, 324. *See also* bureaucracy
advertising, marketing, 213, 274, 294, 298, 300
aesthetics, 7–8, 19, 38–40, 45n31–32, 46n36, 84, 99, 287–90, 305, 311, 321–22
Africa, 147, 150, 152, 163–64, 167–70, 182n40, 246–47, 298
agriculture, 48n39, 204, 216, 218, 227, 266, 277, 283n50
Algeria, 166, 170, 173, 176, 182n44
algorithms, 301, 316, 321
alterity studies, 137, 140–43, 148, 154, 155n2, 159n47
American Revolution, 14, 115, 121–22, 124–26, 133n81–82, 139, 151–52, 160n64
Americas, 5, 8, 89, 100, 126, 134n87, 137–63, 166, 170, 172, 174, 177, 201, 246–47, 272

analogy, 9–10, 21, 34–37, 40, 42–45, 48n47, 49n56, 105, 115, 128n10, 145, 149, 290, 307, 309–10
anatomy, 10, 43–44, 48n47
anthropology, 6–8, 10, 12, 24n11, 42–44, 80–81, 193, 233
anti-imperialism. *See under* imperialism
antiquity, 9, 33, 37, 45, 64, 106n13, 114, 117, 121–22, 127n4, 132n54, 132n56, 134n85, 138–40, 145, 147–48, 150–54, 165, 169, 177, 178n6
aristocracy, 13, 92, 102, 119–20, 123, 145, 216–19, 222–24, 227, 231
Aristotle, 37, 144–45, 158n29, 159n52
art, 3, 5, 9–10, 42, 47n31, 48n39, 59–61, 64–66, 69–70, 74n37, 81, 89, 91–93, 95, 102, 147, 153, 288, 290, 302, 306, 313, 322–23
  history, 10, 17, 26n31, 59–60, 70, 89
Asia, 154, 218, 233, 246–47, 272, 298
Atlantic Ocean, 138, 143, 158–59n36
Australia, 201, 203, 270–71, 308
Austria, 119, 166–67, 201–2
awards. *See* prizes
Aztec Empire, 150

backwardness, 4, 16–17, 96–97, 100, 150, 192, 200. *See also* progress
Baldwin, Peter, 192, 204
Balzac, Honoré de, 9
Baumgarten, Alexander Gottlieb, 33, 40–41, 47n31–32
Belgium, 165, 170, 173, 183–84n77, 196, 202, 249
Bentham, Jeremy, 168, 325
Berlin, 143, 147, 156n9, 198, 248, 315
Bertillon, Jacques, 270, 276

Bhabha, Homi, 137, 157n17
biology, 10, 42, 44, 154, 222
biopolitics, 18, 193, 215
Bismarck, Otto von, 16, 171
Black Legend. *See Leyenda Negra*
Board of Trade (UK), 247–48
Bodin, Jean, 113
Boer Wars, 167, 176
Bohemian rebellion, 115, 125
Bordeaux, 120–21, 125–26, 131n49, 131n51
Bougainville, Louis-Antoine de, 139
Bourdieu, Pierre, 55
bourgeoisie, 92, 102–3, 219, 221–22, 225, 229, 231. *See also* proletariat
Brazil, 143, 196
Britain, 9, 15–16, 19, 89, 93, 101, 109n60, 115, 122–26, 127n3, 133n66, 133n69, 133–34n83, 134n87, 165–77, 182n52, 192, 194–204, 215, 220, 247–49, 252, 258n32, 258n36, 269–71, 277, 280. *See also* United Kingdom (UK)
British Empire, 9, 165–67. 168–69, 171, 174–76, 269
Brooke, James, Rajah of Sarawak, 170, 176, 183n56
Brussels, 247
Buffon, Georges-Louis Leclerc, Comte de, 139, 150–51, 153
Burdach, Karl Friedrich, 43
bureaucracy, 8, 13, 16, 18, 166, 174, 195–96, 223–24, 226, 230, 300, 302. *See also* administration
Burke, Kenneth, 20, 288, 290–92, 294

Calcutta, 273, 276
Calvinism, 116, 128n19, 130n37
Cambridge (UK), 194, 280, 320
Canada, 173, 196, 203, 247, 250, 275, 280
Candolle, Alphonse de, 315
capitalism, 93, 102, 140, 192, 194, 214–16, 221–31, 295
Carus, Carl Gustav, 43
categorization, 5–9, 17–18, 20–21, 23, 40, 54, 57, 80, 88, 144, 157n20, 167–69, 171, 174–75, 242, 269–70, 274, 290, 295–98, 308–10, 317. *See also* classification
Catholic Church, 116, 200, 310
centralization/decentralization, 122, 173, 176–77, 192, 201, 203, 230–31

centre/periphery, 267–69, 270, 275, 280
centres of calculation, 20, 266–71, 277, 280, 281n7
Chakrabarty, Dipesh, 4
Chamberlain, Joseph, 203
Charles I (England), 119–20, 130n36
Chicago School (economics), 229–32, 238n68
Child, Josiah, 218
China, 1–2, 21, 165, 182n52, 196, 226, 252, 254, 269, 273, 278–79, 300
Chodowiecki, Daniel, 91–93, 104
Christianity, 6, 144–46, 150, 153, 158n28, 228
civilization, 3, 8, 94, 105, 192–93, 196, 219, 274, 310
  concept of, 6, 15, 196, 199–202
Clark, Colin, 277–79
class, 15, 81–83, 100–1, 105, 149, 167, 194, 201, 215, 221, 231, 299, 308, 317. *See also* workers, working class
classification, 9–10, 21–23, 33, 38, 40–41, 44, 104, 144–46, 149, 151–52, 154, 175, 200, 250, 270, 276, 293, 295–97, 307–10, 324, 326n3. *See also* categorization
systems, 21, 38, 43, 309–10
Clavijero, Francisco Javier, 139, 150–51, 156n7
climate, 137, 144, 146–47, 149–51, 153
Coase, Ronald, 230–31
Cold War, 193
collectivization, 215, 222, 225–26
colonialism, 6, 8–9, 15, 19, 89, 121, 126, 137–38, 140, 144–46, 148, 150, 164–184, 196, 200, 202–4, 269, 274. *See also* decolonization *and* imperialism *and* postcolonial studies
Columbus, Christopher, 137, 143, 155n1
commensurability/in-/noncommensurability, 4–6, 15, 23, 58, 72n17, 323
commensuration, 5, 17–18, 21, 292, 295, 309, 326n3
commercial society, 217, 219, 220
commonality, 141, 151, 217, 308–9
Commonwealth of England, 114, 118–19, 121, 125–26, 130n33
communism, 221–22, 224, 226, 228, 310
comparability/incomparability, 2, 5–6, 15–20, 22, 42, 54, 57–58, 67, 69, 93–95, 99, 104, 108n36, 120, 129n26, 142,

Index

145, 160n65, 169, 229, 242–44, 246–51, 253–54, 270, 274, 276, 278, 280, 308, 313, 323–24
*comparata.* See under comparison, comparative
comparison, comparative, *passim*
  comparata, 2, 6–9, 17–18, 23, 53–54, 56–59, 67, 70, 138–39, 141–43, 145–46, 152–55, 157n18, 242, 306, 308–11, 323
  concept of, 4–5, 8, 22–23, 33–34, 36, 43, 100, 125, 310–11
  criticism of, 2–10, 22, 34, 39–42, 54–55, 70, 83–84, 93–95, 145
  defence of, 2–7, 10, 217–20, 228–29
  effects of, 1, 4–5, 9–10, 12, 18–21, 23, 36, 54–55, 57–60, 81, 94, 102, 122, 143, 153–54, 221, 227, 292, 298–303, 317
  evaluative, 8, 14, 21, 42, 56–57, 80, 95, 100–1, 140, 144, 146, 153–55, 302, 306–13, 317–18, 321–25
  formalized, 215, 288–304
  functions of, 9, 11–12, 33, 36, 44, 58, 60, 66–67, 105, 139, 154, 164–65, 192–93, 198, 202, 310, 324
  illicit, 13, 82–84, 98
  meta-/second-order, 7, 9, 146, 153, 155, 159n39, 160n65, 164
  methodology of, 2, 4–5, 9–11, 23, 33–38, 41, 43–45, 49n56, 59–61, 70, 154, 193, 204, 307, 317–19
  numerical, 17–19, 72n14, 151, 266, 268, 273, 280, 291, 307, 314, 322–24
  politics of, 8, 12, 18, 53, 143, 204–5, 323–25
  practices of, doing of, 1–5, 8–14, 18, 22–23, 27n54, 41, 53–60, 66, 70, 80–85, 91, 100–2, 104, 137–43, 145, 148, 150, 152–54, 157n18, 159n39, 307, 310, 315
  temporal, 4, 6, 14, 16, 19, 21, 23, 89, 93, 96–97, 100, 104, 242, 310–11 (see also temporalization and time)
  tertium comparationis, 7–9, 15, 34, 53–54, 57–58, 141–43, 145–46, 153–55, 160n65, 242, 308
competition, 13, 22, 80, 82, 93, 100–1, 103, 122, 146, 165–66, 198, 200, 244, 248, 254, 269, 275–77, 294, 297–302. *See also* rivalry

and comparison, 1–2, 9, 11–16, 22–23, 26n33–34, 48n39, 80, 89, 91, 93–97, 100–1, 103–4, 164, 166, 175–76, 197, 204–5, 214–238, 244, 292, 297–303, 307, 317–18
concept of, 217–20
neoliberal, 13, 215–16, 231–34
socialist (*see* emulation: socialist)
computer, 57, 271, 291, 293–94
Comte, Auguste, 44
conceptual history, 23, 36, 140, 192, 201, 260–61n75, 310
Condillac, Étienne Bonnot de, 33, 37–39, 43
conferences, congresses, 8, 15–16, 19–20, 192–93, 195–98, 201, 205, 225, 247–52, 266–84
  of experts (*see under* experts)
  statistical (*see under* statistics, statistical)
Congo, 173, 175
congruence, 53–54, 57, 67, 69
connoisseurship, 10, 21, 55, 60, 66–69, 91–93, 307, 320
conservatism, 120, 124, 126, 170, 201–3, 219, 223, 230
consumerism, 1, 101, 215, 217–18, 220–21, 223, 226, 237n48, 254, 293, 295, 301, 311
copying, 10, 55, 60–61, 64–66, 73n27, 123, 225
corporatism, 198, 228
corruption, 1–2, 39, 54, 92, 116, 129n26, 175
Costa Rica, 273
counterconcepts, 21, 146. *See also* dichotomies
counting, 17–18, 22, 222, 279, 300, 306–7, 309, 314, 318, 321–22, 324, 326n11
credit rating agencies, 2, 306, 315–17
Crimean War, 97
crises, 19–20, 83–84, 96–97, 113–14, 137, 217, 223, 228–29, 233–34, 243–44, 253–54, 274
Crombie, Alistair, 45, 49n56
Cromwell, Oliver, 118
crossed history. *See Histoire croisée*
Cuba, 140, 152
culture, cultural, 4, 6–8, 11–12, 14–15, 18, 37, 39, 42–44, 53, 55, 57, 59, 99–100, 117, 119, 125, 138–39, 145, 150, 152–54, 164, 166, 170–71, 197,

201, 203, 209n47, 215, 223–24, 227, 237n59, 267, 279, 283n50, 291, 295, 304n18, 310–11, 319, 323, 325
concept of, 24n13, 199–202
history, 140, 267
Cuvier, Georges, 43–44, 49n52
Cuzco, 145, 154
Czechoslovakia, 19, 251, 271

Darwin, Charles, 15, 44
Darwinism, 101, 222, 224
data, 2, 17, 19–20, 38, 57, 59, 243, 245–46, 253–54, 267–68, 270, 275, 277–80, 291, 293, 300, 302, 311, 318, 321–22
decolonization, 165, 242. *See also* colonialism *and* postcolonial studies
degeneration, 139, 148, 150–54, 227
democracy, democratization, 123, 131n49, 160n67, 194, 220–21, 224–25, 242
depoliticization. *See* politicization/depoliticization
Descartes, René, 9, 33–37, 40
despotism, 124, 166
Desrosières, Alain, 267, 269
development, 1, 4, 18, 21, 37, 39, 44, 49n56, 57, 95–96, 99–100, 102, 120, 141, 150–53, 159n39, 165, 172–73, 175, 191–92, 194, 200–1, 204, 221, 224, 228, 230, 233–34, 242–43, 246, 251–53, 266–67, 271, 277, 279–80, 293, 307. *See also* evolution
dichotomies, 21, 138, 140–42, 148, 151, 155, 307, 310, 321. *See also* counterconcepts
dictionaries, 83, 146, 150, 217. *See also* encyclopaedias
Diderot, Denis, 139, 149–50, 153
difference, 6–7, 9, 13–18, 21–22, 27n57, 33, 36, 38–40, 44–45, 46n12, 48n39, 49n56, 53–54, 58, 60–61, 64–67, 72n9, 80–82, 84–88, 92–97, 99, 102, 104, 114, 116–117, 119, 122–23, 125, 132n62, 132n65, 138, 140–43, 145–49, 151, 153–55, 158n26, 160n61, 166, 169–70, 173, 175, 192–93, 195–97, 202, 204–5, 214, 216–19, 226, 232, 242, 245, 247, 250, 268, 270, 274, 279, 288, 294–96, 304n18, 308–11, 316–20, 323. *See also* similarity
Dilke, Charles, 174

diplomacy, 164, 169–70, 175, 179n13, 268, 270, 277
Dürer, Albrecht, 66
Durkheim, Émile, 44, 193, 195, 290, 303n5, 326n5, 327n19
Dutch Republic. *See* Netherlands
Dutch Revolt, 14, 114–17, 119, 122, 125
Dvořák, Antonín, 152

early modern period, 6, 10, 13–14, 24n12, 84, 106n13, 113–15, 120, 124–26, 127n4
Econometric Society, 272, 275, 278
economics, economic, 9, 11–13, 19–20, 100, 138, 168, 203, 220–23, 226–28, 230–31, 243–45, 251, 253, 267, 272–73, 278–80, 289, 295, 304n18
neoclassical, 220, 230, 232
statistics (*see under* statistics, statistical)
economy, 13, 15–16, 19–20, 53, 59, 91, 93, 100–2, 116, 138, 140, 150, 192–94, 197, 200–5, 215–18, 220–30, 232–34, 242–46, 250, 252–54, 261n76, 268, 273–74, 277–80, 299, 311, 323–24
global, international, 243–44, 246–47, 253–54, 274
national, 18, 193, 253–54, 269, 280
world, 244, 246, 253–54, 260–61n75
education, 13, 15, 21, 43, 88, 94, 96, 100, 103, 191, 193–95, 220, 231, 266, 277, 283n50, 307
higher, 12, 21, 215, 231 285–304, 310 (*see also* academia *and* university)
elites, elitism, 97, 120, 131n49, 167, 220, 223, 227, 231, 234, 294, 298, 318
emotions, 1–2, 20, 22, 80–81, 94, 104, 205, 290, 292, 295
emulation, 11, 15, 86, 88–89, 91, 93–94, 97, 101, 121, 165, 176, 191, 198, 200, 203–4, 214–16, 221, 224, 293
socialist, 13, 214–16, 224–26, 231
encyclopaedias, 82–83, 146–47, 150. *See also* dictionaries
England, 2–4, 13–14, 84–86, 100, 102, 107n28, 115, 117–20, 123–26, 128n10, 130n35, 133n69, 133n80, 138, 171, 174–76, 183n73, 183–84n77, 197, 200–3, 218, 221, 293
English Revolution, 14–15, 115, 117–22, 125–26, 130n37

Index

Enlightenment, 34, 36, 39, 45, 94, 139, 146, 148, 150–51, 153–54, 158–59n36
entangled history, 8, 138, 140–41, 157n18. *See also Histoire croisée*, crossed history
entrepreneur, 216–17, 222–24, 227–28, 230–31, 234
envy, 1–2, 11, 39, 80, 85, 100–3, 214, 218–19, 222. *See also* jealousy
epistemology, 8–9, 18, 33–34, 36, 38–40, 43–44, 70, 266
equality/inequality, 2–3, 35, 39, 53–54, 82–84, 86, 88–89, 92, 94, 103–4, 139, 141, 145, 151, 194, 215, 221–22, 244, 294, 302, 325
equivalence, 8, 88, 295, 324
Erhard, Ludwig, 228
Esping-Andersen, Gøsta, 191–92, 194
estate, 81–83, 85–86, 88, 92, 99, 115, 117, 119, 123–24, 126, 133n69
Eurocentrism, 6, 144
Europe, 4–6, 8–9, 13, 16, 18, 23, 24n12, 42, 84, 92, 94, 100, 106n13, 117, 121, 137–41, 143–46, 148–55, 154, 156n9, 160n69, 164–77, 192–93, 196, 200, 204–5, 217–18, 221, 246–47, 250, 269, 272, 293
  Central, 120, 251
  continental, 2, 9, 14, 84–85, 89, 168, 175–77, 193, 202
  Eastern, 154, 200, 251, 254
  Western, 4, 83, 120, 128n9, 154, 200–1, 204, 218
evolution, 4, 39, 44, 222, 268. *See also* development
exceptionalism, 15, 94, 143, 152, 160n67, 164, 167–68, 172, 175–76, 324–25
exhibitions, 10, 15, 195, 197
experts, 16, 19–20, 60, 64–66, 139, 192, 196–98, 219, 225, 230, 250–52, 266–84, 295, 304n12, 320–23
  conferences/congresses of, 15–16, 19, 20, 192, 198, 205, 266–84
  networks of, 18, 195, 197, 201, 246, 253, 266–84

Far East, 150, 166, 169
federalism, 15, 118, 121–22, 132n60
fetishism, fetishization, 109n60, 193, 226, 296
Finland, 191, 293

First World War, 19–20, 27n53, 197, 199–201, 208n43, 217, 243, 245–47, 249, 253, 260n75
Florence, 102, 143
Florida, 137, 149, 279
football, 11, 292–93, 315
Fortescue, John (c. 1395–c. 1477), 2–4, 14
Foucault, Michel, 9–10, 34–35, 37, 43–45, 215–16, 229, 231, 293, 310, 324–25, 327n19
Fourcade, Marion, 304n18, 308, 310, 326n10
France, 3, 14–15, 18, 43–44, 83–85, 115–16, 119–25, 131n51, 132n57, 133n83, 138, 147, 152, 165–68, 169–76, 182n40, 182n44, 183n73, 191, 196–98, 200–4, 218, 221, 233, 249, 269–70, 298, 304n12, 313, 315
Franklin, Benjamin, 121, 151
free trade, 220, 222, 269
French Revolution, 14–15, 43, 115, 122–26, 196, 269
Friedman, Milton, 229–30
*Fronde*, 15, 115, 119–21, 125–26, 131n46, 131n49
Furetière, Antoine, 83
Füssli, Johann Caspar, 64
generalization, 16, 146–47, 268–69, 325

Geneva, 116, 246–49, 252, 272–73
genius, 93, 95, 108n34, 173–75, 313, 324
Genoa, 102, 247, 251
Geoffroy Saint-Hilaire, Étienne, 43–44
geography, 5, 115, 122, 125, 154, 164, 243, 246, 254, 269, 279, 289, 310
Gérando, Joseph-Marie de, 43
Gerbi, Antonello, 153, 155n3
Germany, 16, 18, 28n69, 41–43, 81, 85, 88, 91, 94, 99–100, 102, 107n28, 108n34, 109n51, 116, 121, 128n10, 132n56, 132n58, 138, 144, 147, 165–66, 170–72, 174–76, 182n39–40, 183n58, 192, 194–204, 208n43, 217, 228, 245, 247–49, 260n75, 267–69, 271, 281n9, 308, 310, 313, 316
Ghent, 115–116, 128n19, 129n22, 202
Giddens, Anthony, 55, 59, 157n19
Gilpin, William, 64
global history, 158n36, 164, 178n4, 266, 270
Global South, 274, 303
globalization, 18–20, 244, 253, 290

Goethe, Johann Wolfgang von, 10, 55, 59–70, 72n23, 73n29, 74n33, 151–52
Goffman, Erving, 291
Goncharov, Ivan, 97, 100, 105
governmentality, 215–16, 234, 324
governments, 1–2, 8, 13–16, 19–20, 113, 115, 118–19, 121–22, 125–26, 127n4, 129n29, 130n34, 132–33n65–66, 139, 147, 165–66, 168, 172–77, 183n57, 194, 196–97, 199, 228, 230–31, 244, 246–54, 258n36, 267, 269, 271–77, 279–80, 296–97, 300
Greece, 49n56, 132n54, 140, 145, 148, 154, 165
Gross Domestic Product (GDP)/Gross National Product (GNP), 18, 191, 253, 255n6, 278–80, 311

*habitus*, 56, 59
Hamilton, Alexander, 121, 151
Harnack, Adolf von, 60
Harrington, James (1611–77), 118, 130–31n40, 133n67
Hayek, Friedrich August von, 223, 227, 229
Hazlitt, William (1778–1830), 3–4
Hegel, Georg Friedrich Wilhelm, 139, 229
Hembyze, Jan van, 116–17
Henry VIII, 84
Herder, Johann Gottfried, 42–43, 48n39
hermeneutics, 60
heuristics, 22, 56, 289
hierarchy, 20–21, 40, 47n22, 82–84, 86, 88, 99, 123, 146, 152–53, 155, 160n69, 218–19, 226, 230, 290, 293–94, 302, 309
higher education. *See under* education
Hildebrand, Bruno, 269
*Histoire croisée*, crossed history, 8–9, 25n20. *See also* entangled history
history, 3–5, 7, 11–12, 16, 18, 22–23, 33–34, 37, 39, 43, 45, 70, 83, 119, 121, 137–39, 141, 143–45, 150, 153, 164–70, 172, 175, 177, 191–92, 204–5, 215, 242–43, 266–69, 271, 289, 307, 310, 315, 320–21
  art (*see under* art)
  conceptual (*see* conceptual history)
  cultural (*see under* culture, cultural)
  global (*see* global history)
  intellectual, 45, 105n7, 113, 176, 215
  natural (*see* natural history)
  political (*see under* politics, political)

transnational, 18, 140, 164, 171, 195, 201
world, 23, 254, 271, 279
Hobbes, Thomas, 80–81, 218
Hogarth, William, 89–91, 93, 104, 107n26
Horace, 10
humanities, 2, 4–6, 10–11, 23, 26n31, 45, 137, 298, 302, 318, 327n19
Humboldt, Alexander von, 139, 151–52, 155n1, 160n65
Humboldt, Wilhelm von, 43
Hume, David, 139, 147, 150, 153–54, 219

iconology, 17, 60
identity, 9, 46n12, 59, 70, 95, 138, 141, 168, 244, 251, 254, 276, 296, 299
ideology, 164, 166, 215–16, 226, 228–29, 234, 274
images, 10, 17–18, 22, 38, 40, 55, 58, 60–61, 64, 66–70, 75n43, 82, 86, 89–92, 104, 115, 119, 152, 166
immeasurability. *See* measurability/immeasurability
imperialism, 3–6, 8–9, 11, 14–16, 117, 121, 164–84, 197, 199, 201, 203, 222, 224, 242, 269, 280. *See also* colonialism
  anti-, 166, 176–77, 180n21, 184n81
Inca Empire, 138, 140, 145, 152
incommensurability. *See* commensurability/in-/noncommensurability
incomparability. *See* comparability/incomparability
India, 19, 170, 248, 250–52, 254, 269, 273, 278
indicators, 17–20, 22, 101, 231, 253, 298, 309, 311, 315–16, 324–25
indices, 1, 20–21, 142, 244, 252, 322
individualism, individuality, 22–23, 40, 55, 82, 93–97, 99–100, 102–5, 221–22, 226, 228–30
industrialization, 100–1, 192, 222, 224–25, 227, 278, 280
inequality. *See* equality/inequality
insurance, 2, 16, 192–93, 195–99, 201–4, 208n43
intellectuals, 11, 43, 45, 164, 168, 170, 176, 289. *See also* history: intellectual
International Association for Research in Income and Wealth (IARIW), 272, 275, 279
International Biometric Society, 272

Index

International Chamber of Commerce (ICC), 248
International Congresses on Accidents at Work (ICAW), 195–98, 201
International Convention Relating to Economic Statistics (1928), 248, 252–53
internationalism, 244, 246–47, 270–71, 282n28
International Labour Organization (ILO), 16, 19, 27n54, 247, 249–51, 270, 272, 282n27, 283n50
International Monetary Fund, 20, 280
international organizations, 19, 244–45, 249, 253, 266, 269, 271, 275–76, 278–79, 296
International Statistical Institute (ISI), 20, 267, 270–72, 275–77
International Union for the Scientific Study of Population Problems, 272, 275
internet, 1, 22, 81, 280, 296
interventionism, 167, 176, 201–2, 227, 229
interwar period, 19–20, 228, 253, 270–71
Ireland, 129n27, 167, 200
Italy, 10, 16, 26n30, 65, 73n29, 155n3, 165, 192, 196, 201, 203–4, 249

Jakob, Ludwig Heinrich von, 269
Japan, 165, 200, 228, 249, 252, 259n56, 293
jealousy, 39, 94, 171, 219. *See also* envy
Jefferson, Thomas, 132n64, 139, 151–52, 154
Jesuits, 145
Jevons, William Stanley, 220–22, 229
Johnson, Samuel, 217
journalism, 169, 228, 246, 304n12. *See also* press
Judaism, 102, 149
judgement, 3–4, 11, 21–22, 36–37, 41–42, 44, 54, 90, 93, 116, 121, 132n64, 145, 150, 166, 201, 230, 247, 308, 310–11, 313, 317–18, 320–24
Jullien, Marc-Antoine, 43
juxtaposition, 10, 57, 65, 67, 115, 119

Kant, Immanuel, 38, 41–44, 289–90, 303n2
Keynesianism, 228–29, 233, 280
Khrushchev, Nikita, 224
Kitchener, Herbert, 176

knowledge, 8–10, 17–18, 21, 23, 34–38, 40, 42, 45, 54–59, 70, 86, 114, 119, 123, 138, 148, 169, 223, 243, 247–48, 253, 267–69, 289, 292, 309–11, 320, 325
Koselleck, Reinhart, 7, 21
Kropotkin, Petr, 222
Kuznets, Simon, 20, 275, 278–80

La Bruyère, Jean de, 84, 88, 104
Lairesse, Gerard de, 86–88, 104, 107n20
*laissez-faire*, 222, 227–29, 233
Lambert, Johann Heinrich, 38, 47n24, 47n26
Langer, Johann Peter, 61–65, 69, 73n31
language, 6–7, 16–18, 23, 37, 39–40, 48–49n47, 55, 59, 124, 158n28, 192, 194, 196–97, 201–2, 205, 229, 268, 271, 291, 300, 303, 311
Las Casas, Bartolomé de, 138, 144–45, 158n29
Latour, Bruno, 20, 267, 269
League of Nations, 19, 245, 247–52, 270, 277
  Economic and Financial Organization (EFO), 245–46, 248, 251–52
Leipzig, 85
Lenin, Vladimir Ilyich, 224–25
Leonard, William R., 275–76
Leopold II (Belgium), 173
Levellers, 117, 121, 129n29, 131n51
*Leyenda Negra*, 146, 158n35, 160n56, 172
liberalism, 13, 82, 97, 170, 172, 177, 201–3, 216–17, 221–34, 269. *See also* neoliberalism *and* ordoliberalism
Lichtenberg, Georg Christoph, 91, 93, 107n26, 107n28, 108n33
Lie, Trygve, 273–74
linguistics, 7, 10, 43, 57–58, 61, 69
Linnaeus, Carl, 9, 33, 38, 47n22
Lippmann, Walter, 228
List, Friedrich, 269
lists, 200, 249, 251, 277, 306–7, 309, 311, 313, 315–16, 318–19, 321–23
literature, 3, 5, 9, 40, 42–43 64, 82–84, 97, 105, 160n65, 167, 169, 288, 290–91, 316, 323
  comparative, 5, 9, 42, 44, 164
Lloyd George, David, 199, 202
Locke, John, 36–38, 46n12
logic, 9, 14–17, 37–38, 40–42, 45, 47n22, 49n56, 54, 102, 142, 291, 310

London, 89–90, 119, 247–48, 251, 269, 315
Louis XIV, 119
Luzzatti, Luigi, 203–4

Madison, James, 121–22, 132n64, 133n66
Maine, Henry Sumner, 193–94
maps, 20, 144, 200, 291, 314
marginalism, 220–23, 229, 236n27
markets, 11, 13, 82, 89, 93, 168, 194, 215–34, 242, 247–48, 253, 291, 295, 301–3, 304n18
marks, 15, 39, 67, 69, 85–87, 92, 144, 148, 199, 215, 232, 275, 294–95, 298, 302, 313, 315, 317, 319, 324. *See also* scores
Martí, José, 140, 145, 152, 154, 156n15
marxism. *See* Marx, Karl
Marx, Karl, 220–24, 290, 295, 302
mathematics, 17, 34–36, 38, 49n56, 220, 271, 278, 293, 299, 313
Mazarin, Jules, Cardinal, 119–20
meaning, 6–7, 10, 16–17, 23, 57–58, 65–67, 69–70, 98–100, 107n21, 113, 125, 169, 203, 215, 217, 223, 242, 288–89, 291–92, 294–95, 310
measurability/immeasurability, 17, 40, 101, 191, 194, 200, 232, 268, 295, 323
measurement, measuring, 1, 9, 13–14, 18–19, 21, 34, 42, 69, 81, 88–89, 101–3, 124, 138, 143, 195, 221, 243, 245, 253, 269–70, 274–75, 280, 292, 294–96, 298, 300–1, 307–9, 313, 318–22, 324, 326n11
media. *See* print *and* social media
Menger, Carl, 221
mercantilism, 218, 222, 233–34
merchants, 13, 102, 120, 165, 217–20
Merck, Johann Heinrich, 65–66, 74n37–38
merit, 3, 39, 60, 65, 88, 93, 100, 292, 294, 298, 313, 325
metaphor, 37–38, 40, 105, 157n18, 160n65, 291
Mexico, 139, 144–45, 150, 191, 276
Meyer, William Stevenson, 250
Middle Ages, 4, 82, 84, 90, 148, 217, 223
Middle East, 166, 271
Mier Noriega y Guerra, Servando Teresa de, 150
militarism, 11, 14–16, 114, 116, 166, 172–74, 176, 203, 222, 224–25
Mill, John Stuart, 95–97, 193

Mirabeau, Honoré Gabriel Riqueti, Comte de, 133–34n83
Mises, Ludwig von, 220–21, 223
model/countermodel, 8, 15–16, 33, 35–36, 40, 43, 45, 49, 56, 65, 83, 88–89, 93, 95–97, 114–15, 117, 119, 121, 123–25, 132n54, 133–34n83, 164, 172, 176, 191, 193–94, 197–98, 202–3, 214–15, 217, 226, 234, 277, 307, 316, 323–25
modernity, 5, 11–14, 20, 33, 35, 37, 39, 44, 82, 95, 99–102, 104, 115, 121–22, 126, 127n4, 138–39, 159n39, 165–66, 168, 171, 191–96, 198, 200–2, 204–5, 207n16, 217, 223–24, 230, 242–44, 252, 267–68, 290, 310
modernization, 18, 36, 192–94, 207n16, 215, 271
monarchy, 84, 113, 115, 116–23, 125–26, 127n4, 129n29, 130n34, 131n49, 132n60, 132n65, 134n87
Mont Pèlerin Society, 228–29
Montaigne, Michel de, 85
Montesquieu, 139, 146, 150, 219
Montreal, 272
moralism, 82–84, 91, 107n26, 218, 229
Morelli, Giovanni, 67–68

nation, 1, 3, 8, 12, 14–16, 18–20, 42, 48n39, 100, 102, 105, 115, 118, 123, 126, 154, 165, 171–72, 174–75, 192–205, 218, 224, 228, 232–33, 244–48, 250–51, 253–54, 266–69, 271, 275–80, 297, 311, 314
state, 1, 3, 8, 11, 14–16, 18–19, 199, 204, 251, 269, 277
nationalism, 7, 167–68, 218, 222, 228, 234, 244
National Socialism, 226, 271
Native Americans, 137–38, 140, 144–46, 150, 152, 158n28
natural history, 8, 10, 38, 42–44, 139, 145, 153
naturalism, 147–48
naturalization, 57, 143, 147, 155
natural sciences, 9, 18, 43, 48–49n47, 148, 193, 242, 324
nature, 37–39, 44–45, 48n39, 61, 91, 93–95, 101, 103, 144–45, 147, 149, 153–54, 166, 172, 175, 204, 218–19, 222–23, 227, 233, 292, 325
neoclassical economics. *See under* economics

Index                                                                 341

neoliberalism, 13, 21, 214–15, 228–31, 294. *See also* competition: neoliberal
Netherlands, 14–15, 86, 114–19, 120–22, 125–26, 127n5, 128n12, 128n15, 129n26, 129n30, 130n35, 130n37, 132n54, 132n56, 132n60, 130n62, 132n64, 134n86, 139, 165–66, 168–74, 176, 183n57, 201, 218, 280, 315
networks, 18, 34, 171, 178–79n7, 197, 199, 201, 244–47, 253, 291, 320
neutrality, 1, 7, 21, 54, 142–43, 192, 196, 205, 268, 292, 311
New Deal (U.S.), 193, 228
New Public Management, 13, 230–31, 238n70
newspapers. *See* journalism *and* press
New Zealand, 201–3
Nietzsche, Friedrich, 1, 4, 22, 37, 44, 102, 306, 325, 327n21
nobility, 82, 85, 92, 116, 128n15
noncommensurability. *See* commensurability/in-/noncommensurability
Norway, 196, 201, 274
Novalis, 43
numbers, 16–19, 21–22, 143, 151, 157n23, 242, 244, 266–71, 273, 277–80, 283n34, 283n50, 291–93, 296–98, 300–3, 306–7, 309, 313–14, 319–24, 326n3
numerals, 313, 315, 317, 319, 322, 326n3

objectivity, 22, 54, 58, 143, 192, 196, 198, 204–5, 220, 268–69, 292, 295, 313, 320, 322, 324–25
Oken, Lorenz, 43
ordoliberalism, 226–31
Organisation for European Economic Co-operation (OEEC)/Organisation for Economic Co-operation and Development (OECD), 191, 266, 280, 293
orientalism/occidentalism, 4, 140, 170, 177n2
*Ormée*, 119–21, 131n49
Osterhammel, Jürgen, 243, 253
othering, 138, 140–42, 148, 150, 153–54, 155n2, 157n21, 201, 310
Ottoman Empire, 165–66

Paine, Thomas, 121, 132n61, 134n87
palaeontology, 43

pamphlets, 116–17, 131n49, 167, 169, 197, 214. *See also* press
parable, 100, 105
Paris, 43, 120, 126, 131n49, 132n64, 195–96, 221, 228, 269, 315
Parker, Robert, 319
*parlement*, 119, 120, 126
parliamentarism, 119, 125, 196, 200, 202, 209n50
Parliament (Britain), 117–20, 123–26, 130–31n40, 170
  House of Commons, 107n28, 118, 133n69
  House of Lords, 107n28, 118, 123, 130n34
Parsons, Talcott, 291
path dependency, 16, 192, 195
patriotism, 121–22, 132n61
Pauw, Cornelis de, 139, 143, 145–54, 157n24
Pedersen, Susan, 166, 192
performance, 10–11, 13, 17–18, 21–23, 34, 56–57, 59, 66, 91, 95, 104, 140, 142–43, 215, 231, 250, 266, 280, 294, 299–302, 306–7, 310–11, 317, 323–25
periphery. *See* centre/periphery
Pernetry, Antoine-Joseph, 139, 156n12
Perrault, Charles, 139
Peru, 138, 144–45, 158n28, 260n63
Philip II (Spain), 115–16
philosophy, 9, 33–41, 43–44, 54, 87, 95–96, 100, 102, 139, 144–45, 147, 154, 221, 267–69, 288–91, 303
Piles, Roger de, 313–14
Pinochet, Augusto, 229
pictures. *See* images
plantation economy, 138, 140
Plato, 145
Pliny the Elder, 145
poetry, 9–10, 33, 40, 47–48n32, 95, 151, 313
Poland, 19, 91, 121–22, 127n3, 132n56, 250–51
Polanyi, Karl, 194
policy, 2, 21, 95, 165–66, 172–75, 191–205, 227–28, 231–33, 243, 247, 253, 271, 274–75, 277, 280
politicians, 19, 113, 165, 170, 201, 203, 224, 232, 234, 243–44, 246–47, 277, 279, 306–7
politicization/depoliticization, 22, 251, 253

politics, political, 8, 11–12, 14–16, 18, 20–21, 23, 53, 59, 88, 91, 93, 96–97, 103, 114–26, 138, 140, 143–44, 152, 164–77, 191–92, 194, 198–205, 215–16, 220, 224, 226–27, 230, 233–34, 244, 249–52, 266–71, 277–80, 294, 304n18, 307, 311, 323–24
   history, 113, 170, 176, 267, 274
   science, 7, 11, 24n10, 164, 232, 270
polity, 8, 113, 119, 124–25, 132n54, 269
Porter, Michael, 231–33
Porter, Theodore M., 267, 269, 320, 323
Portugal, 143, 165, 168, 171–72, 196, 260n63
postcolonial studies, 3–4, 6–7, 9, 137, 140, 228
post-structuralism, 44
poverty/wealth, 8, 12, 84–86, 91, 93, 101, 103, 116, 118, 172, 195, 216, 218–19, 228, 234, 266, 270, 272, 274–75, 278–80, 293, 311
practice, 6, 13, 18, 55–57, 59, 65, 72n10, 84–85, 117–19, 124, 134n85, 138, 142, 144, 157n19, 170, 172, 175, 192, 203, 267, 274–75, 277, 293, 300, 302, 314
   of comparing (*see* comparison, comparative: practices of, doing of)
practice theory, 20, 55–58, 71–72n7, 141–42
Prague, 271
press, 11, 23, 61, 65–66, 165, 167–70, 179n9, 191, 202, 225, 245–46, 270–71, 279, 293–94, 295–97, 300–1, 322,. *See also* journalism
prestige, 9, 11, 14–15, 19, 91, 93, 100, 109n60, 244, 249, 251, 254
prices, 216, 243, 252, 280, 295, 300–2, 308
pride/shame, 1, 14–16, 39, 83, 85, 103, 126, 201, 204, 218, 225, 306
prizes, 95, 297, 301, 306–7, 316, 318–19, 322–23
Programme for International Student Assessment (PISA), 293, 308
progress, 4, 14–16, 19, 21, 23, 88, 93, 103, 194, 196, 199–202, 204, 229, 273–74, 277, 302, 311. *See also* backwardness
proletariat, 225, 227. *See also* bourgeoisie *and* workers, working class
propaganda, 16, 170, 176, 197, 199, 228

Proudhon, Pierre-Joseph, 221
Prussia, 122, 167
psychology, 11, 26n34, 37, 43, 103, 221, 289
public, 1–2, 11, 14–15, 42–43, 84–85, 100, 103, 114, 123, 160n64, 165, 169–70, 174, 176–77, 199, 201, 215, 227, 254, 277, 294, 302, 308–9, 324–25
public opinion, 9, 118, 272
quantification, 17, 19, 22, 101–2, 104, 205, 232, 243–44, 268, 289, 291–92, 295, 300, 302, 307–9, 313, 318–24, 326n3

*Querelle des anciens et des modernes*, 138–39, 148

race, racism, 9, 102, 105, 139, 147, 154–55, 174, 200–1, 224, 270, 299
railway, 2, 165, 249, 270, 315
Raimondi, Marcantonio, 61–65, 69, 73n27
rank, 12–13, 39, 80–88, 106n13
rankings, 3–5, 12, 17–22, 101, 104, 146, 152, 177, 200–1, 233, 249–51, 288–303, 304n12, 306–25. *See also* ratings
Raphael, 61–64, 73n26–27
ratings, 2, 4, 12, 15, 22, 36, 101, 104, 173, 198, 278, 292, 295, 298, 301, 306–7, 311–12, 315–19, 321–25. *See also* rankings
rational choice, 222–23, 316
rationalism, 38–40, 123–24, 147, 176, 196, 221–22, 226, 268, 274, 292, 294, 303
rationalization, 40, 164, 223
Raynal, Guillaume Thomas François (Abbé Raynal), 139, 146–47, 149–50, 153, 155n4
reactivity, 301, 309, 325
Reagan, Ronald, 231–32
religion, 4–6, 24n12, 64, 91, 117–19, 122, 130n37, 131n45, 146, 150, 153, 192–94
Renaissance, 10, 42
Renan, Ernest, 4
republic, 14, 113–22, 125–26, 127n3, 129n29, 132n54, 132n57, 133n66
republicanism, 14, 113, 115, 117–19, 121, 125–26, 127n4, 130n37, 131n46, 131n49, 132n57, 175
representation, 7, 14, 19, 38, 41, 56–57, 59, 66–67, 86, 89, 91, 117, 123,

131n49, 165, 171, 200–1, 249, 251–52, 272–73, 291, 293, 302
numerical, 17, 57, 192, 268, 277, 279, 292–93, 295, 302, 313, 324
resemblance, 9–10, 13–14, 35, 41, 43, 83, 125, 203, 243, 246, 301
reviews, 21, 61, 64–67, 70, 102, 169, 171, 175, 307, 317–18, 320–22
revolution, 14–15, 88, 113, 125, 170, 172, 224, 226, 245, 252
rhetoric, 4, 9, 21, 33, 37, 40–41, 145, 164, 167, 176, 273, 288, 291–92
Rice, Stuart Arthur, 272, 275–77, 283n37
risk, 4, 196–97, 201, 299
rivalry, 10–11, 13–14, 16, 20, 43, 94, 118, 165, 214–20, 222, 232, 298, 303. See also competition
Rohr, Julius Bernhard von, 88
Romanticism, 3–4, 41–43, 45
Rome, 61, 102, 118, 120, 132n54, 145, 154, 165
Roosevelt, Theodore, 16, 81, 105n6
Röpke, Wilhelm, 227
Rostow, Walt Whitman, 271, 283n35
Rousseau, Jean-Jacques, 37, 39, 41–42, 94–96, 104, 105n1, 123, 219–22, 224, 231, 233–34
routines, 2, 10, 19, 23, 56–57, 59, 142, 224
Russia, 13, 97, 100, 166–67, 200, 202, 214, 217, 298. See also Soviet Union

Said, Edward, 4, 137, 157n17, 157n21
Saint Petersburg, 97–99
Salandra, Antonio, 203–4
scales, 7, 15, 22, 35, 37, 308, 311, 318–19, 322, 324
Scandinavia, 16, 201, 273, 315
Scheler, Max, 102–5
Schelling, Friedrich Wilhelm Joseph, 43
Schlegel, Friedrich, 9, 42–43
Schlözer, August Ludwig, 268–69
Schumpeter, Joseph, 217, 223–24, 227, 231–32, 238n71
science, scientific, 4–5, 8–11, 20, 33–35, 38, 40–45, 53, 56, 60, 105, 147–48, 153, 168, 172, 196, 203, 205, 217, 220–22, 231, 242–43, 252–53, 269, 271–72, 275–77, 293, 300, 307, 310, 315, 324
 method(s), 23, 33, 38, 44, 49n52, 49n56, 154, 192–93, 295, 326n5, 327n19
 natural (see natural sciences)
 social (see social sciences)
scores, 2, 17, 21, 292–93, 296–99, 308, 319–20, 323, 325. See also marks
Scotland, 102, 129n27, 146, 201
Second World War, 20, 165, 193, 228, 243, 248, 251, 253–54, 266–67, 271, 275, 293
Seeley, John Robert, 173
semiotics, 10, 38, 55, 59–60, 66–70, 75n43. See also signals, signs
sensualism, 37–38, 43
Sepúlveda, Juan Ginés de, 138
shame. See pride/shame
Shanghai, 252, 273
Shanghai Ranking of World Universities, 300–1, 319–20, 322
Shils, Edward, 291
Sieyès, Emmanuel Joseph (Abbé Sieyès), 15, 123–24, 133n75, 269
signals, signs, 7, 18, 34, 37–39, 58, 60–61, 67, 69–70, 85, 199, 290. See also semiotics
similarity, 2, 6–7, 10, 12, 17, 19, 21, 34–37, 40, 44, 46n12, 53, 58, 64, 66, 85–86, 96, 103, 105, 114–19, 122, 138, 141–43, 146–50, 153, 155, 157n20, 165, 171, 193, 202–5, 214–15, 217, 227–28, 247–48, 288–89, 295, 306, 308–10, 313–14, 316, 318, 324. See also difference
simile, 9, 40
Simmel, Georg, 11–12, 20, 103, 288–90, 292, 303n2
simplification, 17, 34–35, 92, 150, 290–92, 294, 309
Singapore, 191, 293
singularity, 16, 39–41, 271, 288, 324, 329n56
Skocpol, Theda, 195
Slack, Paul, 14, 314
slavery, 15, 102, 117, 138–40, 144–45, 147–48, 150–51, 158n29, 174, 182n52, 219, 221
Smith, Adam, 219–21, 223, 227, 230–31, 234
Snow, Ernest C., 270, 277
social democracy, 201–2, 228, 233, 274
socialism, 13, 101, 203, 214–17, 219–22, 224–29, 231
social media, 81, 233
social policy, 191–96, 198–205, 243

social sciences, 2, 5–6, 17–18, 43–45, 164, 192–95, 198, 204–5, 242, 268, 280, 298, 308, 318, 321, 323, 327n19
social security, 192–93, 266, 275
sociology, 5, 8, 10–12, 16, 20, 44, 56, 83, 100, 191–92, 204, 267, 288–91, 298, 307–8, 320, 322
Sombart, Werner, 102, 105
*sorevnovanie*. *See* emulation: socialist
South Africa, 176, 182n40, 183n57, 203, 273
Soviet Union (USSR), 13, 193, 215–16, 224–25, 267. *See also* Russia
sovereignty, 80, 84, 117, 119, 123–24, 194, 218, 221, 268, 274, 277
Spain, 115–17, 125, 145–46, 148–50, 154, 155n1, 165, 168, 172, 196, 249, 269
Spencer, Herbert, 15
Spivak, Gayatri Chakravorty, 138, 157n17, 157n21
sports, 11, 26n34, 223, 292, 294, 297, 315, 323
Stakhanovite Movement, 214, 226
Stalin, Iosif, 214–15, 225–26
Stalinism, 13, 215–16, 224, 226, 231
standardization, 2–4, 11, 14, 16, 18–19, 21, 23, 57, 81, 88–89, 91, 93, 96–97, 192, 198, 200–1, 205, 227, 244–45, 247, 251–53, 269–70, 274–76, 279–80, 293–96, 298–99, 311, 315, 317, 320–25
statism, 177, 226, 228–29, 233
statistics, statistical, 5, 16–22, 49n56, 101, 143, 172, 191–92, 196–97, 242–54, 266–98, 293–94, 311, 314, 323
  bureaus, offices, departments, 15, 18–20, 196, 243, 245–48, 251–53, 270, 272–73, 275–76, 280, 307
  conferences, congresses, 20, 247, 251, 266–84
  economic, 19–20, 243–49, 251–54, 255n6, 267, 270, 278–79
  global, 19–20, 243–49, 251, 253–54, 266–84
  method(s), 20–22, 243–45, 247, 251–53, 280
  publications, 19, 168, 242, 245–46, 248, 252
status, 12–13, 145, 153, 194, 199, 204, 218, 226, 288, 293–94, 296–98, 301–2, 304n12

stereotypes, 23, 147, 150, 154, 167, 170–71, 174
Stigler, George, 229
Stone, Richard, 278, 280
subjectivity, 22, 37, 41, 60, 220, 292, 307, 319–20, 322–24
superlative, 22, 306, 325
surveys, 151, 203, 232, 245–48, 253, 293, 297–99
Sweden, 149, 210, 250
Switzerland, 15, 113–19, 120–22, 125–26, 127n6, 128n9, 129n22, 129n26, 132n56, 201–2, 243, 247, 249, 270, 273, 278, 308, 313, 315
symbols, 20–21, 90, 290–91, 294, 302, 315, 317, 319, 326n3

tables, 1–2, 17–18, 21–22, 57, 151–52, 192, 215, 231–32, 242, 245, 252, 280, 292, 294, 311, 313–15, 323
taxation, 14, 123, 194, 299, 311
technocracy, 13, 19–20, 22, 217, 226, 231, 234, 249–50, 270, 274, 282n28
technology, 15, 38, 165, 194, 200, 223, 226, 230, 232, 269, 294, 302, 320, 325
telegraph, 165, 245, 251
temporalization, 37, 39, 89, 93, 96–97, 100, 104. *See also* comparison, comparative: temporal *and* time
*tertium comparationis*. *See under* comparison, comparative
Thatcher, Margaret, 230–31
theology, 43–44, 54
Thierry, Charles de, 175, 183n73
time, 3–5, 13–14, 17, 19, 21, 33, 37, 44, 60–61, 69, 75n46, 80–82, 96, 122, 142, 152, 164, 192, 242, 270, 279, 289, 295, 297, 299–301, 310–11. *See also* comparison, comparative: temporal *and* temporalization
Tocqueville, Alexis de, 152
totalitarianism, 271
trade, 218, 220, 102, 118, 138, 140, 150, 164–65, 174, 217–20, 227, 232–33, 243–44, 246–48, 252, 254, 266, 316. *See also* free trade
trade unions, 202–3, 215
transfer, 64, 120, 123, 145, 165, 192, 201
translation, 7, 17, 64–65, 86, 98, 131n51, 143, 146, 154, 159n45, 194, 197, 201–2, 214, 278, 289, 303n2, 318

Index    345

Truman, Harry, 272, 274
trust, 37, 154, 229–30, 268–69, 301, 320, 322
truth, 2, 9, 34–36, 38, 46n12, 47n24, 121–22, 154
Turing, Alan, 271, 283n35
tyranny, 118–19, 172, 182n52
Tytler, James, 146–47, 150, 154

United Kingdom (UK), 230, 269, 280, 293–94. *See also* Britain
United Nations (UN), 20, 255–56n6, 266–67, 271–76, 280, 281n3, 283n44, 283n50
   Economic and Social Council, 272–73
   Food and Agricultural Organization (FAO), 272, 278
   Relief and Rehabilitation Administration (UNRRA), 277–78
United States of America (U.S.), 15–16, 20–21, 100–2, 109n60, 115, 121–22, 124–25, 127n3, 132n62, 133n66, 133–34n81–83, 139–40, 151–52, 160n67, 165–66, 169, 193, 196, 199, 228–32, 246–47, 249, 267, 269, 271–75, 278–80, 293–94, 297–298, 322
universality/uniqueness, 3, 6–7, 12, 14–15, 17, 22–23, 34, 41–42, 54–56, 58, 60, 92–95, 99, 121, 145, 152–53, 167, 194–95, 205, 228, 276, 289, 291, 297, 303, 310, 323–24
university, 1, 13, 17, 19, 21, 28n69, 215, 226, 273, 280, 291–98, 300–2, 304n12, 306–8, 310, 316–20, 322, 325. *See also* academia, education: higher
uniqueness. *See* universality/uniqueness
*U.S. News and World Reports* (USN), 293, 298–99, 301, 304n12
utilitarianism, 221, 229–30
Utrecht, 115, 128n12, 128n19, 132n65

Valladolid Controversy (1550/51), 138, 144
value(s), 1, 11, 13, 42, 54–55, 64–65, 67, 87–88, 93, 101–3, 139, 191, 201, 216–17, 220, 223, 231–34, 248, 277, 280, 290–92, 295, 302–3, 311, 313, 326n3
Veblen, Thorstein, 100–2, 104
Vega, Inca Garcilaso de la, 138, 145–48, 152, 154, 159n48, 160n69
Venice, 102, 114, 116, 118, 121, 129n26, 132n54, 132n56
Versailles Peace Treaty, 249
Vespucci, Amerigo, 143–44
Victorian era, 9, 97, 100, 164–74, 176–77
Vienna, 167

Wackenroder, Wilhelm Heinrich, 42
Washington, D.C., 20, 224, 266–67, 269, 271–73, 275–76, 278–80
Washington, George, 151
wealth. *See* poverty/wealth
Weber, Max, 194, 223, 227, 289, 302, 308
welfare state, 5, 16–18, 191–95, 198–201, 204–5, 227–29, 233
'the West', 2, 4, 6, 13, 34, 45, 159n39, 224, 228, 233, 269, 303
Wieland, Christoph Martin, 65
Wilhelmine era, 16, 100, 102, 199
William I of Orange (1533–84), 115, 128n8
Winckelmann, Johann Joachim, 64
Wirth, Louis, 291
Wittgenstein, Ludwig, 57
workers, working class, 15, 17, 86, 101, 197, 199–200, 203, 214–15, 221, 224, 225–27, 229, 249, 302. *See also* class *and* proletariat
World Bank, 20, 272, 280
World Economic Forum, 232
world society, 5, 11–12, 267

zero-sum games, 22, 218, 234, 292, 317

www.ingramcontent.com/pod-product-compliance
Lightning Source LLC
Chambersburg PA
CBHW071147070526
44584CB00019B/2697